SO-AFP-375

The **Rough Guide** to

Costa Rica

written and researched by

Jean McNeil

with additional contributions by
Joe Fullman and Andy Symington

ROUGH GUIDES

NEW YORK • LONDON • DELHI

www.roughguides.com

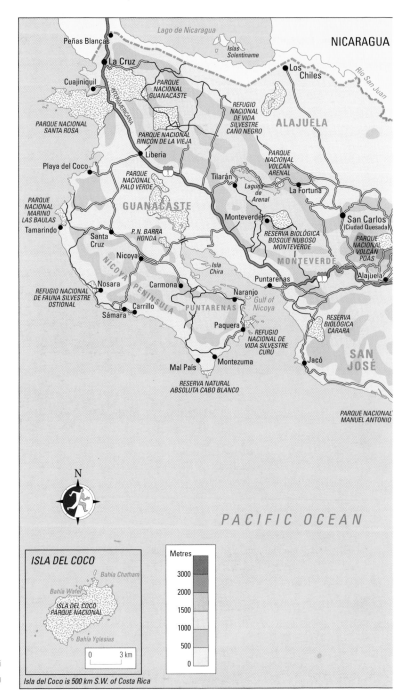

PACIFIC OCEAN

ISLA DEL COCO

Isla del Coco is 500 km S.W. of Costa Rica

Metres

3000
2000
1500
1000
500
0

▲ Surfer, Mal País

Introduction to
Costa Rica

Hemmed in between the Pacific and Atlantic oceans near the narrowest point of the Central American isthmus, the tiny republic of Costa Rica is often pictured as an oasis of political stability in the midst of a turbulent region. This democratic and prosperous nation is also one of the most biodiverse areas on the planet, an ecological treasure house whose varied habitats – ranging from rainforests and beaches to volcanos and mangrove swamps – support a fascinating variety of wildlife, much of it now protected by an enlightened national conservation system which is widely regarded as a model of its kind.

Though this idyllic image might not do justice to the full complexities of contemporary Costa Rican society, it's true that the country's long democratic tradition and complete absence of military forces (the army was abolished in 1948) stand in sharp contrast to the brutal internal conflicts which have ravaged its neighbours, while the country has also largely escaped the natural disasters which have afflicted so many other Central American states. This reputation for peacefulness has been an important factor in the spectacular growth of Costa Rica's tourist industry – more than a million people visit the country annually, mainly from North America. Most of all, though, it's the country's outstanding natural beauty which has made it one of the world's prime eco-tourism destinations, with visitors coming to walk trails beneath the vaulting canopy trees of million-year-old rainforests; to climb the volcanos that punctuate the country's mountainous spine; or to explore the high-altitude cloudforest, home to the jaguar, the lumbering tapir and the resplendent quetzal.

Admittedly, tourism has made Costa Rica less of an "authentic" experience than some travellers would like: it's hard to go anywhere in the country without bumping into whitewater rafters or surfers, and more

v

Fact file

- The Republic of Costa Rica lies on the Central American isthmus between the Atlantic and Pacific oceans, consisting of a mountainous backbone – rising to 3819m at the summit of Mount Chirripó, its highest point – flanked by low-lying coastal strips. Though set in one of the most geologically active regions on Earth, Costa Rica has suffered less from earthquakes and volcanic eruptions than its northern neighbours – the worst incident in modern times was the earthquake which struck near Cartago in April 1910, killing 1750 people.

- The country's population is largely of Spanish extraction, though there's a substantial community of English-speaking Costa Ricans of African origin along the Caribbean coast, along with a few thousand indigenous peoples. Costa Rica is a young country: out of its population of slightly over 3 million, more than a third are aged under 15; men currently enjoy a life expectancy of 72, women of 77.

- Costa Rica's main exports are coffee and bananas, though in recent years income from these products has been overtaken by that from tourism. The country's recent prosperity has also been partly funded by massive borrowing – per capita, Costa Rica's levels of debt are among the highest in the world. Despite widespread poverty, the free and compulsory primary education system means that the country boasts a literacy rate of 90 percent, the best in Central America.

and more previously remote spots are being bought up by foreign entrepreneurs. Still, few Costa Ricans have anything bad to say about their country's popularity as a destination – perhaps simply because they know which side their bread's buttered. But as more hotels open, malls go up, and visitors flock to resorts and national parks, there's no doubt that Costa Rica is experiencing a significant social change, while the darker side of outside involvement in the country – sex tourism, real-estate scams and conflicts between foreign property-owners and poorer locals – are all on the increase.

Despite such problems, revenue from tourism is one of the reasons Costa Ricans – or Ticos, as they are generally known – now enjoy the highest rate of literacy, health care, education and life expectancy in the isthmus. That said, Costa Rica is certainly not the middle-class country that it's often portrayed to be – a significant percentage of people still live below the poverty line – and while it is modernizing fast, its character continues to be rooted in distinct local cultures, from the Afro-Caribbean province of Limón, with its Creole cuisine, games and patois, to the traditional *ladino* values embodied by the *sabanero* (cowboy) of Guanacaste. Above all, the country still has the highest rural population density in Latin America, and society continues to revolve around the twin axes of countryside and family: wherever

▲ Evening street scene, Liberia

you go, you're sure to be left with mental snapshots of rural life, whether it be horsemen trotting by on dirt roads, coffee-plantation day-labourers setting off to work in the dawn mists of the Highlands, or avocado-pickers cycling home at sunset.

Where to go

Though everyone passes through it, hardly anyone falls in love with **San José**, Costa Rica's under-rated capital. Often dismissed as an ugly urban sprawl, the city enjoys a dramatic setting amid jagged mountain peaks, plus some excellent cafés and restaurants, leafy parks, a lively university district and a good arts scene. The surrounding **Valle Central** is the country's agricultural heartland, and also home to several of its finest volcanos, including the huge crater of Volcán Poás and the largely dormant Volcán Irazú, a strange lunar landscape high above the regional capital of Cartago.

Toucans and tapirs

Costa Rica's position as a land bridge between the temperate north and the tropical south has given it a beguiling diversity of animal life, including tropical creatures such as the jaguar, temperate-zone animals like the deer, and some unusual, seemingly hybrid combinations such as the coati and the tapir. It's also home to no fewer than 850 species of bird – more than the US and Canada combined – along with a quarter of the world's known butterflies and thousands of moths, bees and wasps.

While it has an extraordinary wealth of bird and animal life, Costa Rica isn't a zoo. Most animals are very shy – and in some cases, centuries of hunting has driven them to take refuge in the most impenetrable terrain. That said, the average visitor to one of the national parks or reserves has a fair chance of spotting one or two unfamiliar creatures, most likely the bright-beaked toucan, the common paca (a large, harmless rodent which forages on the forest floor) or the coati (which looks like a cross between a raccoon and an anteater), along with a few smaller bird species. You will, however, have to be extremely lucky to get a glimpse of one of the country's larger mammals, such as the jaguar, ocelot or tapir.

Biodiversity under protection

Despite its small size, Costa Rica possesses no less than five percent of the world's total biodiversity, in part due to its position as a transition zone between North and South America, and also thanks to its complex system of interlocking micro-climates, created by differences in topography and altitude. This biological abundance is now safeguarded by one of the world's most enlightened and dedicated conservation programmes – about 25 percent of Costa Rica's land is protected, most of it through the country's extensive system of national parks.

Costa Rica's national parks vary from the tropical jungle lowlands of Corcovado to the grassy volcanic uplands of Rincón de la Vieja, an impressive and varied range of terrain which has enhanced the country's popularity with eco-tourists. Outside the park system, however, land is assailed by deforestation – ironically, there are now no more significant patches of forest left anywhere in the country except in protected areas.

While nowhere in the country is further than nine hours' drive from San José, the far north and the far south are less visited than other regions. The broad alluvial plains of the **Zona Norte** are often overlooked, despite featuring active Volcán Arenal, which spouts and spews within sight of the friendly tourist hang-out of La Fortuna, affording arresting night-time scenes of blood-red lava illuminating the sky. Off-the-beaten-path travellers and serious hikers will be happiest in the rugged **Zona Sur**, home to Mount Chirripó, the highest point in the country. Further south, on the outstretched feeler of the Osa Peninsula, Parque Nacional Corcovado protects the last significant area of tropical wet forest on the Pacific coast of the isthmus and is probably the best destination in the country for walkers – and also one of the few places where you have a fighting chance of seeing some of the more exotic wildlife for which Costa Rica is famed.

In the northwest, the cattle-ranching province of **Guanacaste** is often called "the home of Costa Rican folklore", and *sabanero* culture dominates here, with exuberant ragtag rodeos and large cattle haciendas. **Limón** province, on the Caribbean coast, is the polar opposite to traditional *ladino* Guanacaste, home to the descendants of the Afro-

> **Costa Rica's outstanding natural beauty has made it one of the world's prime eco-tourism destinations**

Caribbeans who came to Costa Rica at the end of the nineteenth century to work on the San José–Limón railroad – their language (Creole English), Protestantism and the West Indian traditions remain relatively intact to this day.

Close to the **Pacific coast**, Monteverde has become the country's number-one tourist attraction, pulling in the visitors who flocked here to walk through some of the last remaining cloudforest in the Americas.

▲ Mangoes

Further down the coast is the popular beach of Manuel Antonio, with its picture-postcard ocean setting, plus the equally pretty but far less touristed beaches of Sámara and Nosara on the Nicoya Peninsula.

When to go

lthough Costa Rica lies between 8° and 11° north of the equator, temperatures, governed by the vastly varying altitudes, are by no means universally high, and can plummet to below freezing at higher altitudes. Local microclimates predominate and make weather unpredictable, though to an extent you can depend upon the **two-season rule**. From roughly May to mid-November

The country with no army

"We are a country with more teachers than soldiers . . . and a country that turns military headquarters into schools." So President Ricardo Jiménez Oreamuno rousingly described Costa Rica in 1922, and his oft-repeated quote still neatly sums up the country's status as an island of relative peace in a turbulent region. The reason for Costa Rica's continued stability whilst so many of its neighbours descended into dictatorship and civil war during recent decades are manifold, and include the comparative lack of ethnic tensions, a long-standing tradition of social equality and democracy, and also the fact, almost unheard of in the modern world, that Costa Rica has no army.

The decision to abolish the country's armed forces was taken by President Figueres in 1948. Figueres' motives were not entirely utopian, representing a pragmatic bid to save valuable resources and to limit the political instability that had been the scourge of so many Latin American countries. Even so, despite the subsequent success of Costa Rica's bold experiment, things are not entirely rosy. Today, to compensate for the absence of a national military body, the police forces are powerful, highly specialized and, in some cases, heavily armed.

you will have afternoon rains and sunny mornings. The rains are heaviest in September and October and, although they can be fierce, will impede you from travelling only in the more remote areas of the country – the Nicoya Peninsula especially – where dirt roads become impassable to all but the sturdiest 4WDs. In the dry season most areas are just that: dry all day, with occasional blustery northern winds blowing in during January or February and cooling things off. Otherwise you can depend on sunshine and warm temperatures.

In recent years Costa Rica has been booked solid during the peak season, the North American winter months, when bargains are few and far between. The crowds peter out after Easter, but return again to an extent in June and July. During peak times you have to plan well in advance, faxing the hotels of your choice, usually prepaying or at least putting down a deposit by credit card, and arriving armed with faxed confirmations and a set itinerary. Travellers who prefer to play it by ear are much better off coming during the low or rainy season (euphemistically called the "green season"), when many hotels offer discounts.

The months of November, April (after Easter) and May are the best times to visit, when the rains have either just started or just died off, and the country is refreshed, green and relatively untouristed.

Temperature and rainfall

	Jan	Feb	Mar	Apr	May	Jun	Jul	Aug	Sep	Oct	Nov	Dec
Caribbean coast												
av. max. temp. (˚C)	27	28	29	30	31	31	31	31	31	30	28	27
av. min. temp. (˚C)	19	21	22	23	24	24	24	24	23	22	20	20
av. rainfall (mm)	137	61	38	56	109	196	163	170	244	305	226	185
San Jose and the Highlands												
av. max. temp. (˚C)	24	26	26	24	27	26	25	26	26	25	25	24
av. min. temp. (˚C)	14	14	15	17	17	17	17	16	16	16	16	14
av. rainfall (mm)	15	5	20	46	229	241	211	241	305	300	145	41
Pacific coast												
av. max. temp. (˚C)	31	32	32	31	30	31	31	30	29	29	29	31
av. min. temp. (˚C)	22	22	22	23	23	23	23	23	23	23	23	23
av. rainfall (mm)	25	10	18	74	203	213	180	201	208	257	259	122

30

things not to miss

It's not possible to see everything that Costa Rica has to offer in one trip – and we don't suggest you try. What follows is a selective and subjective taste of the country's highlights: outstanding national parks, spectacular wildlife, gorgeous beaches and an abundance of fresh tropical fruit. They're arranged in five colour-coded categories which you can browse through to find the very best things to see, do and experience. All highlights have a page reference to take you straight into the Guide, where you can find out more.

01 **Teatro Nacional, San José** Page **81** • Central America's grandest theatre, built in imitation of the Paris Opéra with money raised by a tax on coffee.

02 Monteverde Cloudforest Reserve Page **280** • Experience the bird's-eye view – and a touch of vertigo – from a suspended bridge in the lush Monteverde Cloudforest Reserve.

03 Playa Cocles Page **166** • One of the most appealing beaches on the entire Caribbean coast, with pristine tropical scenery, a soothing atmosphere and excellent accommodation.

04 **Calle Real, Liberia** Page **228** • Now restored to its original nineteenth-century glory, this is the country's finest surviving colonial street.

05 **Sports-fishing** Page **51** • Anglers battle big fish in Costa Rica's coastal waters, teeming with swordfish, marlin, tarpon and snook.

06 **Rara Avis Rainforest Reserve** Page **203** • Costa Rica's premier eco-tourism destination flourishes with palms, primitive ferns, orchids and a vibrant birdlife, from vultures to oropéndolas, whose curious nests are pictured here.

07 Arenal Volcano Page **193** • One of the Western Hemisphere's more active volcanos, Arenal's upper slopes are periodically doused in flows of red-hot lava.

09 Coffee Page **37** • Sample a cup of Costa Rica's most famous export, and the foundation of the country's prosperity.

08 Carnival, Puerto Limón Page **152** • Young bloods and grandparents alike take to the streets during Costa Rica's raciest carnival.

10 Santa Rosa National Park Page **234** • This gorgeous park protects a rare stretch of dry tropical forest.

11 Museo de Jade Page **83** • Admire the nuanced colours – from milky-whites to deep greens – of this ancient stone, once prized more than gold, at the world's largest collection of pre-Columbian jade.

12 Santa Elena Cloudforest Reserve Page **283** • This spectacular reserve features excellent trails through misty and mysterious vegetation.

13 El Sano Banano Page **298** • Swing in a hammock shaded by palms at the secluded *El Sano Banano* hotel, just outside the popular beach village of Montezuma.

14 **Poás Volcano** Page **115** • Poás is one of the world's more easily accessible active volcanos, with a history of eruptions that goes back eleven million years.

15 **Cowboys** Page **217** • Guanacaste is home to Costa Rica's cowboys, or *sabaneros* – iconic figures whose ranching skills and bull-fighting prowess have become part of national legend.

16 Manuel Antonio National Park Page **309** • This perennially popular park boasts four beaches, mangroves, tropical forest and stunning coastal scenery.

17 Xandari Plantation Inn Page **114** • Spend a night at this beautiful spot set in a coffee plantation amidst the scenic heights of the Valle Central.

18 Corcovado National Park Page **352** • This verdant coastal rainforest is one of Costa Rica's finest destinations for walking and wildlife-spotting.

19 Birdwatching Page **52** • Costa Rica is the natural habitat of the most colourful birds in the Americas, including hummingbirds, scarlet macaws, toucans and the resplendent quetzal.

20 **Baird's tapir** Page **382** • Halfway between an elephant and a cow, Baird's tapir is one of Costa Rica's most remarkable – and elusive – inhabitants.

21 **Tortuguero Canal** Page **172** • Ride the boat ride north from Puerto Limón along the Tortuguero Canal, past luxuriant tropical vegetation and colourful wooden houses on stilts.

22 Rincón de la Vieja National Park Page **230** • Clouds of sulphurous smoke and steaming mudpots dot the desiccated slopes of Rincón de la Vieja Volcano, one of the country's more thermally active areas.

23 **Museo de Oro Precolombino** Page **81** • Visit this dazzling display of over two thousand pre-Columbian gold pieces.

24 **Monkeys** Page **384** • Costa Rica is home to four species of monkey, including the white-faced capuchin monkey (pictured here).

25 **Crocodiles and caimans** Page **386** • Along Costa Rica's lush, tropical waterways, crocs and caimans bask on submerged branches and muddy river banks, their fearsome teeth glinting in the sun.

26 **Irazú Volcano** Page **134** • The blasted lunar landscape at the summit of Irazú is a stirring natural sight, with fantastic views on a clear day all the way to the Caribbean.

27 **Whitewater rafting** Page **48** • Whitewater rafting is one of Costa Rica's most popular outdoor activities, with a range of rivers to suit all abilities.

xxiii

28 **Leatherback turtles** Page **249** • Hundreds of these magnificent turtles come ashore near Tamarindo to lay their eggs every year.

29 Fruit Page **36** • Costa Rica's tropical fruit ranges from the ubiquitous banana, papaya and mango to the custard fruit *anona* and the spiny but sweet *mamones chinos*.

30 Sámara Page **258** • Enjoy spectacular sunsets and calm waters at this relaxing Pacific coast beach.

Contents

Using this Rough Guide

We've tried to make this Rough Guide a good read and easy to use. The book is divided into six main sections, and you should be able to find whatever you want in one of them.

Colour section

The front colour section offers a quick survey of Costa Rica. The **introduction** aims to give you a feel for the country, with suggestions on where to go. We also tell you what the weather is like and include a basic country fact file. Next, our authors round up their favourite aspects of Costa Rica in the **things not to miss** section – whether it's the outdoors, amazing sights or a special lodge. Right after this comes a full **contents** list.

Basics

The **basics** section covers all the **pre-departure** nitty-gritty to help you plan your trip. This is where to find out which airlines fly to your destination, what paperwork you'll need, what to do about money and insurance, Internet access, food, public transport, car rental – in fact just about every piece of **general practical information** you might need.

Guide

This is the heart of the Rough Guide, divided into user-friendly chapters, each of which covers a specific region. Every chapter starts with a list of **highlights** and an **introduction** that helps you to decide where to go. Likewise, introductions to the various towns and smaller regions within each chapter should help you plan your itinerary. We start most town accounts with information on arrival and accommodation, followed by a tour of the sights, and finally reviews of places to eat and drink, and details of nightlife. Longer accounts also have a directory of practical listings. Each chapter concludes with **public transport** details for that region.

Contexts

Read **contexts** to get a deeper understanding of what makes Costa Rica tick. We include a brief **history** of the country, an overview of its **environment** and **wildlife**, and a detailed further reading section that reviews dozens of **books** relating to Costa Rica.

Language

The **language** section gives useful guidance for speaking Spanish, Tico-style, and vocabulary you might need on your trip, including a comprehensive menu reader. Here you'll also find a glossary of words and terms particular to Costa Rica.

small print + Index

Apart from a **full index**, which includes maps as well as places, this section covers publishing information, credits and acknowledgements, and also has our contact details in case you want to send in updates and corrections to the book – or suggestions as to how we might improve it.

Map and chapter list

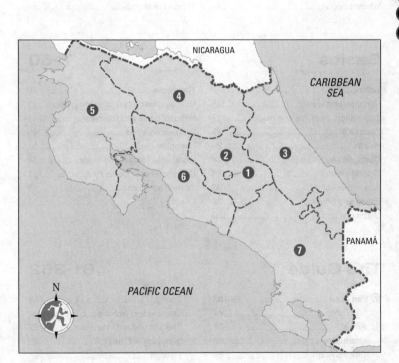

Contents

Colour section

i–xxiv

Basics

7–60

The Guide

61–362

Contexts
363–411

Language

413–424

small print and Index

437–448

CONTENTS

Basics

Basics

Getting there

The easiest way to reach Costa Rica is by air via the US; direct flights head to the capital San José daily from a number of US cities including Miami, Houston, Dallas, Atlanta, New York, Los Angeles and Chicago. Numerous air, hotel and car packages are also available, as well as a variety of tours focusing on nature expeditions, wildlife, ecology or just relaxing on the beach. Alternatively, you can travel overland from the US through Mexico and Central America, though this amounts to a major expedition in its own right.

Costa Rica has two international airports. Juan Santamaría (SJO), just outside San José, receives the majority of flights while Daniel Oduber (LIR), near the northern city of Liberia, handles some flights from the US and Canada. Although there are a few direct flights from Europe to Costa Rica, the vast majority of routes pass through the US. This is an important factor because it means having to comply with US entry requirements, even if you are merely transiting the country.

Airfares always depend on the **season**, with the highest being around July, August and December to mid-January; you'll get the best prices during the dry winter (Dec–April) and the wet summer (May–Nov). Note, too, that although prices are steepest during the Christmas period (mid-December through the first week in January) when flying from the US, in Europe this can be the cheapest time to travel. Also, flying on weekends is usually more expensive; price ranges quoted below assume midweek travel.

You can often cut costs by going through a **specialist flight agent** or a **discount agent**, who in addition to dealing with discounted flights may also offer special student and youth fares and a range of other travel-related services such as travel insurance, rail passes, car rentals, tours and the like. Booking flights well in advance, or taking advantage of Web-only offers and airline frequent-flyer programmes, can often knock a couple of hundred dollars off the price of your flight.

You may even find it cheaper to pick up a bargain **package deal** from one of the tour operators listed below or check the travel sections of the Sunday papers for the latest offers.

Booking online

Many airlines and discount travel websites offer you the opportunity to book your tickets, hotels and holiday packages online, cutting out the costs of agents and middlemen; these are worth going for, as long as you don't mind the inflexibility of non-refundable, non-changeable deals. There are some bargains to be had on auction sites too, if you're prepared to bid keenly. Almost all airlines have their own websites, offering flight tickets that can sometimes be just as cheap, and are often more flexible.

Online booking agents and travel sites

Ⓦ www.cheapflights.co.uk (in UK & Ireland), Ⓦ www.cheapflights.com (in US), Ⓦ www.cheapflights.ca (in Canada), Ⓦ www.cheapflights.com.au (in Australia). Flight deals, travel agents, plus links to other travel sites.
Ⓦ www.cheaptickets.com Discount flight specialists (US only). Also at ☎ 1-888/922-8849.
Ⓦ www.ebookers.com Efficient, easy to use flight finder, with competitive fares.
Ⓦ www.etn.nl/discount A hub of consolidator and discount agent links, maintained by the nonprofit European Travel Network.
Ⓦ www.expedia.co.uk (in UK), Ⓦ www.expedia.com (in US), Ⓦ www.expedia.ca (in Canada). Discount airfares, all-airline search engine and daily deals.
Ⓦ www.flyaow.com "Airlines of the Web" – online air travel info and reservations.

ⓦ**www.gaytravel.com** US gay travel agent, offering accommodation, cruises, tours and more. Also at ☎1-800/GAY-TRAVEL.

ⓦ**www.geocities.com/thavery2000** An extensive list of airline websites and US toll-free numbers.

ⓦ**www.hotwire.com** Bookings from the US only. Last-minute savings of up to forty percent on regular published fares. Travellers must be at least 18 and there are no refunds, transfers or changes allowed. Log-in required.

ⓦ**www.kelkoo.com** Useful Europe-only price-comparison site, checking several sources of low-cost flights (and other goods & services) according to specific criteria.

ⓦ**www.lastminute.com** (in UK), ⓦ**www .lastminute.com.au** (in Australia), ⓦ**www .lastminute.co.nz** (in New Zealand), ⓦ**www .site59.com** (in US). Good last-minute holiday package and flight-only deals.

ⓦ**www.opodo.co.uk** Popular and reliable source of low UK airfares. Owned by, and run in conjunction with, nine major European airlines.

ⓦ**www.orbitz.com** Comprehensive web travel source, with the usual flight, car hire and hotel deals but also great follow-up customer service.

ⓦ**www.priceline.co.uk** (in UK), ⓦ**www .priceline.com** (in US). Name-your-own-price website that has deals at around forty percent off standard fares.

ⓦ**www.skyauction.com** Bookings from the US only. Auctions tickets and travel packages to destinations worldwide.

ⓦ**www.travelocity.co.uk** (in UK), ⓦ**www .travelocity.com** (in US), ⓦ**www.travelocity.ca** (in Canada), ⓦ**www .zuji.com.au** (in Australia). Destination guides, hot fares and great deals for car rental, accommodation and lodging.

ⓦ**www.travelshop.com.au** Australian site offering discounted flights, packages, insurance, and online bookings. **Also on** ☎1-800/108108.

ⓦ**travel.yahoo.com** Incorporates some Rough Guides material in its coverage of destination countries and cities across the world, with information about places to eat and sleep.

ⓦ**www.travelzoo.com** Great resource for news on the latest airline sales, cruise discounts and hotel deals. Links bring you directly to the carrier's site.

From the US and Canada

Daily direct flights depart for San José from numerous cities in the US.

It takes just under three hours to fly from Miami to San José, and around three to

four hours from Houston and Dallas. Flight times from New York and Los Angeles are usually around eight hours, including plane changes.

You can fly **non-stop** to San José from Miami, Dallas or Houston. Lacsa (the Costa Rican carrier) usually offers the cheapest fares **from Miami** and **Dallas** (starting at \$400–500). Continental's flight **from Houston**, starting at around \$330, is the best value. American and Continental both fly from many US cities to Dallas, Miami or Houston to connect with the flight to Costa Rica.

The best fares **from New York** are on Continental via Houston and Lacsa via San Salvador (\$500–600), while American Airlines has a direct flight for about \$750. Continental offers the cheapest fare **from Chicago** (\$600) via Houston. **From the West coast**, the best deals are on TACA (from Los Angeles via Mexico City) and on Mexicana (from San Francisco via Mexico City); flights start at \$500–700.

There are no non-stop flights to San José from Canada. The cheapest fare **from Toronto** is on TACA's thrice-weekly service via Havana (CDN\$700-800; 6hr 45min), while American Airlines' daily flight costs only a little more, but involves a plane change in Miami. **From Montréal**, American is the best bet, with daily flights, also requiring a plane change in Miami (CDN\$820-860; 8hr 45min). The quickest and cheapest flight **from Vancouver** is on American with a change of planes in Dallas (CDN\$900; 10hr). Good deals are offered by the charter operator Air Transat, who fly weekly from Toronto to San José in high season.

Airlines

American Airlines ☎1-800/433-7300, ⓦwww .aa.com. Daily flights from Miami and Dallas to San José.

Continental Airlines ☎1-800/537-9222, ⓦwww.continental.com. Flights from Houston and Newark to San José.

Delta ☎1-800/221-1212, ⓦwww.delta.com. Flights from Atlanta to both San José and Liberia.

Grupo TACA ☎1-800/400-8222. ⓦwww.taca .com. Non-stop flights from Miami and Dallas to San José. Also direct flights from New York, LA, New Orleans, Houston, Washington DC, Chicago, Montréal and Toronto.

Iberia ☎1-800/772-4642, ⓦwww.iberia.com.
Flights from Miami to San José.

Mexicana ☎1-800/531-7921, ⓦwww.mexicana
.com. Flights from LA, San Francisco, San José
(California), Denver, San Antonio, Chicago, Newark
and Miami; all involve a plane change in Mexico City,
and sometimes a stop in Guatemala City.

Air Transat ☎1-866/847-1112, ⓦwww
.airtransat.com. Charter operator with budget flights
to San José from Toronto.

Travel agents

Airtech ☎212/219-7000, ⓦwww.airtech.com.
Standby seat broker; also deals in consolidator fares.

Educational Travel Center ☎1-800/747-5551
or 608/256-5551, ⓦwww.edtrav.com. Low-cost
fares worldwide, student/youth discount offers, car
rental and tours.

Flightcentre US ☎1-866/WORLD-51, ⓦwww
.flightcentre.us, Canada ☎1-888/WORLD-55,
ⓦwww.flightcentre.ca. Rock-bottom fares worldwide.

STA Travel US ☎1-800/329-9537, Canada
☎1-888/427-5639, ⓦwww.statravel.com.
Worldwide specialists in independent travel; also
student IDs, travel insurance, car rental, rail passes
and more.

TFI Tours ☎1-800/745-8000 or 212/736-1140,
ⓦwww.lowestairprice.com. Well-established
consolidator with a wide variety of global fares.

Tico Travel ☎1-800/493-8426, ⓦwww.ticotravel
.com. Costa Rican travel specialists who also offer
discount air fares.

Travel Avenue ☎1-800/333-3335, ⓦwww
.travelavenue.com. Full-service travel agent that
offers discounts in the form of rebates.

Travel Cuts US ☎1-800/592-CUTS, Canada
☎1-888/246-9762, ⓦwww.travelcuts.com.
Popular, long-established student-travel organization,
with worldwide offers.

Travelers Advantage ☎1-877/259-2691,
ⓦwww.travelersadvantage.com. Discount travel
club, with cash-back deals and discounted car rental.
Membership required ($1 for 3 months' trial).

Travelosophy US ☎1-800/332-2687, ⓦwww
.itravelosophy.com. Good range of discounted and
student fares worldwide.

Worldtek Travel ☎1-800/243-1723, ⓦwww
.worldtek.com. Discount travel agency for worldwide
travel.

Tour operators

Adventure Center ☎1-800/228-8747 or
510/654-1879, ⓦwww.adventurecenter.com. Trips
of 9–16 days to Costa Rican rainforests.

Adventures Abroad ☎1-800/665-3998, ⓦwww
.adventures-abroad.com. Adventure specialists,
with 1–3-week trips throughout Costa Rica and other
Central American countries.

Backroads ☎1-800/GO-ACTIVE or 510/527-
1555, ⓦwww.backroads.com. Cycling, hiking and
multi-sport tours designed for the young at heart,
with the emphasis on going at your own pace.
Accommodation ranges from campsites to luxury
hotels. Also family-friendly options and singles trips.

Concord World Travel ☎1-800/235-5222,
ⓦwww.costaricadreamin.com. Specialists in Costa
Rican travel, with guided nature tours and flight, hotel
and car packages.

Elderhostel ☎1-877/426-8056, ⓦwww
.elderhostel.org. Extensive network of educational and
activity programmes, including twelve-day nature-study
trips, birdwatching tours and two-week educational
trips studying environment and history. Participants
must be over 55 (companions may be younger).

GAP Adventures ☎1-800/465-5600, ⓦwww
.gap.ca. Two-week trekking and public-transport
trips along the coast, visiting Costa Rican rain- and
cloudforests and national parks.

Geographic Expeditions ☎1-800/777-8183
or 415/922-0448, ⓦwww.geoex.com. Adventure
travel and cultural tours, including rainforest and
river trips.

Global Exchange ☎415/255-7296, ⓦwww
.globalexchange.org. Human rights organization
offering "Reality Tours" (all subject to political stability)
to meet local activists and participate in educational
workshops. Also offer Costa Rican eco-tourism trips.

Green Tortoise Adventure Travel ☎1-800/867-
8647, ⓦwww.greentortoise.com. Inexpensive
tours (Nov–April) to off-the-beaten-track destinations
throughout Costa Rica and Central America.

Journeys International ☎1-800/255-8735
or 734/665-4407, ⓦwww.journeys-intl.com.
Prestigious, award-winning operator focusing on eco-
tourism and small-group trips, including to national
parks in Costa Rica.

Nature Expeditions International
☎1-800/869-0639, ⓦwww.naturexp.com. Small-
group expeditions led by specialists in anthropology,
biology and natural history; Costa Rican trips offer
optional lectures on the environment and eco-tourism.

REI Adventures ☎1-800/622-2236, ⓦwww.rei
.com. Climbing, cycling, hiking, cruising, paddling/
kayaking and multisport tours.

From the UK and Ireland

There are no direct flights **from the UK** to
Costa Rica but journeys can take as little as
13 hours, including changes.

Continental has flights from the UK via Houston, while American Airlines flies via Miami and United via Chicago or New York. Of the three, Continental generally has the lowest fares (around £525 in low-season, £645 in high) and offers an excellent service, with swift connections in Houston. If you can find a budget fare **to Madrid**, Iberia's direct flights to San José can fall as low as £330 return, but their routing via Miami is more time-consuming. Check the "last-minute" section of Iberia's website, ⓦwww.iberia.com, for good deals from Madrid to San José.

You can often find good fares in the classified ads of newspapers, particularly on Sundays (in London, try *Time Out*, the *Evening Standard* and free magazines like *TNT*), and on the Internet. Another cheap low-season fare from the UK is with Martinair **via Amsterdam** and Orlando or Miami (5–7 weekly) for about £440, but it's a time-consuming and inconvenient routing, with two stopovers and a total flying time of at least 18 hours.

There are no direct flights **from Ireland** to Costa Rica. Your best option is to fly via the US or Madrid, where you can connect with flights to San José (see p.10). Delta has the widest range of flights from Dublin (and several from Shannon) to New York and Atlanta, from where you can get an onward flight to San José, though you'll probably have to change planes at least once more. On Aer Lingus from Dublin and Shannon, you can get same-day connections to San José, via New York (JFK) and Mexico City. Fares from Dublin and Belfast start at around € 700.

Airlines

Aer Lingus Republic of Ireland ☎ 01/886 8888, ⓦ www.aerlingus.com. From Dublin and Shannon to JFK and Mexico City, to connect with San José flights.
American Airlines UK ☎ 0845/7789 789, Republic of Ireland ☎ 01/602 0550, ⓦ www.aa.com. Flights from the UK and Ireland to Costa Rica, with a change in Miami.
British Airways UK ☎ 0870/850 9850, Republic of Ireland ☎ 1-800/626 747, ⓦ www.ba.com. Flights from the UK and Ireland to the US. Connections in Dallas and Miami with American Airlines flights to San José.

British Midland UK ☎ 0345/554 554, Dublin ☎ 01/283 8833, ⓦ www.flybmi.com. Low-cost transatlantic fares from Britain and Ireland.
Continental Airlines UK ☎ 0845/607 6760, Republic of Ireland ☎ 1-890/925 252, ⓦ www.continental.com. From the UK and Ireland to Costa Rica, with a change in Houston.
Delta Belfast ☎ 028/9048 0526, Dublin ☎ 01/407 316 ⓦ www.delta.com. Flights from Dublin and Shannon to Atlanta, with connections to San José.
Iberia UK ☎ 0845/601 2854, Republic of Ireland ☎ 01/407 3017, ⓦ www.iberiaairlines.co.uk. From the UK and Ireland via Madrid and Miami.
Martinair UK ☎ 0870/507 4074, ⓦ www.klm.com. Flights from the UK via Amsterdam and Orlando or Miami.
United Airlines UK ☎ 0845/844 4777, ⓦ www.unitedairlines.co.uk. From the UK and Ireland with a change in Chicago or New York.

Travel Agents

Flightbookers ☎ 020/7757 2000, ⓦ www.flightbookers.net. Low fares on an extensive range of scheduled flights.
Journey Latin America ☎ 020/8747 3108, ⓦ www.journeylatinamerica.co.uk. Latin American specialists, adept at arranging unusual itineraries at competitive fares. They also offer tours (see below).
North South Travel UK ☎ 01245/608 291, ⓦ www.northsouthtravel.co.uk. Friendly, competitive travel agency, offering discounted fares worldwide. Profits are used to support projects in the developing world, especially the promotion of sustainable tourism.
STA Travel UK ☎ 0870/160 0599, ⓦ www.statravel.co.uk. Worldwide specialists in low-cost flights, overland and holiday deals. Good discounts for students and under-26s.
Trailfinders UK ☎ 020/7938 3939, ⓦ www.trailfinders.com, Ireland ☎ 01/677-7888, ⓦ www.trailfinders.ie. One of the best-informed and most efficient agents for independent travellers.

Tour Operators

Exodus ☎ 020/8675 5550, ⓦ www.exodus.co.uk. Experienced adventure-tour operators offering a range of Central American itineraries, including several two-week tours of Costa Rica.
Explore Worldwide ☎ 01252/760 000, brochure requests ☎ 01252/760 100, ⓦ www.explore.co.uk. Competitively priced range of hotel-based tours (14–21 days) in Central America.
Journey Latin America ☎ 020/8747 8315, ⓕ 8742 1312, ⓦ www.journeylatinamerica.co.uk.

Specialist in flights, packages and adventurous, tailor-made trips to Latin America, including two 11-day Costa Rica tours.

Kumuka Expeditions UK ☎0800/068 8855, ⓦwww.kumuka.co.uk. Independent tour operator specializing in overland expeditions, as well as local and private transport tours.

Maxwell's Travel Dublin ☎01/677 9479, ⓕ679 3948. Very experienced Latin American specialist, and the Irish agent for many tour operators.

Reef and Rainforest Tours ☎01803/866 965, ⓕ865 916, ⓦwww.reefandrainforest.co.uk. Eco-tours and "research programmes" on which you can work with scientists, collecting data, photographing animals and the like. The Costa Rican programme includes a humpback whale research project off the Osa Peninsula, plus birding, natural history and adventure tours.

South American Experience ☎020/7976 5511, ⓕ7976 6908, ⓦwww.southamericanexperience. co.uk. Tailor-made itineraries of Latin America – the 19-day tour to Costa Rica takes in San José, Manuel Antonio, Tortuguero, Volcán Poás and Monteverde. Good-value flights too, including tickets with multiple stopovers.

Sunvil Holidays ☎020/8757 4747, ⓦwww .sunvil.co.uk. Flexible fly-drive itineraries, with accommodation in a number of areas including Sámara and Nosara.

The Adventure Company ☎0870/794 1009, ⓦwww.adventurecompany.co.uk. Hotel-based tours for small groups throughout Central America.

Trips Worldwide ☎0117/987 2626, ⓕ987 2627, ⓦwww.tripsworldwide.co.uk. Tailor-made tours to Central America, and particularly strong on Costa Rica, with prices to suit all budgets.

USIT Northern Ireland ☎028/9032 7111, ⓦwww .usitnow.com, Republic of Ireland ☎0818/200 020, ⓦwww.usit.ie. Specialists in student, youth and independent travel – flights, trains, study tours, TEFL, visas and more.

Wildlife Encounters UK ☎01737/218 802, ⓦwww.wildlife-encounters.co.uk. Top-rated wildlife-watching tours around the world, including whale-watching tours with dolphins.

Wildlife Worldwide UK ☎020/8667 9158, ⓦwww.wildlifeworldwide.com. Tailor-made trips for wildlife and wilderness enthusiasts.

Flights from Australia and New Zealand

There are no direct flights from Australia or New Zealand to Costa Rica – the quickest and easiest option is to fly via the US. Note that it's best to book several weeks ahead.

From Australia, the cheapest fares **to San José** are via LA on Air New Zealand–TACA, or with Qantas/Air New Zealand and Continental via LA and Houston (both from around AUS$2400/2900 low/high season). American Airlines' fares to San José via LA are higher (AUS$2699/3150 low/high season). If you only want a ticket **to LA**, the cheapest fares are on United Airlines, Qantas and Air New Zealand (AUS$1400/2499 in low/high season). Air New Zealand can get you **to Mexico City** for AUS$2500–3000; Qantas and United Airlines' fares are more expensive at AUS$2800–3250.

Fares are higher travelling **via Asia,** but include an overnight stop in the carrier's home city, with the best deals on All Nippon Airways (ANA) via Osaka, and Korean Air-lines via Seoul (AUS$1429–1899). The best-value flights to Mexico City are with JAL (AUS$1529–1999), with an overnight stop in Tokyo. Fares from all eastern Australian cities are generally the same; fares from Perth and Darwin are about AUS$200 more.

From New Zealand, as from Australia, the best through-tickets **to San José** are via LA on Air New Zealand–TACA, or with Qantas/ Air New Zealand and Continental via LA and Houston (both from around NZ$2600/3300 low/high season). American Airlines' fares to San José via LA are slightly higher (NZ$2850/3300 low/high season). If you just want a flight **to LA**, the cheapest are on Qantas (NZ$1700–2800), Air New Zealand (NZ$2000–2800), United Airlines (NZ$2000–2800), and American Airlines (NZ$2000–2800). All these airlines also fly **to Mexico City** (NZ$2500–3200). **Via Asia** the best deals to LA are on Korean Air via Seoul (NZ$2200–2800), and to LA and Mexico City on JAL via Tokyo or Osaka (NZ$2000–2800). All the above fares are from Auckland; expect to pay an extra NZ$150 for Christchurch and Wellington departures. Flight Centre and STA Travel generally offer the lowest fares; it's also worth checking ⓦwww.travel.com .au, ⓦwww.travelforless.co.nz and ⓦwww .sydneytravel.com for discounted fares.

Airlines

Air New Zealand Australia ☎13 24 76, ⓦwww .airnz.com.au, New Zealand ☎0800/737 000,

Ⓦ www.airnz.co.nz. Daily flights from Sydney, Brisbane, Melbourne and Adelaide to LA, either direct or via Honolulu, Tonga, Fiji or Papeete; with onward connections to San José on TACA International or via Houston on Continental Airlines.

All Nippon Airways Australia ☎ 1800/001 126 or 02/9367 6711 (no NZ office), Ⓦ www.fly-ana.com. Several flights weekly from Brisbane and Sydney to Los Angeles, with an overnight stop in Osaka included in the fare.

American Airlines Australia ☎ 1300/130 757, New Zealand ☎ 0800/887 997, Ⓦ www.aa.com.

Continental Airlines Australia ☎ 1300/361 400, New Zealand ☎ 09/308 3350, Ⓦ www.continental. com.Onward connections from LA via Houston to San José.

JAL (Japan Airlines) Australia ☎ 02/9272 1111, New Zealand ☎ 09/379 9906, Ⓦ www.jal.com. Several flights weekly from Sydney, Brisbane, Cairns and Auckland to LA and Mexico City, with an overnight stopover in either Tokyo or Osaka included in the fare.

Korean Air Australia ☎ 02/9262 6000, New Zealand ☎ 09/914 2000, Ⓦ www.koreanair.com .au. Several flights weekly from Sydney, Brisbane and Auckland to LA, with an overnight stop in Seoul included in the fare.

Qantas Australia ☎ 13 13 13, New Zealand ☎ 0800/808 767 or 09/357-8900, Ⓦ www.qantas .com. Daily flights to LA from major Australian and New Zealand cities, with onward connections to San José on Continental via Houston or direct on TACA International.

United Airlines Australia ☎ 13 17 77, Ⓦ www .united.com. Daily direct flights to LA from Sydney, Melbourne and Auckland, with onward connections to San José.

Travel agents

Anywhere Travel Australia ☎ 02/9663 0411, Ⓦ www.anywheretravel.com.au. Discount flight agent offering discounted flights, as well as accommodation, tours and car rental.

Holiday Shoppe New Zealand ☎ 0800/808 480, Ⓦ www.holidayshoppe.co.nz. Excellent deals on flights and holidays.

OTC Australia ☎ 1300/855 118, Ⓦ www.otctravel .com.au. Deals on flights and hotels.

Flight Centre Australia ☎ 13 31 33, Ⓦ www .flightcentre.com.au, New Zealand ☎ 0800 243 544, Ⓦ www.flightcentre.co.nz. Rock-bottom fares worldwide.

STA Travel Australia ☎ 1300/733 035, New Zealand ☎ 0508/782 872, Ⓦ www.statravel.com. Worldwide specialists in low-cost flights, overlands

and holiday deals. Good discounts for students and under-26s.

Student Uni Travel Australia ☎ 02/9232 8444, Ⓦ www.sut.com.au, New Zealand ☎ 09/379 4224, Ⓦ www.sut.co.nz. Great deals for students.

Thomas Cook Australia: Sydney ☎ 02/9231 2877, Melbourne ☎ 03/9282 0222, Ⓦ www .thomascook.com.au plus branches nationwide (for the location of your nearest branch call ☎ 131 771; for telesales call ☎ 1800/801 002); New Zealand: Auckland ☎ 09/379 3920, Ⓦ www.thomascook .co.nz. Low-cost flights, plus tours, accommodation and travellers' cheques.

Trailfinders Australia ☎ 02/9247 7666, Ⓦ www .trailfinders.com.au. One of the best-informed and most efficient agents for independent travellers.

USIT Beyond ☎ 09/379 4224 or 0800/788 336, Ⓦ www.usitbeyond.co.nz, plus branches nationwide. Student/youth travel specialists.

Tour operators

Adventure Associates Australia ☎ 02/9389 7466, Ⓦ www.adventureassociates.com.au. Escorted small-group tours from San José, including a seven-day bus, boat and hiking tour through the rainforests of Corcovado National Park and the Isla del Caño. They also arrange independent trekking, mountain-biking, whitewater rafting, canal trips and sports-fishing, plus city stopovers and cruises in and around Costa Rica.

Adventure Specialists Australia ☎ 02/9261 2927 or 1-800/634 465. Excellent agency offering adventure trips (8–22 days) from San José, including whitewater rafting, rainforest hikes, national park visits and horse-riding.

The Adventure Travel Company New Zealand ☎ 09/379 9755, Ⓔ advakl@hot.co.nz. Wide selection of adventure tours throughout Central America.

Birding Worldwide Australia ☎ 03/9899 9303, Ⓦ www.birdingworldwide.com.au. Three-week birdwatching tours offer the chance to discover some of Costa Rica's 850 species of birds.

Contours Australia ☎ 03/9670 6900 or 1800/331 378, Ⓦ www.contourstravel.com.au. Specialists in stopovers in San José and tours to the Caribbean and Central America.

Exodus Australia ☎ 03/9662 2700 & 1300/655 433, Ⓦ www.peregrine.net.au plus branches in Brisbane, Sydney, Adelaide and Perth. Eight-week overland tours trucking between Mexico City and Panamá City; fourteen-day coast-to-coast off-road cycling adventures through Costa Rica's jungles; plus wildlife-spotting and rainforest boat tours.

Intrepid Travel Australia ☎ 1300/360 667 or 03/9473 2626, Ⓦ www.intrepidtravel.com.

Small-group tours with the emphasis on cross-cultural contact and low-impact tourism.
Kumuka Expeditions Australia ☎ 1800/804 277 or 02/9279 0491, ⓦ www.kumuka.com. Independent tour operator specializing in overland expeditions, as well as local and private transport tours.
Wiltrans Australia ☎ 02/9255 0899, ⓦ www .maupintour.com. Agents for Maupin, who offer all-inclusive seven-day guided tours from San José (Oct–July) including rafting, rainforest hikes through Carara Reserve and a descent of Volcán Irazú by bike.

Overland to Costa Rica

Costa Rica's international bus company, Ticabus (ⓦ www.ticabus.com), runs a good **overland bus** service between Guatemala, Honduras, El Salvador, Nicaragua and Costa Rica and on south into Panamá.

Ticabus leaves **Guatemala City** daily for San José at 1pm. It's a two-and-a-half-day trip, entailing nights (at your own expense) in San Salvador and Managua. A one-way fare is $44. From **Tegucigalpa** in Honduras, Ticabus leaves daily at 9.15am for San José ($31), arriving 48 hours later (with an overnight stop in **Managua**, again at your own expense). From Managua, you can also get a Nicaraguan SIRCA bus (daily at 6am) or, more comfortably, a Ticabus (daily at 5.45am & 7am); in both cases the journey takes ten hours ($11). Additionally, a deluxe service run by Transnica leaves Managua daily at 7am, taking only eight hours. From Panamá City, a Ticabus leaves daily at 11am, getting to San José at a rather inconvenient 3am ($25).

The main northern border crossing with Nicaragua is at Peñas Blancas (see p.241) on the Interamericana Highway. Further east, another crossing at Los Chiles (see p.198) involves a boat trip (and usually an overnight stop to catch it in the morning) to/from San Carlos on the shores of Lake Nicaragua, although a bridge is planned. The main route south to and from Panamá is again on the Interamericana, at Paso Canoas (see p.361). On the Caribbean coast, Sixaola is a smaller crossing, while in the southern highlands, two little used routes link San Vito with the border towns of Río Sereno and Cañas Gordas.

Red tape and visas

Citizens of the US, Canada, the UK and most Western European countries can obtain a ninety-day entry stamp for Costa Rica without needing a visa. Citizens of Australia, New Zealand and Ireland do not need a visa either, but are only issued a thirty-day entrance stamp. Whatever your nationality, you must in theory show your passport, a valid onward (or return) air or bus ticket, a visa for your next country (if applicable) and proof of "sufficient funds" (around $400 per month), but if you arrive by air the last is rarely asked for. Most other nationalities need a visa; always check first with a Costa Rican consulate concerning current regulations. The website www.rree.go.cr gives up-to-date requirements. For most nationalities, a thirty-day visa will cost about $25.

Your **entrance stamp** is very important: no matter where you arrive, make sure you get it. You have to carry your passport (or a photocopy) with you at all times in Costa Rica. If you are asked for it and cannot produce it, you may well be detained and fined.

The easiest way to **extend your entry permit** is to leave Costa Rica for 72 hours – to Panamá or Nicaragua, say – and then re-enter, fulfilling the same requirements as on your original trip. You should, although it is at the discretion of the immigration officer, be given another ninety- or thirty-day stamp. If you prefer not to leave the country, you can apply for a permit or visa extension at the **Departamento de Migración** in San José (see p.98; ℮dmigracion@ns .migracion.go.cr), a time-consuming and often costly business. You'll need to bring all relevant documents – passport and three photographs, onward air or bus ticket – as well as proof of funds (credit cards and/or travellers' cheques). If you do not have a ticket out of Costa Rica you may have to buy one in order to get your extension. Bus tickets are more easily refunded than air tickets; some airlines refuse to cash in onward tickets unless you can produce or buy another one out of the country. Note that you will pay approximately ten percent tax on all air tickets bought in Costa Rica.

If, for whatever reason, you overstay your ninety- or thirty-day limit, you must get an **exit visa** in order to be allowed to leave the country. This involves going to the Departamento de Migración in San José with your passport and onward ticket. The exit visa, normally granted within one to three days, gives you thirty days in which to leave the country and costs $40; you will also have to pay overstayers' fees of $1.50 per month. These fees have been subject to abrupt change (always upwards) recently, so make sure you ask exactly how much you will be required to pay and ensure that you have sufficient funds – either in colones or dollars – to fork out when you leave. Any reputable tour operator (see p.32) should be able to help you through the red tape, although this will cost a further $15–20.

Costa Rica has no such thing as a working holiday visa. If you plan to stay for a long period, you need a **Resident's Permit**, which is extremely difficult to get a hold of – you'll need to appoint a Costa Rican resident (friend, family or a lawyer) to act on your behalf, fill in stacks of paperwork and then wait as long as six months for your application to be processed. Be warned that the Costa Rican government is currently cracking down heavily on illegal residents; without a permit you risk being deported and not allowed to re-enter the country for ten years. If you're **studying**, or on a **volunteer programme** (see p.54), the organization or school may sort out visas for you; check in advance. If you are planning to live or work in Costa Rica, the Residents' Association of Costa Rica (℡233-8068, ℗www.casacanada.net/arcr) is an invaluable first point of contact.

Costa Rica's stringent regulations governing **the stay of children** were put in place to counteract the number of people bringing children into the country from the US to defy custody arrangements or trials. Officially, if one parent, rather than both, is travelling with their child, that child is not permitted to remain in Costa Rica for more than thirty days unless the travelling parent asks permission, in person, supported by the other parent's request in writing, from the Costa Rican Child Protection Agency, the Patronato Nacional de la Infancia, C 19, Av 6, San José (in the Tribunales de la Justicía complex). That said, the Costa Rican authorities take a very dim view of this method, preferring that both parents are with the child when permission to stay is requested. It becomes even more tricky if a child is coming to Costa Rica without his or her parents: in this case you have to contact the Costa Rican embassy or consulate in your home country to get a notarized permit.

Costa Rican embassies and consulates abroad

Australia Consulate-General, 11/30 Clarence St, Sydney, NSW 2000 ℡02/9261 1177.
Canada 325 Dalhousie St, Suite 407, Ottawa, Ontario, K1N 7G2 ℡613/562-2855, ℗www .costaricaembassy.com.
Ireland no representation; contact the UK embassy
New Zealand no representation; contact the Australian consulate-general.
UK 14 Lancaster Gate, London W2 3LH ℡020/7706 8844, ℮costaricanembassy @btconnect.com.
US 2112 S St NW, Washington, DC 20008 ℡202/234-2945, ℗www.costarica-embassy.org.

Information, websites and maps

Costa Rica has no tourist office in North America, the UK or Australasia. US and Canadian residents can call a toll-free tourist information hotline (☎1-800/343-6332), which is answered by English-speaking ICT (see p.68) staff in San José.

Information

The best source of information about Costa Rica is the **Instituto Costarricense de Turismo** (ICT), Apartado 777, San José 1000, Costa Rica (☎506/223-1733 or 223-1090, ☏223-5452, ⓦwww.visitcostarica.com). You can write to them from abroad for information, although it may take awhile to receive a reply, and you'll probably receive pretty but not particularly informative glossy pamphlets and brochures.

You're better off going in person to the ICT office (see p.68), located in the unprepossessing bunker underneath the Plaza de la Cultura in central San José, where the friendly bilingual staff will do their best to answer any queries you may have. On request, they'll give you a free city map plus a very useful comprehensive bus timetable with recent additions and changes corrected on the spot. The office can also provide a list of museums and their opening hours, details of many San José restaurants and bars as well as a brochure produced by the *Cámara Costaricense de Hoteles* (Costa Rican Hotel Association) with contact details for many of the country's hotels. The small ICT booths at the three main entry points to the country – in San José's Santamaría International Airport, Peñas Blancas on the Nicaraguan border and Paso Canoas on the Panamanian border – can provide the map and hotel brochure but not the timetables. Otherwise, there are no official tourist offices offering independent (unbiased) information outside the capital. As a rule you have to rely on locally run initiatives, often set up by a small business association or the chamber of commerce, or hotels and tourist agencies.

A number of Costa Rican **tour operators**, based in San José, can offer information and guidance when planning a trip around the country, though these may not be as objective as they could be; see p.32 for details.

Useful websites

ⓦ**www.centralamerica.com** Costa Rica-based travel specialists, also with information on Central America.

ⓦ**www.apc.org** Website of the Association of Progressive Communication (APC), this deals with issues relating to global development and human rights.

ⓦ**www.costaricabureau.com** The official view – the website of the Costa Rican Tourism and Travel Bureau.

ⓦ**www.costaricanet.net** Links to thousands of Costa Rican websites including sites set up by Costa Rica aficionados in the US.

ⓦ**www.costaricatourism.co.cr** Website of the Costa Rican National Chamber of Commerce.

ⓦ**www.1costaricalink.com** Huge tourist web resource.

ⓦ**www.infocostarica.com** Chat forum and hotel reservation service.

ⓦ**www.nacion.co.cr** Costa Rica's leading Spanish language daily newspaper online.

ⓦ**www.terra.co.cr** Spanish language site – good source of listings for upcoming events, exhibitions and more.

ⓦ**www.ticotimes.net** Weekly news about Costa Rica (in English).

ⓦ**www.tourismconcern.org.uk** Devoted to promoting low-impact, eco-tourism.

ⓦ**www.roughguides.com** Site contains complete text from the guidebooks, links to travel journals and photos as well as a catalogue of the guides and maps.

Note that many Costa Rican hotels and businesses now have email. If you don't know their email address, it's worth trying the establishment's name followed by @racsa.co.cr or @sol.racsa.co.cr – the most common suffixes for email addresses in Costa Rica. Beware real-estate advertisements on the Internet. Costa Rica is property scam heaven, and there are lots of shady deals around; if you have any intention of buying property in the country, wait until you arrive.

Maps

The **maps** dished out by Costa Rican embassies and the ICT are basic and somewhat out-of-date; it's best to arm yourself with general maps before you go. The best **road map**, a colourful spread with all the major routes and national parks, is the *Costa Rica Road Map* (1:650,000; Berndtson & Berndtson), available from map stores or by mail from Hauptstr. 1a, D-82256 Fürstenfeldbruck, Germany (℉49/8141 16280). Other maps with clearly marked contour details, gas stations, national parks and roads include Costa Rica (1:500,000) available from World Wide Books and Maps, and the Globetrotter Travel Map – Costa Rica (1:470,000), which also has very useful city centre maps for San José, Alajuela, Cartago and Heredia on the reverse. It's available from New Holland Publishers, Garfield House, 86–88 Edgware Road, London W2 2EA, UK (℡44(0)20 7724 7773). Road and park markings are less distinct on Nelles Verlag's large Central America Map (1:900,000), but it's handy if you are travelling throughout the isthmus. Buy it at specialist travel or map stores or write direct to Nelles Verlag, Schleissheimer Str. 371b, D-80935 München, Germany.

In Costa Rica, it's a good idea to go to one of San José's two big downtown bookstores, Librería Universal or Librería Lehmann (see p.97) and look through their stock of **maps**, which are contoured and show major topographical features like river crossings and high-tide marks. You buy them in sections; each costs about $2. You can also go to the government maps bureau, the **Instituto Geográfico Nacional**, in San José at Av 20, C 5/7, which sells more lavishly detailed colour maps of specific areas of the country.

Considering it's such a popular hiking destination, there are surprisingly few good maps of Costa Rica's **national parks**. Those given out at ranger stations are very general; your best bet is to get a hold of the book *Parques Nacionales de Costa Rica/National*

Parks of Costa Rica (separate editions in Spanish and English), published by the National Parks Service and usually available in San José bookshops such as Librería Universal or Librería Lehmann. Although rather cramped, not too detailed and of little practical use for walking the trails, these maps (of all the parks currently in existence) do at least show contours and give a general idea of the terrain, the animals you might see and the annual rainfall.

Map outlets

In the US and Canada

Book Passage 51 Tamal Vista Blvd, Corte Madera, CA 94925 and in the historic San Francisco Ferry Building ℡1-800/999-7909 or 415/927-0960, ⓦwww.bookpassage.com.

Distant Lands 56 S Raymond Ave, Pasadena, CA 91105 ℡1-800/310-3220, ⓦwww.distantlands .com.

Globe Corner Bookstore 28 Church St, Cambridge, MA 02138 ℡1-800/358-6013, ⓦwww.globecorner.com.

Longitude Books 115 W 30th St #1206, New York, NY 10001 ℡1-800/342-2164, ⓦwww .longitudebooks.com.

Map Town 400 5 Ave SW #100, Calgary, AB, T2P 0L6 ℡1-877/921-6277 or 403/266-2241, ⓦwww.maptown.com.

Rand McNally ℡1-800/333-0136, ⓦwww .randmcnally.com. Thirty stores around the US; check the website for nearest location.

Travel Bug Bookstore 3065 W Broadway, Vancouver, BC, V6K 2G9 ℡604/737-1122, ⓦwww .travelbugbooks.ca.

Wide World Books and Maps 4411A Wallingford Ave N, Seattle, WA 98103 ℡206/634-3453, ⓦwww.travelbooksandmaps.com.

World of Maps 1235 Wellington St, Ottawa, ON, K1Y 3A3 ℡1-800/214-8524 or 613/724-6776, ⓦwww.worldofmaps.com.

World Wide Books and Maps 736 Granville St, Vancouver, BC, V6Z 1E4 ℡604/687-3320.

In the UK and Ireland

Stanfords 12–14 Long Acre, London WC2E 9LP ℡020/7836 1321, ⓦwww.stanfords.co.uk. Also at 39 Spring Gardens, Manchester ℡0161/831 0250, and 29 Corn St, Bristol ℡0117/929 9966.

Blackwell's Map Centre 50 Broad St, Oxford OX1 3BQ ℡01865/793 550, ⓦwww.maps .blackwell.co.uk. Branches in Bristol, Cambridge,

Cardiff, Leeds, Liverpool, Newcastle, Reading and Sheffield.

John Smith and Sons University Avenue, Glasgow G12 8PP ☎0141/339 1463, ⓦwww .johnsmith.co.uk.

The Map Shop 30a Belvoir St, Leicester LE1 6QH ☎0116/247 1400, ⓦwww.mapshopleicester.co.uk.

National Map Centre 22–24 Caxton St, London SW1H 0QU ☎020/7222 2466, ⓦwww.mapsnmc .co.uk. In Ireland: 34 Aungier St, Dublin ☎01/476 0471, ⓦwww.mapcentre.ie.

The Travel Bookshop 13–15 Blenheim Crescent, London W11 2EE ☎020/7229 5260, ⓦwww .thetravelbookshop.co.uk.

Traveller 55 Grey St, Newcastle-upon-Tyne NE1 6EF ☎0191/261 5622, ⓦwww.newtraveller.com.

In Australia and New Zealand

Map Centre ⓦwww.mapcentre.co.nz.
Mapland (Australia) 372 Little Bourke St, Melbourne ☎03/9670 4383, ⓦwww.mapland .com.au.
Map Shop (Australia) 6–10 Peel St, Adelaide ☎08/8231 2033, ⓦwww.mapshop.net.au.
Map World (Australia) 371 Pitt St, Sydney ☎02/9261-3601, ⓦwww.mapworld.net.au. Also at 900 Hay St, Perth ☎08/9322 5733, Jolimont Centre, Canberra ☎02/6230 4097 and 1981 Logan Road, Brisbane ☎07/3349 6633.
Map World (New Zealand) 173 Gloucester St, Christchurch ☎0800/627 967, ⓦwww.mapworld .co.nz.

Insurance

It's always sensible to take out an insurance policy before travelling. Before paying for a new one, however, it's worth checking whether you are already covered: some **all-risks home insurance policies** may cover your possessions when overseas, and many private medical schemes include cover when abroad. In Canada, **provincial health plans** usually provide partial cover for medical mishaps overseas, while holders of official student/teacher/youth cards in Canada and the US are entitled to meagre accident coverage and hospital in-patient benefits. Students will often find that their student health coverage extends during the vacations and for one term beyond the date of last enrolment.

After checking out the possibilities above, you might want to contact a **specialist travel insurance** company, or consider the travel insurance deal we offer (see p.20). A typical travel insurance policy usually provides cover for the loss of baggage, tickets and – up to a certain limit – cash or cheques, as well as cancellation or curtailment of your journey. Most exclude so-called **dangerous sports** unless an extra premium is paid: in Costa Rica this can mean scuba-diving, whitewater rafting, windsurfing and trekking, though probably not kayaking or jeep safaris. Many policies can be chopped and changed to exclude coverage you don't need – for example, sickness and accident benefits can often be excluded or included at will. If you do take **medical coverage**, ascertain whether benefits will be paid as treatment proceeds or only after you return home, and if there is a **24-hour medical emergency number**. When **securing baggage** cover, make sure that the per-article limit – typically under £500/$750 and sometimes as little as £250/$400 – will cover your most valuable possession. If you need **to make a claim**, you should keep receipts for medicines and medical treatment, and in the event you have anything stolen, you must obtain an official statement from the police.

Rough Guides travel insurance

Rough Guides Ltd offers a low-cost **travel insurance** policy, especially customized for our statistically low-risk readers by a leading British broker, provided by the American International Group (AIG) and registered with the British regulatory body, GISC (the General Insurance Standards Council). There are five main Rough Guides insurance plans: **No Frills** for the bare minimum for secure travel; **Essential**, which provides decent all-round cover; **Premier** for comprehensive cover with a wide range of benefits; **Extended Stay** for cover lasting four months to a year; and **Annual multi-trip**, a cost-effective way of getting Premier cover if you travel more than once a year. Premier, Annual Multi-Trip and Extended Stay policies can be supplemented by a "Hazardous Pursuits Extension" if you plan to indulge in sports considered dangerous, such as scuba-diving or trekking. For a policy quote, call the Rough Guides Insurance Line: toll-free in the UK ☏0800/015 09 06 or ☏+44 1392 314 665 from elsewhere. Alternatively, get an online quote at www .roughguides.com/insurance.

Health

Health-wise, travelling in Costa Rica is generally very safe. Food tends to be hygienically prepared, so bugs and upsets are normally limited to the usual "travellers' tummy". Water supplies in most places are clean and bacteria-free, and outbreaks of serious infectious diseases such as cholera are rare.

In general, as in the rest of Latin America, it tends to be local people, often poor or without proper sanitation or access to health care, who contract infectious diseases. If you do fall ill or have an accident, medical treatment in Costa Rica is very good but very expensive: extensive health insurance is a must.

Inoculations

No compulsory **inoculations** are required before you enter Costa Rica unless you're traveling from a country that has Yellow Fever, such as Colombia, in which case you must be able to produce a current inoculation certificate. You may, however, want to make sure that your polio, typhoid and hepatitis A and B jabs are up-to-date, though none of the diseases is a major risk. Rabies, a potentially fatal illness, should be taken very seriously. There is a vaccine comprising a course of three injections that has to be started at least a month before departure and which is effective for two years – though it's expensive and serves only to shorten the course of treatment you need. If you're not vaccinated, stay away from dogs, monkeys and any other potentially biting or scratching animals. If you do get scratched or bitten, wash the wound at once, with alcohol if possible, and seek medical help immediately.

The sun

Costa Rica is just 8°–11° north of the Equator, which means a blazing-hot sun directly overhead. To guard against **sunburn** take at least factor-15 sunscreen and a good hat, and wear both even on slightly overcast days, especially in coastal areas. Even in places at higher altitudes where it does not feel excessively hot, such

A traveller's first-aid kit

Among the items you might want to carry with you, especially if you're planning to go hiking, are:

- Antiseptic cream
- Plasters/Band-Aids
- Imodium (Lomotil) for emergency diarrhoea treatment
- Paracetamol/aspirin
- Rehydration sachets
- Calamine lotion
- Hypodermic needles and sterilized skin wipes
- Iodine soap for washing cuts (guards against humidity-encouraged infections)
- Insect repellent
- Sulphur powder (fights the sand fleas/chiggers that are ubiquitous in Costa Rica's beach areas)

Note that most of Costa Rica's major towns have well-stocked pharmacies (*farmacias* or *boticas*) where trained pharmacists are licensed to dispense a wide range of drugs (essentially anything other than antibiotics or psychotropic drugs for which you'll need a prescription). Pharmacies often offer competitive prices because they tend to stock generic rather than name-brand drugs.

as San José and the surrounding Valle Central, you should protect yourself. **Dehydration** is another possible problem, so keep your fluid level up, and take rehydration salts (Gastrolyte is readily available). **Diarrhoea** can be brought on by too much sun and heat sickness. It's a good idea to bring an over-the-counter remedy like Lomotil from home – it should only be taken for short periods, however, as extensive use leads to constipation, which is equally uncomfortable and inconvenient while travelling.

Drinking water

The only areas of Costa Rica where it's best not to drink the tap water (or ice cubes, or drinks made with tap water) are the port cities of **Limón and Puntarenas**. Bottled water is available in these towns; drink from these and stick with known brands, even if they are more expensive. Though you'll be safe drinking tap water elsewhere in the country, it is possible to pick up **giardia**, a bacterium that causes stomach upset and diarrhoea, by drinking out of streams and rivers – campers should pick up their water supplies from the national parks waterspouts, where it's been treated for drinking.

The time-honoured method of **boiling** will effectively sterilize water, although it will not remove unpleasant tastes. A minimum boiling

time of five minutes (longer at higher altitudes) is sufficient to kill micro-organisms. Boiling water is not always convenient, however, as it is time-consuming and requires supplies of fuel or a travel kettle and power source. **Chemical sterilization** can be carried out using either chlorine or iodine tablets or a tincture of iodine liquid. When using tablets it is essential to follow the manufacturer's dosage and contact time. Tincture of iodine is better; add a couple of drops to one litre of water and leave to stand for twenty minutes. **Pregnant women** or people with **thyroid problems** should consult their doctor before using iodine sterilizing tablets or iodine-based purifiers. Inexpensive iodine removal filters are recommended if treated water is being used continuously for more than a month or if it is being given to babies.

Malaria and dengue fever

Although some sources of information – including perhaps your GP – will tell you that you don't need to worry about **malaria** in Costa Rica, it is a risk, although admittedly very small. Around 800 cases of malaria are reported annually, with about half of these being tourists. If you want to make absolutely sure of not contracting the illness, and intend to travel extensively anywhere on the **Caribbean coast**, especially in Puerto Limón and south towards Cahuita and Puerto Viejo, you should take a course of prophylactics (usually chloroquine rather than mefloquine), available from your doctor or clinic.

Dengue fever is perhaps more of a concern, although by no means a major one. Despite regular scare stories in the local papers about outbreaks in San José's suburbs and the area immediately south of Puerto Limón, there are fewer than a thousand reported cases a year, most of which occur during the rainy season when the mosquito population is at its height. The symptoms are similar to malaria, but with extreme aches and pains in the bones and joints, along with fever and dizziness. The only cure for dengue fever is rest and painkillers, and the only way to avoid it is to make sure you don't get bitten by mosquitos. On rare occasions, the illness may develop potentially fatal complications, though this usually only affects people who have caught the disease more than once.

Snakes

Snakes abound in Costa Rica, but the risk of being **bitten** is incredibly small – there has been no instance of a tourist receiving a fatal bite in recent years. Most of the victims of Costa Rica's more venomous snakes are field labourers who do not have time or the resources to get to a hospital. Just in case, however, travellers hiking off the beaten track may want to take specific **antivenins** plus sterile hypodermic needles. If you're worried, you can buy antivenin at the University of Costa Rica's snake farm in Coronado, outside San José, where herpetologists (people who study snakes) are glad to talk to visitors about precautions.

If you have no antivenin and are unlucky enough to get bitten, the usual advice is to catch or kill the specimen for identification (since administering the wrong antivenin can cause death), though in practice it's usually impossible to do this – indeed it's probably best not to try, especially if faced with one of the larger vipers.

In general, **prevention** is better than cure. As a rule of thumb, you should approach rainforest cover and grassy uplands – the kind of terrain you find in Guanacaste and the Nicoya Peninsula – with caution. Always watch where you put your feet and, if you need to hold something to keep your balance, make sure the "vine" you're grabbing isn't, in fact, a surprised snake. Be particularly wary at dawn or dusk – before 5.30am or after 6pm. Many snakes start moving as early as 4.30pm, particularly in dense cloudforest cover. In addition, be careful in "sunspots", places in dense rainforest cover where the sun penetrates through to the ground or to a tree; snakes like to hang out there, absorbing the warmth. Above all, though, don't be too alarmed. Thousands of tourists troop through Costa Rica's rainforests and grasslands each year without encountering a single snake.

HIV and AIDS

HIV and **AIDS** (in Spanish, SIDA) is present in the country, but isn't prevalent (travelling around you'll see government-sponsored educational directives, such as billboards aimed at persuading husbands to "be faithful to your wife and save both your lives"). That said, the same common-sense rules apply here as all over the world: sex without a condom, especially in some of the popular beach towns, is a serious health risk. **Condoms** sold in Costa Rica are not of the quality you find at home; best bring them with you. Though hospitals and clinics in Costa Rica use sterilized equipment, you may want to bring sealed hypodermic syringes anyway.

Medical resources for travellers

Websites

ⓦ **health.yahoo.com** Information on specific diseases and conditions, drugs and herbal remedies, as well as advice from health experts.
ⓦ **www.cdc.gov** The US government's official site for travel health.
ⓦ **www.istm.org** The website of the International Society for Travel Medicine, with a full list of clinics specializing in international travel health. Publishes outbreak warnings, suggested inoculations, precautions and other background information for travellers.

@ www.tmvc.com.au Contains a list of all Travellers Medical and Vaccination Centres throughout Australia, New Zealand and Southeast Asia, plus general information on travel health.
@ www.tripprep.com Travel Health Online provides an online-only comprehensive database of necessary vaccinations for most countries, as well as destination and medical service provider information.

In the US and Canada

Canadian Society for International Health 1 Nicholas St, Suite 1105, Ottawa, ON, K1N 7B7 ☎613/241-5785, @ www.csih.org. Distributes a free pamphlet, "Health Information for Canadian Travellers", containing an extensive list of travel health centres in Canada.

Centers for Disease Control 1600 Clifton Rd NE, Atlanta, GA 30333 ☎1-800/311-3435 or 404/639-3534, @ www.cdc.gov. Publishes outbreak warnings, suggested inoculations, precautions and other background information for travellers. Useful website plus International Travelers Hotline on ☎1-877/FYI-TRIP.

International Association for Medical Assistance to Travellers (IAMAT) 417 Center St, Lewiston, NY 14092 ☎716/754-4883, @ www .iamat.org, and 1287 St. Clair Avenue West, Suite #1, Toronto, Ontario M6E 1B8 ☎416/652-0137. Non-profit organization supported by donations, which can provide a list of English-speaking doctors in Costa Rica, climate charts and leaflets on various diseases and inoculations.

International SOS Assistance Eight Neshaminy Interplex Suite 207, Trevose, PA, USA 19053-6956 ☎1-800/523-8930, @ www.intsos.com. Members receive pre-trip medical referral info, as well as overseas emergency services designed to complement travel insurance coverage.

Travel Medicine ☎1-800/872-8633, @ www .travmed.com. Sells first-aid kits, mosquito netting, water filters, reference books and other health-related travel products.

In the UK and Ireland

British Airways Travel Clinics 213 Piccadilly, London W1 (Mon–Fri 9.30am–5.30pm, Sat 10am–4pm, no appointment necessary; ☎0845/600 2236); 101 Cheapside, London EC2 (Mon–Fri 9am–4.30pm, appointment required; ☎0845/600 2236); @ www.britishairways.com/travel /healthclinintro. Vaccinations, tailored advice from an online database and a complete range of travel healthcare products.

Dun Laoghaire Medical Centre 5 Northumberland Ave, Dun Laoghaire, County Dublin ☎01/280 4996, ⨍01/280 5603. Advice on medical matters abroad.

Hospital for Tropical Diseases Travel Clinic 2nd floor, Mortimer Market Centre, off Capper St, London WC1E 6AU (Mon–Fri 9am–5pm by appointment only; ☎020/7388 9600, @ www .masta.org; a consultation costs £15, which is waived if you have your injections here). A recorded Health Line (☎0906/133 7733; 50p per min) gives hints on hygiene and illness prevention as well as listing appropriate immunizations.

Liverpool School of Tropical Medicine Pembroke Place, Liverpool L3 5QA ☎0151/708 9393, @ www.liv.ac.uk/lstm/lstm. Walk-in clinic Mon–Fri 1–4pm; appointment required for yellow fever, but not for other jabs.

MASTA (Medical Advisory Service for Travellers Abroad) 40 regional clinics (call ☎0870/606 2782 for the nearest). Also operates a pre-recorded 24-hour Travellers' Health Line (UK ☎0906/822 4100, 60p per min), giving written information tailored to your journey by return of post.

The Travel Doctor @ www.thetraveldoctor.com. A wealth of information on all matters relating to travel health including a directory of UK travel health clinics.

Travel Health Centre Department of Inter-national Health and Tropical Medicine Royal College of Surgeons in Ireland, Mercers Medical Centre, Stephen's St Lower, Dublin 2 ☎01/402 2337. Expert pre-trip advice and inoculations.

Travel Medicine Services PO Box 254, 16 College St, Belfast BT1 6BT ☎028/9031 5220. Offers medical advice before a trip and help afterwards in the event of a tropical disease.

Tropical Medical Bureau Grafton Buildings, 34 Grafton St, Dublin 2, ☎1850/487 674, @ www .tmb.ie.

In Australia and New Zealand

Travellers' Medical and Vaccination Centres 27–29 Gilbert Place, Adelaide, SA 5000 ☎08/8212 7522, @ www.tmvc.com.au; 1/170 Queen St, Auckland ☎09/373 3531; 5/247 Adelaide St, Brisbane, Qld 4000 ☎07/3221 9066; 5/8–10 Hobart Place, Canberra, ACT 2600 ☎02/6257 7156; 270 Sandy Bay Rd, Sandy Bay Hobart Tas, 7005 ☎03/6223 7577; 2/393 Little Bourke St, Melbourne, Vic 3000 ☎03/9602 5788; Level 7, Dymocks Bldg, 428 George St, Sydney, NSW 2000 ☎02/9221 7133; Shop 15, Grand Arcade, 14–16 Willis St, Wellington, New Zealand ☎04/473 0991.

Costs, money and banks

Costa Rica is the most expensive country in Central America. Just about everything – from ice-cream cones and groceries to hotel rooms, meals and car rental – costs more than you might expect. Some prices, especially for upper-range accommodation, are comparable with those in the US, which never fails to astonish American travellers and those coming from the cheaper neighbouring countries. That said, prices have dropped from their peak of a few years ago, when Costa Rica developed a reputation as being overpriced, and you can, with a little foresight, travel fairly cheaply throughout the country. The US dollar has long been the second currency of Costa Rica and is accepted almost everywhere. We quote dollar prices throughout the Guide. Note, however, that the vast majority of Costa Ricans get paid in colones, and buy and sell in colones, so it's still a good idea to get the hang of the currency.

Average costs

The high cost of living is due in part to the **taxes** (16–25 percent) which are levied in restaurants and hotels, and also, more recently, to the International Monetary Fund, whose restructuring policies of balancing the country's payments deficit have raised prices. Even on a rock-bottom budget, you're looking at spending $25 a day for lodging, three meals and the odd bus ticket. Campers and hardy cyclists have been known to do it on $15 a day, but this entails sleeping either in a tent or somewhere pretty dire. You'll be far more comfortable if you count on spending at least $20 a day for accommodation and $15 for meals.

The good news is that **bus travel**, geared towards locals, is always cheap – about 25¢ to $1 for local buses, and around $4 to $5 for long-distance buses (3hr or more). For notes on **tipping** in Costa Rica, see the Directory, p.60.

Youth and student discounts

Full-time students are eligible for the International Student ID Card (ISIC, @www .isiccard.com), which may entitle the bearer to some discounts at museums in Costa Rica. For Americans, there's also a health benefit, providing up to $3000 in emergency medical coverage and $100 a day for 60 days in the hospital, plus a 24-hour hotline to

call in the event of a medical, legal or financial emergency. The card costs $22 in the USA; Can$16 in Canada; AUS$18 in Australia; NZ$20 in New Zealand; £7 in the UK; and €13 in the Republic of Ireland. More useful is the local **student card** which may offer discounts to museums and theatres – they're available to visitors on language courses and other education programmes (see p.55).

Currency

The official currency of Costa Rica is the **colón** (plural colones), named after Colón (Columbus) himself. There are two types of coins in circulation: the old silver ones, which come in denominations of 5, 10 and 20, and newer gold coins, which come in denominations of 5, 10, 25, 50, 100 and 500. The silver and gold coins are completely interchangeable, with the exception of public payphones, which don't accept all gold coins. Notes are available in 1000, 2000, 5000 and 10,000. You'll often hear colones colloquially referred to as "pesos"; in addition, the 1000 is sometimes called the "rojo" (red). The colón floats freely against the American dollar, which in practice has meant that it devalues by some 10% per year; at the time of writing it was around 430 colones to the $1. Obtaining colones outside Costa Rica is virtually impossible: wait until you arrive and get some at the airport or border posts.

Exchange and banks

Outside San José there are effectively no official **bureaux de change** in Costa Rica – the Juan Santamaría airport does have one, but service is very slow and rather surly. In general, legitimate moneychanging entails going to a bank, a hotel (usually upper-range) or, in outlying areas of the country, to whoever will do it – a tour agency, the friend of the owner of your hotel who has a Chinese restaurant . . . That said, it's unlikely that you'll need to change US dollars into colones, as dollars are accepted almost everywhere. If you do, or if you are changing other currencies such as sterling or euros, you'll find that the efficient and air-conditioned private banks (most of which are in San José) are much faster but charge scandalous commissions. Private banks in San José include Banco Mercantil, Banco Metropolitano, Banco Popular, Banco de San José, BANEX and Banco del Comercio. The state banks such as the Banco Nacional don't charge such high commissions but are slow and bureaucratic.

When heading for the more remote areas, try to carry sufficient colones with you, especially in small denominations – you may have trouble changing a 5000 bill in the middle of the Nicoya Peninsula, for example. Going around with stacks of mouldy-smelling colones may not seem safe, but you should be all right if you keep them in a money belt, and it will save hours of time waiting in line. Some banks may not accept bent, smudged or torn dollars, although street traders usually will. It's also worth noting that, due to a recent influx of counterfeit **$100 bills**, some shops, and even banks, are unwilling to accept them. If you bring any into the country, make sure that they are in mint condition. For more on banking hours, see Opening hours box on p.42.

Travellers' cheques

One of the safest ways to carry your money is **travellers' cheques**, which should be brought in US dollars only. Costa Rican bank tellers will only stare blankly at other currencies, although a couple of the private banks in San José grudgingly accept euro or sterling cheques. North American brands of travellers' cheques, including Amex, Citibank and Visa are most familiar to Costa Rican banks; they'll change Barclays' US-dollar cheques too, although they might look askance for a minute before deciding they're legit. Don't expect to use travellers' cheques as cash in Costa Rica except in mid- or top-range hotels and guest houses that regularly cater to foreigners.

The usual **fee** for travellers' cheque sales is one or two percent, and it pays to get a selection of denominations. Make sure you keep the purchase agreement and a record of cheque serial numbers safe and separate from the cheques themselves. In the event that cheques are lost or stolen, the issuing company will expect you to report the loss forthwith to their office in San José; most companies claim to replace lost or stolen cheques within 24 hours.

Debit and credit cards

By far the easiest way to travel in Costa Rica is with a **debit card**. Nearly all towns and resorts have at least one bank with an **ATM** that accepts foreign debit and credit cards. Many banks have machines that take Visa/Plus; Banco Nacional also accepts Mastercard/Cirrus, as do several others. Some machines will issue US dollars as well as colones. Make sure you have a **personal identification number (PIN)** that's designed to work overseas. Even so, getting money out can sometimes be a trial and error process and may require several attempts. Debit cards (unlike credit cards) are not liable to interest payments, and the flat transaction fee is usually quite small – your bank will be able to advise on this.

Credit cards are a very handy backup source of funds, and can be used over the counter or in ATMs, provided you have a PIN number; make sure you get one before leaving your home country. Credit cards are especially useful in Costa Rica for making deposits for hotels via fax or phone and for renting a car. In outlying areas, however, like the Talamanca coast, Quepos and Manuel Antonio and Golfito, some businesses may levy a six percent charge for credit card transactions; you may be better off taking plenty of cash. In general, **Visa** is widely accepted, and **Mastercard** somewhat less so; retailers tend to accept only one or the other, so it's handy to have both. **American Express** is not as commonly accepted, though you certainly won't have any problem using it in the higher-class hotels or to pay for air tickets and rental cars. Some retailers and hotels only accept the local Costa Rican credit card, called "Su Tarjeta" (ST).

Both state and private banks in Costa Rica can give you **cash advances** on your credit card (in either colones or dollars, provided they have enough dollars on hand) with relative ease. Bring your passport as identification. Remember that all cash advances are treated as loans, with interest accruing daily from the date of withdrawal; there may be a transaction fee on top of this.

A compromise between travellers' cheques and plastic is **Visa TravelMoney**, a disposable pre-paid debit card with a PIN which works in all ATMs that take Visa cards. You load up your account with funds before leaving home, and when they run out, you simply throw the card away. You can buy up to nine cards to access the same funds – useful for couples or families

travelling together – and it's a good idea to buy at least one extra as a back-up in case of loss or theft. The card is available in most countries from branches of Travelex and AAA. For more information, check the Visa TravelMoney website at Ⓦusa.visa.com /personal/cards/visa_travel_money.

Wiring money

Having **money wired** from home is never convenient or cheap, and should be considered a last resort only. In Costa Rica you can have money wired to Western Union, in San José at C 9, Av 2/4 (☎283-6336 or toll-free 800/777-7777, Ⓦwww.westernunion.co.cr), or the Costa Rican company, Servicios Internacionales Unigiros SA in San José at Av 1, C 1/3 (☎255-1033). Both companies' fees depend on the destination and the amount being transferred. The funds should be available for collection at the office within minutes of being sent. You can also have money wired directly from a bank in your home country to a bank in Costa Rica; a cumbersome process, because it involves two separate institutions. The person wiring the funds to you will need to know all the details of the bank the funds are being wired to. Expect the transfer to take several days to clear.

Getting around

Costa Rica's public bus system is excellent, cheap and quite frequent, even in remote areas. Taxis regularly do long- as well as short-distance trips and are a fairly inexpensive alternative to the bus, at least if you're travelling in a group.

Car rental is more common here than in the rest of Central America, but is fairly expensive. Note, too, that Costa Rica has one of the highest accident rates in the world, and driving can be quite a hair-raising experience. **Domestic airlines** are reasonably economical and can be quite a time-saver,

especially since Costa Rica's difficult terrain makes driving distances longer than they look on the map. A number of **tour operators** in San José organize individual itineraries and packages with transport included, well worth checking out before making any decisions about heading out on your own.

By bus

Travelling by **bus** is by far the cheapest way to get around Costa Rica. **San José** is the hub for virtually all bus services in the country; indeed, it's often impossible to travel from one place to another without backtracking to the capital. The most expensive journey in the country (from San José to Paso Canoas on the Panamanian border) costs $6, while fares in the mid- to long-distance range vary from $2.50 to $4. Some popular buses, like the service to Golfito, ought to be **booked in advance**, though you may be lucky enough to get on without a reservation. **Tickets** on most mid- to long-distance and popular routes are issued with a date and a seat number; you are expected to sit in the seat indicated. Make sure the date is correct; even if the mistake is not yours, you cannot normally change your ticket or get a refund. Neither can you buy **return** bus tickets on Costa Rican buses, which can be quite inconvenient if you're heading to very popular destinations like Monteverde, Jacó and Manuel Antonio at busy times – you'll need to jump off the bus as soon as you arrive and buy your return ticket immediately to assure yourself a seat. For updated information on bus timetables check ⓦ www.costaricamap .com/ing/infotbuslocal; for more details on bus companies and terminals, see p.99.

The majority of the country's buses are in fairly good shape, although they're usually not air-conditioned and there's very little room for luggage, or long legs. Most comfortable are the **Ticabuses** – modern air-conditioned buses with good seats, adequate baggage space and very courteous drivers – that run from San José to Panamá or to Managua. Most buses in Costa Rica have buzzers or bells to signal to the driver that you want to get off, though you may still find a few people using the old system of whistling, or shouting "*¡parada!*" ("stop!"). The atmosphere in Costa Rican buses is generally friendly, and if the driver starts to drive away while you're halfway out the back door trying to get off, your fellow passengers will erupt in spontaneous help. Though there are no **toilets** on the buses, drivers make (admittedly infrequent) stops on longer runs. Often a lunch or dinner stop will be made at a roadside restaurant or gas station; failing that, there is always a bevy of hardy food and drinks sellers who leap onto the bus proffering their wares.

In recent years, travellers have begun to make much use of the network of air-conditioned **minibuses** that connect most of Costa Rica's main tourist destinations. While these cost five or more times as much as the public buses, they are

Finding your way around Costa Rican towns

In Costa Rica there is only one vision of urban planning: the grid system. However, there are a number of peculiarities that are essential to come to grips with if you want to find your way around with ease. The following rules apply to all cities except Limón.

Typically, you'll see **addresses** written as follows: Bar Esmeralda, Av 2, C 5/7 (abbreviated from Avenida 2, Calles 5/7). This means that Bar Esmeralda is on Avenida 2, between Calles 5 and 7. Bar Lotto, C 5, Av 2, on the other hand, is on the corner of Calle 5 and Avenida 2. Apartado (Aptdo) means "postbox", and bis means, technically, "encore": if you see "Av 6 bis" in an address it refers to another Avenida 6, right next to the original one.

Many **directions**, in both written and verbal form, are given in terms of metres rather than blocks. In general, one block is equivalent to 100m. Thus "de la Escuela Presidente Vargas, 125 metros al sur, cincuenta metros al oeste", translates as "from the Presidente Vargas School, 125 metres south [one block and a quarter] and 50 west [half a block]". More confusingly, verbal directions are commonly given in relation to **landmarks** which everyone – except the visitor – knows and recognizes. Frustratingly, too, some of these landmarks may not even exist any longer. This is something to get the hang of fast: taxi drivers will often look completely bewildered if given street directions, but as soon you come up with a landmark, the proverbial light bulb goes on.

significantly faster, more comfortable and will pick up and drop off at hotels. The main operator is **Interbus** (☎283-5573, ⓦwww .interbusonline.com), with comprehensive routes across the country; they charge $25–40 for a mid- to long-range journey. The similar but cheaper **Fantasy Bus Gray Line** (☎220-2126, ⓦwww.fantasy.co.cr) runs direct services between several San José hotels and many tourist spots. Fares are about $25 one-way.

By car

Although there's little traffic outside the Valle Central, the common perception of **driving** in Costa Rica is of endless dodging around cows and potholes, while big trucks nudge your rear bumper in an effort to get you to go faster around that next blind bend. The reality is somewhat different. While many roads are indeed badly potholed, driving is relatively easy, and with your own vehicle you can see the country at your own pace

without having to adhere to bus and plane schedules. Citizens of the US, Canada and the UK need only a **valid driver's licence** to operate a vehicle in Costa Rica. Residents of other countries should check with their nearest Costa Rican consulate, although in practice both police and rental agencies readily accept Australian and New Zealand licences. In **Australia**, international drivers' licences can be obtained from state motoring organization offices in major towns and cities, or contact the Australian Automobile Association, 212 Northbourne Ave, Canberra ACT 2601 (☎02/6247 7311, ⓦwww.aaa .asn.au). In **New Zealand**, contact the New Zealand Automobile Association at 17/99 Albert St, Auckland (☎09/377 4660, ⓦwww .aa.co.nz) or your local AA office.

In recent years, a system of fines (*multas*) for infractions like **speeding** has been introduced in Costa Rica. The limit on the highways is either 75km/hr or 90km/hr and is marked on the road surface or on signs.

Car safety in Costa Rica

The **road traffic accident** rate in Costa Rica is phenomenal – and rising. Most tourists see at least one accident on the roads during their time in the country, and though Costa Ricans blame bad road conditions, the real cause is more often poor driving – you're advised to drive extremely defensively. Sections of washed out, unmarked or unlit road add to the hazards, as do mechanically unsound buses and big trans-isthmus trucks.

Another hazard of driving in Costa Rica involves **car crime**. A recent scam involves thieves entering car rental companies' parking lots and making slow punctures in the tyres of hire cars. Unsuspecting drivers then take these cars out onto the road until the puncture eventually forces them to pull over, at which point the thieves (who have been following) stop to offer help before robbing you on the roadway or hard shoulder. Drive to the nearest public area and call for the police.

- Keep your doors locked and windows shut, especially in San José.
- If someone suspicious approaches your vehicle at a red light or stop sign, blow your horn.
- Do not pull over for flashing headlights. Note that an emergency or police vehicle has red or blue flashing headlights.
- If you become lost, find a public place, like a service station, to consult your map or ask for directions.
- If someone tells you something is wrong with your vehicle do not stop immediately. Drive to the nearest service station or other well-lit public area.
- Keep valuables in the trunk or out of sight, and your car locked at all times.
- Do not pick up hitchhikers.
- Do not leave the keys in your vehicle or the motor running when you stop to fill up; use the telephone or the ATM.
- If you suspect you are being followed, go to the nearest well-lit public area and call the police.
- In case of emergency call 911.

Car rental essentials

You have to exercise caution when **renting a car** in Costa Rica, where it is not uncommon for rental companies to claim for "damage" they insist you inflicted on the vehicle. It is by far the best policy to rent a car through a Costa Rican **travel agent**. If you are travelling on a package, your agent will sort this out. Otherwise, go into an ICT-accredited travel agent in San José and ask them to arrange rental for you. This should be no more expensive than renting on your own and will help guard against false claims of damage and other accusations; rental companies will be less willing to make trouble with an agent who regularly sends them clients than with individual customers who they may not see again.

Make sure to **check the car** carefully before you sign off the damage sheet. Check the oil, brake fluid, fuel gauge (to make sure it's full) and that there is a spare tyre with good air pressure and a jack. Look up the Spanish for "scratches" (rayas) and other relevant terminology first, so you can at least scrutinize the rental company's assessment. Keep a copy of this document on you.

Take the maximum **insurance** (around $15-20 per day); because of the country's high accident rate, you need to be covered for damage to the vehicle, yourself, any third party and public property.

Speed traps are very common, and if you're caught speeding you may have to pay up to $150. If a motorist – especially a trucker – in the oncoming direction flashes his headlights at you, you can be almost certain that traffic cops with speed-trapping radar are up ahead. Although traffic cops routinely accept bribes to tear up tickets, it's a very serious offence and should not be attempted under any circumstances.

Petrol is positively cheap by European standards: about $15 a tank on a medium-sized car or about $30 for a big 4WD. If you're unlucky enough to have an **accident** in Costa Rica, don't attempt to move the car until the traffic police arrive: call the National Insurance Institute (☎800/835-3467), who will send an inspector to check the vehicles involved to assess who caused the accident – vital if you're using a rental car.

If you intend to drive in the rainy season (May–Nov), especially on the Nicoya Peninsula, or to Santa Elena and Monteverde, or anywhere at all off the beaten track, you'll need to rent a **four-wheel drive** (4WD).

Car rental

Car rental in Costa Rica is expensive. Expect to pay about $350 per week (including insurance) for a regular vehicle, and up to $500 for a large 4WD. Rental days are calculated on a 24-hour basis: thus, if you pick up your car

on a Tuesday at 3pm for a week, you have to return it before that time the following Tuesday. The minimum age for rental is usually 25, and you'll need a credit card, either Mastercard or Visa, which has sufficient credit for the entire cost of the rental. There are rental offices in all the major tourist spots, and you can arrange to pick up your car in another part of Costa Rica and drop it off at the airport when you leave – this normally entails a charge of $20–30, but this may be waived if you're taking the vehicle for more than a few days. It's also worth knowing that most tour operators in Costa Rica can arrange car hire much more cheaply than if you organize it yourself through one of the overseas operators listed below.

If you're planning to visit the Nicoya Peninsula, national parks, or other remote spots, it's definitely worth paying the extra money for a 4WD. In smaller vehicles, punctures are a depressingly regular experience, and although getting them repaired is a matter of a couple of minutes' hammering at the rim at the local garage, it's not the best way to spend a holiday.

Most car rental companies in Costa Rica are located in San José, at the international airport, and at the new airport in Liberia; you can also rent cars in various towns around the country – of the Costa Rican rental agencies, Elegante and ADA have the largest network of regional offices.

Renting outside San José is often a bit more expensive, but it can save you the drive on the tricky Interamericana Highway from the capital to your destination. Prices vary considerably from agency to agency (Europcar, Payless and Adobe are all recommended). During peak season (especiallyChristmas, but any time from December to March) it's wise to reserve a car before you arrive.

Car rental companies in San José

In all the following, where two numbers are given, the first is the company's downtown office, the second the airport office.
ADA Av 18, C 11/13 ☏ 233-7733, ☏ 441-1260.
Adobe C 7, Av 8/10 ☏ 221-5425, ⊛www .adobecar.com.
Avis C 42, Av Las Americas ☏ 293-2222, ⊛www .avis.co.cr.
Budget Paseo Colón, C 30 ☏ 223-3284, ⊛www .budget.com.
Elegante C 10, Av 13/15, Barrio México ☏ 221-0066, ☏ 233-8605, ⊛www .eleganterentacar.com.
Europcar/Prego C 36/38, Paseo Colón ☏ 257-1158, ⊛www.europcar.co.cr.
Hertz C 38, Paseo Colón ☏ 221-1818, ⊛www.hertz.com.
Hola In front of the *Best Western Irazú* on the airport highway ☏ 231-5666, ⊛www.hola.net.
National C 36, Av 7 ☏ 233-4044, ⊛www.natcar .com.
Payless C10, Av 13/15, Barrio México ☏ 257-0026, ☏ 441-9366, ⊛www.payless.co.cr.
Thrifty C 3, Av 13 ☏ 257-3434, ⊛www.thrifty.com.

Car rental companies abroad

In North America

Avis ☏ 1-800/331-1084, ⊛www.avis.com.
Budget ☏ 1-800/800-6000, ⊛www.budget.com.
Dollar ☏ 1-800/421-6868, ⊛www.dollar.com.
Hertz ☏ 1-800/654-3001 in the US, ☏ 1-800/263-0600 in Canada, ⊛www.hertz.com.
National ☏ 1-800/CAR-RENT, ⊛www.nationalcar .com.

In the UK

Avis ☏ 0870/606 0100, ⊛www.avis.co.uk.
Budget ☏ 0800/181 181, ⊛www.budget.com.
Europcar ☏ 0345/222 528, ⊛www.europcar.co.uk.
Hertz ☏ 0870/844 8844, ⊛www.hertz.co.uk.

Holiday Autos ☏ 0870/400 0011, ⊛www .holidayautos.com.
Thrifty ☏ 01494/442 110, ⊛www.thrifty.co.uk.

In Australia

Avis ☏ 13 6333, ⊛www.avis.com.
Budget ☏ 1300/362 848, ⊛www.budget.com.
Dollar ☏ 02/9223 1444 or 1800/358 008, ⊛www.dollarcar.com.au.
Hertz ☏ 1800/550 067, ⊛www.hertz.com.

In New Zealand

Avis ☏ 09/526 5231 or 0800/655 111, ⊛www .avis.com.
Budget ☏ 0800/652 227 or 09/375 2270, ⊛www.budget.com.
Hertz ☏ 09/309 0989 or 0800/655 955, ⊛www .hertz.com.

By air

Costa Rica's two **domestic air carriers** offer reasonably economical flights between San José and many beach destinations and provincial towns. Sansa is the state-owned domestic airline; NatureAir is its commercial competitor. Both fly small twin-propeller aircraft, and service more or less the same destinations. These flights can be very handy, saving many hours of bus travel better spent on the sand.

Of the two, **NatureAir** (☏ 220-3054, ☏ 220-0413, ⊛www.natureair.com), which flies from Tobías Bolaños airport in Pavas, 7km northwest of San José, is more reliable and has more frequent services on some runs. **Sansa** (☏ 221-9414, ☏ 255-2176, ⊛www.flysansa .com) flies from Juan Santamaría airport, 17km northwest of San José, and is cheaper but less dependable than NatureAir. On both airlines, make your reservations as far as possible in advance, and even then be advised that a booking means almost nothing until the seat is actually paid for. Reconfirm your flight in advance of the day of departure and again on the day of travel, if possible, as schedules can change at short notice.

If you're planning to cover a lot of ground in a limited amount of time, Sansa's **Costa Rica Air Pass** ($199/249 for 1/2 weeks; $50 surcharge if you arrived in Costa Rica on an airline other than one affiliated with Grupo TACA) gives you unrestricted use of all their services. If you're travelling throughout

Central America, a **TACA regional airpass** (ⓦ www.tacaregional.com) offers unlimited travel on the domestic airlines of Guatemala, Honduras, Nicaragua and Panamá, as well as Costa Rica. For a rundown of Sansa and NatureAir **schedules**, along with their addresses and phone numbers, see p.103.

While it's both convenient and exhilarating to fly around the country in the small aircraft operated by domestic airlines and air-charter companies, the **accident rate** for light aircraft in Costa Rica has been worryingly high in recent years. There are signs, however, that this is being remedied. In 2001, stricter safety checks and more rigorous flying procedures were implemented, and the number of incidents has declined since then. While fares will be at least double that of Sansa and NatureAir, **air charter taxis** (journeys can cost anywhere from $125 to $550 per planeload) can prove a reasonably cheap way to get to the beaches and more remote areas if several people split the expense. Most charter planes operate from Tobías Bolaños airport in Pavas.

Air-charter companies

As well as these below, Sansa and NatureAir also offer charter services.
Aerobell Tobías Bolaños airport, Pavas
ⓣ 290-0000, ⓦ www.aerobell.com. Professional operation with friendly and efficient staff; they have charter flights all over the country in twin-engine planes ($320 an hour to charter a 5-seater plane).
Alfa Romeo Aero Taxi Puerto Jiménez, opposite the cemetery ⓣ 735-5112. Zona Sur air charter company specializing in local short-hop trips.
Paradise Air Tobías Bolaños airport, Pavas ⓣ 231-0938, ⓦ www.flywithparadise.com. They run charter flights all over Costa Rica and internationally and also arrange customized aero-safari tours.

By bicycle

Costa Rica's terrain makes for easy **cycling** compared with neighbouring countries and, as there's a good range of places to stay and eat, you don't need to carry the extra weight of a tent, sleeping bag and stove. Always bring warm clothes and a cycling jacket, however, wherever you are. As for **equipment**, rear panniers and a small handlebar bag (for maps and camera) should be enough. Bring a puncture repair kit, even if your tyres are supposedly unbustable. You'll need a bike with a triple front gear – this gives you 15 to 21 gears, and you will really need the low ones. Make sure, too, that you carry and drink lots of water – five to eight litres a day in the lowlands.

There is very little **traffic** outside the Valle Central, and despite their tactics with other cars (and pedestrians), Costa Rican drivers are some of the most courteous in Central America to cyclists. That said, however, bus and truck drivers do tend to forget about you as soon as they pass, sometimes forcing you off the road. **Roads** are generally good for cyclists, who can dodge the potholes and wandering cattle more easily than drivers. Bear in mind that if you cycle up to Monteverde, one of the most popular routes in the country, you're in for a slow trip: besides being steep there's not much traction on the loose gravel roads. Although road signs will tell you that cycling on the Interamericana (Pan-American Highway, or Hwy-1) is not permitted, you will quickly see that people do anyway.

San José's best **cycle shop** is Bicimania, at the corner of Paseo Colón and C 26. They have all the parts you might need, can fix your bike and may even be able to give you a bicycle carton for the plane.

Tour operators

The Costa Rican tourist boom of the last ten years has led to a proliferation of **tour operators**. Market research shows that about fifty percent of travellers to Costa Rica arrive with only their return flight and the first few nights of accommodation booked; they then set about planning tours and travel once they've arrived in the country.

Wandering around the city, you face a barrage of tour agencies and advertisements: if you want to shop around it could take some time to sort yourself out. The following is not a comprehensive list of tour operators in Costa Rica, but all those that we've listed are experienced and recommended, offering a good range of services and tours. They're all licensed (and regulated) by the ICT.

There are scores of others – be especially wary of fly-by-night operators, of which there are plenty. You often see, for instance, posters advertising cheap "packages" to Tortuguero or to Monteverde, both for about $80–100 – less than half the price of a regular package. These cut-price tours are not packages at all, and never worth the price: in some cases you will be responsible for your own transport, accommodation will be the most basic, and no tours, orientation or guidance will be given – something you can easily arrange on your own, for the same price or less.

Tour operators in Costa Rica

Camino Travel C 1, Av 0/1 ☎234-2530, ⓦwww .caminotravel.com. A young, enthusiastic staff with high standards (and a mainly European clientele) offers upmarket and independent travel, including individual tours with quality accommodation. They can also help with bus and transport information and car rental. Convenient downtown office.

Costa Rica Expeditions C Central, Av 3 ☎257-0766, ⓦwww.costaricaexpeditions.com. The longest-established and most experienced of the major tour operators, with superior accommodation in Tortuguero, Monteverde and Corcovado, a superlative staff of guides and tremendous resources. You can drop into the busy downtown office and talk to a consultant about individual tours.

Costa Rican Trails Av 15, C 23/25, ☎221-3011, ⓦwww.costaricantrails.com. Small, friendly and very professional agency who will visit you in your hotel room to discuss their range of tailor-made and flexi-drive holidays in all price ranges. They're also experts in adventure sports, including rafting and motorbike tours.

Ecole Travel C 7, Av 0/1 ☎223-2240, ⓦwww .ecoletravel.com. Small agency, popular with backpackers, offering well-priced tours to Tortuguero and hiking trips to Chirripó (4 days) and the Osa Peninsula (3 days). They also run boats from the Moín docks near Puerto Limón to Tortuguero.

Expediciones Tropicales Av 11/13, C 3 bis ☎257-4171, ⓦwww.costaricainfo.com. Well-regarded agency with knowledgeable guides who run

popular "Four-in-One" day-tour of Volcán Poás and nearby sights ($79; 11hr), as well as a host of other trips from San José at competitive prices.

Horizontes Nature Tours C 28, Av 1/3 ☎222-2022, ⓦwww.horizontes.com. Highly regarded agency concentrating on rainforest walking and hiking, volcanos and birdwatching, all with an emphasis on natural and cultural history. Specialists in mountain biking and horse-riding as well.

OTEC C 3, Av 1/3 ☎256-0633, ⓦwww .travelvouch.com (Spanish only). This large agency specializes in adventure tours including fishing, trekking, surfing and mountain biking, plus hotel reservations and car rentals. They're particularly focused on student travel, and offer discounts to ISIC card holders.

RainForest World Turrialba ☎556-2678, ⓦwww.rforestw.com. Recommended eco-tourism outfit that offers a range of rafting, kayaking and hiking trips as well as customized itineraries.

Ríos Tropicales C 38, Av 0/2 ☎233-6455, ⓦwww.riostropicales.com. Agency specializing in whitewater sports around the country.

Serendipity Adventures Turrialba 93 ☎556-2592, ⓦwww.serendipityadventures.com. This superior travel agency offers individual custom-made tours for self-formed groups with a sense of adventure. Serendipity make a point of searching out undiscovered parts of Costa Rica. They're experts in canyoning and rappelling, and are the only ones in Costa Rica to offer hot-air balloon trips.

Simbiosis Tours Apt 6939-1000, San José ☎259-3605, ⓔcooprena@racsa.co.cr. Tour company offering package tours to one of six cooperatives in Costa Rica. The cooperatives are composed of low-income rural families living a modest lifestyle and sharing a common goal of exploring new and sustainable land uses. Projects managed by the co-ops and featured in various packages include lodges, restaurants, private reserves, nature trails, horseriding and organic farms.

Specops ☎232-4028, ⓦwww.specops.com. Adventure education group, comprising US Special Forces veterans and expert Costa Rican guides which specializes in white-knuckle thrills, jungle survival courses and adventure film and photography.

Accommodation

Most towns in Costa Rica have a wide range of places to stay, and even the smallest settlements usually have basic lodgings. Prices are higher than you'd pay in most other Central American countries, but they're by no means exorbitant, and certainly not when compared with the US or Western Europe. Budget accommodation runs the gamut from the extremely basic, where $10–20 will get you little more than a room and a bed, to reasonably well-equipped accommodation with a clean, comfortable en-suite room, a fan and possibly even a TV for around $20–30 a night. In the middle and upper price range, facilities and services are generally of a very good standard throughout the country. When looking at prices, remember that not all hotels list the hotel tax in the published price; be sure to check first. At the time of writing, the tax stood at 16.39 percent, including a 3 percent "tourist tax".

The larger places to stay in Costa Rica are usually called **hotels**. **Posadas**, **hostals**, **hospedajes** and **pensiones** are smaller, though posadas can sometimes turn out to be quite swanky, especially in rural areas. **Casas** tend to be private guesthouses, while **albergues** are the equivalent of lodges. **Cabinas** are common in Costa Rica, particularly in coastal areas: they're usually either a string of motel-style rooms in an annex away from the main building or, more often, separate self-contained units. Usually – although not always – they tend toward the basic, and are most often frequented by budget travellers. More upmarket versions may be called "villas" or "chalets". Anything called a **motel** – as in most of Latin America – is not likely to be used for sleeping.

Few hotels except those at the upper end of the price range have double beds, and it's more common to find two or three single beds. **Single travellers** will generally be charged the single rate even if they're occupying a double room, though this is sometimes not the case in popular beach towns and at peak seasons.

Incidentally, wherever you're staying, don't expect to get much reading done in the evenings. Light bulbs are very wan, even in good hotels, and avid after-dark readers may want to bring their own reading lamp (plus adaptor). Also bear in mind that in Costa Rican hotels, the term **hot water** can be misleading. Showers are often equipped with squat plastic nozzles: these are water heaters. Inside is an electric element that heats the water to a warm, rather than hot, temperature. Some of the nozzles have a button that actually turns on the element. Under no circumstances should you touch this button or get anywhere near the nozzle when wet – these contraptions may not be quite as bad as their tongue-in-cheek name of "suicide showers" suggests,

---

Accommodation price codes

All the accommodation in this book has been graded using the following price codes. The prices quoted are for the **least expensive double room in high season**, and do not include the 16.39 percent national tax which is automatically added onto hotel bills.

- ❶ less than $10
- ❷ $10–20
- ❸ $20–30
- ❹ $30–50
- ❺ $50–75
- ❻ $75–100
- ❼ $100–150
- ❽ over $150

but there's still a distinct possibility you could get a nasty shock. The trick to getting fairly hot water is not to turn on the pressure too high. Keep a little coming through to heat the water more efficiently.

Reservations

Costa Rica's hotels tend to be chock-full in high season (Nov–April), especially at Christmas, New Year and Easter, so **reserve well ahead**, particularly for youth hostels and good-value hotels in popular spots. Many hotels, even the budget ones, have faxes, and email is also becoming increasingly common, so the easiest and surest way to reserve in advance is with a credit card by fax or email. Once on the ground in Costa Rica, phone or fax again to reconfirm your reservation. Some establishments will ask you to reserve and pay in advance – the more popular hotels and lodges require you to do this as far as thirty days ahead, often by money transfer (though they'll accommodate you if there's space).

For many travellers, this level of preplanning is impractical. If you prefer to be a little more spontaneous, you should travel in the low season, from roughly after Easter to mid-November, when you can safely wait until you arrive in the country to make reservations. During these months it's even possible to show up at hotels on spec – there will probably be space, and possibly even a low-season discount of as much as fifty percent. Another budget option is to arrange to **stay with a Tico family** (see box, p.56).

Pensiones and hotels

When travelling, most Costa Ricans and nationals of other Central American countries stick to the bottom end of the market and patronize traditional **pensiones** (a fast-dying breed in Costa Rica, especially in San José) or established Costa Rican-owned hotels. If you do likewise you may well get a better price than at the tourist or foreign-owned hotels, although this is not a hard and fast rule. Though standards are generally high, at the **lower end** of the scale, you should expect to get what you pay for – usually clean but dim, spartan rooms with cold-water showers. If you

think you might have a choice or like to shop around, it's perfectly acceptable to ask to see the room first.

The majority of accommodation catering to foreigners is in the **middle range**, and as such is reasonably priced – although still more expensive than similar accommodation in other Central American countries. Hotels at the lower end of this price range will often be very good value, however, giving you private bath with hot water, perhaps towels, and maybe even air conditioning (which, it has to be said, is not really necessary in most places; a ceiling fan generally does fine). At the upper end of this price range a few extras, like TV or breakfast, may be thrown in.

Resorts, lodges and B&Bs

There are many **resorts** scattered throughout Costa Rica, ranging from swanky hotels in popular areas like Manuel Antonio to lush **rainforest lodges** in areas of outstanding natural beauty – the sort of places that have their own Jacuzzis, swimming pools, spas, gourmet restaurants and stretches of jungle. Prices can fall dramatically out of season when you might be able to get yourself a night or two of luxury for as little as $120–145.

Until recently many hotels offered breakfast in their room rates as a matter of course, but this is becoming less common and, if breakfast is offered at all, it will probably cost extra. However, a new breed of **B&Bs** (often owned by expats) has sprung up in recent years. Costa Rican B&Bs are similar to their North American or UK counterparts, offering rooms in homes or converted homes with a "family atmosphere" and a full breakfast. For more information, contact the Established Bed and Breakfast Group, ☎289-8638, ℗228-1405, ⊛www.catch22.com/~vudu/bliss2.

Camping

Though **camping** is fairly widespread in Costa Rica, gone are the days when you could pitch your tent on just about any beach or field. With the influx of visitors to Costa Rica, local residents (especially in small beachside communities) are getting upset with campers leaving rubbish on the beach. You'll have a far better relationship with locals if you ask politely whether it's OK to camp; if you're directed to a nearby campsite, this is simply because locals are trying to keep their environment clean.

In the beach towns, you'll usually find at least one well-equipped **private campsite**, with good facilities including lavatories, drinking water and cooking grilles; staff may also offer to guard your clothes and tent while you're at the beach. You may also find hotels, usually at the lower end of the price scale, where you can pitch your tent on the grounds and use the showers and washrooms for a fee – ask around. Though not all **national parks** have campsites, the ones that do usually offer high standards and at least basic facilities, with lavatories, water and cooking grilles – all for around $2 per person per day. In some national parks you can bunk down at the **ranger station** if you call well in advance; for more details, see p.45.

There are three general rules of camping in Costa Rica: first, never leave your tent (or anything of value inside it) unattended, or it may not be there when you get back. Second, never leave your tent open except to get in and out, unless you fancy sharing your sleeping quarters with snakes, insects, coati or toads. Finally, take your refuse with you when you leave.

Youth hostels

Costa Rica has a small network of 23 good and reasonably priced **youth hostels** affiliated with Hostelling International, many of them in prime locations. They usually cost around $10–20 per night ($8–16 if you're an HI member) and can be conveniently booked from the Toruma hostel in San José (see p.77). As with all accommodation in Costa Rica, bookings should ideally be made several months in advance if you're coming in high season.

All 23 hostels can be reached by public transport and follow conservation regulations based on the sustainable development principle. Most of them have a range of double, triple and family rooms and some offer additional services including Internet access (often for free), laundry and luggage storage. Bed linen, towels and soap are included in the price.

Youth hostel associations

In Costa Rica

Hostelling International Costa Rica Toruma Hostel, Av Central, C 29/31, San José ☎ & ℱ224-4085, ⓦwww.toruma.com or ⓦwww.hicr.org.

In the US and Canada

Hostelling International–American Youth Hostels ☎301/495-1240, ⓦwww.hiayh.org. Annual membership for adults (18–55) is $28, for seniors (55 or over) is $18, and for under-18s and groups of ten or more, is free. Life memberships are $250.
Hostelling International Canada ☎1-800/663 5777 or 613/237 7884, ⓦwww.hihostels.ca. Rather than sell the traditional 1- or 2-year memberships, the association now sells one Individual Adult membership with a 28- to 16-month term. The length of the term depends on when the membership is sold, but a member

---

What to bring when camping in Costa Rica

- Groundsheet
- Backpack
- Lightweight (summer) sleeping bag, except for climbing Chirripó, where you may need a three-season bag
- Rain gear
- Mosquito net
- Maps
- Torch
- Knife

- Matches, in a waterproof box
- Firelighter
- Compass
- Insect repellent
- Water bottles
- Toilet paper
- Sunglasses
- Sunblock
- Plastic bags (for wet clothes/ refuse)

can receive up to 28 months of membership for just $35+tax. Membership is free for under-18s and you can become a lifetime member for $175.

In the UK and Ireland

Youth Hostel Association (YHA) ☎0870/770 8868, ⓦwww.yha.org.uk. Annual membership £13.50; under-18s £6.70; lifetime £195 (or five annual payments of £41).
Irish Youth Hostel Association ☎01/830 4555, ⓦwww.irelandyha.org. Annual membership €25; under-18s €10.50; family €50; lifetime €75.

In Australia and New Zealand

Australia Youth Hostels Association ☎02/9261 1111, ⓦwww.yha.com.au. Adult membership rate AUS$52 (under-18s, AUS$19) for the first twelve months and then AUS$37 each year after.
Youth Hostelling Association New Zealand ☎0800/278 299 or 03/379 9970, ⓦwww.yha .co.nz. Adult membership NZ$40 for one year, NZ$60 for two and NZ$80 for three; under-18s free; lifetime NZ$300.

Eating and drinking

The best way to describe most Costa Rican food – called *comida típica* ("native" or "local" food) by Ticos – is to apply that evasive adjective "unpretentious". Simple it may be, but tasty nonetheless, especially when it comes to the interesting regional variations found along the Caribbean coast, with its Creole-influenced cooking, and in Guanacaste, where there are vestiges of the ancient indigenous peoples' use of maize. For more on the cuisine of these areas, see the relevant chapters in the Guide.

Típico dishes you'll find all over Costa Rica include rice and some kind of meat or fish, often served as part of a special plate with coleslaw salad, in which case it's called a **casado** (literally, "married person"). The ubiquitous **gallo pinto** ("painted rooster"), often described as the national dish of Costa Rica, is a breakfast combination of red and white beans with rice, sometimes served with *huevos revueltos* (scrambled eggs). The heavy concentration on starch and protein reveals the rural origins of Costa Rican food: *gallo pinto* is food for people who are going out to work it off.

Of the dishes found on menus all over the country, particularly recommended are **ceviche** (raw fish "marinated" in lime juice

with coriander and peppers), **pargo** (red snapper), **corvina** (sea bass) and any of the ice creams and **desserts**, though these can be too sickly-sweet for many tastes. The fresh **fruit** is especially good, either eaten by itself or drunk in *refrescos* (see p.41). Papayas, pineapple and bananas are all cheap and plentiful, along with some less familiar fruits like *mamones chinos* (a kind of lychee), *anona* (which tastes like custard) and *marañón*, whose seed is the cashew nut.

Eating out

Eating out in Costa Rica will cost more than you might think, and has become even more expensive over the past few

See p.418 in Contexts for a Spanish/English glossary of food and drink terms.

years. Main dishes can easily run between $7 and $9, and then there's those sneaky **extra charges**: the service charge (10 percent) and the sales tax (15 percent), which bring the meal to a total of 25 percent more than the menu price. Add this all up, and dinner for two can easily come to $20 or even $25 just for a single course and a couple of beers. **Tipping** (see p.60) is not necessary, however. Costa Rica's best restaurants are on the outskirts of San José, and in popular tourist destinations such as Tamarindo and Manuel Antonio, where demand has created some excellent gourmet options.

The cheapest places to dine in Costa Rica – and where most workers eat lunch, their main meal – are the ubiquitous **sodas**, halfway between the North American diner and the British greasy café. Sodas offer filling set *platos del día* (daily specials) and *casados* for about $3. Most do not add sales tax (although restaurants masquerading as sodas, like *El Parque* in San José, do). You usually have to go to the cash register to get your bill. Sodas also often have takeout windows where you can pick up snacks such as the delicious little fingers of bread and sugar called *churros*. Many sodas are vegetarian, and in general **vegetarians** do quite well in Costa Rica. Most menus will have a vegetable option, and asking for dishes to be served without meat is perfectly acceptable.

Because Costa Ricans start the day early, they are less likely to hang about late in restaurants in the evening, and establishments are usually empty or **closed** by 10 or 10.30pm. Non-smoking sections are uncommon, to say the least, except in the most expensive establishments, but in general Ticos don't smoke much in restaurants.

Drinking

Costa Rica is famous for its **coffee**, and it's usual to end a meal with a small cup, traditionally served in a pitcher with heated milk on the side. Most of the best blends are exported so premium coffee is generally only served in high-end restaurants and sold in shops.

Always popular are **refrescos**, cool drinks made with milk (*leche*) or water (*agua*), fruit and ice, all whipped up in a blender. You can buy them at stalls or in cartons, though the latter tend to be sugary. You'll find **herb teas** throughout the country; those served in the Caribbean province of Limón are especially good. In Guanacaste you can sample distinctive **corn-based drinks** *horchata* and *pinolillo*, made with milk and sugar and with a grainy consistency.

Costa Rica has several local brands of lager beer, a godsend in the steamy tropics. Most popular is Imperial with its characteristic eagle logo, but Bavaria Gold is the best of the bunch, with a cleaner taste and more complex flavour; they also produce a decent dark beer. Pilsen and Rock Ice are other worthwhile tipples; of the local low-alcohol beers, Bavaria Light is the best-tasting.

Coffee in Costa Rica

There are two types of coffee available in Costa Rica: **export quality** (grano d'oro), typically packaged by either Café Britt or Café Rey and served in good hotels and restaurants; and the **lower-grade blend**, usually sold for the home market. Costa Rica's export-grade coffee is known the world over for its mellowness and smoothness. The stuff produced for the domestic market, however, is another matter entirely. Some of it is even **pre-sweetened**, so if you ask for it with sugar (*con azúcar*), you'll get a saccharine shock. Among the best coffees you'll find in Costa Rica are **La Carpintera**, a smooth, rich, hard bean grown on Cerro de la Carpintera in the Valle Central, and **Zurqui**, the oldest cultivated bean in the country, grown for 150 years on the flanks of Volcán Barva. Strong, but with a silky, gentle taste, **Café el Gran Vito**, grown by Italian immigrants near San Vito in the extreme south of the country, is an unusual grade of export bean, harder to find than those grown in the Valle de El General and the Valle Central.

Wine, once a rare commodity, has become far more common in mid- and top-range restaurants, where you'll often find good Chilean varieties on offer. **Spirits** tend to be associated with serious drinking, usually by men in bars, and are rarely consumed by local women in public. There is an indigenous hard-liquor drink, **guaro**, of which Cacique is the most popular brand. It's a bit rough, but good with lime sodas or in a cocktail. For an after-dinner drink, try Café Rica, a creamy liqueur made with the local coffee.

Bars

Costa Rica has a variety of **places to drink**, from shady macho domains to pretty beachside bars, with some particularly cosmopolitan nightspots in San José. The capital is also the place to find the country's last remaining **boca bars**, atmospheric places that serve *bocas* (tasty little snacks like tapas) with drinks; though historically these were free, nowadays even in the most traditional places you'll probably have to pay for them (for more on San José's boca bars, see p.94). In even the smallest town with any foreign population – either expat or tourist – you'll notice a sharp split between the places frequented by locals and those

that cater to foreigners. Gringo grottoes abound, especially in beach towns. These places tend to have a wide bar stock, at least compared to the limited *guaro*-and-beer menu of the local bars. In many places, especially port cities like Limón, Puntarenas and Golfito, there is the usual contingent of rough, rowdy bars where testosterone-fuelled machos go to drink gallons and fight; it's usually pretty obvious which ones they are – they advertise their seediness with a giant Imperial placard parked right in front of the door so you can't see what's going on inside.

Most bars typically **open** in the morning, any time between 8.30 and 11am, and **close** at around 11pm or midnight. **Sunday** night is usually dead: many bars don't open at all and others close early, around 10pm. Though Friday and Saturday nights are the busiest, the **best nights** to go are often those during the week, when you can enjoy live music, happy hours and other specials. Karaoke is incredibly popular, and if you spend much time in bars, you'll soon pick out the well-loved Tico classics. The drinking age in Costa Rica is 18, and many bars will only admit those with a *cédula* (ID). A photocopy of your passport page is acceptable.

Communications

Costa Rica's privatized postal system (@www.correos.go.cr) is reasonably efficient, though you may have problems sending and receiving letters from remote areas. The Costa Rican state electronics company, the ICE (Instituto Costarricense de Electricidad) provides international telephone, fax and Internet services via RACSA, the telecommunications subsidiary.

Mail

Even the smallest Costa Rican town has a **correo** (post office), but the most reliable place to mail overseas is from San José's lime-green Correo Central (main post office; see p.98). Airmail letters to the US cost 90 colones, 110 colones to Canada and take about ten days to arrive; letters to Europe cost 130 colones and take two weeks or more; letters to Australasia cost 170 colones and take three or four weeks.

Most post offices have a **lista de correos** (Poste Restante, General Delivery) – an efficient and safe way to receive letter mail, especially at the main office in San José. They will hold letters for up to four weeks for a small fee (though in smaller post offices you may not be charged at all). Bring a photocopy of your passport when picking up mail, and make sure that correspondents address letters to you under your name exactly as it appears on your passport.

One thing you can't fail to notice is the paucity of **mailboxes** in Costa Rica. In the capital, unless your hotel has regular mail pickup, the only resort is to hike down to the Correo Central. In outlying or isolated areas of the country, you will have to rely on hotels or local businesses' private mailboxes. In most cases, especially in Limón Province, where mail is very slow, it's probably quicker to wait until you return to San José and mail correspondence from there. For hours of correos, see Opening hours box on p.42.

Although letters are handled fairly efficiently, **packages** are another thing altogether – the parcels service both coming and going gets snarled in paperwork and labyrinthine customs regulations, besides being very expensive and very slow. If you must send parcels, take them unsealed to the correo for inspection.

Telephones

The **country code** for all of Costa Rica is @506. There are no area codes, and all phone numbers now have seven digits. Calls **within Costa Rica** are inexpensive and **calling long-distance** can work out very reasonably if you ring directly through a public telephone network, and avoid calling from your hotel or other private business. The cheapest rates run from 10pm to 7am nightly. The easiest way to make an **international call** is to purchase a phone card (*tarjeta telefónica*), available from most grocery stores, street kiosks and pharmacies. You'll need card number 199 (card number 197 is for domestic calls only) which comes in two denominations: 3000 colones (giving you 17 minutes of talk time to the US and 12 minutes to Europe) and 10,000 colones. To use, insert the card into a payphone, dial @199 and then 2 for instructions in English. Holders of AT&T, MCI, Sprint, Canada Direct or BT calling-cards can also make calls from payphones. Simply dial the relevant access code (see box); charges will automatically be billed to your calling-card account. Many pay phones also accept credit cards. You can also call collect to virtually any foreign country from any phone or payphone in Costa Rica; simply dial @09 or @116 to get an English-speaking operator, then tell them the country code, area code and number; note that this method costs twice as much as dialling direct.

If you want to pay for a call on the spot, the most convenient way is to use a private line in a hotel (though this can be expensive; check before you go ahead), at a local *pulpería* (general store; usually more reasonably priced) or from the San José Radiográfica office (see p.98), where you can also make overseas calls, send and receive faxes and use directories.

Email

Most Costa Rican towns have at least one **Internet café**, while places popular with tourists usually have m any more; charges are low, around $1–1.50 per hour in major towns and around $3–5 in more remote areas where they rely on (rather slow) satellite link-up. Additionally, all Costa Rican post offices – even the most rural – now offer Internet access

Useful phone numbers

International information ☏124
International operator (for collect calls) ☏116 or 09
Calling-card access codes
AT&T ☏0800/011-4114
BT ☏0800/044-1044
Canada Direct ☏0800/015-1161
MCI ☏0800/012-2222
Sprint ☏0800/013-0123
   For all other countries, look in the White Pages (the Costa Rican phone book).

with prepaid cards that you can buy in the post office (300 colones for 30min, 500 for 1hr).

The media

Though the Costa Rican media generally pumps out relatively anodyne and conservative coverage of local and regional issues (shadowing the antics of the president and the political elite with dogged tenacity), it's possible to find good investigative journalism, particularly in the daily La Nación. There are also a number of interesting local radio stations, though TV coverage leaves something to be desired.

Newspapers

In San José, all **domestic newspapers** are sold on the street by vendors. Elsewhere you can find them in newsagents and *pulperías* (general stores). All are tabloid format, with colourful, eye-catching layout and presentation.

   Though the Costa Rican press is free, it does indulge in a certain follow-the-leader journalism. Leader of the pack is the daily **La Nación**, voice of the (right-of-centre) establishment and owned by the country's biggest media consortium; other highbrow dailies and television channels more or less parrot its line. Historically, *La Nación* has featured some good investigative reporting, as in the Banco Anglo corruption scandal

and Costa Rica's continuing drug-trafficking problems. It also comes with a useful daily pull-out arts section, **Viva**, with listings of what's on in San José, and the classifieds are handy for almost anything, including long-term accommodation.

   Also quite serious is **La República**, even if they do have a tendency to slap a football photo on the front page no matter what's happening in the world. **Al Día** is the populist "body count" paper, which will give you a feel for the kind of newspaper read by most Costa Ricans. Alternative voices include **El Heraldo**, a small but high-quality daily, and **La Prensa Libre**, the very good left-leaning evening paper. **Mesoamerica**, based in San José, gives a solid weekly review and impartial analysis of politics, economics and society in Central America. You can consult it in libraries or take out a subscription by writing to ICAS, Aptdo 1524-2050, San Pedro, Costa Rica. The weekly **Semanario Universidad**, the voice of the University of Costa Rica, certainly goes out on more of a limb than the big dailies, with particularly good coverage of the arts and the current political scene. You can find it on or around campus in San José's university district of San Pedro, and also in libraries.

Costa Rica's version of *Newsweek*, **Rumbo**, is a rather dull weekly, featuring thinly researched articles on sociological themes such as jealousy and infidelity alongside features on current politics in the region. Owned by the same group as *La Nación*, it also produces a dreadful women's magazine called **Perfil**.

Local English-language papers include the venerable and serious **Tico Times** (⊛www.ticotimes.net), which comes out on Fridays, and the **Central America Weekly**, intended for tourists, with articles on holiday activities. Both can be a good source of information for travellers, and the ads regularly feature hotel and restaurant discounts, as do the various other glossies produced by the tourist board. As for the **foreign press**, you can pick up recent copies of the *New York Times*, *International Herald Tribune*, *USA Today*, *Miami Herald*, *Newsweek*, *Time* and sometimes the *Financial Times* in the souvenir shop beside the *Gran Hotel Costa Rica* in downtown San José and La Casa de Revistas on the southwest corner of Parque Morazán. Of the San José bookstores, Librerías Lehmann and Universal keep good stocks of mainstream and non-mainstream foreign magazines; the Mark Twain Library at the Centro Cultural Costarricense-Norteamericano (see p.86) also receives English-language publications.

Radio

There are lots of **commercial radio stations** in Costa Rica, all pumping out techno and house, along with a bit of salsa, annoying commercials, and the odd bout of government-sponsored pseudo-propaganda

promoting the general wonder that is Costa Rica. Some of the more interesting **local radio stations** have only a limited airtime, such as Radio Emperador (104.7FM) and Radio Costa Rica (930AM). Radio Alajuela (98.3FM/1280AM) features Costa Rican singers, along with some talk spots, from 8.30pm to midnight. Radio America Latina (780AM) has a fascinating advice show (10.30–11pm) – how to live your life better, be happy, find God – while Radio Monumental (93.5FM/670AM), broadcast from the Burger King Palace in central San José, is a politically themed talk show. Another fascinating programme is El Club del Taxista Costarricense – the "Costa Rican taxi driver's club" – broadcast by Radio Columbia (98.7FM/760AM) from 9.30 to 11pm. This social and political talk show, now in its 22nd year, was initially directed only at taxi drivers, but its populist appeal has led to it being adopted by the general population. Radio Dos (99.5FM) has an English language morning show, Good Morning Costa Rica, which runs from 6-8am.

Television

Most Costa Rican households have a **television**, beaming out a range of wonderfully awful Mexican or Venezuelan *telenovelas* (soap operas) and some not-bad domestic news programmes. On the downside, Costa Rica is also the graveyard for 1970s American TV, the place where *The Dukes of Hazzard* and other such delights, dubbed into Spanish, come back to haunt you.

Channel 7 is the main national station, particularly strong in local and regional news. Other than its news show, Telenoticias, Costa Rica has few home-grown products, and Channel 7's programming comprises a mix of bought-in shows from Spanish-speaking countries plus a few from the US. **Channel 6** is the main competitor, very similar in content; **Channel 19** has mostly programmes and movies from the US dubbed into Spanish. The Mexican cable channels are good for news, and even have reports from Europe. Many places also subscribe to **CNN** and other cable channels, like HBO, Cinemax and Sony Entertainment, which show wall-to-wall reruns of hit comedy shows and films.

Holidays, festivals and opening hours

Though you shouldn't expect the kind of colour and verve that you'll find in fiestas in Mexico or Guatemala, Costa Rica has its fair share of lively holidays and festivals, or *feriados*, when all banks, post offices, museums and government offices close. In particular, don't try to travel anywhere during Semana Santa, Holy (Easter) Week: the whole country shuts down from Holy Thursday until after Easter Monday, and buses don't run. Likewise, the week from Christmas to New Year is invariably a time of traffic nightmares, overcrowded beach towns and suspended transport services.

Provincial holidays, like Independence Day in Guanacaste (July 25) and the Limón Carnival (the week preceding October 12) affect local services only, but nonetheless the shutdown is drastic: don't bet on cashing travellers' cheques or mailing letters if you're in these areas at party time.

January 1 New Year's Day. Celebrated with a big dance in San José's Parque Central.

February Puntarenas Carnival. A week of parades, music and fireworks at the end of the month.

March Monteverde Music Festival. National and international musicians gather in the cloudforest town for a month of song and dance.

March 19 St Joseph's Day (El día de San José). The patron saint of the San José Province is celebrated with fairs, parades and church services.

Ash Wednesday Countrywide processions; in Guanacaste they're marked by horse, cow and bull parades, with bullfights (in which the bull is not harmed) in Liberia.

Holy Week (Semana Santa) Dates vary annually but businesses will often close for the entire week preceding Easter weekend.

April International Arts festival. San José plays host to two weeks of theatre shows, concerts, dance performances and art exhibitions.

April 11 Juan Santamaría Day. Public holiday to commemorate the national hero who fought at the Battle of Rivas against the American adventurer William Walker in 1856.

May 1 Labour Day (Día de los trabajadores). The president delivers his annual "state of the nation" address while everyone else heads to the beach.

May 29 Corpus Christi Day.

June 20 St Peter's and St Paul's Day.

July 25 Independence of Guanacaste Day (Guanacaste province only). Celebrations mark the annexation of Guanacaste from Nicaragua in 1824.

August 2 Virgin of Los Angeles Day. Patron saint of Costa Rica. Worshippers make a pilgrimage to the Basilica in Cartago to venerate the miraculous Black Virgin of Los Angeles (La Negrita).

August 15 Assumption Day and Mother's Day.

September 15 Independence Day, with big patriotic parades celebrating Costa Rica's independence from Spain in 1821. The highlight is a student relay race across the entire Central American Isthmus carrying a 'freedom torch' from Guatemala to Cartago (the original capital of Costa Rica).

October 12 El día de la Raza (Columbus Day; Limón Province only). Centred on the carnival, which takes place in the week prior to October 12.

November 2 All Souls' Day. Families visit cemeteries to pay their respects to their ancestors.

Christmas Week The week before Christmas is celebrated in San José with fireworks, bullfights and funfairs.

December 25 Christmas Day. Family-oriented celebrations with trips to the beach and much consumption of apples and grapes.

December 27 San José Carnival.

Opening hours in Costa Rica

Banks are generally open Monday to Friday 8.30am to 3.30pm; **correos**, Monday to Friday 7.30am to 5.30 or 6pm, and Saturdays 7.30am to noon; government offices, Monday to Friday 8am to 5pm; and **stores**, Monday to Friday 9am to 6 or 7pm, and often on Saturday mornings, as are a few banks. In rural areas shops generally close for lunch. Practically everything is closed on Sundays.

National parks and reserves

Costa Rica protects some 27 percent of its total territory under the aegis of a carefully structured system of national parks, wildlife refuges and biological reserves – in all there are currently more than 75 designated protected areas. Gradually established over the last thirty years, the role of these parks in protecting the country's rich fauna and flora is generally lauded.

In total, the parks and reserves protect approximately four percent of the world's total **wildlife species** and **life zones**, among them rainforests, cloudforests, *páramo* (high-altitude moorlands), swamps, lagoons, marshes and mangroves, and the last remaining patches of tropical dry forest in the isthmus. Also protected are areas of historical significance, including a very few pre-Columbian settlements, and places considered to be of immense scenic beauty – valleys, waterfalls, dry lowlands and beaches. Costa Rica has also taken measures to protect beaches where marine turtles lay their eggs, as well as a number of active volcanos. For a **history** of the park system in Costa Rica, see Contexts.

Definitions

A **national park** (*parque nacional*) is typically a large chunk of relatively untouched wilderness – usually more than 2500 acres – dedicated to preserving features of outstanding ecological or scenic interest. These are the most touristy of the protected areas, typically offering walking, hiking or snorkelling opportunities, while a couple even have historical exhibits. Though habitation, construction of hotels and hunting of animals is prohibited in all national parks, "buffer zones" are increasingly being designated around them, where people are permitted to engage in a limited amount of agriculture and hunting. In most cases, park boundaries are surveyed but not demarcated – rangers and locals know what land is within the park and what is not – so don't expect fences or signs to tell you where you are.

Although it also protects valuable ecosystems and conserves areas for scientific research, a **biological reserve** (*reserva biológica*) generally has less of scenic or recreational interest than a national park, and hunting and fishing are usually prohibited. A **national wildlife refuge** (*refugio nacional de vida silvestre* or *refugio nacional de fauna silvestre*) is designated to protect the habitat of wildlife species. It will not be at all obviously demarcated, with few, if any, services, rangers or trails, and is generally little visited by tourists.

There are also a number of **privately owned reserves** in Costa Rica, chief among them community-initiated projects such as the now famous reserves at Monteverde and nearby Santa Elena. While the money you pay to enter these reserves does not go directly to the government, they are almost never money-grabbing places; the vast majority are conscientiously managed and have links with national and international conservation organizations. For more on how national parks and protected areas link up in Costa Rica's conservation strategy, see Contexts.

Visiting Costa Rica's parks

All national parks have entrance **puestos**, or ranger stations, often little more than a small hut where you pay your fee and pick up a general map. Typically the main ranger stations – from where the internal administration of the park is carried out, and where the rangers sleep, eat and hang out – are some way from the entrance puesto. At some parks you will only deal with the entrance puesto, while at others it's a good idea to drop by the main administration centre, where you can talk to rangers (if your Spanish is good)

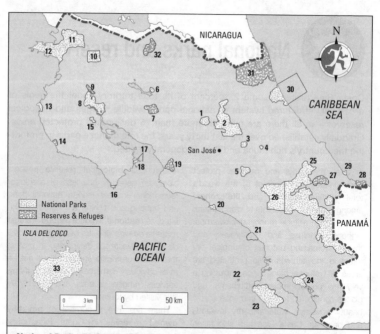

National Parks, Biological Reserves, Wildlife Refuges & Principal Private Reserves

1. Parque Nacional Volcán Poás
2. Parque Nacional Braulio Carrillo
3. Parque Nacional Volcán Irazú
4. Monumento Nacional Guayabo
5. Parque Nacional Tapantí
6. Parque Nacional Volcán Arenal
7. Reserva Biológica Bosque Nuboso
   Monteverde & Reserva Santa Elena
8. Parque Nacional Palo Verde
9. Reserva Biológica Lomas Barbudal
10. Parque Nacional Rincón de la Vieja
11. Parque Nacional Guanacaste
12. Parque Nacional Santa Rosa
13. Parque Nacional Marino las Baulas
14. Refugio Nacional de Fauna Silvestre
    Ostional
15. Parque Nacional Barra Honda
16. Reserva Natural Absoluta Cabo Blanco
17. Reserva Biológica de Guayabo y Negritos
18. Refugio Nacional de Fauna
    Silvestre Curú
19. Reserva Biológica Carara
20. Parque Nacional Manuel Antonio
21. Parque Nacional Marino las
    Ballenas
22. Reserva Biológica Isla del Caño
23. Parque Nacional Corcovado
24. Refugio Nacional de Fauna
    Silvestre Golfito
25. Parque Internacional la Amistad
    (Costa Rica & Panamá)
26. Parque Nacional Chirripó
27. Reserva Biológica Hitoy-Cerere
28. Refugio Nacional de Vida Silvestre
    Gandoca-Manzanillo
29. Parque Nacional Cahuita
30. Parque Nacional Tortuguero
31. Refugio Nacional de Fauna
    Silvestre Barra del Colorado
32. Refugio Nacional de Vida Silvestre
    Caño Negro
33. Parque Nacional Isla del Coco

about local terrain and conditions, enquire about drinking water and use the bathroom. In some parks, such as Corcovado, you can sleep in or camp near the main stations. Usually these provide basic but adequate accommodation, be it on a campsite or a bunk, and a friendly atmosphere.

Outside the most visited parks – Volcán Poás, Volcán Irazú, Santa Rosa and Manuel Antonio – **opening hours** are erratic. Many places are open daily, from around 8am to 3.45pm, though there are exceptions, while other parks may open a little earlier in the morning. Unless you're planning on camping or staying overnight, there's almost no point in arriving at a national park in the afternoon. In all cases, especially the volcanos, you should aim to arrive as early in the morning as possible to make the most of the day and, in particular, the weather (especially in the wet season). You'll usually find a ranger somewhere, even if he or she is not at the puesto. If you hang around for a while and call "¡Upe!" (what people say when entering houses and farms in the countryside), someone will usually appear.

The only central office where you can make reservations and get detailed, up-to-date **information** or buy **permits**, where required, is the Fundación de Parques Nacionales (FPN; Av 15, C 23/25, San José, ☎257-2239, ⓦwww.minae.go.cr/accvc), who will contact those parks for which you sometimes need reservations, chiefly Santa Rosa, Corcovado and Chirripó (see the individual accounts in the Guide for more details). Other parks can be visited on spec.

Most parks now charge an **entrance fee** of $6 per day. If you want to camp overnight in any park, you'll sometimes have to pay for both days – $12 in total.

Park organization

In order to decentralize the national park system and to shift some of the administrative and day-to-day responsibilities to the areas in which the parks are located, Costa Rica was formally divided in 1994–95 into **eight conservation areas**.

In the middle of the country, the **CENTRAL VOLCANIC MOUNTAIN RANGE** contains the most accessible nationalparks, near San José and easily visited on a day-trip. Closest to the capital is **Braulio Carrillo National Park**, protecting tropical wet forest and cloudforest and containing its own volcano, Volcán Barva. The little-known **Juan Castro Blanco National Park** sits above **Volcán Poás National Park**, one of the most visited in the country; **Irazú National Park**, centred on another volcano, lies to the southeast. Nearby is the archeological site of **Guayabo National Monument**, a pre-Columbian settlement on the slopes of the Cordillera Central.

The tiny **ARENAL** conservation area, in the west of the Zona Norte, comprises the relatively new **Volcán Arenal National Park**, established to protect the lava trails and the flora and fauna on the slopes of Volcán Arenal. You can still watch the night-time eruptions, when lava streams down the sides of the mountain.

LA AMISTAD conservation area, located largely in the extreme south of the country and continuing east to encompass parts of the Caribbean province of Limón, includes giant **La Amistad International Park** – a joint venture between Costa Rica and Panamá that protects large areas of mammalian habitat and huge tracts of virtually impenetrable montane forests. Popular with hikers and backpackers, **Chirripó National Park** is named for Mount Chirripó, at 3819m the highest point in Costa Rica. The wet and dense **Tapantí National Park** lies close to the Valle Central, while in the east, Limón Province is home to the little-visited **Hitoy-Cerere Biological Reserve**, tiny **Cahuita National Park**, established to conserve some of the last remaining coral reef in Costa Rica, and, in the southeast, **Gandoca-Manzanillo Wildlife Refuge**, an area of protected mangroves and low-lying swamps.

In the northeast corner of the country the **TORTUGUERO PLAINS** conservation area covers an enormous expanse of 1330 square kilometres and comprises **Tortuguero National Park**, established to protect the nesting grounds of several species of marine turtle, and the wet lowland tropical forest of **Barra del Colorado Wildlife Refuge**. Largely impenetrable except by water, this area protects an enormous range of mammal and marine life, as well as some 400 different species of birds.

GUANACASTE conservation area, in the northwest of the country, includes the national parks of **Guanacaste**, **Rincón de la Vieja** and **Santa Rosa.** It covers a wide variety of altitudes, from sea level to nearly 2000m at the top of Rincón de la Vieja Volcano. Of most interest here are the surviving pockets of tropical dry forest and the good hiking trail up Rincón de la Vieja.

Straddling the Nicoya Peninsula and southern Guanacaste, **TEMPISQUE** covers

National parks

National park	Location	Topography	Wildlife	Activities
LA AMISTAD	border with Panamá	rainforest	mammals, birds	hiking
VOLCÁN ARENAL	136km NW of San José	volcanic	birds, mammals	volcano-watching, hiking
BALLENA	192km SW of San José	marine coral	mammals, fish	diving, snorkelling
BARRA HONDA	330km E of San José	subterranean caves	bats, reptiles, birds	caving (via Liberia)
LAS BAULAS	301km NW of San José	beach, marine	turtles	turtle-watching
BRAULIO CARRILLO	20km N of San José	cloudforest, rainforest	birds, reptiles, mammals	hiking, birding
CAHUITA	195km SE of San José	marine, beaches	coral, reptiles, mammals	swimming, walking, snorkelling
CHIRRIPÓ	151km S of San José	mountain peaks, páramo	mammals, birds (incl. quetzal)	hiking, climbing
CORCOVADO	380km SW of San José	rainforest	mammals, amphibians, reptiles	hiking
GUANACASTE	250km NW of San José	rainforest, tropical dry forest	butterflies, moths, birds, mammals	hiking
GUAYABO NAT. MONUMENT	84km SE of San José	rainforest	mammals, birds	archeology, history, walking
VOLCÁN IRAZÚ	54km SE of San José	volcanic	birds	volcano-watching
ISLA DEL COCO	500km offshore	volcanic, rainforest	marine life	diving
MANUEL ANTONIO	132km SW of San José	rainforest, mangroves, beaches	mammals, marine life, reptiles	hiking, swimming
PALO VERDE	240km NW of San José	limestone hills, savannah	birds, mammals	bird-watching, hiking
VOLCÁN POÁS	56km N of San José	volcanic, dwarf cloudforest	mammals, birds	volcano-watching
RINCÓN DE LA VIEJA	253km NW of San José	rainforest, savannah	birds	hiking, volcano-watching
SANTA ROSA	261km NW of San José	tropical dry forest	mammals, turtles	hiking, history, turtle-watching
TAPANTÍ	40km SW of San José	primary montane forests	mammals, birds	hiking
TORTUGUERO	254km NE of San José	rainforest, beach	turtles, mammals, birds	turtle-watching (via road/water)

Guardaparques

A **guardaparque** is a park ranger, working long hours and long shifts – often twenty days on and eight days off – for basic pay. You will sometimes see guardaparques in the more remote areas of the country setting out on foot to patrol the park against poaching. Poaching of birds and animals, including famous and endangered species such as the quetzal and the jaguar, for sale to zoos or individuals is common, as is the hunting of animals for meat. Guardaparques also often go on patrol at night, alone and armed only with a torch.

Many are locals, and extremely knowledgeable about their patch of terrain, while others are university students of biology, botany or ecology who may have studied abroad and who are working for the parks service as part of their education.

The service also relies on a cadre of dedicated international **volunteers** to help out at the more remote ranger stations. If you fancy volunteering, see p.54 for more details; you have to be pretty brave to do this, as you are expected to do everything that a ranger does.

In general, visitors to Costa Rica's national parks will find *guardaparques* friendly and very informative. Though only part of their job is to provide tourist information, if gently encouraged they will sometimes tell you about their encounters with fearsome bushmasters or placid tapirs. Independent travellers and hikers might want to ask about the possibility of joining them on patrol during the day (you'll probably have to speak some Spanish). Although frowned upon by the powers that be, this can be a great and educational experience.

Palo Verde National Park, Las Baulas National Marine Park, Barra Honda National Park, Isla de Guayabo, Negritos, and **Pájaros Island Biological Reserves** and **Lomas Barbudal Biological Reserve**. This is a tremendously varied, if little visited, collection of protected areas, varying from subterranean caves in Barra Honda and turtles in Las Baulas to seasonal wetlands in Palo Verde – well worth the effort of getting off the beaten track.

The **OSA** conservation area in the extreme southwest of Costa Rica protects some of the most diverse tropical forest in the Americas. Comprising **Corcovado National Park** on the Osa Peninsula, the **Golfito Wildlife Refuge** and the **Piedras Blancas National Park** on the mainland, it also encompasses the **Marine National Park**

Ballena and **Caño Island Biological Reserve**, both excellent snorkelling and scuba-diving destinations.

There's also a satellite category of parks that do not fit neatly into geographical or biological areas: **Manuel Antonio National Park** on the Pacific coast, protecting an area of astounding scenic beauty, including beaches and jungle trails; the Pacific lowland **Carara Biological Reserve**, a haven for crocodiles and other reptiles and amphibians; the unique and very localized habitat of **Cabo Blanco Absoluta Nature Reserve** on the tip of the Nicoya Peninsula; and the remote **Isla del Coco National Park**, 500km off the Costa Rican coast in the Pacific Ocean, which safeguards marine life and many endemic land-living species of reptiles and birds.

Outdoor activities

Costa Rica is famous for year-round adventure tourism and outdoor activities, with numerous well-organized packages and guided outings (see p.32 for details of tour operators). For further information on sporting activities in Costa Rica pick up the twice-monthly Costa Rica Outdoors magazine or visit ⑩www.costaricaoutdoors.com – they specialize in fishing, but cover other sports too.

Hiking and walking

Almost everyone who comes to Costa Rica does some sort of **hiking** or **walking**, whether it be through the rainforest, on grassy uplands or drylands, or ambling along beaches or trails in parks with less demanding terrain.

From lowland tropical forest to the heights of Mount Chirripó, there are opportunities for walking in all kinds of terrain, often for considerable distances. Make sure to **bring** sturdy shoes or hiking boots and a hat, sunblock, umbrella and lightweight rain gear. It helps to have binoculars, too, even if you don't consider yourself an avid birder or animal-spotter; it's amazing what they pick up that the naked eye misses. In certain areas, like Corcovado – where you'll be doing more walking than you've ever done before, unless you're in the Marines – most people also bring a tent. In the high *páramo* of Chirripó, you'll need to bring at least a sleeping bag.

There are a number of things you have to be careful of when hiking in Costa Rica. The chief danger is **dehydration**: always carry lots of water with you, preferably bottled, or a canteen. In 1992, two hikers died in Barra Honda National Park when they ventured along unfamiliar trails in the midday heat without sufficient water and became lost. Bring a hat and sunscreen to protect yourself against sunstroke, and use both, even if it's cloudy.

Each year many hikers **get lost**, although they're nearly almost always found before it's too late. If you're venturing into a remote and unfamiliar area, bring a map and compass and make sure you know how to use both. To lessen anxiety if you do get lost, make sure you have matches, a torch and, if you are at a fairly high altitude, warm clothing. It gets cold at night above 1500m, and it would be ironic (and put quite a damper on your holiday) to end up with hypothermia in the tropics.

Whitewater rafting

After hiking and walking, **whitewater rafting** is probably the single most popular activity in Costa Rica. Some of the best rapids and rivers to be found south of Colorado are here, and there's a growing mini-industry of rafting outfitters, most of them in San José. Elsewhere in the country your hotel or lodge might provide a guided rafting trip as an inclusive or extra tour.

Whitewater rafting entails getting in a rubber dinghy with about eight other people (including a guide) and paddling, at first very leisurely, down a river, and then negotiating exhilarating rapids of varying difficulty. Overall it's very safe, and the ample life jackets and helmets help. **Wildlife** you are likely to see from the boat includes crocodiles, caimans, lizards, parrots, toucans, herons, kingfishers, iguanas and butterflies. Most trips last a day, though some companies run overnight or weekend excursions. They **cost** between $60 and $90 for a day, including transport, equipment and lunch. Dress to get wet, with a bathing suit, shorts and surfer sandals or gym shoes.

Rafters classify their rivers from Class I (easiest) to Class V (pretty hard – don't venture onto one of these until you know what you're doing). The **most difficult** rivers in Costa Rica are the Class III–IV Ríos Reventazón and Pacuaré (both reached from the Valle Central via Turrialba), the

Class IV Río Toro (Zona Norte) and some sections of the Río Naranjo around Manuel Antonio National Park. **Moderately easy** Río Sarapiquí (Zona Norte) is a Class II river with some Class III rapids, and a fearsome class IV-V section. The gentlest of all is Corobicí in Guanacaste, a Class I flat water.

Whitewater rafting outfitters

Aguas Bravas Aptdo 1500-2100, San José ☎ 292-2072, ⌂ www.aguas-bravas.co.cr. Small company operating mostly on the Río Sarapiquí and specializing in summer camps for kids aged 10–17 and family-orientated rafting excursions. They also offer kayaking tours and trips in non-motorized dinghies. Their day-trip to the Class IV-V section of the Sarapiquí is for the reasonably fit only.
Aventuras Naturales Aptdo 10736-1000, San José ☎ 225-3939, ⌂ www.adventurecostarica .com. Wide choice of tours and levels including day-trips on the Ríos Reventazón, Sarapiquí and Corobicí, two-day trips on the Río Pacuaré (with an overnight stay at the Pacuaré Jungle Lodge) and three- or four-day expeditions on the Río General near Chirripó.
Costa Rica Whitewater C Central, Av 3, San José ☎ 257-0766, ⌂ www.costaricaexpeditions.com. Part of the long-established Costa Rica Expeditions (see p.32), this company has been rafting for over twenty years, with a good selection of day-trips and longer excursions, most of them fairly difficult.
Costa Sol Rafting Aptdo 8-4390-1000, San José ☎ 293-2150, ⌂ www.costasolrafting.com. Day-trips on the more difficult rivers, some overnighters, and ocean kayaking.
Ríos Tropicales Aptdo 472-1200, San José ☎ 233-6455, ⌂ www.riostropicales.com. One of the larger outfitters, with challenging trips on the Ríos Reventazón, Pacuaré and Corobicí – a good choice for experienced rafters.

Kayaking

More than twenty rivers in Costa Rica offer good **kayaking** opportunities, especially the Sarapiquí, Reventazón, Pacuaré, General and Corobicí. The small towns of Turrialba, in the Valle Central, and Puerto Viejo de Sarapiquí, in the Zona Norte, are good bases for customized kayaking tours, with a number of specialist operators or lodges that rent boats, equipment and guides. Costa Sol Rafting (see above) run "kayaking clinics", crash courses lasting

from half a day or more where you can learn how to handle a kayak.

Sea kayaking has become increasingly popular in recent years. This is an activity for experienced kayakers only, and should never be attempted without a guide. The number of rivers, rapids and streams pouring from the mountains into the oceans on both coasts can make currents treacherous, and any kind of boating, especially kayaking, is potentially dangerous without proper supervision.

Swimming

Costa Rica has many lovely **beaches**, most of them on the Pacific coast. You do have to be careful swimming at many of them, however, as more than 200 **drownings** occur each year – about four or five a week. Most are unnecessary, resulting from **rip tides**, strong currents that go from the beach out to sea in a kind of funnel. Rip tides are created by an excess of water coming into the beach and seeking a release for its extra energy. When the water finds an existing depression on the ocean floor, or creates one from its own force, it forms a kind of swift-moving current, much like a river, over this depression. Rip tides are always found on beaches with relatively **heavy surf**, and can also form near river estuaries. Some are permanent, while some "migrate" up and down a beach. People who die in rip tides do so because they panic – it is undeniably unnerving when you find yourself being carried at what seems an alarming rate, 6 or 10km an hour, out into the wide blue ocean. They try to swim against the current, which is a useless enterprise. The combination of panic and an intense burst of energy exhausts people fast, causing them to take in water. Tragically, many people who die as a result of rip currents do so in water that is no more than waist-high. The important thing to know about rip tides is that, while they may drag you out to sea a bit, they won't take you far beyond the breakers, where they lose their energy and dissipate. They also won't drag you under – that's an undertow – and there are far fewer of those on Costa Rica's beaches. The best advice if you get

Rip tides in Costa Rica

Some of the most popular and frequented beaches in Costa Rica are, ironically, also the worst for **rip tides**:

Playa Doña Ana (Central Pacific)

Playa Jacó (Central Pacific)

Manuel Antonio's Playa Espadilla (Central Pacific)

Playa Tamarindo (Guanacaste)

Playa Avellana (Guanacaste)

Playa Junquillal (Guanacaste)

Playa Bonita (Limón)

Punta Uva (Limón)

Cahuita, the first 400m of beach (Limón)

caught in rip currents is to relax as much as possible, float, call for help and wait until the current dies down. Then swim back towards the beach at a 45° angle; not straight in. By swimming back at an angle you'll avoid getting caught in the current again.

It's also important to be aware of fairly heavy **swells**. These waves might not look that big from the beach but can have a mighty pull when you get near their break point. Many people are hurt coming out of the sea, backs to the waves, which then clobber them from behind. Best come out of the sea sideways, so that there is minimum body resistance to the water.

In addition to the above precautions, never swim alone, don't swim at beaches where turtles nest (this means, more often than not, sharks), never swim near river estuaries (pollution and rip tides) and always ask locals about the general character of the beach before you swim.

Diving and snorkelling

Though **diving** is less of a big deal in Costa Rica than in Belize or Honduras's Bay Islands, there are a few worthwhile dive sites, the best of them along the extreme northwest of the **Pacific coast**, such as Santa Elena Bay's Murciélago and Catalina Islands.

You can also theoretically **snorkel** all along the Pacific coast – Playa Flamingo in northern Guanacaste has clear waters but not a

lot to see, while Playa Panamá and Bahía Ballena also have good snorkelling. For people who want to see an abundance of underwater life, the small **reef** near Manzanillo on the Caribbean coast is the best; the nearby reef at Cahuita has suffered in recent years from erosion and is now dying.

Diving outfitters in Costa Rica

Aquamor Adventures Manzanillo ☎391-3417, ⓦwww.greencoast.com/aquamor. Excellent dive operation situated within the Gandoca-Manzanillo Marine Refuge, with night dives, certification courses and tours. Employs local captains and works in alliance with the Talamanca Dolphin Foundation.

Bill Beard's Diving Safaris Playa Hermosa ☎ & ⓕ672-0012, ⓦwww.billbeards.com. Experienced operator in the northern Guanacaste region. PADI certification courses.

Costa Rica Adventure Divers Bahía Drake ☎385-9541, ⓦwww.costaricadiving.com. Boat dives, dive courses and snorkelling around Bahía Drake and the pristine reef of nearby Isla de Caño.

Ocotal Beach Resort and Marina Playa Ocotal ☎670-0321, ⓦwww.ocotaldiving.com. PADI certification courses and five- and seven-day dive trips to offshore islands.

Rich Coast Diving Playas del Coco ☎670-0176, ⓦwww.richcoastdiving.com. Snorkelling and scuba-diving trips.

Surfing

Surfing is very good on both of Costa Rica's coasts, although there are certain beaches that are suitable during only parts of the year. You can surf all year round on the **Pacific**: running north to south the most popular beaches are Boca de Barranca, Naranjo, Tamarindo, Jacó, Hermosa, Quepos, Dominical and, in the extreme south near the Panamá border, Pavones. On the **Caribbean** coast the best beaches are at Puerto Viejo and Punta Uva further down the coast.

The **north Pacific Coast and Nicoya Peninsula** is the country's prime surfing area, with a wide variety of breaks and lefts and rights of varying power and velocity. Within Santa Rosa National Park, **Playa Naranjo** gives one of the best breaks in the country (Dec–March) and has the added attraction of good camping facilities, though you'll need your own 4WD to reach them. **Playa Potrero Grande**, only accessible by boat from Playa del Coco, offers a very fast right point break.

Moving down to the long western back of the Nicoya Peninsula, **Playa Tamarindo** has three sites for surfing, though parts of the beach are plagued by rocks. While they don't offer a really demanding or wild ride, Tamarindo's waves are very popular due to the large number of hotels and restaurants in the town nearby. **Playa Langosta**, just south of Tamarindo, offers right and left point breaks, a little more demanding than Tamarindo. **Playa Avellanas** has a good beach break, locally called the *Guanacasteco*, with very hollow rights and lefts, while **Playa Nosara** offers a fairly gentle beach break, with rights and lefts. Remote and difficult to reach, **Playas Coyote**, **Manzanillo** and **Mal País** have consistent lefts and rights and several points.

Near Puntarenas on the **Central Pacific Coast**, **Boca Barranca** is an estuary with a very long left, while **Puerto Caldera** has a good left. **Playa Jacó** is not always dependable for good beach breaks, and the surf is not too big. Further south, **Playa Hermosa** is better, with a very strong beach break. The adjacent **Playas Esterillos Este**, **Oeste** and **Bejuco** offer similarly good beach breaks.

On the south Pacific coast, **Playita Manuel Antonio** is good when the wind is up, with beach breaks and left and right waves. Southwards, **Dominical** offers great surfing, with strong lefts and rights and beautiful surroundings. Down at the very south of the country, past Golfito, **Playa Pavones** boasts one of the longest left points in the world, very fast and with a good formation.

The best surfing beaches on the **Caribbean coast** lie towards the south, from Cahuita to Manzanillo villages. **Black-Sand Beach** at Cahuita has an excellent beach break, with the added bonus of year-round waves. **Puerto Viejo** is home to "La Salsa Brava", one of the few legitimate "big waves" in Costa Rica, a very thick, tubular wave formed by deep water rocketing towards a shallow reef. Further south, **Manzanillo** has a very fast beach break in lovely surroundings and with good camping.

Further north towards Puerto Limón are a couple of beaches that, while not in the class of Puerto Viejo, can offer experienced surfers a few good waves. **Playa Bonita**, a few kilometres north of Limón, is known for its powerful and dangerous left; only people who really know what they are doing should try this. Similarly, the left-breaking waves at **Isla Uvita**, just off the coast from Puerto Limón, are considered tricky.

If you're interested in **learning to surf**, Alvaro Solano (☎643-2830 or 643-1308), Costa Rica's national surfing champion, gives lessons at Playa Jacó on the Central Pacific coast. There are also several popular surf schools in Tamarindo (see p.253 for details). *The Surfer's Guide to Costa Rica* by Mike Parise, available from Amazon. com, is an invaluable guide for the serious surfer.

Fishing and sports-fishing

Costa Rica has hit the big time in the lucrative **sports-fishing** game. Both coasts are blessed with the kind of big fish serious anglers love – marlin, swordfish, tarpon and snook among them. The most obvious characteristic of sports-fishing is its tremendous **expense**: some three- or four-day packages run upwards of $3000. **Quepos** and **Golfito** have long been good places to do some fishing, while **Barra del Colorado** in the northeast and **Playa Flamingo** in Guanacaste have turned into monothematic expensive sports-fishing destinations. Although good fishing is possible all year round, **January** and **February** are the most popular months.

Sports-fishing is just that: sport. The vast majority of fish are returned to the sea alive. Marty Bernard's No Frills Sports-fishing Tours (☎228-4812, ⓦwww.nofrillsfishing .com) is famous in Costa Rica for teaching total amateurs how to snag huge tarpon and *guapote* (rainbow bass) in a day; it offers all-inclusive two-day tours for $790, which is an excellent price. See the accounts of Barra del Colorado in Limón province (p.169), Los Chiles in the Zona Norte (p.198), Quepos in the Central Pacific (p.309) and Golfito in the Zona Sur (p.343) for local sports-fishing opportunities. The *Tico Times* has a fishing columnist, Jerry Ruhlow, who regularly reports on the current best fishing spots.

Casual anglers can find cheaper and more low-key fishing opportunities in the country's many trout-rich **freshwater rivers**, or in **Laguna de Arenal**, where rainbow bass fishing is especially good.

Birdwatching

One oft-repeated statistic you'll hear about Costa Rica is that the country boasts more than 850 species of birds (including migratory ones), a higher number than all of North America. Consequently, the **birding** is impressive, and it's likely that you'll spot hummingbirds, scarlet macaws, toucans, kingfishers and a variety of trogons. The resplendent quetzal, found in the higher elevations of Monteverde, Braulio Carrillo National Park and the Talamanca mountain range, is elusive, but can still be spotted. The tiny hamlet of San Gerardo de Dota, close to the Cerro de la Muerte and signposted from the stretch of Interamericana which runs between Cartago and San Isidro de El General, is by far the best place to see quetzals.

Serious birders have a few **tour operators** to choose from, all of them in San José. Of those listed on p.32, Horizontes and Costa Rica Expeditions are the best. The *Albergue de Montaña Talari* in Rivas (see p.332) runs weekly tours through the south of Costa Rica guided by professional ornithologists ($660 per person all-inclusive).

Mountain biking

Only certain places in Costa Rica lend themselves well to **mountain biking**. In general, the best areas for extensive biking are Corcovado National Park, Montezuma village to Cabo Blanco Absoluta Nature Reserve on the Nicoya Peninsula, and Santa Rosa National Park in Guanacaste. The La Fortuna and Volcán Arenal area is also increasingly popular: you can bike to see the volcano (although not up it) and around the pretty Laguna de Arenal.

There are plenty of bike **rental shops** throughout the country; you may also be able to rent one from local tour agencies. Prices are generally around $5 an hour or $25 for the day. See "Getting Around"

for more on independent cycling around Costa Rica.

Biking tours in Costa Rica

Bi.Costa Rica ☏ 258-0303, ✆ www.bruncas .com/bicostarica.html. Expert bike tour operators who organize guided custom-made tours throughout the country for experienced cyclists only. Hotel stop-overs are well chosen and itineraries are both challenging and imaginative.
Ríos Tropicale ☏ 233-6455, ✆ www .riostropicales.com. This whitewater rafting specialist also arranges bike rides up and around Poás and Irazú volcanos and a ten-day coast-to-coast tour on demand.

Horse-riding

Almost everywhere you go in Costa Rica, with the exception of the waterlogged northern Limón Province, you should be able to hook up with a **horseback tour**. Guanacaste is probably the best area in the country for riding, with a cluster of excellent haciendas (working cattle ranches) that also cater to tourists, offering bed, breakfast and horse hire. They're covered in detail in our chapter on Guanacaste.

Riding **on the beach** on the Nicoya Peninsula, especially in Montezuma in the south and Sámara on the west coast, is also very popular. Horses are rented by the hour. However, there has been a history of mistreatment of horses in these places. Don't expect the animals here to be in as good shape as sleek thoroughbreds back home, but if you see any extreme cases of mistreatment complain to the local tourist information centre or local residents.

Horse-riding tours

Buena Vista Lodge 31km northeast of Liberia ☏ 661-8158, ✆ www.buenavistacr.com. Horseriding tours in the Rincón de la Vieja area.
Desafío Tours Santa Elena, Monteverde ☏ 645-5874, ✆ www.monteverdetours.com. Trips on well-cared-for horses around Monteverde. They can also arrange bespoke horse tours across the country.
Finca Los Caballos Montezuma, Nicoya ☏ 642-0124, ✆ www.naturelodge.net. Riding tours for guests only, with horses for all levels and

trips along beaches, to waterfalls and through rainforest.

Hacienda Barú Between Quepos and Dominical on the Caribbean coast ☎787-0003, ⓦwww .haciendabaru.com. Rides and horseback tours into the rainforest and around the hacienda's private reserve.

Mr Big J Cahuita ☎755-0328 Friendly tour company that organizes rides through Cahuita National Park, the jungle and along the lovely black sand beach.

Volcán Turrialba Lodge Near Turrialba ☎273-4335, ⓦwww.volcanturrialbalodge.com. Five-hour rides up to the volcano and through remote and spectacular cloudforest.

Shopping

Compared with many Latin American countries, Costa Rica does not have an impressive crafts or artisan tradition. However, there are some interesting souvenirs, such as carved wooden salad bowls, plates and trays. Wherever you go, you'll see hand-painted wooden replica ox-carts, originating from Sarchí in the Valle Central (see p.118) – perennial favourites, especially when made into drinks trolleys.

Reproductions of the pre-Columbian pendants and earrings displayed in San José's Museo Nacional, the Museo de Oro and the Museo de Jade are sold both on the street and in shops. Much of it isn't real gold, however, but gold-plated, which chips and peels: check before you buy.

Costa Rican **coffee** is one of the best gifts to take home. Make sure you buy export brands Café Britt or Café Rey and not the lower-grade sweetened coffee sold locally. It's often cheaper to buy bags in the supermarket rather than in souvenir shops, and cheaper still to buy beans at San José's Mercado Central. If you want your coffee beans roasted to your own taste, go to the *Café Gourmet* in San José for excellent beans and grinds. For more on coffee, see p.37.

In the absence of a real home-grown crafts or textile tradition, generic **Indonesian** dresses and clothing – batiked and colourful printed cloth – are widely sold in the beach communities of Montezuma, Cahuita, Tamarindo and Quepos (near Manuel Antonio). In some cases this craze for all things Indonesian extends to slippers, silver and bamboo jewellery – and prices are reasonable.

If you have qualms about buying goods made from **tropical hardwoods**, ask the salesperson what kind of wood the object is made from, and avoid mahogany, laurel and purple heart. Other goods to avoid are coral, anything made from tortoise shells, and furs such as ocelot or jaguar.

Work, volunteering and study

Costa Rica's all-round appeal makes it a good place to learn Spanish, and language-study tours and volunteer work projects (many of which are tax-deductible for travellers from the US) are extremely popular.

Volunteer work and research projects

There's a considerable choice of **volunteer work** and **research projects** in Costa Rica – some include food and lodging, and many can be organized from the US. As an example, University Research Expeditions sends teams each year on two-week expeditions to replant lost trees and measure soil and plant characteristics. The team shares a rented house in a rural area of southern Costa Rica.

A good resource **in the US** for language study and volunteer work programmes is *Transitions Abroad*, a bimonthly magazine focusing on living and working overseas available from Dept TRA, PO Box 745, Bennington, VT 05201 (T802/442 4827, Wwww.transitionsabroad.com). Prospective **British** volunteers should contact the Costa Rican Embassy in London (see p.16). In **Australia**, details of current student exchanges and study programmes are available either from the Costa Rican consul (see p.16) or from the AFS, PO Box 5, Strawberry Hills, Sydney (T02/9215 0077, Wwww.afs.org.au). In **New Zealand**, contact the AFS, PO Box 5662, Level 3, 125 Featherstone Street, Wellington (T04/494 6020, Wwww.afsnzl.org.nz).

Volunteer programmes

Amigos de las Aves 32-4001 Rio Segundo de Alajuela T441-2658, E richmar@racsa.co.cr. This organization works on breeding pairs of scarlet and great green macaws. Volunteers are required for 2–3-month placements and help with their education programme.
ANAI Aptdo 170–2070, Sabanilla T224-6090 or 3570, Wwww.anaicr.org. Based in southern Talamanca, ANAI trains people to farm organically and manage forests sustainably. There are also volunteer programmes to help protect the Gandoca-Manzanillo

Refuge and the turtles that come to the Caribbean coast each year (May–July). Minimum six weeks.
APREFLOFAS Aptdo 917-2150, San José T240-6087, Wwww.preserveplanet.org. Runs a host of wildlife preservation schemes and reforestation programmes around the country and helps local communities set up sustainable eco-tourism projects. Minimum three months.
ASVO (Association of Volunteers for Service in Protected Areas); contact the director of International Voluntary Programmes T223-4989, Wwww.asvocr.com. Government-run association enabling volunteers to work in the national parks, helping guard protected areas, write reports and give environmental classes. Minimum one month.
Caribbean Conservation Corp PO Box 2866, Gainesville, FL 32602 T1-800/678-7853, in Costa Rica T225-7516, Wwww.cccturtle.org. Volunteer research work on marine turtles at Tortuguero.
Earthwatch Wwww.earthwatch.org. In the US: 3 Clock Tower Place, Suite 100, Maynard, MA 01754 T1-800/776-0188. In the UK: 267 Banbury Road, Oxford OX2 7HT T01865/318 838, F01865/311 383. Leatherback turtle study in Tamarindo, helping with a turtle hatchery and relocating threatened nests.
Genesis II Cloud Forest Reserve PO Box 655, 7050, Cartago T & F381-0789, Wwww .genesis-two.com. Accepts physically-fit volunteers for four-week placements helping with reforestation and wildlife preservation projects in a Talamancan mountain reserve.
Global Service Corps 300 Broadway, Suite 28, San Francisco, CA 94133-3312 T415/788-3666 ext 128, Wwww.globalservicecorps.org. Service programmes in Costa Rica.
Global Volunteers 375 E Little Canada Rd, St Paul, MN 55117, US T1-800/487-1074 or 651/407-6100, Wwww.globalvolunteers.org. Volunteer programme helping to maintain the Santa Elena Cloud Forest Reserve.
Monteverde Institute Aptdo 69–5655, Monteverde T & F645-5053, Wwww.mvinstitute .org. Volunteer projects in the Monteverde cloudforest including teaching, fieldwork on trails and other conservation efforts. Volunteers must know Spanish and commit for six weeks.

Proyecto Campanario Near Sierpe on the Osa Peninsula ☎ 258-2778, ⓕ 256-0374, ⓦ www.campanario.org. Research station and eco-tourist project which sometimes offers free or discounted lodging and meals in exchange for work on and around the reserve. Must be able to swim.

University Research Expeditions University of California, Berkeley, CA 94720-7050 ☎ 510/642-6586, ⓦ www.berkeley.edu. Environmental and animal behaviour studies.

Volunteers for Peace 43 Tiffany Rd, Belmont, VT 05730 ☎ 802/259-2759, ⓦ www.vfp.org. Volunteer projects in Costa Rica and other Central American countries.

Study programmes and learning Spanish

San José offers a wealth of Spanish courses. Though you can arrange a place through organizations based in the US (see below), the best way to choose is to visit a few, perhaps sit in on a class or two, and judge the school according to your own personality and needs. This is not always possible, though, especially in high season (Dec–April), when many classes have been booked in advance. At other times, the drop-in method should be no problem at the majority of the schools we've listed. Note that courses in Costa Rica generally cost more than in Mexico or Guatemala.

Some of the **language schools** listed here are Tico-run; some are branches of international (usually North American) education networks. Instructors are almost invariably Costa Ricans who speak some English. School noticeboards are an excellent source of information and contact for travel opportunities, apartment shares and social activities. Most schools have a number of Costa Rican families on their books with whom they regularly place students for **homestays**. If you want **private tuition**, any of the schools listed below can recommend a tutor. Private rates run from $15 to $30 an hour.

Language schools in Costa Rica

Academia Latinoamericana de Español Aptdo 1280-2050, San Pedro, San José ☎ 224-9917, ⓦ www.alespanish.com. Friendly school near the Toruma Youth Hostel in San José. Small groups (4–6) and intensive courses (20hr weekly; $155),

with morning or afternoon schedules; homestay programmes cost a further $135 per week. There's a 15 percent discount for Hostelling International cardholders; all materials included.

Central American Institute for International Affairs (ICAI) Aptdo 10302, Otoya 1000, San José ☎ 233-8571, ⓦ www.educators.com. Spanish tuition, cultural events and field trips, with an emphasis on learning through conversation. Good resources include a reference library, international directories and a travel office that can arrange weekend excursions. Two- or four-week programmes (4hr daily), with a minimum of six students per class ($300 per week for lessons plus $150 per week for accommodation).

Centro Lingüístico Conversa C 38, Av 3/5, San José ☎ 221-7649, ⓦ www.conversa.net. Well-established institute that also teaches English to Ticos. Classes have a minimum of six students (5hr 30min daily for a super-intensive course) with thorough teaching that puts the emphasis on grammar. The four-week programme includes accommodation either with a Tico family, in a separate lodge with private bath and bedrooms, or at the centre's five-acre farm, 10km outside San José.

Cultural Costarricense-Norteamericano, Spanish Programme Aptdo 1489-1000, San José ☎ 207-7500, ⓦ www.cccncr.com. Primarily a centre for cross-cultural exchange, but also offers Spanish lessons. The unrivalled facilities include a theatre, a gallery and the Mark Twain Library, which has an excellent stock of English and Spanish publications.

Costa Rica Spanish Institute (COSI) PO Box 1366-2050, San Pedro ☎ 234-1001, ⓦ www.cosi.co.cr. Small classes in San Pedro, as well as a "beach and rainforest programme" in Manuel Antonio National Park. Homestays are arranged, as are private lessons and cultural activities.

Costa Rican Academy of Language Av 0, C 25/27 ☎ 233-8938 or 233-8914, ⓦ www.crilang.com. Small, friendly and Costa Rican-owned school, with a multinational clientele (including many Germans and Swiss) and a conversational approach to learning, based on current affairs. There are also Latin dance classes every afternoon, and trips to discos to practise the steps.

Institute for Central American Development Studies (ICADS) ☎ 234-1381, ⓕ 234-1337, ⓦ www.icadscr.com. Month-long Spanish immersion programmes including lectures and activities emphasizing environmental issues, women's studies, economic development and human rights, with optional afternoon internships in grassroots organizations.

Instituto Británico Aptdo 8184, San José, 1000 ☎ 225-0256, ⓦ www.institutobritanico.co.cr.

Courses for all levels of proficiency, including tailor-made courses focusing on specific vocabulary (like business Spanish) and one-week express courses in basic "survival" Spanish. You can also study in Liberia, Guanacaste.

Instituto Profesional de Español para Extranjeros Aptdo 562-2050, San Pedro, San José ☎283-7731, ⓦwww.ipee.com. Small school that prides itself on a cosy atmosphere, total-immersion methodology and small groups (maximum six people). All ages and levels of Spanish are catered for, and courses run year-round, from one week to six months or more. Facilities include free Internet access, and they can also arrange field trips, excursions and homestays.

Montaña Linda Language School Orosí ☎ & ⒻEdit 533-2153, ⓦwww.montanalinda.com. Popular school in a gorgeous location southeast of San José run by a friendly and knowledgeable couple. Tuition is either one-to-one or in tiny classes up to a maximum of three people, with the choice of grammar or conversation. Accommodation is provided in a nearby hostel ($99 for five nights, including four three-hour classes and two meals daily; $119 for five classes;

$220 for ten), and a wide range of tours and sightseeing activities are available.

Universal de Idiomas Aptdo 751-2150, Av 2, C 9, San José ☎223-9662, ⓦwww.universal-edu .com. Well-established school with three-day crash courses and month-long programmes (3–4 hrs of tuition daily). Homestays, tours and dancing and cooking lessons can also be arranged.

Universidad Veritas Aptdo 1380-1000, Zapote, San Pedro ☎283-4747, Ⓕ225-2907, ⓦwww .uveritas.ac.cr. Intensive month-long ($500) and 12-week ($1380) courses catering to all levels of Spanish, with 20 hours' tuition weekly, plus courses in other subjects including Costa Rican history, culture and literature. Homestays, student residences and tours available.

Contacts for study programmes in Costa Rica

Bernan Associates 4611-F Assembly Dr, Lanham, MD 20706 ☎1-800/274-4447, ⓦwww .bernan.com. Distributes UNESCO's encyclopedic *Study Abroad*.

Staying with a Costa Rican family

There's no better way to experience life off the tourist trail and to practise your Spanish than staying with a Tico family. Usually enjoyable, sometimes transformative, this can be a fantastic experience, and at the very least is sure to provide some genuine contact with Costa Ricans.

Most homestay programmes are organized by the country's various language schools and cater mainly to students. However, some schools may be willing to put you in contact with a family even if you are not a student at the school in question. The **Ilisa Language School** (☎280-0700, ⓦwww.ilisa.com), one of San José's largest, is particularly helpful in this regard. Stays can last from one week to several months, and many travellers use the family home as a base while touring the country. You'll have your own key, but in most cases it would be frowned upon if you brought someone home for the night. The one rule that always applies is that guests and hosts communicate in Spanish. Costs, which include meals and laundry, average about $550 a month.

For a non-study based option, try **Bell's Home Hospitality** (☎225-4752, Ⓕ224-5884, ⓦwww.homestay.thebells.org), run by a long-time resident of Costa Rica, Vernon Bell, and his wife Marcela, who arrange for individuals, couples and families to stay in private rooms in a family home, with private or shared bath. Breakfast is included in the price, with evening meals and airport transfers available for a small additional cost. The Bells also run tours, mostly day-trips, to places like Volcán Poás, Sarchí and even one-day island cruises. Another recommended organization is **Monteverde Homestays** (☎645-6627, ⓦwww .monteverdehomestay.com), which has a range of family homes near the Santa Elena and Monteverde nature reserves.

Other points of contact for homestays as well as longer-term **apartment rentals and houseshares** include adverts in the *Tico Times* (although homestays and flats listed here tend to be expensive), the (Spanish) classifieds in *La Nación* and the noticeboards of hostels and guesthouses.

Council on International Educational Exchange (CIEE) 205 E 42nd St, New York, NY 10017 ☏ 1-888-COUNCIL, ⓦ www.ciee.org. The non-profit parent organization of Council Travel, CIEE runs summer, semester and academic-year programmes in Costa Rica.
Eurolingua Eurolingua House, 61 Bollin Dr, Altrincham, WA14 5QW, UK ☏ 0161 972 0225, ⓦ www.eurolingua.com. Links to language study courses worldwide, including Costa Rica.
Payaway ⓦ www.payaway.co.uk Huge resource for students looking to study or work abroad. The site features a "Jobs Abroad" bulletin board.
STA Travel UK ☏ 0870/160 0599, Australia ☏ 1300/733-035, New Zealand ☏ 0508/782-872, ⓦ www.statravel.com. The low-cost travel service

offers a wealth of links and contacts for students wishing to study abroad.
Studyabroad.com 1450 Edgmont Ave, Suite 140, Chester, PA 19013 ☏ 610/499-9200, ⓦ www .studyabroad.com. A useful website on studying abroad, with listings and links to programmes worldwide.
World Learning Kipling Road, PO Box 676, Brattleboro, VT 05302 ☏ 802/257-7751, ⓦ www .worldlearning.org. Runs a "School for International Training" which organizes accredited college semesters abroad, comprising language and cultural studies, and other academic work. It also has a summer programme for high-school students called "Experiment in International Living".

Gay and lesbian Costa Rica

Costa Rica has a good reputation among gay and lesbian travellers, and contin-ues to be generally hassle-free for gay and lesbian visitors. The country has a large gay community by Central American standards, and to a smaller extent a sizeable lesbian one too, though it's pretty much confined to San José; there's also a large community of transvestite/transsexual prostitutes (travestís) in the capital.

Although there have been some incidents of police harassing gays in bars, in general you will be met with respect, and there's no need to assume, as some do, that everyone is a raving hetero-Catholic poised to dis-criminate against gays. Part of this tolerance is due to the subtle tradition in Costa Rican life and politics summed up in the Spanish expression "quedar bien", which translates roughly as "don't rock the boat" or "leave well alone". People don't ask you about your sexual orientation or make assump-tions, but they don't necessarily expect you to talk about it unprompted, either.

Where once it was difficult to find an entrée into gay life (especially for women) without knowing local gays and lesbians, there are now several points of contact in Costa Rica for gay and lesbian travellers. On the web, try the Gay and Lesbian Guide to

Costa Rica (ⓦ www.gaycostarica.com); Pur-ple Roofs Gay and Lesbian Travel directory (ⓦ www.purpleroofs.com/centralamerica/ costarica/costaricaregion), which provides information about gay-friendly accommoda-tion and nightlife, or Tiquicia Travel (ⓦ www .tiquiciatravel.com), a travel agent that specializes in gay and lesbian holidays to Costa Rica. In the country itself, you can pick up Gayness, the monthly newspaper for Costa Rica's gay community from down-town newsstands in San José. To find out about gay-oriented events, you can also head to the University of Costa Rica in San José and check in with the Vida Estudantíl office on the fourth floor of Building A. For a more informal introduction to the scene head to Déjà Vu, a mainly gay disco in San José (see p.95 for this and other gay bars).

Women travellers

Educated urban women play an active role in Costa Rica's public life and in the workforce, while woman in more traditional positions are generally accorded the respect due to their role as mothers and heads of families. Despite this, however, women may be subjected to a certain amount of machismo.

In general, people are friendly and helpful to solo women travellers, who get the *pobrecita* (poor little thing) vote, because they're *solita* (all alone), without family or man. Nonetheless, Costa Rican men may throw out unsolicited comments (*piropos*) at women in the street: "*mi amor*", "*guapa*", "*machita*" ("blondie") and so on. If they don't feel like articulating a whole word, they may stare or hiss – there's a saying used by local women: "Costa Rica's full of snakes, and they're all men."

Blonde, fair-skinned women are in for quite a bit of this, whereas if you look remotely Latin you'll get less attention. This is not to say you'll be exempt from these so-called compliments, and even in groups, women are targets. Walk with a man, however, and the whole street theatre disappears as if by magic. The accepted wisdom is to pass right by and pretend nothing's happening. If you're staying in Costa Rica for any time, though, you may want to learn a few responses in Spanish; this won't gain you any respect – men will look at you and make *loca* (crazy) whirligig finger gestures at their temples – but it may make you feel better.

None of this is necessarily an expression of sexual interest: it has more to do with a man displaying his masculinity to his buddies than any desire to get to know you. Sexual assault figures in Costa Rica are low, you don't get felt up or groped, and you rarely hear *piropos* outside the towns. But for some women, the machismo attitude can be endlessly tiring, and may even mar their stay in the country.

In recent years there has been a spate of incidents allegedly involving Rohypnol, the so-called **date-rape drug** (legal and available over the counter in Costa Rica), whereby women have been invited for a drink by a man, or sent a drink from a man in a bar, which turns out to be spiked with the drug (often by the bartender, who's in on the game). In the worst cases, the women have woken up hours later having no recollection of the missing time, and believe they were raped. This is not to encourage paranoia, but the obvious thing to do is not accept opened drinks from men and be careful about accepting invitations to go to bars with unknown men. If you do, order a beer and ask to open the bottle yourself.

Directory

DANCING Costa Ricans love to dance, and it's common to see children who have barely learned to stand up grooving and bopping, much encouraged by their parents. Consequently, there are many good discos, mainly in San José. Your popularity at discos or house parties will have something to do with how well you can dance; if you're really keen you might want to take salsa and merengue lessons before you come. Fitting in at a disco is easier for women, who simply wait to be asked to dance. Men, however, are not only expected to go out and hunt down female dance partners, but also to lead, which means they actually have to know what they're doing. For a list of dance schools in San José, see p.93.

DEPARTURE TAX Currently $26 if leaving by air, but check with your travel agent or airline in Costa Rica before you depart. The tax is not included in the price of your air ticket. You must leave sufficient funds in dollars or colones to pay it, and will be expected to show the stamp that confirms payment to the *migración* officer when you leave. If you're leaving overland there is no departure tax.

DISABLED TRAVELLERS While public transport isn't wheelchair-accessible, an increasing number of hotels and restaurants are. Two good contacts are The Foundation for Universal Access to Nature (℡771-7482, ℮chabote@racsa.co.cr), who can suggest places to visit, and the tour agency Vaya Con Silla de Ruedas (℡454-2810, ⓦwww .gowithwheelchairs.com), who have a tour bus designed for making trips around the country with wheelchair users on board. The Costa Rica Deaf Travel Corporation (℡289-4812, ⓦwww.cdtcsa.com) can arrange for tour guides who are certified in sign language.

ELECTRICITY The electrical current in Costa Rica is 110 volts – the same as Canada and the US – although plugs are two-pronged, without the round grounding prong.

EMERGENCIES The national emergency number is ℡911.

GAMBLING Casinos have sprung up in many (usually upmarket) hotels, and are increasingly found even in smaller beach or provincial hotels, generally ruining the landscape and ambience with their red carpets, fake wood, orange lighting and besuited dealers. Slot machines, card games and roulette wheels are among the games on offer in these palaces of kitsch.

LANGUAGE The language of Costa Rica is Spanish. Although tourists who stay in top-end hotels will find that "everyone speaks English" (a common myth perpetrated about Costa Rica), your time here will be far more meaningful if you arm yourself with at least a 100-word Spanish vocabulary. Communicating with *guardaparques* and people at bus stops, asking directions and ordering *bocas* – not to mention finding salsa partners – is facilitated by speaking the language. For more on Costa Rican Spanish, see p.414.

LAUNDRY There are very few launderettes in Costa Rica, and they're practically all in San José (see p.98 for a list). Furthermore, launderettes are rarely self-service – someone does it for you – and charge by the kilo. Most hotels will have some kind of laundry service, although charges are often outrageously high.

PHOTOGRAPHY Film is extremely expensive in Costa Rica, so bring lots from home. Although the incredibly bright equatorial light means that 100ASA will do for most situations, remember that rainforest cover can be very dark, and if you want to take photographs at dusk you'll need 400ASA or even higher. San José is the main place in the country where you can process film; for a list of outlets, see p.97.

PROSTITUTION Prostitution is legal in Costa Rica. While there is streetwalking (largely confined to the streets of San José, especially those in the red-light district immediately west and south of the Parque Central), many prostitutes work out of bars.

59

Bars in San José's "Gringo Gulch" (more or less on C 7, Av Central/5) tend to cater to and attract more foreign customers than the bars in the red-light district, which are frequented by Ticos. Streetwalkers around C 12 look like women but are not. *Travestís* are transsexual or transvestite prostitutes; they don't take kindly to being approached by jokers. In recent years Costa Rica has gained a reputation as a destination for sex tourism, and more specifically for child-sex tourism. The government is trying to combat this with a public information campaign and strict prison sentences for anyone caught having sex with a minor.

TIME Costa Rica is in North America's Central Standard time zone (the same as Winnipeg, New Orleans and Mexico City) and six hours behind GMT.

TIPPING Unless service has been exceptional, you do not need to leave a tip in restaurants, where a ten percent service charge is automatically levied. Taxi drivers are not usually tipped, either. When it comes to nature guides, however, the rules become blurred. Many people – especially North Americans, who are more accustomed to tipping – routinely tip guides $3–10 per day. If you are utterly delighted with a guide it seems fair to offer a tip, although be warned that some guides may be made uncomfortable by your offer – as far as many of them are concerned, it's their job.

TOILETS The only place you'll find so-called "public" conveniences – they're really reserved for customers – is in fast-food outlets in San José, petrol stations and roadside restaurants. When travelling in the outlying areas of the country you may want to take a roll of toilet paper with you. Note that except in the poshest hotels – which have their own sewage system/septic tank – you should not put toilet paper down the toilet. Sewage systems are not built to deal with paper, and you'll only cause a blockage. There's always a receptacle provided for toilet paper.

Guide

Guide

Guide

San José

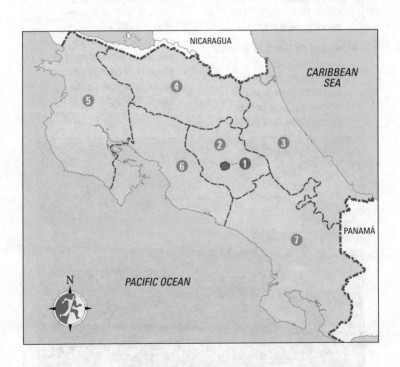

NICARAGUA

CARIBBEAN
SEA

④

⑤

②

③

⑥ ①

PANAMÁ

⑦

N

PACIFIC OCEAN

CHAPTER 1 # Highlights

* **Teatro Nacional** San José's most elegant building, and a little piece of Europe in the heart of the tropics. See p.81

* **Museo de Jade** Visit this compelling exhibit of jade artefacts created by Costa Rica's indigenous peoples. See p.83

* **Grano de Oro** San José's finest gourmet restaurant has a lovely, leafy patio and is the only place in town for piña colada cheesecake. See p.91

* **Cielo** Groove to lively tunes until the wee hours with trendy Josefinos at this hip, festive club. See p.93

* **Mercado Central** Enormous, labyrinthine food market where crimson sides of beef and crispy *chicharrones* (deep-fried pork skins) share the aisles with teetering mounds of papaya and sacks of pungent coffee beans. See p.80

△ Parque Central, San José

San José

Sprawling smack in the middle of the fertile Valle Central, **SAN JOSÉ**, the only city of any size and administrative importance in Costa Rica, has a spectacular setting, ringed by the jagged silhouettes of soaring mountains – some of them volcanos – on all sides. On a sunny morning, the sight of the blue-black peaks piercing the sky is undeniably beautiful. At night, from high up on one of these mountains, the valley floor twinkles like a million Chinese lanterns.

That's where the compliments end, however. Costa Ricans who live outside the capital are notoriously hard on the place, calling it, with a mixture of familiarity and contempt, "**Chepe**" – the diminutive of the name José – and writing it off as a maelstrom of stress junkies, rampant crime and other urban horrors. Poor Chepe is much maligned by just about everyone: you're hard pressed to find one among the 800,000 odd Josefinos willing to say much good about their city's pothole-scarred streets and car-dealership architecture, not to mention the choking black diesel fumes, kamikaze drivers and chaotically unplanned expansion. Travellers, meanwhile, talk about the city as they do about long lines at the bank or immigration offices: it's a pain, but it's unavoidable. The gridlocked **centre** is hectic, with vendors of fruit, lottery tickets and cigarettes jostling one another on street corners, and shoe stores seemingly crammed into every block. Though you can sometimes sense an underlying order behind the chaos, walking around town means, more often than not, keeping your eyes glued to the ground to avoid stepping in deep open drains

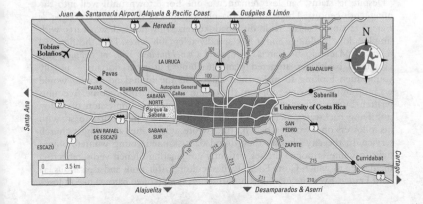

or in one of the boxes of clucking chicks sold by street-corner hopefuls. **Street crime** is on the rise, and pedestrians adopt the defensive posture (bags clutched securely, knapsacks worn on the front, determined facial expression) that you see in so many other big cities. All in all, walking in San José is a stressful experience, which is a shame, because exploring on foot is really the best way to get around.

Despites its many ills, if you have the time it is definitely worth getting to know Chepe a bit better – many people even end up perversely fond of the place, modern malls, fast-food outlets, neon billboards and all. San José has a sprinkling of excellent **museums** – some doubly memorable for their bizarre locations – a couple of elegant buildings and landscaped parks. Cafés and art galleries dot the streets, and as you wander amid the colonial-era wooden houses in the leafy barrios of **Amón** and **Otoya**, you could be in an old European town.

Today, one in four Costa Ricans lives within the San José metropolitan area, and the capital is beginning to suffer from pressure on land due to the population density in the Valle Central and to rural migration. Most Josefinos live in the **suburbs**, now awash with the mega-supermarkets and American-style malls that have colonized San José in the last few years, though some districts, like comfortable **Escazú** and hip **San Pedro** (home to the University of Costa Rica), still merit a visit in their own right.

Some history

San José was established in 1737 at the insistence of the Catholic church in order to give a focal point to the scattered populace living in the area. For the next forty years, **Villa Nueva de la Boca del Monte**, as it was cumbersomely called, remained a muddy village of a few squalid adobe houses, until coffee was first planted in the Valle Central in 1821 (see p.111), triggering the settlement's expansion.

The single most crucial event in determining the city's future importance, however, was Costa Rica's **declaration of independence** from the Spanish crown in 1821. Following the declaration, Mexico's self-proclaimed "emperor", General Agustín de Iturbide, ordered Costa Rica's immediate annexation, a demand which caused a rift between the citizens of Heredia and Cartago, who supported the move, and those of Alajuela and San José, who saw it for what it was: a panicky imperialist attempt to stifle Latin America's burgeoning independence movements. A short **civil war** broke out, won in 1823 by the *independentistas*, who moved the capital from Cartago to San José in the same year.

Despite its status, San José remained a one-horse town until well into the nineteenth century. The framed sepia photographs in the venerable *Balcón de Europa* restaurant show wide dirt roads traversed by horse-drawn carts, with simple adobe buildings and a few spindly telegraph wires. Like the fictional town of Macondo in García Marquez's *One Hundred Years of Solitude*, this provincial backwater attracted piano-teaching European flotsam – usually young men looking to make their careers in the hinterland – who would wash up in the drawing rooms of the country's nascent bourgeoisie. Accounts written by early foreign tourists to San José give the impression of a tiny, stultifying backwater society: "The president of the republic has to sit with his followers on a wooden bench," they wrote, aghast, after attending a church service. In the city's houses they found dark-skinned young women, bound tight in white crinoline dresses, patiently conjugating French verbs, reflecting the degree to which Costa Rica's earliest cultural affiliations and aspirations lay with France. Even the mansions of former *finqueros* (coffee barons) in San José's

Barrio Amón – especially the Alianza Francesa – resemble mansions in New Orleans or Port-au-Prince, with their delicate French ironwork, Moorish-influenced lattices, long, cool corridors of deep-blooded wood and brightly painted exteriors.

By the 1850s, fuelled largely by the tobacco boom, the city had acquired the trappings of bourgeois prosperity, with leafy parks, a few paved avenues and some fine examples of European-style architecture. Grand urban houses were built to accommodate the new class of burgeoning burghers, coffee middlemen and industrialists; these Europhile aspirations culminated in 1894 with the construction of the splendid **Teatro Nacional** – for which every molecule of material, as well as the finest craftsmen, were transported from Europe.

During the twentieth century, San José came to dominate nearly all aspects of Costa Rican life. Not only the seat of government, since the 1970s it has become the Central American headquarters for many foreign non-governmental organizations which has considerably raised its international profile. Multinationals, industry and agribusiness have based their national and regional offices here, creating what at times seems to be a largely middle-class city, populated by an army of neatly suited, briefcase-toting office and embassy workers.

Arrival

Arrival in San José, whether by plane or bus, is straightforward, even if you don't speak Spanish, since all the machinery to get you into town is well oiled and there's less opportunistic theft than at most other Central and South American arrival points.

By air

Most international **flights** arrive at the modern new terminal at Juan Santamaría International Airport (☎443-2622), 17km northwest of San José and 3km southeast of Alajuela. The **ICT office** here (Mon–Fri 9am–5pm; ☎443-1535 or 443-2883) can supply maps and give advice on accommodation. There's also a **correo** (Mon–Fri 8am–5pm), an **ATM** machine (handily situated next to the departure tax desk), and a **bank**, downstairs on the departure level (Mon–Fri 6.30am–6pm, Sat & Sun 7am–1pm); colones are not necessary for taxis, but you'll need them for the bus. The departure tax is $26; Visa (but not MasterCard) is accepted.

The best way to get into central San José from the airport is by **taxi**, which takes about twenty to thirty minutes in light traffic and costs $12–14. After 9pm, it's about $20. Official airport taxis are orange and line up outside the terminal. You'll have no problems getting a cab, as the drivers will stampede for your business when you're practically still in customs. Take a deep breath and make sure to agree on the fare before you get in the cab. Some taxi drivers take travellers who haven't made accommodation bookings to hotels where they get commission – these are often more expensive than you were bargaining for, so be firm about where you want to go. Taxi drivers accept dollars as well as colones, although they tend not to accept notes larger than $20.

The Alajuela–San José **bus** (every 3min between 5am & 10pm; every 15min at other times) stops right outside the airport's undercover car park. Though it's much cheaper than a taxi, there are no proper luggage racks inside and the buses are nearly always full – you can just about get away with it if you're carrying only a light backpack or small bag. Drivers will indicate which buses are on their way to San José (a thirty-minute journey) and which to Alajuela. The fare is 220 colones (about 50¢) – payable in local currency; pay the driver. The bus drops passengers in town at Av 2, C 12/14 near the Hospital de San Juan de Dios, where there are plenty of taxis.

By bus

Most **international buses** from Nicaragua, Honduras, Guatemala and Panamá pull into the Ticabus station, Av 4, C 9/11 (☎221-8954), next to the yellow Soledad Church. Since buses can arrive at odd hours, you may want to take refuge at one of the 24-hour eating spots nearby on Av 2 before looking for a room. One of the cheapest is the *Casa del Sandwich* on the corner of C 9, and there's a taxi rank around the corner on Av 2 between C 5 and 9. Coming from Managua on Transica, you'll arrive at the terminal at C 22, Av 3/5; taxis can be flagged down on Av 3.

The closest thing San José has to a **domestic bus station** is **La Coca-Cola**, five blocks west of the Mercado Central at Av 1/3, C 16/18 (the main entrance is on C 16). Named after an old bottling plant, La Coca-Cola not only applies to the station proper – which is quite small and the arrival point for only a few buses, principally those from Jacó and Quepos – but also the surrounding area, where many more buses pull in. Like many bus stations, La Coca-Cola is well on its way to being an irredeemable hellhole – noisy, hemmed in by small, confusing streets crammed with busy market traders, and invariably prowled by pickpockets. Lugging your bags and searching for your bus stop around here makes it very hard not to look like a confused gringo, thus increasing the chances that you'll become the target of opportunistic theft: best to arrive and leave in a taxi. Be especially careful of your belongings around the **Tilarán terminal** (C 12, Av 7/9), which is also used by buses to Monteverde: people waiting here for the 6.30am bus to Monteverde seem to be particularly at risk of attempted theft.

For details on getting out of the city from La Coca-Cola, see "Moving on from San José" on p.98.

Information

San José's **Instituto Costarricense de Turismo** (**ICT**) **office** (Mon–Fri 9am–5pm; ☎223-1733 or 223-1090, ℱ223-5452, ⓦwww.visitcostarica.com) is underneath the eastern edge of the Plaza de la Cultura, C 5, Av 0/2. It has free maps, hotel brochures and – most crucially – free leaflets detailing the national bus schedule. They also hand out the free monthly *Culture Calendar*, which details concerts and festivals throughout the country.

The Sistema Nacional de Areas de Conservación (National System of Conservation Areas), or SINAC, operates a free phone information line in English and Spanish about Costa Rica's **national parks** – call ☎192 Monday to Friday 8am to 5.30pm. They can provide information on individual parks, transport and camping facilities. For info on opening hours, entrance tariffs and background on the national parks system, log on to ⓦwww.minae.go.cr. In San José you can get information, buy entrance tickets and make reservations for park shelters at the **Fundación de Parques Nacionales** office, Av 15, C 23/25, Barrio Escalante (☎257-2239, ℱ222-4732, ⓔazucena@ns.minae .go.cr).

City transport

Once you've gotten used to the deep gutters and broken pavements, San José is easily negotiated **on foot**. Several blocks in the city centre around the Plaza de la Cultura have been completely pedestrianized. There is little need to take **buses** within the city centre, though the suburban buses are useful, particularly if you are heading out to Parque la Sabana, a thirty-minute walk west along Paseo Colón. Escazú is a twenty-minute ride to the west, and the University of Costa Rica and San Pedro are a ten-minute ride to the east.

Buses stop running between 10–11pm and **taxis** become the best way to get around. These days street crime is noticeably on the rise, and most Josefinos advise against walking alone after dark, women especially.

Buses

Fast, cheap and frequent buses connect the centre of the city with virtually all of San José's neighbourhoods and suburbs, and generally run from 5am until 10–11pm. **Bus stops** in the city centre seem to change every year. Currently, most buses to San Pedro, Tres Ríos and other points east leave from the stretch of Avenida Central between C 9 and C 15. You can pick up buses for Paseo Colón and Parque la Sabana (labelled "Sabana-Cementerio") at the bus shelters on Av 2, C 5/7. In an enlightened move, city authorities are hoping to move the bus stops out of the centre proper in order to cut traffic and pollution (most city buses belch depressingly black streams of diesel fumes from their exhaust pipes).

All buses have their routes clearly marked on their windshields, and usually the **fare** too. These are payable either to the driver or his helper when you board and are usually 100 colones, though the faster, more comfortable *busetas de lujo* (luxury buses) to the suburbs cost upwards of 150 colones. The traditional method of stopping the bus to get off is for men to whistle and women to call out *¡Parada!* (stop), but bus drivers have recently taken to putting up testy signs saying "*los monos gritan, los pájaros silvan, por favor toca el timbre*" ("monkeys yell, birds whistle, please use the bell").

San José's street system and addresses

San José, along with most Costa Rican towns of any size, is planned on a grid system. It's intersected by east–west **Avenida Central** (called Paseo Colón west of La Coca-Cola bus station) and north–south **Calle Central**. From Av Central, parallel avenidas run to the north (odd numbers) and to the south (even numbers). From Calle Central, even-numbered calles run to the west and odd numbers to the east. Avenidas 8 and 9, therefore, are actually quite far apart. Similarly, Calles 23 and 24 are at opposite ends of the city. When you see **bis** (literally "encore" – again) in an address it denotes a separate street, usually a dead end (calle sin salida), next to the avenida or calle to which it refers. Av 8 bis, for example, is between Av 8 and 10. "**0**" in addresses is shorthand for "Central": thus Av 0, C 11 is the same as Av Central, C 11.

Most times, locals – and especially taxi drivers – won't have a clue what you're talking about if you try to use street numbers to find an address. When possible, give directions in relation to local **landmarks**, buildings, businesses, parks or institutions. In addition, people use **metres** to signify distance: in local parlance 100 metres equals one city block. There are precious few street signs, so it's helpful to count streets as you go along so as not to miss your turn. Note that most roads are one-way, usually (but not always) the alternate direction to the previous road.

The following is a rundown of the main inner-city routes, all of which stop along Av Central or Av 2 in the centre of town. If in doubt, ask "¿dónde está la parada para...?" ("Where is the stop for...?").

Sabana–Cementerio buses travel west along Paseo Colón to Parque la Sabana, and are ideal for going to any of the shops, theatres and restaurants clustered around Paseo Colón, the Museo de Arte Costarricense or Parque la Sabana.

Sabana–Estadio services run basically the same route, with a tour around Parque la Sabana. Good for the neighbourhoods of Sabana norte and Sabana sur.

Sabanilla–Bethania buses run east through Los Yoses and beyond to the quiet residential suburb of Sabanilla.

San Pedro (also **La U**) or **Tres Ríos** buses will also take you east through Los Yoses and on to the University of Costa Rica and the hip neighbourhood of San Pedro. Other buses serving San Pedro are: Vargas Araya, Santa Marta, Granadilla, Curridabat and Cedros.

Taxis

Taxis are cheap and plentiful, even at odd hours of the night and early morning. Licensed vehicles are red with a yellow triangle on the side, and have "SJP" ("San José Público") licence plates. A ride anywhere within the city costs $1.50–2.50, and about double that to get out to the suburbs. The starter fare – about 50¢ – is shown on the red digital read-out, and you should always make sure that the meter is on before you start (ask the driver to *toca la maría, por favor*). Some drivers may claim that the meter doesn't work – if this is the case, it's best either to agree on a fare before you start out or to find another taxi whose meter is working. Many drivers are honest – don't immediately assume everyone's trying to cheat you. After midnight, taxis from the El Pueblo centre charge forty percent extra. These are institutionalized higher fares, and you shouldn't attempt to negotiate. Tipping is not expected. To book a taxi, call ☏254-0533 or 254-3211.

By car and bike

There's no need to **rent a car** specifically for getting around San José – indeed, most Josefinos advise foreigners against driving in the city, at least until they're familiar with the aggressive local style of driving. In addition, most of the city's streets are one-way, though sometimes unmarked as such. Cars left on the street anywhere near the city centre are almost guaranteed to be broken into or stolen. Secure **parqueos** (guarded parking lots) dot the city; if you do rent a car, use them. Most close at 8 or 8.30pm, although there are some 24-hour lots, including one on the corner of A 0, C 19. Some hotels have on-site parking. If you have to leave your car on the street, most areas have a man whose job is to guard the cars – look for the fellow with the truncheon and expect to pay around 300 colones. If driving in the centre of the city, keep your windows rolled up and your doors locked so no one can reach in. For a list of car **rental companies**, see p.30.

It's generally not a good idea to cycle in San José. Diesel fumes, potholes and un-cycle-conscious drivers don't make for pleasant cycling, although riding in the suburbs or Parque la Sabana is easier and less hazardous to your health.

△ San José advertisement

Safety in San José

Be particularly wary, even during the day, in the streets around La Coca-Cola bus terminal and Parque Central, Av 2. A few places have a bad reputation day and night, including Barrio México in the northwest of the city and the red-light districts of C 12, Av 8/10, and Av 4/6, C 4/12, just southwest of the centre. The **dangers** are mainly mugging, purse-snatching or jewellery-snatching rather than serious assault, and many people walk around without encountering any problems at all. However, taxis are cheap enough that it's probably not worth taking the risk.

You have to be careful when crossing the street in San José, as drivers are very aggressive, and pedestrian fatalities (you'll see lots of stories about "atropellados" in the national newspaper) are distressingly common. There are a few ground rules, however, that can help minimize your chances of ending up in hospital.

• If possible, always try to cross the street at an official crossing point alongside other pedestrians; note that there are only a handful of pedestrian lights in the entire city.
• You can't see the traffic lights easily (they're hung about 5m above your head), so watch the traffic and other pedestrians.
• Take particular care negotiating the city's very wide roadside storm drains.
• Run if it looks like the light is changing.
• Don't expect anyone to stop for you under any circumstances. You have to get out of their way, not vice versa.

Accommodation

After a period of rapid growth – and high prices – in the hotel business during the 1990s tourism boom, San José is at last getting more quality hotel rooms, with fairer prices in all categories. The budget-to-moderate sector has improved markedly with several new guesthouses and family-run hotels. Rock-bottom hotels, however, still tend, with a few exceptions, to be depressing cells that make the city seem infinitely uglier than it is. San Jose also has its fair share of international **hotel chains**, many of whose names (and generic facilities) – *Radisson*, *Holiday Inn* and *Best Western* – will be familiar to North Americans and Europeans. While some are comfortable and have excellent service, they don't offer much in the way of local colour. It's also worth noting that while these hotels employ Costa Ricans, most of their profits are repatriated to the company's home country.

If you are coming in **high season** (Dec–May), and especially over busy periods like Christmas and Easter, be prepared to reserve (and, in some cases, even pay) in advance. Places that require money in advance may give you a bank account number in Costa Rica for you to wire money to, although credit card transactions are becoming increasingly common. Room **rates** vary dramatically between high and low seasons – the prices we quote are for a double room in peak season, and you can expect to get substantial discounts at less busy times.

Many of San José's rock-bottom hotels have cold-water showers only. Unless you're very tough, you'll want some form of **heated water**, as San Jose can get chilly, especially from December to March. At the budget end of the spectrum, so-called "hot" water is actually often no more than a tepid trickle, produced by one of the eccentric electric contraptions you'll find fitted over showers throughout the country (see Basics, p.33) – it's still better than cold water, however.

Though staying in one of the budget hotels in the **city centre** is convenient, the downside is noise and pollution – Avenida 2 and parts of Avenidas 1, 3 and 5 can be noisy, but this is not a hard-and-fast rule, as the city authorities seem to like to change bus routes (the source of most street noise) every few years. The very cheapest rooms are in the insalubrious area immediately around La Coca-Cola, and while there are a couple of clean and well-run budget places here, the area is generally best avoided unless you've got an early bus to catch or are an aficionado of seedy hotels.

Not too far from downtown, in quieter areas such as **Paseo Colón**, **Los Yoses** and **Barrios Amón** and **Otoya**, is a group of more expensive hotels, many of them in old colonial homes.

To the west of the city is Escazú, the stomping grounds of American expats, and popularly known as "Gringolandia". The vast majority of B&Bs here are owned by foreign nationals, with higher prices than elsewhere in town. Street names and addresses are particularly confusing in this area so get clear directions or arrange to be picked up. East of the city and closer to the centre is studenty San Pedro, with better connections to downtown and a more cosmopolitan atmosphere. It's a great place to stay, but unfortunately there are only a couple of hostels in the area.

La Amistad Av 11, C 13 ☎258-0021, ⓕ258-4900, ⓦwww.centralamerica.com/cr/hotel/amistad. Set a large house in historic Barrio Otoya, this hotel has forty rooms all with cable TV, phone, private bath and queen-sized beds; there are also seventeen deluxe rooms with a/c and two apartments ($86 for four people) with a/c. Good single rates ($37). Breakfast included. ❹–❺

Ara Macao C 25 bis, Av 0/2, 50m south of *Pizza Hut* in Barrio California ☎233-2742, ⓕ257-6228, ⓦwww.hotels.co.cr/aramacao. Small and pleasant B&B with eleven rooms (six with kitchenettes for longer stays), just outside the city centre but near the restaurants of Barrio California and Los Yoses. Rooms are airy and have private bath and cable TV. Breakfast included. ❹–❺

Aranjuez C 19, Av 11/13 ☎256-1825, from the US & Canada call toll-free 1-877/898-8663, ⓕ223-3528, ⓦwww.hotelaranjuez.com. In quiet Barrio Aranjuez yet still close to the centre, the rooms of this hotel are in converted houses that have been joined with communal sitting areas. Relax in the pretty garden around the back. The 23 rooms either have shared bath (❹) or private bath and TV (❸). A good buffet breakfast and free email are available, and they can arrange tours to Laguna Lodge in Tortuguero. Be sure to reserve ahead.

Bellavista Av 0, C 19/21 ☎223-0095. Friendly, central hotel with lively murals of *Caribeña* life. Rooms are a bit dark and musty, and walls are thin, but all have private bath with hot water, and ceiling fans do what they can to provide a semblance of fresh air. It's close to the Limón bus

stop, and rooms at the front get lots of noise from buses. ❸

Le Bergerac C 35, Av 0 ☎234-7850, ⓕ225-9103, ⓦwww.bergerac.co.cr. For luxury without the price tag, this elegant and relaxing top-end hotel is a good bet. The eighteen spacious rooms all have cable TV and phone, and some also have their own private gardens. A superb French restaurant, *L'lle de France*, is prettily set next to an interior courtyard, and there's a travel service that arranges tours. Continental breakfast included. ❺–❼

Cacts C 28–30, Av 3 bis ☎221-2928, ⓕ221-8616, ⓦ www.tourism.co.cr/hotels/cacts/index. Recently expanded, *Cacts* has 25 rooms, all with ceiling fans and TV; all but four have private bath. A sunny roof terrace, tropical garden, swimming pool and Jacuzzi add to its charm. Enjoy a complimentary breakfast buffet of fresh fruits and baked goods. The friendly owners run a travel agency and can help with tours and reservations. ❹

Casa Hilda Av 11, C 3 & 3 bis, house no. 353 ☎221-0037, ⓕ221-2881, ⓔc1hilda@racsa.co.cr. Small and affordable hotel in an old-style wooden house on a quiet street near the city centre. The five rooms are basic but comfortable and have private bath with hot water and fans. Rooms with outside-facing windows are best; the others are a bit dark. There's also a patio garden and communal sitting areas with cable TV. Good single rates. ❸–❹

Casa León Av 6 bis, C 13/15 ☎222-9725. A good alternative if the *Costa Rica Backpackers* (see below) is full, this small guesthouse has dorms

SAN JOSÉ

Centro
Costarricense
de la Cienca
y la Cultura

SABANA
NORTE

AVENIDA 7

AVENIDA 5

Museo de
Arte
Costarricense

AV 3 BIS

AVENIDA 3

AVENIDA 1

PASEO COLÓN

AVENIDA 2

AVENIDA 4

AVENIDA 6

SABANA
SUR

Escazú ▶

La
Coca-Cola

Mercado
Central

San Juan de
Dios Hospital

AVENIDA 2

Parque Central

AVENIDA 4

AVENIDA 10

AVENIDA 12

See Central San
José map

AVENIDA 16

AVENIDA 18

AVENIDA 20

N

★ BUS STOPS

Alajuela, Volcán Poás & International Airport	Los Chiles & Zarcero	C
	Nicoya, Sámara & Tamarindo	I
	Peñas Blancas & La Cruz	J
Cahuita, Puerto Viejo de Talamanca & Sixaola	L	
	Puerto Jiménez	B
Cartago	A	Puntarenas	M
Golfito	N	Puerto Viejo de Sarapiquí	A
Guápiles	F	Santa Cruz, Playa Hermosa	
Jacó,Quepos	A	& North Guanacaste Beaches	G
Liberia & Playa del Coco	K	San Isidro de El General	O
Limón	E	Sarchí	H
	A	Tilarán & Monteverde	D

($10 per person in a mixed-sex dorm) and basic private rooms with spotlessly clean shared bath and kitchen. There is laundry service and luggage storage. The house can be hard to find; look for it next to the train tracks and tell your taxi driver it's a *calle sin salida*. ❷

Casa Ridgway C 15, Av 6 bis between Av 6/8 ☎ & ℻ 233-6168 or 222-1400, ✉friends@racsa .co.cr. Near the Ticabus stop, this homely Quaker guesthouse is a good budget choice with several clean, single-sex dorms ($10 per person), plus a few private singles ($12) and doubles ($24) with communal bathrooms. There's also a shared kitchen, laundry and luggage storage. Note that alcohol is banned and there's a "quiet time" after 10pm. Reserve ahead in high season, and try not to arrive after 8pm except by prior arrangement. ❸

Casa Verde de Amón Corner of C 7 & Av 9 ☎ & ℻223-0969, ✉casaverde@racsa.co.cr. Set in a historic late 19th-century mansion house, this quiet, beautifully restored hotel is filled with antiques and oriental rugs. Well-furnished rooms and suites have wooden floors and fittings – and some even have Victorian bathtubs. Prices are very reasonable, particularly in low season, and there are weekly discounts. Rooms ❺, suites ❼.

Cinco Hormigas Rojas C 15, Av 9/11, 200m east of the back of the INS building and then 25m north ☎ & ℻ 257-8581. The "five red ants" is a small, quirky B&B in a private house in quiet Barrio Otoya, decorated with vibrant paintings by owner Mayra Güell. The six, bright rooms share two bathrooms while a small tropical garden attracts butterflies and hummingbirds. Breakfast included. No smoking. ❹

Costa Rica Backpackers Av 6, C 21/23 ☎221-6191, ℻223-2406, ⓦ www .costaricabackpackers.com. A great place to meet fellow travellers, this is one of the city's best budget guesthouses with both single- and mixed-sex dorms ($9 per person) plus a few private double rooms ($20). Facilities include a fully

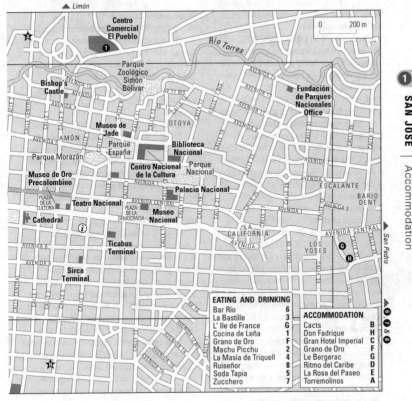

Map labels:

▲ Limón

Centro Comercial El Pueblo

Río Torres

Parque Zoológico Simón Bolívar

AV 11 BIS

Bishop's Castle

AVENIDA 11

AVENIDA 9

Fundación de Parques Nacionales Office

AVENIDA 15

AVENIDA 13

OTOYA

Museo de Jade

AMÓN

Parque España

Biblioteca Nacional

Parque Morazán

Centro Nacional de la Cultura

Parque Nacional

Museo de Oro Precolombino

AVENIDA 1

Palacio Nacional

ESCALANTE

BARIO DENT

PLAZA DE LA CULTURA

Teatro Nacional

AVENIDA CENTRAL

AVENIDA 5

AVENIDA 3

Cathedral

PLAZA DE LA DEMOCRACIA

Museo Nacional

AVENIDA 1

AVENIDA CENTRAL

San Pedro

Ticabus Terminal

LA CALIFORNIA

AVENIDA 2

LOS YOSES

G

AVENIDA 6

Sirca Terminal

H

AVENIDA 8

AV 10

AVENIDA 14

AVENIDA 16

0   200 m

EATING AND DRINKING	
Bar Río	6
La Bastille	3
L' Ile de France	G
Cocina de Leña	1
Grano de Oro	F
Machu Picchu	2
La Masía de Triquell	4
Ruiseñor	8
Soda Tapia	5
Zucchero	7

ACCOMMODATION	
Cacts	B
Don Fadrique	H
Gran Hotel Imperial	C
Grano de Oro	F
Le Bergerac	G
Ritmo del Caribe	D
La Rosa del Paseo	E
Torremolinos	A

equipped kitchen, a garden with swimming pool, luggage storage, laundry service, a TV room, free Internet access and free parking. ②

Don Carlos C 9, Av 7 & 9 ☏221-6707, ⓕ255-0828, ⓦwww.doncarlos.co.cr. Elegant landmark hotel filled with replicas of pre-Columbian art and a lovely kitsch breakfast terrace/cocktail lounge with a fountain and a pretty tiled mural of the city hand-painted by Costa Rican artist Mario Aroyabe. All rooms have cable TV and safe (some also have private patios) and there's free Internet access, plus an excellent souvenir shop and travel agency. ⑤

Don Fadrique C 37, Av 8, Los Yoses ☏225-8186, ⓕ224-9746, ⓔfadrique@centralamerica.com. Upmarket hotel with restaurant, bar and tropical gardens, located in the former villa of Don Fadrique Gutierrez, early twentieth-century architect, general and philosopher. The hotel's halls are hung with Costa Rican art, and each of the twenty nicely furnished rooms comes with TV

and private bath with hot water. Good low-season discounts. Breakfast included. ⑥

Europa C 0, Av 3/5 ☏222-1222, ⓕ221-3976, ⓦwww.hoteleuropacr.com. Mid-range casino-hotel in the heart of downtown, with a restaurant, bar, indoor pool, lots of bright communal areas and a 24-hour Egyptian-themed gaming room. Outside rooms tend to get street noise but more light while inside rooms are quieter but less airy. There's a helpful tour desk inside the hotel with good contacts throughout the country. ⑤

Fleur de Lys C 13, Av 2/6 ☏223-1206, ⓕ257-3637, ⓦwww.hotelfleurdelys.com. Victorian mansion hotel in a pleasant and fairly quiet part of downtown, near the Ticabus stop and the Museo Nacional. Each floor has a sunny and plant-filled atrium and each of its 31 prettily decorated rooms has TV and private bath. There's also a recommended restaurant and small bar. Rooms vary: some are a bit dark, some have a bathtub. Good low-season rates (⑤), and under-12s stay free, though high-season prices (⑦) are a bit expensive.

La Gema Av 12, C 9/11 ☎257-2524, ⒡222-1074. This small, light hotel south of the centre surrounds an open courtyard planted with leafy trees. Rooms are a good size, though walls are a bit thin – the sunnier upstairs rooms are best. ④

Gran Hotel Costa Rica Av 0/2, C 3 ☎ & ⒡ 256-8585, ⓦwww.granhotelcr.com. This elegant hotel has over 100 spotlessly clean but rather unimaginatively furnished rooms – some are enormous, some are small, but all have TV, phone and 24-hour room service. The central location – overlooking the Plaza de la Cultura, and with a popular terrace café below – can be noisy, especially when the buskers are in full swing. Discounts are often available in low season. ⑤

Gran Hotel Imperial C 8, Av 0/1 ☎222-8463, ⒡257-4922. Near the bus station, the dark and frankly scary entrance belies a secure but basic hotel, popular with backpackers and offering some of the cheapest rooms in San José (singles from $4). The downside is that it's rather noisy, there are no private bathrooms (and hot water in the mornings only), and there have been reports of people getting ill from the attached restaurant. ①

Grano de Oro C 30, Av 2/4 ☎255-3322, ⒡221-2782, ⓦwww.hotelgranodeoro.com. Elegant converted mansion in a quiet area west of the centre, with 32 comfortable rooms and suites furnished in faux-Victorian style, with wrought-iron beds and polished wooden floors – they're popular with honeymooners and older Americans. Several of the deluxe rooms have lovely private gardens and all rooms have cable TV, minibar, phone and fax. A new rooftop sun terrace is equipped with twin hot tubs. An excellent breakfast is served in the highly recommended restaurant. ⑥–⑧

Hotel 1492 Jade y Oro Av 1, C 31/33 ☎256-5913 or 225-3752, ⒡280-6206, ⓦwww .hotel1492.com. On a quiet stretch of Avenida 1, this comfortable hotel has ten well-appointed rooms, some surrounding an elegant antique- and art-filled atrium and others adjoining a small tropical garden. All have private shower and TV. The friendly staff can arrange tours. ⑤

Kap's Place C 19, Av 11/13 ☎221-1169, ⒡256-4850, ⓦwww.kapsplace.com. One of city's best budget choices, this family-friendly hotel is run by the unstintingly helpful Karla Arias who is a bottomless source of information on all things San José. The fourteen en-suite rooms (two with shared bathroom) are colourfully decorated. There's a fully equipped communal kitchen plus a large two-floor apartment (with its own kitchen). Tours arranged on request. ③–④

Pensión de la Cuesta Av 1, C 11/15 ☎ & ⒡ 255-2896, ⒠ggmbner@racsa.co.cr. Tranquil rooms – though some are a bit gloomy – in a pink, colonial-style wooden house, with a plant-filled lounge area, gold masks on walls and decorated bedsteads. All rooms have shared bath, plus there's a communal kitchen, laundry service and luggage storage. Staff can arrange tours and car rental. ③

Rincón de San José Av 9, C 13/15 ☎221-9702, ⒡222-1241, ⓦwww.hotelrincondesanjose.com. This renovated Dutch-owned hotel in pretty Barrio Amón has clean rooms (all with cable TV), wooden floors and piping hot showers, plus the use of a computer and safe. The excellent *Café Mundo* restaurant is just across the street. Breakfast included. ⑤–⑥

Ritmo del Caribe Paseo Colón C 32/34 ☎ & ⒡ 256-1636, ⓦwww.ritmo-del-caribe.com. Converted modern house with nicely decorated singles and doubles, some with TV and balcony; double-glazed windows muffle most of Paseo Colón's round-the-clock traffic. There are also a couple of mixed-sex dormitories ($9 per person). A tasty German breakfast is included, and the helpful owners can advise on tours and travel. ④

Ritz C 0, Av 8/10 ☎233-1731, ⒡222-8849. Very clean and fairly large (25 rooms, some with private bathroom) central hotel with its own tour service. It's popular with European travellers, and is a good place to meet other backpackers. Management is friendly and the communal areas are pleasant, though rooms are rather dark. Rooms with private bath are $5 more than those without. ②

La Rosa del Paseo Paseo Colón, C 28/30 ☎257-3213, ⒡223-2776, ⒠rosadelp@racsa .co.cr. Converted late 19th-century house on busy Paseo Colón. Rooms have nice touches – sparkling bathrooms, wooden floors and Victorian fittings – and all come with private bath and cable TV. Breakfast included. ⑤

Santo Tomás Av 7, C 3/5 ☎255-0448, ⒡222-3950, ⓦwww.hotelsantotomas.com. In quiet, elegant Barrio Amón, near downtown, this is one of San José's best boutique hotels. It occupies an old mansion awash in soft lighting and decorated with burnished wood and Persian rugs. Rooms vary widely in size, character and price, though all have TV and telephone. There's a small swimming pool, hot tub, an excellent open-air restaurant, a travel service and free Internet access. ⑤

Torremolinos C 40, Av 5 bis ☎222-5266, ⒡255-3167, ⒠torrehtl@sol.racsa.co.cr. Now part of the Occidental hotel chain, this well-maintained hotel is in a quiet area just two blocks east from Parque la

Sabana. Smallish rooms are comfortably furnished, and all have TV, radio and telephone; a/c (not really necessary) costs more. Facilities include a nice pool, Jacuzzi, gym and sauna, and there's a good bar and restaurant. Good low-season discounts. **❻**

Toruma Av 0, C 29/31 ⊤ & ⨍ 224-4085, ⨂ www .toruma.com. Costa Rica's main HI hostel, this beautiful establishment has a Neoclassical exterior and high ceilings. It's a good place both to meet people and to make onward hostel, tour and travel reservations. Accommodation is in single-sex dorms ($8 per person for HI members, $10 for non-members – membership is available at the front desk) and a few singles (HI members $16, non-members $20). There's luggage storage, a safe, laundry, free Internet access and free parking. Book well in advance in high season. Non-smoking.

San Pedro

D'Galah Opposite the University of Costa Rica, in front of the Facultad de Farmacia ⊤ 280-0614, ⨍ 280-8092, ⨂ dgalah@racsa .co.cr. Despite a characterless exterior, inside there are two plant-filled courtyards, a small swimming pool and hot tub and bright, quiet and fairly spacious rooms, some with kitchenette (about $10 more). Ideal if you want to be near the university. **❹**

La Granja Off Av 0 in Barrio La Granja, San Pedro ⊤ & ⨍ 225-1073. This eight-room guesthouse is 50m south of the *antiguo higuerón*, the former site of a now disappeared tree which still serves as a local landmark. It's built in a converted family house with a pretty garden, near the university, bars and restaurants. Most rooms have shared showers. Also has some cheap singles ($15), a TV lounge, communal kitchen and laundry service. **❷**

Maripaz 350m southeast of the *antiguo higuerón* tree ⊤ & ⨍ 253-8456, ⨂ maripaz@racsa.co.cr. Five-room B&B (two with private bath) in the home of a welcoming Costa Rican family. Located in a quiet, pleasant area near the university and several language schools. **❸–❹**

Hotel Milvia 250m northeast of the Muñoz y Nanne supermarket ⊤ 225-4543, ⨍ 225-7801, ⨂ www.novanet.co.cr/milvia. Mid-range hotel

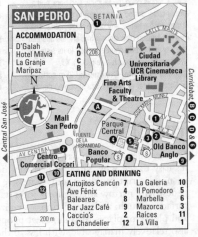

in a lovely old Caribbean-style plantation house beautifully decorated with antiques and modern Costa Rican art. Located in a residential area, with a soothing fountain, garden, sun terrace and mountain views, plus TV lounge and games room. Lunch and dinner available on request. **❺**

Escazú

Casa de las Tías San Rafael de Escazú, southeast of the El Cruce Shopping Centre; take the east turn by the *Restaurante Cerutti* ⊤ 289-5517, ⨍ 289-7353, ⨂ www.hotels.co.cr/casatias. Set on a garden estate, this quiet, friendly hotel has just five rooms, each individually decorated with private bath and hot water. No under-12s allowed. **❺–❻**

Park Place B&B On the left-hand side of the road up Escazú hill ⊤ 228-9200, ⨍ 289-8638. Small, nicely decorated, American-run B&B with lounge, fireplace, communal kitchen, and a good view from the upstairs verandah. No children allowed. **❺**

Posada del Bosque Bello Horizonte de Escazú ⊤ 221-7319, ⨍ 257-3525. Quiet, homely place on landscaped grounds. Comfortable no-smoking rooms with shared bath. The friendly owners can arrange tennis, swimming and horse-riding. **❹–❺**

Posada El Quijote 800m south of the El Cruce Shopping Centre, just east of Chango's restaurant

T289-8401, F289-8729, Wwww.quijote.co.cr.
Eight spacious rooms, renovated in Spanish
colonial style and comfortably furnished with bath,

hot water and cable TV. Breakfast is served in the
lovely garden. ❺

Around San José

Best Western Irazú Off the Autopista General
Cañas between San Jose and the airport, 4km
northwest of downtown T232-4811, in the US
1-800/528-1234, F232-4549, Wwww
.bestwestern.com. Big rooms with TV, telephone and
all the facilities of a resort hotel – swimming pool,
sauna, tennis court, restaurants and bars, and a
rather tacky casino. If you want to escape San José
it's as good a bet as any of the large hotels. There
are low-season discounts, a free shuttle bus into
the city and a daily shuttle service to its sister Best
Western at Jacó Beach (see p.307). ❺
Camino Real Inter-Continental 2km north
of Escazú, near the Multiplaza shopping centre

T289-7000, F289-8930, Wwww.interconti
.com. If you like big fancy hotels, this is one of the
best, with a large pool (and pool bar), sauna, gym,
two restaurants and a free shuttle bus into town.
Rooms have piping-hot water, cable TV and phone.
Breakfast is included in the price. ❽
Kalexma B&B La Uruca, 5km northwest of
downtown T290-2624, F231-0638, Wwww
.kalexma.com. Twelve comfortable rooms with
shared or private bath. There's a communal
kitchen, two TV lounges, laundry service and
Internet access. Staff can arrange transport, tours,
and Spanish classes. Breakfast included.
❷ without bathroom, ❹ with bathroom.

The City

Few travellers come to San José for the sights, and going by first impressions
it's easy to see why. San José certainly doesn't exude immediate appeal, with
its nondescript buildings and aggressive street life full of umbrella-wielding
pedestrians, narrow streets, noisy food stalls and homicidal drivers. Scratch the
surface, though, and you'll find a civilized city, with museums and galleries
and plenty of places to walk, meet people, enjoy a meal, and go dancing. It's
also relatively manageable, with less of the chaos and crowds that plague most
other Latin American cities. San José is a surprisingly green and open city:
small, carefully landscaped parks and paved-over plazas punctuate the centre of
town. All the attractions lie near each other, and you can cover everything of
interest in a couple of days.

Of the city's museums, the major draws are the exemplary **Museo de Oro
Precolombino,** featuring over 2000 pieces of pre-Columbian gold, and
the **Museo de Jade**, the Americas' largest collection of the precious stone.
Less visited, the **Museo Nacional** offers a brutally honest depiction of the
country's colonization and some interesting archeological finds. The **Museo
de Arte y Diseño Contemporáneo** displays some of the most striking
contemporary works in the Americas.

The centre itself is subdivided into little neighbourhoods (barrios) that flow
seamlessly in and out of one another. **Barrios Amón** and **Otoya,** in the north,
are the prettiest, lined with the genteel mansions of former coffee barons. To
the west are **La California** and **Los Yoses**, home to the *Toruma* youth hostel,
most of the embassies and the Centro Cultural Costarricense Norteamericano.
The esteemed University of Costa Rica rises amid the lively student bars and
cafés of the **San Pedro** barrio, just east of the city centre.

Parque Central

Dominating the city centre is Parque Central, Av 2, C 0/2, a landscaped square
punctuated by tall royal palms and centred on a weird Gaudí-esque bandstand.

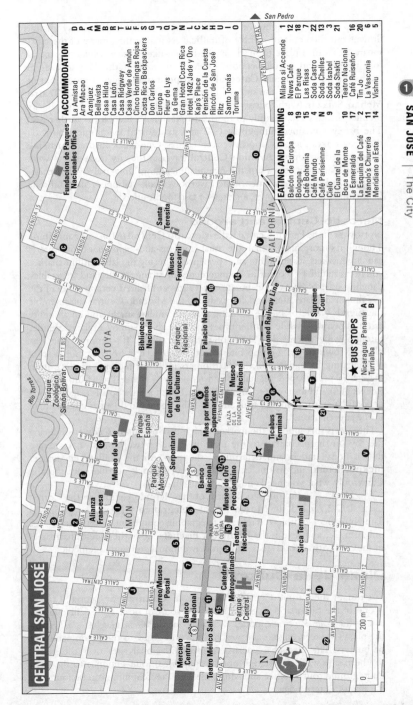

CENTRAL SAN JOSÉ

▲ San Pedro

SAN JOSÉ | The City

1

ACCOMMODATION

La Amistad	D
Ara Macao	P
Aranjuez	A
Bellavista	M
Casa Hilda	B
Casa León	R
Casa Ridgway	T
Casa Verde de Amón	E
Cinco Hormigas Rojas	F
Costa Rica Backpackers	S
Don Carlos	G
Europa	J
Fleur de Lys	Q
La Gema	V
Gran Hotel Costa Rica	N
Hotel 1492 Jade y Oro	L
Kap's Place	C
Pensión de la Cuesta	K
Rincón de San José	H
Ritz	U
Santo Tomás	I
Toruma	O

EATING AND DRINKING

Balcón de Europa	8
Bologna	19
Café Bohemia	15
Café Mundo	4
Café Parisienne	N
Cielo	9
El Cuartel de la Boca de Monte	10
La Esmeralda	17
La Esquina del Café	2
Manolo's Churrería	11
Meridiano al Este	14
Milano si Accende	1
News Café	12
El Parque	18
Las Risas	7
Soda Castro	22
Soda Chelles	13
Soda Isabel	3
Soda Shakti	21
Teatro Nacional	16
Café Ruiseñor	20
Tin Jo	6
La Vasconia	5

★ **BUS STOPS**

Nicaragua, Panamá A
Turrialba B

79

0 200 m

Green parrots roost nightly in the palms; come twilight, their noisy chatter drowns out the constant rumble of traffic. Less frantic than many of the city's squares, it's a nice place to snack on the lychee-like *mamones chinos* or papayas sold by the nearby fruit vendors. Directly in front of the Parque Central looms the huge columnar **Catedral Metropolitaneo**, nicely restored but of little interest inside. At the square's northeast corner, the Neoclassical **Teatro Mélico Salazar** (with touristy but worthwhile shows) is one of Costa Rica's premier theatres, second only to the Teatro Nacional a few blocks further east. The barely contained hubbub of C 2 and its assorted electronics and shoe shops overtakes the park's northwestern corner. One block further north, the pleasant, pedestrianized **Avenida Central** traverses the city from east to west. Useful department stores dot the Avenida, including Universal (with a particularly good book department), the cavernous book–stationery shop Librería Lehmann and, further down, a clutch of fast-food outlets.

Mercado Central and around

Northwest of the Parque Central is the **Mercado Central** (Mon–Sat 5am–5pm). Though it's more orderly than the usual chickens-and-*campesinos* Latin American city markets, it's still quite an experience. Entering the labyrinthine market, you're assaulted by colourful arrangements of strange fruits and vegetables, dangling sides of beef and elaborate, silvery rows of fish. At certain times of the day (lunch and late afternoon, for example) the Mercado Central can resemble the Eighth Circle of Hell – choking with unfamiliar smells and an almighty crush of people – while at other times you'll be able to enjoy a relaxed wander through wide uncrowded alleys of rural commerce. It's certainly the best place in town to get a cheap bite to eat, and the view from a counter stool is fascinating, as traders and their customers jostle for regional produce from *chayotes* (a pear-shaped vegetable) and *mamones* (a lychee-type fruit) to *piñas* (pineapples) and *cas* (a sweet-sour pale fruit.) With a little Spanish, and a pinch of confidence, shopping for fruit and vegetables here can be miles cheaper than in the supermarket.

The streets surrounding the market, which can look quite seedy even during the day (in sharp contrast to the roads just one or two blocks east), are also full of noisy traders and determined shoppers. All this activity encourages **pickpocketers**, and in this environment tourists stick out like sore thumbs. Carry only what you need and be on your guard.

Two blocks east and one block north of the Mercado Central, in the Correo Central, C 2, Av 1/3, the **Museo Postal, Telegráfico y Filatélico** (Mon–Fri 8am–4pm; free) exhibits old relics of telegraphic equipment, of interest to buffs only. On C 2 and Av 3 is the **Farmacia Fischel**, one of the oldest pharmacies in the city, with a good stock of both conventional and herbal remedies.

Plaza de la Cultura

Just east of the Parque Central, **Plaza de la Cultura** (Av Central, C 3/5) is one of the few places in San José where you can sit at a pleasant outdoor café – the *Café Parisienne,* under the arches of the *Gran Hotel Costa Rica* on the plaza's western edge – and watch the world go by to the accompaniment of buskers. The elegant Neoclassical Teatro Nacional rises over the plaza's southern side while the (rather poorly signposted) joint-entrance to the city's underground tourist office and Museo de Oro Precolombino can be found on the plaza's eastern edge.

Museo de Oro Precolombino

The Plaza de la Cultura cleverly conceals one of San José's treasures, the Banco Central-owned **Museo de Oro Precolombino**, or Pre-Columbian Gold Museum (Tues–Sat 10am–4pm; $5; ☏243-4202, ⓦwww .museosdelbancocentral.org). The bunker-like underground museum is unprepossessing but the gold on display is truly impressive – all the more extraordinary if you take into account the relative paucity of pre-Columbian artefacts in Costa Rica (compared with Mexico, say, or Guatemala). Most of the exquisitely delicate goldwork is by the **Diquis**, ancient inhabitants of southwestern Costa Rica.

The delicate gold pieces are hung on transparent wires, giving the impression of their floating in space, mysteriously suspended in their perspex cases. Most of the gold pieces are small and unbelievably detailed, with a preponderance of disturbing, evil-looking animals. Information panels (in English and Spanish) suggest that one of the chief functions of these portents of evil – frogs, snakes and insects – was to protect the bearer against illness. The Diquis believed that sickness was transmitted to people through spirits in animal form. The *ave de rapiña*, or bird of prey, seems to have had a particular religious relevance for the Diquis: hawks, owls and eagles, differing only fractionally in shape and size, are depicted everywhere. Watch out, too, for angry-looking arachnids, ready to bite or sting; jaguars and alligators carrying the pathetic dangling legs of human victims in their jaws; grinning bats with wings spread; turtles, crabs, frogs, iguanas and armadillos; and a few spiny lobsters. Museum displays highlight the historical and geographical context of Costa Rican gold. Maps pinpoint gold production centres and there are models of gold-making settlements.

Sharing the building is the marginally interesting **Museo de Numismática** (free with admission to Gold Museum, and same opening hours) with a collection of Costa Rican coins. Look out for the old five-colón note, decorated with a delicate, brightly coloured panorama of Costa Rican society.

Teatro Nacional

Reputedly designed after the Paris Opéra, San José's heavily colonnaded, grey-brown **Teatro Nacional** sits on the corner of C 5 and Av 2, tucked in behind the Plaza de la Cultura. The theatre's marbled stairways, gilt cherubs and red velvet carpets would look more at home in Europe than in Central America. You won't find such impressive elegance anywhere else between here and the Manaus Opera House in deepest Amazonia.

Teatro Nacional's story is an intriguing one, illuminating the industrious, no-nonsense attitude of the city's coffee bourgeoisie, who demonstrated the national pride and yearning for cultural achievement that came to characterize Costa Rican society in the twentieth century. In 1890, the world-famous prima donna Adelina Patti was making a tour through the Americas, but could not stop in Costa Rica as there was no appropriate theatre. Mortified, and determined to raise funds for the construction of a national theatre, the wealthy coffee farmers responded by levying a tax on every bag of coffee exported. Within a couple of years the coffers were full to bursting; European craftsmen and architects were employed, and by 1897 the building was ready for its inauguration, a stylish affair with singers from the Paris Opéra performing *Faust*.

The theatre itself is lavishly done in red plush, gold and marble, with richly detailed frescoes and statues personifying "Dance," "Music", and "Fame". The upstairs "salons" are decorated in mint and jade-green, trimmed with gold, and lined with heavy portraits of former bourgeoisie. In the main lobby, look for the mural depicting the coffee harvest (once featured on the

Costa Rican gold

Little, if anything, is known of the prehistory of the **Diquís**, who were responsible for most of the goldwork at the Museo de Oro Precolombino. However, the history of goldworking in the New World is fairly well documented. It was first recorded (around 2000 BC) in Peru, from where it spread northwards, reaching Mexico and the Central American isthmus by 700–900 AD. All the ancient American peoples favoured more or less the same methods and styles, using a gold-copper alloy (called *tumbaga*) and designs featuring extremely intricate shapings, with carefully rendered facial expressions and a preference for ingenious but rather diabolical-looking zoomorphic representations – growling peccaries, threatening birds of prey, and a two-headed figure, each mouth playing its own flute. The precise function of these intricately crafted creations is still the subject of some debate since many of the objects show no sign of having been worn (there are no grooves in the pendant links to indicate they were worn on chains). Archeologists believe they may have been intended for ceremonial burial and, indeed, some were even "killed" or ritually mutilated before being entombed. Others may have been worn as charms protecting the bearer against illness and evil spirits.

The Diquís would have obtained the gold by panning in rivers, and it is speculated that in Osa, at least, the rivers routinely washed up gold at their feet. Diquís *caciques* (chiefs) and other social elites used their gold in the same way it is used today – to advertise wealth and social prestige. Ornaments and insignias were often reserved for the use of a particular *cacique* and his family, and these special pieces were traded as truce offerings and political gifts between various rulers, maintaining contacts between the *caciques* of distant regions. Indeed, it was the removal of native distinctions of social rank following the Spanish Conquest of the country in the seventeenth century that heralded the almost immediate collapse of the Costa Rican gold-making industry.

Although the Diquís were the undisputed masters of design, archeological digs in the Reventazón Valley suggest that gold-working could also be found among the peoples of the Atlantic watershed zone. When Columbus first came ashore in 1502, he saw the local (Talamancan) peoples wearing gold mirror-pendants and headbands and rashly assumed he had struck it rich – hence the country's name. An early document of a subsequent expedition to the Caribbean coastal region of Costa Rica, now housed in archives in Cartago, contains the impressions of native wealth recorded by one gold-crazed Spaniard in Diego de Sojo's 1587 expedition: "The rivers abound with gold . . . and the Indians extract gold with calabashes in very large grains . . . from these same hills Captain Muñoz . . . took from the tombs of the dead . . . such a great quantity of gold as to swell two large chests of the kind in which shoes and nails for the cavalry are brought over from Castile."

five colón note), a gentle reminder of the agricultural source of wealth that made this urban luxury possible. All in all, the building remains in remarkably good condition, despite the dual onslaught of the climate and a succession of earthquakes. The latest, in 1991, closed the place for two years – until recently, the huge marble staircases on either side of the entrance still had wooden supports strapped onto them like slings. Above all it is the details that leave a lasting impression: plump cherubim, elegantly numbered boxes fanning out in a wheel-spoke circle, heavy hardwood doors and intricate glasswork in the washrooms.

Even if you're not coming to see a performance (see p.95) you can wander around the post-Baroque splendour, though you'll be charged $3 for the privilege (guided tours offered). Just off the foyer is an elegant café serving good coffee, juices, and European-style cakes.

Parque España and around

Lined with tall trees, the verdant **Parque España** (three blocks east and two blocks north of Plaza de la Cultura) is surrounded by several excellent museums. On the western corner, facing Av 5, stands the **Edificio Metálica** (Metal Building, also known as the "Escuela Metálica"), so-called because its exterior is made entirely out of metal plates shipped from France over one hundred years ago. Though the prospect sounds dour, the effect – especially the bright multi-coloured courtyard as seen from the **Museo de Jade**, high above – is very pretty, if slightly military. Just west of Parque España lies **Parque Morazón**, more a concrete-paved square than a park proper. It's centred on the landmark grey-domed bandstand floridly known as the Templo de Música.

Museo de Jade

On the north side of the Parque España rises one of the few office towers in San José: the INS, or Institute of Social Security, building. The eleventh floor of this uninspiring edifice contains one of the city's finest museums, the **Marco Fidel Tristan Museo de Jade** (Jade Museum; Mon–Fri 8.30am–3pm; $2; ☎287-6034), home to the world's largest collection of American jade

As in China and the East, jade was much prized in ancient Costa Rica as a stone with religious or mystical significance, and for Neolithic civilizations it was an object of great power. It was and still is considered valuable because of its mineralogical rarity. Only slightly less hard than quartz, it's well known for its durability, and is a good material for weapons and cutting tools like axes and blades. As no quarries of the stone have been found in Costa Rica, the big mystery is how the pre-Columbian societies here got hold of so much of it. The reigning theories are that it came from Guatemala, where the Motagua Valley is home to one of the world's six known jade quarries, or that it was traded or sold down the isthmus by the Olmecs of Mexico. This also would explain the Maya insignia on some of the pieces – symbols that had no meaning for Costa Rica's pre-Columbian inhabitants.

The museum displays are ingenious, subtly back-lit to show off the multi-coloured and multi-textured pieces to full effect. Jade exhibits an extraordinary range of nuanced colour, from a milky-white green and soft grey to a deep green; the latter was associated with agricultural fertility and particularly prized by the inhabitants of the Americas around 600 BC. No two pieces in the collection are alike in hue and opacity, though, as in the Museo de Oro, you'll see a lot of **axe-gods**: anthropomorphic bird-cum-human forms shaped like an axe and worn as a pendant, as well as a variety of ornate necklaces and fertility symbols.

Incidentally, the **view** from the museum windows is one of the best in the city, taking in the sweep of San José from the centre to the south and then west to the mountains.

Museo de Arte y Diseño Contemporáneo

Sprawling across the entire eastern border of the Parque España, the former National Liquor Factory, dating from 1887, today houses an arts complex that includes the Centro Nacional de la Cultura, Juventud y Deportes (Ministry of Culture, Youth and Sports), known as CENAC. Many Josefinos still refer to the buildings as the old *Liquoría;* indeed you can still see a massive old distilling machine in the grounds, complete with the nameplate of its Birmingham manufacturers. The main attraction here is the cutting-edge **Museo de Arte y Diseño Contemporáneo**, or Museum of Contemporary Art and Design

(Tues–Sun 10am–5pm; $2; ☏257-7202, ⊛www.madc.ac.cr), entered from the corner of C 15 and Av 3. Opened in 1994 under the direction of dynamic artist Virginia Pérez-Ratton, it's a highly modern space, with a cosmopolitan, multimedia approach – there's a space specially designed for outdoor installations by up-and-coming Central American artists. The CENAC complex also houses two theatres, a dance studio (wander around during the day for glimpses of dancers and musicians rehearsing) and an amphitheatre.

Barrios Amón and Otoya

Weaving its way north up the hill from the Parque España, the historic **Barrio Amón** leads into another old barrio, **Otoya**. Lined with historic buildings and the former homes of the Costa Rican coffee gentry, these two neighbourhoods are among the most attractive in San José. After decades of neglect they are currently undergoing something of a rediscovery by hoteliers, café and restaurant owners. More than one hundred years old, Amón is home to fine examples of "neo-Victorian" tropical architecture. Low-slung wooden houses are girthed with wide verandahs and iron railings. Striking examples include the **Alianza Francesa** building (C 5 & Av 7), the turreted **Bishop's Castle** (Av 11 bis & C 3), and the grand old **Casa Verde de Amón** hotel (C 7 & Av 9).

Two blocks north of Parque España, in Barrio Otoya, at Av 11 and C 7/9, is the entrance to the **Parque Zoológico Simón Bolívar** (Tues–Fri 8am–4pm, Sat & Sun 9am–5pm; $2). There are plans to move it to a location outside San José sometime in the future, but until then the zoo, with its pitifully cramped conditions, should be avoided by animal lovers. Nevertheless, it continues to draw Tico families on Sundays and gaggles of schoolchildren on weekdays. If you do visit and want to do something about the facilities, the zoo operates an "adopt-an-animal" programme – ask at the entrance kiosk or the museum office.

El Pueblo and the Centro de la Ciencia y la Cultura

The cluster of shops, restaurants, bars and discos that make up the **Centro Comercial El Pueblo** – generally known simply as "El Pueblo" – lies about 200m north of the zoo across the Río Torres. For a tourist complex, El Pueblo is well designed and a sensible initiative that gives both tourists and Josefinos – who love it – an attractive, atmospheric place to shop, eat, drink and dance, all within the same complex. El Pueblo's whitewashed adobe buildings with wooden staircases evoke a type of colonial architecture that has found it hard to survive in Costa Rica, due to the successive tremors of earthquakes. Walking to El Pueblo means running a gauntlet of pedestrian-unfriendly traffic, however, and most people take a taxi, which costs around $2.50 from the Plaza de la Cultura. The adjacent **Spirogyra Jardín de Mariposas** (daily 8am–4pm; $5) has a wide variety of butterflies fluttering about, with daily guided tours pointing out particularly unusual and pretty ones.

Near El Pueblo, at the end of Calle 4, is the **Centro Costarricense de la Ciencia y la Cultura** (Tues–Fri 8am–4pm, Sat & Sun 10am–4pm; $5). Located in a former prison, this complex devotes most of its space to the mildly interesting **Museo de los Niños** (Children's Museum), where Costa Rican kids learn about their country's history, culture and science through interactive displays. The complex also houses the **Museo Histórico Penitenciario** (Penitentiary History Museum), with original prison cells restored to their nineteenth-century condition, and some rather anodyne accounts of the country's penal history.

The Parque Nacional and around

San José's **Parque Nacional**, the city's finest open space, marks the heart of downtown San José. Bordered by Av 1 and 3 and C 15 and 19 and overlooked by rows of mop-headed palms and thick deciduous trees, it's popular among courting couples and older men discussing the state of the nation. After gaining notoriety as a hang-out for muggers and prostitutes, it was equipped with tall lamps to add extra light – a tactic which has apparently succeeded in drawing the courting couples back to its nocturnal benches. Even so, it's still probably not a good idea to wander around here after dark.

Immediately north of the park, the modernist **Biblioteca Nacional** is Costa Rica's largest and most useful library, at least for readers of Spanish (Mon–Fri 8.30am–4.30pm). Anyone can rifle through the newspaper collection to the right of the entrance on the ground floor. At the library's southwest corner, the **Galería Nacional de Arte Contemporáneo** (Mon–Sat 10am–1pm & 2–5pm; free; ☎257-5524) features small and often quirky displays of work by local artists.

You can hear government debates Costa Rican-style at the **Palacio Nacional**, home to Costa Rica's Legislative Assembly, just south of the park at the corner of C 15 and Av Central. The fun starts at 4pm, but check first if the Legislature is in session. East of the Palacio, at the top end of Av 3 between C 21/23, the **Museo Ferrocarríl**, or Railway Museum (Mon–Fri 9am–4pm; $1), was the terminus for the old "Jungle Train" (see p.146). Today it holds a largely photographic collection dedicated to the famed train that once ran from San José to Limón before being dealt two blows in quick succession: one by the April 1991 earthquake and another by the government, who made the decision not to finance its repair. It's worth a look if you're in the area, especially for railway enthusiasts, but doesn't merit a trip in its own right.

Plaza de la Democracía

A block southwest of the Parque Nacional sits the concrete **Plaza de la Democracía**, yet another of the city's soulless squares which is just one aesthetic notch up from a paved parking lot. Constructed in 1989 to mark President Oscar Arias's key involvement in the Central American Peace Plan, this expanse of terraced concrete slopes up towards a fountain. At its western end is a row of **artisans' stalls** selling hammocks, thick Ecuadorian sweaters, leather bracelets and jewellery. You can also buy Guatemalan textiles and decorative *molas* (patchwork textiles in vibrant colours) made by the Kuna people of Panamá, though at steeper prices than elsewhere in Central America. Other stalls sell T-shirts and wooden crafts and trinkets. The traders are friendly and won't pressure you; a bit of gentle bargaining is a must.

The Museo Nacional

The north end of the square is crowned by the impressive **Museo Nacional** (Tues–Sat 8.30am–4.30pm, Sun 9am–4.30pm; $2; ☎257-1433, ⓦwww .museocostarica.com), occupying the renovated former Bellavista Barracks. Bullet holes from the 1948 insurrection (see Contexts) can still be seen on the north side of the building's thick walls. More than a century old (and that *is* old for Costa Rica), the museum's collection, though rather haphazard, gives a fascinating introduction to the story of Costa Rica's **colonization**. A grisly series of drawings, deeply affecting in their simplicity, tells the story of the fate of Costa Rica's **indigenous** people at the hands of the Spanish settlers. Violence, it appears, was meted out in both directions, including beheadings, hangings, clubbings, shooting of priests and the pouring of liquid gold down throats. Infanticide and suicide as a means of resistance in the indigenous community are also mercilessly depicted. Displays explain (in both English and Spanish) how the arrival of the Spanish forever disturbed the balance of social and political power amongst the indigenous groups. There's also an explanation on the function of gold in the indigenous social hierarchy, with descriptions on which objects were used to identify warriors, chiefs and shamans.

The museum's **colonial-era** section is dominated by the massive but spartan furniture and cheesy Spanish religious iconography. Exhibits make clear how slowly culture and education advanced in Costa Rica, giving a sense of a country struggling to extricate itself from terrible cultural and social backwardness – in European terms – until well into the twenty-first century. In the same room are examples of **colonial art**, which replaced indigenous art forms with scores of lamentable gilt-and-pink Virgin Marys.

Other highlights include petroglyphs, pre-Columbian stonework, and wonderful anthropomorphic gold figures in the **Sala Arqueológica**. This is the single most important archeological exhibition in the country; the grinding tables and funerary offerings, in particular, show precise geometric patterns and incredible attention to detail, but the really astounding pieces are the "flying panel" **metates**, corn-grinding tables used by the Chorotega peoples of present-day Guanacaste, each with three legs and meticulously sculpted from a single piece of volcanic stone.

Los Yoses and La California

The neighbourhoods of **Los Yoses** and **La California** face one another from opposite sides of Avenida Central as it runs east from the Museo Nacional to San Pedro. Mainly residential, Los Yoses is home to foreign embassies and a few hotels. The commercial La California runs into Barrio Escalante and Barrio Dent, two of San José's nicest residential districts. Walking through Barrio Escalante is the way to head east, and much more pleasant than bus-choked Avenida Central.

Homesick North American tourists should head to the **Centro Cultural Costarricense Norteamericano**, 100m north of the Am-Pm supermarket on the corner of Av Central and C 37 in Barrio Dent (Mon–Fri 7am–7pm, Sat 9am–noon; ☏255-9433 for library, ⓦwww.cccncr.com). The library has English-language publications – the *Miami Herald*, *New York Times* and *USA Today* – as well as all the main Costa Rican dailies. There's also an art gallery, the Eugene O'Neill Theater, with jazz festivals and English-language theatre performances, a pleasant café and CNN beamed out on the communal TV.

About 300m northeast of the Centro Cultural is San José's best bookstore, **Librería Internacional** (Mon–Sat 9.30am–7pm; ☏253-9553), with a well-stocked Latin American literature section, including Costa Rican authors, and a good selection of both fiction and non-fiction in English as well as maps and tourist guides. At the very end of Barrio Dent, where Avenida Central runs into the fountain-roundabout that separates San José proper from San Pedro, is the truly ugly but wildly popular **San Pedro Mall**. A ceramic-coloured multi-storey building festooned with plants and simulated waterfalls, inside it's a jumble of American chain stores and fast-food outlets. If anything, it offers a glimpse into the dating rituals and shopping habits of upper-class Costa Rican teenagers.

San Pedro

First impressions of **San Pedro** (see map on p.77) can be off-putting. Avenida Central (known here also as Paseo de los Estudiantes) appears to be little more than a strip of gas stations, broken-up sidewalks and shopping malls. Walk just a block off the Paseo, however, and you'll find a lively university student quarter, plus a few elegant old residential houses. The area has traditionally been home to some of the city's best restaurants and nightlife, but an increasing proliferation of dark bars filled with shouting college students means that it's often not the most relaxing spot to be on a Friday or Saturday night, at least during term time.

Theoretically it's possible to walk to the campus from Los Yoses, but this entails dealing with the huge, threatening Fuente de la Hispanidad roundabout. This is not recommended, as there are no provisions at all for pedestrians; it's much better to take any university-bound bus from Los Yoses. Buses to San Pedro from the centre of town stop opposite the small **Parque Central**, with its bubblegum-orange bandstand and monument to John F. Kennedy. Walking north from the *parque*, through three blocks of solid sodas, bars and bookshops you come to the cool, leafy campus of the **University of Costa Rica**, one of the finest in Central America, and certainly the most prestigious educational institution in the country. Founded in 1940, the university has in the past been accused of being too rigidly academic and elitist, but the overall campus atmosphere is busy, egalitarian and stimulating.

The best places to hang out on **campus** and meet both young Josefinos and students from other countries are the frenzied and cheap cafeteria in the building immediately to the right of the library (there's also an excellent **bookstore** across from the back entrance of the cafeteria), the Comedor Universitario, or **dining hall**, and the Facultad de Bellas Artes, which has a wonderful open-air **theatre** used for frequent concerts. Noticeboards around campus, particularly in front of the *Vida Estudiantíl* office (Student Life office, Building A, fourth floor), keep you up to date with what's going on; try also to get hold of a copy of *Semana Universitaria*, the campus newspaper, which is sold in most restaurants and bookshops in the area and lists upcoming events. The three or four blocks surrounding the university are lined with lively bars and restaurants, though in most of them you'll feel more comfortable if you're under thirty. For Spanish-speakers this is a great place to meet people, watch movies and browse around the several well-stocked bookstores. One of the best is Librería Macondo, 100m before you come to the university proper; look for the lime-green storefront.

Paseo Colón and Parque la Sabana

Clustered around the main entrance to La Coca-Cola, off C 16 near Av 1, shops selling women's underwear, cosmetics and luggage compete for space with a variety of cheap snack bars and drinks stalls. Two blocks south, however, the atmosphere changes, as Av Central turns into **Paseo Colón**, a wide boulevard of upmarket shops, restaurants and car dealerships. At the very end of the *paseo*, a solid expanse of green today known as **Parque la Sabana** was until the 1940s San José's airport, and is now home to the country's key art museum, the **Museo de Arte Costarricense**. To get to the *parque*, take the Sabana Cementerio bus from Av 2, or walk (20–30min from downtown).

Parque la Sabana

Enjoy an afternoon stroll in **Parque la Sabana**, a verdant park with leafy trees shading a central lake and colourful modern art scattered about. On Sunday afternoons, hordes of local families come to feed the resident geese and eat ice cream. It's also one of the best places in San José to **jog**. The cement track is usually full of serious runners in training, but you can also run quite safely throughout the park.

The bright white Neocolonial edifice of the old air terminal at the eastern end of **Parque la Sabana** has been converted into the attractive **Museo de Arte Costarricense** (Tues–Sun 10am–4pm; $5, free Sun 10am-2pm; ☏222-7155), with a fine collection of mainly twentieth-century Costa Rican paintings. Highlights among the permanent exhibits include the outstanding landscapes of **Teodorico Quirós**, with their Cézanne-inspired palettes of russets and burnt siennas, along with Enrique Echandi, Margarita Berthau, abstract painter Lola Fernández and a scattershot selection of foreign artists including Diego Rivera and Alexander Calder. The remarkable **Salon Dorado** upstairs features four full walls of bas-relief wooden carvings overlaid with sump-tuous gold, portraying somewhat idealized scenes of Costa Rica's history since the Spanish arrived. On the western wall are imagined scenes from the lives of the indigenous peoples, followed on the north wall by Columbus's arrival, to which the indigenous peoples improbably respond by falling to their knees and praying solemnly. Other golden representations include the Costa Rican agrarian gods of horses, oxen and chickens, and an image of this very building when it was San José's airport, little biplanes buzzing around it like mosquitoes.

On the southwest corner of Sabana Park, across the road in the Ministry of Agriculture and Livestock complex, is the quirky natural science museum **Museo de Ciencias Naturales La Salle** (Mon–Fri 8am–3pm; $1). Walk in, and after about 400m you'll see the painted wall proclaiming the museum; the entrance is at the back. It's an offbeat collection, with displays ranging from pickled fish and snakes coiled in formaldehyde to some rather forlorn taxidermy exhibits – age and humidity have taken their toll. Highlights include the model of the huge **baula**, or leatherback turtle, the biggest reptile on earth, and the **dusky grouper** fish, a serious contender for first prize in the Ugliest Animal in the World contest. Tons of crumbly fossils and an enormous selection of pinned butterflies (twelve cases alone of titanium-bright Blue Morphos) finish off the collection. Live turtles, virtually motionless, doze in the courtyard garden. The Sabana–Estadio **bus** (see p.70) stops right outside the museum. Note, on your left as you go by on the way to the museum, the futuristic air traffic control tower shape of the **Controlaría de la República**: this is the government's administrative headquarters.

Eating

It used to be that nobody went to Costa Rica for the food, and, while it's still true that in most of the country you'll eat nothing more exotic than rice and chicken, the standard of cuisine in the capital has improved dramatically over the last few years. For a Central American city of its size, San José has a surprising variety of **restaurants** – Italian, Thai and even macrobiotic – along with simple places that offer dishes beginning and ending with rice (rice-and-shrimp, rice-and-chicken, rice-and-meat). For excellent *típico* cooking, try the upmarket restaurants specializing in grills or barbecues (*churrascos*).

Many of the city's best restaurants are in the relatively wealthy and cosmo-politan neighbourhoods of **San Pedro**, along **Paseo Colón**, and in **Escazú**. Wherever you choose, eating out in San José can set your budget back on its haunches. Prices are generally steep, and the 23 percent tax on restaurant food (which includes a 10 percent "service charge") can deliver a real death-blow. The cheapest places are in the centre, especially the snack bars and **sodas**, where the restaurant tax doesn't apply. Sadly, however, the best of these are disappearing at an alarming rate because of competition from fast-food outlets. The sodas that remain are generally cheap and cheerful. A *plato del día* soda lunch will rarely set you back more than $5. They also have *empanadas* and sandwiches to take out – combine these with a stop at one of the fruit stalls on any street corner and you've got a quick, cheap lunch. The pieces of papaya and pineapple sold in neatly packaged plastic bags have been washed and peeled by the vendors and should be safe, but if in doubt, wash again. Snacks sold at the **Mercado Central** are as tasty as anywhere, and there's a good cluster of sodas hidden away in the Galería shopping arcade, Av 2, C 5/7.

Fast-food outlets in San José are proliferating so rapidly that at times it can look like a veritable jungle of *Pizza Huts*, *Taco Bells* and *KFCs*, not to mention *McDonald's*. **Cafés** also abound; some, like *Giacomín*, have old-world European aspirations; others, such as *Spoon*, are resolutely Costa Rican, with Josefinos piling in to order birthday cakes or grab a **coffee**. Most cafés serve exclusively export Costa Rican coffee which has a mild, soft flavour. For more variety, try *La Esquina del Café*, with numerous blends and roasts. (For more on coffee, see Basics, p.37.) As is the case with shops and restaurants, some of the best cafés are in the **shopping malls** outside San José. **Bakeries** (*pastelería*, *repostería*) on every corner sell cakes, breads and pastries, most of them heavy with white refined flour. Worthwhile bakery chains include *Musmanni*, *Spoon*, *Schmidt* and *Giacomín*. The city's fantastic **ice cream** is another source of woe to dieters. *Pops* is the best of the major chains, with particularly good fruit flavours.

Working Josefinos eat their main meal between noon and 2pm, and at this time sodas especially get very busy. Many of the more upmarket restaurants close at 3pm and open again in the evening. In the listings below we have given a phone number only for places where you might need to **reserve** a table.

Cafés and bakeries

Café Bohemia Teatro Mélico Salazar, Av 2, C 0. Upmarket café adorned with historic photos of San José and filled with theatregoers discussing the city's latest cultural offerings over steaming cups of coffee and flaky pastries.

Café Parisienne Gran Hotel Costa Rica, Av 2, C 3/5. The closest thing in San José to a European street café, complete with wrought-iron chairs and trussed-up waiters. Laze away the afternoon over coffee and cake while taking in the tunes and antics of buskers and performers on Plaza de la Cultura. It's one of the few cafés that serves continental breakfast.

La Esquina del Café C 3 bis, Av 9. Small, quiet, aromatic café with excellent coffee and freshly roasted beans. The friendly staff will answer questions about the entire coffee process, from bean to cup. They serve a good cappuccino with proper frothed milk, tasty desserts (you can try before you buy) and lunches of soups, salads and sandwiches. You can also buy little bags of beans from Costa Rica's various coffee-producing regions.

Giacomín Branches next to the Automercado in Los Yoses, in San Pedro, and in Escazú. Comfort-able café for chocolate and cake lovers, with lots of seasonal cakes such as *stollen* and *panettone*.

News Café Av 0, C 7/9. Refuel over a cup (or two) of Costa Rica's potent coffee at this midtown café. Find a comfortable perch on the balcony and people-watch to your heart's content. Inside, the walls are adorned with pictures that tell the story of Costa Rica's coffee-growing industry.

Ruiseñor 150m east of the Automercado in Los Yoses. Upmarket café serving sandwiches and pastries on a pleasant outdoor terrace. The old-fashioned, European-style atmosphere and service are a treat, but you pay for it.

Spoon Av 0, C 5/7, and other branches throughout San José and the Valle Central. Packed with Josefinos ordering birthday cakes. Coffee is somewhat bitter but served with mix-it-yourself hot milk; the choices of cookies and cakes are endless.

Sodas

Bologna Av 8, C 17. An Italian version of a traditional Costa Rican soda. Fill up on ciabattas and focaccias washed down with super-strong Italian coffee.

Castro Casa 279, Av 10, C 2/4. The 1970s fluorescent and vinyl decor and surrounding rough neighbourhood belie the treats inside. Definitely not on the tourist trail, this huge soda is where local families take their kids for a Sunday ice-cream treat (there's also a play area) and to sample the excellent fruit salads.

Chelles Av 0, C 9. Open 24 hours, this spartan bar, with bare fluorescent lighting and a TV blaring away in the corner, is a San José institution and a great place to sit and watch your fellow customers or the street action outside. Aproned waitresses serve up cold, cheap beer, snacks and *casados*.

Isabel C 19, Av 9. Permanently filled (or so it seems) with locals shooting the breeze, downing endless cups of coffee and munching on tortillas and *casados*. A street kiosk just outside sells snacks to those too busy to stop. Open Mon–Sat from 7am–10pm.

Manolo's Churrería Av 0, C 0/2. A 24-hour soda that's become an institution with Josefinos as a late-night hangout. It's not cheap, but it's safe after hours and the sinful pastries and hearty sandwiches hit the spot after a few too many *cervezas*. The downstairs café is less expensive and perfect for people-watching.

El Parque C 2, Av 4/6. This 24-hour soda caters to everyone from businessmen grabbing a cup

Teatro Nacional Café Ruiseñor Av 2, C 3/5. Coffee, fruit drinks, sandwiches and fantastic cakes served amid a Neoclassical decor of marble, crystal and dark wood. Settle in at a table by the window and check out the goings-on in Plaza de la Cultura.

Zucchero C 33, Av 5, just north of Los Yoses. Excellent coffee and French-style pastries and cakes served up in quiet, residential Barrio Escalante.

of coffee on their way to work and retail workers popping out for a quick lunchtime snack to late-night bar hoppers looking to eat themselves sober. Try the *pinto con huevo* (rice, beans and eggs), a bargain at just $1.

Shakti C 13, Av 8. The self-proclaimed "home of healthy food" offers filling *platos del día* of *sopa negra* or salad, hearty vegetarian *casado*, a *refresco* and tea or coffee, all for only $2.50. Tasty breakfast specials include granola, fruit juice and coffee or tea for only $2. It's popular for lunch, so go early or late for a seat. Open Mon–Fri lunch only.

Tapia Southeast corner of Parque la Sabana. Huge place, open to the street with views (across the busy ring road) of Parque la Sabana. Especially handy for late-night snacks, with sandwiches and burgers for those weary of *casados*.

La Vasconia Av 1, C 3/5. Get off the tourist trail and dig into cheap breakfasts, *ceviche* and *empanadas* alongside Costa Rican workers at this casual soda. Adorning the walls are thousands of photos of the national soccer team (some dating back to 1905).

Vishnu Three branches at Av 1, C 1/3; Av 3, C1; Av 8, C 9/11. These cheery vegetarian sodas are an obligatory pit stop for healthy fare in San José. Enjoy delicious, reasonably priced *platos del día* with brown rice and also generous vegetable dishes and soups. The vegetarian club sandwich with chips will set you back a mere $3; fruit plates with yoghurt are around $1.50.

Restaurants

Antojitos Cancún In the Centro Comercial Cocorí, 50m west of the Fuente de la Hispanidad roundabout, Los Yoses. Cheap, filling Mexican food, not wholly authentic, but good for late-night snacks and cheap all-you-can-eat buffets. Draught beer and an outside terrace where you can sit and watch the 4WDs whiz round the fountain. Mariachi Fri and Sat from 10pm.

Ave Fénix San Pedro, Av 0, 150m before Parque Central as you come in on Av Central from the

west ☎225-3362. No-nonsense, dependable Szechuan Chinese place, serving tasty dishes and frequented by the Chinese community. Dinner costs $15 or so.

Balcón de Europa C 9, Av 0/1 ☎221-4841. The pasta and other Italian staples are nothing special at this city landmark, but the atmosphere is great. Sepia photos of San José's early days line the wood-panelled walls, along with treacly snippets of "wisdom". Monster cheeses dominate the dining room, as does the game strummer who serenades each table. Closed Sat.

La Bastille Av 0, C 22 ☎255-4994. Swanky restaurant-cum-art gallery with a dining room bedecked in garishly coloured modern art, including some strange Gaudí-esque chairs. Though the decor is strictly "love it or hate it", the French-Italian cuisine is some of the finest in the city – the ravioli is particularly recommended. Around $50 for two with wine.

Cabernet Outside San José in Rancho Redondo, Camino a Las Nubes de Coronado ☎229-1113. Perched high above San José with breathtaking views, this cosy gourmet restaurant serves superb French dishes. Lamb, steak and sea bass figure prominently. The multilingual proprietor can take you through what is probably the best wine list in San José. About $50 for two with wine and dessert, while the taxi will set you back about $15. Closed Mon.

Café Mundo Av 9, C 15, Barrio Otoya ☎222-6190. One of the finest restaurants in San Jose, though lately the service has been less than stellar. Still, the Italian-influenced cuisine continues to delight and is served in a beautiful dark-wood dining room or, if the weather is nice, on a leafy terrace. The Caesar ($5) and niçoise ($10) salads are large but a bit overpriced. If you're on a budget, go for the pizza, or just come for a cappuccino ($2). At night the bar attracts a largely gay clientele. Closed Sat & Sun.

La Cascada Behind the Centro Comercial Trejos Montalegre, Escazú ☎228-0906. This difficult-to-find restaurant (there's no sign) with ho-hum decor is actually the best steakhouse in San José. Hugely popular, it's often full of Tico families, especially on Sunday afternoon. The hunks of beef are fantastic, and the terrifically filling plates all come with rice and veggies.

Le Chandelier 100m west and 100m south of the ICE (Instituto Costarricense de Electricidad) building in Los Yoses ☎225-3980. Exquisite French food prepared by the restaurant's Swiss owner. Try the lobster in pastry or the delicious trout with almonds. A homely decor of exposed ceiling beams and a crackling fireplace. Dinner for two costs about $35–45. Closed Sun.

Cocina de Leña Centro Comercial El Pueblo ☎255-1360. Some see this as an example of Tico food at its best, superb meals cooked in a wooden oven and served in faux rustic surroundings. Others see it as a glorified soda selling overpriced staples to gullible tourists. The truth lies somewhere in between. The succulent chicken dishes are recommended and it's certainly handy if you're making a night of it among the bars and discos of El Pueblo. Dinner for two costs around $40.

La Galería 50m west of *Spoon*, behind the Aparthotel Los Yoses ☎234-0850. Popular, though expensive, restaurant with Josefinos on a special night out. A variety of European dishes in heavy sauces; cheese-lovers will swoon over the fondue. Classical music adds to the upscale atmosphere. Closed Sat & Sun.

Grano de Oro C 30, Av 2/4 ☎253-3322. Upmarket restaurant with beautiful hacienda-style decor and a changing menu. Breakfast (from 6am) includes fresh fruit, eggs benedict and banana macadamia pancakes. The salads are excellent – try the spinach, avocado and gorgonzola – while the main courses feature Costa Rican takes on international staples, such as filet mignon stuffed with tropical fruits. Amazing desserts, including tiramisu and piña colada cheesecake. Book ahead and bring plenty of funds.

L'Ile de France Hotel Le Bergerac, C 35, Av 0 ☎234-7850, ⓕ225-9103, ⓦwww.bergerac.co.cr. Set next to a pleasant courtyard adorned with tropical greenery, this popular Los Yoses stalwart has been serving up French specialities for over a quarter of a century – onion soup, rabbit liver paté, duckling *Landais*-style, salmon in basil sauce etc. It's a little pricey (around $50 for two with wine) but the food is superbly presented. Closed lunch and Sun.

Machu Picchu C 32, Av 1 ☎222-7384. Velvet llamas hang on the walls at this San José favourite, the only true South American restaurant in town. The appetizers, including *ceviche* and Peruvian *bocas*, tend to be more interesting than the main dishes. Around $30 for two with beer or wine. Closed Sun.

Marbella In the Centro Comercial Calle Real, San Pedro ☎224-9452. Spanish cuisine, including excellent veal dishes and delicious paella ($15 for two) with real rabbit (otherwise unknown in Costa Rica). Closed Sun evening & Mon.

La Masía de Triquell Av 2, C 40 ☎296-3524. When the desire for paella and other fresh Mediterranean fare hits you, this is the spot for consistently dependable Catalan cuisine. Count on spending at least $35–40 on dinner for two. Closed Sun.

Mazorca 200m east and 100m north of San Pedro Church; just east of the entrance to UCR. Inexpensive macrobiotic meals served amid a simple, homely decor. The tasty bread, soups, peanut-butter sandwiches and macrobiotic cakes are a welcome change from greasy *arroz con pollo*. Lunch is $5; takeaways are also available. Closed Sun.

Meridiano al Este Av 0, C 21 ☎256 2705. Opposite the La California gas station (but don't let that put you off), this reasonably priced restaurant draws a young, hip crowd with its quality international cuisine, including pastas, steaks, pizzas and tapas. Nightly entertainment features everything from live music by local bands to poetry recitals and comedy performances.

Il Pomodoro San Pedro 150m east of the entrance to the University ☏283-1010. Dig into the best pizza in San José at this large, cheerful restaurant popular with the university crowd. Specials include the tasty vegetarian pizza. Wash it all down with cheap draught beer. Around $20 for two.

Tin Jo C 11, Av 6/8 ☏221-7605. Quiet, popular and fairly formal Asian restaurant with a choice of Chinese, Indian, Indonesian, Thai, Burmese and Japanese. The lemongrass soup, bean-thread noodle salad in lime juice and coconut milk curries are particularly recommended. Dinner with wine is around $40 for two; skip the alcohol, or go for lunch, and you'll get away with half that.

Drinking and nightlife

San José pulsates with the country's most diverse nightlife, with scores of **bars, clubs** and **live music** venues. Most young Josefinos, students and foreigners in the know stay away from the centre of town and head, instead, to Los Yoses or San Pedro. Av Central in **Los Yoses** is a well-known "yuppie trail" of bars, packed with middle- and upper-middle-class Ticos imbibing and conversing. It starts roughly at the terribly fashionable *Cielo*, packed with a young hip crowd, and reaches its peak at the hugely popular American-style *Río* bar with an outdoor terrace overlooking the Avenida Central.

Note that prostitution (see Directory in Basics) is legal in Costa Rica and particularly prevalent in downtown San José. Many of the city centre "bars" are, in reality, little more than pick-up joints for professional prostitutes. The cluster of casinos and bars on Avenida Central between Calles 5 and 11 fall mainly into this category. At any time of day or night (most are open 24 hours), these bars are full of scantily clad young ladies trying to attract the attention of glassy-eyed gringos and Europeans. They're best avoided unless you want to spend every few minutes explaining why you're not interested in doing a little "business."

San Pedro nightlife is geared more towards the university population, with a strip of studenty bars to the east of the UCR entrance. Those looking for local atmosphere should head to a **boca bar** (see box p.94) or seek out places to hear **peñas**, slow, acoustic folk songs from the Andean region that grew out of the revolutionary movements of the 1970s and 1980s.

Even if you don't dance, it's entertaining to watch the Ticos burn up the floor at one of the city's **discos**. Because locals are usually in couples or groups, the atmosphere at most places isn't a "scene". In general, the **dress code** is relaxed: most people wear smart jeans and men need not wear a jacket. **Cover charges** run up to about 700 colones ($2), though the big mainstream discos at El Pueblo charge slightly more than places downtown.

Many bars don't offer **music** during the week, but change character drastically come Friday or Saturday, when you can hear jazz, blues, up-and-coming local bands, rock and roll, or South American folk music. That said, activity is not relentlessly weekend-oriented. It's possible, with a little searching, to hear good live music on a Wednesday, or find a packed disco floor on a Monday or Tuesday. People do stay out later on the weekends, but even so, with the exception of the studenty bars in San Pedro, most places close by 2 or 3am, and earlier on Sunday.

San José is one of the best places in Central (possibly Latin) America for **gay** nightlife. Establishments come and go – those in our listings are the best established places – and it helps if you have a local lesbian or gay contact to help you hunt down small local clubs.

Salsa like a Josefino

One of the best ways to meet people and to prepare yourself for San José nightlife is to take a few salsa lessons at one of the city's many *academias de baile*. You don't necessarily need a partner, and you can go with a friend or in a group. The tuition is serious, but the atmosphere is usually relaxed. The best classes in San José are at Bailes Latinos, in the Costa Rican Institute of Language and Latin Dance, Av 0, C 25/27 (☎233-8938, ☎233-8670); at Malecón, C 17/19, Av 2 (☎222-3214); and at Merecumbé, which has various branches, the most central of which is in San Pedro (☎224-3531 or 234-1548).

For full details of **what's on**, check the *cartelera* in the *Tiempo Libre* section of *La Nación*, which lists live music along with all sorts of other activities, from swimming classes to cultural discussions.

Bars and live music

Baleares In San Pedro, 50m west of the Más por Menos supermarket. Live rock (Thurs–Sat) in a dark and cavernous bar popular with students and locals. Usually a $2 cover charge.

Bar Jazz Café In San Pedro, near the Banco Popular ☎253-8933. The best bar in San José for live jazz, with an intimate atmosphere and consistently good groups. Cover charge varies from $5 to $10 (sometimes including a glass of wine) and it's usually worth it. Music starts after 10pm.

Bar México Barrio México, opposite the church. Strictly off the tourist trail but well worth hunting out, this traditional bar serves tasty *bocas* to its largely working-class clientele. Full of atmosphere, it's a great place to mix with locals. Live Latin music on Wed.

Bar Río Boulevard Los Yoses. Wildly popular Los Yoses sports bar with a large terrace. Inside, eight (count 'em) TV screens, each usually showing a different football match and in the back is a large dance area. Live music on Tuesdays and the occasional weekend. The starchy fast-food menu is a good way to soak up the alcohol.

Caccio's 200m east and 25m north of San Pedro Church. A great spot to meet Ticos is this insanely popular student hangout where guys wearing baseball caps sing along loudly to outdated songs. Knock back cheap, cold beer while munching on pizza. Open till 2am. Closed Sun.

Chelles Av 0, C 9 ☎221-1369. This simple, brightly lit, 24-hour bar, with football on TV and cheap beers and *bocas,* pulls in an eclectic crowd of weary businessmen and late-night revellers.

Cielo Av 1, C 21. Wildly popular, two-storey club packed nightly from 8pm with young Josefinos and a smattering of tourists. Conversing gives way to dancing as the night progresses.

El Cuartel de la Boca del Monte Av 1, C 19/21 ☎221-0327. Lively, long-established bar – with great lunch, dinner and bocas – that still packs in Josefinos, particularly on Mondays and Wednesdays when there's live music (Latin, rock and reggae) by up-and-coming bands. Open until 2am Wed–Sat.

La Esmeralda Av 2, C 5/7 ☎221-0530. Colourful, landmark bar that doubles as the headquarters of the union of Mariachi bands, who whoosh by your table in a colourful swirl of sombreros and sequins before dashing off in a taxi to serenade elsewhere in San José. Closed Sun.

Meridiano al Este Av 0, C 21 ☎256-2705. One of San José's best new restaurants – and an outstanding venue for live music as well as poetry recitals and comedy. The programme changes often, but Sunday nights usually feature the pick of San Jose's up-and-coming jazz and Latin performers.

Milano si Accende Av 11, C 3 bis. Self-consciously European bar with Italian food and oh-so comfortable sofas. On Mondays, groove to European dance and electronica.

Raíces Av 2, C 45. Dedicated reggae bar with a booming sound system and hordes of dreadlocked Ticos packing the small dance floor. Closed Mon & Tues.

Las Risas C 1, Av 0/1 ☎223-2803. One of the best downtown bars, on three floors. A young crowd packs the small dance floor at the popular top-floor disco. Bring ID – a copy of your passport will suffice — or the bouncers won't let you in. The cover charge of $2 will usually get you two drinks or a tequila. Saturday is ladies' night.

Shakespeare Av 2, C 28. Quiet, friendly bar. Popular with people who pop in for a drink before

Boca bars

In Costa Rica, *bocas* (appetizers) are the tasty little snacks traditionally served free in bars. Boca bars are a largely urban tradition, and although you find them in other parts of the country, the really famous ones are all in San José. Because of mounting costs, however, and erosion of local traditions, few places serve *bocas* gratis any more. Several bars have a *boca* menu, among them El Cuartel de la Boca del Monte (see p.93) near Los Yoses and La Villa in San Pedro, but the authentic *boca* bars are concentrated in suburban working- or lower-middle-class residential neighbourhoods. They have a distinctive convivial atmosphere – friends and family spending the evening together – and are very busy most nights. Saturday is the hardest night to get a table; get there before 7.30pm. You'll be handed a menu of free *bocas* – one beer gets you one *boca*, so keep drinking and you can keep eating. The catch is that the beer costs about twice as much as elsewhere ($2 as opposed to $1) but even so, the little plates of food are generous enough to make this a bargain way to eat out. You'll do better if you speak Spanish, but you can get by with point-and-nod. Typical *bocas* include deep-fried plantains with black-bean paste, small plates of rice and meat, shish kebabs, tacos or empanadas; nothing fancy, but the perfect accompaniment to a cold beer.

One of the most authentic and well-known is the working-class, longtime Bar México (Mon–Fri 3pm–midnight, Sat 11am–midnight), opposite the church in Barrio México, northwest of the city. Barrio México is a pretty rough neighbourhood, so go by taxi. You'll find a varied clientele – but conspicuously few foreigners – at Los Perales and El Sesteo (both Mon–Sat 7pm–midnight). They're about 100m from each other on the same street in the eastern suburb of Curridabat – hard to find on your own, but taxi drivers will know them.

heading to a performance at the adjacent Sala Garbo cinema or Laurence Olivier theatre. Occasionally has live jazz.

La Villa In San Pedro, 150m north of the old Banco Anglo ☏ 280-9541. San José's best bar for beer, tasty *bocas*, and conversation is in this old house plastered with political and theatrical posters. Frequented by students who hold forth on politics and literature to the tunes of Mercedes Sosa on the CD player and occasional live *peñas*. Closed Sun.

Discos

Cocoloco El Pueblo. Smart, well-dressed clientele, small dance floors, and the usual Latin techno-pop/reggae/merengue mix.

Ebony 56 El Pueblo. One of the most popular among El Pueblo's glut of discos. Several large dance floors with salsa and US and European dance music with the odd 1980s/1990s pop hit thrown in. Closed Sun.

Infinito El Pueblo. Similar to *Cocoloco*, with three dance floors and booming salsa, US and European dance music, and 1970s romantic hits spun by excellent DJs. Attracts an older, smarter crowd. Closed Sun.

Salsa 54 C 3, Av 1/3. Downtown alternative to the El Pueblo discos, this lively joint plays the favoured mix of Latin and American tunes but, as the name implies, also goes heavy on the salsa and merengue. The best place to dance in San José proper, attracting the most talented *salseros*.

Planet Mall San Pedro Mall. Central America's largest disco (apparently) with the same slightly soulless atmosphere of US and European mega-clubs. Still, it's wildly popular (if a little pricey at $10) with young Josefinos. DJs spin European dance and Latin rhythms.

Terra U San Pedro, one block east of San Pedro Church. With three open-air levels and a heaving dance floor, this is a one of San José's weekend hot spots. Latin and Jamaican dance hits predominate. Music videos (and occasional soccer match highlights) play on the TV.

Gay and lesbian nightlife

La Avispa C 1, Av 8/10. Landmark San José lesbian disco-bar (men are also welcome) with a friendly atmosphere, three dance floors and several pool tables. Thursday night is karaoke night. There's a $5 cover charge Thursday to Sunday. Closed Mon & Wed.
Café Mundo Av 9, C 15, Barrio Otoya ☎222-6190. In the restaurant (see p.91) of the same name, this low-key bar-restaurant attracts a mainly gay clientele.

Déjà Vu C 2, Av 14/16 ☎236-6332. A mixed crowd – gay, lesbian and straight – come for the hot and happening atmosphere and music, mostly house and techno with some salsa and reggae. Two large dance floors plus a quiet bar and a café. The neighbourhood is pretty scary, so best to take a taxi. Cover charge varies from $3 to $5, though drinks are cheap. Closed Sun & Mon.

The arts and entertainment

Bearing in mind the decreasing financial support from the national government, the quality of the arts in San José is very high. Josefinos especially like **theatre**, and there's a healthy range of venues for a city this size, staging a variety of inventive productions at affordable prices. If you speak even a little Spanish it's worth checking to see what's on.

Costa Rica's **National Dance Company** has an impressive repertoire of classical and modern productions, some by Central American choreographers, arranged specifically for the company – again, ticket costs are low. The city's premier venues are the Teatro Nacional and the Teatro Mélico Salazar; here you can see performances by the **National Symphony Orchestra** and **National Lyric Opera Company** (June–Aug), as well as visiting orchestras and singers, usually from Spain or other Spanish-speaking countries. The Teatro Mélico Salazar occasionally stages performances of traditional Costa Rican singing and dancing.

Going to the **cinema** in San José is a bargain ($3–5 a ticket), though many venues have decamped to the suburbs, particularly to shopping malls, such as the Cinemark in Escazú's Multiplaza, which you can only reach by car or taxi. There are still a few good downtown cinemas left, however, several of which retain some original features, along with plush, comfortable seats. Most cinemas show the latest American movies, which are almost always subtitled. The few that are dubbed will have the phrase "hablado en Español" in the newspaper listings or on the posters. For Spanish-language art movies, head to Sala Garbo.

For **details of all performances**, check the *Cartelera* section of the *Tiempo Libre* supplement in *La Nación* on Thursday and the listings in the *Tico Times*, which also distinguish between English- and Spanish-language films and productions.

Cinemas

Alianza Francesa Barrio Amón, Av 7, C 5 ☎222-2283. Occasional French-language films, usually dubbed or subtitled in Spanish.
Cine Omni C 3, Av 0/1 ☎221-7903. Downtown cinema showing US blockbusters.

Colón Paseo Colón, C 38/40 ☎221-4517. Plush, US mall-style cinema, with mainstream Hollywood films.
Multcines San Pedro In San Pedro Mall ☎280-9585. American-style multiplex with ten screens, full surround-sound and popcorn on tap.

Facultad de Derecho Cinema Law School
Cinema, University of Costa Rica, San Pedro
☏207-5322. Occasional European and arthouse
films.
Sala Garbo Av 2, C 28 ☏223-1960. Popular
arthouse cinema showing independent films from

around the world usually in the original language
with Spanish subtitles.
Variedades C 5, Av 0/1 ☏222-6104. Old but
well-preserved downtown movie house with
rococo-style decor showing good foreign and
occasionally Spanish-language films.

Theatres

Bellas Artes Facultad de Bellas Artes
University of Costa Rica, San Pedro ☏207-4095.
Generally excellent and innovative student
productions with new spins on classical and
contemporary works.
Eugene O'Neill Centro Cultural Costarricense-
Norteamericano, Los Yoses ☏225-9433. Works
by modern playwrights in innovative independent
productions.
Laurence Olivier In the Sala Garbo building, Av

2, C 28 ☏222-1034. Modern theatre specializing
in contemporary productions, plus occasional jazz
concerts and film festivals.
Mélico Salazar C Central, Av 2 ☏ 221-4952.
San José's "workhorse" theatre stages occasional
performances of traditional Costa Rican song and
dance.
Teatro Nacional C 5, Av 2 ☏252-0863. The city's
premier theatre hosts opera, ballet and concerts,
as well as drama.

Shopping and markets

San José's **souvenir and crafts shops** are well stocked and in general fairly
pricey; it's best to buy from the larger shops run by government-regulated
crafts cooperatives, from which more of the money filters down to the artisans.
You'll see an abundance of pre-Columbian gold jewellery copies, Costa Rican
liqueurs (Café Rica is the best known), T-shirts with jungle and animal scenes,
weirdly realistic wooden snakes, leather rockers from the village of Sarchí (see
p.118), walking sticks, simple leather bracelets, hammocks and a vast array
of woodcarvings, from miniature everyday rural scenes to giant, colourfully
hand-painted Sarchí ox-carts. Look out too for *molas,* handmade and appliquéd
clothes, mostly shirts, occasionally from the Bahía Drake region of southwestern
Costa Rica, but more usually made by the Kuna peoples of Panamá.

A good place to buy any of these handicrafts is at San José's **street
craftmarket** in the Plaza de la Democracía (see p.85). Also on sale are regional
leather and silver jewellery and a selection of crafts from other Latin American
countries, including Ecuadorian sweaters. It's worth bargaining, although the
goods are already a little cheaper than in shops.

Atmósfera C 5, Av 1. Elegant gallery-like outlet
selling jewellery, furniture and woodwork.
CANAPI C 11, Av 1. Big shop with a good stock of
wooden bowls, walking sticks and boxes.
Hotel Don Carlos C 9, Av 9. Good pre-Columbian
artefacts and jewellery reproductions.
La Casona C 0, Av 0/1. Large two-floor
marketplace with stalls selling the usual local
stuff along with Guatemalan knapsacks and
bedspreads. It's great for browsing, and the traders
are friendly, but quality at some stalls is pretty
poor, and there's not one good T-shirt in evidence.
Mercado Central Av 0/1, C 6/8. *The* place to buy
coffee beans, but make sure they're export quality
– ask for Grano d'Oro ("Golden Bean").

Mercado Nacional de Artesanía C 22, Av 2 bis.
One of the country's largest retailers of souvenirs
and crafts, featuring Sarchí ox-carts, jewellery,
woodwork and all the usual T-shirts.
Plaza Esmeralda La Uruca, Pavas, about 5m
northwest of city centre. Craft cooperative run by
local artisans where you can watch cigars being
rolled, necklaces being set and the ubiquitous
Sarchí ox-carts being painted. Closed Sun.
Sol Maya Paseo Colón C 18/20. Rather pricey
indigenous and Guatemalan arts and crafts.
Tienda de la Naturaleza Curridabat Av 0, 1km
east of San Pedro. The shop of the Fundación
Neotrópica, this is a good place to buy the posters,
T-shirts and other paraphernalia painted by

English artist Deirdre Hyde that you see all over the country. She specializes in the landscapes of tropical America and the animals that live there, jaguars in particular.

Listings

Airline offices Alitalia, C 38, Av 3 (☎295-6870); American, Paseo Colón, C 26/28 (☎257-1266); Continental, C 19, Av 2 (☎296-4911); Copa, C 1, Av 5 (☎222-6640); Delta, at the airport (☎257-8946); Iberia, C 40, Paseo Colón (☎257-8266); Lacsa, C 1, Av 5 (☎222-9383); LanChile, Sabana Oeste (☎290-5222); Lufthansa, C 5, Av 7/9 (☎243-1818); Mexicana, C 1, Av 2/4 (☎295-6969); SAM, Av 5, C 1/3 (☎233-3066); Sansa, Av 5, C 1/3 (☎221-5774); TACA, C 1, Av 1/3 (☎296-9353); United Airlines, Sabana Sur (☎220-4844); Varig, Av 5, C 1/3 (☎290-5222).

Banks State-owned banks in San José include the Banco de Costa Rica, Av 2, C 4/6 (Mon–Fri 9am–3pm; Visa only) and Banco Nacional, Av 0/1, C 2/4 (Mon–Fri 9am–3pm; Visa only). Private banks include Banco Mercantil, Av 3, C 0/2 (Mon–Fri 9am–3pm; Visa only); Banco Metropolitano, C 0, Av 2 (Mon–Fri 8.15am–4pm; Visa only); BANEX, C 0, Av 1 (Mon–Fri 8am–5pm; Visa only); Banco Popular, C 1 Av 2/4 (Mon–Fri 8.30am–3.30pm, Sat 9am–1pm; Visa & MasterCard); and Banco de San José, C 0, Av 3/5 (Visa & MasterCard). There's an American Express office at C1, Av 0/1 (Mon–Fri 8.30am–5pm; ☎257-1792; ⊚www .americanexpress.com).

Bookstores Mora Books, Av 1, C 3/5, in the Omni building (☎255-4136), is a pleasant shop with a good selection of secondhand English-language books, CDs, guidebooks, magazines and comics. Chispas, C 7, Av 0/1 (☎223-2240) sells new and secondhand books, and has the best selection of English-language fiction in town. It also sells a good array of guidebooks and books about Costa Rica (in English and Spanish), plus the *New York Times*, *El País* and several English-language magazines. Lehmann, Av 0, C 1/3 (☎223-1212), has a good selection of mass-market Spanish-language fiction and non-fiction, as well as maps, children's books and a small (mainly secondhand) collection of English language books. The Librería Internacional, with branches 300m west of Taco Bell in Barrio Dent (☎253-9553) and in the Multiplaza Escazú (☎298-1138), has the best selection of international fiction; they also stock travel books and Spanish-language fiction, as well as books in English and German. Macondo, opposite the entrance to the library at the university campus in San Pedro, is probably the best bookshop in town for literature in Spanish, especially from Central America, as well as academic disciplines such as sociology and women's studies. Librería Universal, Av 0, C Central/1 (☎222-2222), is strong on Spanish fiction, books about Costa Rica (in Spanish), and country maps. Librería y Bazar Guillen at La Coca-Cola bus terminal is a good place to browse for reading material before leaving on a long trip. 7th Street Books, C 7 Av 0/1 (☎256-8251), has both new and used books, including English literature, and also a wide selection of books and maps on Costa Rica in English and Spanish.

Car rental see p.29.

Embassies and consulates Argentina, 400m south of McDonald's in Curridabat (☎234-6520 or 234-6270); Belize, 400m east of the Iglesia Santa Teresita, Rohrmoser (☎253-5598); Bolivia, in Rohrmoser (☎232-9455); Brazil, Paseo Colón, C 20/22 (☎223-1544); Canada, C 3, Av 1 (☎296-4149); Chile, 50m east and 225m west of the Automercado, Los Yoses (☎224-4243); Colombia, 175m west of Taco Bell, in Barrio Dent (☎283-6861); Ecuador, 100m west and 100m south of the Centro Comercial Plaza Mayor, in Rohrmoser (☎232-1503); El Salvador, Av 10, C 33/35, Los Yoses (☎256-4047); Guatemala, 100m north and 50m east of Pizza Hut, in Curridabat (☎283-2557); Honduras, 300m east and 200m north of ITAN, in Los Yoses (☎234-9502); México, Av 7, C 13/15 (☎257-0633); Nicaragua, Av 0, C 25/27 (☎222-2373 or 233-8747); Panamá, C 38, Av 5/7 (☎281-2442); Peru, 100m south and 50m west of the San José Indoor Club, in Curridabat (☎225-1786); UK, 11th floor, Edificio Centro Colón, Paseo Colón, C 38/40 (☎258-2025); US, opposite the Centro Comercial in Pavas – take the bus to Pavas from Av 1, C 18 (☎220-3939); Venezuela, Av 2, C 37/39, Los Yoses (☎225-5813 or 8810). There is no consular representative for Australia or New Zealand.

Film processing San José is the only place in the country you should try to get film processed. That said, it's expensive and the quality is low; wait until you get home if you can. Bearing in mind these caveats, try Universal, Av 0, C 0/1, which only processes Fuji; IFSA, Av 2, C 3/5, which only processes Kodak; or Dima, Av 0, C 3/5, which processes both Kodak and Fuji.

Hospitals The city's public (social security) hospital is San Juan de Dios, Paseo Colón, C 14/16 (☏ 257-6282). Of the private hospitals, foreigners are most often referred to Clínica Biblica, Av 14, C 0/1 (☏ 257-5252; emergency and after-hours number ☏ 257-0466), where basic consultation and treatment (for example, a prescription for a course of antibiotics) starts at about $100. San José has many excellent medical specialists – your embassy will have a list – and private health care is not expensive.

Immigration Costa Rican *inmigración* (Mon–Fri 8am–4pm; ☏ 220-0355) is on the airport highway opposite the Hospital México; take an Alajuela bus and get off at the stop underneath the overhead walkway. Get there early, if you want visa extensions or exit visas. Larger travel agencies, such as Tikal Tours can take care of the paperwork for you for a fee (roughly $10–25).

Internet access Most of the hotels and guesthouses in San José now offer Internet access, often for free. You'll also find plenty of Internet cafés in town. Expect to pay around 300 colones per half hour (sometimes less). Many cafés also serve a range of drinks and snacks. Try Café Digital, Av 0, C 5/7, which also has a snack bar, a cigar shop and a balcony overlooking Avenida Central; Neotopia Cyber Café, Av 1, C11 or Internet Café Costa Rica, Av 0, C 0/2.

Laundry Burbujas, 50m west and 25m south of the Mas por Menos supermarket in San Pedro, has coin-operated machines and sells soap; Lava y Seca, 100m north of Mas por Menos, next to Autos San Pedro, in San Pedro, will do your laundry for you, as well as dry-cleaning. Other places include Lava Más, C 45, Av 8/10, next to *Spoon* in Los Yoses; Lavamatic Doña Anna, C 13, Av 16; and Sixaola (one of a chain), Av 2, C 7/9. Many hotels and guesthouses also offer a laundry service.

Libraries and cultural centres The Alianza Francesa, C 5, Av 7 (Mon–Fri 9am–noon & 3–7pm; ☏ 222-2283) stocks some French publications; the Quaker-affiliated Friends' Peace Center, C 15, Av 6 bis (Mon–Fri 10am–3pm; ☏ 221-8299) has English-language newspapers, plus weekly meetings and discussion groups. Other libraries/ cultural centres include the Biblioteca Nacional, C 15, Av 3 (Mon–Sat 9am–5pm) and the Centro Cultural Costarricense-Norteamericano, 100m north of the Am-Pm supermarket in Barrio Dent (Mon–Fri 7am–7pm, Sat 9am–noon; ☏ 207-7500, Ⓦ www.cccncr.com).

Pharmacies Clínica Biblica, Av 14, C 0/1 (open 24hr; ☏ 257-5252); Farmacia del Este, on Av Central near Mas por Menos in San Pedro (open until 8pm); Farmacia Fischel, Av 3, C 2; there are many pharmacies in the blocks surrounding the Hospital Calderon Guardia, 100m northeast of the Biblioteca Nacional, in Barrio Otoya.

Post office The Correo Central, C 2, Av 1/3 (Mon–Fri 7am–5pm, Sat 7am–noon; ☏ 258-8762) is two blocks east and one block north of the Mercado Central. They'll hold letters for up to four weeks (10 colones per letter; you'll need a passport to collect your post).

Sports The sports complex behind the Museo de Arte Costarricense on Parque la Sabana has a gym, Olympic-size pool and a recently refurbished running track. The park itself has tennis courts, and is as good a place as any for jogging, with changing facilities and showers. There are lots of runners about in the morning, though there have been reports of assaults on lone joggers in the evening and it's wise to stay away from the heavily wooded northeastern corner of the park. Parque de la Paz in the south of the city is also recommended for running and has a velodrome and a roller hockey rink; in San Pedro you can jog, swim and play basketball at the UCR campus. The Club Deportivo Cipresses (☏ 253-0530), set in landscaped grounds 700m north of the La Galera gas station in Curridabat offers $7 day memberships which give access to weights, machines, pools and aerobics classes. The nearest public pool to San José is at Ojo de Agua, 17km northwest of town; you can get a bus there from AV2, C 20/22 (15min).

Telephone offices Radiográfica, C 1, Av 5 (daily 7.30am–9pm; ☏ 287-0087) is the state-run office where you can use directories, make overseas calls and send or receive faxes. Unfortunately, it charges a flat fee of $3 for the use of its phones on top of the price of the call.

Moving on from San José

San José is the **transport hub** of Costa Rica. Most bus services, flights and car rental agencies are located here. Wherever you are in the country, you're technically never more than nine hours by highway from the capital, with the majority of destinations being much closer than that. Eventually, like it or not, all roads lead to San José.

By bus

Thefts from the luggage compartments of long-distance bus services are becoming more common, especially on the Monteverde and Manuel Antonio routes. The accepted wisdom is, if possible, to take your luggage onto the bus with you. Even then, make sure all compartments are locked and that you have nothing valuable inside easily unzipped pockets. If you have to put your bags in the luggage hold, make sure only the driver or his helper handles them, and get a seat from where you can keep an eye on the luggage compartment during stops.

The tables on the following pages deal with **express bus services** from San José. Regional bus information is covered in the relevant accounts in the Guide. As schedules are prone to change, exact departure times are not given here, though some details are given under individual destinations elsewhere in the book. If you're going to be travelling by bus, your best bet is to get a complete timetable at the ICT office (see p.68) when you arrive.

Bus companies in San José

A bewildering number of **bus companies** use San José as their hub. The following is a rundown of their head office addresses and/or phone numbers, and the abbreviations that we use in the tables overleaf.

ATC	Autotransportes San José-San Carlos	(☏255-4318 or 256-8914)
BL	Autotransportes Blanco-Lobo, C 12, Av 9	(☏771-4744)
BM	Buses Metropoli	(☏530-1064)
EA	Empresa Alfaro, C 14, Av 3/5	(☏222-2666)
EG	Empresarios Guápileños	(☏710-7780)
EM	Empresa Esquivel	(☏666-1249)
EU	Empresarios Unidos	(☏222-0064)
ME	Transportes MEPE, Av 11, C 0/1	(☏257-8129)
MO	Transportes Delio Morales, C 16, Av 1/3	(☏223-5567)
MRA	Microbuses Rapiditos Heredianos, C1, Av 7/9	(☏223-8392)
MU	MUSOC, C 16, Av 1/3	(☏222-2422)
Nica	Nicabus	(☏223-0293)
PA	Panaline	(☏256-8721)
PU	Pulmitan, C 14, Av 1/3	(☏222-1650)
SA	SACSA, C 5, Av 18	(☏551-0232)
TC	Transportes Caribeños	(☏221-2596)
Tica	Ticabus, C 9, Av 4/6	(☏221-8954)
TIL	Transportes Tilarán, C 14, Av 9/11	(☏222-3854)
TJ	Transportes Jacó	(☏223-1109)
TRA	TRALAPA, C 20, Av 1/3	(☏221-7202)
TRC	Tracopa-Alfaro, Av 18, C 2/4	(☏221-4214)
TRN	Transnica	(☏223-4242)
TRS	Transtusa, Av 6, C 13	(☏556-4233)
TU	TUASA, C 12, Av 2	(☏442-6900)
Tuan	Tuan	(☏441-3781)

Domestic bus services from San José

In the table below, the initials in the ☎ column correspond to the bus company that serves this route; see p.99 for telephone numbers. Where advance purchase is mentioned, it is advised, and strongly recommended in the high season (HS), or on weekends (WE) – from Friday to Sunday. You need buy your ticket no more than one day in advance unless otherwise indicated. NP = National Park; WR = Wildlife Refuge; NM = National Monument.

TO	FREQUENCY	BUS STOP	DISTANCE	DURATION	☎	ADV. PURCHASE
Alajuela (and airport)	every 5min	Av 2, C 12/14	17km	35min	TU	no
Braulio Carrillo NP see Guápiles						
Cahuita	4 daily	C 0, Av 11/13	195km	4hr	ME	yes (HS)
Caño Negro WR see Los Chiles						
Cartago	every 5min	C 5, Av 18/20	22km	45min	SA	no
Chirripó NP see San Isidro						
Corcovado NP see Puerto Jiménez						
Fortuna	12 daily	C16, Av 1/3	130km	4hr 30min	ATS	yes (HS)
Golfito	2 daily	C 14, Av 3/5	339km	8hr	TRC	yes (3 days)
Guápiles	every 45min	C 0, Av 11/13	30km	35min	EG	no
Guayabo NM see Turrialba						
Heredia	every 5min	C 1, Av 7/9 & Av 2, C12/14	11km	25min	TU/MRA	no
La Selva/Selva Verde see Puerto Viejo de Sarapiquí						
Liberia	17 daily	C 24, Av 5/7	217km	4hr	PU	no
Limón	25 daily	C 0, Av 11/13	162km	2hr 30min	TC	no
Los Chiles	2 daily	C 12, Av 7/9	217km	5hr	ATS	no
Manuel Antonio NP see Quepos						
Monteverde	2 daily	C 12, Av 7/9	167km	3hr 30min	TIL	yes (3–5 days)

Destination	Frequency	Departs	Distance	Duration	Company	Reservations
Nicoya	6 daily	C 14, Av 3/5	296km	6hr	EA	no
Nosara	1 daily	C 14, Av 3/5	361km	6hr	EA	no
Palmar	7 daily	C 14, Av 5	258km	5hr	TRA	no
Playa Brasilito	2 daily	C 20, Av 3/5	320km	6hr	TRA	yes (WE)
Playa Coco	3 daily	C 24, Av 5/7	251km	5hr	PU	yes (WE)
Playa Flamingo	2 daily	C 20, Av 3/5	320km	6hr	TRA	yes (WE)
Playa Hermosa	1 daily	Av 5, C 20/22	265km	5hr	EM	no
Playa Jacó	5 daily	C 16, Av 1/3	102km	2hr 30min	TJ	yes (WE)
Playa Junquillal	1 daily	C 20, Av 3/5	298km	5hr	TRA	no
Playa Panamá	1 daily	Av 5, C 20/22	265km	5hr	EM	no
Playa Potrero	2 daily	C 20, Av 3	320km	6hr	TRA	yes (WE)
Puerto Jiménez	2 daily	C 12, Av 7/9	378km	8hr	BL	yes
Puerto Viejo de Talamanca	4 daily	C 0, Av 13	210km	4hr 30min	ME	yes
Puntarenas	15 daily	C 16, Av 10/12	110km	2hr	EU	no
Quepos	4 daily	C 16, Av 3/5	145km	3hr 30min	MO	yes (3 days)
Sámara	1 daily	C 14, Av 3/5	331km	6hr	EU	yes (WE)
San Carlos/Ciudad Quesada	15 daily	C 12, Av 7/9	110km	3hr	ATS	no
San Isidro de El General	14 daily	C 0, Av 22/24	136km	3hr	MU	no
Santa Cruz	9 daily	Av 3, C 18/20	274km	5hr	TRA	no
Sarchí	30 daily	Av 3, C 16/18	152km	1hr 30min	Tuan	no
Tamarindo	2 daily	C 14, Av 5	320km	6hr	EA	yes (WE)
Turrialba	17 daily	C 13, Av 6/8	65km	1hr 40min	TRS	no
Volcán Arenal see Fortuna						
Volcán Irazú	1 Sat & Sun	Av 2, C 1/3	54km	2hr	BM	no (but go early)
Volcán Poás	1 daily	Av 2, C12/14	55km	1hr 30min	TU	no (but go early)

International bus services from San José

Codes given under the ⊤ column correspond to the relevant bus company (see p.99). Advance purchase – at least a week in advance, particularly for Managua and Panamá City – is necessary for all routes.

TO	FREQUENCY	BUS STOP	DISTANCE	DURATION	⊤
David	1 daily	Av 3/5, C 14	400km	9hr	TRC
Guatemala City	2 daily	Av 4, C 9/11	1200km	60hr	Tica
(overnight in Managua & El Salvador)					
Managua	3 daily	Av 4, C 9/11	450km	11hr	Tica
Managua	3 daily	C 22, Av 3/5	450km	11hr	TRN
Managua	1 daily	C 0, Av 11	450km	11hr	Nica
Panamá City	2 daily	Av 4, C 9/11	903km	18hr	Tica
Panamá City	1 daily	C 16, Av 3–5	903km	18hr	PA
Paso Canoas	7 daily	C 14, Av 5	349km	8hr	TRC
(for Panamá)					
Sixaola	2 daily	C 0, Av 9/11	250km	6hr	M/E
(for Panamá)					
Tegucigalpa	2 daily	Av 4, C 9/11	909km	48hr	Tica
(overnight in Managua)					

By air

Domestic flights from San José are run by Sansa, the state airline, and NatureAir, a commercial company. Sansa flies from Juan Santamaría International airport, 17km northwest of the city. They change their schedules frequently, so it's best to phone ahead or double-confirm when booking. NatureAir, more reliable in terms of schedules, flies from Pavas airport, 7km west of the city. Although the table gives as accurate a rundown of the routes as possible, flight durations are subject to change at the last minute. Some of the routings, particularly those to the Nicoya Peninsula, tend to be roundabout, often with one or two stops. Note that advance purchase (14 days) is necessary to ensure yourself a seat during the high season, especially for Quepos, Sámara and Tamarindo. Both companies have offices and agents throughout the country in most of the destinations they serve, or you can book and pay for tickets at a travel agent. Sansa check-in is at their San José office one hour before departure; they run a free bus to get you to the airport, and in some cases offer free transfers to your hotel at the other end. Fares range from $35 one-way to $70–80 return for most destinations. NatureAir is typically $10–15 more expensive.

Domestic flights from San José

Sansa, C 24, Paseo Colón/Av 1
(☎221-9414, reservations ☎257-9444,
🅕255-2176, Ⓦ www.flysansa.com)

TO	FREQUENCY	DURATION
Barra del Colorado	1 daily	30min
Drake Bay	2 daily	50min
Golfito	4 daily	45min
Nosara	2 daily	55min
Palmar Sur	2 daily	50min
Puerto Jiménez	3 daily	50min
Quepos	6 daily	30min
Sámara	2 daily	55min
Tamarindo	7 daily	40min
Tambor	2 daily	20min
Tortuguero	1 daily	35min

NatureAir, Tobías Bolaños airport,
Pavas (☎220-3054 or 296-1102, 🅕220-0413,
Ⓦ www.natureair.com)

Barra del Colorado	1 daily	30min
Drake Bay	2 daily	45min
Golfito	1 daily	1hr 10min
Liberia	4 daily	1hr 10min
Palmar Sur	2 daily	1hr 15min
Quepos	4 daily	25min
Sámara	1 daily	1hr 5min
Tamarindo	3 daily	50min
Tambor	2 daily	30min
Tortuguero	1 daily	30min

SAN JOSÉ | Moving on from San José

2

The Valle Central and the highlands

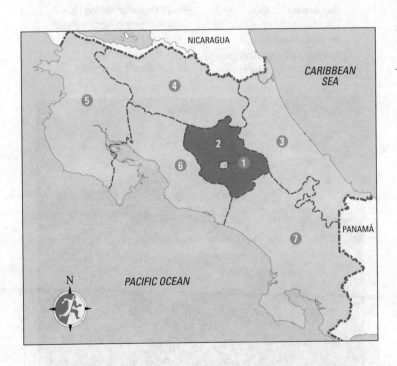

CHAPTER 2 # Highlights

* **Xandari Plantation Hotel** Relax at this enchanting hotel set amidst the cool, coffee-studded hills of the Valle Central. See p.115

* **Volcán Poás** Trek to the stunning summit of Volcán Poás. See p.115

* **CODECE** Spend a day at the CODECE community tourism project, meeting local families and sampling the traditional culture, cuisine and music of highland Costa Rica. See p.116

* **Volcán Irazú** Enjoy unforgettable views from the blasted-out crater of mighty Volcán Irazú, dominating the landscape north of Cartago. See p.134

* **Whitewater rafting** Raft the churning white waters of the Ríos Reventazón and Pacuaré, near Turrialba. See p.138

△ Volcán Poás

2

The Valle Central and the highlands

osta Rica's Valle Central ("Central Valley") and the surrounding highlands form the cultural and geographical fulcrum of the country. Rising between 3000 and 4000m, this wide-hipped inter-mountain plateau – often referred to as the Meseta Central, or "Central Tableland" – has a patchwork-quilt beauty, especially when lit by the early-morning sun, with staggered green coffee terraces set in sharp contrast to the blue-black summits of the surrounding mountains. Many of these are volcanos: the Valle Central is edged by a chain of volcanic peaks, running from smoking Poás in the north to precipitous Irazú in the east. Though there have been no genuine eruptions since Irazú blew its top in 1963, Poás and Irazú periodically spew and snort, raining a light covering of fertile volcanic ash on the surrounding farmland.

Although it occupies just six percent of the country's total landmass, the fertile Valle Central supports roughly two-thirds of Costa Rica's population. Here you'll find the country's four most important cities: San José (covered in Chapter One), **Alajuela**, **Heredia** and **Cartago**. The tremendous pressure on land is noticeable even on short forays from San José: urban areas, suburbs and highway communities blend into each other, and in some places, every spare patch of soil sprouts coffee bushes, fruit trees or vegetables.

In addition to the volcanos and their surrounding national parks, the region boasts **whitewater rafting** on the Río Reventazón near Turrialba, and rainforest hiking at **Parque Nacional Tapantí**, south of Cartago. Most people use San José as a base for forays into the Valle Central; while the **provincial capitals** each have their own strong identity, with the exception of Alajuela they have little to entice you to linger. If you do want to get out of the city and stay in the Valle Central, relax at one of the lodges and inns scattered throughout the countryside.

Mountainous terrain and narrow, winding, unlit roads can make **driving** difficult, if not dangerous. Many Ticos commute from the Valle Central and the surrounding highlands to work in San José via an efficient **bus** network. However, some interesting areas – notably Irazú and Tapantí – remain frustratingly out of reach of public transport. In many cases the only (expensive) recourse is to rent a car or take a taxi from the nearest town, or join an organized tour from San José.

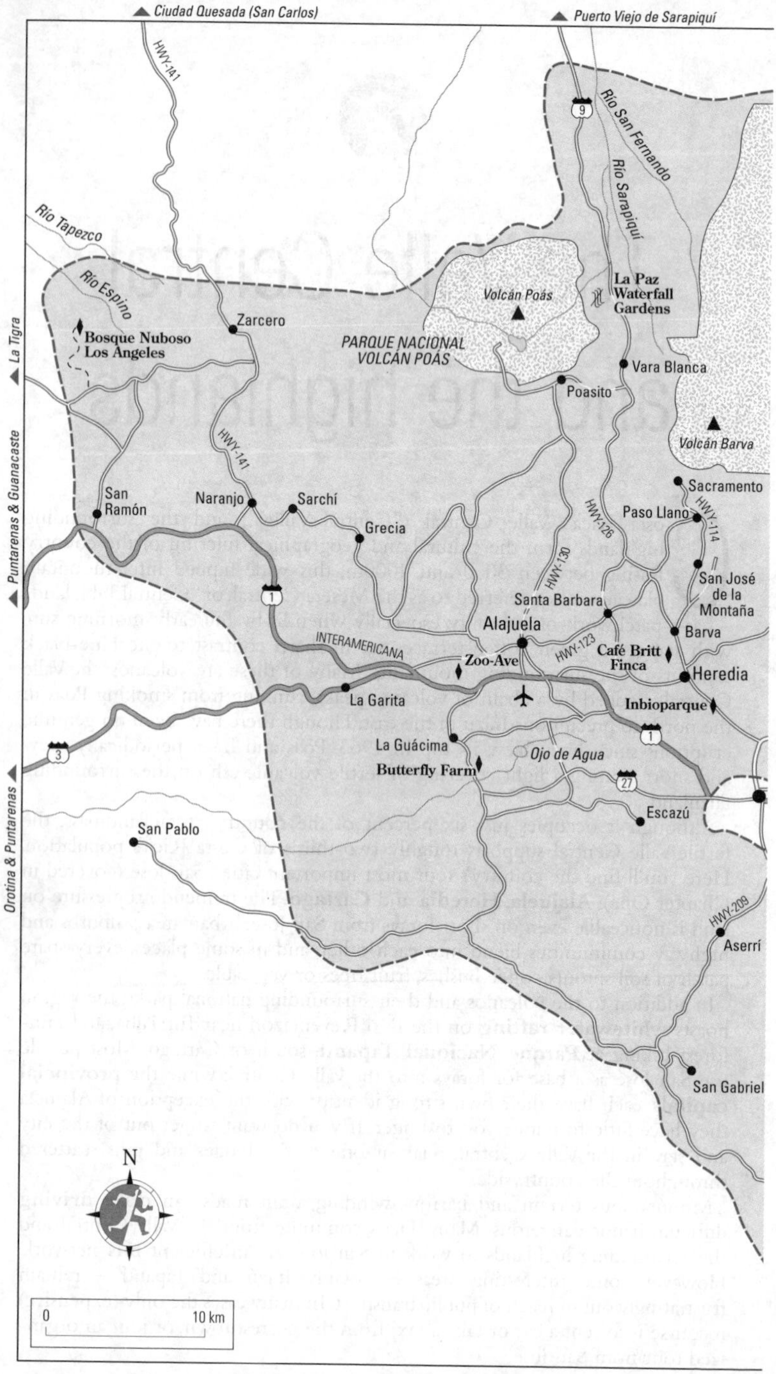
Ciudad Quesada (San Carlos)
Puerto Viejo de Sarapiquí
HWY-141
9
Río San Fernando
Río Sarapiquí
Río Tapezco
Río Espino
La Tigra
Puntarenas & Guanacaste
Orotina & Puntarenas
Zarcero
Bosque Nuboso Los Angeles
Volcán Poás
La Paz Waterfall Gardens
PARQUE NACIONAL VOLCÁN POÁS
Vara Blanca
Poasito
Volcán Barva
Sacramento
HWY-114
Paso Llano
HWY-126
HWY-130
San Ramón
Naranjo
Sarchí
Grecia
San José de la Montaña
1
Santa Barbara
Alajuela
Barva
INTERAMERICANA
HWY-123
Café Britt Finca
Zoo-Ave
Heredia
La Garita
Inbioparque
3
La Guácima
Ojo de Agua
Butterfly Farm
27
Escazú
San Pablo
HWY-209
Aserrí
San Gabriel
N
0
10 km

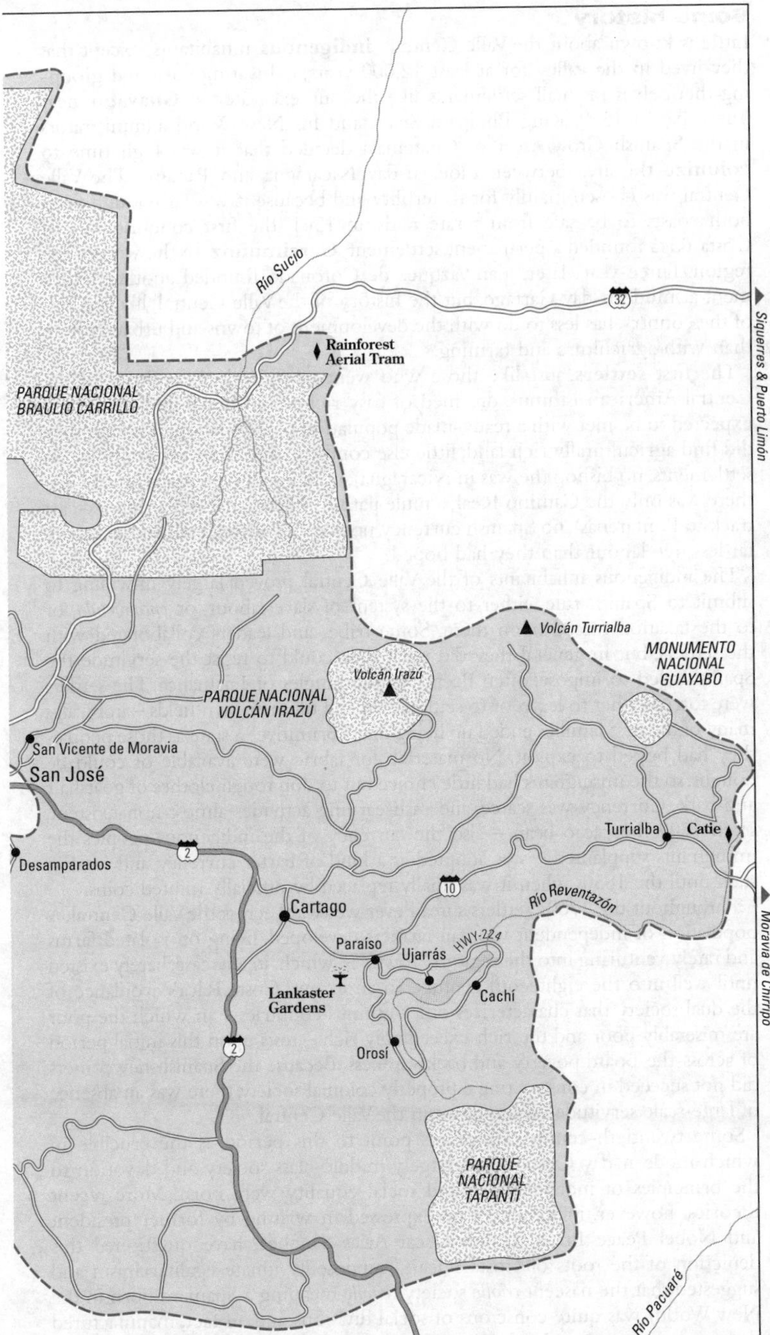

Rainforest Aerial Tram

PARQUE NACIONAL BRAULIO CARRILLO

Río Sucio

▲ Volcán Turrialba

MONUMENTO NACIONAL GUAYABO

Volcán Irazú ▲

PARQUE NACIONAL VOLCÁN IRAZÚ

● San Vicente de Moravia
San José

● Desamparados

Turrialba ● Catie ◄

● Cartago

Río Reventazón

Paraíso
Ujarrás
Lankaster Gardens
Cachí

Orosí

PARQUE NACIONAL TAPANTÍ

► Siquerres & Puerto Limón

► Moravia de Chiripó

HMY-224

Río Pacuaré

▼ San Isidro & Zona Sur

Some history

Little is known about the Valle Central's **indigenous** inhabitants, except that they lived in the valley for at least 12,000 years, cultivating corn and grouping themselves in small settlements like the one excavated at **Guayabo**, near Turrialba. In 1559, King Philip of Spain and his New World administrators in the Spanish Crown seat of Guatemala decided that it was high time to **colonize** the area between modern-day Nicaragua and Panamá. The Valle Central was chosen mainly for its fertility and because it was far enough from both coasts to be safe from pirate raids; in 1561, the first conquistadors of Costa Rica founded a permanent settlement, **Garcimuñoz**, in the west of the region. Three years later, Juan Vazquez de Coronado founded another settlement at modern-day Cartago, but the history of the Valle Central, like the rest of the country, has less to do with the development of towns and urban culture than with agriculture and farming.

The first **settlers**, just like those who went to the other countries of the Central American isthmus, dreamed of easy riches and newfound status, and expected to be met with a ready-made population of slave labour. Though they did find agriculturally rich land, little else conformed to their expectations: no settlements, no bishop (he was in Nicaragua), no churches, no roads (until 1824 there was only the Camino Real, a mule path to Nicaragua, and a thin ox-cart track to Puntarenas), no Spanish currency, no way of earning cash and, crucially, far less free labour than they had hoped.

The indigenous inhabitants of the Valle Central proved largely unwilling to submit to Spanish rule, either to the system of slave labour, or *encomienda,* or to the taxation forced upon them. Some tribes and leaders collaborated with the settlers, but in general they did what they could to resist the servitude the Spanish tried to impose, often fleeing to the jungles of Talamanca. The settlers were forced either to leave, or to settle down and till their own fields – ironically, many of the first families ended up living in as "primitive" a state as those peoples they had hoped to exploit. No materials for fabric were available or could be bought, so the immigrants had little choice but to don rough clothes of goatshair and bark. Currency was scarce, and cash-earning activities almost non-existent, so in 1709 the cacao bean – also the currency of the indigenous peoples the immigrants supplanted – was adopted as a kind of barter currency and used as such until the 1850s when it was finally replaced by officially minted coins.

Throughout the 1700s, settlers spread ever westward across the Valle Central. A population of independent yeoman farmers developed, living on isolated farms and rarely venturing into the region's "towns" – which, in any case, barely existed until well into the eighteenth century. To an extent, Costa Rica's avoidance of the dual society that characterizes other isthmus countries – in which the poor are miserably poor and the rich exceedingly rich – rests upon this initial period of across-the-board poverty and backwardness. Because the Spanish newcomers did not succeed in constructing a properly colonial society, there was an absence of large-scale servitude on big farms in the Valle Central.

Some twentieth-century historians point to this period as the crucible in which modern-day Costa Rica's largely middle-class society and devotion to the principles of independence and social equality were born. More recent theories, however, including those expressed in writing by former president and Nobel Peace Prize winner Oscar Arias Sánchez, have questioned this depiction of the roots of Costa Ricans' supposedly innate egalitarianism and suggested that the nascent *criollo* society (*criollo* meaning a Spaniard born in the New World) was quite conscious of social divisions and, in fact, manufactured them where none existed. Though many of the *conquistadors* were from

Extremadura, the poorest region in Spain, and had acquired their titles by conquest rather than by inheritance, they and their descendants thought themselves superior to the waves of poor peasants coming from Andalucía. In turn, settled families looked with contempt upon new arrivals, and there is evidence to show that, had economic conditions permitted, they would have imposed a system of indentureship on the local *mestizo* (mixed-race) population, as happened in the highlands of Nicaragua, El Salvador and Guatemala.

In 1808, Costa Rica's governor, Tomás de Acosta, brought **coffee** here from Jamaica; a highland plant, it flourished in the Valle Central. Legislators, keen to develop a cash crop, offered incentives to farmers – in 1821, San José's town council gave free land and coffee seedlings to the settlers, while families in Cartago were ordered to plant 20 to 25 coffee bushes in their back yards. In 1832, there were enough beans available for export, and real wealth – at least for the exporters and coffee brokers – came in 1844, when the London market for Costa Rican coffee opened up. It was the country's main source of income until war and declining prices devastated the domestic market in the 1930s.

The Heredia and Cartago provinces still earn much of their money from coffee and today the Valle Central remains the most economically productive region in Costa Rica. The huge black tarpaulins you see from the air as you fly in are flower nurseries. Fruit, including mangoes and strawberries, is cultivated in Alajuela; vegetables thrive in the volcanic soil near Poás and Irazú; and on the slopes of Irazú and Barva, Holstein cattle provide much of the country's milk. Venture anywhere outside the urban areas and you will see evidence of the continued presence of the yeoman farmer, as small plots and family holdings survive despite the population pressure that continues to erode the available farmland.

Alajuela and around

Alajuela Province is vast, extending from **Alajuela** town, 20km northwest of San José, all the way north to the Nicaraguan border and west to the slopes of Volcán Arenal. The account here deals only with that part of the province on the south side of the Cordillera Central, spanning the area from Alajuela itself to Zarcero, 59km northwest, up in the highlands. The area's principal attraction, **Parque Nacional Volcán Poás**, features great trails, lakes on its slopes and spectacular summit views of the densely populated, heavily cultivated province. En route to the top, you'll pass flower-growing fincas, fruit farms and the occasional coffee field. The region is blessed with a pleasant, temperate climate; Alajuela is considerably warmer than San José, and two of the province's towns – Atenas and La Garita – have been deemed by the National Geographic Society to have the best climate in the world.

The crafts factories at **Sarchí**, famous for its coloured wooden ox-carts, lure many visitors, as does **Zoo-Ave**, the exceptional bird sanctuary and zoo just outside town on the way to La Garita, and the **Butterfly Farm** at La Guácima. Alajuela also boasts the little-visited **Los Angeles Cloudforest**, a miniature version of the better-known cloudforest at Monteverde, and **Ojo de Agua**, a thermal water-fed swimming and recreation complex near the Juan Santamaría airport, popular with Josefinos as a place to escape the city.

Alajuela

At first sight, it may be hard to distinguish **ALAJUELA** from San José, until the pleasant realization dawns that you can smell bougainvillea rather than dieselas you walk down the street. Alajuela was founded in 1657 and remains a largely agricultural centre, with a **Saturday market** that draws hundreds of farmers who come to sell fruit, vegetables, dairy products and flowers.

Alajuela's most cherished historical figure is the drummer-boy-cum-martyr **Juan Santamaría**, hero of the Battle of 1856, who sacrificed his life to save the country from the avaricious American adventurer William Walker (see p.238). Today, Santamaría is celebrated in his own **museum** (see p.114), about the only formal attraction in town. All in all, Alajuela can be seen in half a day, but it makes a convenient base for visiting the arts-and-crafts village of **Sarchí** or the butterfly farm at **La Guácima**. Above all it's a useful place to stay for travellers who have to catch early-morning flights: the **Juan Santamaría International Airport** is less than 3km away, about five minutes by bus, compared to about forty minutes from San José.

the patron saint of Alajuela, which takes place on the 16th. It's a very dignified affair, with well-ordered, flower-strewn parades and performances by schoolkids' orchestras in the Parque Central.

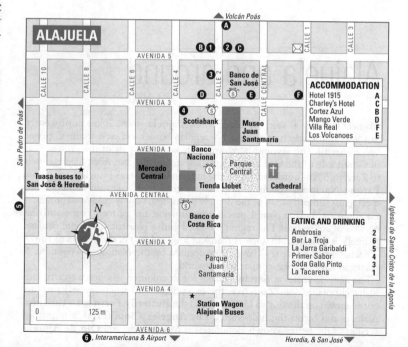

Arrival, orientation and information

Red-and-black Tuasa **buses from San José** arrive on C 8, four blocks west of the Parque Central, amid an inhospitable confusion of bus stops, supermarkets and shoe stores. The beige-and-orange Station Wagon Alajuela bus from San José drops you off on Av 4, just west of Parque Juan Santamaría, a few minutes' walk from the centre. If you're **driving** from San José, head in the direction of the airport on the *pista* (officially, the Autopista General Cañas) which is also the road to Puntarenas. The turnoff to Alajuela is 17km northwest of San José – don't use the underpass or you'll end up at the airport. **Taxis** line up on the south side of the Parque Central.

Alajuela's peaceful **Parque Central** (officially called Plaza del General Tomás Guardia) marks the focal point of Alajuela's grid of streets and is skirted by Avenida Central and Calle Central, the town's main thoroughfares. As in San José, the numbers of calles and avenidas go up by twos, although no one pays any attention to street numbers, instead giving directions in relation to known **landmarks**, the most popular being the Parque Central; the Mercado Central, two blocks to the west; the Tienda Llobet department store at Av Central and C 4; and the correo.

Alajuela has no **tourist office** and the town's **banks** are all clustered around the Parque Central: to change **travellers' cheques**, you can choose between Banco Nacional and Banco de Costa Rica, both just west of the park, and Scotiabank, C2, Av 3, opposite the entrance to the Museo Histórico Cultural Juan Santamaría. The Banco de Costa Rica and Scotiabank have **ATMs** that accept Visa and MasterCard. The small and efficient **correo** (Mon–Fri 7.30am–5pm, Sat 7.30am–noon) is north of the centre, at the corner of C 1 and Av 5, and has inexpensive **Internet access**.

Accommodation

Since the opening of the large *Hampton Inn* near the airport, Alajuela's few **hotels** are now much less booked up by people with early-morning flights to catch. However, the town's budget **hostels** still fill up very quickly, and it's important to reserve ahead even in the rainy season. You'll also find several attractive and comfortable places to stay outside town including the *Xandari Plantation Inn,* one of Costa Rica's loveliest hotels.

In town

Charley's Hotel Av 5, 200m north of Parque Central ☏ & ⓕ441-0115, ⓔilyhotel@latinmail .com. This friendly hotel attracts a gringo crowd who often fill up the eleven large clean rooms, some with private bath and hot running water. You can hang out with fellow travellers in the TV lounge and also book tours to local attractions such as Volcán Poás. ④
Cortez Azul Av 5, C 2/4 ☏443-6145, ⓔhostelcorteazul@yahoo.com. Comfortable hostel run by a local artist (whose works hang on the walls) with 5 small rooms (some with private bath), communal kitchen and laundry facilities. Bike rental and guided tours to Volcán Poás also offered. ②
Hotel 1915 C 2, Av 5/7 ☏440-7163, ⓕ441-0495. Set in an old house, Alajuela's finest hotel over-

looks an attractive patio filled with rocking chairs and plants. All rooms have private bath, plenty of hot water and TV. ④
Mango Verde Av 3, C 2/4 ☏ & ⓕ441-6330, ⓔmangover@racsa.co.cr. Alajuela's top budget spot, this small and cheerful hostel has simple rooms, all with private bath, plus a pretty TV lounge and breakfast bar, communal kitchen and attractive blue-walled yard. ②
Villa Real C 1, Av 3 ☏441-4022, ⓔvillarealcr@hotmail.com. Basic backpackers' hang-out with friendly English-speaking staff. The TV room is often full of travellers who've just arrived in or are about to leave Costa Rica. The smallish but comfortable rooms have shared bathrooms. ②

Los Volcanoes Av 3, C 0/2 ⊤441-0525,
Ⓕ440-8006. One of Alajuela's oldest buildings,
this former Red Cross centre built in 1920 now
houses a charming budget hotel. Basic, comfortable rooms have shared ($35) and private ($45)
bathrooms. There's a travel agency and free
shuttle service to and from the airport. ❹

Around Alajuela

Orquideas Inn 5km outside Alajuela on the road
to Poás ⊤443-9346, Ⓕ443-9740, Ⓦwww
.orquideasinn.com. This Spanish hacienda-style
country inn has kitsch flourishes (check out the
Marilyn Monroe-themed restaurant), large rooms
and landscaped gardens with volcano views.
There's also a pool, a newly refurbished restaurant,
tour desk and gift shop.❺–❻
Siempreverde Lodge A well-signed left turn at
the school in San Isidro, 8km north of Alajuela on
the main Poás road ⊤449-5152, Ⓕ449-5003,
Ⓦwww.dokaestate.com. Small, comfortable
four-room B&B on the slopes of Volcán Poás
next to the lush Doka Coffee estate (daily tours
available). ❹–❺

Xandari Plantation Hotel 6.5km north of
Alajuela, clearly signposted from the main road
to Poás ⊤443-2020, in the US 805/684-7879,
Ⓕ442-4847,Ⓦwww.xandari.com. A beautifully
decorated luxury hotel with 17 spacious villas,
Xandari sits high above the city, with splendid
views of the Valle Central. Pamper yourself at the
full spa, splash about in their three swimming
pools, or wander through the spacious grounds,
complete with waterfalls and a verdant coffee
plantation. The top-notch restaurant serves a
constantly changing set menu of international
cuisine (with at least one vegetarian option) featuring vegetables grown in their greenhouses. Airport
pick-up is included. ❻

The Town

Alajuela's few attractions can be found near **Parque Central**. Old colonial
buildings rise up around the park, though the historical aesthetic effect is spoiled
somewhat by the storefronts festooned with Pepsi-Cola banners. Most impressive
is the sturdy whitewashed former jail that now houses the **Museo Juan
Santamaría (**Av 3, C Central/2; Tues–Sun 10am–6pm; free), entered
through a pretty tiled courtyard garden lined with long wooden benches.
The curiously monastic atmosphere of the exhibition rooms is almost
more interesting than their small collection, which runs the gamut from
mid-nineteenth-century maps of Costa Rica to crumbly portraits of
figures involved in the Battle of 1856, including one of a victorious
Juan Santamaría holding aloft a torch. A modern auditorium hosts lectures and conferences (in Spanish) on regional topics. The white-domed
Catedral de Alajuela flanks the eastern end of the Parque Central.
Reopened after being badly damaged in a 1990 earthquake, it possesses no great
architectural merit, though it does have pretty floor tiles, round stained-glass
windows and a large cupola bizarrely decorated with *trompe l'oeil* balconies. One
block south of the Parque Central, the small and empty **Parque Juan Santamaría**
features a statue of the ubiquitous local hero.

Outside the centre, the town is leafy, quiet and residential, with occasional views
of the blue mountain ridges and bright-green carpet of the Valle Central. The
Iglesia de Santo Cristo de la Agonía, five blocks east of the Parque Central,
was constructed in 1935, but looks much older, with a Baroque exterior painted
in two-tone cream. Head inside for a look at the lovely wooden, gilt-edged altar,
with naive Latin American motifs and gilt-painted columns edging the bright
tiled floor. Realist murals, apparently painted from life, show various stages in the
development of Christianity in Costa Rica, depicting monsignors and indigenous
people gathering with middle-class citizens to receive the Word.

Eating, drinking and nightlife

Josefinos often deride Alajuela for its lack of **nightlife** – many people live in and around the centre, so pressure from residents means that bars close relatively early, at around 11pm. Even so, Alajuela has several decent **restaurants** and you can dig into particularly tasty *ceviche* and *casados* at the friendly Mercado Central. The Museo Juan Santamaría occasionally features classical or jazz concerts and theatrical events and the local forty-piece band plays orchestral and local favourites at the Parque Central bandstand every Sunday morning.

Ambrosia Av 5, C 2. Outdoor terrace-café with sticky cakes, an extensive selection of coffees and tasty *casados*.

Bar La Troja 10–15min (about 1km) walk south of the centre along C 4. The only vaguely lively spot in town, this rooftop bar has a chill atmosphere and decent Latin music.

La Jarra Garibaldi Av Central, 10 blocks west of Parque Central. Vast Mexican restaurant with a garden and "ranchito" bar serving potent tequila-based cocktails; there's live music on Wed, Thurs and Fri. It's cheesily entertaining and a big hit with the swanky older crowd.

Primer Sabor Av 3, C2/4. Enjoy surprisingly tasty Chinese fare at this family-friendly restaurant just west of the museum.

La Tacarena Av 5, C 2. One of the few places open on Sundays, this quiet corner restaurant with wooden booths offers a simple but varied menu of pizza, burgers and typical Costa Rican dishes ($2–5) like *arroz con pollo* and *casados*.

Soda Gallo Pinto C2, Av 3/5. Popular soda where you can fill up on cheap tortillas, tacos, and, of course, hearty *gallo pinto*, Costa Rica's national dish of beans and rice.

Around Alajuela

The most popular excursions in the Valle Central all lie within 30km of Alajuela. Closest to town are the unabashed tourist attractions of **La Guácima Butterfly Farm** and the aviary at **Zoo-Ave**. Head slightly further afield to the north of the province to visit the crafts-making enclave of **Sarchí**, the lovely mountain town of **Zarcero**, and **Volcán Poás**, one of the most visited national parks in the country.

Parque Nacional Volcán Poás

PARQUE NACIONAL VOLCÁN POÁS (daily 8am–3.45pm; $7), just 37km north of Alajuela, is home to one of the world's most accessible active volcanos, with a history of eruptions that goes back eleven million years. Poás's last gigantic blowout was on January 25, 1910, when it dumped 640,000 tons of ash on the surrounding area, and from time to time you may find that the

---

Moving on from Alajuela

Alajuela doesn't have a main bus terminal. Instead, there's a loose collection of bus stops just south of Av 1 between C 8 and 10. Other than San José and Heredia services, all buses depart from around here, including regular departures for Naranjo, Sarchí, Grecia and La Guácima Abajo (for the Butterfly Farm). It's a confusing area, and the departure points are not well marked, so ask around to make sure you are waiting at the right place.

Fast and frequent Tuasa **buses to San José** and **Heredia** leave from a stop on C 8 between Av 1 and Central. Note that even if the bus says "Alajuela–San José," you'll need to check with the driver if it goes direct to San José or to Heredia first.

volcano is off limits due to sulphurous gas emissions, so check conditions with the ICT in San José before you set off.

Getting to the Park

Most visitors get to the park on a pre-arranged **tour** from San José (approximately $45 per person for a 4–5 hour trip, including return transport and guide – see p.32 for details of tour operators). All kinds of combination packages with other Valle Central sites exist. The popular "Four-in-One" tour organized by Expediciones Tropicales ($79 per person including breakfast, lunch and guide; 11hr; ℡257-4171, ⊛www.costaricainfo.com) takes in the La Paz Waterfall Gardens, the Parque Nacional Braulio Carrillo and a boat ride on the Sarapiquí river. Otherwise, a Tuasa bus leaves daily from C 12/14, Av 2 in San José at 8.30am, travelling via Alajuela and returning from the volcano at 2pm (2hr; 885 colones). If you want to reach Poás before tour buses and dense cloud cover arrive, you'll need to either drive or take a **taxi** from Alajuela (roughly $30) or San José ($45–50) – reasonably affordable if split between a group of people.

The park's **visitor centre** shows videos of the volcano and has a snack shop; they serve hot coffee but otherwise supplies are limited and you're probably better off packing a picnic lunch. Make sure you bring a sweater and wet-weather gear with you in the rainy season. No **camping** is allowed in the park.

The Park

Try to get to the volcano before the clouds roll in, which they invariably do at around 10am, even in the dry season (Dec–April). Poás has blasted out three craters in its lifetime, and due to the more or less constant volcanic activity, the appearance of the **main crater** changes regularly – it's currently 1500m wide and filled with milky turquoise water from which sulphurous gases waft and bubble. Although it's an impressive sight, you only need about fifteen minutes' viewing and picture-snapping.

The 65-square-kilometre park features a few very well-maintained, short and unchallenging **trails**, which take you through a strange, otherworldly landscape, dotted with smoking *fumaroles* (steam vents) and tough ferns and trees valiantly surviving regular scaldings with sulphurous gases (the battle-scarred *sombrilla de pobre*, or poor man's umbrella, looks the most woebegone). You'll also see a rare version of cloudforest called **dwarf** or **stunted cloudforest**, a combination of

---

CODECE

An exemplary agro-ecological community tourism project is underway in the mountain town of San Antonio de Escazú, just west of San José. Here a group of local families, with help from the Dutch government and a couple of Canadian universities, have established CODECE (Association for the Conservation and Development of the Mountains of Escazú). **CODECE** offers an authentic experience of Costa Rican *campesino* life, including a visit to a working *trapiche*, or old-fashioned sugar mill, and a five-acre forest preserve, which includes an organic vegetable garden. Guests spend time with community families and are served *típico* food and drink. Depending on your interests, the community can arrange for marimba music or for a retired local schoolteacher to narrate local history and legends. CODECE works mostly with groups of at least twelve people, but can sometimes accommodate smaller groups or couples. A day tour starts at around $15, and accommodation can also be arranged with local families for two-day trips ($50). Ring the CODECE office (℡228-0183, ℮codece@racsa.co.cr), preferably several days in advance, and speak to the project coordinator about details.

The strawberry trail

A deep whiff tells all: The area around Volcán Poás abounds with **strawberry fields**, and it's hard to resist stopping en route from Alajuela to the volcano to sample the fresh, glistening *fresas* (strawberries). *Chubascos* (closed Tues), about 15km north of Alajuela on the road to Poás, makes the very best strawberry *refresco* in the country and also draws crowds for its superlative local cuisine, including succulent *casados* and large lunch plates made with extra-fresh ingredients. *Las Fresas* (closed Wed), a twenty-minute drive from Alajuela on the road to San Pedro de Poás, also specializes in strawberry dishes, as well as excellent wood-oven pizzas.

pine-needle-like ferns, miniature bonsai-type trees, and bromeliad-encrusted ancient arboreal cover, all of which has been stunted through an onslaught of cold (temperatures can drop to below freezing), continual cloud cover, and acid rain from the mouth of the volcano.

The **Crater Overlook Trail**, which winds around the main crater along a paved road, is only 750m long. A side trail (1km; 20–30min) heads through the forest to the pretty, emerald Botos Lake that fills an extinct crater and is a lovely spot to picnic. Named for the pagoda-like tree commonly seen along its way, the **Escalonia Trail** (about 1km; 30min) starts at the picnic area (follow the signs), taking you through ground cover less stunted than that at the crater. Birds ply this temperate forest, from the colourful but shy quetzal to the robin and several species of hummingbird. Although a number of large mammals live in the confines of the park, including coyotes and wildcats such as the margay, you're unlikely to spot them around the crater. One animal you'll come across, however, is the small, green–yellow **Poás squirrel**, unique to the region.

Accommodation

If you want to get a really early start to guarantee a view of Poás's crater, you'll find plenty of places to stay in the vicinity, including a couple of comfortable **mountain lodges** on working dairy farms (though you'll need a car to get to them) and other, more simple and inexpensive places that can be reached on the daily bus to Poás. If you want **to camp**, the *Mountain View Campground* (T482-2196; $5 per tent per night), just before the *Chubascos* restaurant on the main road to Poás, has a pleasant garden site with hot showers.

La Providencia Ecological Reserve 1km south of the park entrance on the slopes of Poás T 232-2448. Relax in charming rustic cabinas on a working dairy farm near the top of Poás, with spectacular views of Volcán Arenal and the Talamanca mountains. The owners prepare excellent local food, rent out horses for trots up the volcano ($20 for 3 hours) and organize trout fishing trips. ❹
Lo Que tu Quieras 5km south of the park entrance T 482-2092. Run by a friendly couple, the wishfully named "Whatever You Want" hotel has three small cabinas with heated water and fireplaces. The decent restaurant serves local dishes and boasts huge picture windows with staggering views across the valley; stop by for a drink on your way back from the volcano. There's

also a small butterfly garden (Tues–Sun 9am–2.30pm; $3), horses for hire ($3/hr) and camping for a nominal fee. ❷
Poás Volcano Lodge 6km north of the small village of Poasito which is 10km before the entrance to Poás on the main mountain road from Alajuela and San José; take a right fork towards Varablanca T 482-2194, F 482-2513, W www .poasvolcanolodge.com. Set on a working dairy farm, this rustic lodge has nine rooms (with private and shared bathrooms), a comfortable communal eating area with a sunken fireplace, extensive forest grounds with walking trails, and a basement games room with pool and ping-pong tables. They also have mountain bikes for hire and offer horse-riding tours of the nearby Braulio Carillo Parque Nacional. ❺

La Paz Waterfall Gardens

One of Costa Rica's most popular attractions, the **La Paz Waterfall Gardens** (daily 8.30am–5.30pm; $21; Ⓦwww.waterfallgardens.com), lie 15km east of Poás. An immaculate series of riverside trails links five waterfalls on the Río La Paz, meandering through a large, colourful garden planted with native shrubs and flowers. You can also visit a butterfly observatory and hummingbird garden, home to sixteen different species. From the reception centre, visitors take one of several self-guided tours that wind prettily through the site and along the river. Viewing platforms at various points along the way place you both above and underneath the waterfalls. **Magia Blanca**, the highest waterfall, crashes deafeningly nearly 40m down into swirling white water. The marked trails conclude at the top of the **La Paz Waterfall**, Costa Rica's most photographed cascade (it can also be seen from the public highway that runs over a large rickety bridge below). The gardens and trails are attractive, but rather sterile – there's little danger of stumbling across any wildlife here. If you're feeling hungry, pop into the decent café in the reception area (set lunch $11) serving typical Costa Rican cuisine with an upper level that overlooks the lovely gardens.

There's currently no public transport to the gardens, and most people visit the gardens as part of an organized tour from San José. Expediciones Tropicales (see p.32) includes La Paz as part of their "Four-in-One" highlights tour. You can also stay at Expediciones Tropicales' new, luxurious **Peace Lodge** (Ⓣ225-0643, Ⓕ225-1082; Ⓞ). Handsome rooms feature handmade canopy beds, stained-glass windows, private bathrooms, hot tubs and balconies overlooking the gardens. Staying in the lodge entitles you to entry to the gardens before and after official opening hours when you can explore its lush expanses away from the otherwise constant crowds. If you're driving, take a right at the junction in Poasito towards Vara Blanca and, on reaching the village, take a left at the gas station and follow the well-marked signs for about 5km.

Sarchí and around

Touted as Costa Rica's centre for arts and crafts, especially **furniture making**, **SARCHÍ**, 30km northwest of Alajuela, is an overly commercialized village, firmly on the tourist trail but with little or no charm. The setting is pretty enough, between precipitous verdant hills, but don't come expecting to see picturesque scenes of craftsmen sitting in small historic shops, blowing glass, sculpting marble or carving wood. The **fábricas de carretas** (ox-cart factories)and the **mueblerías** (furniture factories) are rather large, soulless factory showrooms; in a few of them, however, you can watch carts and furniture being painted and assembled. At the very least, the ox-carts and leather rocking chairs are less expensive here than anywhere else in the country; most people come on half-day shopping trips from the capital or stop on their way to Zarcero and the Zona Norte.

The **Sarchí ox-cart** was first produced by enterprising local families for the immigrant settlers who arrived at the beginning of the twentieth century to run the coffee plantations. The original designs featured simple geometric shapes, though the ox-carts sold today are kaleidoscopically painted square carts built to be hauled by a single ox or team of two oxen. Moorish in origin, the designs can be traced back to immigrants from the Spanish provinces of Andalucía and Granada. Full-scale carts ($1000-plus) are rarely sold, but many smaller-scale coffee table-sized versions are made for tourists ($150–350). Faced with the

Fábricas de carretas and craft shops in Sarchí

The village crafts shops abound with Sarchí tables, bedsteads and leather rocking chairs and also wiggly wooden snakes, hand-polished wooden boxes, bowls and walking sticks, T-shirts and, and the ubiquitous hokey "home sweet home" wall hangings.

Fábrica Chaverrí Sarchí Sur, on the left-hand side of the road as you enter the village ☎454-4411, ℱ454-4944, ⓦwww.sarchicostarica.com. Wander around the painting workshop and see hundreds of ox-carts in progress at Sarchí's largest ox-cart factory. They'll arrange shipping and transport for souvenirs, and credit cards are accepted. The new restaurant, with an attached conservatory dining area, serves good, basic Costa Rican cuisine.

Fábrica Jorge Quesada Alfaro At the north end of Sarchí Norte, on the main road ☎454-4586, ℱ454-2890, ℯquesada@racsa.co.cr. Here you'll find the classiest selection of rocking chairs and stools in Sarchí – plus, it's the only furniture factory where you can watch them being made. Also on sale are children's highchairs and furry animal hides.

Plaza de la Artesanía Sarchí Sur ☎454-3430, ℱ454-2396. A roadside mall of snazzy, pricey shops and restaurants arranged around a courtyard, with everything from Guatemalan vests to gold jewellery. You'll find ox-carts at Habanos and Fábrica el Rancho Sarchipeño, both of whom arrange freight transport ($60–80 to the US or Europe). Take an ice-cream break at the *heladería* or tuck into tasty Mexican fare at the restaurant *Helechos*. The Banco Nacional here can change dollars.

question "But what, exactly, am I going to do with this at home?" the salespeople in Sarchí deftly whip off the top of the miniature cart to reveal a bar with room for several bottles, a serving tray and an ice section. They sell like hotcakes. Many of the *mueblerías* will freight-mail your ox-cart if you arrange it in advance.

The village itself is spread out and divided into two halves. Large *fábricas* line the main road from **Sarchí Sur**, in effect a conglomeration of *mueblerías*, to the residential area of **Sarchí Norte**, which climbs the hill. Besides the shops and factories, the only thing of interest is Sarchí Norte's pink-and-turquoise **church**, atop the hill. Inside, the tiles are delicate pastel shades of pink and green; in the little park fronting the church, stone benches are painted with the same colourful designs you see on the ox-carts.

Practicalities

If you intend to buy a large item, it's best not to come to Sarchí by public transport, as buses are always crowded and seats are tiny. However, if you have no choice, local **buses** from Alajuela run approximately every thirty minutes from 5am to 10pm. Buses back (via Grecia) can be hailed on the main road from Sarchí Norte to Sarchí Sur. From **San José** a daily express service (1hr–1hr 30min) runs from La Coca-Cola every thirty minutes from 5am to 10pm; the return schedule is the same. You can also take the bus to Naranjo from La Coca-Cola, every 25 minutes, and switch there for a local service to Sarchí. Call the Tuan bus company (see p.99) for information.

Sarchí has just a few hotels, of which the best is the small *Hotel Daniel Zamora* (on a side street opposite the soccer field, ☎454-4596; ❸–❹) with clean rooms and hot water. For **lunch** or a snack, try the decent Mexican restaurant *Helechos*, inside the Plaza de la Artesanía, or *La Finca* restaurant (to the right of the Mercado de Artesanía souvenir shop as you drive north out of town), which serves excellent maize soup and grilled steak.

The Banco Nacional on the main road beyond the church changes dollars and travellers' cheques, as does a smaller branch in the Mercado de Artesanía. Call **taxis** on ☎454-4028 or hail one on the street.

Grecia and Llano del Rosario

If you have time on the way to Sarchí, stop off to see the remarkable *fin-de-siècle* church in the small town of **GRECIA**, some 18km northwest of Alajuela. After their first church burned down, the prudent residents of Grecia decided to take no chances and built the second out of pounded sheets of metal, imported from Belgium. The white-trimmed rust-coloured result is surprisingly beautiful, with an altar that's a testament to Latin American Baroque froth, made entirely from intricate marble and rising up into the eaves of the church like a wedding cake. A couple of kilometres outside the centre of Grecia on the Alajuela road, **El Mundo de las Serpientes** (daily 8am–4pm; $12; ☎494-3700) is a small collection of forty species of snakes from around the world housed in large glass boxes. The entrance fee includes a highly informative guided tour (in English or Spanish), during which you learn all kinds of strange snake information, such as the fact that they are completely deaf, and that they frequently die of stress. From San José there's a **bus** to Grecia every half hour from La Coca-Cola (5.30am–10pm; 1hr).

Four kilometres northwest of Sarchí, at **LLANO DEL ROSARIO** (follow a left-fork road signposted just south of Naranjo), you can try Costa Rica's only **bungee jump**. Tropical Bungee (☎248-2212, ⓦwww.bungee.co.cr; $60) organizes leaps from the bridge over the Río Colorado; they can also arrange pick-ups from San José.

Los Angeles Cloudforest Reserve

Some 40km by road northwest of Alajuela, **LOS ANGELES CLOUDFOREST RESERVE** (8am–5pm; ⓦwww.villablanca-costarica.com) is a less crowded alternative to the Monteverde Cloudforest (see p.280). Climbing from 700m to nearly 2000m, Los Angeles' twenty square kilometres contains a number of habitats and microclimates, including dark, impenetrable cloudforest, often shrouded in light misty cloud and resounding with the calls of monkeys.

There's no official puesto in the reserve, and entrance fees ($12 self-guided; $24 with guide) must be paid at the *Hotel Villablanca* reception which can also provide details on birdwatching tours, night tours and horseback rides (all $24) in the reserve. From here, two rather short, easy **trails** provide a good introduction to the reserve, following along wooden boardwalks covered with non-slip corduroy. A third, much longer trail (8km), for which a guide is obligatory, takes you to the junction of the rivers Balsa and Espino. This trail follows paths that are not fitted with corduroy (and therefore quite slippery) through changes in elevation and correspondingly different vegetations.

The hotel grounds also contain a small chapel called **La Mariana**, built by the reserve's owner, ex-president Rodrigo Corazon, to celebrate his long and happy marriage by honouring the Virgin Mary. The building, plain on the outside, has a unique, colourful ceiling covered with 840 hand-painted tiles depicting traditional and religious ceremonies throughout Latin America. You can learn all about the chapel with an audiotour (in English; 30 min; $5).

Practicalities

Los Angeles lies roughly 40km northwest of Alajuela by road, and is best reached via San Ramón, 30km from Alajuela on the Interamericana (Hwy-1).

From San Ramón, take a right fork opposite the hospital towards La Fortuna and follow the road until you reach the hamlet of Los Angeles Norte, from where the *Hotel Villablanca* and reserve are well signed. If you don't have your own transport, hourly **buses** go from Alajuela to San Ramón; a taxi from here to the reserve costs approximately $10. You can **stay** in the reserve at the *Hotel Villablanca* (☎461-0300, ℱ461-0301; ❻), which has 48 comfortable en-suite *casitas*, or chalets, plus a restaurant and a TV lounge.

Zarcero

ZARCERO, 52km northwest of Alajuela on Hwy-141, sits almost at the highest point of this stretch of the Cordillera Central in an astounding landscape where precipitous inclines plunge into deep gorges, and contented Holstein cattle munch grass in the valleys. A pleasant mountain town, Zarcero has crisp fresh air and ruddy-faced inhabitants. Head for the central plaza for a different view of this small town. In front of a pretty white church stands a collection of fabulous, Doctor Seuss-like topiary sculptures – an elephant, a light bulb, a strange bird, along with Gaudí-esque archways of vines and hedges, all the work of Costa Rican landscape gardener Evangelisto Blanco.

Discover the spectacular mountainous countryside around Zarcero with its verdant hills and valleys on a **horse-riding tour** run by Laguna Horseback Riding ($30 for 3–4hr; ☎463-3437, ⓦ www.cabinaslapradera.com) at *Cabinas la Pradera* in nearby Laguna. Zarcero is also famous for its fresh, white, relatively bland **cheese**, called *palmito* (heart-of-palm, which is what it looks like). You can buy it from any of the shops near the bus stop on the south side of the central plaza.

Practicalities

Buses from San José to Zarcero leave hourly between 5am and 7.30pm from La Coca-Cola (1hr 30min), arriving in Zarcero on the northern side of the *zócalo*. The bus stop for San Carlos/Ciudad Quesada and the Zona Norte is on the northwest corner of the central plaza (hourly; 1hr). For town and regional info, head to the **tourist office** (☎463-2120, ℮catuzar@costarricense.com) on the main street near the high school. The small, friendly *Hotel Don Beto* (☎ & ℱ463-3137; ❸) is on the northern corner of Zarcero's main square. You'll find only a few places to eat, most near the central plaza. *Restaurante El Higaron*, and *Pizzeria Galería* serve decent, inexpensive local food. Next door to the pizzeria, a bakery and sweet shop, *Panadería la Marinita,* sells delicious fresh cookies and cakes. Banco de Costa Rica on Zarcero's main street changes **travellers' cheques** and has an ATM. Surprisingly, Zarcero also boasts a large, semi-olympic **swimming pool**, Piscinas Apamar (450m uphill to the east of Parque Central; $2; ☎463-3674,) along with thermal baths and a Jacuzzi.

Southwest of Alajuela

Butterfly and bird enthusiasts will be rewarded by visits to two sites southwest of Alajuela. **La Guácima Butterfly Farm** (daily 8.30am–5pm, last tour at 3pm; $15; ☎438-0440, ⓦwww.butterflyfarm.co.cr), 14km southwest of Alajuela, breeds valuable pupae for export to zoos and botanical gardens all over the world. Tours begin with an audiovisual exhibit introducing the processes involved in commercial butterfly breeding, after which guides explain all aspects of butterfly life, including their cruelly short lifespans, while flashes of bright colours flutter prettily around the mesh-enclosed breeding area. Look out, in particular, for the Blue Morpho, one of Costa Rica's rarest and most beautiful butterflies. The farm also has beautiful views over the Valle Central; in the wet season, be sure to go early, as the rain drives the butterflies to hide, and clouds obscure the views. If you call the farm in advance, pick-ups can be arranged from hotels in San José.

Buses from San José to La Guácima leave from Av 1, C 20/22, daily except Sunday at 11am and 2pm; the trip takes two hours, so get the earlier service. Return buses to the capital leave at 12.15pm and 3.15pm from Av 2, C 8, where you can also pick up the **Alajuela** service to La Guácima – look for buses marked "La Guácima Abajo" at 6.20am, 9am, 11am and 1pm; the Butterfly Farm is practically the last stop, and they will let you off at the gates. Return buses pass the gates of the farm at about 11.45am, 1.45pm, 3.45pm and 5.45pm; get to the stop a little early just to make sure.

The largest aviary in Central America, **Zoo-Ave** (daily 9am–5pm; $9; ☎433-8989, ⓦwww.zooave.org), at Dulce Nombre, 5km west of Alajuela, is just about the best place in the country – besides the wild – to see Costa Rica's fabulous birds. The exceptionally well-run exhibition has large, clean cages and carefully tended grounds. Many of the birds fly free, fluttering around in a flurry of raucous colours: look out for the kaleidoscopic *lapas* – **scarlet macaw** – and wonderful blue **parrots**. Other birds include chestnut mandibled **toucans** and the fluffy **tropical screech owls**. You'll also see **primates**, from monkeys to marmosets and while a sign in one of the enclosures says, "There are fifty iguanas in this area. Can you find any?", you're unlikely to spot one of these shy creatures. Ideally, you need a minimum of an hour to see everything. The La Garita bus from Alajuela leaves from the area southwest of the main terminal and passes right by Zoo-Ave (15min).

The small hamlet of **La Garita**, known for having one of the most clement climates in the world, lies 5km west of Zoo-Ave. Fruits, ornamental plants and flowers flourish here, but the only reason to stop, really, is if you happen to be going through to **Playa Jacó** (see p.304) on the weekends when *Restaurante Fiesta del Maíz* ("Corn Party Restaurant") is open. The restaurant (open Fri–Sun & holidays) sits just east of Atenas as you head toward the Pacific coast. It draws swarms of Ticos, who come for the tasty under-$5 main courses and snacks, all made from corn. While the Costa Rican fare is authentic, the restaurant itself is disappointingly reminiscent of a fast-food joint, with bolted-down tables and long queues at the till.

Heredia and around

Heredia Province stretches northeast from San José all the way to the Nicaraguan border, skirted on the west by Hwy-9, the old road from San José to Puerto Viejo de Sarapiquí, and to the east by the Guápiles Highway (Hwy-32), which provides access to Braulio Carrillo and to Limón on the Caribbean coast. The moment you leave San José for the provincial capital of **Heredia**, the rubbery leaves of coffee plants spring up on all sides.

In the Valle Central, the chief attraction is the dormant **Volcán Barva**. A good day's climb up its dense forested slopes brings you to superb views at the top.

Nearby, the **Rainforest Aerial Tram** (see p.127) offers vistas of primary rainforest canopy from above, causing minimal disturbance to the animals and birds.

Heredia

Just 11km northeast of San José lies the lively city of **HEREDIA,** boosted by the student population of the Universidad Nacional (UNA), at the eastern end of town, and famed for its **soccer team**, one of the best and most popular in the country. The town centre is prettier than most, though a little rundown, with the Parque Central flanked by tall palms and a few historical buildings. Small and easy to navigate, Heredia is a natural jumping-off point for excursions to the nearby historical hamlet of **Barva** and to the town of **San José de la Montaña**, a gateway to **Volcán Barva**. Many tourists also come for the **Café Britt Finca tour**, hosted by the nation's largest coffee exporter, about 3km north of the town centre.

Arrival and information

During the day, **Tuasa buses** leave San José for Heredia every five–ten minutes from C 1, Av 7/9. Microbuses Rapiditos Heredianos depart with the same frequency from Av 2, C 12/14; between midnight and 6am, they leave San José hourly. All buses pull into Heredia at the corner of C Central and Av 4, a stone's throw south of the Parque Central. Banco Nacional at C 2, Av 2/4 and Scotiabank at Av 4, C Central/C2 both have ATMs, and change currency and **travellers' cheques**. The **correo** (Mon–Fri 7.30am–5.30pm) is on the northwest corner of the Parque Central. **Taxis** line up on the east side of Mercado Central, between Av 6 and 8, and on the southern side of the Parque Central.

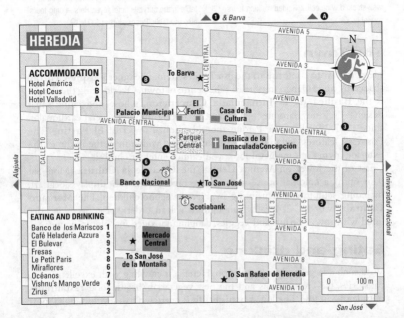

Accommodation

While decent accommodation in downtown Heredia is pretty sparse, it's unlikely, in any case, that you'll need to stay in town; San José is within easy reach, and there are several country resort-type hotels nearby, including *Finca Rosa Blanca*, one of the finest in the country. All are accessible by bus, though a car does offer more flexibility.

Central Heredia

Hotel America C Central, opposite the San José bus stop ☎ 260-9292, ℱ 260-9293, ⓦ www .hotelamerica.net. Clean if soulless rooms, some of which are rather dark; all come with bathroom, fan, TV and hot water. Breakfast is included. ❹
Hotel Ceus Av 1 ☎ 262-2628, ℱ 262-2639, ⓦ www.hotelamerica.net. Quiet hotel with spotless but no-frills rooms with private bathrooms and

hot water. For meals, try out the hotel's decent seafood restaurant. ❷
Hotel Valladolid C 7, Av 7 ☎ 260-2905, ℱ 260-2912, ⓔ valladolid@racsa.co.cr. This upmarket five-storey hotel located in the town's northeast corner near the university has spacious, comfortable rooms, a roof terrace (good views), Jacuzzi and sauna. ❺

Around Heredia

Chalet Tirol North of Heredia, well signposted on the road to Los Angeles via San Rafael ☎ 267-6222, ℱ 267-6228, ⓦ www.chalet-tirol.com. This incredibly kitsch hotel with ten alpine chalets sits in a lovely pine forest on the edge of the Parque Nacional Braulio Carrillo. Also on the grounds is a reproduction Tirol (traditional Austrian-style) village church for concerts and events and a square with a fountain. Dine at the renowned gourmet French restaurant complete with linen napkins and well-stocked wine cellar. Guided walking tours available. ❻

Finca Rosa Blanca On the road between San Pedro de Barva and Santa Bárbara de Heredia ☎ 269-9392, ℱ 269-9555, ⓦ www.finca-rblanca .co.cr. One of the top accommodations in Costa Rica, this classy hotel roosts like a giant white bird above the coffee fields, with six suites and two villas, plus a gorgeous tiled pool that seems to drip over the hillside. An excellent four-course dinner, prepared from organic produce grown in the lovely gardens, is served family-style around the large table in the fairytale hotel foyer. Horse-riding tours also available. Prices start at $175. ❽

The Town

Heredia's layout conforms to the usual grid system. The quiet **Parque Central,** shaded by huge mango trees, marks the centre of town. Overlooking the Parque is the **Basílica de la Inmaculada Concepción**, whose unexciting squat design – "seismic Baroque" – has kept it standing through several earthquakes since 1797. North of the Parque, the old colonial tower of **El Fortín**, "The Fortress", features odd gun slats that fan out and widen from the inside to the exterior, giving it a medieval look: you cannot enter or climb it.

East of the tower on Avenida Central, the **Casa de la Cultura** (Mon–Sat 9am–6pm), a colonial house with a large breezy verandah, displays local art, including sculpture and painting by Heredia schoolchildren. The **Mercado Central** (Av 6/8, C 2/4; daily 5am–6pm) is a clean, orderly place, its wide aisles lined with rows of fruits and veggies, dangling sausages and plump prawns.

Eating and drinking

With such a large student population, Heredia is crawling with excellent cafés, patisseries, ice-cream joints and the best vegetarian/health food **restaurants** outside of San José. The low-key **nightlife** is restricted to a few local salsa spots and some great bars, the best of which are clustered around the four blocks immediately to the west of the Universidad Nacional, in the east of Heredia.

Banco de los Mariscos In Santa Bárbara, 6km north of Heredia ☏269-9090. Huge, upmarket restaurant serving delicious fresh seafood, including lobster. It's a touch pricey – around $50 for two – but well worth it.

Café Heladeria Azzura Southwest corner of Parque Central. Indulge in superior Italian ice cream, excellent *refrescos*, fresh sandwiches and real cappuccino and espresso at this upmarket café.

Chalet Tirol In *Chalet Tirol* hotel, north of Heredia, well signposted on the road to Los Angeles Cloudforest Reserve via San Rafael ☏267-6222. One of Costa Rica's most acclaimed French restaurants, with an elegant dining area adorned with murals and a large and eclectically-stocked wine cellar. Try the excellent bean-heavy cassoulet. Meal cost is around $20 per head.

El Bulevar Av 4, C 5/7. The "in" place for Heredia's student population, this lively bar opens to the street so you can people-watch while downing inexpensive beer-and-*boca* specials.

Fresas C 7, Av 0. This large, popular American-style restaurant with outdoor seating serves tasty soda meals for about $5. Strawberries are the speciality; don't miss the delicious strawberry fruit salads.

Le Petit Paris C 5, Av 2/4 ☏262-2564. Dine on excellent French cuisine (the crêpes are a speciality) at this oasis of calm with tables in a small garden and a lunch menu that changes daily. Enjoy live jazz on Wednesdays. Expect to pay around $10–15 for a full meal. Closed Sun.

Miraflores Av 2, C 2/4. Heredians dance salsa and merengue at this lively disco and bar that attracts a slightly older crowd. Groove to live music on Tuesdays.

Océanos C 4, Av 2/4. Hang out with students at this bar decorated with an assortment of fishing paraphernalia and surfboards. The tasty *bocas* hit the spot.

Vishnu's Mango Verde C 7, Av Central. One of a chain of vegetarian eateries, this rustic, plant-filled restaurant has a pretty back garden and serves good vegetarian food, including yoghurts and sandwiches made to order. Lunch only Mon–Fri.

Zirus Centro Comercial Plaza Cibeles, Av 1, C 5/7 ☏262-5959. Popular pizza restaurant with takeaway service and a friendly atmosphere.

Around Heredia

North and east of Heredia the terrain climbs to higher altitudes, reaching its highest point at **Volcán Barva**, at the western entrance of the wild, rugged **Parque Nacional Braulio Carrillo**. Temperatures are notably cooler around here, the landscape dotted with dairy farms and conifers. Though the area in general gives a good picture of coffee-oriented agriculture and provincial Costa Rican life, none of the villages surrounding Heredia town offers much to detain you. Aficionados of religious architecture, however, can make jaunts out to a number of pretty **churches**, from the old colonial structure in **Barva** to **San Rafael**'s white and silver church, set high above the Valle Central, to the jolly twin-towered churches of **Santa Bárbara de Heredia** and **San Joaquín de Heredia**.

Moving on from Heredia

Heredia has no central bus terminal, but a variety of well-signed **bus stops** are scattered around town, with a heavy concentration around the Mercado Central. Buses **to San José** depart from C Central, Av 2/4 (about every 5–10min during the day). From the Mercado Central, C 4, Av 6/8, local buses leave for **San José de la Montaña**, **San Joaquín de Heredia**, **San Isidro de Heredia** and the swimming complex at **Ojo de Agua**. Buses to **San Rafael de Heredia** depart from near the train tracks at Av 10 and C 0/2 and buses to **Barva** and **Santa Bárbara de Heredia** depart from C Central, Av 1/3. All buses leave fairly regularly, about every thirty minutes.

Parque Nacional Braulio Carrillo

The **PARQUE NACIONAL BRAULIO CARRILLO** (8am–3.45pm; $7), 15km northeast of Heredia, covers 325 square kilometres of virgin rain- and cloudforest, but still draws few visitors on account of its sheer size and lack of facilities. Most tourists experience the majestic views of cloud and foliage only from the window of a bus on their way to the Caribbean coast. The park is named after Costa Rica's third, and rather dictatorial, chief of state, who held office in the mid-1800s. It was established in 1978 to protect the land from the possible effects of the Guápiles Highway, then under construction between

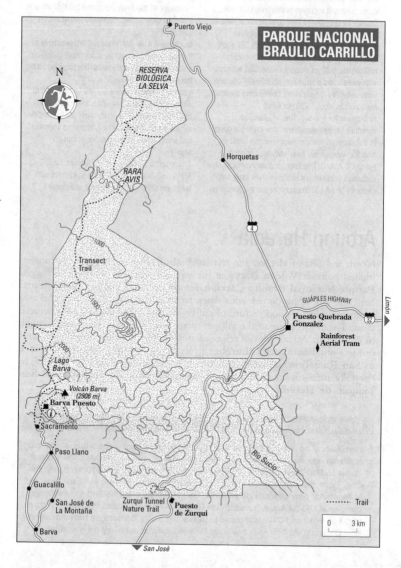

San José and Limón, a piece of intelligent foresight without which this whole stretch of countryside might have been turned into a solid strip of gas stations and motels.

Even when only seen from the highway, Braulio Carrillo's dense forested cover gives you a good idea of what much of Costa Rica used to look like about fifty years ago, when approximately three-quarters of the country's total terrain was virgin rainforest. The rare and shy quetzal has been sighted in the higher altitudes of the park, as have toucans, trogons and eagles, while large mammals such as the jaguar and ocelot skulk in the dense undergrowth. In addition, Braulio Carrillo is one of the few places in the country where the bushmaster (matabuey), Central America's largest venomous snake, makes its home, along with the equally poisonous fer-de-lance (terciopelo).

The park has three staffed **puestos**, one at Volcán Barva (see p.128) and the others on the main Guápiles Highway at Zurquí, just before the Zurquí Tunnel, and at Quebrada Gonzalez, 2km east of the Sucio River bridge. You'll find picnic facilities and well-marked trails leading from the puestos into the forest. Camping is not permitted and there's no accommodation within this section of the park except for very basic huts at the Volcán Barva puesto.

Rainforest Aerial Tram

The brainchild of American naturalist Donald Perry, the **RAINFOREST AERIAL TRAM** (Mon 9am–4pm, Tues–Sun 6am–4pm; $49.50,) lies just beyond the northeastern boundary of Braulio Carrillo, 1.5km from the Guápiles Highway. Funded by private investors, and the product of many years' research, the tram was, when it opened in the mid-nineties, the first of its kind in the world. (There are now two others in Costa Rica; one near Jacó on the Pacific coast, the other on the island of Dominica.) Its premise is beautifully simple: twenty overhead cable cars, each holding five passengers and one guide, run slowly along the 1.7km aerial track skirting the tops of the forest and passing between trees, providing eye-level encounters along the way. The ride (45min each way; the entrance fee allows you unlimited rides) affords a rare glimpse of birds, animals and plants, including the epiphytes, orchids, insects and mosses that live inside the upper reaches of the forest and, as it's largely silent, cuts down the chances of animals being frightened by the oncoming thudding of feet. Torch-lit night rides (until 9pm) examine the canopy's nocturnal inhabitants. More conventionally, you can also explore the park via a network of ground-level trails.

In his book, *Life Above the Jungle Floor* (see Contexts, p.408), Perry tells how he risked life and limb to get the project started. Committed to protecting the rainforest canopy and the jungle floor, he refused to allow the construction firm erecting the tram's high-wire towers to use tractors; they were unable to secure a powerful enough helicopter in Costa Rica, but Nicaragua's Sandinistas came to the rescue, loaning one of their MI-17 combat helicopters (minus the guns) to help erect the poles.

Practicalities

Less than an hour from San José, the turn-off for the aerial tram is on the right-hand side of the highway, 5.3km beyond the (signed) bridge over the Río Sucio. From the turn-off it's another 1.5km walk or drive. To get there **by bus**, catch the Guápiles service from San José (C 0, Av 11) and ask the driver to drop you at the turn-off. The return Guápiles–San José bus will stop when flagged down, unless it's full. Alternatively, and much more conveniently, you can organize a **tour** ($65 per person) with the tram's San José office on C 7, Av 7 (☎257-5961, ℱ257-6053, ⓦwww.rainforesttram.com), which includes transport to and from your hotel, a guided aerial excursion and hiking on nature trails. At a slightly higher price, San José travel agencies offer similar trips, as well as tours combining the tram with other regional attractions such as the La Guácima butterfly farm. The tram's new jungle lodge comprises ten luxury bungalows, all with bathrooms and views of the forest. Room rates of $95 include unlimited tram rides and access to the trails as well as three meals a day. For tram trips, it's advisable to wear a hat and insect repellent and to bring binoculars, camera and rain gear.

North of Heredia: Café Britt and Barva

Just north of Heredia on the road to Barva, you'll see signs off the highway directing you to the **Café Britt Finca** (tours daily at 9am & 11am; also at 3pm mid-Dec to April; $15; ☎261-0707, ⓦwww.coffeetour.com), where you can get an idea of how the modern-day coffee industry operates. The Finca grows one of the country's best-known brands and is the most important exporter of Costa Rican coffee to the world. Guides take you through the history of coffee growing in Costa Rica, demonstrating how crucial this export crop was to the development of the country, with a rather slick multimedia presentation and thorough descriptions of the processes involved in harvesting and selecting the beans. Once you've toured the plantation, roasting factory and drying patios, it's back for a free tasting and, of course, the inevitable stop in the gift shop. The Finca will pick up visitors and return them to most San José hotels ($30, including transport and tour), and also offers day-trips combining a tour of the Finca and lunch with visits to La Guácima butterfly farm ($60) and the Rainforest Aerial Tram ($99). They also arrange a "coffee-lover's" tour, including a session on how to make the perfect cappuccino ($50).

If Cafe Britt piques your interest in fincas, the unusual **Museo de la Cultura Popular** (Mon–Fri 9am–4pm, Sat & Sun 10am–5pm; $1.50; ☎260-1619, ⓦwww.ilam.org/cr/museoculturapopular), a couple of kilometres beyond the turn-off, recreates coffee plantation life from the late nineteenth and early twentieth century. Set in a large house with verandahs surrounded by coffee fields, the museum features rooms recreated in the style of that time. The museum **restaurant** (closed weekends) serves authentic food of the period, including *torta de arroz* (layered rice casserole), *pan casero* (a type of sweet bread) and *gallos picadillos* (a mixture of meat, vegetables and rice).

A kilometre further north, the colonial village of **BARVA** is worth a brief stop on the way to Volcán Barva to see the huge cream Baroque **church**, flanked by tall brooding palms, and the surrounding adobe and tile-roofed houses. Though Barva was founded in 1561, most of what you see today dates from the 1700s. The village also boasts an excellent Mexican restaurant, *El Charro de Fofo,* that serves all the usual Mexican staples like tortillas and refried beans in a cheerful corner spot 300m south of the village's main square on the road to Heredia. There are several decent sodas near the church; **buses** to San José de la Montaña (for the volcano) stop opposite the soccer field.

Volcán Barva

Just beyond Barva, a turn-off on the right-hand side of the highway heads towards **VOLCÁN BARVA**. Although it's not far from Heredia, the volcano is difficult to reach due to the lack of public transport and a bad stretch of

△ Raking drying coffee

unpaved road just before the entrance – you'll need a 4WD even in the dry season. The park entrance fee is $7 and from here trails wind up the slope of this long-dormant volcano to a small, pristine crater.

The **main trail** (3km; about 1hr) begins from the puesto, ascending through dense deciduous cover, climbing to 3000m before reaching the cloudforest at the top. Along the way, you'll get panoramic views over the Valle Central and southeast to Volcán Irazú; if you're lucky – bring binoculars – you might see the elusive, jewel-coloured quetzal (though these nest-bound birds are usually only seen at their preferred altitude of 3600m or more). At the summit, you'll find the green-blue lake that fills the old crater, surrounded by dense forests that are often obscured in cloud. Take a compass, water and food, a sweater and rain gear, and leave early in the morning to enjoy the clearest views of the top. Be prepared for serious mud in the rainy season.

Practicalities

Daily **buses** (at around 6.30am, noon & 4pm) run from Heredia to the tiny hamlet of Sacramento, from where it's a three-kilometre walk up a steep track to the Barva puesto. **Buses** from Sacramento to Heredia leave daily at 7.30am, 1pm and (most conveniently, but on weekends only) 5pm. Otherwise, you'll need to get a taxi – ask in either of the restaurants mentioned below, or try ringing local driver Lizandro Cascante (⊕224-2400).

If you want **to stay** near the volcano, you'll find basic **huts** ($2 per night) and **camping** facilities (reserve in advance on ⊕283-5906) at the Barva puesto. The hamlet of Guacalillo, 8km south of the volcano, has surprisingly good accommodation. *Hotel de Montaña El Portico* (⊕237-6022, ⓕ260-6002; ❹) offers enormous, simply furnished rooms with private bath, and also rents out attractive self-catering cabins ($70 per night for up to five people). Relax in pretty cabinas with wall hangings and fireplaces at the adjacent *Hotel Las Ardillas* (⊕260-2172, ⓔardillas@racsa.co.cr; ❹). Tuck into a healthy selection of soups and salads along with meat cooked over a coffee-wood fire at the on-site cosy restaurant and then pamper yourself at the tiled spa with mud treatments, massage and hypnotherapy ($20–50/hr).

In preparation for your climb, dine on *típico* food at the *Campesino* restaurant, about 3.5km north of Paso Llano en route to Volcán Barva, at the *Sacramento* another 500m further north, or at *Soda El Bosque* in Sacramento, a picturesque little café stuffed with junk-shop objects collected by its owner; they serve traditional *gallos* with various toppings, as well as breakfast and *casados*.

East and south of Heredia

Once a mass of coffee fields, the area south of Heredia has, in recent decades, become increasingly urbanized by the San José suburban sprawl. There are still a few spots worth checking out, however. The small village of **San Vicente de Moravia**, about 10km southeast of Heredia, is a well-known centre of handicrafts, from ceramics and leather to wooden bowls and jewellery. You'll find a dozen or so shops in town, most of them spread along the aptly named Calle de la Artesanía, just north of the Parque Central. Most sell the same items you'll find all over the country – wooden walking sticks, snakes, serving bowls and mini ox-carts – but a few specialize in unique crafts. Check out Artesanía Bribrí, with its collection of balsa and cedar wood masks (usually depicting supernatural beings) and leather goods (satchels, purses and belts) made by the **Bribrí** indigenous peoples of the Talamanca coast (see p.167); Hidalgo la Rueda, with leather goods and a workshop you can tour; and Artesanías Zurqui, with a large collection of attractive handmade ceramics with blue glazed finishes.

About 6km east of San Vicente, in a cluster of villages known commonly as Coronado, lies the village of **Dulce Nombre de Coronado**. Budding herpetologists will want to stop by the **Instituto Clodomiro Picado**, or "snake farm" (Mon–Thurs 8am–4pm by group reservation only, Fri 2–3pm for the general public; ☎229-0344), where a variety of poisonous species are bred for research, their venom used in the commercial production of antivenin. Most of the action occurs at feeding time, when you can watch live mice and toads being guzzled by the hungry reptiles; Friday-afternoon visitors have a special treat, as this is when the snakes' venom is extracted. The institute also sells pre-prepared antivenin which you can take on the road with you, but in general the serum needs to be refrigerated; ask the staff for instructions. To get to the snake farm **by bus**, a local *serviceto* bus *Dulce Nombre* leaves San José hourly from Av 3, C 3/5. Staff at the institute will know current return bus times.

Four kilometres south of Heredia is **Inbioparque** (daily 7.30am–4pm; $18; ☎507-8107, Ⓦwww.inbio.ac.cr/inbioparque), a small educational and recreational centre set up by the Instituto Nacional de Biodiversidad to explain in simple terms how biodiversity works and exactly why it is so important. The park comprises a projection room with an audiovisual presentation on Costa Rican biodiversity, storyboards and displays explaining biodiversity in action, and **guided trails** (30min–2hr) through four small botanical gardens filled with plants and animals from the country's four main ecosystems – Valle Central forest, humid forest, tropical dry forest and wetland – as well as a small butterfly garden. Although mostly aimed at schoolchildren and students, the park is a good place for budding naturalists to learn to identify native species – it's home to 51 species of bird and over five hundred native plant species. You'll find a café on site, and transport from San José can be arranged for $10; alternatively, take the local bus from San José to the village of Santo Domingo.

Cartago and around

With land made fertile by deposits from Volcán Irazú, **Cartago Province** extends east of San José and south into the Cordillera de Talamanca. The section covered in this chapter is a heavily populated, farmed and industrialized region, centred on **Cartago**, a major shopping and transport hub for the southern Valle Central. Dominated by the soaring form of **Volcán Irazú**, the varied and pretty landscape is patched with squares of rich tilled soil and pockets of pine forest. Though home to Costa Rica's most famous church, the fat, Byzantine **Basílica de Nuestra Señora de Los Angeles**, the town itself is not really worth staying in, and many of the region's attractions are best visited on day-trips from San José. The most popular excursion is to the volcano, but there's also the mystically lovely **Valle Orosí**, the orchid collection at **Lankester Gardens**, and the wild, little-visited **Parque Nacional Tapantí**.

It takes about forty minutes to reach Cartago on the good (toll) highway from San José. From Cartago there are road connections to Turrialba on the eastern slopes of Irazú, Parque Nacional Tapantí and the **Valle Orosí**, and south via the Interamericana over the hump of the Cordillera Central to San Isidro and the Valle del General.

Cartago

Founded in 1563 by Juan Vazquez de Coronado, **CARTAGO**, meaning "Carthage", was Costa Rica's capital for three hundred years before the centre of power was moved to San José in 1823. Like its ancient namesake the city has been razed a number of times, although in this case by earthquakes instead of Romans – two, in 1823 and 1910, almost demolished the place. Most of the town's fine nineteenth-century and *fin-de-siècle* buildings were destroyed, and what has grown up in their place – the usual assortment of shops and haphazard modern buildings – is not particularly appealing. Nowadays Cartago functions mainly as a busy market and shopping centre, with some industry around its periphery. The star attraction is its soaring cathedral, or *basílica*, dedicated to La Negrita, Costa Rica's patron saint.

Arrival, information and accommodation

SACSA buses depart frequently from San José on C 5, Av 18/20 for Cartago; after 8.30pm, buses leave from in front of the *Grand Hotel Costa Rica*. Arriving in Cartago, buses sometimes do a bit of a tour of town, stopping at virtually every block; wait until Parque Central, where you'll be dropped off right in front of the ruined church, Las Ruinas.

Like the other provincial capitals in the Valle Central, Cartago has no **tourist office**. Banco de Costa Rica (Av 4, C 5/7), Banco Nacional (C 1, Av 2) and Banco Popular (Av 1, C 2/4) have **ATMs** and will change **travellers' cheques**. The **correo** is ten minutes from the town centre at Av 2, C 15/17 (Mon–Fri 7.30am–6pm, Sat 7.30am–noon). **Taxis** leave from the rank at Las Ruinas.

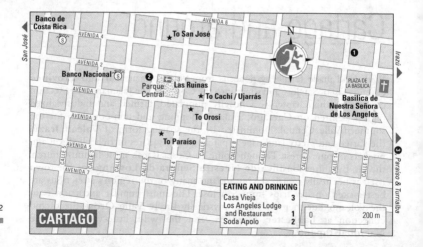

EATING AND DRINKING
Casa Vieja 3
Los Angeles Lodge and Restaurant 1
Soda Apolo 2

0   200 m

CARTAGO

You'll find few hotels in Cartago; one of the more decent ones is the *Los Angeles Lodge* (Av 4, C14/16, ☎591-4169, ℱ591-2218; ❸–❹) with six clean, if slightly shabby, rooms (all with bath and TV) and a reasonable restaurant. Most accommodation in town is extremely basic and frequented only by commercial travellers – best avoided. In any case, getting stuck in Cartago overnight is unlikely, as there's a 24-hour bus service to San José.

The Town

The ruined Iglesia de la Parroquía, known as **Las Ruinas**, dominates the dour, paved **Parque Central**. Originally built in 1575, the church was repeatedly destroyed by earthquakes but stubbornly rebuilt every time, until eventually the giant earthquake of 1910 vanquished it for good. Only the elegantly tumbling walls remain, enclosing pretty subtropical gardens; unfortunately the gardens are locked more often than not, but you can peer through the iron gate at the fluffy blossoms flowering inside. If you inspect the sides and corners of the ruins carefully, you'll see where the earthquake dislodged entire rows of mortar, sending them several centimetres beyond those above and below.

From the ruins it's a five-minute walk east to Cartago's only other attraction: the Cathedral, properly named the **Basílica de Nuestra Señora de Los Angeles**. Built in a decorative Byzantine style after the previous basilica was destroyed in an earthquake of 1926, this huge cement-grey structure with its elaborate wood-panelled interior is home to **La Negrita**, the representation of the Virgin of Los Angeles, patron saint of Costa Rica. On this spot on August 2, 1635, the Virgin reportedly showed herself to a poor peasant girl in the form of a dark doll made of stone. Each time the girl took the doll away to play with it, it mulishly reappeared on the spot where she had found it; this was seen as a sign, and the church was built soon after. August 2 is now one of the most important days in the Costa Rican religious calendar, when hundreds of pilgrims make the journey to Cartago to visit the tiny black statue of the Virgin, tucked away in a shallow subterranean antechamber beneath the crypt. It is a tradition in this grand, vaulting church for pilgrims to shuffle all the way down the aisle towards the altar on their knees, rosaries fretting in their hands as they whisper a steady chorus of Hail Marys (on August 2, many of them will have shuffled from as far as San José to pay their respects). In the left-hand antechamber of the cathedral you'll see silver *ex votos* (devotional sculptures) of every imaginable shape and size, including horses, planes, grasshoppers (representing plagues of locusts), hearts with swords driven through them, arms, fingers and hands. This is a Latin American tradition stretching from México to Brazil, whereby the faithful deposit representations of whatever they need cured, or whatever they fear, to the power of the Almighty.

Eating and drinking

You'll find a few basic **restaurants** in Cartago, and a handful of **sodas** where you can fill up for under $5. Your best bet may be to pop into one of the excellent **pastry shops** and enjoy lunch on a bench in front of the basilica.

Casa Vieja 4km from Cartago on the main road to Paraíso ☎591-1165. Easily the best place to eat in the area, with an elegant dining room set in a grand colonial house and an extensive international menu. Closed Mon.

Restaurant Los Angeles In *Los Angeles Lodge*,

Av 4, C 14/16. The interior may be a bit gloomy, but this restaurant is still a cut above most of the others in town because of the wide range of seafood dishes it serves.

Soda Apolo Av 2, C 2. Its bar permanently propped up by locals, this lively street-corner soda is a good source of solid, *típico* food and (if your Spanish is up to it) gossip.

Around Cartago

Volcán Irazú, forming part of the mighty Cordillera Central, dominates the landscape north of Cartago and is the most popular excursion in the province. Southeast of Cartago you can visit the **Parque Nacional Tapantí**, one of the closest places to San José for rainforest hiking. If you have your own transport, it makes for a good day excursion or weekend trip. The park lies in the pretty **Valle Orosí**, which boasts a couple of interesting churches at Ujarrás and Orosí.

On the eastern slopes of the Cordillera Central, the small town of **Turrialba** is a local hub for watersports. The nearby Ríos Reventazón and Pacuaré boast the best **whitewater rafting** in the country. The town is also the gateway to the **Monumento Nacional Guayabo**, the most important ancient site in Costa Rica. Turrialba and the Monumento Nacional Guayabo both lie two hours east of San José, and are best reached via Cartago.

Parque Nacional Volcán Irazú

The blasted lunar landscape of **PARQUE NACIONAL VOLCÁN IRAZÚ** (daily 8am–3.45pm; $7) reaches its highest point at 3432m and, on clear days, offers fantastic views all the way to the Caribbean coast. Famous for having had the gall to erupt on the day President John F. Kennedy visited Costa Rica on March 19, 1963, Irazú has been more or less calm ever since. But while its **Diego de la Haya crater** is far less active, in terms of bubblings and rumblings, than that of Volcán Poás, its deep depression and the strange algae-green lake that fills it create an undeniably dramatic sight.

Looming 32km north of Cartago, the volcano makes for a long and entirely uphill but scenic trip, especially in the early morning before the inevitable **clouds** roll in. Up at the top you'll see very little vegetation, and what does grow has an otherworldly quality, struggling to survive in this strange environment. There's not much to do around here after viewing the crater from the mirador – no official trails cut through the park, though you can clamber up the scraggly slopes of a few outcrops and scramble among the grey ash dunes. Whatever you do, watch your step, as volcanic ash crumbles easily, and you could end up falling into the ominous-looking lake.

Moving on from Cartago

To get back to **San José**, hop on whichever bus happens to be loading up in the covered area on Av 4, C 2/4. Buses leave every ten minutes between 5am and midnight, and about every hour otherwise. Local buses are frequent and reliable: for **Paraíso**, use the stop on Av 5, C 2/4 (6am–10pm Mon–Fri every 10min; Sat & Sun hourly); for **Orosí**, catch a bus at C 6, Av 1/3 (6am–10pm Mon–Fri every 30min; Sat & Sun hourly); for **Cachí** and **Ujarrás**, buses leave roughly every hour from C 6, Av 1/2.

Practicalities

A visit to Irazú is strictly for day-trippers, since there's nowhere to stay or camp in the park. Only one public **bus** runs to the park, leaving from San José's *Gran Hotel Costa Rica* at 8.15am on weekends and public holidays only; get there early in high season to get a seat. The bus stops to pick up passengers at Cartago (from Las Ruinas) at 8.45am. The round-trip fare is about 1550 colones ($3.75), which doesn't include the park entrance fee.

At the crater parking area, you'll find toilets, an information board and a **reception centre** with a snack bar that serves *tamales*, cakes and hot drinks. A small gift shop rents out waterproof ponchos ($2) – it can get cold at the summit, so bring a sweater. The bus returns to San José at about 12.30pm. You can also get to Irazú on any number of half-day **tours,** run by travel agencies in San José, that whisk you back and forth in a modern minibus for around $35, not including the entrance fee.

Lankester Gardens

Orchids are the chief attraction at the tropical garden and research station **LANKESTER GARDENS** (daily 8.30am–3.30pm; $5), 6km southeast of Cartago. The large, attractive gardens are covered with a bewildering array of tropical plant and flower species, including orchids, heliconias and bromeliads – ostentation elaborate blooms that thrust out from the undergrowth. The most rewarding time to visit is the dry season, particularly in March and April, when the garden explodes with virulent reds, purples and yellows.

To get to the gardens by **bus from San José**, take the Cartago service, get off at Las Ruinas, and change to a Paraíso bus. Get off when you see the *Casa Vieja* restaurant, about ten minutes out of town, and take the road to your right, signposted to the gardens, then turn right at the fork – a total walk of about 1km.

Valle Orosí

West of the small town of **Paraíso**, 8km southeast of Cartago, the road drops down a ski-slope hill into the deep bowl of the **VALLE OROSÍ**. The pretty villages of **Orosí** and **Ujarrás**, each with their own lovely church, are accessible by bus via Paraíso; annoyingly, although they lie less than 8km apart, you can't get directly from one to the other, and have to backtrack to Paraíso. Southeast of these lies the wildlife-rich, but little-visited, **Parque Nacional Tapantí**.

Near Paraíso, you'll find the *Albergue Linda Vista* (☎574-5534; ❷), a friendly B&B with beautiful views; coming into Paraíso, turn right at the Parque Central and drive straight on as if to leave town until you see the sign to the *albergue* on your right. A further kilometre east along the same road is the family-run *Mirador Sanchiri* (☎574-5454, ℉574-8586, ⒲www.sanchiri.com; ❹) with comfortable cabins that sit in a stupendous position high above the valley. The restaurant serves tasty meals made from locally grown produce and the hotel's friendly staff can help with local information and tours.

Ujarrás and around

The tiny agricultural hamlet of **UJARRÁS**, about 10km southeast of Cartago, sits in a flat basin at the foot of precipitous hills in a beautiful corner of the Valle Orosí. Here you can visit the ruins of the **Iglesia de Nuestra Señora de la Limpia Concepción**, originally built in 1693 on the site of a shrine erected by a local fisherman who claimed to have seen the Virgin in a tree trunk. The church was abandoned in 1833 after irreparable damage from flooding. Today the orange-ish limestone ruins are lovingly cared for, with a full-time gardener who tends to the landscaped grounds. The ruined interior, reached through what used to be the door, is now a grassy, roofless enclosure fluttering with birds; despite its dilapidated state, you can identify the fine lines of a former altar. Ujarrás has its own microclimate and can get quite hot, so after a walk around the ruins, head to the small outdoor **swimming pool** across the road, popular with local families and perfect for a cool swim. Avocados grow nearby, and you'll see plantation workers cycling home at the end of the day with bulging sacks of avocados and other produce slung over their backs.

To get to Ujarrás by **bus from Cartago**, take one of the hourly services from Las Ruinas that goes via Paraíso to Cachí. Cachí is some 6km east of Ujarrás; ask to be dropped at the fork for Ujarrás, from where it's a one-kilometre walk to the ruins. To get back to Paraíso and Cartago just flag the bus down at the same spot – the bus currently passes the fork for Ujarrás at about fifteen minutes past the hour. **Driving**, take Hwy-224 south from Cartago, signed to Paraíso and Cachí, which makes a circular trip around Lake Cachí. Extremely steep and winding, this route affords fantastic views over the valley as you descend the last few kilometres.

The best local restaurant, *La Casona del Cafetal,* is at Cachí, several kilometres east of the ruins on the looped valley road. The Ujarrás **mirador** (entrance 50¢; take a right-hand fork uphill from the road back to Paraíso) is a relaxing spot for a cold beer, though the drinks are pricey.

Just south of Cachí you'll come to the charming **Casa del Sonador**, a wooden and bamboo cottage decorated with local woodcarver Macedonio Quesada's lively depictions of rural people – gossiping women, musicians and farmers – and religious scenes. Quesada's sons now use the house as their workshop, where they create and sell their wood carvings (about $5), mostly figures carved from coffee-bush roots. If you're interested, they might also take you on an informative walk around the area, explaining the coffee-growing process and the use of local medicinal herbs.

Orosí

One of the most picturesque small villages in Costa Rica, **OROSÍ** nestles in a little topographical bowl between gloomy, thick-forested hills. It also boasts the **Iglesia de San José de Orosí** (built in 1735), which sits squat against the rounded pates of the hills behind. This simple, low-slung adobe structure, single-towered and roofed with red tiles, has an interior devoid of the hubris and frothy excess of much of Latin American religious decor. The adjacent **Religious Art Museum**, also called the **Museo Franciscano** (Tues–Sat 1–5pm, Sun 9am–5pm; $1) exhibits fascinating *objectos de culto* such as icons, religious paintings and ecclesiastical furniture, along with a faithful recreation of a monk's tiny room.

If the sun's out, check out the two **swimming pools** in the village. Both are fed by hot springs at the foot of the Volcán Rincón de la Vieja and maintain a constant temperature of 30°C. Balneario Thermales Orosí (daily 7.30am–4pm; $1.25) is attractively framed by forest-clad hills and is the better maintained of the two. You'll find several lovely **walking trails** around the village, with waterfalls and swimming spots en route; the *Albergue Montaña Linda* (see opposite) offers a wide range of reasonably priced tours, as well as Spanish lessons at its popular language school (see Basics, p.56) and community projects; the knowledgeable owners can provide heaps of info about the area.

Practicalities

Regular **buses** leave from the stop on C 6, Av 1/3 in Cartago for the forty-minute journey to Orosí (6am–10pm; Mon–Fri every 30min, Sat & Sun hourly). The last service back to Cartago via Paraíso leaves at 5pm from the stop on the main street in front of the church. By **car**, take the road from Cartago to Paraíso, then turn right and drive straight ahead until you begin to descend the precipitous hill to the village. For a **taxi**, ask at the *Restaurante Coto* (see below) or go to the rank on the north side of the main square; a 4WD taxi up the hill to Paraíso costs about $7 and to Parque Nacional Tapantí (see below) about $10. Note that there are no banks in Orosí, so be sure to bring all the money you need with you.

Orosí offers surprisingly good **accommodation**. The *Orosí Lodge* (☎ & ℱ533-3578, ⓦwww.orosilodge.com; ❹), adjacent to the Balneario Thermales Orosí, is a lovely, small hotel with comfortable rooms equipped with coffeemaker, minibar and ceiling fan. The nearby *Cabinas Media Libra* (☎533-3838; ❸) has clean rooms with TV, telephone and private bathroom. For those on a budget, you can't do better than *Albergue Montaña Linda* (☎533-3640, ℱ533-2153, ⓦwww.montanalinda.com) with two pretty eleven-bed single-sex dormitory rooms ($6.50 per person/per bed), some private doubles (❷) and camping space ($3 with own tent, $4 with hostel tent). They also have an on-site language school and hire out bikes.

Grab a bite **to eat** at *Restaurante Coto* (☎533-3032) on the main road, with an inviting terrace that faces the church. The café in the *Orosí Lodge* offers a good breakfast menu and decent coffee and cakes, plus a vintage Costa Rican jukebox.

Parque Nacional Tapantí

Rugged, pristine **PARQUE NACIONAL TAPANTÍ** (daily 8am–3.45pm; $7) receives one of the highest average annual rainfalls (a whopping 5600mm) in the country – if you really want to get wet, go in October. Altitude in this watershedarea ranges from 1220m to 2560m above sea level and contains two life zones: low mountain and premontane rainforest. It's chock-full of **mammals**; about 45 species live here, including the tapir (*danta*), the brocket deer (*cabro de monte*), the mountain hare (*conejo de monte*) and wildcats, along with **birds** such as the golden oriole, falcons, doves, hawks and the quetzal. Because of the wet, frogs, salamanders and snakes abound.

Tapantí's **trails** are relatively short and densely wooded. The wide, 4km **Camino Principal**, or main road, leads off from the puesto at Quebrada Segunda (Second Creek), 12km south of Orosí. Leading off from this are three walks under much denser cover: the **Sendero Natural Arboles Caídos** to the east, and the **Senderos Oropendola** and **Pantanoso** to the west. All provide anywhere from ninety minutes' to three hours' walking. Towards the end of the main trail, **Sendero La Pava** leads to the Río Grande de Orosí and a mirador with views of a waterfall. Whenever you go, bring rain gear and dress in layers. If the sun is out it can be blindingly hot, whereas at higher elevations, when overcast and rainy, it can feel quite cool. Despite its low numbers of visitors, Tapantí has good services, with toilets and drinking water at regular intervals along the trails.

Practicalities

Getting to Tapantí by public transport is difficult. From Cartago, take the bus to Orosí, from where you can catch a jeep taxi ($10) to the park. Alternatively, but less conveniently, stay on the bus until its final stop at the tiny hamlet of

Río Macho and then walk the 9km to the park. **Driving** from Orosí, turn right at the coffee factory Beneficiadora Renex and continue for 10km along a bad road (you'll need a 4WD in the rainy season).

You can **stay** near the park at the *Kiri Mountain Lodge* (☏ & ℱ551-5523, ✉kirilodge@hotmail.com; ❸) with comfortable rooms and a restaurant and bar; they can also arrange guided walks, trout-fishing and horse-riding. To **camp**, head for the *Finca Los Maestros* (☏533-3312; $1 per person), 800km before the park. It's run by friendly local schoolteacher Mireya Aquilar who will cook on request ($1.50 for breakfast; $2 for an evening meal). For **lunch** try *Truchas de Purisol*, a trout farm at the end of a bumpy track signposted from the hamlet of Purisol, 3km back north from the park towards Orosí. You can catch your own lunch ($5 per kilo) from a series of beautifully landscaped ponds and cook it over one of the picnic area's barbecues; alternatively, the site's restaurant serves a delicious lunch with grilled trout ($8). There are well-signposted trails through the surrounding woods.

Turrialba and around

The pleasant agricultural town of **TURRIALBA**, 45km east of Cartago on the eastern slopes of the Cordillera Central, boasts sweeping views over the rugged eastern Talamancas. Most visitors come through Turrialba en route to **Guayabo** or on the way to a **whitewater rafting** or **kayaking** trip on the Ríos Reventazón or Pacuaré. Recommended Turrialba rafting operators include Ticos River Adventure (☏556-1231, ⓦwww.ticoriver.com), Jungla Expeditions (☏556-2639, ⓦwww.junglaespeditions.com) and Costa Rica Ríos Adventures (☏434-0776, ⓦwww.costaricarios.com), one of Central America's largest watersports specialists. Most of the local hotels offer guided walks or horseback rides up the dormant **Volcán Turrialba**, which, with its lack of trails, is otherwise inaccessible to visitors.

In town you'll find the **Proyecto Viborana** (daily 9am–5pm; $5), a small snake centre run by renowned herpetologist Minor Camacho, who gives fascinating educational talks, focusing on the deadly fer-de-lance snake, a native (although thankfully not a very common one) of the area. For a memorable view from above, take a ride on a **hot-air balloon** with Serendipity Adventures (☏556-2592, ⓦwww.serendipityadventures.com), who also organize pricey but unique holidays in Costa Rica – see Basics (p.32) for details.

Practicalities

The Banco Popular on the town's main street has an ATM and changes **travellers' cheques**, as do the Banco Nacional and the Banco de Costa Rica, both opposite the disused railway line; the **correo** is just north of the centre, directly above the square. San José buses leave every hour between 5am–10pm from C 13, Av 6/8.

Turrialba isn't really a tourist town, but has some perfectly decent places to stay, from simple hotel rooms in town to picturesque mountain lodges, some of which sit at **higher altitudes**. Turrialba's best budget option is the **Interamericano** (☏556-0142, ℱ556-7790, ⓦwww.hotelinteramericano .com; ❸), in the southeast corner of town near the old train station. It's basic, clean and friendly and an excellent place to meet other travellers. There's hot water, Internet access and a kitchen for guests' use, and they can organize kayaking and other tours. About 7km from Turrialba on the road to Limón is the *Turrialtico Lodge* (☏ & ℱ556-1111, ⓦwww.turrialtico.com; ❺), a cosy lodge with fourteen wood-panelled rooms, all with private bath and hot water; some have balconies overlooking the gorgeous surrounding countryside. They organize tours to Irazú and the Río Reventazón. A further half a kilometre along the road to Limón, perched atop a mountain, is the *Hotel de Montaña Pochotel* (℡538-1515, ℻538-1212, ⓦwww.pochotel.com; ❸) with comfortable rooms, stunning volcano views and a restaurant that serves traditional mountain fare including heavy stews and grilled meat platters. There are also camping facilities on the grounds. Further out still, some 15km northwest of Turrialba along a poorly maintained road a couple of kilometres north of Esperanza, the quiet, modern *Volcán Turrialba Lodge* (℡273-4335, ℻273-0703, ⓦwww.volcanturrialbalodge.com; ❺) is a simply furnished farmhouse that sits on the very flanks of Volcán Turrialba – it advertises itself as "the only hotel with a volcano in its garden". The fourteen rooms all have wood-burning stoves and private bath; diversions include ox-cart rides and horseback tours to the Turrialba crater. You can arrange for a pick-up from San José; otherwise you'll need a 4WD to get here over the badly rutted access road (call for directions).

Several sodas around the main square in Turrialba offer inexpensive, *típico* fare. The **restaurant** *La Feria,* next to the *Wagelia* hotel, serves decent regional cuisine. The excellent alfresco restaurant at *Turrialtico Lodge* (see p.138) is renowned for its local specialities, including barbecued meats and *pozol,* a tasty corn and pork soup.

Monumento Nacional Guayabo

The most accessible ancient archeological site in Costa Rica, the **MONUMENTO NACIONAL GUAYABO** (℡556-9507; daily 8am–3.45pm; $7) lies 19km northeast of Turrialba and 84km east of San José. Discovered by explorer Anastasio Alfaro at the end of the nineteenth century, the remains of the town of Guayabo were only excavated in the late 1960s. Administered by Mirenem, the Ministry of Mines and Resources (which also controls Costa Rica's national park system), Guayabo today suffers from an acute shortage of funds, and only a small part of the site has been excavated. With the withdrawal of the annual US aid grant, the prospects for further exploration look bleak.

The site is visually disappointing compared to the magnificent Maya and Aztec cities of Mexico or Guatemala – cultures contemporaneous with Guayabo – though it's well to remember that civilizations should not necessarily be judged on their ability to erect vast monuments. Facing the considerable difficulties posed by the density of the rainforest terrain, the Guayabo managed not only to live in harmony with an environment that remains hostile to human habitation, but also constructed a complex system of water management, social organization, and expressed themselves through the "written language" of petroglyphs.

Archeologists believe that Guayabo was inhabited from about 1000 BC to 1400 AD; most of the heaps of stones and basic structures now exposed were erected between 300 and 700 AD. The central mound is the tallest circular base unearthed so far, with two staircases and pottery remains at the very top. The people of Guayabo brought stones to the site from a great distance – probably from the banks of the Río Reventazón – and petroglyphs have been found on 53 of these stones. Other than this, little is known of the people who lived here, though excavations have shown that they were particularly skilled in water conducting. At the northern end of the site you can see the stone *tanque de captación,* where they stored water conducted by subterranean aqueducts from nearby springs. It's also thought that this community was led by a chief, a *cacique*, who had both social and religious power. There are no clues as to why Guayabo was abandoned, though hypotheses include an epidemic or war with neighbouring tribes.

At the **entrance hut** you can pick up a leaflet, written in the "voice" of Brúl, a Bribrí word for armadillo, that points out orchids, a petroglyph and guarumo trees. Other than this, there's no official guided tour to help you interpret what can otherwise look like random piles of stone. You can, however, organize your own private guide; ask at your hotel or try locally based Loco's Tours (T 556-6035, E riolocos@whitwh20.com) with guided trips to the monument for $40. You can also visit the small exhibition space that has fragments of pottery and a model showing how the city would have looked.

Daily **buses** to Guayabo from Turrialba leave from Av 2, C 0/2 (Mon–Sat at 11am & 5.15pm, returning at 12.30 & 5.30pm; Sun at 9am, returning at 4pm), though the inconvenient timetable means you may either have not enough or too much time at the site. Alternatively, you can walk back to the main road, a 4km downhill hike, and intercept the bus that goes back from the hamlet of Santa Teresita to Turrialba. It passes by at about 1.30pm, but you should double-check the times with the *guardaparques* or you might be left standing at the crossroads for 24 hours. If you're stuck, you can always bed down at the monument's small campsite ($2 per person). **Driving** from Turrialba takes about thirty minutes. The last 4km is on a bad gravel road; it's passable with a regular car, but watch your clearance. **Taxis** charge $12 from Turrialba.

Travel details

Buses

Alajuela to: La Guácima Abajo, for the Butterfly Farm (4 daily; 20min); San José (every 5–10min; 20min); Sarchí (every 30min; 1hr); Volcán Poás (1 daily; 2hr); Zoo-Ave (every 30min; 15min).
Braulio Carrillo to: San José (every 30min; 35min).
Cartago to: Orosí (every 1hr 30min Mon–Fri, hourly Sat & Sun; 30min); Paraíso (every 5–10min Mon–Fri, hourly Sat & Sun; 30min); Río Macho, via Orosí, for Tapantí (every 30min Mon–Fri, hourly Sat & Sun); San José (every 10min; 40min); Ujarrás (hourly; 30min).
Heredia to: San José (every 5–10min; 15min); Volcán Barva, via San José de la Montaña (3 daily Mon–Sat, 2 daily Sun; 1hr).

Orosí to: Cartago (every 30min Mon–Fri, hourly Sat & Sun; 30min).
San José to: Alajuela (constant; 20min); Braulio Carrillo (every 30min; 35min); Cartago (every 20min; 40min); Heredia (every 5–10min; 15min); Sarchí (17 daily; 1hr 30min); La Guácima Abajo for the Butterfly Farm (2 express daily except Sun; 40min); Turrialba (16 daily; 1hr 30min); Volcán Irazú (1 Sat & Sun; 1hr 30min); Volcán Poás (1 daily; 2hr); Zarcero (12 daily; 2hr).
Sarchí to: Alajuela (every 30min; 1hr); San José (17 daily; 1hr 30min).
Turrialba to: Guayabo (2 daily Mon–Fri; 1hr+).
Ujarrás to: Cartago, via Paraíso (every 1hr 30min Mon–Fri, hourly Sat & Sun; 30min).

3

Limón Province and the Caribbean coast

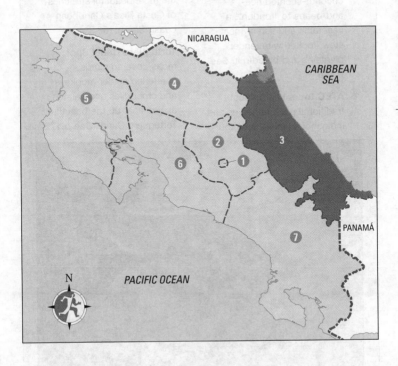

NICARAGUA

CARIBBEAN
SEA

④

⑤

②

⑥

①

3

PANAMÁ

⑦

N

PACIFIC OCEAN

✱ **Carnival, Puerto Limón**
Revellers in Afro-Caribbean
costumes and spangly tops
parade through the streets to
a cacophony of tambourines,
whistles and blasting sound-
systems. See p.152

✱ **Caribbean Cuisine** Sample
the region's traditional
Caribbean cooking, from
coconut-scented rice-
and-beans to "rondon", a
vegetable and fish or meat
stew cooked with tender
plantains and breadfruit. See
p.148

✱ **ATEC tours** Learn about
traditional plant remedies and
indigenous history on a tour

to the Bribrí and Cabécar
villages, led by the grassroots
organization ATEC and locals
whose families have been in
the area since the eighteenth
century. See p.167

✱ **Playas Cocles, Uvita and
Manzanillo** The idyllic
beaches of Cocles, Uvita
and Manzanillo dot one of
the most beautiful stretches
of Costa Rica's Caribbean
coast. See p.166

✱ **Tortuguero Canal** Spot
moss-covered sloths,
chattering spider monkeys
and crocodiles and caiman
as you float up the beautiful
Tortuguero Canal. See p.172

△ Coastal cuisine

Limón Province and the Caribbean coast

We were at the shore and travelling alongside a palmy beach. This was the Mosquito Coast ... Massive waves were rolling towards us, the white foam vivid in the twilight; they broke just below the coconut palms near the track. At this time of day, nightfall, the sea is the last thing to darken: it seems to hold the light that is slipping from the sky; and the trees are black. So in the light of this luminous sea, and the pale still-blue eastern sky, and to the splashings of the breakers, the train racketed on towards Limón.

Paul Theroux, *The Old Patagonian Express*

The Caribbean or "Miskito" coast (in Spanish, Mosquito) forms part of the huge, sparsely populated Limón Province, which sweeps south in an arc from Nicaragua to Panamá. Hemmed in to the north by dense jungles and swampy waterways, to the west by the mighty Cordillera Central and to the south by the even wider girth of the Cordillera Talamanca, Limón can feel like a lost, remote place.

Those seeking palm-fringed sands and tranquil crystalline waters that the word "Caribbean" conjures up will be disappointed. Limón has very few really good **beaches** to speak of and most are battered, shark-patrolled shores, littered with driftwood, and huge, bucking skies stretching out to sea. However, you can watch gentle giant sea **turtles** lay their eggs on the wave-raked beaches of **Tortuguero**; snorkel coral reefs at the unspoilt **Cahuita** or Punta Uva; go surfing at **Puerto Viejo de Talamanca**; or go animal- and bird-spotting in the region's many **mangrove swamps**. The interior of Limón Province is crisscrossed by the powerful Río Reventazón and Río Pacuaré, two of the best rivers in the Americas for **whitewater rafting**.

Although Limón remains unknown to the majority of visitors – especially those on package tours – it holds much appeal for eco-tourists and travellers off the beaten track. The province has the highest proportion of **protected land** in the country, from the **Refugio Nacional de Fauna Silvestre Barra del Colorado**, on the Nicaraguan border, to the **Refugio Nacional de Vida Silvestre Gandoca-Manzanillo** near Panamá in the extreme south. That said, however, the wildlife reserves and national parks still offer only partial resistance to the considerable ecological threats of full-scale fruit farming, logging, mining and tourism.

The Caribbean coast exudes a greater sense of **cultural diversity** than anywhere else in Costa Rica – a feeling of community and a unique and complex local history. **Puerto Limón**, the only town of any size, is one of several established "black" Central American coastal cities, like Bluefields in Nicaragua and Lívingston in Guatemala. A typical Caribbean port, it has a large, mostly Jamaican-descended **Afro-Caribbean** population. In the south, near the Panamanian border, live several communities of indigenous peoples from the **Bribrí** and **Cabécar** groups, none of whom has been well served by the national government.

Options are limited in **getting around** Limón Province. From San José to Puerto Limón, you have a choice of just two roads, while from Puerto Limón south to the Panamá border at Sixaola there is but one decent route (not counting the few small local roads leading to the banana fincas). North of Puerto Limón there is no public land transport at all: instead, private *lanchas* ply the coastal **Tortuguero canal**, dug in the late 1960s in order to bypass the treacherous breakers of the Caribbean. The canal connects the port of Moín, 8km north of Puerto Limón, to the Río Colorado near the Nicaraguan border.

Daily **flights** travel from San José to Barra del Colorado and Tortuguero. A reliable **bus** network operates in the rest of the province, with the most efficient and modern routes running from San José to Puerto Limón and on to Sixaola. Gas provision is generally poor, except on the highway from San José; take a spare can with you if you plan to do much driving south of Puerto Limón or down into Panamá. **Language** can be a problem when travelling around Limón. While English is spoken widely along the coast (in Puerto Limón, Tortuguero and Barra del Colorado), don't expect everyone to know it. Your best bet is to make your first approaches in Spanish, if you can; people can then choose in which language to answer you.

The area's diverse microclimates mean there is no best **time to visit** the Caribbean coast. In Tortuguero and Barra del Colorado, you'll encounter wet weather all year round, with a small dry spell in January and February. South of Limón, September and October offer the best chance of rain-free days.

Some history

Although the coast has been populated for at least ten thousand years, little is known of the ancient indigenous **Bribrí** and **Cabécar** people who inhabited the area when Columbus arrived just off the coast of present-day Puerto Limón, on his fourth and last voyage to the Americas in 1502. Well into the mid-eighteenth century, the only white people the Limón littoral saw were British **pirates**, rum-runners and seamen from the merchant vessels of the famous Spanish Main, plying the rich waters of the Caribbean, and bringing with them commerce and mayhem. Nefarious buccaneers often found refuge on Costa Rica's eastern seaboard, situated as it was between the two more

---

Ethnicity in Limón Province

In his book *Tekkin a Waalk*, journalist and travel writer Peter Ford uses the ingenious term "an anthropological Galápagos" to describe the ethnic and cultural oddities encountered in Limón, where the Caribbean meets Central America. There's no doubt that the province provides a touch of multiculturalism lacking in the rest of Costa Rica's relatively homogeneous Latin, Catholic society. In Limón, characterized by intermarriage and racial mixing, it's not unusual to find people who are of combined Miskito, Afro-Caribbean and Nicaraguan ancestry. Though the first black inhabitants of the province were the slaves of the British pirates and mahogany-cutters who had lived in scattered communities along the coast since the mid-1700s, the region's ethnic diversity stems largely from the influence of Minor Keith (see p.146), who brought in large numbers of foreign labourers to work on the construction of the Jungle Train. They were soon joined by turtle fishermen who had settled in Bocas del Toro, Panamá, before migrating north to escape the Panamanian war of independence from Colombia in 1903. The settlers brought their respective religions with them – unlike in the rest of Costa Rica, most Afro-Caribbeans in Limón Province are Protestant.

Regardless of race or religion, the coastal settlers were resourceful and independent. They not only planted their own crops, bringing seeds to grow breadfruit, oranges, mangoes and ackee, all of which flourished alongside native coconuts and cocoa, but also made their own salt, charcoal, musical instruments and shoes and brewed their own spirits – red rum, *guarapo*, cane liquor and ginger beer.

Limón's diversity has never been appreciated by the ruling and economic elite of the country. Until 1949, blacks were effectively forbidden from settling in the Valle Central or the Highlands, and while the indigenous communities have a degree of autonomy, their traditional territories have long since been eaten up by government-sanctioned mining and banana enterprises. Official discrimination against the province's Afro-Caribbean inhabitants ended in 1949 with a new constitution that granted them full citizenship. Black *Limonenses* now make up around 30 percent of the province's population.

lucrative provinces of Panamá and Nicaragua, from which there was a steady traffic of ships to raid. Their presence, along with the difficult terrain, helped deter full-scale settlement of Limón.

Traditionally neglected and underfunded by the government, Limón suffered a further blow in the 1991 **earthquake**, which heaved the Caribbean coast about 1.5 metres up in the air. Already badly maintained roads, bridges and banana railroads were destroyed, including the track for the **Jungle Train** from San José to Puerto Limón, one of the most scenic train rides in the world. While much has been rebuilt, an air of neglect still hangs over parts of the province, from housing and tourist infrastructure to basic sanitation.

The province's development was inextricably linked to two things, themselves related: the **railway** and **bananas**. In 1871 it was decided that Costa Rica needed a more efficient export route for its coffee crop than the long, meandering river journey from Puerto Viejo de Sarapiquí to Matina (midway between Tortuguero and Puerto Limón) from where the beans were shipped to Europe. From the other main coffee port – Puntarenas on the Pacific coast – boats had to go all the way round South America to get to Europe. **Minor Keith**, an American, was contracted to build a railroad across the Cordillera Central from San José to Puerto Limón; to help pay for the laying of the track, he planted bananas along its lowland stretches. Successive waves of Highlanders, Chinese, East Indian (still locally called Hindus) and Italian immigrant labourers were brought in for the gruelling construction work, only to succumb to yellow fever. At least four thousand people died while laying the track for the Jungle Train. In the final stages, some ten thousand Jamaicans and Barbadians, thought to be immune to the disease, were contracted, many of them staying on to work on further railroad expansion or in the banana plantations. In 1890, the first **Jungle Train** huffed its way from San José via Turrialba and Siquerres to Limón, bringing an abrupt end to the Caribbean coast's era of near-total isolation. This also marked the beginning of Costa Rica's **banana boom**. Initially planted as a sideline to help fund the railroad, the fruit prospered amid this ideal climate, leading Keith to found the United Fruit Company, whose monopoly of the banana trade throughout Central America made him far wealthier than the railroad ever could.

San José to Puerto Limón

Two land routes head from the capital to Puerto Limón. Though the main route, the **Guápiles Highway** (Hwy-32), remains one of the best-maintained roads in the country, it's still half-jokingly referred to as the "Highway to Heaven" because of its high accident and fatality record. Nevertheless, the vast majority of buses and cars take this road, which begins in San José at the northern end of C 3 and climbs out of the Highlands to the northeast. This opening section of the highway is the most impressive, with Barva and Irazú volcanos looming on either side. In general, however, the road doesn't offer quite the scenery you might expect because it's hewn from sheer walls of mountain carpeted with thick, intertwining vegetation. While one side is solid rock, the other side, in places, makes a sheer phantasmagoric drop that you can't quite see, with only the enormous, common huge-leaf plant known as "poor man's umbrella" (*sombrilla de pobre*) growing by the roadside to break the monotony.

The older, narrower and slower route, Hwy-10, often called the **Turrialba Road**, runs through Turrialba on the eastern slopes of the Cordillera Central before following the old switchbacking San José–Limón train tracks through a dense and pristine mountainous landscape, gutted by the deep cuts of the Pacuaré and Reventazón rivers. It joins the Guápiles Highway near **Siquerres**, about three-quarters of the way to Limón, beyond which the road passes through a final 80km of low flatlands to the coast. Considered dangerous and difficult to drive, the Turrialba Road now carries very little traffic, as it takes about four hours as opposed to two-and-a-half to three hours on the Guápiles Highway.

Guápiles

GUÁPILES, about 50km east of San José, is the first town of any size on the Guápiles Highway and functions as a supply point for the Río Frío banana plantations and a waystation for the *bananero* workers. The only reason to pause here is to break your trip. The few **hotels** in town cater mainly to plantation workers and have cold water and thin walls. The one exception is the comparatively swish *Hotel Suerre* (℡710-7551, ℗710-6376, ⓦwww.suerre.com; ❻), a country club with pool, gym and exercise room and poolside bar (all of which non-guests are welcome to use for a fee) and also a good restaurant. Just outside Guápiles, following a well-marked right turn from the highway at the *Ponderosa* restaurant, sits the *Casa Río Blanco* (℡ & ℗710-4124, ⓦwww.casarioblanco.com; ❺), a rainforest lodge with comfortable cabinas and lush hiking trails down to the river and its waterfalls.

Siquerres

Many of the package tours to Tortuguero (see p.172) make a brief stop at **SIQUERRES**, 1km northeast of the Guápiles Highway at Km-99 from San José, en route to picking up the boat at the small village of Hamburgo de Siquerres on the Río Reventazón. As the rusted hulks of freight cars and track-scarred streets show, Siquerres – which means "reddish colour" in a Miskito dialect – used to be a major railway hub for the Jungle Train that carted people, bananas and cacao to the Highlands. Along with Turrialba, this is where black train drivers, engineers and maintenance men would swap positions with their "white" (Spanish, *mestizo*, European or Highland) counterparts, who would then take the train into the Valle Central, where blacks were forbidden from travelling until 1949. Though the Jungle Train no longer runs, trains still haul bananas and machinery to and from Siquerres, mainly servicing the innumerable banana towns or fincas nearby (easily recognizable on maps from their factory-farm names of Finca 1, 2, a, b and so forth). You won't find much in the way of sights in sleepy Siquerres except for the completely **round church** on the western side of the soccer field. Built to mirror the shape of a Miskito hut, its authentic indigenous shape shelters a plain, wood-panelled interior.

From Siquerres, it's a relatively easy sixty-kilometre drive east to Puerto Limón on a well-maintained road. Truck and bus drivers love to make up time by speeding and overtaking on these stretches. The countryside unfolds with macadamia nut farms set alongside small banana plots, flower nurseries and bare agricultural land dotted with humble roadside dwellings.

Puerto Limón and around

To the rest of the country, **PUERTO LIMÓN**, more often simply called Limón, is Costa Rica's *bête noire*, a steamy port raddled with slum neighbourhoods, bad

Creole cuisine in Limón Province

Creole cuisine is known throughout the Americas, from Louisiana to Bahía, for its imaginative use of African spices and vegetables, succulent fish and chicken dishes and fantastic sweet desserts. Sample Limón's version at any of the locally run restaurants dotted along the coast. These are often family affairs, usually presided over by respected older Afro-Caribbean women. Sitting down to dinner at a red gingham tablecloth, with a cold bottle of Imperial beer, reggae on the boombox and a plate heaped with coconut-scented rice-and-beans is one of the real pleasures of visiting this part of Costa Rica. Note that many restaurants, in keeping with age-old local tradition, feature Creole dishes on weekends only, serving simpler dishes or the usual Highlands rice concoctions during the week.

Everyone outside Limón will tell you that the local speciality, **rice-and-beans** (in the lilting local accent it sounds like "rizanbin"), is "*comida muy pesada*" (very heavy food). However, this truly wonderful mixture of red or black beans and rice cooked in coconut milk is no more *pesada* – and miles tastier – than traditional Highland dishes like *arroz con camarones*, where everything is fried; it's the coconut milk that gives this dish its surprising lift. Another local speciality is **pan bon**, sweet bread glazed and laced with cheese and fruit which is often eaten for dessert, as are ginger biscuits and plantain tarts. Pan bon doesn't translate as "good bread", as is commonly thought; "bon" actually derives from "bun", brought by English-speaking settlers. **Rundown** (said "rondon" – to "rundown" is to cook) is a vegetable and meat or fish stew in which the plantains and breadfruit cook for many hours, very slowly, in spiced coconut milk. It may be hard to find, mainly because it takes a long time, at least an afternoon, to prepare. Though some restaurants – *Springfield* in Limón, *Miss Junie's* in Tortuguero and *Miss Edith's* in Cahuita – have it on their menus as a matter of course, it's usually best to stop by on the morning of the day you wish to dine and request it for that evening.

Favoured **spices** in Limonese Creole cooking include cumin, coriander, peppers, chillies, paprika, cloves and groundspice, while the most common vegetables are those you might find in a street market in West Africa, Brazil or Jamaica. Native to Africa, **ackee** (in Spanish *seso vegetal*) was brought to the New World by British colonists, and has to be prepared by knowledgeable cooks because its sponge-cake-like yellow fruit, enclosed in three-inch pods, is poisonous until the pods open. Served boiled, ackee resembles scrambled eggs and goes well with fish. **Yucca**, also known as manioc, is a long pinkish tuber, similar to the yam, and usually boiled or fried. Local yams can grow as big as 25kg, and are used much like potato in soups and stews. Another native African crop, the huge melon-like **breadfruit** (*fruta de pan*), is more a starch substitute than a fruit, with white flesh that has to be boiled, baked or grated. **Pejiballes** (*pejibaye* in Spanish – English-speaking people in Limón pronounce it "picky-BAY-ah") are small green or orange fruits that look a little like limes. They're boiled in hot water and skinned – and are definitely an acquired taste, being both salty and bitter. You'll find them sold on the street in San José, but they're most popular in Limón. Better known as heart-of-palm, **palmito** is served in restaurants around the world as part of a tropical salad. **Plantains** (*plátanos* in Spanish), the staple of many Highland dishes, figure particularly heavily in Creole cuisine, and are deliciously sweet when baked or fried in fritters. Right at the other end of the health scale are **herbal teas**, a speciality of the province and available in many restaurants: try wild peppermint, wild basil, soursop, lime, lemon grass or ginger.

sanitation and drug-related crime. The traveller may be kinder to the city than the Highland Tico, although Paul Theroux's first impressions in *The Old Patagonian Express* are no encouragement:

The stucco fronts had turned the colour and consistency of stale cake, and crumbs of concrete littered the pavements. In the market and on the parapets of the crumbling buildings there were mangy vultures. Other vultures circled the plaza. Was there a dingier backwater in all the world?

Not much has changed in the twenty-five years or so since Theroux went through town, though the vultures have disappeared. Many buildings, damaged during the 1991 earthquake (the epicentre was just south of Limón) lie skeletal and wrecked, still in the process of falling down. Curiously, however, with its washed-out, peeling oyster-and-lime hues, Limón can be almost pretty, in a sad kind of way, with the pseudo-beauty of all Caribbean "slums of empire", as St Lucian poet Derek Walcott put it.

Limón has never been in the same league as the Caribbean ports of Veracruz in Mexico or Cartagena in Colombia, lacking those cities' architecture and dilapidated elegance. It's a working port but a neglected one, because most of the big-time banana boats now load at the deeper natural harbour of **Moín**, 8km up the headland toward Tortuguero. Generally, tourists come to Limón

PUERTO LIMÓN

ACCOMMODATION
Acón	F
Apartments Cocorí	B
Cabinas Maeva	C
Caribe	G
Maribú Caribe	A
Miami	H
Park	D
Teté	E

EATING AND DRINKING
Brisas del Caribe	8
Centro Turístico Piuta	4
Maribú Caribe	3
Park Hotel	6
Queenies	7
Quimbambu	2
El Ranchito	A
Soda La Estrella	5
Springfield	1

PORTETE & PLAYA BONITA

Playa Bonita

Main Docks

Tortuguero Canal

Lanchas to Tortuguero

PORTETE

Puerto Limón

Isla Uvita

Moín

0   2 km

Malecón (Sea Wall)

AVENIDA 6

AVENIDA 5

CALLE 6   CALLE 5   CALLE 4   CALLE 3   CALLE 2

AVENIDA 4

Buses to Cahuita, Puerto Viejo & Sixaola

Supermarket

Scotiabank

AVENIDA 3

Mercado Central

Banco Costa Rica

CARIBBEAN SEA

AVENIDA 2

Town Hall

Coopelimón Buses to San José

CALLE 1

Mural

Parque Vargas

AVENIDA 1

Docks

0   100 m

Cahuita, Puerto Viejo & San José

for one of three reasons: to get a **boat to Tortuguero** from Moín, to catch a bus south to the **beach towns** of Cahuita and Puerto Viejo or to join in the annual **El Día de la Raza** (Columbus Day) carnival during the week preceding October 12.

Arrival, information and orientation

Arriving in Limón after dark can be unnerving – get here in daylight if possible. Transportes Caribeños **buses** (see p.99) make the two-and-a-half-hour trip between **San José** (departing from C 0, Av 11) and **Limón** roughly every half-hour from 5am until 7pm. San José buses arrive at Limón's new Gran Terminal del Caribe on C 7, Av 1/2, from where you can also catch a bus to Moín. You should buy your ticket several days in advance during the El Día de la Raza Carnival, even though extra buses go into service at this time. Arrivals **from the south** – Cahuita, Puerto Viejo de Talamanca and Panamá (via Sixaola) – terminate at the Transportes MEPE stop at C 3, Av 4, 100m north of Mercado Central.

For **information** about the Caribbean coast, you'll need to contact the San José ICT (223-1733), as there's no official tourist office in the entire province. The Banco de Costa Rica, on Av 2, C 1, offers **money exchange**, as does Scotiabank, on Av 3, C 2; both banks have ATMs that accept Visa and Cirrus. You'll find the **correo** (Mon–Fri 7.30am–5pm, Sat 8am–noon) on Av 2, C 4, though the mail service from Limón is dreadful – you're better off posting items from San José. The correo does offer **Internet access** however, as does the *Net Café* on Av 4, C 5/6. Note that during El Día de la Raza Carnival, everything shuts for a week, including all banks and the post office.

While Limón isn't quite the mugger's paradise as portrayed by the Highland media, you shouldn't linger on the sidewalk looking lost nor carry valuables while on the street – most of the hotels listed below have safes. When trying to **find your way around**, bear in mind that even more so than in other Costa Rican towns, nobody refers to *calles* and *avenidas* in Limón. The city does have street numbers, but virtually no signs. To confuse things further, unlike other towns in Costa Rica, *calles* and *avenidas* in Limón run sequentially, rather than in separate even- and odd-numbered sequences. Though the city as a whole spreads quite far out, central Limón covers no more than about ten blocks.

Limón patois

Limón patois combines **English phrases**, brought by Jamaican and Barbadian immigrants to the province in the last century, with a Spanish slightly different to that spoken in the Highlands. Though used less these days, the traditional greeting of "What happen?" ("Whoppin?") remains a stock phrase, equivalent to the Spanish "*¿Qué pasa?*" ("What's going on?"). In Limón, you'll also hear the more laconic "Okay" or "All right" (both hello and goodbye) taking the place of the Spanish "*Adiós*" ("hello" in Costa Rica rather than goodbye; see p.421), "*Que le vaya bien*" and "*Que Díos le acompañe*".

Yet, English might be spoken at home, and among the older Limón crowd, but Spanish is the language taught at school and used on the street, particularly among the younger generation. Older *Limonenses* sometimes refer to Spanish speakers as "Spaniamen" (which comes out sounding like "Sponyaman").

Accommodation

It's worth shelling out a bit extra for a **room** in Limón, especially if you're travelling alone – the comfort and safety of your hotel makes a big difference to your peace of mind. In midweek, the town's hotels fill up quickly with commercial travellers; try to get to Limón as early as possible if you're arriving on a Wednesday or Thursday.

Staying **downtown** puts you in the thick of things, and many hotels have communal balconies, perfect for relaxing with a cold beer and checking out the lively street activity below. The downside is the noise, especially at night; if you prefer to hear gentle waves lapping, try the *Park Hotel*, which stands alone on a little promontory close to sea. There's a group of quieter hotels outside town (about 4km up the spur road to Moín) at **Portete** and the small, somewhat misnamed **Playa Bonita**. A taxi to here costs less than $1.50, and the bus to and from Moín runs along the road every twenty minutes or so. Allow an hour to walk into town. In all but the most upmarket places, avoid drinking the **tap water**, or use a filter or iodine tablets.

Hotel prices rise by as much as fifty percent for **carnival** week, and to a lesser extent during Semana Santa, or Easter week. The least expensive times to stay are when rainfall is at its highest, between July and October, and December to February, which (confusingly) are considered high season in the rest of the country.

Limón has its share of dives, which tend to get booked when a big ship has docked. None of the places listed below is rock-bottom cheap. If this is what you're after, you'll find it easily enough, but always ask to see the room first and inspect the bathroom in particular.

In town

Acón Av 3, C 2/3 ☎758-1010, ℱ758-2924. This large, central hotel has rather gloomy but well-equipped rooms with TV and a/c, plus hot water in the somewhat small private bathrooms. There's also parking. ❸–❹

Hotel Caribe Av 2, C 1, above *Brisas del Caribe* restaurant ☎758-0138. Bed down in these plain but spacious rooms with TV and fan, just beware that it can get noisy at night. ❷–❸

Miami Av 2, C 4/5 ☎ & ℱ758-0490. This friendly spot near the central market offers large, clean rooms with ceiling fans, cable TV and private bathrooms. ❷–❸

Park Av 3, C 1, by the malecón ☎798-0555 or 758-4364, ℮irlixie@sol.racsa.co.cr. Popular with Ticos and travellers alike, this well-appointed hotel offers a range of rooms: the more expensive ones come with a sea view, slightly less expensive rooms have a street view, and the cheapest, *plana turista*, have no view at all. There's a good restaurant on site and note that it's important to book in advance. ❹

Teté Av 3, C 4/5 ☎758-1122, ℱ758-0707. One of the best downtown hotels in this price range, friendly *Teté* has clean, well-cared-for rooms; those on the street have balconies but can be noisy, while the darker inside rooms are quieter. ❷

Portete and Playa Bonita

Apartments Cocorí Playa Bonita ☎795-1670, ℱ795-2930. Relax in these comfortable self-catering apartments, with fan or a/c, amid a beautiful leafy setting overlooking the ocean. Pluses include a friendly staff and a swimming pool. The lively outdoor bar-restaurant, right by the sea, has lovely views. ❸

Cabinas Maeva Portete; look for the blue-and-white sign ☎758-2024. Cute, yellow hexagonal cabinas with small private bathrooms nestle among palm trees, a beautiful pool and Neoclassical statues. ❷

Maribú Caribe Portete ☎795-4010, ℱ795-3541, ℮maricari@racsa.co.cr. A favourite among banana-company executives, this luxurious seaside complex of round, thatched-roof huts has a 1960s decor, a pool and a pleasant but pricey bar-restaurant overlooking the sea. ❻

The Town

Stroll around Puerto Limón for about fifteen minutes and you've pretty much seen it all. **Avenida 2**, known locally as the "market street" and for all purposes the main drag, runs along both the north edge of Parque Vargas and the south side of the **Mercado Central**. At times, the market seems to contain the entire population of Limón – dowager women mind their stalls while men clutch cigarettes, chattering and gesticulating. The produce looks fresh: chayotes, plantains, cassava, yucca, beans and the odd banana (most of the crop is exported) vie for space with bulb-like cacao fruit, baseball-sized tomatoes and huge carrots. For an inexpensive, quality bite to eat, try the market's sodas and snack bars.

Limón, often noisy and chaotic, becomes pleasantly languid in the heat of the day, with workers drifting towards **Parque Vargas** and the malecón at lunch to sit under the shady palms. The park features a sea-facing **mural** (at the easternmost end of C 1 and Av 1 and 2) by artist Guadalupe Alvarea. The mural swarms with colourful, evocative images of the province's tough history. On the left of the semicircular wall, indigenous people are shown making crafts, which were later destroyed by the Catholic missionaries. Moving right, you'll note the era of Columbus, with ships being loaded with coffee and bananas by women wearing vibrant African cloth. Finally, the arrival of the Jungle Train is depicted with a wonderful Chinese dragon to symbolize the Chinese labourers who worked on it.

El Día de la Raza carnival

Though carnivals in the rest of Latin America are usually associated with the days before Lent, the Limón Carnival celebrates Columbus's arrival in the New World on October 12. The idea first came to Limón by Arthur King, a local who had been away working in Panamá's Canal Zone. He was so impressed with that country's Columbus Day celebrations that he decided to bring the merriment home to Limón. Today, **El Día de la Raza** (Day of the People) basically serves as an excuse to party. Throngs of Highland Ticos descend upon Limón – buses fill to bursting, hotels brim, and revellers hit the streets in search of this year's sounds and style. Rap, rave and ragga – in Spanish and English – are hot, and Bob Marley lives, or at least is convincingly resurrected, for carnival week.

Carnival can mean anything you want it to, from noontime displays of Afro-Caribbean dance to Calypso music, bull-running, children's theatre, colourful *desfiles* (parades) and massive firework displays. Most spectacular is the **Grand Desfile**, usually held on the Saturday before October 12, when revellers in Afro-Caribbean costumes – sequins, spangles and fluorescent colours – parade through the streets to a cacophony of tambourines, whistles and blasting sound systems.

Instead of taking place in Limón's streets as it has in years past (the national press reported on "sanitation" problems that threatened to bring the whole event to a halt), most of the carnival's nighttime festivities now occur within the fences of the harbour authority JAPDEVA's huge docks and parking lot. This might sound like a soulless location, but it's a well-managed affair, and while you may not be dancing in the streets, you're at least dancing. The overall atmosphere – even late at night – remains unthreatening, with teens and grandparents alike enjoying the music. Kiosks dispense steaming Chinese, Caribbean and Tico food, and on-the-spot discos help pump up the volume. **Cultural Street**, which runs from the historic Black Star Line (the shipping company that brought many of the black immigrants here), is an alcohol-free zone, popular with family groups. Kids can play games at small fairgrounds to win candyfloss and stuffed toys. Elsewhere, bars overflow onto the street, and the impromptu partying builds up as the night goes on.

A small colony of **sloths** live in the park's tall royal palms. At the end of the central promenade rises a shrine to sailors and fishermen, and also a dilapidated bandstand, the site of occasional concerts. From here, the **malecón** (a thin ledge where it's hardly possible to walk, let alone take a seaside promenade) winds its way north. Avoid it at night when muggings have been reported. On the northern end of the park is the slightly run-down **municipalidad** (town hall), with a pale facade and peeling Belle Epoque grillework. Opposite, on the shore, sits an elegant modern sculpture in the shape of a ship's prow. A small amphitheatre and stage have been cleverly built into its framework, and here you can enjoy the occasional concert or outdoor theatre performance.

The only other building of note in Limón is the landmark **Radio Casino** (corner of C 4 and Av 4), home to an excellent community-service station, broadcast by and for Limonenses, with call-in chat shows, international news and good music, including local and imported reggae. As for **swimming** in town, forget it: one look at the water from the tiny spit of sand next to the *Park Hotel* is discouragement enough. Pollution, sharks, huge banana-carrying ships and sharp, exposed coral make it practically impossible to swim anywhere nearby; the nearest possibility is at **Playa Bonita**, though even that is plagued by dangerous rip tides.

Eating, drinking and entertainment

Though Limón has a surprising variety of places to eat, only one restaurant in town, *Springfield*, serves completely authentic **Caribbean and Creole cuisine**. It's best to heed the warnings and not sit outside at the restaurants in the town centre, particularly around the Mercado Central, where tourists are prime targets for often aggressive beggars. Inside the market, however, it's quite safe and you'll find a host of decent sodas serving tasty *casados*. Gringos in general and women especially should avoid most **bars**, especially those that have a large advertising placard blocking views of the interior, which are often less than salubrious. For a drink, stick to places like *Restaurante Mares* or *Brisas del Caribe*. When you tire of the town, head to relaxing **Playa Bonita** for lunch or an afternoon beer.

In town

Brisas del Caribe C 1, Av 2, in *Hotel Caribe*. Enjoy views of Parque Vargas from this clean bar-restaurant with a soothing ambiance, except when they blast the sound system. The varied menu includes Chinese fare, sandwiches, snacks and a tasty *medio casado* (half *casado*) for around $2.

Park Hotel Av 3, C 1, by the malecón. The only restaurant in town where you feel you might actually be in the Caribbean – warm breezes float in through large slatted windows that look out onto vistas of blue seas and clouds as far as the eye can see. Dine on excellent, though pricey, breakfast and standard Costa Rican fare, including *elote* (corn on the cob) and *arroz con pollo*.

Queenies Av 3, C 2. Come to this excellent hole-in-the-wall café for home-made cakes, *tamales* and delicious coffee.

Soda La Estrella C 5, Av 3/4. The best lunch in town features excellent soda staples, delicious *refrescos*, coffee, and snacks like *arreglados* (filled puff pastries), all accompanied by cordial service.

Springfield North of the end of the malecón, across from the hospital. *The* place in Limón for genuine Caribbean cuisine, starring coconut-flavoured rice-and-beans with a choice of chicken, beef or fish ($5). Try to arrive early, as the restaurant gets very full. On the weekend, a Reggae disco heats up the outdoor dance floor. Credit cards accepted.

Portete and Playa Bonita

Centro Turístico Piuta Portete. Revellers come for drinks and dancing at this vast barn-like bar

with a deafening reggae disco on weekends.

Quimbambu Playa Bonita. Dine on excellent

Shallow-bottomed private *lanchas* make the trip up the coastal canal from the docks at Moín to **Tortuguero** (3hr). It's best to arrive at the docks early (7–9am) although you may find boatmen willing to take you until 2pm. Expect to pay around $50 round-trip for a group of four to six people; if you're travelling alone or in a couple, try to get a group together at the docks. Buses for **Moín** depart from the main bus terminal at C 7, Av 1/2, but the bus has no set schedule and leaves when it's full (more or less every thirty minutes), so a taxi ($2–3) may be a better option.

Buses to San José run by Transportes Caribeños (see p.99) start running at 5am from the main bus terminal and continue hourly until 7pm. Prosersa buses (T222-0610) depart from the main bus terminal to **Siquerres** and **Guápiles**, where you can make a bus connection to the capital.

Transportes MEPE buses (C 3, Av 4, T221-0524), 100m north of the Mercado Central, serve the area **south of Limón**. Buses operate from 7am to 6pm, four times daily to Cahuita (1hr) and five times daily to Puerto Viejo (1hr 30min–2hr). The **Sixaola** bus also stops in both places. Two daily buses at 6am and 2.30pm go direct to **Manzanillo** village (2hr) in the heart of the Gandoca-Manzanillo Wildlife Refuge, via Puerto Viejo.

Taxis line up on Av 2 and around the corner from the main bus terminal: they do long-haul trips to Cahuita and Puerto Viejo ($30–40), and to the banana plantations of the Valle de Estrella ($20), where you can pick up another taxi to the **Reserva Biológica Hitoy-Cerere**. Prices are per car, so if you're in a group, renting a taxi can be far more convenient than taking the bus, and almost as cheap.

There are few day-trips worth doing from Limón. You could try to make the trip up the canal to Tortuguero and back in a day, though you'd have almost no time to see either the turtles or the village. Quite manageable, however, is a short boat trip up the **Río Matina** from Moín – and with a guide, you might spot sloths, monkeys, iguanas and caiman. Friendly, knowledgeable local guide Bernardo R. Vargas (T798-4322, F758-2683) offers a packed one-day tour that takes in a walk in the rainforest at Aviarios de Caribe, Parque Nacional Cahuita, a tour of local banana and coffee plantations and a city tour of Limón (4–5hr; $40).

– though pricey – fresh fish cooked to order at this hopping beach-bar. Live music on the weekends.

El Ranchito Portete. Peaceful, friendly poolside bar-restaurant high above the sea, with excellent food and *refrescos*.

South of Puerto Limón

Twenty kilometres south of Limon, the eight-square-kilometre private **Reserva Selva Bananito** unfolds alongside the Parque Nacional La Amistad and protects an area of mountainous, virgin rainforest. The reserve is reached via an inland road from the main coastal highway that goes through the banana town of Bananito and then along a very rough track across several rivers (you'll need a 4WD). The reserve owners offer a slew of activities from horse-riding and tree-climbing to hiking and bird-watching (toucans, orioles and kingfishers have all been spotted in the reserve); prices range from $15 to $45. A wonderfully peaceful spot to wind down is the reserve's **lodge** (T253-8118, F280-0820, Wwww.selvabananito.com; $132 per person per night including three meals). Eleven attractive, spacious cabins have large verandahs overlooking the forest and meals and drinks are served in the main ranch. Owned and run by the environmentally conscious children of a pioneering German farmer, the lodge is built from secondhand wood discarded by loggers, has solar-powered hot water (though no electricity) and donates a percentage of its profits to the Fundación Cuencas de Limón, which helps protect the local area and to develop educational programmes. If you don't have your own transport, you can call the lodge and arrange to be picked up from Bananito, reachable by bus or taxi from Limón.

Ten kilometres further south along the coast road, and one kilometre before it crosses the wide Río Estrella, the small wildlife sanctuary **Aviarios del Caribe** (8am–5pm; $5) sits on a small island in the river's delta. The sanctuary functions as an important rehabilitation and research centre for injured and orphaned sloths, and, not surprisingly, is the best place in Costa Rica to see them up close. Several walking trails traverse the grounds and there's an observation platform for birdwatching (an incredible 312 species have been sighted here – bring binoculars). You may also spot whitefaced, howler and spider monkeys. On the three-hour **kayak tour** (departure at 6am; $30) through the delta you might catch a glimpse of caiman, river otters and all kinds of birds. The sanctuary's lodge (℡750-0775, ℻750-0725, ⓦwww.ogphoto.com/aviarios; ⑤) has comfortable B&B accommodation in seven rooms with fans and hot-water bath – it's often full, so book ahead. To reach Aviarios del Caribe by bus from Limón, take the Cahuita service and ask to be dropped off at the entrance, just before the Puente Río Estrella.

Reserva Biológica Hitoy-Cerere

Sixty kilometres, and a three-hour road-trip, south of Limón is one of Costa Rica's least visited national reserves, the **RESERVA BIOLÓGICA HITOY-CERERE** (daily 8am–4pm; $6; ℡758-3996). Sandwiched between the Tanyí, Telier and Talamanca indigenous reservations, this very rugged, isolated terrain – ninety-one square kilometres of it – has no campsites or washrooms, though there is a ranger station at the entrance with a small dormitory where you can bed down for the night ($6 per person).

In the Bribrí language, *hitoy* means "woolly" (the rocks in its rivers are covered with algae, and everything else has grown a soft fuzz of moss); and *cerere* means "clear waters", of which there are many. One of the wettest reserves in all of Costa Rica, it receives a staggering 4m of **rain** per year in some areas, with no dry season at all. Its complicated biological profile reflects the changing altitudes within the park. The top canopy trees loom impressively tall – some as high as 50m – and epiphytes, bromeliads, orchids and lianas grow everywhere under the very dense cover. **Wildlife** is predictably abundant, but most of the species are nocturnal and rarely seen, although you might spot three-toed sloths, and perhaps even a brocket deer. You'll probably hear howler monkeys, and may glimpse whitefaced monkeys. Pacas and rare frogs abound, many of them shy and little-studied. More visible are the 115 species of **birds**, from large black vultures and hummingbirds to trogons and dazzling blue kingfishers.

Hitoy-Cerere's **Sendero Espavel,** a tough nine-kilometre hike, leads south from the ranger station through lowland and primary rainforest past clear streams, small waterfalls and beautiful vistas of the green Talamanca hills. Only **experienced tropical hikers** should attempt it, and bring a compass, rubber boots, rain gear and water. The trail begins at a very muddy hill; after about 1km, in the area of secondary forest, you'll notice the white-and-grey wild cashew trees (*espavel*) for which the trail is named. Follow the sign here; it leads off to the right and cuts through swathes of thick forest before leaving the reserve and entering the Talamanca reservation, which is officially off-limits. At the reserve's boundary, take the trail leading up a steep hill. This ends at the Río Moín, 4.5km from the start. All you can do now is turn back, taking care to negotiate the numerous fallen trees, tumbled rocks and boulders. Many of them were felled by the 1991 earthquake; older casualties are carpeted in primeval plants and mosses. The only possible respite from very dense jungle terrain are the small dried-up river beds that follow the streams and tributaries of the Ríos Cerere and Hitoy.

Having a car is the most convenient way to get to **Hitoy-Cerere**. Take the right fork towards Penhurst from the coastal Limón–Cahuita Road and follow the signs to the reserve. Using public transport, you'll need to take the bus from Limón to Valle de Estrella, and get off at the end of the line at a banana town called (confusingly) both **Fortuna** and **Finca Seis** (Finca Six). It's 15km from here to the reserve, most of it through banana plantation. A local 4WD taxi – ask at the plantation office – can take you there, and will return to pick you up at a mutually agreed time for $15–20. The nearest **accommodation** is at the Selva Bananito Lodge (see p.154) or Aviarios del Caribe (see p.155).

Cahuita village and the Parque Nacional Cahuita

Head down the paved Hwy-36, which runs from Limón to Sixaola on the Panamanian border, 43km southeast of Limón and you'll come across the tiny village of **CAHUITA**. Like other villages on the Talamanca coast, Cahuita has become a byword for relaxed, inexpensive Caribbean holidays, with a laid-back atmosphere and great Afro-Caribbean food, not to mention top surfing beaches further south along the coast. The local "dry" season is between March and April, and from September to October, though it's pretty wet all year round. Close to the village, the largely marine **PARQUE NACIONAL CAHUITA** was created to protect one of Costa Rica's few living coral reefs; many people come here to snorkel and take glass-bottomed boat rides.

The sheltered bay was originally filled with *cawi* trees, known in Spanish as *sangrilla* ("bloody") on account of the tree's thick red sap – Cahuita's name comes from the Miskito words *cawi* and *ta*, which means "point". Most of the inhabitants descend from Afro-Caribbean settlers of the Bocas del Toro area of Panamá and from workers brought to help build the Jungle Train. Older residents remember when fishing, small-scale farming and some quadrille-dancing formed the mainstay of local life. These days, Cahuita – along with the rest of the Talamanca coast – has become very popular with backpackers and surfers, its semi-Rasta culture offering an escape from the cultural homogeneity of Highland and Pacific Costa Rica. Yet while tourism has undoubtedly brought prosperity to the village, it has also created problems in its wake – at one point Cahuita was known for its drug scene and bouts of opportunistic theft. In recent years, though, the community has made huge and largely successful efforts to clean up the village, with extra policemen drafted in to patrol the sandy streets. Still, it's worth being cautious: lock your door and windows, never leave anything on the beach and avoid walking alone in unlit places at night. Nude or topless bathing is definitely unacceptable, as is wandering though the village in just a bathing suit.

Arrival and information

Before the Puente Río Estrella was built in the mid-1970s, a journey from Limón to Cahuita involved a train ride, a canoe ferry across the Río Estrella and a bus over a dirt road. Access has also become dramatically easier since the

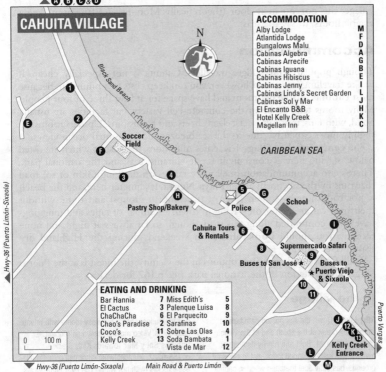

CAHUITA VILLAGE

N

ACCOMMODATION

Alby Lodge	M
Atlantida Lodge	F
Bungalows Malu	D
Cabinas Algebra	A
Cabinas Arrecife	G
Cabinas Iguana	B
Cabinas Hibiscus	E
Cabinas Jenny	I
Cabinas Linda's Secret Garden	L
Cabinas Sol y Mar	J
El Encanto B&B	H
Hotel Kelly Creek	K
Magellan Inn	C

Black Sand Beach

Soccer Field

CARIBBEAN SEA

Hwy-36 (Puerto Limón-Sixaola)

Pastry Shop/Bakery

Police

School

Cahuita Tours & Rentals

Supermercado Safari

Buses to San José ★

Buses to ★ Puerto Viejo & Sixaola

EATING AND DRINKING

Bar Hannia		7 Miss Edith's	5
El Cactus	3	Palenque Luisa	8
ChaChaCha		6 El Parquecito	9
Chao's Paradise	2	Sarafinas	10
Coco's		11 Sobre Las Olas	4
Kelly Creek	13	Soda Bambata	1
		Vista de Mar	12

0   100 m

Puerto Vargas

Kelly Creek Entrance

Hwy-36 (Puerto Limón-Sixaola)   Main Road & Puerto Limón

opening of the Guápiles Highway in 1987. Nowadays, the easiest way to get to Cahuita from San José is by **bus** on the comfortable direct Transportes MEPE service (4 daily; 4hr) which goes on to Puerto Viejo. Taking a bus from San José to Puerto Limón (3hr) and then changing for Cahuita (4 daily) is only marginally less expensive than taking the direct bus and increases travel time by at least an hour. In Cahuita, buses stop at the central crossroads opposite the *Sarafinas* bar-disco. Current timetables are posted in front of the Cahuita Tours office, 200m north along the village's main street.

If you're coming to Cahuita **from Puerto Viejo**, be sure to pick up a copy of the free *Costa Rican Caribbean Info Guide*, with local maps and a directory of accommodation and businesses in both villages. The tour companies provide the only visitor **information** in the village itself. Mr Big J's (☎755-0328), towards the Parque Nacional Cahuita puesto and beach, is particularly friendly and has a book exchange and laundry facilities. Cahuita Tours (☎755-0000) has two public phones outside the office and one inside where you can make international calls. Turística Cahuita (☎755-0017) sells the *Tico Times*. For Internet access, stop by the CyberNet café, opposite *Cabinas Safari*. There are no banks in town – the nearest are in Bribrí, 20km away, or in Limón. Your best bet for **changing money**, travellers' cheques and obtaining cash advances on credit cards is the efficient cambio (7am–4pm) at *Cabinas Safari;* the Safari Supermarket changes cash only. The small *guardia rural* (police station) is on the last beach-bound road at the north end of the village; the **correo** next door (theoretically Mon–Fri 7.30am–5pm) keeps erratic hours, to say the least.

Accommodation

Though popular with budget travellers, Cahuita is not especially cheap. If you're travelling in a group, however, you can keep costs to a minimum because most **cabinas** charge per room and have space for at least three or four people. Many rooms tend to be of the concrete-cell variety, but facilities are usually good, with fans, mosquito nets, clean sheets and bathrooms. Upstairs rooms are slightly more expensive, due to the sea breezes and occasional ocean views.

The **centre of the village** has scores of options, the best of which are listed below; staying here is convenient for restaurants, bars and the national park. There's also accommodation in all price ranges on the long (3km or so) road that runs by the sea north along **Playa Negra**. It's quieter here, and the beach is not bad, though women (even if travelling in groups) and those without their own car are better off staying in town; a number of rapes and muggings have been committed along this road, though so far always at night and none recently. You should **book ahead** on weekends during the Highland dry season (Dec–April).

You'll find several **camping** options in the vicinity; the nicest is at the Puerto Vargas ranger station in the national park (see p.162 for details).

In the village

Alby Lodge Down the signposted path behind *Hotel Kelly Creek* at the south end of the village ⓣ & ⓕ755-0031. Built and run by its Austrian owners, this well-equipped lodge, set in pleasant grounds, has individual thatched wooden cabins with porch, hammock and private bathroom. ④

Cabinas Arrecife On the seafront just north of the police station ⓣ755-0081. This relaxed, back-packer-style accommodation has cheap, simply furnished rooms (some with sea views), hammocks slung on the porch and snorkelling gear for hire. ②

Cabinas Jenny On the beach ⓣ755-0256. Beautiful rooms (especially the more expensive ones upstairs) have high wooden ceilings, sturdy bunks, mosquito nets, fans and wonderful sea views. Deck chairs and hammocks are provided, and there are good stout locks on all doors. ②

Cabinas Linda's Secret Garden Near *Alby Lodge* ⓣ755-0327. Set in a charming rock garden, this

popular budget choice has cosy rooms with private bathrooms. Video movies shown on request. ③

Cabinas Sol y Mar Towards Kelly Creek ⓣ755-0237, ⓔcabsolymar@hotmail.com. Small, basic rooms (with hot water) run by friendly locals who also manage the neighbouring soda; clean and safe. ②

El Encanto B&B Past the police station in the north of the village ⓣ & ⓕ755-0113, ⓦwww.elencantobedandbreakfast.com. Highly recommended B&B, with a gorgeous garden, three beautifully decorated doubles and a delicious breakfast included in the room rate. There's also a self-contained house that sleeps up to six. ④

Hotel Kelly Creek Beside the national park beach at Kelly Creek ⓣ755-0007, ⓔkellycr@racsa.co.cr. Four vast, wood-panelled rooms right by the park entrance, with mosquito nets and a good Spanish restaurant on site. ④

Playa Negra

Atlantida Lodge Next to the soccer field on the road to Playa Negra, about 1km from the village ⓣ755-0115, ⓕ755-0213, ⓦwww.atlantida.co.cr. This friendly spot is the best of the village's pricier options with pretty grounds, good security and the nicest pool in town, complete with Jacuzzi and poolside bar. The cool rooms are decorated in tropical yellows and pinks, with heated water, and

there's free coffee and bananas all day. Bike rental available. ④–⑤

Bungalows Malu Beyond the soccer field ⓣ755-0006. Five pretty individual thatched-roof cabinas in a large tropical garden facing the sea, with an Italian restaurant on site. ③

Cabinas Algebra 2km or so up the Playa Negra Road ⓣ & ⓕ755-0057, ⓔalansa@racsa.co.cr.

Run by a friendly Austrian couple, these funky, attractive cabinas are some distance from town, but the owners offer free pick-up from the village, as well as haircuts and laundry service. Enjoy tasty meals at the *Bananas Restaurant* on site. ❸

Cabinas Iguana 200m south of *Soda Bambata* on a small side road ☎755-0005, ⊕755-0054, ⓦwww.cabinas-iguana.com. One of the best budget spots in town, with lovely wood-panelled cabinas on stilts set back from the beach, a large screened verandah, laundry service, book exchange and a small swimming pool. The friendly owners also rent out two apartments and a three-bedroom house with kitchen. ❷

Chalet Hibiscus 2.5km north of village on the right ☎755-0021, ⊕755-0015, ⓔhibiscus@racsa.co.cr. Two luxury houses (both sleeping up to ten) and several separate chalets sit on a small point by the sea with beautiful views, good security and friendly owners. The larger house is open and breezy, with a verandah and hammock, rustic wooden decor, an unusual wood-and-rope spiral staircase and comfortable rooms. There's also a swimming pool, games room and a garden sloping down to the sea. ❹

Magellan Inn 3km up Playa Negra, on a small signposted road leading off to the left ☎ & ⊕755-0035, ⓔmagellaninn@racsa.co.cr. Comfortable, quiet hotel with beautiful gardens dotted with pre-Columbian sculptures and a small pool. The hacienda-style rooms have rattan furniture and hot water. Rates include continental breakfast, and there's also a bar and an excellent French Creole restaurant. ❺

The Village

Cahuita comprises just two puddle-dotted, gravel-and-sand streets running parallel to the sea, intersected by a few cross-streets. Though it seems like anything nailed down has been turned into some kind of small business, you'll still see a couple of private homes among the haphazard conglomeration of

---

Pirates and ghosts

According to local history, in the 1800s the coastal waters of the Caribbean crawled with pirates. Two **shipwrecks** in the bay on the north side of Punta Cahuita are believed to be pirate wrecks, one Spanish and one French. You can sometimes see the Spanish wreck on glass-bottomed boat tours to the reef (contact one of the town's tour companies on p.157) although it has been (illegally) picked over and the only thing of interest that remains are encrusted manacles – an indication of the dastardly motives of the ship's crew.

In her excellent collection of local folk history and oral testimony, *What Happen*, sociologist Paula Palmer quotes Selles Johnson, descendant of the original turtle hunters, on the pirate activity on these shores:

. . . them pirate boats was on the sea and the English gunboats was somewhere out in the ocean, square rigger, I know that. I see them come to Bocas, square rigger. They depend on breeze. So the pirate boats goes in at Puerto Vargas or at Old Harbour where calm sea, and the Englishmen can't attack them because they in Costa Rican water . . . so those two ships that wreck at Punta Cahuita, I tell you what I believes did happen. Them was hiding in Puerto Vargas and leave from there and come around the reef, and they must have stopped because in those days the British ship did have coal. You could see the smoke steaming in the air. So the pirate see it out in the sea and they comes in here to hide.

Where you find pirates you also find pirate ghosts, it seems, doomed to guard their ill-gotten treasure for eternity. Treasure from the wrecks near Old Harbour, just south of Cahuita, is said to be buried in secret caches on land. One particular spot, supposedly guarded by a fearsome headless spirit dressed in a white suit, has attracted a fair share of treasure hunters; no one has yet succeeded in exhuming the booty, however, all of them fainting, falling sick or becoming mysteriously paralysed in the attempt.

signs advertising cabinas and restaurants. Few locals drive (bicycles are popular), so most of the vehicles you see kicking up the dust belong to tourists.

Cahuita's main street runs from the national park's entrance at Kelly Creek to the northern end of the village, marked more or less by the soccer field. Beyond here it continues two or three kilometres north along Playa Negra. The small park at the central crossroads downtown, with its three small busts of Cahuita's founding fathers, is the focal point of the village, where locals wait for buses to San José and catch up on recent gossip. Opposite, *Coco's* disco and bar is *the* place to hang out at night, especially on the weekends when its breezy verandah crams with partygoers from the city and gaggles of young backpackers soaking up the atmosphere.

You can swim at either of the village's two **beaches**, although neither is fantastic: the first 400m or so of the narrow **Playa Cahuita** (also known as the White Sand Beach and as Kelly Creek), just south of the village in the national park, is particularly dangerous because of rip tides. At the northern end of the village, **Playa Negra** (or Black Sand Beach) is safe for swimming in most places but also littered with driftwood. The beach south of Punta Cahuita – sometimes called **Playa Vargas** – is better for swimming than those in the village. It's protected from raking breakers by the coral reef and also patrolled by lifeguards. It does, however, take some effort to reach it – you need to follow a trail for half a kilometre or so through thick vegetation and mangrove swamps that back the shore.

The principal daylight activity in Cahuita involves taking a boat trip out to the Parque Nacional Cahuita's coral reef to **snorkel** – try the town's three tour companies see p.157; $15–20) – or you can snorkel off the beach at Playa Vargas (see above). Though you can **surf** at Cahuita, Puerto Viejo (see p.163) has better waves – Cahuita Tours and Turística Cahuita both rent out boards. Wherever you swim, either in the park itself or on Playa Negra, don't leave possessions unattended, as even your grubby T-shirt and old shorts may be stolen. If you don't fancy snorkelling, Mr Big J's organizes **horse rides** along the beach and jungle hikes ($20–30), and all three tour agencies in Cahuita offer combined jeep trips to local villages and the beach ($40).

Eating

Cahuita has plenty of places **to eat** fresh local food, with a surprisingly cosmopolitan selection. As with accommodation, prices are higher than elsewhere in Costa Rica – dinner starts at around $5.

Cha Cha Cha Next door to Cahuita Tours. Fantastic, reasonably priced gourmet cuisine – exotic salads, grilled squid, seafood and Tex-Mex – prepared by a French-Canadian chef and served in a pretty setting with fresh flowers on the tables and fairy lights at night.

Chao's Paradise Playa Negra. Groovy little joint serving up posh Creole cooking including excellent "rondon" made with the freshest ingredients.

El Cactus Signed down a side street at the northern end of the village. Friendly, informal pizzeria also offers other Italian staples like cannelloni and lasagna.

El Parquecito Behind the village park. This excellent breakfast spot in the village features fresh juices, pancakes and French toast.

Kelly Creek Next to *Hotel Kelly Creek*. Classy restaurant with tasty Spanish fare including gazpacho, fried chorizo and paella, plus a good wine list.

Miss Edith's Northern end of village. Justifiably popular among tourists, *Miss Edith's* dishes up Cahuita's best Creole food. Dig into tasty rice-and-beans, rundown, pan bon and a wide range of vegetarian dishes. Top off the meal with home-made ice cream and herbal teas. The service is notoriously slow, especially at dinner, and no alcohol is served.

Palenque Luisa In the middle of the village opposite *Bar Hannia*. This popular restaurant offers an extensive menu of *casados* and fish and Creole dishes. Enjoy live calypso music on Saturday nights.

Sobre Las Olas At the northern end of the village, right on the beach. Atmospheric, classy hangout with first-rate seafood – the lobster is particularly delicious – and the sound of lapping waves in the background. Closed Tues.

Vista del Mar Near *Kelly Creek*. Known by locals as "El Chines", this barn-sized backpackers' favourite with a vast menu features Chinese food, inexpensive rice-and-bean combos and fish dishes.

Nightlife and entertainment

Nightlife in Cahuita revolves around listening to music over a cold beer. On weekends, the village's two discos get sweaty – cranked-up sound systems play until the wee hours and revellers dance and spill out onto the street.

Bar Hannia In the village centre. Small, friendly bar with ice-cold beer and a relaxed atmosphere.
Coco's In the centre of the village. *The* place to party in Cahuita, with a pleasant balcony over the main street, a dance floor inside and reggae tunes. If you're a single woman you'll inevitably be chatted up by the resident dreadlocked hustlers, though they're harmless enough.

Sarafinas Next to *Coco's*. The village's other disco, with a large, rather dark interior and powerful sound system, operates somewhat erratic opening times but it's nearly always heaving at the weekend and for other 'special occasions'.
Soda Bambata Playa Negra. Laid-back reggae bar directly opposite the beach.

Parque Nacional Cahuita

One of Costa Rica's smallest national parks, 10.7-square-kilometre **PARQUE NACIONAL CAHUITA** covers a wedge-shaped piece of land that encompasses the area between Punta Cahuita and the main highway and, most importantly, the **coral reef** (*arrecife*) about 500m offshore. On land, Cahuita protects the coastal rainforest, a lowland habitat of semi-mangroves and tall canopy cover that backs the gently curving white-sand beaches of

Cahuita coral

Arcing around Punta Cahuita, the *arrecife de Cahuita*, or **Cahuita reef**, comprises six square kilometres of coral, and is one of just two snorkelling reefs on this side of Costa Rica (the other is further south at the Refugio Nacional de Vida Silvestre Gandoca-Manzanillo; see p.168). **Corals** are actually tiny animals, single-celled polyps, that secrete limestone, building their houses around themselves. Over centuries the limestone binds together to form a multilayered coral reef. The coral thrives on algae, which, like land plants, transform light into energy to survive; reefs always grow close to the surface in transparent waters where they can get plenty of sun. The white-sand beaches along this part of the coast were formed by shards of excreted coral.

Unfortunately, Cahuita's once-splendid reef is dying, soured by agricultural chemicals from the rivers that run into the sea (the fault of the banana plantations), and from the silting up of these same rivers caused by topsoil run-off from logging, and the upheaval of the 1991 earthquake. The species that survive are common **brain coral**, grey and mushy like its namesake, **moose horn coral**, which is slightly red, and sallow grey **deer horn coral**. In water deeper than 2m, you might also spot fan coral wafting elegantly back and forth.

This delicate **ecosystem** shelters more than 120 species of fish and the occasional green turtle. Lobsters, particularly the fearsome-looking spiny lobster, used to be common but are also falling victim to the reef's environmental problems. Less frail, and thus more common, is the blue parrotfish, so called because of its "beak"; actually teeth soldered together. Unfortunately, the parrotfish is causing a few environmental problems of its own as it uses its powerful jaws to gnaw away at the coral's filigree-like structures and spines.

Playa Vargas to the south and Playa Cahuita to the north. Resident **birds** include ibis and kingfishers, along with whitefaced monkeys, sloths and snakes, but the only animals you're likely to see are howler monkeys and, perhaps, coati, who scavenge around the northern section of the park, where bins overflow with rubbish left by day-trippers.

Puerto Viejo (15 km) ▼

There are two **entrances** to the park, one at **Kelly Creek** at the southern end of Cahuita village (open during daylight hours; voluntary donation) and another at **Puerto Vargas** (8am–5pm; $7), 4km south of Cahuita along the Limón–Sixaola Road.

The park's one **trail** (7km), skirting the beach, offers a very easy, level walk, with a path so wide it feels like a road, covered with leaves and other brush, and a few fallen trees and logs. Stick to the trail, as snakes abound here. The Río Perzoso, about 2km from the northern entrance, or 5km from the Puerto Vargas trailhead, is not always fordable, unless you like wading through chest-high water when you can't actually see how deep it is. Similarly, at high tide the beach is impassable in places: ask the ranger at the Puerto Vargas entrance about the tide schedules. Walking this trail can be unpleasantly humid and buggy: best to go in the morning. It's also very likely to rain and, despite the dense cover of tall trees, you'll still get wet.

If you want to go **snorkelling** on your own, you have to enter the park at the Puerto Vargas entrance and swim the 200 to 500m out to the reef from Playa Vargas. Note the signs indicating treacherous currents, wear shoes (you will have to walk over exposed coral) and watch out for prickly black sea urchins.

You'll find good **camping** facilities ($2 per day) at the Puerto Vargas entrance, complete with barbecue grill, pit toilets and showers, but you'll need to bring your own drinking water, insect repellent and a torch. Be careful, too, not to pitch your tent too close to the high-tide line; check with the rangers. Theft is also a problem: don't leave anything unattended and ask the rangers for advice – they may be able to look after your belongings.

Moving on from Cahuita

Nine daily buses head from Cahuita to **Limón**, where you can connect for **San José**. If you're in a hurry to reach the capital, it's faster and easier to take the direct non-stop service (4 daily; 4hr) run by Transportes MEPE. For **Puerto Viejo** (40 min) the local bus leaves Cahuita eight times daily (first bus at 6am, last at 7pm), continuing on from Puerto Viejo to **Bribrí** and then **Sixaola**.

Puerto Viejo de Talamanca and around

The twelve-kilometre coastal stretch between the languorous hamlet of **PUERTO VIEJO DE TALAMANCA**, 18km southeast of Cahuita, and Manzanillo village is among the loveliest in Costa Rica. Though not great for swimming, the **beaches** – Playa Chiquita, Punta Uva and Manzanillo – are the most picturesque on the Caribbean coast. You'll also find plenty of accommodation – plus a lively social scene.

It's **surfing** that really pulls in the crowds; the stretch south of *Stanford's* restaurant at the southern end of Puerto Viejo offers some of the most challenging waves in the country and certainly the best on the Caribbean coast. Puerto Viejo's famous twenty-foot wave "**La Salsa Brava**" crashes ashore between December and March and from June to July; September and October, when La Salsa Brava disappears, are the quietest months of the year.

Arrival

All buses **from San José** to Puerto Viejo (4 daily; 4hr 30min) stop first in **Limón** and **Cahuita** and then continue to **Sixaola**; the first bus leaves San José at 6am and the last at 3.30pm. The last bus back to San José from Puerto Viejo departs at 4pm. Taking a bus from San José to Limón (25 daily) and changing there is only slightly less expensive and adds on at least an hour to travel time. Three daily buses (at 7.15am, 3.45pm & 7.15pm) go from here

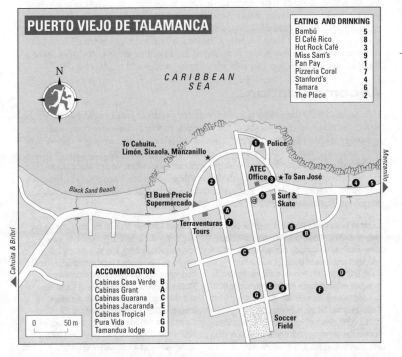

PUERTO VIEJO DE TALAMANCA

N

CARIBBEAN SEA

EATING AND DRINKING	
Bambú	5
El Café Rico	8
Hot Rock Café	3
Miss Sam's	9
Pan Pay	1
Pizzeria Coral	7
Stanford's	4
Tamara	6
The Place	2

To Cahuita, Limón, Sixaola, Manzanillo

Police

ATEC Office ★ To San José

Manzanillo

Black Sand Beach

El Buen Precio Supermercado

Surf & Skate

Terraventuras Tours

Cahuita & Bribri

ACCOMMODATION	
Cabinas Casa Verde	B
Cabinas Grant	A
Cabinas Guarana	C
Cabinas Jacaranda	E
Cabinas Tropical	F
Pura Vida	G
Tamandua lodge	D

0   50 m

Soccer Field

along the coast to **Manzanillo** (45min). If you're driving, be aware that the coast road south of Puerto Viejo is unpaved and very bumpy.

Information

Puerto Viejo has no **tourist information** office but the village's tour operators can give you advice, maps and so on. The most helpful operator is Puerto Viejo Tours (Tues–Sun 8am–noon & 2–6pm; ⊤ & ⊕750-0411, ⊜puertoviejotours@yahoo .com), opposite the bus stop on the seafront; they offer a wide range of tours, including rafting, horse-riding, snorkelling and bird-watching. They'll also change dollars and travellers' cheques, as will the nearby Comisaratio store. Terraventuras Tours (⊤750-0426, ⊜terraventuras@hotmail.com), on the main street, rents out snorkelling equipment at very reasonable rates, and the surf shop **Surf & Skate** rents out surf and boogie boards and can organize surfing lessons. If you're interested in ecology, the proprietor of *Cabinas Tropical,* author and biologist Rolf Blancke (⊤750-0283, ⊜rblancke@racsa.co.cr), takes people out on excellent trips into the Gandoca Rainforest ($45 for a twelve-hour trip).

The **correo** (Mon–Fri 7.30am–6pm, Sat 7.30am–noon) sits in the small commercial centre two blocks back from the seafront. You can get **petrol** at the east end of the village, across the road from the disco *Bambú.* The **ATEC** office on the main road (daily 8am–9pm; ⊤ & ⊕750-0191, ⊛www .greencoast.com/atec) has Internet access, telephones for international calls and a fax; there's also an Internet café, Video Mundo, next door.

The ATEC office arranges exemplary tours of the local Bribrí communities (see p.167) plus **Afro-Caribbean tours** with a historical and educational bent. Locals whose families have been in the area since the eighteenth century take you on walks through the villages and the jungle, telling you about old farming techniques and traditional plant remedies. Some tours include time in the Refugio Nacional de Vida Silvestre Gandoca-Manzanillo (see p.168). The ATEC office can also recommend local diving and snorkelling experts and they have a small library of books on the area, plus nature guides and guidebooks.

Accommodation

Due to its rapidly increasing popularity, places to stay in and around Puerto Viejo have mushroomed and you shouldn't have any problem finding accommodation, although it's still best to reserve a room in advance during high season and surfing-season weekends (Dec–March, June & July). The vast majority of places in the **village** are simple cabinas, some without hot water, while more upmarket establishments line the **coast** south of the village. You can **camp** on the beaches, but rock-bottom budget travellers usually forsake their tents and stay at the excellent *Tamandua Lodge.*

Cabinas Casa Verde One block south of the main drag ⊤ & ⊕750-0047, ⊛www.cabinascasaverde .com. Fourteen comfortable cabinas, decorated with shell mobiles and pieces of washed-up coral, with sparkling clean showers, ceiling fans, mosquito nets and space to sling hammocks. Bike hire and parking available. ❸–❹

Cabinas Grant On the main road ⊤750-0292. Spotless, locally run hotel with basic but serviceable rooms; those on the first floor have balconies and cost slightly more. ❷–❸

Cabinas Guarana South of the main drag on the way to the soccer field ⊤750-0244, ⊛www .cabinasguarana.com). Run by a friendly Italian couple, this lovely small hotel has attractive rooms, tiled bathrooms, hammocks and a communal kitchen. Check out the treehouse in the garden and climb up for great views over the village. Internet access and parking available. ❹

Cabinas Jacaranda Just north of the soccer field ⊤750-0069. Basic but very clean budget option, with cabinas decorated in lively

Guatemalan fabrics and set amid a lush tropical garden. ❷–❸

Cabinas Tropical On the eastern edge of the village ☎ & ⓕ 750-0283, ⓦ www.cabinastropical .com. Small, quiet and scrupulously clean hotel with five large, comfortable rooms, and pet birds in the garden. ❸

Pura Vida Near the soccer field ☎ 750-0002, ⓕ 750-0296. This popular budget hotel has ten rooms (with both private and shared baths), ceiling

fans, mosquito nets, a pleasant verandah and garden. It tends to fill quickly. ❸

Tamandua Lodge Two blocks back from the main street ☎ 750-0479, ⓔ tamandualodge@racsa.co.cr. Aimed squarely at backpackers, this new budget lodge offers three private rooms ($20), a mixed dorm ($15) and, by far the cheapest option, camping space in the garden ($3) as well as Internet access and parking. ❷

The village

The **village** itself lies between the thick forested hills of the Talamanca Mountains and the sea, where locals bathe and kids frolic with surfboards in the waves. It's a dusty little place in daylight hours but reasonably well cared for, with bright hand-painted signs pointing the way to cabinas, bars and restaurants. The main drag through the centre, potholed and rough, is crisscrossed by a few dirt streets and an offshoot road that follows the shore. As in Cahuita, many Europeans have been drawn to Puerto Viejo, and have set up their own businesses; you'll find lots of places offering health foods and New Age remedies. Also similar to Cahuita, most locals are of Afro-Caribbean descent. In recent years Puerto Viejo has become a byword for backpacker and surf-party culture, with a surprisingly vibrant nightlife and an attendant drugs scene, though this is fairly low-key and shouldn't adversely affect your stay. Nevertheless, make sure your room is well secured at night and avoid wandering alone through the quiet fringes of the village in the small hours. The best way to negotiate Puerto Viejo's dirt-track streets is by bicycle. You'll find several bike rental shops in town and many of the local hotels and cabinas also rent out bikes for about $3–4 a day.

Theoretically, you could walk along the beach from Cahuita to Puerto Viejo (a good 15km, and a whole day's walk), but this is not wise. Tides cut you off from time to time, leaving you the grim option of crashing through the jungle that backs the beach; there's also a creek to be forded, and robberies have been reported.

Signs of **indigenous culture** are more evident here than in Cahuita; the **KéköLdi** Reserve, inhabited by about two hundred Bribrí and Cabécar peoples, skirts the southern end of Puerto Viejo, and ATEC (see p.167) has a strong presence in the town.

Eating, drinking and nightlife

Puerto Viejo offers a surprisingly cosmopolitan range of **places to eat**, and ATEC can put you in touch with village women who cook typical regional meals on request. Although relatively quiet during the day, Puerto Viejo begins thumping at **night**. If you're looking for a quiet drink, try the spacious verandah in front of the Comisaratio store – buy your beer from the shop and sip it while watching the sun slide prettily into the sea.

Bambú On the eastern edge of town. This beachfront reggae disco with good sunset views from its terrace gets absolutely packed on Mondays and Fridays; great fun.

El Café Rico Opposite *Cabinas Casa Verde*. Dutch-run café with the best coffee in town, tasty

sandwiches, crepes and breakfast. Nice rooms (❸), bike hire and laundry service also available.

Hot Rock Café On the junction of the main street and the road leading to the police station. One of the town's more openly touristy places, this lively café-bar shows a movie

(7pm nightly), usually followed by live Latin or reggae music.

Miss Sam's Three blocks back from the seafront. Tuck into wonderful Caribbean home cooking including rice and beans and "rondon" – at very reasonable prices.

Pan Pay On the seafront near the police station. This popular breakfast spot and bakery offers croissants, cakes and delicious Spanish tortilla.

Pizzeria Coral Just south of the main street, near the correo. Succulent, if pricey, pizzas ($4) served on a lively outdoor terrace.

Stanford's Just east of the main street. Very popular on weekends, this restaurant-bar serves a small range of snacks and has a large outdoor disco where you can dance to the sounds of reggae and waves crashing on the shore.

Tamara On the main street opposite the ATEC office. Dine on a wide range of Caribbean and international fare, including pizza and pasta, and fresh seafood served up in a pleasant alfresco dining area.

The Place One block back from the bus stop. This attractive café specializes in vegetarian dishes, seafood and tasty coconut-flavoured curries, particularly popular with tourists sick to death of rice, beans and pizza.

South from Puerto Viejo to Manzanillo

The fifteen-kilometre stretch of coast south of Puerto Viejo features the most appealing beaches on the entire Caribbean coast. All the trappings of a pristine tropical paradise are here, with palm trees leaning over calm beaches, purples, mauves, oranges and reds fading into the sea at sunset and a milky twilight mist wafting in from the Talamancas. You'll find excellent accommodation along the Puerto Viejo–Manzanillo Road, but public transport is infrequent, so it's much easier with a car, especially if you want to explore the **Refugio Nacional de Vida Silvestre Gandoca-Manzanillo**, which borders the area. Note that you'll need a 4WD to negotiate the numerous potholes. The road from Puerto Viejo to Manzanillo was only built in 1984 – electricity came five years later – and despite the mini-invasion of hotels and cabinas, local life remains much the same as ever, with subsistence householders fishing for still-abundant lobster and supplementing their income with tourism-oriented activities. There are four hamlets on this stretch of coast. The first two, heading south from Puerto Viejo, are **Playa Cocles** (2km south) and **Playa Chiquita** (4km south) which, owing to the amount of recent development, now more or less blend into one another. Playa Cocles offers perhaps the best surfing in the entire region and is patrolled by lifeguards while Playa Chiquita has a nice collection of bars and cafés. **Punta Uva**, 5km further on, has a pristine white-sand beach set in a protected cove making it particularly good for swimming. **Manzanillo**, another 2km further on, almost at the end of the coastal road, has a large shelf of coral reef just offshore that teems with marine life and offers some of the best snorkelling in Costa Rica. The village itself is small and charming, with laid-back locals and a couple of great places to eat and hang out.

Practicalities

Incredibly, you'll find over twenty-five places to stay on the road from Puerto Viejo to Manzanillo – mostly mid-range options, plus a couple of elegant boutique hotels and several smart self-catering places. One of the best is the *Cariblue* (Playa Cocles, ☎ & ⓕ750-0057, ⓦwww.cariblue.com; ❻) which has luxurious individual cabinas, all with balconies and hammocks, set amid a well-maintained jungle setting with a top-notch Italian restaurant, a swimming pool (with pool bar) and souvenir shop. Run by an effusive New Yorker, the adjacent *La Costa de Papito* (Playa Cocles ☎ & ⓕ750-0080, ⓦwww.greencoast.com/papito .htm; ❹) offers much of the same, albeit of a slightly less luxurious standard. Its pretty gardens are home to ten bungalows, all with bamboo beds and balconies. Bike rental is available. The *Miraflores* (Playa Chiquita ☎750-0038, ⓕ272-2220,

About two hundred Bribrí and Cabécar peoples live in the **KéköLdi Indigenous Reserve**, which begins just south of Puerto Viejo and extends inland into the Talamanca Mountains. The reserve was established in 1976 to protect the indigenous culture and ecological resources of the area, but the communities and land remain under constant threat from logging, squatters, tourism and banana plantations. The worst problems arise from lax government checks on construction in the area which, inhabitants claim, has led to several hotels being built illegally on their land. The main obstacle between the indigenous peoples and their neighbours has been, historically, their irreconcilable views of land. The Bribrí and Cabécar see the forest as an interrelated system of cohabitants all created by and belonging to Sibö, their god of creation, while the typical *campesino* view is that of a pioneer – the forest is an obstacle to cultivation (and therefore civilization), to be tamed, conquered and effectively destroyed.

The best way to visit the reserve is on one of the **tours** ($20 for a half day, $33 for a full day with meal) organized by the Asociación Talamanqueña de Ecoturismo y Conservación, or ATEC (T & F750-0191, Wwww.greencoast.com/atec), a grass-roots organization set up by members of the local community – Afro-Caribbeans, Bribrí indigenous peoples and Spanish-descended inhabitants. If you're spending even just a couple of days in the Talamanca region, an ATEC-sponsored trip is a must; to reserve a tour, go to their Puerto Viejo office on the main road at least one day in advance. The organization's main goal is to give local people a chance to demonstrate their pride in and knowledge of their home territory, and to teach them how to make a living off tourism without selling their land or entering into more exploitative business arrangements. In this spirit, ATEC has trained about fifteen local people as guides, who get about ninety percent of the individual tour price. Whereas many of the hotel-organized excursions use cars, ATEC promotes horseback and hiking tours. They also visit places on a rotating roster, so that local hamlets don't deteriorate from foreigners traipsing through daily.

The tour does not take you, as you might expect, to villages where indigenous peoples live in "primitive" conditions. The Bribrí speak Spanish (as well as Bribrí) and wear Western clothes. But underneath this layer of assimilation lie the vital remains of their culture and traditional way of life. Although the area has seen some strife between the reserve dwellers, their neighbours, and foreign hotel developments, these altercations remain largely on the level of policy. As a visitor, you won't see any overt ill-feeling between the groups. Treks usually last about four hours, traversing dense rainforest and the Talamanca Mountains. They start near the road to Puerto Viejo – where **Bribrí crafts**, including woven baskets and coconut shell carvings, are on sale – and pass cleared areas, cocoa plantings and small homesteads, and then into secondary, and finally primary, cover. In this ancient forest the guide may take you along the same trails that have been used for centuries by Bribrís on their trips from their mountain homes down to the sea, pointing out the traditional medicinal plants that cure everything from malaria to skin irritations. A tour may also involve discussions about the permanent reforestation programme or a visit to the iguana breeding farm established by the local community.

Wwww.mirafloreslodge.com; ❹), opposite the beach, is a rustic, comfortable lodge set on an old cacao plantation. Festooned with tropical flowers, the lovely decor includes Bribrí paintings and carvings. The upstairs rooms are brighter – with mosquito nets, mirrors and high bamboo ceilings – and there's an outside breakfast area. The owner has excellent contacts with the local Bribrí community and runs imaginative tours, including trips to Panamá in a motorized dugout. Actually within the KéköLdi Indigenous Reserve, the *Villas del Caribe*

(Playa Chiquita ☎750-0202, ℱ750-0203, ⓦwww.villasdelcaribe.com; ⑥) offers comfortable two-storey self-catering accommodation, with a terrace, hot water, fans and organic garbage disposal. The grounds are right on the beach, with great sunset views. Several kilometers further south, the *Almonds and Corals* luxury tent lodge (☎222-2024, ℱ272-2220, ⓦwww.almondsandcorals.com; ⑥) lies amid a lush rainforest setting in the Gandoca-Manzanillo Refuge. Each of the stilt-set tents has comfortable furniture and an adjoining bathroom. There's also a restaurant, Jacuzzis and a laundry service, and bike rental and tours are available.

Eating and drinking

There's plenty of choice. Just a couple of kilometres south of Puerto Viejo in Playa Cocles, the *Big Breakfast* café-bar offers a combined Caribbean-American menu (including free coffee) as well as Internet access. Happy hour is from 5pm–7pm. Just beyond the *Miraflores* lodge, 5km south of Puerto Viejo, is **Elena's**, a long-established soda-cum-restaurant serving succulent local fish and chicken dishes, as well as inexpensive lunchtime specials and snacks. The bar closes at 2am. About 8km south of Puerto Viejo, you'll find *Selvin's*, a perennially popular restaurant-bar where locally caught fish is served with coconut-flavoured rice-and-beans. In Manzanillo, look out for *Maxis*, a large upstairs restaurant with great views over the beach and renowned seafood, notably lobster. It gets packed on the weekends. Cabinas are also available for rent here.

Refugio Nacional de Vida Silvestre Gandoca-Manzanillo

Covering over fifty square kilometres of land and a similar area of sea, the little-visited but fascinating **REFUGIO NACIONAL DE VIDA SILVESTRE GANDOCA-MANZANILLO** sits in the southeast corner of the country. The refuge, which includes the small hamlets of Gandoca and Manzanillo, borders Río Sixaola and the frontier with Panamá. It was established to protect some of Costa Rica's last few **coral reefs**, of which **Punta Uva** is the most accessible and offers great snorkelling. There's also a protected **turtle-nesting beach** south of the village of Manzanillo, along with tracts of mangrove forests and the last *orey* **swamp** in the country. More than 358 **bird** species have been identified, many of them rare – ten years ago there were sightings of the endangered harpy eagle, believed to be extinct in the rest of the country due to deforestation. Other species found in the refuge include the *manatí*, tapir and American crocodile, who hang out along the river estuary, though you're unlikely to see them.

If you're interested in exploring the refuge, all Puerto Viejo's tour companies (see p.164) offer trips. One of the best is the excellent Aquamor Adventures (☎759-0612, ✉aquamor@racsa.co.cr) in Manzanillo. Although principally a scuba-diving outfit, the friendly Aquamor also offers a wide range of marine activities including dolphin tours and they can put you in touch with knowledgeable local guides who lead hikes through the refuge. **Camping** is permitted within the refuge, but is really only feasible on the beach, due to the mosquitoes, snakes and other biting creatures inland.

Gandoca-Manzanillo has one fairly demanding but rewarding **trail** (5.5km each way), that passes primary and secondary forest as well as some pretty, secluded beaches on its way from Manzanillo to **Monkey Point** (Punta Mona). It can get extremely hot, and mosquitoes are usually out in force, so carry plenty of water, sunscreen and repellent. Beginning at the northeast end of Manzanillo village, the trail proceeds along the beach for 1km. After crossing a small creek and entering a grove of coconut trees, it becomes poorly marked and easy to lose, but should be just about visible as it climbs up a small bluff. The trail then drops to lower ground and skirts a few small shark-infested beaches before heading inland. Some of these up-and-down sections are quite steep, and if it has been raining (as it invariably has) then mud and mosquitoes can make the trip unpleasant. However, the trail does offer great opportunities for spotting birds and wildlife; you're almost guaranteed a sight of chestnut-mandibled and keel-billed **toucans**. The tiny flashes of colour darting about on the ground in front of you are **poison dart frogs**; watch where you're stepping, and avoid touching them. Punta Mona, at the end of the trail, is flanked by a shady beach, from where you can see across to Panamá, only about 8km to the south. From here you return to Manzanillo the same way.

Four kilometres from Manzanillo down a rough track, **Gandoca** provides access to the estuary of the Río Gandoca, a bird-spotters' delight with boat-trips organized from the village. You can get here by walking from Manzanillo, or there's access from the Sixaola Road – if you have a 4WD – via the banana fincas of Daytonia, Virginia and Finca 96.

Bribrí and the Panamanian border

From Puerto Viejo, the paved road (Hwy-36) continues inland to **BRIBRÍ**, about 10km southwest, arching over the Talamancan foothills to reveal the green valleys stretching ahead to Panamá. This is banana country, with little to see even in Bribrí itself, which is largely devoted to administering the affairs of indigenous reserves in the Talamanca Mountains. If you are stopping on your way into Panamá, Bribrí has a couple of basic **places to stay** including *Cabinas El Mango* (no telephone; ❶) and Cruz Roja (❶759-0612; ❷), a few simple **restaurants** and a **bank**, the Banco Nacional, which changes money and travellers' cheques.

There are several **indigenous reserves** near Bribrí. You can't visit them without special permission both from the communities themselves and from the government, but if you're interested, anthropologist Fernando Cortés (❶766-6800) leads small groups through the Talamanca Mountains on officially sanctioned visits to Cabécar communities. Trips (lasting around a week) begin near Cartago, from where you walk into the Talamanca region, and cost about $100 per person.

From Bribrí, a dusty gravel road winds for 34km through solid banana fincas to **Sixaola**. Locals cross the border here to do their shopping in Panamá, where most things are less expensive. The majority of foreigners who cross into Panamá do so simply because their tourist visa for Costa Rica has expired and they have to leave the country for 72 hours, though the pristine Panamanian island of **Bocas del Toro** just over the border offers an inviting prospect even for those who don't need an extension.

Refugio Nacional de Fauna Silvestre Barra del Colorado

Created to preserve the area's abundant fauna, the **REFUGIO NACIONAL DE FAUNA SILVESTRE BARRA DEL COLORADO** lies at the

3

The border and on into Panamá

Sixaola–Guabito is a small crossing that doesn't see much foreign traffic, and for the most part formalities are simple, but you should still arrive as early in the morning as possible. There's nowhere decent to stay before you get to Bocas del Toro – and you should leave time to look for a hotel once there. Also, bus connections in Panamá can be tricky.

The Sixaola–Guabito border is open daily from 8am to 5pm Panamá time (one hour ahead of Costa Rica). Tourists leaving Costa Rica need to buy a **Red Cross exit stamp** (about $2 from the pharmacy in Sixaola); citizens of some nationalities may require a **tourist card** to enter Panamá (valid for 30 days); the Panamanian Consulate in San José issues them, as does the San José office of Copa, the Panamanian airline (see p.97). Immigration requirements often change; check with the Panamanian Consulate (see p.97).

There's nowhere to **stay** in Guabito, the tiny hamlet on the Panamanian side of Río Sixaola, so your best option is to catch the bus (7am–5pm; every 30min) to the banana town of Changuinola, further into Panamá, or arrange a taxi (ask at the border post), which makes the thirty-minute trip for about $15. The bus continues on to Almirante – though you may need to change at Changuinola – from where you can get a water taxi to **Bocas del Toro**, the main settlement in a small archipelago of little-inhabited islands, with beautifully clear water, great for snorkelling and swimming. **Hotels** include the friendly Hotel Angela (℡757-9813, @www.hotelangela.com; ❹), right on the waterfront, and the rather swanky Swan's Cay (℡757-9090, @www.swanscayhotel.com; ❻).

Connections with the **rest of Panamá** from this northeast corner are tenuous. From Almirante, you'll need to take the ferry fifty kilometres southeast to the banana town of Chiriquí Grande, from where there are road connections to the rest of the country, and a bus service across the Cordillera Central to Chiriquí on the Interamericana, where you can get bus connections to Panamá City and back to San José.

---

northern end of Costa Rica's Caribbean coast, 99km northeast of San José near the border with Nicaragua. This ninety-square-kilometre, sparsely populated (by humans, at least) tract of land is crossed by the Río Colorado, which debouches into the Caribbean next to the village of Barra del Colorado. The grand Río San Juan marks the park's northern boundary, which is also the border with Nicaragua. The river continues north of the border all the way to the Lago de Nicaragua and almost all traffic in this area is by water.

The small, quiet village of **Barra del Colorado**, the area's only settlement of any size, is inhabited by a mixed population of Afro-Caribbeans, Miskitos, Costa Ricans and a significant number of Nicaraguans, many of whom spilled over the border during the Civil War. The village is divided into two halves: Barra Sur and the larger Barra Norte, which stand opposite each other across the mouth of the Río Colorado. Tropical hardwoods are still under siege from illegal logging around here – you may see giant tree trunks being towed along the river and into the Caribbean, from where they are taken down to Limón. There are no public services in town (no correo, police station, Internet café or hospital) except for a couple of public phones outside the souvenir shop next to the airport and near the Los Almendros bar.

Very few people come to Barra on a whim. As far as tourism goes, **sportsfishing** is its *raison d'être*, and numerous lodges offer packages and transportation from San José. Large schools of tarpon and snook, two big-game fish prized for their fighting spirit, ply these waters, as does the garfish, a primeval throwback that looks something like a cross between a fish and a crocodile. The sports-fishing season runs from January to May, and September to October.

Because of the impenetrability of the cover, activities for non-fishing tourists are limited to bird- or crocodile-spotting from a boat in one of the many waterways and lagoons. The usual sloths and monkeys are in residence, and you'll certainly hear the wild hoot of howler monkeys shrieking through the still air. If you are really lucky, and keep your eyes peeled, you might catch sight of a *manatí* (manatee, or sea cow) going by underneath. These large, benevolent seal-like creatures are on the brink of becoming an endangered species. This is **shark** territory so you shouldn't swim here – even though you may see locals taking that risk.

It is extremely **hot** and painfully **humid** around Barra. Wear a hat and sunscreen and, if possible, stay under shade during the hottest part of the day. It rains throughout the year, though February, March and April are the driest months.

Getting to Barra

In terms of the time it takes you to get there, Barra is one of the most **inaccessible** places in the country. Most people arrive either by **lancha** from Tortuguero (1hr) or Puerto Lindo (45min). For the latter you'll need to catch the 2pm bus from Cariari (2hr) which will drop you at the small dock in Puerto Lindo where a *lancha* will be waiting to pick up passengers for Barra. A somewhat irregular *lancha* service also departs from Puerto Viejo de Sarapiquí, although it only operates when there are enough people to make the journey. Ask around the public dock or at the *Hotel El Bambú* to find out when the next one is leaving. *Lanchas* arrive in Barra Sur, or, if you ask, will take you directly to your accommodation. The **flight** from San José to Barra (landing at Barra

The Río San Juan and the Nicaraguan border

Heading to or from Barra from the Sarapiquí area in the Zona Norte entails a trip along the Río Sarapiquí to the mighty **Río San Juan**. Flowing from Lago de Nicaragua to the Caribbean, the San Juan marks most of Costa Rica's border with Nicaragua, and the entire northern edge of the Barra del Colorado Wildlife Refuge. Though it's theoretically in Nicaraguan territory (the actual border is the bank on the Costa Rican side, not the midpoint of the river), Costa Ricans have the right to travel on the river. There isn't however, an official entry point between the two countries so it's technically illegal to cross into either country along this stretch. For more details on crossing into Nicaragua see p.199.

One bizarre phenomenon local to this area is the migration of **bull sharks** from the saltwater Caribbean up the Río San Juan to the freshwater Lago de Nicaragua. They are unique in the world in making the transition, apparently without trauma, from being saltwater to freshwater sharks.

You'll notice much evidence of **logging** in the area, especially at the point where the Sarapiquí flows into the Río San Juan – the lumber industry has long had carte blanche in this area, due to the non-enforcement of existing anti-logging laws. The **Nicaraguan side** of the Río San Juan, part of the country's huge Indio Maíz Reserve, looks altogether wilder than its southern neighbour, with thick primary rainforest creeping right to the edge of the bank. Partly because of logging, and the residual destruction of its banks, the Río San Juan is silting up, and even shallow-bottomed *lanchas* get stuck in this once consistently deep river. It's a far cry from the 1600s and 1700s, when pirate ships used to sail all the way along the Río San Juan to Lago de Nicaragua, from where they could wreak havoc on the Spanish Crown's ports and shipping.

Refugio Nacional Barra del Colorado

Sur) affords stupendous views of volcanos, unfettered lowland tropical forest and the coast. Both Sansa and NatureAir operate daily flights from San José at, respectively, 6am and 6.15am.

Accommodation

Because of Barra's inaccessibility and its emphasis on fishing, hardly anyone comes here for just one night. Most lodges are devoted exclusively to **fishing packages**, although you could, theoretically, call in advance and arrange to stay as an independent, non-fishing guest. The lodges can provide details on their individual packages; generally they comprise meals, accommodation, boat, guide and tackle, and some may offer boat lunches, drinks and other extras. Even *Samay Laguna*, one of the area's few lodges that doesn't cater to sportsfishers, still brings most of its guests on packages from San José. The only place geared up at all for **independent travellers** is *Tarponland*, which has a few cabinas. While all of the accommodation in this area is comfortable, some tends toward the positively rustic, and you should certainly not expect frills like air conditioning.

Casamar Across the river from Barra del Colorado ☎0800/543-0282, ℱ0800/367-2299, ⍈www .casamarlodge.com. Luxurious, elegant cabins set in lovely gardens with hiking trails through jungle to the beach. Fishing packages only, at around $2675 for seven nights.

Río Colorado Fishing Lodge Barra Sur ☎232-4063, ℱ231-5987, ⍈www .riocoloradolodge.com. Built on walkways over the river, this well-known lodge (the oldest in town) has lots of character. Comfortable wooden rooms are homely and come with a/c, cable TV and bathrooms. Enjoy good food and pretty Barra Norte views in the dining room, where local musicians often perform in the evenings. Tours of the rainforest and Tortuguero are also offered and a tame tapir wanders the grounds. Packages from $1500 for six nights. ❻

Samay Laguna Lodge 15min by *lancha* south of Barra Sur ☎390-9062, ℱ384-7047, ⍈www .samay.com. A real away-from-it-all experience, this lodge sits on a deserted stretch of beach (take plenty of mosquito repellent) between Barra and Tortuguero and offers simple rooms

with hot-water private bathrooms plus boat tours, jungle hikes, horse rides on the beach and tours to Tortuguero. The lodge has several packages with boat or plane transfers, the most popular being a round-trip from San José up the Río Sarapiquí and through southern Nicaragua along the Río San Juan (3 days; $278). Prices include all meals. ❽

Silver King Lodge ☎381-1403, ℱ293-7916, ⍈www.silverkinglodge.com. Efficient, well-equipped fishing lodge, with big rooms, a bar, restaurant, swimming pool, Jacuzzi and TV with US channels. Daily rate including fishing $550; without fishing $130 (in the UK, book with Leslies of Luton, ⍈www.leslies-luton.co.uk). ❽

Tarponland Bar and Restaurant Next to the airstrip in Barra Sur ☎710-2141, ℱ710-6592. Large old lodge, moderately priced, with simple screened rooms with fans and private or shared baths – there are several more basic, budget cabinas attached. It's also one of the few places in town where you can get a reasonably priced meal and a cold drink. Fishing from $140 per day, rooms from $20. ❷

Parque Nacional Tortuguero

Despite its isolation – 254km from San José by road and water – **PARQUE NACIONAL TORTUGUERO** (☎710-2929; $7) is among the most visited national parks in Costa Rica. *Tortuguero* means turtle-catcher in Spanish, and turtle-catchers have long flourished in this area, one of the most important nesting sites in the world for the **green sea turtle**, one of only eight species of marine turtle. Along with the hawksbill turtle, the green sea turtle lays its eggs here between July and October.

First established as a protective zone in the 1960s, Tortuguero officially became a national park in 1975. It encompasses 190 square kilometres of protected land, including not only the beach on which turtles nest, but also the surrounding impenetrable tropical rainforest, coastal mangrove swamps and lagoons, and canals and waterways. Except for a short dry season during February and March the park is very wet, receiving over 6000mm of rain a year. This soggy environment hosts a wide abundance of species – fifty kinds of **fish**, numerous **birds**, including the endangered green parrot and the vulture, and about 160 **mammals**, some under the threat of extinction. Due to the waterborne nature of most transport and the impenetrability of the ground cover, it's difficult to spot them, but howler, whitefaced and spider monkeys lurk behind the undergrowth. The park is also home to the fishing bulldog bat, which fishes by sonar, and a variety of large rodents, including the window rat, whose internal organs you can see through its transparent skin. Jaguars used to thrive here, but are slowly being driven out by the encroaching banana plantations at the western end of the park; you may also spot the West Indian manatee, or sea cow, swimming underwater. It's the **turtles**, however, that draw all the visitors. The sight of the gentle beasts tumbling ashore and shimmying their way up the beach to deposit their heavy load before limping back, spent, into the dark phosphorescent waves can't fail to move.

As elsewhere in Costa Rica, logging, economic opportunism and fruit plantations have affected the parkland. Sometimes advertised by package tour brochures as a "Jungle Cruise" along "Central America's Amazon", the journey to Tortuguero is indeed Amazonian, taking you past tracts of **deforestation** and lands cleared for cattle – all outside the park's official boundaries but, together with banana plantations, disturbingly close to its western fringes.

The most popular way to see Tortuguero is on one of literally hundreds of **tour packages**, many of which are two-night, three-day affairs that use the expensive lodges across the canal from the village. Accommodation, meals and transport (which otherwise can be a bit tricky) are taken care of, and guides point out wildlife along the river and canal. The main difference between tours comes in the standard of accommodation; check the reviews of the lodges on p.177 for more details.

With a little planning, you can also get to Tortuguero **independently** and stay in cabinas in the village. Basing yourself in the village allows you to explore the beach at leisure – though you can't swim – and puts you within easy reach of restaurants and bars.

AROUND TORTUGUERO

Barra del Colorado

Cerro Tortuguero (119 m)

CARIBBEAN SEA

Casa Verde Research Station

Airstrip

Caño Chiquero

Park Entrance

Tortuguero

Tortuguero Canal

CARIBBEAN SEA

Agua Fria Puesto

PARQUE NACIONAL TORTUGUERO

N

ACCOMMODATION
Jungle Lodge	3
Laguna Lodge	5
El Manatí	2
Mawamba Lodge	4
Pachira Lodge	6
Tortuga Lodge	1

0   3 km

Jalova Puesto

Parismina, Moín & Siquerres ▼

Getting to Tortuguero

Until the 1991 earthquake, tour boats and a weekly cargo boat traveled from Moín up the **Tortuguero Canal** towards Nicaragua. Although the earthquake made the canal impassable in some areas to all but the most shallow-bottomed of boats, *lanchas* still go up the canal from Moín and elsewhere. Expect a three- or four-hour trip (sometimes longer) by *lancha*, depending upon where you embark – if you're on a package tour, it will probably be **Hamburgo de Siquerres** on the Río Reventazón; travelling independently, you'll find it logistically easier to leave from **Moín**. Either way, the *lanchas* glide through mirror-calm waters past palm and deciduous trees and small, stilt-legged wooden houses, brightly painted and poised on the water's edge. The canal hums with human activity, with scores of *lanchas*, *botes* (large canoes) and *pangas* (flat-bottomed outboard-motored boats) plying the glassy waters. You may spot crocodiles and caiman basking on the canal banks, moss-covered and immobile sloths clinging to a tree or perhaps even a troupe of spider monkeys making their leaping, chattering way through the waterfront canopy.

If you're travelling **independently**, you ought to be able to find a boat at Moín willing to take you up the canal any time from 6am until as late as 2pm (depending on the tides), although the earlier you travel the better – see p.154 for full details. You can arrange with your boatman your return day and time; get a phone number if possible, so you can call from Tortuguero village if you change return plans. The *lanchas* drop you at Tortuguero dock, from where you can walk to the village accommodation or take another *lancha* across the canal to the more expensive tourist lodges. If you haven't booked a hotel, be aware that accommodation in the village can fill up quickly during the turtle-nesting seasons (March–May & July–Oct).

Alternatively, you can do as the locals do and take a 9am bus from San José to **Cariari**, and then switch to a bus for the **Geest banana plantation**, from where a boat departs daily around 1.30pm to Tortuguero. The journey is long, but the boat ride costs only $10 each way, so you'll save a lot, particularly if you're travelling alone. The return boat to San José leaves daily at 7am.

Tour operators to Tortuguero

Several companies offer all-inclusive packages to Tortuguero, usually including accommodation at one of the upmarket lodges lining the canal. Budget options tend to involve some form of bus/boat transfer while the more expensive tours fly direct from San José.

Costa Rica Expeditions C Central, Av 3, San José (☎257-0766, ☏257-1665, ⓦwww.costaricaexpeditions.com). They offer upscale Tortuguero packages including flights from San José, accommodation at the comfortable Tortuga Lodge and three meals a day. Prices start at $300 per person for a three-day, two-night package. They also offer trips to Barra del Colorado.

Ecole Travel C 7, Av 0/1, San José (☎223-2240, ☏223-4128, ⓦwww.ecoletravel.com). One of the longest established companies offering Tortuguero tours, Ecole has excellent budget tours popular with students and backpackers. Tours ($125 for two days and one night) start from Moín dock near Puerto Limón.

Riverboat Fracesca Tours (☎226-0986, ⓦwww.tortuguerocanals.com). Riverboat Fracesca features two-day, one-night tours of the Tortuguero canals for $175. The price includes bus transportation from San José to Moín (where you embark on the canal tour), meals and lodging.

△ Tortuguero National Park

Sansa (☎221-9414, ☎225-2176) and NatureAir (☎220-3054, ☎220-0413) fly daily from San José (flight time 35–50 minutes) departing between 6 and 7am. The return fare costs around $130. The airstrip lies about 4km north of the village. There are no taxis from here to the village, though the more upscale lodges will come and pick you up; otherwise, you'll have to walk.

The village

The peaceful village of **TORTUGUERO**, with a small population of around 700, lies at the northeastern corner of the park, on a thin spit of land between the sea and the canal. The exuberant foliage of wisteria, oleander and bougainvillea imbues the village with a tropical garden feel. Tall palm groves loom over patchy expanses of grass dotted with zinc-roofed wooden houses, often elevated on stilts. This is classic Caribbean style: washed-out, slightly ramshackle and pastel-pretty, with very little to disturb the torpor until after dark.

A dirt path – the "main street" – runs north–south through the village, from which narrow paths lead to the sea and the canal. Smack in the middle of the village stands one of the prettiest churches you'll see anywhere in Costa Rica, tiny and pale yellow, with a small spire and an oval doorway.

At the north end of the village is the **Natural History Museum** (daily 10am–5.30pm; $1) run by the Caribbean Conservation Corporation (Ⓦwww.cccturtle.org), with a small but informative exhibition explaining the life cycle of sea turtles. You can watch a rather portentous twenty-minute video explaining the history of turtle conservation in the area and, before you leave, you'll be invited to 'adopt a turtle' for $25 for which you'll receive an adoption certificate and information so that you can track the migratory progress of your chosen beast on the Internet as it makes its slow, purposeful way across the ocean.

Practicalities

A small, somewhat faded display on the turtles' habits, habitat and history surrounds the **information kiosk** in the village centre. This is the official place to buy tickets for turtle tours; the park rangers sell the tickets at the kiosk from 5pm to 6pm. Here you can also get contact info for local guides. Canadian naturalist and local resident Darryl Loth (☎709-8011, ☎709-8094, Ⓦcasamarbella.tripod.com), who runs the nearby *Casa Marbella* (see opposite), has a small information centre in the village and can arrange tours, including boat trips and hikes up Cerro Tortuguero (see p.180).

There are no bank or money-changing facilities in Tortuguero – bring all the cash you'll need with you – and though there's a correo in the middle of the village, mail may take three or four weeks just to make its way to Limón. If villagers are heading to Limón they might offer to carry letters for you and post them from there, which can be useful if you're staying here for any length of time. Tortuguero has a weekly medical service; otherwise emergencies and health problems should be referred to the park's administration headquarters, north of the village, near the airstrip. The purple Paraíso Tropical souvenir shop in the middle of the village doubles as the village's NatureAir agent, and sells tickets to San José.

Village accommodation

Staying at Tortuguero on the cheap entails bedding down in one of the independent **cabinas** in the village. **Camping** on the beach is not allowed, though you can set up a tent for about $2 per day at the mown enclosure near the **ranger station** at the southern end of the village, where you enter the park. It's in a sheltered situation, away from the sea breezes, and there's drinking water and toilets. Bring a groundsheet and mosquito net, and make sure your tent is waterproof.

Cabinas Aracari South of the information kiosk and soccer field ☎798-3059 (in Limón). Run by a local family, these clean, comfortable cabinas, all with private bath, cold water and fan, sit amid a beautiful tree-filled garden. ②

Cabinas Mary Scar East of the *pulpería*, before the beach ☎220-1478 (in San Jose). Newer cabins come with private bathrooms, while the older, slightly gloomy but clean cabinas have shared spic-and-span bathrooms. There's a friendly atmosphere and you can order simple meals for about $3. ②

Cabinas Tortuguero South of the village, towards the entry to the national park. No phone, ℮tinamon@racsa.co.cr. Five simple en-suite rooms sit in a lovely garden. Tasty meals are offered, including Italian food, because one of the owners is from Bologna. You can also rent canoes. ②

Casa Marbella In front of the Catholic church, next to the information kiosk ☎709-8011, ℱ709-8094, ℮casamarbella.tripod.com. Managed by a committed Canadian environmentalist, an inexhaustible source of info on the regional flora and fauna, this friendly B&B has four large, comfortable en-suite rooms. Enjoy the free breakfast on a small terrace overlooking the canal. Tours offered. ②–③

Miss Junie's At the north end of the village, just before you reach the Natural History Museum ☎710-0523. Tortuguero's most popular cook (see p.178) also offers refurbished, simply decorated, comfortable rooms with hot-water private bath and fans. Excellent breakfast included in the price. ②

The lodges

Staying at Tortuguero's **lodges**, most of which are across the canal from the village, has its drawbacks. Though convenient, and in some cases quite luxurious, life as a lodger can be a rather regimented affair. Guests are shuttled in and out of the lodges with stop-watch precision and there's precious little nightlife. If you want to explore the village and the beach on your own you have to get a *lancha* across the canal (free, but inconvenient). Note, however, that outside the turtle-watching season, most lodges don't operate their boats at night. Owing to Tortuguero's perennial popularity with package tourists, the lodges seldom have space for independent travellers.

Jungle Lodge 1km north of the village, across the canal ☎233-0155, ℱ233-0778. Owned and operated by the tour operator, Cotur, this friendly, comfortable, unpretentious lodge, set in its own gardens, has en-suite rooms, a good restaurant, games room, small disco, swimming pool, free canoes and a lagoon. ②

Laguna Lodge ☎225-3740, ℱ283-8031, ℮www.lagunatortuguero.com. This well-equipped lodge has a riverside bar, swimming pool, beach access and a new conference centre (which looks like a giant turtle as envisaged by Gaudí). For some, the lodge's regime, with set meal and tour times, may be a bit too constraining. Nevertheless, the rooms are perfectly comfortable and the tour guides extremely knowledgeable. This is one of the few lodges that offers hiking trips through the jungle as well as canal tours. ②

El Manatí 1.5km north of the village, across the canal ☎ & ℱ383-0330. One of Tortuguero's best budget options, this peaceful family-run accommodation has basic but clean rooms with hot-water private bath and fans, as well as several attractive two-bedroom cabinas. Breakfast is included. ②

Mawamba Lodge 1km north of the village ☎293-8181, ℱ239-7657, ℮www.grupomawamba.com. This large, ritzy, gregarious lodge has a daily slide show, environmentally friendly boats and round-the-clock cold beers from room service. The cabina-style rooms come with ceiling fans and private bathrooms, there's a large pool and Jacuzzi and the village and ocean are just a short walk away. ②

Pachira Lodge Opposite the village ☎256-7080, ℱ223-1119, ℮www.pachiralodge.com. One of Tortuguero's newer lodges, this luxurious establishment has spacious, attractive rooms in wood cabins, linked by covered walkways, with large en-suite, hot-water bathrooms, along with a pool and imaginative tour options. ②

Tortuga Lodge ☏257-0766, ℱ257-1665, ⓦwww.costaricaexpeditions.com. Owned by Costa Rica Expeditions, this is the plushest lodge in the area (but furthest from the village) with large, attractive en-suite rooms, exemplary (if somewhat over-attentive) service, excellent food, a riverside swimming pool and elegantly landscaped grounds crisscrossed with walking trails. ❷

Eating, drinking and nightlife

Tortuguero village offers homely Caribbean food with a wide selection of fresh **fish**. Expect to pay up to twice as much for a meal as you'd pay in other parts of Costa Rica. For entertainment, the Centro Social La Culebra has a nightly **disco**, though the clientele can be a bit rough. *Bar Brisas del Mar* (known to the locals as *El Bochinche*) is better, with a large, semi open-air dance floor and a sound-and-light system (when it's not in Limón). You can hear the sea from your table and the atmosphere is low-key except on Saturday nights, when the lively weekly disco attracts a large local crowd and goes on well into the wee hours.

El Muellecito Next to the *pulpería*. Tortuguero's best breakfast spot, with tasty pancakes and fruit salad. Closes at 8pm.

Miss Junie's North end of village path, 50m before the Natural History Museum. Operating out of a new dining hall, the town's best restaurant offers solid Caribbean food – red beans, jerk chicken, rice, chayote and breadfruit, all on the same plate – dished up by local Miss Junie. Wash it down with an ice-cold beer.

Miss Miriam's Adjacent to village soccer pitch (and a good spot to watch the village teams in action). This cheerful, immaculate restaurant serves Caribbean food, including chicken with rice and beans cooked in coconut milk, at very reasonable prices. Rooms also available.

The Vine Café run by the owners of the Jungle Souvenir Shop opposite, with good coffee, cheesecake and brownies. Closed during the rainy season.

Tropical Lodge Bar Mid-village on the path to the park entrance. Noisy and entertaining village bar with perfect sunset views over the river. They also have rooms with hot-water private bath and TV.

Visiting the park

Most people come to Tortuguero to see the **desove**, or egg-laying of the turtles. Few are disappointed, as the majority of tours during **laying seasons** (March–May & July–Oct) result in sightings of the surreal procession of the reptiles from the sea to make their egg-nests in the sand. While turtles have been known to lay in the daylight (the hatchlings wait under the cover of sand until nightfall to emerge), it is far more common for them to come ashore in the relative safety of night. Nesting can take place turtle-by-turtle – you can watch a single mother come ashore and scramble up the beach just south of the village or, more strikingly, in groups (*arribadas*) when dozens emerge from the sea at the same time to form a colony, marching up the sands to their chosen spot, safely above the high-tide mark. Each turtle digs a hole in which she lays eighty or more eggs; the collective whirring noise of sand being dug away is extraordinary. Having filled the hole with sand to cover the eggs, the turtles begin their course back to the sea, leaving the eggs to hatch and return to the waves under the cover of darkness. Incubation takes some weeks; when the hatchlings emerge they instinctively follow the light of the moon on the water, scuttling to safety in the ocean.

Tortuguero is one of the best spots in Costa Rica to observe marine turtles nesting, as three of the largest kinds of endangered sea turtles regularly nest here in large numbers. Along with the **green** (*verde*) turtle, named for the colour of soup made from its flesh, you might see the **hawksbill** (*carey*), with its distinctive hooked beak, and the ridged **leatherback** (*baula*), the largest turtle in the world, which can easily weigh 300kg – some are as heavy as 500kg and reach 5m in length. The green turtles and hawksbills nest mainly from July to October (August is the peak month), while the leatherbacks may come ashore from March to May.

Turtle tours, led by certified guides, leave at 8pm and 10pm every night from the information kiosk in the village. If you're not going with an organized group from one of the lodges, you'll need to buy park entrance tickets ($7) from the kiosk, which is staffed by park rangers from 5pm to 6pm every afternoon. Be sure to get there early because the number of visitors is strictly limited. No more than 200 people are allowed on the beach at any one time and visitors must wear dark clothing, refrain from smoking, and aren't allowed to bring cameras (still or video) or flashlights. Everyone must be off the beach by midnight. There are over a hundred certified guides in Tortuguero; they charge $10 for a turtle tour (roughly half the price of a lodge tour) – if you haven't already sorted one out, they conveniently tend to hang around the ticket kiosk at 5pm in search of customers.

A single, generally well-maintained, self-guided **trail** (1km), the **Sendero Natural,** starts at the ranger station at the park entrance, passes two ranger huts and skirts west around the *llomas de sierpe* (swamp). As for the long, wild **beach**, you can amble for up to 30km south, spotting crabs and birds along the way,

Turtling

For hundreds of years the fishermen of the Caribbean coast made their living culling the seemingly plentiful turtle population, selling shell and meat for large sums to middlemen in Puerto Limón. Initially, turtles were hunted for local consumption only, but during the first two decades of the 1900s, the fashion for turtle soup in Europe, especially England, led to large-scale exportation.

Turtle-hunting was a particularly brutal practice. Spears were fashioned from long pieces of wood, taken from the apoo palm or the rawa, and fastened with a simple piece of cord to a sharp, barbed metal object. Standing in their canoes, fishermen hurled the spear, like a miniature harpoon, into the water, lodging the spear in the turtle's flesh. Pulling their canoes closer, the fishermen would then reel in the cord attached to the spear, lift the beasts onto the canoes and take them ashore dead or alive. On land, the turtles might be beheaded with a machete or put in the holds of ships, where they could survive a journey of several weeks to Europe if they were given a little water.

Today, turtles are protected, their eggs and meat a delicacy. Locals around Tortuguero are officially permitted to take two turtles a week during nesting season for their own consumption – the unlucky green turtles are considered the most delicious. The recent sharp decline in the populations of hawksbill, green and leatherback turtles has been linked, at least in part, to **poaching**. This has prompted the national parks administration to adopt a firm policy discouraging the theft of turtle eggs within the park boundaries and to arm park rangers. Meanwhile, should you find a turtle on its back between July 10 and September 15, do not flip it over, as in most cases it is being tagged by researchers, who work on the northern 8km of the thirty-five-kilometre-long nesting beach.

It is not just the acquisitive hand of humans that endangers the turtles. On land, a cadre of **predators**, among them coati and raccoons, regularly ransack the nests in order to eat the unborn reptiles. Once the hatching has started – the darkness giving them a modicum of protection – the turtles really have their work cut out, running a gauntlet of vultures, barracudas, sharks and even other turtles (the giant leatherback has been known to eat other species' offspring) on their way from the beach to the sea. Only about sixty percent – an optimistic estimate – of hatchlings reach adulthood, and the survival of marine turtles worldwide is under question.

and also looking for turtle tracks, which resemble the two thick parallel lines a truck would leave in its wake. Swimming is not a good idea, due to heavy waves, turbulent currents and sharks. Remember that you need to pay **park fees** to walk on either the beach or along the trail.

Other activities around Tortuguero

Almost as popular as the turtle tours are Tortuguero's **boat tours** through the *caños*, or lagoons, to spot animals, including monkeys, caiman and Jesus Christ lizards, and birds like dignified-looking herons, cranes and kingfishers. Most lodges have **canoes** (some also have hydro-bikes) that you can take out on the canal – a great way to get around if you're handy with a paddle, but stick to the main canal as it's easy to get lost in the complex lagoon system northwest of the village. In the south of the village, 50m north of the ranger station and right by the water, Ruben Aragón rents traditional Miskito-style boats and canoes for about $8 an hour, or $15 with a guide-paddler.

You can also climb **Cerro Tortuguero**, an ancient volcanic deposit looming 119m above the flat coastal plain 6km north of the village. A climb up the gently sloping sides leads you to the "peak", where you can enjoy good views of flat jungle and inland waterways. Accessible only by *lancha*, this is a half-day hike, and you must go with a guide. Of the lodges, only the Laguna Lodge offers the guided climb as part of its package.

Travel details

Buses

Cahuita to: Puerto Limón (9 daily; 1hr); Puerto Viejo de Talamanca (8 daily; 1hr 30min–2hr); San José (4 daily; 4hr); Sixaola (4 daily; 2hr).
Puerto Limón to: Cahuita (4 daily; 1hr); Manzanillo (3 daily; 2hr); Moín (every hour; 1hr 30min); Puerto Viejo de Talamanca (5 daily; 1hr 30min); San José (every 30min; 2hr 30min–3hr); Sixaola (1 daily; 3hr).
Puerto Viejo de Talamanca to: Cahuita (8 daily; 1hr 30min–2hr); Manzanillo (3 daily; 45min); Puerto Limón (4 daily; 1hr 30min); San José (4 daily; 4hr 30min); Sixaola (4 daily; 2hr).
San José to: Cahuita (4 daily; 4hr); Puerto Limón (25 daily; 2hr 30min–3hr); Puerto Viejo de Talamanca (4 daily; 4hr 30min); Sixaola (4 daily; 6hr).
Sixaola to: Cahuita (4 daily; 2hr); Puerto Limón (1 daily; 3hr); Puerto Viejo de Talamanca (4 daily; 2hr); San José (4 daily; 6hr).

Boats

Barra del Colorado to: Puerto Viejo de Sarapiquí (private *lanchas* only; 3–4hr). Note that the return trip from Puerto Viejo de Sarapiquí to Barra takes 6hr.
Moín docks to: Tortuguero (private *lanchas* only; 4hr).

Flights

Sansa and NatureAir both fly the following routes:
San José to: Barra del Colorado (2 daily; 35min)
Barra del Colorado to: San José (2 daily; 35min)
San José to: Tortuguero (2 daily; 35min)
Tortuguero to San José (2 daily; 35min).

The Zona Norte

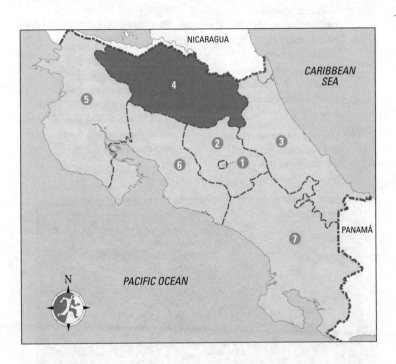

NICARAGUA

CARIBBEAN SEA

4

5

2

3

6

1

PANAMÁ

7

N

PACIFIC OCEAN

CHAPTER 4 # Highlights

✳ **Volcán Arenal** Stunning by day, and even more memorable by night, when flows of incandescent lava illuminate its slopes. See p.193

✳ **Caño Negro** This seasonal floodland offers some of the best birdwatching and wildlife-spotting in Central America, with hundreds of indigenous and migratory species. See p.200

✳ **Laguna de Arenal** Relax in an intimate lodge on the shores of this serene lake, whose sparkling surface reflects the looming volcano. See p.195

✳ **Rara Avis** This private and utterly remote rainforest reserve offers one of the most thrilling and authentic eco-tourism experiences in Costa Rica. See p.203

✳ **Selva Verde** Explore the premontane forest at Selva Verde in the company of knowledgeable guides who will introduce you to the mysteries of the reserve's flora and fauna. See p.208

△ Green iguana

The Zona Norte

Costa Rica's Zona Norte (Northern Zone) spans the hundred-odd kilometres from the base of the Cordillera Central to just short of the mauve-blue mountains of southern Nicaragua. Historically cut off from the rest of the country, the Zona Norte has developed a distinct character, with independent-minded farmers and Nicaraguan refugees making up large segments of the population. Neither group journeys to the Valle Central very often, and many people of the north have a special allegiance to and pride in their region. The far north, especially, for years mauled by fighting in the Nicaraguan civil war, feels more like Nicaragua than Costa Rica.

Topographically, the Zona Norte separates neatly into two broad, river-drained plains (*llanuras*), which stretch all the way to the Río San Juan on the Nicaraguan–Costa Rican border. In the west, the **Llanura de Guatusos** is dominated by Volcán Arenal, while to the east the **Llanura de San Carlos** features the tropical jungles of the **Sarapiquí** area. Less obviously picturesque than many parts of the country, the entire region nonetheless has a distinctive appeal, with lazy rivers snaking across steaming plains, and flop-eared cattle, originally imported from India, languishing beneath riverside trees. The area is vast – at least by Costa Rican standards – with huge tracts of empty space dotted by a number of top-notch tourist attractions. Most people use the small town of **La For tuna** as a gateway to the active **Volcán Arenal,** often staying in one of the lodges around Laguna de Arenal. This and the Sarapiquí area, with its tropical-forest eco-lodges and the research stations of **Selva Verde** and **Rara Avis**, draw the most visitors in the Zona Norte. In the north, the remote flatlands are home to the increasingly accessible wetland national park of **Refugio Nacional de Vida Silvestre Caño Negro**, with an extraordinary number of migratory and indigenous birds. Few visitors venture further, though a steady trickle passes through the small border town of **Los Chiles** en route to Nicaragua. Note that between Boca de Arenal and Los Chiles there is a real shortage of accommodation, though other essentials – fuel and food – are in good supply.

One of the prime agricultural areas in the country, the Zona Norte is carpeted with rice fields, vast banana, pineapple and sugarcane plantations, dairy-cattle farms and the huge factories of TicoFrut, Costa Rica's major domestic fruit grower. The worst excesses of slash-and-burn **deforestation** are all too visible from the Zona Norte's roadsides and riverbanks, with the matchstick corpses of once-tall hardwoods scattered all over stump-scarred fields patrolled by a few cattle. There are plans to establish an international park, Sí-a-Paz ("Yes to Peace"), which would link the wetlands of Caño Negro with those south of Lago de Nicaragua, about 14km from the

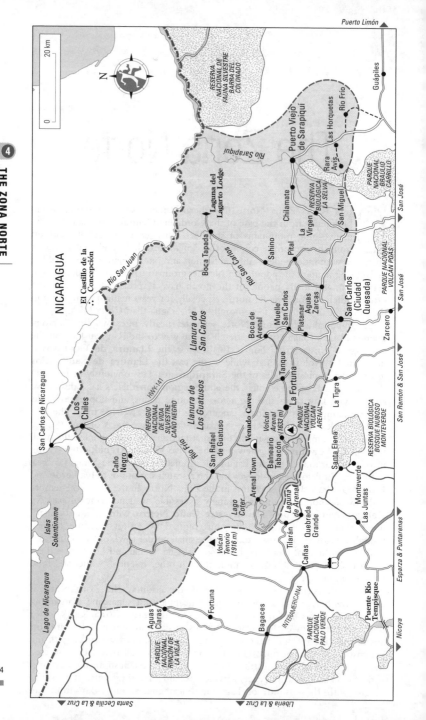

Nicaraguan–Costa Rican border, preserving much of the existing rainforest and wetlands in both regions.

The Zona Norte's **climate** is hot and wet, more so in the east than in the west near Guanacaste, where there is a dry season. You'll be drenched by regular downpours, but the rain is always warm, and makes for an enjoyable respite from the heat. Although many roads in the region are seriously pot-holed, **getting around** the Zona Norte is easy enough and there's a good bus network around the La Fortuna and Puerto Viejo areas. If you plan on travelling outside these areas, then you're better off with a car. The highway infrastructure is relatively new, and both the western (via Heredia) and eastern (via the Guápiles Highway) routes from San José to Puerto Viejo de Sarapiquí are in good condition, as well as incredibly scenic. It's possible to travel cross-country between La Fortuna and Puerto Viejo in about two hours.

Some history

For thousands of years before the Conquest, the original inhabitants of the Zona Norte were tribal groups – chief among them the **Corobicí** and **Guatusos** – who made contact with one another via the great rivers. The **Spanish presence** first made itself felt in the early 1600s, when galleons meandered up the Río San Juan and into Lago de Nicaragua, looking for a route to the east. Pirates (mainly British) soon followed, wreaking havoc on the riverside communities. It was two hundred years before the Spanish made a **settlement** of any size; the Quesada family from San Ramón came down from the highlands of the Valle Central in the nineteenth century to found a village at present-day San Carlos, or Ciudad Quesada, as it's also known. In the meantime, Nicaraguan–Zona Norte communication and commerce car-ried on as it had for thousands of years via the Ríos San Juan, Frío, Sarapiquí and San Carlos. The **Río Sarapiquí** in particular remained a more important highway than any road well into the 1800s, carrying coffee for export from the Heredia Highlands out to the Caribbean ports of Matina and Limón.

Volcán Arenal and around

That the Arenal region attracts such large numbers of tourists is largely due to the **volcano** itself, one of the most active in the Western Hemisphere. The plain and tranquil village of **La Fortuna** sits beneath it, and is now a thriv-ing base for the area's transport, tours and activities including sportfishing, windsurfing and boating on **Laguna de Arenal**, hiking through pockets of remaining rainforest, soaking in steaming natural thermal springs and scrab-bling through subterranean **caves** to explore ancient geological formations. Another possible base, and rather less touristy, is the agricultural town of **San Carlos**, southeast of La Fortuna and two hours away by bus.

It can **rain** a lot in this area, and when it does, prepare to be deluged. The year-round temperature is around 20°C, which accounts for the huge diversity of crops grown here – you'll pass *fincas* growing papaya and oranges, ginger and sugarcane, and beans and cassava, and the area is also home to a nascent cut-flower industry. It's tourism, however, that provides by far the most revenue.

San Carlos and around

Perched on the northern slopes of the Cordillera Central, 650m above sea level, **SAN CARLOS** (also known as **Ciudad Quesada**, or simply Quesada) has a decidedly rural atmosphere. Fresh produce overflows from market stalls onto the streets, and *campesinos* with weathered faces hang out in the main square in front of the church. There's little to actually do: locals only come into town to have a drink on Friday night or to sell their wares at the Saturday market, and most tourists base themselves at La Fortuna or one of the luxurious resorts nearby (see p.190). It's for this very reason that San Carlos is such a likeable spot, and it's well worth visiting just to stroll about and observe a prosperous agricultural hub at work. You get a real feel for what drives Costa Rica's economy: much of the nation's milk, beef, citrus fruit and rice comes from the large-scale agricultural holdings in these parts.

The beautiful country around San Carlos is still largely untouristed territory, with the precipitous slopes of the Cordillera Central hiding pockets of rainforest before gradually giving way to the flatlands of the Llanura de San Carlos and the wide rivers that cut through them. Volcán Arenal dominates, and there are stupendous views of it from the northern slope of the Cordillera Central. The sleepy villages of Muelle, Platanar and Aguas Zarcas, all within about 20km of San Carlos, are devoid of any real sights but handy if you want to get a snack at one of village's roadside restaurants or to fill up with petrol.

Most travellers arrive in San Carlos from San José **via Hwy-141**, the switchback road that climbs through Zarcero and over the hump of the Cordillera Central. Another approach is via the spectacular **mountain road** between the town of San Ramón, perched above the Valle Central, and La Tigra, in the lower reaches of the Zona Norte. This winding route passes through isolated and deep-cut valleys, passing the Los Angeles Cloudforest en route. Though rather indirect – taking you almost to La Fortuna before a right turn heads to San Carlos via El Tanque, Jabillos and Florencia – it's much less busy than the road to San Carlos via Zarcero.

Arrival and information

Buses for San Carlos depart from San José's La Coca-Cola bus terminal daily every hour on the hour from 5am until 7.30pm. It's quite a long haul; even the so-called *directo* services take three hours or more, and stop frequently. The bus station sits 1km north of Parque Central; incoming buses stop in the centre of town before heading to the bus station. Frequent local buses run from the bus station to the centre (85 colones); buses heading to the station are labelled "Terminal". You can change cash and **travellers' cheques** at the Banco Nacional, among other banks close to the Parque Central. Surf the web at Café Internet, one block north and half a block east of the park. For **medical emergencies**, the Hospital de San Carlos (☎460-1176) is the best in the Zona Norte.

Accommodation

You'll find plenty of budget options in San Carlos but if you're looking for more luxurious accommodation, try one of the lodges outside town.

La Garza Opposite the sports field in Platanar, 15km northeast of San Carlos ☎475-5222, ⌨www .hotellagarza.com. Named for the herons (*garzas*) that nest on the grounds, this hotel is part of a working dairy farm. Rustic, comfortable polished-floor bungalows have fans or a/c and are decorated in Guatemalan fabrics. Verandahs look out onto the river, home to a variety of frogs. There's also a restaurant and pool, and breakfast is included. ❹

Hotel Central On the west side of Parque Central ☎460-0766, ✉hcentral@racsa.co.cr. The hospitable *Hotel Central* sits above a casino in the heart of town. Though slightly institutional, the refurbished rooms boast a clean, modern bathroom and come with fan and cable TV. ❸
Hotel Conquistador 700m south of Parque Central ☎ & ⓕ460-6311. Looking much grander than it actually is, the hotel's imposing peach

façade gives way to simple but comfortable, clean rooms with tiled floors, TV, fan and hot-water bath – and some have views over the valley. Those with a car will appreciate the free and secure parking behind. ❷

Hotel del Valle Two blocks north of Parque Central ☎ 460-0718. Handily situated on a quiet central street, this little hotel has rooms with TV, bathroom and fan (though rooms can still get mighty hot). The mattresses are a bit too submissive for some tastes, but comfy nonetheless. ❷

Hotel Don Goyo A block south of Parque Central ☎ 460-1780. One of the most pleasing options in town, these clean, quiet, brightly painted rooms, all with private bath and fan, are in a modern building near the centre. There's also secure parking. Call ahead, because an upcoming change of management means the hotel may close. ❸

La Mirada 4km north of San Carlos ☎ 460-2222. Hillside cabinas, with phone and hot-water bath, overlook the northern plains and offer some of the most beautiful vistas in the area. Take your meals in the open-air restaurant with stupendous views. Parking available. ❷

Occidental El Tucano 8km east of San Carlos on the road to Aguas Zarcas ☎ 460-6000, in the US 1-800/858-2258, Ⓦ www.occidental-hoteles.com. The plushest accommodation in the San Carlos area, this upmarket European-style resort complex sits amid a series of thermal springs in landscaped grounds flourishing with tropical flowers. There's also a swimming pool, Jacuzzi, tennis courts and mini-golf. The spa treatments and natural saunas attract a mainly older-European clientele; non-residents can use the springs for $12. Breakfast included. ❻

La Quinta 15km north of San Carlos on the southern outskirts of the village of Platanar after the sugar mill ☎ 475-5260, Ⓦ www.laquintalodge .com. The best budget option in the area (and accessible by bus from San Carlos), this family-run accommodation has smart, dorm-style shared cabinas ($10 per person), attractive doubles (❸), fully equipped self-catering apartments and a huge pool with a slide. The helpful English-speaking owners also make meals on request. ❸

Tilajari Resort Hotel 1km west of Muelle, 22km north of San Carlos ☎ 469-9091, Ⓦ www.tilajari .com. This quiet, beautifully situated resort hotel sits on an out-of-the-way working cattle ranch by the Río San Carlos (which many of the rooms overlook). Double rooms have bathroom, a/c, terrace and satellite TV and there's a restaurant, conference room, pool and tennis courts. Iguanas roam the landscaped grounds and horse-riding and rainforest walks can be arranged. Buffet breakfast included. ❻

The town

San Carlos fans out around the attractive **Parque Central**, dominated by a startling modern church, with just a few streets trailing away on either side. Within a few blocks of here you'll find most of the shops, restaurants and accommodation. On the north side of the park, the cooperative **Mercado de Artesanía de San Carlos** sells leatherwork and other crafts in a less touristy atmosphere than in the big Sarchí souvenir shops (see p.118). San Carlos is also a **saddlery** centre, and you can watch local leatherworkers making intricate Costa Rican saddles in any of the *talabarterías* dotted around town.

Eating and drinking

San Carlos has several cheap, cheerful **sodas** and **restaurants** and you can also eat very well within the food market itself on the north side of Parque Central. The best of the market's budget sodas is the friendly *Restaurante Plaza*, with a long wooden counter where they serve up meals and snacks, including *gallos*, soups and excellent *batidos*. The Chinese restaurant Imperio, a block south of the square, serves filling rather than inspiring dishes – their chicken and corn soup is a meal in itself. On the west side of the Parque Central is *Coca Loca*, a steakhouse that does a good slab of beef for around $7. On weekend evenings, San Carlos offers a genuine Tico experience far removed from the tourist-oriented nightlife in other parts of the country. Start your bar crawl at *Los Geranios*, a hopping two-level bar a block south of the Parque, with breezy upstairs seating overlooking the street. Later action focuses on the *Iguana* **discoteca**, just north of the northeast corner of the Parque Central, or the sleazier *Titanic*, a block south of it.

San Carlos is a transport hub, with frequent buses to a range of destinations. All buses leave from the bus station, 1km north of Parque Central. Services depart hourly for **San José** until 7.15pm, some non-stop. Twelve a day head for **Los Chiles**, and five (4.40am, 6am, 10am, 3pm & 5.30pm) head for **Puerto Viejo de Sarapiquí** (2hr 30min). Six buses travel daily to **La Fortuna** – some faster than others – and two to Tilarán at 6.30am and 4pm. For other destinations, check at the bus station.

❹ La Fortuna and around

LA FORTUNA (or La Fortuna de San Carlos, as it's officially named) was once a simple agricultural town dominated by the majestic conical form of Volcán Arenal, just 6km away. Nowadays, true to its name, La Fortuna is booming. Despite all the air-conditioned tour buses whizzing through town, however, it remains a pleasant, inviting community, and the locals are patient and warm.

Looming at 1633m, Arenal seems to sit directly on top of the town. On a clear day you can bask in the mesmerizing sight of lava oozing down the lip of the volcano like juice from a squashed fruit. But when it's rainy and foggy – which is more often than not – the volcano is almost totally obscured, its summit hidden behind a sombrero of cloud. In fact, locals estimate that one in two visitors never actually get a glimpse of the summit or lava. Nevertheless, its brooding presence remains palpable, and even if you can't actually see it, you'll almost certainly hear its rumblings and splutterings.

The area west of La Fortuna offers a variety of outdoor activities, from fishing and windsurfing on the **Laguna de Arenal** to hiking forested trails and bathing in steaming hot springs at **Tabacón**. Between La Fortuna and Laguna de Arenal, the spectacularly varied landscape includes pockets of rainforest-like vegetation that open up into wide grassy fields.

La Fortuna has excellent bus connections, making it one of the region's main transport hubs and also a prime setting-off point for tours to the remote wildlife refuge of **Caño Negro**. Note that as the town becomes increasingly popular, **theft** is on the rise; never leave anything unattended, especially in a car, and be careful about walking around alone late at night. Also be wary of "guides" who offer their services on the street.

Arrival

Three direct buses depart **from San José** to La Fortuna (4hr), leaving the Atlántico Norte bus terminal (Calle 12, Avenida 7) at 6.15am, 8.40am and 11.30am. You can also take a direct bus from San José to San Carlos, where there are frequent buses to La Fortuna (40km; 1–2hr). Buses **from Tilarán** to La Fortuna (3hr) depart at 7am and 12.30pm. Most buses pull in at the Parque Central (until recently a soccer field) in the middle of the village.

It's never hard to **orient** yourself: the volcano is west. Most places accept dollars but if you need to **change money**, hotels will do it for about the same rate as the Banco Nacional on the east side of the Parque Central. This and other banks in town all have **ATMs** and change **travellers' cheques**. If it's high time that you wash your smellies, stop by the **laundry** 300m east of the Parque Central, on the main road.

To **rent a car**, try Alamo (☎479-9090), a block west of the church, or Poas (☎479-8027), just one block further south. The Aguas Bravas **tour agency** on the main road opposite the Parque Central sells *La Nación*, the *Tico Times* and the *New York Times* and rents sturdy **mountain bikes** for around $10 a day.

Taxis line up on the south side of Parque Central – they rarely (if ever) use their meters, so agree to a price before getting in and be wary of overcharging. If in doubt, ask locals what they pay.

Accommodation

People with their own transport and a bit of money tend to head to the **lodges** on the road leading west from La Fortuna and the Parque Nacional Volcán Arenal or stay in one of the many pleasant hotels that border Laguna de Arenal. Budget travellers usually stay in the simple **cabinas** in town. Competition means that you may be greeted by **hotel touts** as you stumble off the bus. There's no hard-and-fast rule about whether or not to take them up on their offer, but be aware that if the tout isn't the actual owner, they're being paid on commission, which you'll be paying via a higher room rate.

The scenic **lodges** and **hotels** around Laguna de Arenal are hugely popular so you should book ahead in the dry season; some hotels require advance booking all year round. Most of the more expensive places are often part of all-inclusive packages from San José, including meals and outdoor activities. If you are staying at any of the lodges below you'll find life much easier if you have a car, as they are quite remote and public transport is erratic. Wherever you stay, almost every hotel can fix you up with tours of the volcano and other local attractions.

In La Fortuna

Cabinas Mayol 50m south of the San José bus stop ☏479-9110. Good budget rooms in an old La Fortuna house, all with fans and private bath. ➋

Cabinas Sissy 100m south and 125m west of the Parque Central ☏479-9256, ℻479-9931. Friendly and clean, this basic budget travellers' hang-out has a variety of rooms with fan and private or shared hot-water bath and some have cable TV.

There's also a simple shared kitchen and you can camp here for $4. ➋

Cabinas Las Tinajas 100m north and 25m west of Parque Central ☏479-9308, ℻479-9145. This small complex has four clean, well-furnished, airy cabinas, each equipped with hot-water bathroom, fan and cable TV. While away the hours on the terrace rocking chairs. ➌

Hotel Carmela Opposite the church on the main road ⊕ & Ⓕ479-9010. Inviting and clean, this long-established family-run hotel has rooms with a/c, fridge, cable TV and terrace. Also available are two rooms with disabled access; there's secure parking and breakfast is included. ④

Hotel Dorothy Just south of the bridge at the south end of town ⊕479-8068, Ⓔnoelsamuels douglas@hotmail.com. Basic, simple rooms with colourful decor and hot-water bathroom. The staff speak English and there's Internet access and free coffee on hand. ②

Hotel La Fortuna 75m south and 100m east of Parque Central ⊕479-9197. This recently refurbished hotel offers clean, simple rooms with fan, private bath and little else. The exterior rooms are airier – but expect to be awakened early by traffic noise. Breakfast in the pleasant café-restaurant is included in the price and the cheerful staff can organize tours and transfers. ③

Hotel San Bosco 100m northeast of the Parque Central ⊕479-9050, ⓦwww.arenal-volcano.com. Quiet hotel built around a garden on the north side of town. Rooms, which come with a/c and spacious hot-water bathroom, vary in price and size so if you don't like the first one you see, ask for another. Enjoy lovely views of Arenal from the pool and Jacuzzi as well as from the upper level terrace.

Hotel Villa Fortuna On the main road, 500m east of the Parque Central ⊕479-9139. Slightly outside of town, but quieter because of it, this hotel has large clean rooms with a/c, fridge and hot-water bath. There's also a swimming pool and breakfast is included. ③

Luigi's Lodge 200m west of the church ⊕479-9898, ⓦwww.luigislodge.com. Basic rooms come with a/c, hot-water bath and views of the volcano. There's Internet access, a laundry service, a pool and a restaurant. Breakfast is included. ⑤

Around La Fortuna

Albergue Ecoturístico La Catarata 1km from La Fortuna on the road to Arenal, then 1.5km down a signed turn-off to the left ⊕479-9522, Ⓔcatarata@racsa.co.cr. Sitting amid fertile farmland between La Fortuna and the waterfall, this eco-lodge offers nine rustic but comfortable cabinas, all with fan and hot-water bath. The restaurant serves simple local food made with organic produce from its garden, and a hearty, complimentary breakfast is included. A local initiative funded in part by the Canadian World Wildlife Fund, the lodge also has a butterfly farm, an experimental project to breed pacas and a medicinal herb farm. ③

Arenal Lodge 18km west of La Fortuna and 2km up a side road, just after crossing the dam ⊕460-1881, ⓦwww.arenallodge.com. Remote and leafy, this classy, peaceful retreat offers stunning views of the volcano and a variety of rooms, of which the refined junior suites are the best, with an old-style tropical decor, cane furniture, balcony with rocking chairs and polished wooden floors. They also come with fridge, microwave and coffee-making facilities. The on-site restaurant has lovely vistas. ⑦

Arenal Country Inn 1km south of La Fortuna on the road to San Ramón ⊕479-9670, ⓦwww .arenalcountryinn.com. This quiet hotel with twenty bright rooms set in small bungalows sits amid spacious grounds with volcano vistas. A superb breakfast is included and there's a swimming pool. ⑥

Arenal Observatory Lodge 16km from La Fortuna, then a further 9km down the road to the

park entrance – follow the signs ⊕692-2070, ⓦwww.arenal-observatory.co.cr. Just 1.8km from the crater, this is considered the area's best base for serious volcano watchers. The superior class rooms (⑦) have big comfortable beds and huge windows looking out at the volcano, which seems awesomely close. Standard rooms are rustic and comfortable (⑥), while cheaper rooms are in the La Casona farmhouse (⑤). The extensive grounds include primary rainforest with trails, a small museum, pool and spa. There's a $4 charge for non-guests to enter the grounds, though this is waived if you eat at the restaurant, which is overpriced – but you're really paying for the vista.

Las Cabañitas 1km from La Fortuna on the road to San Carlos ⊕479-9400, ⓦwww.cabanitas.com. Within walking distance of La Fortuna (though much easier by car), these comfortable, wooden cabinas come with a/c, private bath, their own balconies and rocking chairs. The days get hot, so cool off in the pool – there's one for adults and one for kids. Breakfast is included. ⑥

Hotel Arenal Paraíso 7km outside La Fortuna en route to the volcano ⊕460-5333, ⓦwww .arenalparaiso.com. This attractive, unobtrusive hotel has cabinas built of varnished wood, all with hot-water bath (some also have fridges) and huge porches that look out directly onto the volcano. The more upmarket cabinas sit further up the hill, with better views, a/c and private balcony. The pool has a swim-up bar, and a fine breakfast buffet is included. ⑤

Lost Iguana Resort 18km west of La Fortuna, across the dam, then 1.5km down a signed road to the right ☎461-0122, ⓦwww.lostiguanaresort.com. This peaceful jungle lodge has rooms with balconies offering volcano vistas, large, comfortable beds with cheerful cotton sheets, and a/c, minibar and satellite TV. The resort has several jungle trails, and they can also arrange any sort of local activity. Save money by booking online – and keep your eyes peeled for special offers on their website. ❼

Montaña de Fuego Inn 9km west of La Fortuna, on the road to Arenal ☎460-1220, ⓦwww .montanadefuego.com. Dark-wood bungalows have terrace, a/c, fridge and a safe. The higher-end rooms have rocking chairs, perfect for basking in spectacular light shows from the volcano opposite. You have to be comfortable with being face to face with the volcano here – it seems very close indeed. The pool has a swim-up bar and breakfast is included. ❻–❼

Tours from La Fortuna

Price competition between tour agencies in La Fortuna is fierce, but bear in mind that although you may save a few dollars by going with the cheapest agency, you could end up on a badly organized tour with under-qualified guides, or no lunch. Get as many details as possible before handing over your cash and go with a reputable tour operator, such as those listed below, and not with one of the freelance "guides" who may approach you, some of whom have been involved in serious incidents over the years.

By far the most popular excursion is the late-afternoon hike around **Volcán Arenal**, followed by a night-time soak in the thermal pools at **Balneario Tabacón** (see p.194). The volcano hike involves a walk through rainforest, much of it uphill, and a final scramble over lava rocks. Take care, as they're particularly sharp, and few guides carry a medical kit. Bring a torch, too. The volcano in action is an amazing sight if you're lucky enough to be there on a clear night when there's activity. Scarlet rivers of lava pour from the top, and you can hear the crunch of boulders landing as they are spewed from the mouth of the volcano.

The recently constructed **Arenal Hanging Bridges** (☎479-9686, ⓦwww .hangingbridges.com) let you walk among the treetops in a private forest reserve near the dam across Laguna de Arenal. In another development, and to the concern of some environmentalists and volcanologists, an Arenal cable car is now under construction that will no doubt give spectacular views of the volcano. The "jeep–boat–jeep" transfer from La Fortuna to Monteverde (see p.280), offered by a number of tour agencies, is a popular way of reaching the cloudforest and saves a lengthy and bumpy bus trip via Tilarán.

Sunset Tours (☎479-9801, ⓦwww.sunsettourcr.com), near the *Rancho la Cascada* restaurant, is pricier than other tour operators, but has professional, well-qualified guides. Their volcano tours ($22) include the entrance fee to the national park, but not to Balneario Tabacón. They offer a good day-trip to Caño Negro ($52), as well as taxi transfers to Monteverde ($22). Trips run by the professional **Aventuras Arenal**, 150m east of the Parque Central (☎479-9133, ⓦwww.arenaladventures.com), are almost identical and slightly cheaper, and they can also offer transport to just about anywhere in the country.

Desafío Tours (☎479-9464, ⓦwww.desafiocostarica.com), west of the church, are friendly, efficient, community-aware rafting specialists who run day-tours ($65) on the Class IV Río Toro as well as trips in inflatable kayaks on the Río Arenal ($55). You can also take a demanding guided hike up Cerro Chato, the smaller volcanic peak that clings to Arenal's skirts ($45). Their transfer to Monteverde includes a lakeside ride on well-cared-for horses ($65), and they can sort out flights, tours and accommodation anywhere in the country.

Jacamar (☎479-9767, ⓦwww.arenaltours.com), next to the *Lava Rocks* restaurant, runs an Arenal night tour ($25), trips to Caño Negro ($50) and gentle rafting excursions on the Río Peñas Blancas. Their boat-and-taxi transfer to Monteverde costs $19 and takes two to three hours.

The town

Despite its rapid growth in recent years, La Fortuna remains a small, likeable town, where you can stroll about with ease. Most of the town is taken up by agencies selling tours, and visitors wander between them comparing prices, while gazing keenly towards the volcano and popping into sodas for much-needed *refrescos* to cope with the humidity.

Eating and drinking

Considering the number of tourists passing through, **restaurant** prices in La Fortuna are quite fair, catering to locals as much as visitors. The food is pretty much the same everywhere: the inevitable *casados*, *platos del día* and *arroz-con-*whatever. The no-frills but friendly **bar** *Twins*, a block east and half a block south of the Parque Central, draws tourists and locals for beer and karaoke. *Vagabondo* (see below) has a large American-style **discoteca** in the back that stays open late most nights. On the weekends, the *Volcán Look*, 4km west of town, is the liveliest discoteca.

Choza de Laurel 200m west of Parque Central on the main road. Very much on the tourist-bus circuit, but atmospheric nevertheless, with succulent meat entrees (around $8), some of which are slowly roasted on a spit outside, and are impressive both for tenderness and size. Wash it all down with an ice-cold beer.

La Parada Directly opposite the bus stop on Parque Central. Watch the world go by at this popular *soda* with large, filling *casados* for only $2 and a variety of pizzas – all served up by an enthusiastic staff.

Rancho La Cascada At the northeast corner of Parque Central. It's hard to miss this cavernous thatched *palenque* hung with flags from around the world. Though long a tourist favourite, prices remain reasonable and entrees of hefty steaks and house rice with prawns and vegetables hit the spot.

Vagabondo 1km west of town. This attractive, open-air restaurant serves up authentic Italian wood-fired pizzas ($6–8). In the back, a large convivial bar with pool tables stays open late.

La Catarata de La Fortuna

The higher of Río Fortuna's two **waterfalls** (daily 9am–5pm, $6) is the epitome of the picturebook cascade – a tall, thin stream plunging prettily from a narrow aperture in the rocky heights 75m above, and forming a foaming pool among rocks and rainforest vegetation below. Although just 6km south of La Fortuna, it's a fairly stiff uphill walk, or a horse-ride across the fields. Make sure you wear waterproof shoes, and be aware that the paths can be slippery.

To get to the waterfalls, take the road heading south from La Fortuna across the bridge, then turn west down a driveable gravel road (it's the only turn-off in sight). Walk along this track in the morning and you'll spot plenty of birds, if you have the patience to stop and look for them – bring binoculars.

A sign points to the *cataratas*; enter the woods on the left to hike the steep trail leading down to the waterfall. It's tricky when wet, and not that easy when dry, either, although ropes are provided to help you scramble down. The river's current has to be traversed before you reach the base of the falls. You'll see the first of the waterfalls at the head of this stream; the higher, more spectacular one is another minute's walk along the trail. If in doubt, just follow the roar. Swimming is not recommended, due to flash floods, although a lot of people do. There's a *mirador* (signposted) for those who would rather look from a distance, giving great views across the steep valley and its heavily forested floor to the thin finger of the cascade.

La Fortuna has good bus connections, and with a little planning you can get from here to Guanacaste, Puntarenas, Monteverde and Puerto Viejo de Sarapiquí without backtracking to San José. For **Puerto Viejo de Sarapiquí**, take a bus to **San Carlos** (also called Ciudad Quesada; 10 daily; 1–2hr), where you can pick up a service east to Puerto Viejo. Buses depart from San Carlos for Puerto Viejo at 4.40am, 6am, 10am, 3pm and 5.30pm, but always double-check bus times. For **Monteverde**, two daily buses leave from La Fortuna (at 8am and 5pm) to **Tilarán** (3hr), at the head of Laguna de Arenal. If you take the 5pm bus, you'll have to spend the night in Tilarán. You can connect in Tilarán with the Santa Elena service (for the Monteverde Cloudforest Reserve; 3–4hr), which leaves at 12.30pm. Note that many people now opt for the "jeep–boat–jeep" transfer to Monteverde offered by various agencies; it saves time and the boat trip across the lake is spectacular. Frequent local services connect Tilarán with **Cañas** and the Interamericana, where you can pick up buses north to **Liberia** and the beaches of **Guanacaste**, or south to **Puntarenas**. To head to **San José** from La Fortuna, take the *directo* service (2 daily; 4hr 30min), which departs at 12.45pm and 2.45pm, or go to San Carlos from where you can connect with hourly buses to the capital.

For those **driving**, the roads are good, with the exception of a perennially difficult patch between La Fortuna and Arenal Town. La Fortuna's airport has been closed ever since a tragic plane crash in September 2000 on the side of Volcán Arenal.

Parque Nacional Volcán Arenal

Volcán Arenal was afforded protected status in 1995, becoming part of the national parks system as the **Parque Nacional Volcán Arenal** (daily 8am–4pm; $6). The park has some good **trails**, some of them across lava fields; the four-kilometre Tucanes Trail takes you to the part of the forest that was flattened by an eruption in 1968. On your hikes, you may see some **wildlife**; birds (including oropéndolas and tanagers) and agoutis are particularly common. Although the park has a simple café, it's best to take a picnic lunch and plenty of water if you intend to walk extensively. Hiking any distance up the volcano's sides has always been energetically discouraged, and fences now stop you from doing so.

Though Volcán Arenal is one of the most active volcanos in the Americas, whether you see any lava flow depends very much on the weather. In the rainy season the spectacular night flows are very elusive, hidden by shrouds of mist and cloud. If you can't see the summit, the park's visitor centre has video displays of the volcano's more spectacular activity and if nothing else, you'll certainly hear unearthly rumbling and sporadically feel the ground shake, especially at night.

You can't visit the park after dark except by taking one of the **night tours**, which leave La Fortuna every afternoon at about 3–4pm. Most operators run them even when it's cloudy, in the hope that the clouds will lift or the opposite side of the volcano will be clear. None offers you a refund if you don't see anything, so you might want to wait for a clear evening before signing up. Aventuras Arenal (see p.191) run a sunset **boat tour** on which you can watch the action from Laguna de Arenal.

The **park entrance** is 14km from La Fortuna; look for the well-signed driveway off to the left. If you don't have your own vehicle, you can take a **taxi** from La Fortuna to the west side of the volcano (around $35 round-trip per car, including waiting time of a few hours), but unless you're in a large group, it's cheaper – and less bother – to take a tour. The **bus** from La Fortuna drops you off at the entrance to the park and is by far the cheapest option, though the return journey can be tricky – unless you manage to connect with the bus coming from Tilarán or Arenal Town, your only option is to try to get a ride back with other park visitors. Hitching on the main road is quite easy.

Balneario Tabacón, Las Fuentes and Baldi Termae

The volcano's magma heats various underground streams; diverted into pools, these provide the perfect relaxing vantage-point for observing the pyrotechnics with drink in hand. Most of the volcano evening tours end up at one spring or another, but you can easily visit them independently.

The glitzier of the two main springs and the destination for most tourists is **BALNEARIO TABACÓN** (Tabacón Hot Springs; daily 10am–10pm; $29, $19 after 7pm), 10km west of La Fortuna. Fed by a magma-boiled underground thermal river originating in the nether parts of Volcán Arenal, the hot springs complex comprises five pools, some with Jacuzzis, slides and sculpted waterfalls, as well as several artificial hot tubs, warm streams and ponds. The water in the warmest of the pools is about 40°C, while others are closer to 25°C. There's also a small system of trails winding up through the grounds, some of which are lit at night. If it's a clear night, you can watch the erupting volcano's fireworks from the swim-up bar inside one of the hot pools or from the restaurant or one of the many terraces; the atmosphere, with cocktail bar and bikini-clad tourists, makes you feel like you've just stepped into a 1970s James Bond film. They also offer massages ($60 per hour) and health and beauty treatments (mud masks are $20). Note that you shouldn't leave valuables in your car as thefts are common.

If you want to **stay the night**, try the upscale *Tabacón Lodge* (☎256-1500, ⓦwww.tabacon.com; ⑧), 100m down the road from the springs, with

---

The geological history of Volcán Arenal

Volcán Arenal is the youngest **stratovolcano** – the term for a steep, conical volcano created by the eruption of thick lava flows – in Costa Rica, and also the most active. Stratovolcanos are responsible for nearly half the planet's volcanic activity. Of the 1511 volcanos known to have erupted in the past 10,000 years, 699 are stratovolcanos. Geologists have determined that Arenal is no more than 2900 years old; by comparison, Volcán Chato, which flanks Arenal to the south, is much older, and last erupted in the late Holocene period, around 10,000 years ago. Arenal is so active because, geologists speculate, it directly taps a magma chamber located on a fault about 22km below the surface.

Arenal's growth over the ages has been characterized by massive eruptions every few centuries. It is thought to have erupted around 1750, 1525 and 1080 AD, and 220 and 900 BC. The most recent eruption occurred a quarter of a century ago. At that time, Arenal seemed to be nothing but an unthreatening mountain, and locals had built small farms up its forested sides (take a look at Volcán Chato and you get the idea). On **July 29, 1968**, an earthquake shook the area, blasting the top off Arenal and creating the majestic, lethal volcano you see today.

Arenal killed 78 people on that day. Fatalities were caused by a combination of shockwaves, hot rocks and poisonous gases – what volcanologists describe as "Strombolian activity", a volcanic eruption characterized by fountains of fluid basalt lava being ejected from a central crater. The explosion created three craters, and Arenal has been continuously active ever since, with almost daily rumblings and shakings.

luxurious rooms (all equipped with a/c and TV), an efficient and friendly staff and regular live music in the hotel's bar. Rates include unlimited access to the hot springs.

A cheaper, more basic thermal spring, **LAS FUENTES** (open weekdays only; $8) has opened across the road. The main disadvantage is that you can't see the volcano from here. There are showers and changing rooms (although no towels or lockers). Note that there have been reports of assaults on tourists here, so it's probably not the place to go alone for a night soak.

Four kilometres west of La Fortuna, **BALDI TERMAE** (☎479-9651; 10am–10pm; $14) is more accessible than Tabacón if you don't have your own transport. While it lacks the classy touches of its rival, Baldi Termae is significantly cheaper and offers many of the same facilities. There are no lockers, but the atmosphere is friendly and relaxed and there's a swim-up bar with more reasonably priced drinks. Baldi Termae boasts nine pools, the hottest of which gets up to an whopping 67°C. The views of the volcano aren't quite as dramatic as Tabacón, but are still impressive on a fiery night.

Laguna de Arenal and Arenal Town

The waters of **Laguna de Arenal** make what would otherwise have been a pretty area into a very beautiful one – a fact exploited by the tourist board's promotional posters that show a stately and serene Volcán Arenal rising preternaturally out of the lake. Actually a man-made body of water created when the original lake was dammed, the resulting Arenal Dam, built in 1973, now generates much of the country's hydroelectricity. The lake is excellent for fishing rainbow bass (*guapote*), an iridescent fish found only in freshwater lakes and rivers in Costa Rica, Nicaragua and Honduras. The lake is also ideal for windsurfing (Dec–March only) and many of the area hotels rent boards. Tourism is on the rise, bringing with it a sizeable colony of year-round foreign residents,

Tragedy at Volcán Arenal

Just before 10am on August 23, 2000, Volcán Arenal emitted larger than usual pyroclastic flows (lava flows accompanied by clouds of hot gas and ash). The toxic, superheated cloud surprised and engulfed a Costa Rican tour guide and his two charges, an American woman and her 8-year-old daughter, who were on a walking tour in the Los Lagos tourist complex only 2.3km from the crater. Despite having suffered severe burns, the tour guide managed to get his clients off the volcano. All three were taken to hospital in San José, where the guide died that same night. The young girl succumbed to her injuries after being airlifted to hospital in the US.

This was the first time since 1988 that the volcano had claimed a life. The tragedy highlights the fact that Arenal is an active volcano, and gas emissions, incandescent avalanches and ash columns are all regular occurrences. Despite being constantly monitored by volcanologists and geologists, volcanos are notoriously unpredictable, a fact reiterated by the August 2000 tragedy: previous eruptions had always taken place to the west, in the direction of Laguna de Arenal, and the Los Lagos trails where the guide and his charges were walking that day face the east, and were thought to be totally safe. These trails are now closed, choked by the lava flows that streamed down Arenal's flanks in the wake of the outburst.

Danger is part of the appeal: the atavistic thrill of a night-time lava flow or merely the sound of its deep, planetary rumble is undeniable. It's imperative, though, that you never veer from trails or guided tours, and do not to attempt to hike anywhere near the crater, since lethal gases, ballistic boulders and molten rock can appear or change direction without warning.

many of them Germans or Austrians, perhaps attracted by the combination of a rather European-looking landscape with the added benefit of a volcano and year-round tropical temperatures.

You can't actually make a full circuit of the lake, but you can drive along its northeast and west sides, from where there are beautiful views of the volcano and of gentle hills, some of them given over to wind-farming – look for the giant white windmills on the hills above the north edge of the lake. About midway between La Fortuna and Tilarán is the lakeside **ARENAL TOWN**, also known as **Nuevo Arenal** (the original Arenal was flooded when the dam was built). It's a quiet, pleasant town, with numerous accommodation options overlooking the lake. At *Tom's Pan*, on the town's main road, you can stock up on everything from rye and pumpernickel to cakes and gingerbread, or tuck into German sausages while enjoying views of the lake from the outdoor terrace. For lunch and dinner, the *Restaurante Tramonti* (closed Mon) serves traditional thin-crust pizzas ($5–8), cooked in a wood oven. Three kilometres west of town is the excellent *El Caballo Negro*, with delicious vegetarian fare as well as schnitzels ($5–9). **Arenal Botanical Gardens** (daily 9am–5pm, closed Oct; $8), 5km east of Arenal Town, features a pretty collection of tropical plants, including orchids of all shapes and sizes, as well as butterflies and serpents.

Accommodation around Arenal Town

La Ceiba Tree Lodge 6km from Arenal Town on the road to La Fortuna ☎692-8050, 🌐www.ceibatree-lodge.com. A romantic, relaxing lodge just above Laguna de Arenal, with good views. The five cabinas have private bath with hot water, beautiful carved wooden doors, big beds and tasteful artwork, but best of all is the big shady communal terrace for sunset viewing. Named for the massive 500-year-old tree in the grounds, the lodge also has an excellent apartment, perfect for a couple (❻). There are walking trails and mountain-biking, horse-riding, fishing and sailing can be arranged. Breakfast is included. ❺

Chalet Nicholas 2km northwest of Arenal Town, on the road to Tilarán ☎694-4041, 🌐www.chaletnicholas.com. Small, beautifully kept hotel with just three rooms, all with private bathroom and hot water, looking out to the lake and distant volcano. You'll get a warm welcome from the charming hosts, not to mention their five massive Great Danes, who have their own suite. Horse-riding and birdwatching tours can be arranged – and you'll also spot plenty of birds in the hotel grounds. Non-smoking. ❺

Los Héroes Hotel and Restaurant 15km east of Arenal Town on the road to La Fortuna ☎692-8012, 🌐www.hotellosheroes.com. This small Swiss-style hotel perched above Laguna de Arenal looks like it was transported straight from an Alpine meadow. Rooms are comfortable and there's a Jacuzzi, pool, alpine decor with gingerbread woodwork and a restaurant serving cheese fondue. No credit cards accepted. ❹

Lago Coter Ecoadventure Lodge On Lago Coter, 4km north of Arenal Town; follow the westbound road from Arenal Town, then turn right 3km up a rough track. ☎440-6768, 🅕440-6725. Somewhat isolated, this well-equipped lodge is set up for outdoor activities. Rooms are simple and clean if a bit dingy, but the communal areas are more promising, with a cheerful lounge and pool table. The staff are a mine of information about local fauna and flora and you can explore nature trails in a small section of cloudforest. The lodge also arranges canopy tours and hikes to local indigenous communities. ❺

La Rana de Arenal 5km west of Arenal Town ☎694-4031. Set on a large grassy lawn, complete with tennis court, this German-run place is a good hideaway. The seven rooms are small but clean and comfortable, and boast great views over the lake. There's also an apartment available (❺). The upstairs restaurant serves hearty dishes such as goulash soup and excellent schnitzel. Room rates available with or without breakfast. ❹

Villa Decary 2km east of Arenal Town, on the lake ☎383-3012, 🌐www.villadecary.com. Beautifully furnished rooms and bungalows have big beds decorated with colourful Guatemalan fabrics, and balconies with lovely forest and lake views. The hospitable hosts, who are experts on regional flora and fauna, serve up a delicious breakfast with home-made jams. Lots of birds flutter about the grounds, and there's a good hike to the rear of the hotel. No credit cards. ❻–❼

The Venado Caves

About 30km northwest of La Fortuna, on a paved road near the tiny mountain town of **Venado** ("Deer"), are the **Venado Caves** ($6, though there may be no one to collect it). This small network of subterranean caverns is quite accessible, provided you aren't afraid of bats and don't mind getting wet. Inside is a spooky and unique tangle of stalactites and smoothed-out rock formations. Some of the passages from cave to cave are so narrow that you should measure whether or not you are going to fit before you begin the crawl. Using the services of a guide is a very good idea – the caves are labyrinthine – and you should bring a torch and rubber boots (you may be able to rent them from your hotel if you're staying locally). The caves are closed in the wet season.

Several companies in La Fortuna offer day-trips to the caves, including guide and entrance fee. A daily **bus** heads from San Carlos via La Fortuna to Venado, but it leaves at 2pm and returns at 4.30pm, which doesn't give enough time to explore the caves. More frequent buses from La Fortuna to Guatuso will drop you off at a private farm (owned by Sr Solis). From here to the mouth of the caves it's a walk of several kilometres along a gravel road and marked trail.

San Rafael de Guatuso

Historically part of the Corobicí tribal group, the present-day Guatusos are a community of interrelated clans that have inhabited northwestern Costa Rica and southern Nicaragua for thousands of years. Now numbering about four hundred, their history and the story of their steady decline is a familiar one for tribal peoples in the area. Victims of disease, intertribal kidnapping and slavery to Spanish settlers in Nicaragua, they were dealt further blows in the 1700s and 1800s by the efforts of the Nicaraguan and Costa Rican Catholic Churches to convert them to Christianity.

The Guatuso communities today live on three **reserves**, established by the government in the 1960s. The reserves are not obviously demarcated, and you will pass through them en route to the village of **SAN RAFAEL DE GUATUSO** – known locally as **Guatuso** – 10km north of Venado. Though they speak their own language – Maleku, broadcast by Radio Sistema Cultural Maleku and taught in schools – don't expect to see native dress or any outward signs of tribal identity: the locals wear western clothes and the town looks much like any other in Costa Rica. There are, however, several places to buy Guatuso **crafts** – rather folksy, with a preponderance of decorated drums covered in snakeskin and small wooden carvings. Excavations of old Guatuso **tombs** in the area sometimes turn up jade and pottery artefacts, which you can see in San José's Museo Nacional (see p.85).

There's no compelling reason to stay longer than a couple of hours, but if you decide to spend the night, try *Cabinas El Milagro* (☏464-0037), a friendly spot with spick and span basic rooms with cold-water bathroom. Irregular buses (about 2 daily; 90min) travel to Guatuso from La Fortuna. Several buses also travel daily to Guatuso (2hrs) from Tilarán and San Carlos.

The far north

The **far north** of the Zona Norte is an isolated region, culturally as well as geographically, closer to Nicaragua than to the rest of the country and mostly devoted to sugar-cane. Years of conflict during the Nicaraguan civil war made the region more familiar with CIA men and arms runners than with tourists, but it's all quiet now. Los Chiles, near the Nicaraguan border, is the only village of any size: the drive up here, along the stretch of good tarmac road from San Carlos, takes you through a flat landscape broken only by roadside shacks, many inhabited by Nicaraguan economic migrants. Tourist facilities are practically non-existent, and between the small village of Muelle, 8km from San Carlos, and Los Chiles there's 74km of virtually empty highway, with the Llanura de Guatusos stretching hot and interminably to the west.

Most tourists come here to see the **Refugio Nacional de Vida Silvestre Caño Negro**, a vast wetland, and one of the most remote wildlife refuges in the country. No longer a well-kept secret, it's possible to visit Caño Negro on a day-trip from the capital, on an excursion from La Fortuna or one of the larger hotels in the Zona Norte, or to go independently.

During the Nicaraguan civil war, **Los Chiles**, right next to the border, was a Contra supply line. Nowadays, though, there is a climate of international cooperation, helped by the fact that many of the residents are of Nicaraguan extraction, and the area is gently opening up to tourism. A committed group of local hoteliers, restaurateurs and boatmen have formed a local tourism association with help from the national tourist board, and crossing the border is straightforward as long as your documents are in order. Despite these initiatives, bear in mind that you will have a hard time finding people who speak English; the further north you head, the more Spanish you'll need.

Incidentally, the **Río San Juan** is technically Nicaraguan territory – the border is on the Costa Rican bank – though Costa Rica is allowed free use of the river under the terms of a treaty between the two countries.

Los Chiles

Few tourists make it to **LOS CHILES**, a border settlement just 3km from the Nicaraguan frontier, and other than soaking up the town's end-of-the-world atmosphere, there's little to do, except perhaps try to rent a boat or horse to go to **Caño Negro**, 25km downstream on the Río Frío (see p.200). The only other reason you might come to Los Chiles is to cross the Nicaraguan border, although the majority of travellers still cross at Peñas Blancas, further west on the Interamericana.

Arrival

Until 1982, when the current highway was built, Los Chiles was cut off from the rest of Costa Rica. These days, two luxury **buses** daily run from **San José** (C12, Av 7/9) to Los Chiles (5.30am & 3.30pm; 5hr). Return buses to San José leave Los Chiles at 5am and 3pm, but be sure to check these times in advance. Buses depart almost hourly from San Carlos (Ciudad Quesada) stopping in Los Chiles at the small bus station, just west of where the main road takes a right-angled left down to the port.

Driving from San Carlos, Hwy-141 heads north along a reasonable road through the tiny settlements of Florencia and Muelle, and then along the sixty-six-kilometre stretch, potholed in places, from Boca de Arenal through to Los Chiles. There are few service stations north of Muelle: make sure you have lots of petrol. The only other way to get there is to charter an **air-taxi** from San José (see p.31); the airstrip is next to the *guardia civil* post on the edge of town.

Information

Although Los Chiles has no official **tourist information**, everyone in town knows the current bus schedules and the times of the river-boat to the

Nicaraguan border, though you'll need Spanish to ask around. Servicios Turísticos Caño Negro (☎471-1438), based at the *Cabinas Jabirú,* a block west and north of the bus station, has general tourist information and they also run trips to Caño Negro and Nicaragua and can arrange local fishing excursions. Though Los Chiles is quite isolated, it has most of the facilities you'll need: you can **change dollars** and travellers' cheques at the Banco Nacional on the north side of the soccer field (Mon–Fri 8am–3.30pm); it also has an ATM. Full postal services, including fax, are offered at the **correo** in the Mercado Central (Mon–Fri 8am–4pm). For **supplies**, head for the Dos Piños general store 50m east of the docks.

Accommodation

If you're intending to cross the border, you may well need to **stay the night** in Los Chiles, as the boats often leave quite early in the morning. The best budget lodging in town is the simple, clean and comfortable *Cabinas Jabirú*

Crossing into Nicaragua

The border at Los Chiles between Nicaragua and Costa Rica has a turbulent history. During the Nicaraguan civil war, US-sponsored Contras were supplied through here, and it was not unusual to see camouflaged planes sitting on the airstrip, disgorging guns. In the past, the border was closed to foreigners, and for a period also to Nicaraguans and Costa Ricans, though it's now possible for anyone to **enter Nicaragua** from here.

Work has begun on a road bridge across to Nicaragua, but the project is continually plagued by delays. Currently, the only way to reach Nicaragua is by boat on the Río Frío: one to three daily services leave the docks in Los Chiles, with the time of departure depending on demand and tides. From the border control point it's a fourteen-kilometre trip up the Río Frío to the small town of **San Carlos de Nicaragua** (just over an hour; $7) on the southeast lip of the huge Lago de Nicaragua. The Los Chiles *migración* officials are relatively friendly, and you may be able to confirm boat times with the groups of Nicas or Ticos who hang around the office. Make sure that the **Nicaraguan border patrol**, 3km upriver from Los Chiles, stamps your passport, as you will need proof of entry when leaving Nicaragua. There is also a **police check** south of Los Chiles on the highway to San Carlos and La Fortuna. Don't worry if they signal you over – this is mainly to guard against Nicaraguans entering or staying in Costa Rica illegally. Few nationalities need a visa for Nicaragua, but if you do, this has to be done at the Nicaraguan consulate in San José. Note also that if you needed a visa to enter Costa Rica, make sure you've got a double-entry stamp if you do this trip, otherwise you won't be allowed back into Costa Rica.

You'll need some cash upon arrival in San Carlos de Nicaragua; change a few colones for córdobas at the Los Chiles bank. From San Carlos de Nicaragua it's possible to cross the lake to **Granada** and on to **Managua**, but check with the consulate in San José because this is an infrequent boat service and without forward planning you could end up stuck in San Carlos for longer than you'd hoped.

In the current atmosphere of relative political stability in Nicaragua, you can go on organized day-trips from Los Chiles to Nicaraguan San Carlos, Lago de Nicaragua and even the Solentiname islands in the lake. Visitors may even be able to see the fortress San Juan (also called the Castillo de la Concepción or Fortaleza) on Lago de Nicaragua, one of the oldest Spanish structures (1675) in the Americas, built as a defence against the English and pirates (often one and the same) plying the Río San Juan. For more details, contact Servicios Turísticos Caño Negro (☎471-1438), based at the *Cabinas Jabirú* in Los Chiles.

(T 471-1438; **②**), a block west and half a block north of the bus station. It offers rooms with private bath, hot water and fan, plus laundry service and Internet access. Another good option is the *Rancho EcoDirecta* (T 471-1414, E cocas34@hotmail.com; **③**), whose air-conditioned rooms are large and come with hot water. On the southern edge of town, check out the *Complejo Turístico El Gaspar* (T 471-1422, F 471-1033; **③**) with quiet, rustic rooms with fan (**③**) or air-conditioning (**④**) and TV. There's an open-air restaurant, swimming pools and horse-riding, and breakfast is included. Next door, *El Alamo* (T 228-4812, W www.nofrillsfishing.com; **④**) offers modern, uninspiring rooms and is mainly although not exclusively a lodge for sport-fishing groups.

The Town

Los Chiles is laid out on a small grid of dusty, uneventful streets. The highway peters out just beyond the town in the direction of the Río San Juan, leaving nowhere to go but the river. There's no traffic to speak of – just a few *campesinos* ambling along on their horses, huge workhorse trucks rumbling by caked with the red dust of the tropical forest soil and children nipping past on creaky bikes. Probably the most excitement you'll encounter are the clumps of youths sitting in the middle of the road idly chatting.

There is little to see around the usually deserted **main square** (more accurately, an ill-kempt soccer field), although the faded, tumbledown houses lining the right-hand side of the road to the river have a certain atmospheric melancholy, embellished with wooden latticework of surprising delicacy and French doors opening off tall, narrow porches. These were some of the first buildings to be built in the area, forty to fifty years ago, and they now evoke a forlorn, France-in-the-tropics feel. If there's any activity, you'll find it at the *migración* and the adjacent docks, where children frolic in the river or at the bunker-like **Mercado Central**, 200m northeast of the soccer field. Apart from the Dos Piños general store east of the docks, this is the only place in town to buy fresh food.

Los Chiles is a great spot for **tarpon-fishing**, and many locals offer fishing trips in their own *lanchas* (except during Jan–April, when fishing is not permitted). Enquire at the dock or at the *El Alamo* hotel, near the southern edge of town. Provision of rods and tackle varies, and you'll need a licence, which the hotel can arrange.

Eating and drinking

A number of decent, inexpensive sodas dot the town. Friendly *Soda Pamela*, by the bus station, serves up excellent *batidos*, cool shakes that are a godsend in the heat. Attractive, welcoming *Doña Sonia*, on the main road, offers *casados* for a mere $2, and it's the best spot in town for a cold beer. *Complejo Turístico El Gaspar* (see above) serves *comida típica* in an open, thatched dining area.

Refugio Nacional de Vida Silvestre Caño Negro

The largely pristine **REFUGIO NACIONAL DE VIDA SILVESTRE CAÑO NEGRO** ($4), 25km southwest of Los Chiles by road, or 35km by boat, is one of the top places in the Americas to view enormous concentrations of both migratory and indigenous **birds**, along with mammalian and reptilian **river wildlife**. Until recently, its isolation kept it well off the beaten tourist track, though nowadays, numerous tours are offered from San José and La Fortuna.

Caño Negro is created by the seasonal flooding of the Río Frío so depending on what time of year you go, you may find yourself whizzing around a huge lake in a motorboat or walking along mud-caked riverbeds. There's a three-metre difference in the water level between the rainy season (May–Nov), when Caño Negro is at its fullest, and the dry season (Dec–April); note that the rainy season is not necessarily the best time to see wildlife, because while the mammalian population of the area stays more or less constant, the birds vary widely. In the dry season you'll see enormous flocks of birds mucking about in the mud together or washing their feathers; the **best time** for birders to visit is between January and March, when the most migratory species are in residence.

Unless you're an expert in identifying wildlife, the most rewarding way to enjoy the diverse flora and fauna of Caño Negro is to use the services of a **guide** who knows the area and can point out animals and other features of river life. If you come independently call the ranger station in advance to arrange this. You can also ask around in the village of Caño Negro near the park entrance.

Getting to Caño Negro

An increasing number of **tour companies** run trips to Caño Negro from San José, La Fortuna and the more upmarket Zona Norte hotels. Prices vary widely, but in general the trip to Caño Negro is a little more expensive than many expeditions because of the distances involved and – in the wet season

---

Wildlife in Caño Negro

Migratory birds such as storks, ducks, herons and cormorants join an abundance of permanent residents including iguanas, snakes, osprey eagles, kingfishers, "Jesus Christ" lizards, yellow turtles, "yellow-footed" birds (*patas amarillas*) and egrets (*garças*). The largest colony of the Nicaraguan **grackle** also makes regular appearances here, the only place in Costa Rica where it nests. Large animals including **pumas**, **jaguars** and **tapirs** have also been spotted – there are thought to be considerable numbers in the reserve, though it's rare that you'll actually see them.

Among the more unusual inhabitants of Caño Negro in the wet season is the **garfish**, a kind of in-between creature straddling fish and mammal. This so-called "living fossil" is a fish with lungs, gills and a nose, and looks oddest while it sleeps, drifting along in the water; again, it's rare to see one. The **tarpon** can grow to truly huge dimensions – up to 2m in length – and you'll often see its startling white form splashing out of the water, arching its enormous fin and long body.

Other creatures to watch out for include the ubiquitous pot-bellied **iguanas**; **swimming snakes**, heads held aloft like periscopes, bodies whipping out behind (don't get too close and do not touch – in most cases they will be fleeing from you); the elegant, long-limbed **white ibis** that rests on river-level branches and banks; and the sinuous-necked **anhingas** (snakebirds), who impale their prey with the knife-point of their beaks before swallowing. **Crocodiles** and **caimans** also live here, the latter far more common than the former.

Howler monkeys (*monos congos*) will often sound the alarm as you approach. To see them, look up into the taller branches of riverside trees. It helps to have binoculars to distinguish their black hairy shapes from the densely leaved trees. Equally, the **sloth**'s resemblance, from a distance, to a dense clump of leaves makes them very difficult to spot. Not only do they move very little during the day, they are also very well camouflaged by the green algae that often covers their brown hair. For the best chances of catching sight of one, use binoculars to scan the middle and upper branches of eucalyptus trees (the ones with the big, light-green leaves growing in umbrella-patterns) and especially the V-shaped intersections between branches, keeping an eye out for what will initially look like a dark mass. The rows of small grey triangles you might see on riverside tree trunks are **bats**, literally hanging out during the day.

– the amount of time spent in the boat simply getting there. See La Fortuna (p.191) and Basics (p.32) for contact info of some of the many tour operators that run this trip. Expect to pay $40–70 per person for a long day-trip, including entrance fee, lunch and guided visit.

The road from Los Chiles to Caño Negro has improved, and is serviced by two daily buses, leaving Los Chiles at 5am and 2pm year-round, and returning from Caño Negro at 7am and 6pm. If the road isn't passable during the wet season, a boat regularly runs up the river – ask at the docks. You can also hire your own boat ($60–100) but you'll likely save little money over taking a guided tour from Los Chiles itself. If you do it this way, note that the first 25km of the trip down the Río Frío (taking an hour or more by *lancha*) does not take you through the wildlife refuge, which begins at the mouth of the large flooded area and is marked by a sign poking out of a small islet. Make sure your boatman takes you right into Caño Negro.

If you take a tour, the **entrance fee** is included. If not, you should pay at the **ranger station** on the north side of the lake, provided you can find someone to collect the money. You can also **stay** at the ranger station (T460-6484; ❷), though facilities are minimal. Call from the public telephone at Caño Negro to reserve. You may be able to buy a meal, but bring your own supplies just in case. There are also a handful of accommodation options in the village of Caño Negro, including the *Caño Negro Fishing Club* (T656-0071, Wwww.canonegro.com; ❺). Bungalow rooms, set in spacious grounds, have big beds, fans and private bath, and the price includes breakfast. **Camping** is permitted in Caño Negro, but no formal facilities are provided and there's a charge of around $4, payable to the ranger.

La Laguna del Lagarto Lodge

Poised midway between Caño Negro and Tortuguero, 70km from either, **La Laguna del Lagarto Lodge** (T289-8163, Wwww.lagarto-lodge-costa-rica .com; ❹–❺) is one of the most remote in the country. Set in an extensive area of virgin tropical rainforest, the lodge is home to an incredible variety of trees, plants and animals and offers some of the best birdwatching in the country – it's one of the very few places in Costa Rica where you might still see the highly endangered great green macaw, as well as a large resident colony of more common oropéndolas. The lodge is only 16km from the Nicaraguan border and can arrange horse-riding tours and river excursions on the Río San Juan – not usually very accessible to tourists – as well as hiking and canoeing. The lodge also has its own network of jungle trails.

Rooms are rustic but comfortable, and have peaceful views from their balconies; rooms have shared (❹) or private (❺) bath including breakfast. To reach the lodge **by car** from San José or Ciudad Quesada you have to drive east through Aguas Zarcas, then turn left (signed) to Pital. From here, head northwest to Sahino and Boca Tapada on good gravel roads. The lodge is 10km to the east of Boca Tapada, also on a reasonable road, although 4WD is recommended. **Buses** leave from Av 9, C12 in San José daily at 12.30pm, and hourly from San Carlos to Pital, from where you can connect with buses north to Boca Tapada. The lodge will pick you up from here and can also arrange transfers from San José or La Fortuna.

The Sarapiquí region

Northwest of the Las Horquetas turn-off on the Guápiles Highway, the **Sarapiquí region** stretches around the top of Braulio Carrillo National

Park (see p.126) and west to the village" of San Miguel, from where Volcán Arenal and the western lowlands are easily accessible by road. Steamy, tropical and carpeted with fruit plantations, the area bears more resemblance to the hot and dense Caribbean lowlands than the plains of the north and, despite the large-scale deforestation, still shelters some of the best-preserved **premontane rainforest** in the country.

South of Puerto Viejo de Sarapiquí, the area around the small town of **Las Horquetas** is home to the biggest *palmito* (heart-of-palm) plantations in the world. This and banana cultivation form the core of the local economy, alongside more recent eco-tourism initiatives such as the research station **La Selva**, and the rainforest lodges of **Rara Avis** and **Selva Verde**. These lodges are the region's chief tourist attractions and offer access to some of the last primary rainforest in the country. The largest settlement, sleepy **Puerto Viejo de Sarapiquí**, attracts few visitors and is primarily a river transport hub and a place for the banana, coconut and pineapple plantation workers to stock up on supplies, prop their machetes at the bar and have a beer or two.

There are two options when it comes to getting **from San José or the Valle Central** to Puerto Viejo. The western route, which takes a little more than three hours, goes via Varablanca and the La Paz waterfall, passing the hump of Volcán Barva. Characterized by winding mountain roads and plenty of potholes, this route offers great views of velvety smooth green hills clad with coffee plantations, which turn, eventually, into rainforest. Faster (1hr–1hr 30min) and less hair-raising, although somewhat less scenic, is the route via the **Guápiles Highway** through Braulio Carrillo National Park, heading off to the left at the Las Horquetas/Puerto Viejo turn-off at the base of the mountain pass. If you're on an all-inclusive package to one of the lodges and have transport included, your driver will take this route.

Unsurprisingly, the region receives a lot of **rain** – as much as 4500mm annually, and there is no real dry season (although less rain is recorded from January to May), so rain gear is essential year-round.

Rara Avis

RARA AVIS, a private rainforest reserve 17km south of Puerto Viejo and about 80km northeast of San José, offers one of the most thrilling and authentic eco-tourism experiences – if not *the* best – in Costa Rica, featuring both primary rainforest and some secondary cover dating from about thirty years ago. This general area, bordering the northeast tip of pristine Braulio

Carrillo National Park, is home to a number of unique **palm species**. You'll also see huge ancient hardwood trees smothered by lianas, "walking" palms (that shift a metre or so in their lifetime), primitive ferns and mosses and orchids.

Established in 1983 by American Amos Bien (a former administrator of the Estación Biológica La Selva) and Trino (a local squatter *campesino*), Rara Avis combines the functions of a tourist lodge and a private rainforest reserve, and is dedicated to the conservation, study and farming of the area's biodiversity. Its ultimate objective is to show that the rainforest can be profitable for an indefinite period, giving local smallholders a viable alternative to clearing the land for cattle. Rara Avis supports a number of endemic plants that have considerable economic potential, including *geonoma epetiolata*, or the stained-glass palm, which was until recently believed to be extinct. Another significant part of the Rara Avis mandate is to provide alternative sources of employment in Las Horquetas, 15km away, where most people work for the big fruit companies or as day-labourers on local farms.

Rara Avis also functions as a **research station**, accommodating student groups and volunteers whose aims, as well as studying the bird, plant and animal life, include development of rainforest products – orchids, palms and so forth – as crops. For more on rainforest management and sustainability, see Contexts.

Getting to Rara Avis

Because of its isolation you'll have to spend at least one night in the reserve, though two or three would be preferable and it's necessary to reserve accommodation (see opposite) in advance. If time is short, a **package** to Rara Avis

---

What to see at Rara Avis

Rara Avis's **flora** is as diverse as you might expect from a premontane rainforest. The best way to learn to spot different flowers, plants, trees and their respective habitats is to go on a walk with one of the knowledgeable guides, most of whom have lived at Rara Avis or nearby for some time. Especially interesting plants include the **stained-glass palm tree**, a rare specimen much in demand for its ornamental beauty, and the **walking palm**, whose tentacle-like roots can propel it over more than a metre of ground in its lifetime as it "walks" in search of water. **Orchids** are numerous, as are non-flowering bromeliads, heliconias, lianas, primitive ferns and other plants typically associated with dense rainforest cover.

A mind-boggling number of **bird species** have been identified at Rara Avis, and it's likely that more are yet to be discovered. As well as the fearsome black, turkey and king vultures and the majestic osprey eagle, you might see four types of kites, ten types of hawk owls, nearly thirty species of hummingbird, pretty Amazon and green kingfishers, woodpeckers, both chestnut-mandibled and keel-billed toucans, robins, warblers, great-tailed grackle and the unlikely named black-crested coquette, great potoo and tiny hawk. The endangered great green macaw also nests here, and trogons and quetzals can be spotted in the December–February season.

Among the more common **mammals** are opossums, monkeys, armadillos, tamanduas, bats, anteaters, tapirs, ocelots and jaguars, though the last three are rarely seen. Along with other vipers, the **fer-de-lance** and **bushmaster snakes**, two of the most venomous in the world, may lie in wait, so take extra care on the trails, and look everywhere you step and put your hand. **Boa constrictors** also hang out around here; ask if any have been spotted lately. If you do see one, be careful: boas are generally quite torpid, but can get aggressive if bothered.

that includes transport from San José may be worth considering (see p.32 for tour agents), but with a little planning it's perfectly possible – and more economical – to go on your own.

To get to Rara Avis **independently**, take the Río Frío/Puerto Viejo de Sarapiquí bus from San José to the turn-off (*cruce*) for the small village of Las Horquetas (1hr–1hr 30min); ask the driver to let you off. From the turn-off, it's a five-minute walk to the **Rara Avis office** in the village (since all accommodation at the lodge must be pre-booked, they'll know you're coming). You'll then be loaded onto a tractor-pulled cart, which laboriously ascends the arduous final 15km of the journey. The tractor leaves daily for Rara Avis at 9am, so you'll have to take the 7am bus from San José. Make sure you get the express (*directo*) service via the Guápiles Highway (the bus via Heredia leaves thirty minutes earlier and takes the long western route to Puerto Viejo).

If you come with your own transport, there's a car park at the office, where you can leave your vehicle. If you stay the previous night in Puerto Viejo, the twenty-minute taxi ride to the Rara Avis reception costs $7–8; there are also several buses.

Getting to Rara Avis from Las Horquetas is at least half the fun, though not exactly comfortable. The uphill flatbed-tractor journey to the lodges takes two to four hours depending both on the condition of the road (actually, a muddy, rutted track) and on where you're staying. The pluses of this mode of transport include the sheer excitement – there's much multilingual cheering when the driver revs up the tractor and, squelching and spluttering, gets to the top of each slippery hill – and an exhilarating open-air view of the surrounding landscape, with plenty of time for toucan-spotting. Minuses include bumps and bruises, choking diesel fumes and a few worrying moments as the tractor slithers and slides up and down pitted hills.

If you miss the tractor, **horses** are available for hire from the villagers until about 1pm ($25) – any time after that is pushing it, as the trip takes four hours, including walking the last 3km on a rainforest trail.

Leaving Rara Avis, the tractor departs at about 2pm, in time to catch the last bus for San José, which passes at about 6pm. If by chance you miss this bus, the Rara Avis office in Las Horquetas can arrange for a taxi (about $25 per carload) to the Guápiles Highway, from where you can flag down a Guápiles–San José bus, which pass by hourly until 7pm.

Accommodation

There are three **places to stay** at Rara Avis (bookable on ☎253-0844 or 764-3131, ⓕ764-4187, ⓦwww.rara-avis.com; ⑥–⑦). Rates include all meals, transport by tractor to and from Las Horquetas and guided walks.

The main accommodation complex is the comfortable *Waterfall Lodge* ($140 for a double, including taxes and meals). Set above a picture-perfect cascade, it has rooms with running hot water, private baths, spacious balconies with hammocks and fantastic views of utterly pristine rainforest and the hot, flat lowland plains stretching towards the Caribbean. It's an idyllic place to stay; the only sounds heard at five or six in the morning are the echoing shrieks of birds and *monos congos* (howler monkeys), and the light, especially first thing, is sheer and unfiltered, giving everything a wonderfully shimmering effect. Meals, cooked by local women and served three times a day, are delicious: breakfasts consist of heaped platters of eggs and cheese, *gallo pinto*, corn muffins, fresh fruit and wonderful coffee, while lunches and dinners are filling, delicately flavoured dishes with a variety of meat and vegetables. Vegetarians are well catered for, and beer and snacks are kept in a small "tuck shop": you take your own and keep track of your bill. There's no electricity, but there's solar-powered lighting and a generator for the kitchen and (happily) the drinks fridge. There's a telephone available for guests (☎710-8032), but you'll need a credit card to use it.

About 500m away, *River-Edge Cabins* ($160 for a double, including taxes and meals) is even more isolated and peaceful – if you stay here, though, you'll have to be unfazed by walking through the forest at night with only a torch or a lamp.

Five minutes from *Waterfall Lodge* is the centre's cheapest accommodation, *Las Casitas* ($45 per person including taxes and meals), consisting of six rooms each sleeping four people in bunk beds. Facilities are comfortable enough, with shared bathroom, and the rate includes all three meals and guided walks.

Rara Avis activities

Rara Avis has a network of excellent **trails**. From the *Waterfall Lodge*, nine or so trails weave through fairly dense jungle cover, not including the two steep ones ("Atajo" and "Catarata") that you can choose to ascend in place of the last leg of the tractor journey. All the trails are well marked and offer walks of thirty minutes to several hours, depending upon your pace. The guided walks are fun and informative, although guests are welcome to go it alone: you'll be given a map at the lodge reception, but you should always let the staff know which trail you are following and about how long you intend to be. Rain gear is essential at all times, and take plenty of insect repellent.

Just below the *Waterfall Lodge*, a fifty-metre-high waterfall on the Río Atelopus plummets into a deep pool before continuing the river's slide down towards lower ground. **Swimming** in the ice-cold pool, shrouded in a fine mist, is a wonderful experience, and an alarm system has now been installed to give early warning of any approaching floodwaters – an occasional hazard up here.

Estación Biológica La Selva

The fully equipped research station **ESTACIÓN BIOLÓGICA LA SELVA** (☎766-6565; in San José ☎240-6696, ℱ710-6535, ⓦwww.ots.ac.cr), 93km northeast of San José and 4km southwest of Puerto Viejo de Sarapiquí, is one of the best places in the region to visit if you're a botany student or have a special interest in the scientific life of rainforests. It's also a superb birder's spot, with more than four hundred species of indigenous and migratory birds. An equally staggering number of tree species – some 450 – have been identified, as well as 113 species of mammals, including anteaters, coatimundi and monkeys. Many leading biologists from various countries have at one time studied here, and its facilities are extensive – a large swath of premontane rainforest shouldering the northern part of Braulio Carrillo National Park forms the natural laboratory, while the research facilities include lecture halls, extensive labs and accommodation for the scientists and students.

La Selva's ground cover extends from primary **forest** – sixty percent of the reserve's total area – through abandoned plantations to pastureland and brush, crossed by an extensive network of about 25 **trails** varying in length from short to more than 5km long and covering a total of nearly 60km. Most are in very good condition, clearly and frequently marked, though some are pretty rough, and many can get very muddy indeed. Only visitors staying at the complex are allowed to walk the trails unsupervised; day visitors will have to take one of the two daily guided walks. Tourists tend to stick to the main trails within the part of La Selva designated as the **ecological reserve**, next to the Río Puerto Viejo. These **trails**, the Camino Circular Cercano, the Camino Cantarrana and the Sendero Oriental, radiate from the river research station and take you through dense primary growth, the close, tightly knotted kind of tropical forest for which the Sarapiquí area is famous.

Practicalities

Though tourists are secondary to research at La Selva, visitors are welcome, provided there's space, either to stay at the centre or to take a guided walk during the day. It's impossible to overstate La Selva's popularity; in the high season (Nov–April) you need to **reserve** months in advance by fax. Visiting in the low season (roughly May–Oct) is a safer bet, but even then you should call first.

The least expensive way of getting to La Selva **from San José** is to take the 7am Río Frío/Puerto Viejo de Sarapiquí bus (marked "Río Frío"), which, if you ask, will drop you off at the entrance to the road leading to the station. Note, however, that it's a two-kilometre walk down the road from the junction. If you

New views on the rainforest

Many people unaccustomed to the **rainforest** approach it with the kind of awe reserved for great architectural or engineering feats. The idea that a rainforest is like a cathedral, to be admired in hushed and humble silence, intermingles with its metaphorical role as the epitome of the pristine – a latter-day Eden. Regeneration and decay is quick in tropical climes, but it has always been assumed that the highly complex and intertwined mechanisms that make a rainforest take centuries, even millennia, to regenerate themselves.

The tropical rainforest in the Sarapiquí region, and especially that within La Selva's natural laboratory, has long been thought to be representative of premontane, or ancient and relatively untouched, rainforest cover. But recent research into the history of La Selva's forests has raised new theories about the **regenerative capacities** of rainforests – ideas that are bound to be considered controversial by conservationists.

Unlike temperate-zone deciduous trees, those that make up the tropical rain-forest do not form internal rings, so traditionally scientists have had to resort to other tactics to determine the age of a given piece of forest, like examining the soil layer. Recent findings unearthed in La Selva include pottery pieces, two-thousand-year-old charcoals, burial sites, an ancient hearth and tools used to cultivate crops like maize and yucca. These suggest, in the broadest sense, that early rainforests around here may have been slashed, burned and inhabited by generations of indigenous peoples. Meanwhile, contemporaneous evidence provided by scientists working in the Darién Gap and in the Amazon basin presents the possibility that rainforests throughout the Americas may be more resilient to disturbances than previously thought.

At the 1993 Ecological Society of America conference, La Selva researchers announced new data illustrating that between about 2000 and 800 years ago the reserve's forest was put under the scythe by indigenous people to make space for, typically, corn plantations, small villages and patches of *pejibaye* (a kind of miniature coconut). For rainforest scientists, the chief benefit of this information is that certain puzzles surrounding seemingly natural patterns of plant distribution may be solved. But in a wider sense it suggests that, far from being static repositories of untouched biodiversity, rainforests may be the products of constant change and adaptation.

Scientists at La Selva and elsewhere are quick to say that these findings do not sanction clear-cutting or any other modern form of rainforest destruction. While admitting that it may be possible to cultivate the land in a sustainable or regenerative fashion, the scientists insist that the kind of agriculture they believe pre-Columbian people to have practised in the rainforest in no way resembles the massive plantation-style cultivation, logging, large squatter settlements and other threats to the rainforest that we witness today.

don't fancy the walk, continue in the bus on to **Puerto Viejo de Sarapiquí**, from where you can backtrack the four kilometres in a taxi for about $2.50.

If you want to **stay** at La Selva, you *must* book in advance by calling the office. The simple but comfortable student-residence–style **accommodation** at La Selva is overpriced at $135 for two, but it's the only way to gain access to the impressive network of trails and it helps subsidize research. Rates include three meals a day, served in the communal dining hall, and one free guided walk per stay. The walks last more than three hours and are led by highly qualified, extremely informative guides. If you're just visiting, the guided walk costs $26 and, again, should be reserved beforehand.

Selva Verde Lodge

One of the most luxurious rainforest lodges in Costa Rica and a mecca for birdwatching, the **SELVA VERDE LODGE** sits amid two square kilometres of preserved forest alongside the Río Sarapiquí, near the village of Chilamate, 5km west of Puerto Viejo and 103km northeast of San José. Owned and operated by a US-based company that specializes in ecological and adventure holidays, Selva Verde comprises an impressive complex of accommodation blocks, dining hall, lecture rooms and a lovely riverside bar-patio where monkeys chatter above and the Sarapiquí bubbles below. The lodge is set in landscaped tropical gardens rather than dense overgrowth, and appears to have mastered its environment to the extent that even the animals – among them the dreaded fer-de-lance snake – behave themselves and don't bother the tourists. And while it's run very professionally, and has some of the most knowledgeable naturalist guides in Costa Rica, the atmosphere is rather *Sheraton*-in-the-jungle, with super-comfortable rooms and very tasty food. Despite the slightly sanitized jungle experience, however, the hiking, wildlife-spotting and birdwatching opportunities are undeniably excellent, as are the refreshing swims in the Sarapiquí. Whitewater rafting, horse-riding, riverboat rides and visits to a banana plantation are among the many other activities offered.

Getting to Selva Verde

Taxis from Puerto Viejo to Selva Verde cost about $4 per car. If you're driving, watch for a green gate and a large orange building (the lodge's library and community centre) on the left-hand side of the road from Puerto Viejo. Buses running from Puerto Viejo westwards, or from San José to Puerto Viejo via Heredia will drop you off at the entrance. The lodge can arrange transfers from San José's airport.

Accommodation

Accommodation at the **Selva Verde Lodge** (☎766-6800, in the US ☎1-800/451-7111, ⓦwww.selvaverde.com, ⓦwww.holbrooktravel.com; ➐) is in two complexes of elevated bungalows: the *River Lodge* – from which the Sarapiquí's gentle gurglings can be heard – and the *Creek Lodge*, named for a dried-up creek nearby. The former is slightly more expensive because of its tranquil location; the rooms with river views are best. The bungalows are nicely spread out and the comfortable rooms have dark wood floorboards contrasting with bright walls. You can lounge on hammocks and there's electric light after dark, so night owls have the option of reading (everybody at Selva Verde seems to go to bed early – the bar and barbecue area empties out by 9pm). Bear in mind that much of the time the lodge is full of tour groups or study groups (it's often possible to join one of their fascinating evening talks). Rates include all meals (which are served buffet-style), good showers with hot water and full mosquito netting. All rooms are non-smoking, and reservations should be made at least thirty days in advance; the first night must be pre-paid. Children under 12 stay for free.

Selva Verde activities

Selva Verde's expanse offers an excellent variety of walks along well-marked trails through primary and secondary forest, riverside, swamps and pastureland. Unless you've come as part of a pre-paid, all-inclusive package, you'll need to pay for the activities below: these cost from $15 (for guided walks) to $45 (for a half-day of whitewater rafting); there's also a free birdwatching tour daily at 6am.

You can take a **self-guided walk** in the section of secondary rainforest across the road from the lodge – ask for a map at reception. While you might not see much in terms of animal life, birding is rewarding here – recent sightings have included a family of toucans. For experienced rainforest walkers or botany enthusiasts, the **guided walks** through the denser section of premontane forest across the Río Sarapiquí are more rewarding. The informative guides are absolutely top-notch and can make uncannily authentic bird calls to get the attention of trogons and toucans and will point out poison-dart frogs, primitive ferns and complex lianas.

After birdwatching, the most popular activity at Selva Verde is **whitewater rafting** on the Class III (easy–moderate) Río Sarapiquí (May–Nov only). The trip is exciting enough, though experienced rafters might regret the lack of any really scary rapids. You can also take **riverboat rides** from Puerto Viejo, which give a good introduction to wildlife in the area – though, admittedly, animal-watching is better in more pristine spots like Caño Negro (see p.200) or Tortuguero (p.172). The banks of the Sarapiquí are, at least in Costa Rican terms, heavily populated, and on one side are packed for long stretches with banana plantations – you'll be able to observe at first hand the problems caused by the plastic pesticide bags used in the plantations, which get caught up in the water or tangled around the lower branches of trees, poisoning the river and its wildlife.

Puerto Viejo de Sarapiquí

Just short of 100km northeast of San José, **PUERTO VIEJO DE SARAPIQUÍ** (known locally as Puerto Viejo, not to be confused with Puerto Viejo de Talamanca on the Caribbean coast) is an important hub for banana plantation workers and those who live in the isolated settlements between here and the Caribbean coast. The Río Sarapiquí is the focal point for the six thousand local inhabitants, and most cargo, both human and inanimate, is still carried by river to the Río San Juan and the Nicaraguan border in the north, and to the canals of Tortuguero and Barra del Colorado in the east. Puerto Viejo de Sarapiquí is a lazy, humid jungle outpost as well as a jumping-off point for visiting the nearby rainforest lodges. Everything focuses on the main street through town, lined with coconut trees. Weary *campesinos* trudge along, wielding the machetes they use in the pineapple and banana plantations surrounding the town.

Arrival

Numerous **buses** leave San José's Gran Terminal del Caribe for Puerto Viejo and the small settlement of Río Frío (they may be marked with the latter name); the **fast service**, via the Guápiles Highway and Las Horquetas, departs nine times a day from 6.30am to 6pm, completing the ninety-seven-kilometre trip in under two hours. Buses from San José to Puerto Viejo **via Heredia** (ask the driver if you're unsure which bus you're on – there's nothing on the front indicating which route it takes) take more like three hours and leave at 6.30am, 1pm and 5.30pm, returning from Puerto Viejo at 6am, 7.30am, 11am and 4.30pm.

Accommodation

Puerto Viejo de Sarapiquí's **accommodation** is quite varied considering the town's size, though Friday and Sunday nights can get booked up with plantation workers. To really get to know the dense rainforest in the region, however, you may prefer to stay at one of the nearby **jungle lodges**, or at one of the good, privately owned hotels near the town (see below).

Right by the football field on the main road in Puerto Viejo is *Mi Lindo Sarapiquí* (℡766-6074; ❸), with well-scrubbed rooms with fan and private bath above a good restaurant; buses stop right across the street. It's the best budget accommodation in town, but failing this, *Cabinas Monteverde* (℡766-6236; ❷), on the main street next to the *Monteverde* restaurant, has small and very basic (though clean) rooms with cold-water shower and fans. Also on the main street is *El Bambú* (℡766-6005, ✇www.elbambu.com; ❺), the plushest accommodation in town, with nicely decorated rooms (all with fans, colour TV and hot water), pretty potted tropical plants, a bar and restaurant set around the massive stand of bamboo that gives the place its name, a pool, tour service and a gym.

The town

A strange mixture of tropical languor and industriousness, Puerto Viejo is a relatively clean and well-ordered town, though it gets a bit more lively on Friday evenings, when the banana and palmito plantation workers are paid. The town's one main street runs from the Cruz Roja at the entrance to the town and curves around towards the river and the small dock. The town centre lies across from the large, manicured soccer field, where well-dressed schoolchildren gather to watch the local team practise. The best source of general **information** is Souvenirs Río Sarapiquí (daily 8am–5.15pm; ℡766-6727), diagonally across from the Banco Nacional. It's run by the knowledgeable and affable Luís Alberto Sánchez, who can make reservations for area lodges and hotels and arrange transfers to La Fortuna, rafting trips and boat rides on the Río Sarapiquí (from $15 per person), plus tours to the Tortuguero/Barra del Colorado area.

The Banco Nacional has an ATM and there's a correo (Mon–Fri 7am–5pm) on the corner where the main street joins the road to the dock, as well as a couple of supermarkets. You can surf the net at Internet Sarapiquí, 500m from the football field in the direction of the intersection with the main road. There's a taxi rank next to the soccer field. Drivers will take you anywhere, and prices are more or less fixed, about $2.50 per person to La Selva and around $7–8 per person to Rara Avis. Ken Upcraft (℡841-5341), based 3km east of the village of San Ramón de Sarapiquí and 6km above La Virgen, runs good kayaking expeditions designed for beginners. The trips cost $75 and include free accommodation in a rustic Tico farm. He also has an exquisite stained-glass workshop that's well worth a visit.

Eating and drinking

Mi Lindo Sarapiquí on the main street is the place **to eat**, with an extensive menu of good, freshly prepared *típico* food. The atmospheric restaurant in the *Hotel Bambú* is also good and the best spot in town to kick back with a beer. The busy and surprisingly smart bus station has an excellent cheap **snack bar**,

Moving on from Puerto Viejo

Puerto Viejo is a transport hub for the entire Zona Norte and eastern side of the country. From here, it's possible to travel back to the **Valle Central**, either via the Guápiles Highway (1hr 30min or more) or via Varablanca and Heredia (3hr or more). You can also cut across the country west to **San Carlos** (five buses daily; 2hr 30min) and on to **La Fortuna** (4hr) and Volcán Arenal, from where it's easy to continue, via Tilarán, to **Monteverde** and **Guanacaste**. By river, it's possible to continue north from Puerto Viejo along the Río Sarapiquí to the Nicaraguan border and then east along the Río San Juan to Barra and Tortuguero on the Caribbean coast. You'll have to rent a private lancha to do this pleasant journey, which can take anywhere between four and seven hours (you're going upstream). It's fairly pricey, unless you're in a group of eight or so – about $300 (8–10 maximum capacity). Ask at Souvenirs Río Sarapiquí, on the main road just before the Banco Nacional, or phone ☎766-6846.

To visit the surrounding area, numerous buses run along the Heredia road, bound for the small settlement of La Virgen. These can be hailed from any roadside bus stop and will cost 25–50 cents, depending on distance travelled.

while the soda near the dock by the river serves drinks, *empanadas* and other snacks – a pleasant spot to while away an hour with a cold beer, watching the activity at the docks. Another decent soda is the lunchtime-only *La Sarapiqueña*, 50m south of *Mi Lindo Sarapiquí*, with good *gallos* and *pintos* for less than $2. A few **fruit stalls** on the main street sell seasonal treats such as *mamones chinos*, the spiky lychees that look like sea anemones.

Two kilometres south of the road junction, the *Lapa Verde* restaurant distracts attention, as it's set in an enormous airy *palenque* looming over the road. Its Peruvian chef cooks excellent mid-priced dishes – the *ceviche* is particularly tasty, and different from the Costa Rican equivalent. There's sometimes live music or dancing in the evenings, and it's generally open daily until pretty late.

Accommodation around Puerto Viejo de Sarapiquí

Although La Selva, Selva Verde and Rara Avis are the area's prime tourist destinations, a number of attractive **hotels** and **lodges** dotted around Puerto Viejo also offer **rainforest** experiences. In general they're reasonably priced and accessible, and some offer packages from San José. If you're travelling by bus and the accommodation is west of Puerto Viejo, you can either take the San José–Río Frío bus via Heredia (see p.123), or get the fast bus to Puerto Viejo and hop on one of the regular local buses heading towards La Virgen and Chilamate. Anything in Puerto Viejo itself or east of it can be reached more quickly by the service to Río Frío/Puerto Viejo via the Guápiles Highway.

Albergue Islas del Río 5km west of Puerto Viejo, 1km west of Chilamate; look for the Aguas Bravas sign. ☎766-6524. This simple, friendly hostel on the Río Sarapiquí is one of the few budget options along this stretch of road. Three rooms have bunk beds ($8 per person) and cold-water bathrooms. It's a good base for outdoor activities, and biking, rafting and horse-riding can all be arranged. Rafting costs $50 for a day including lunch. ❷

Gavilán Lodge 1km south of the Puerto Viejo intersection and 1km down a signed dirt road, ☎766-6743, ⓦwww.gavilanlodge.com. By the Río Sarapiquí, this tranquil lodge surrounds a sunny lawn. The colourful cabin rooms have fans and comfy beds as well as tiny hot-water bathrooms. There's a small Jacuzzi, restaurant and shady lounge area and you can also cool off in the river. ❹
Hotel Ara Ambigua 1.5km from Puerto Viejo, 400m down a signed gravel road to the right

①766-7101, ⓦwww.hotelaraambigua.com. Lovely rustic cottages, nicely furnished and impeccably clean. Rooms come with private bath, hot water and a/c and are beautifully decorated with pastel shades and pictures of birds. There's a swimming pool, frog garden and a few resident crocs. It's worth a visit alone for the tasty food – try the chicken brochettes – dished up by the owners in the hotel's pseudo-Baroque restaurant, complete with giant gold-painted wooden chandelier. ❸

Posada Andrea Cristina 1km west of Puerto Viejo ① & ⓕ766-6265. Simple rooms with fan and private bath – go for the nice A-frame cabins, with high wooden ceilings – along with the best breakfasts, coffee and conversation around. Many people stay here for the family atmosphere and use it as a base to explore the area, including Tortuguero; one of the owners is a qualified nature guide and can offer much advice on what to do and where to go. ❹

La Quinta Lodge 7km west of Puerto Viejo, and 5km east of La Virgen, 1.5km up a side road served by the occasional bus ①761-1052, ⓦwww.quintasarapiqui.com. On the banks of the Río Sardinal, this comfortable lodge has 26 rooms, all with ceiling fans and hot water, set in bungalows scattered throughout the property and equipped with balconies and rocking chairs. Activities include swimming in the pool or river and exploring the lodge's own cultivated lands, its butterfly garden and the on-site exhibition, "Jewels of the Rainforest", with displays of colourful forest insects. There's a pleasant outdoor restaurant, and biking, horse-riding and birdwatching can all be arranged by the cheerful staff. ❺

Sarapiquis Centro Neotrópico 2km east of La Virgen ①761-1004, ⓦwww.sarapiquis.org. Although part-funded by the Belgian government and set up as both a hotel and non-profit educational centre, there's more than a whiff of money-making in this peculiar place. The hotel has its own museum of indigenous culture, pre-Columbian tombs and replica village, but the entrance fee isn't cheap (at $12, it's more expensive than the Louvre). The 24 rooms are housed in large *palenques* (round buildings based on an indigenous design); all have a private terrace and bath with solar-heated hot water (waste water is recycled, and there's even an organic biological sewage treatment, the only one in Costa Rica). Next door is a rainforest reserve with hanging bridges; guided or self-guided walks are available. The hotel has a bar, restaurant and pricey Internet access. ❻

Sueño Azul 2km west of the village of Las Horquetas; look for the signposted road ①764-4244, ⓦwww.suenoazulresort.com. Reached from Las Horquetas over a couple of swaying suspension bridges, this competently run *finca* is designed for luxurious relaxation. The large, commodious rooms happily lack TV; the emphasis here is on enjoying a peaceful stay and they offer informative guided walks and horseback excursions and also feature resort facilities such as pool, yoga and massage rooms. A peaceful terrace restaurant overlooks the junction of the San Rafael and Puerto Viejo rivers. Take advantage of the ample bird and wildlife watching opportunities. It's a good idea to book well in advance. ❻

Travel details

Buses

La Fortuna to: San Carlos (6 daily; 1–2hr); San José (3 daily; 5hr); San Rafael de Guatuso (2 daily; 1hr); Tilarán (2 daily; 3hr).
Los Chiles to: San Carlos (10 daily; 2hr 30min), San José (2 daily; 5hr).
Puerto Viejo de Sarapiquí to: San Carlos (5 daily; 2hr30min); San José (via Guápiles Highway, 7 daily; 1hr 30min–3hr; via Heredia, 4 daily; 3–4hr).
San Carlos to: La Fortuna (6 daily; 1–2hr); Los Chiles (10 daily; 2hr 30min); Puerto Viejo de Sarapiquí (5 daily; 2hr 30min); San José (14 daily; 3hr); Tilarán (1 daily; 4hr).
San José to: La Fortuna (3 daily; 5h); Los Chiles (2 daily; 5hr); Puerto Viejo de Sarapiquí (via Guápiles Highway, 7 daily; 1hr 30min–2hr; via Heredia, 3 daily; 3–4hr); San Carlos (14 daily; 3hr); Tilarán (4 daily; 4–5hr).
Tilarán to: La Fortuna (2 daily; 2hr); San Carlos (1 daily; 4hr); San José (4 daily; 4–5hr); Santa Elena, for Monteverde (1 daily; 3–4hr).

Guanacaste

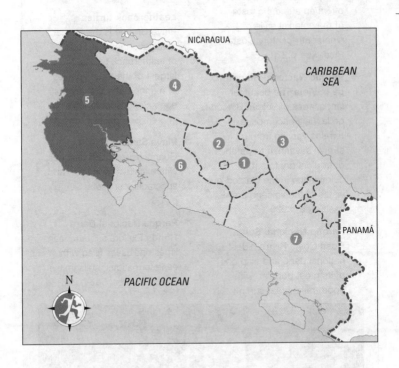

CHAPTER 5

Highlights

* **Cowboys** Skilful and self-reliant, Guanacaste's cowboys – or *sabaneros* – encapsulate the history of Costa Rica's vibrant rural communities. See p.217

* **Calle Real, Liberia** The lovely, historic Calle Real offers an authentic taste of the colonial style of nineteenth-century Costa Rica. See p.228

* **Parque Nacional Rincón de la Vieja** The beautiful landscapes of Volcán Rincón de la Vieja encompass terrains varying from rock-strewn savannah to patches of tropical dry forest, culminating in the blasted-out vistas of the volcano crater itself. See p.230

* **Parque Nacional Santa Rosa** Costa Rica's oldest national park, and also one of its most popular, with good trails, great surfing and plenty of turtle-spotting opportunities. See p.234

* **Fiestas** Lively community fiestas celebrate Guanacaste's livestock heritage with bullfights, rodeos, processions and traditional dancing. See p.262

* **Leatherback turtles** Playa Grande is the annual destination for hundreds of leatherback turtles, the largest of the three species of marine turtle that lay their eggs along Costa Rica's shores. See p.249

* **Playa Sámara** One of Guanacaste's finest beaches, with excellent swimming and spectacular sunsets. See p.258

* **Parque Nacional Barra Honda** Explore subterranean, limestone caves filled with eerie formations, stalagmites and stalactites. See p.265

△ Fruit stand

5

Guanacaste

For the majority of the Tico population, the **Guanacaste Province**, hemmed in by mountains to the east and the Pacific to the west, and bordered on the north by Nicaragua, is distinctly apart. Guanacastecos still sometimes refer to Valle Central inhabitants as "Cartagos", an archaic term dating back to the eighteenth century when Cartago was Costa Rica's capital. Though little tangible remains of the dance, music and folklore for which the region is distinct, there is undeniably something special about the place. Granted, much of the **landscape** has come about through the slaughter of tropical dry forest, but it's still some of the prettiest you'll see in the country, especially in the wet season, when wide-open spaces, stretching from the ocean across savannah grasses to the brooding humps of volcanos, are awash in earth tones, blues, yellows and mauves.

The dry heat, relatively accessible terrain and panoramic views make Guanacaste the best place in the country for **walking** and **horse-riding**, especially around the mud pots and stewing sulphur waters of the spectacular **Parque Nacional Rincón de la Vieja** and through the tropical dry forest cover of **Parque Nacional Santa Rosa**. For many travellers, however, Guanacaste means only one thing: **beaches**. Most are found where the **Nicoya Peninsula** joins the mainland. Roughly two-thirds of the mountainous peninsula is in Guanacaste, while the lower third belongs to the Puntarenas Province, covered in Chapter 6. Beaches range from simple hideaways such as quiet Nosara to large resorts aimed at the North American winter market. Several beaches are also nesting grounds for marine turtles – giant leatherbacks haul themselves up onto Playa Grande, near Tamarindo, and Parque Nacional Santa Rosa is the destination for Olive Ridley turtles. The only **towns** of any significance for travellers are the provincial capital of **Liberia**, and **Nicoya**, the main town on the peninsula. If you are overnighting on the way to **Nicaragua**, La Cruz makes a useful base.

Highland Ticos tend to describe Guanacaste as a virtual desert, liberally applying the words *caliente* (hot) and *seco* (dry). Certainly it is dry, in comparison to the rest of the country: parts of it receive only 500mm of rain a year, ten times less than the Caribbean coast. To some extent irrigation has helped, but in summer (Dec–April), Guanacaste still experiences some drought. This is when you'll see an eerie landscape of bare, silver-limbed trees glinting in the sun, as many shed their leaves in order to conserve water. The province is significantly greener, and prettier, in the wet season (May–Nov), which is generally agreed to be the **best time** to come, with the added benefit of fewer travellers and lighter rainfall than the rest of the country receives during these months.

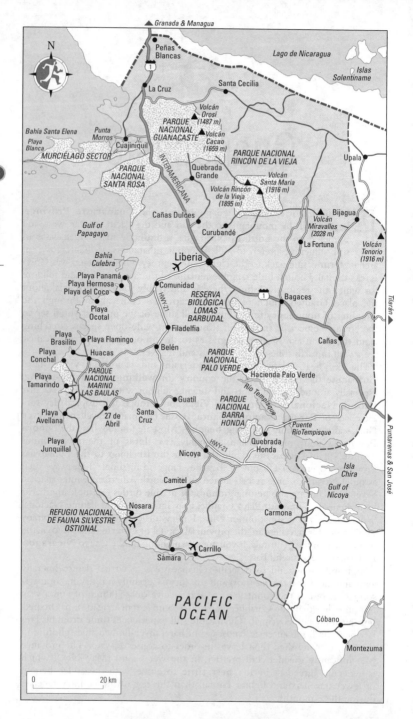

Cowboy culture in Guanacaste

Much of Guanacaste has long been turned into pasture for cattle ranching, and a huge part of the region's appeal is its **sabanero** (cowboy) culture. As in the US, the *sabanero* has acquired a mythical aura – industrious, free-spirited, monosyllabic, and a skilful handler of animals and the environment – and his rough, tough body, clad in jeans with leather accoutrements symbolizes "authenticity" (women get assigned a somewhat less exciting role in this rural mythology: the *cocinera*, or cook). In reality, however, the life of the *sabaneros* is hard; they often work in their own smallholdings or as *peones* (farmworkers) on large haciendas owned by relatively well-off ranchers.

To witness the often extraordinary skills of the *sabaneros*, head for the smaller towns – particularly on the Nicoya Peninsula – where during the months of January and February weekend **fiestas** are held in the local *redondel de toros* (bullring). More a rodeo than a bullfight, unlike in Spain, no gory kills are made: the spectacle comes from amazing feats of bull riding and roping. You'll see cowboys riding their horses alongside the Interamericana highway, too, often towing two or three horses behind them as big transport trucks steamroll past on their way to Nicaragua. This dependence on cattle culture has its downside. Much of Guanacaste is degraded pastureland, abandoned either because of its exhaustion by grazing or as a result of continually poor domestic and foreign markets for Costa Rican meat. Although impressive efforts to regenerate former tropical dry forest are under way – at Parque Nacional Santa Rosa and Parque Nacional Guanacaste, for example – it is unlikely that this rare life-zone will recover its original profile.

These days, Guanacaste is changing fast. An enormous number of hotels, some all-inclusive resorts, are being built on the Pacific coast, and with the opening of the Liberia airport to international traffic, winter charter tourism has truly arrived. Inland, mass tourism is less evident, and, despite the presence of *McDonald's* in its dignified streets, Liberia itself remains one of the most charming towns in the country. There seems to be no getting away from "progress", however, and the province may become many tourists' first, and perhaps only, glimpse of the country.

Access to most of Guanacaste from the Valle Central is easy via the Interamericana, which runs right through to the Nicaraguan border at Peñas Blancas. Still, this is Central America, and common hazards include falling mangos, dead monkeys, iguanas, cyclists and schoolchildren. Follow the road rules because plenty of traffic cops patrol this road. Modern, comfortable **buses** ply the highway, with good services to Cañas, Liberia and the border. The national parks of Rincón de la Vieja and Santa Rosa are trickier to reach, however, and bus travellers may have to walk, hitch or take a taxi for part of the journey. All the beaches are accessible by bus and car, though the roads are not in fantastic shape, and journeys from San José can take several hours. The new bridge over the Río Tempisque has significantly speeded up access to places such as Playa Sámara on the Nicoya Peninsula.

Some history

Due to significant excavations in the area and some contemporaneous Spanish accounts, Guanacaste's **pre-Columbian** history is better documented than in the rest of Costa Rica. Archeologists have long been interested in the **Chorotegas**, considered to have been the most highly developed of all Costa Rica's scattered and isolated pre-Columbian peoples, but whose culture predictably went into swift decline after the conquest. In archeological terms it belongs to the **Greater Nicoya Sub-area**, a pre-Columbian designation that includes some of western Nicaragua, and which continues to yield buried clues to the extent of communication between the Maya and Aztec cultures to the north and smaller groups inhabiting Mesoamerica from the fifth to the fifteenth centuries.

Following the conquest, the region became part of the administrative entity known as the **Capitanía General de Guatemala**. Guanacaste was annexed by Nicaragua in 1787, but in 1812 the Spanish rulers about-faced and donated the province to Costa Rica, so that its territory became large enough for it to be officially represented in the Captaincy. When the modern-day Central American nations declared independence from Spain, and the Captaincy was dissolved in 1821, Guanacaste found itself in the sensitive position of being claimed by both Costa Rica and Nicaragua. In an 1824 vote the province's inhabitants made their allegiances clear: the Guanacastecos in the north, traditionally cattle ranchers with familial ties to Nicaragua, voted to join that country, while the inhabitants of the Nicoya Peninsula wished to maintain links with Costa Rica. The peninsular vote won out, by a slim margin.

As the nineteenth century progressed, **cattle ranching** began to dominate the landscape, providing the mainstay of the economy until well into the 1900s. Despite the continuing presence of the cattle culture and the *sabanero* (see box p.217) in Guanacaste, however, beef prices have been dropping in Costa Rica for some years now, after the boom years of the '60s and '70s when deforestation was rife. In contrast, as in the rest of the country, the **tourist industry** is becoming increasingly important to the local economy.

The Río Tempisque area: north to Liberia

From San José, the Autopista General Cañas leads 95km to the Puntarenas turn-off and the Interamericana (Hwy-1). For Guanacaste and Nicaragua, head north on the highway. Eventually, neat white fences of cattle *fincas* begin to appear, with stretches of cleared land on both sides of the road. Heading north to Liberia you pass the turn-off for Las Juntas de Abangares on your right, one possible route to Monteverde and Santa Elena (see p.273), while on the left

---

The flowering trees of Guanacaste

Guanacaste's many flowering trees dot the landscape with pastel puffs of colour. Trees blossom in a strange way in the dry lands of Guanacaste, flowering literally overnight and then, just as suddenly, shedding their petals to the ground, covering it in a carpet of confetti colours. The **corteza amarilla** bursts into a wild Van Gogh-like blaze in March, April and May, and is all the more dramatic being set against a landscape of burnt siennas, muted mauves and sallow yellows. The **guanacaste** tree itself, also called the 'elephant ear', is a majestic wide-canopied specimen and an emblem of the nation. Its cream-coloured flowers appear in May, and its curious seed pods feed the cattle and horses.

In November the deciduous **guachipelín** tree blooms, with its delicate fern-like leaves; in January it's time for the pastel-pink floss of the **poui**, followed in March by the equally pretty **tabebuia rosea**. By the end of the dry season the red flowers of the **malinche** explode into colour.

runs the road to the Río Tempisque, Guanacaste's principal drainage river with a newly constructed bridge across its estuary (see box p.258). Beyond Cañas, protected areas administered by the **Area de Conservación Tempisque** (ACT) encompass **Parque Nacional Palo Verde**, an important site for migratory birds, **Reserva Biológica Lomas Barbudal**, and the deep underground caves of **Parque Nacional Barra Honda** on the Nicoya Peninsula, just across the Río Tempisque.

The **ACT regional office** (Mon–Fri 8am–4pm; ☎671-1455), on the Interamericana across from the turn-off to Parque Nacional Palo Verde, is not set up for tourists, though staff can advise on current road conditions. For general information, it's best to head to Palo Verde itself or contact the head office in Nicoya (☎686-4967).

Volcán Miravalles and Volcán Tenorio

North of the Interamericana beyond the town of Cañas – and clearly visible from the hot Guanacaste lowlands – loom **VOLCÁN MIRAVALLES** and **VOLCÁN TENORIO**. From the Reserva Biológica Privada La Pacífica, 7km north of Cañas, turn north off the Interamericana onto the road to Upala, a paved and reasonably maintained fifty-eight-kilometre stretch that runs between the two volcanos, and from which you can contemplate the spectacular colour changes and cloud shadows on their flanks. Miravalles, at 2028m the highest volcano in Guanacaste, is home to an important forest reserve with abundant wildlife and birds, though it's not open to the public.

An active volcano, although so far without spectacular eruptive displays, Tenorio was designated a national park in 1995. Marked trails lead to the top of the volcano from the entrance hut, located 8km off the Upala road. Don't wander from the trails, for the area is geothermically active; there are *fumaroles* (little columns of hot vapour escaping from the ground) and mud pots – one false move and you could step into skin-stripping superheated volcanic soil. The ICE (Costa Rican Electricity Institute) signs hereabouts point towards several geothermal plants where geologists are successfully exploiting heat vents far below the surface to tap much-needed new sources of energy.

About 35km along the road to Upala is the small hamlet of **Bijagua**, where you can **stay** in the *Albergue Ecoturística Heliconia* (☎286-4203, ℗226-6027; ④). The lodge is located on a private forest reserve set right between the volcanos, with hiking trails, waterfalls and natural hot springs. Rooms are in six cabins, all with private bath, and there's a restaurant and stunning views throughout. Breakfast is included. Bijagua itself is an impressively enterprising community, home to a number of eco-tourism projects, including an ecology centre, organic farms and a collective of women artisans. The lodge can arrange walking tours of the Tenorio National Park as well as trips to the Refugio Natural Caño Negro (see p.200), travelling via the spectacular road to Upala, from where you can glimpse Lago Nicaragua and the Solentiname Islands shimmering in its blue waters.

The rustic *La Carolina Lodge*, 6km east from Bijagua, in the hamlet of San Miguel (☎380-1656, ⓦwww.lacarolinalodge.com; ⑥), is set in a working farm well off the beaten path amid extremely quiet surroundings. There are private or shared rooms (one sleeping up to seven people). By the lodge is a (swimmable) river where toucans, green parrots and hummingbirds nest, and where you might also catch a glimpse of sloths and anteaters. Included in the very reasonable price are delicious home-style meals, a guided walk and a horseback ride. Trips to Tenorio National Park can be arranged, and the owners offer

Greater Nicoya (modern-day Guanacaste) was an archeological and cultural buffer zone between the complex cultures of the Aztecs and the Maya to the north, and the simpler agrarian cultures to the south, who had more in common with the prehistoric peoples of the Amazon basin. Greater Nicoya was occupied from an indeterminate date by the **Nicoyans**, about whom little is known, but most of the historical and archeological facts discovered about the region relate to the peoples known as the **Chorotegas**, who arrived in Nicoya in 800 AD, though some sources date their arrival as later, fleeing social and political upheavals far to the north.

The central Mexican empire of Teotihuacán, near the Mexico City of today, had fallen into disorganization by about 650 AD, and was abandoned about one hundred years later, at the same time that the Classic Maya civilisations of modern-day Yucatán and northern Guatemala also collapsed. New **fragmented groups** were created, some of whom forged migratory, militaristic bands. In the eighth century, harassed by their territorial enemies the Olmecs, groups of Maya and Aztecs migrated south. Among them were the people who would become known as Chorotegas. The word Chorotega derives from either their place of origin, Cholula, or from two words in the Chorotegan language: *cholol* (to run or escape) and *teca* (people) – "the people who escaped".

Evidence of immediate and long-term cultural upheaval in the area after 800 AD includes a significant increase in the number of Nicoyan **burial sites** found dating from around this time. The use of objects associated with elites – like ceremonial skulls, jades and elaborate metates – suddenly declined almost to the point of disappearing completely, and populations seem to have migrated from the interior toward the coasts. While this evidence could suggest a natural disaster (a volcanic eruption, perhaps) it also bears the hallmarks of what could be termed an invasion.

The Chorotegas' first contact with the **Spanish** was calamitous. The 1522 Spanish expedition from Panamá up the Pacific coast to Nicaragua brought smallpox, the plague and influenza to the indigenous people of Greater Nicoya. Imprisonment and slavery followed, with coastal peoples raided, branded and sold into slavery in Panamá and Peru. The demise of the Chorotegas from the sixteenth century was rapid and unreversed.

Excavations in Guanacaste and the Nicoya Peninsula reveal something of the Chorotegas' **belief systems** and social arrangements. Near Bahía Culebra, anthropologists unearthed pottery shards, utensils and the remains of hearths, along with a

transport from Liberia ($75 per carload); alternatively, there are five buses daily from Cañas to Bijagua, from where a taxi to the lodge costs about $12.

You can also stay near Volcán Miravalles on the side facing Volcán Rincón de la Vieja (see p.230).

Parque Nacional Palo Verde

About 30km west of Cañas on the northern bank of the Río Tempisque lies the **PARQUE NACIONAL PALO VERDE** (daily 8am–4pm; $6), created in 1982 to preserve the habitat of the **migratory birds** that nest in the estuary of the Tempisque and a large patch of relatively undisturbed lowland dry forest. With a distinctive topography featuring ridged limestone hills – unique to this part of the country, and attesting to the fact that certain parts of Guanacaste were once under water – the park shelters about fifteen separate ecological habitats. From December to May, Palo Verde can dry out into baked mud flats, while in the wet season, extensive flooding gives rise to saltwater and freshwater lakes and swamps. Following the wet season, the great floodplain drains slowly, creating marshes, mangroves and other habitats favoured by migratory birds. Little visited by tourists, the park is mainly of interest to serious burial ground holding twenty females, children and infants. Chorotega villages were made up of longhouse-type structures – common to many indigenous cultures of the Americas – inhabited by entire extended families, and centred on a large square, site of religious ceremonies and meetings.

Like the Maya and Aztecs, the Chorotegas had a belief system built around **bloodletting** and the **sacrifice** of animals and humans. Although it is not known if beating hearts were ripped from chests, virgins were definitely thrown into volcano craters to appease their gods, about whom little is known. Chorotegas also believed in **yulios**, the spirit alter ego that escaped from their mouths at the moment of death to roam the world for ever. Although pagan, Chorotega priests shared a number of duties and functions with the Catholic priests who worked to destroy their culture. Celibate, they may also have heard confessions and meted out punishments for sins.

Few Chorotega **rituals** are documented. One known practice was the formation of a kind of human maypole, consisting of *voladores*, or men suspended "flying" (actually roped) from a post, twirling themselves round and round while descending to the ground. Originating with the Aztecs, the ritual was dedicated to the Morning Star, considered to be a deity; the four *voladores* represented the cardinal points. While no longer displayed in Costa Rica, it is still performed in the Mexican state of Veracruz and in certain villages in Guatemala.

The Chorotega **economy** was based on maize (corn). They also cultivated tobacco, fruit, beans and cotton, using cacao beans as currency, and the marketplace was run by women. All land was held communally, as was everything that was cultivated and harvested, which was then distributed throughout the settlement. This plurality did not extend to social prestige, however. Three strata characterized Chorotega society: at the upper echelon were chieftains (*caciques*), warriors and priests; in the middle were the commoners, and at the bottom were the slaves and prisoners of war. The Chorotegas were the only indigenous peoples in Costa Rica to have a written **language**, comprising hieroglyphs similar to those used by the Maya. They were also skilled artisans, producing ornamental jewellery and jade, and colouring cotton fabrics with animal and vegetable dye. It was the Chorotegas who made the bulk of the distinctive **ceramics** so celebrated in the country today, many of which can be seen in San José's Museo Nacional (for more on Chorotega pottery, see p.257).

birders, but what you see depends on the time of year – by far the **best months** are at the height of the dry season (Jan–March), when most of the 250 or so migratory species are in residence. In the wet season, flooding makes parts of the park inaccessible.

The park is home to one of the largest concentrations of **waterfowl** in Central America, both indigenous and migratory, with more than three hundred species of birds, among them the endangered Jabirú stork and black-crowned night heron. Further from the river bank, in the tree cover along the bottom and ridges of the limestone hills, you may spot toucans, and perhaps even one of the increasingly rare scarlet macaws. At evening during the dry season, many birds and other species – monkeys, coatis and even deer – congregate around the few remaining waterholes; bring binoculars and a torch. Note, though, that you shouldn't swim in the Río Tempisque (or anywhere else), as it's home to particularly huge crocodiles – some, according to the park rangers, are as much as five metres long.

From the administration building (see p.232), two **trails** lead up to the top of hills, from where you can see the expansive mouth of the Río Tempisque to the west and the broad plains of Guanacaste to the east. A number of other **loop trails**, none more than 4km long, run through the park. The shortest

△ Horseman, Guanacaste

of the trails, at just 300m, is **Las Calizas**; others include **El Manigordo** ("ocelot"; 1.5km), **El Mapache** ("raccoon"; 2km) and **El Venado** ("deer"; 2km), all of which give you a good idea of the landscape and a chance of viewing the animals after which they're named. You've also got a good chance of seeing collared peccaries, abundant in this area, or a coatimundi, which you may see or hear foraging in the undergrowth. White-tailed deer also live here, but they're very shy and likely to dart off at the sound of your approach.

For longer treks, try the **Bosque Primario** trail (about 7km), through, as the name suggests, primary forest cover. You can also walk the 6km (dry season only) to the edge of the Río Tempisque from where you'll see the aptly named **Isla de los Pájaros** (Bird Island). Square in the mouth of the river, the island is chock-full of our feathered friends all year, with black-crowned night herons swirling above in thick dark clouds. Many hotels and tour agencies in the province offer boat trips around the island, but landings are not permitted, so you have to content yourself with bird-spotting and taking photographs from the boat.

Check with rangers regarding conditions before walking on any of the trails: access is constantly subject to change, due to flooding and sometimes bee colonies. The Río Tempisque walk in particular can be muddy and unpleasantly insect-ridden in all but the driest months. You should bring plenty of water, as the heat and humidity are considerable. A note on **safety** in Palo Verde: in recent years swarms of **Africanized bees** – sometimes sensationally termed "killer bees" – have taken to colonizing the area. Africanized bees are aggressive, and may pursue – in packs – anyone who unwittingly disturbs one of their large, quite obvious, nests. The usual advice is to cover your head and run in a zigzag pattern so that you can dodge the cloud of pursuing bees. Although, luckily, this occurs very rarely, you should take special care if you are sensitive to stings, and ask the rangers about the presence of nests on or around trails. Bees are also found in the Lomas Barbudal Reserve (see p.224).

Practicalities

Getting to Palo Verde takes a while, though it is possible with a regular non-4WD vehicle in the dry season. From the well-signed turn-off from the Interamericana at Bagaces (opposite the ACT regional office, where you can check out current road conditions), it's a thirty-kilometre drive to the entrance hut, and a further 9km to the administration building. There are signs all along the road to the park, but at long intervals, and the road forks unnervingly from time to time without indicating which way to go. If in doubt, follow the tyre tracks made by the rangers. This road is theoretically passable year-round without a 4WD.

The Organization for Tropical Studies (OTS) has a field station at Palo Verde, originally set up for comparative ecosystem study and research into the dry forest habitat. If you contact their San José office (℡240-6696, ℱ240-6783, ℗www.ots.ac.cr) in advance you may be able to stay in their rustic field station, next door to the administration building providing it's not full of scientific researchers. Accommodation (◎) is in clean dormitories, and meals are included in the rate. There's also a basic but perfectly comfortable *albergue* at the ranger station, about 10km from the entrance. The six rooms here each contain six bunk beds ($15 per person), including mosquito nets and fans, and meals are available (breakfast $3; lunch and dinner $6). You can also camp (℡671-1290 or 671-1062; $2 per day) at the small site next to the administration building, where there are lavatories, but it's best to call ahead to check that there's space. If there's not, there are several accommodation options along the Interamericana in and around Bagaces.

Reserva Biológica Lomas Barbudal

The **RESERVA BIOLÓGICA LOMAS BARBUDAL** (daily 8am–4pm; $6) is an impressive, though small-scale, initiative about 20km west of Bagaces, just north of Parque Nacional Palo Verde. Home to some of the last vestiges of true **tropical dry forest** in the region, Lomas Barbudal means "bearded hills" and that's just what they look like, with relatively bare pates surrounded by sideburns of bushy deciduous trees. Stretches of savannah-like open grassland

Tropical dry forest

With its mainly deciduous cover, Guanacaste's **tropical dry forest**, created by the combination of a Pacific lowland topography and arid conditions, looks startlingly different depending upon the time of year. In the height of the dry season, almost no rain falls on lowland Guanacaste, the trees are bare, having shed their leaves in an effort to conserve water, and the landscape takes on a melancholy, burnt-sienna hue. In April or May, when the rains come, the whole of Guanacaste perks up and begins to look comparatively green, although the dry forest never takes on the lush look of the rainforest.

The story of the demise of the tropical dry forests in Mesoamerica is one of nearly wholesale destruction. In all, only about two percent of the region's pre-Columbian dry forest survives, and what was once a carpet stretching the length of the Pacific side of the isthmus from southern Mexico to Panamá now exists only in besieged pockets. Today, dry forests cover just 518 square kilometres of Costa Rica, almost all in Guanacaste, concentrated around the Río Tempisque and, more significantly, north in the Parque Nacional Santa Rosa. Due to deforestation and climatic change, tropical dry forests are considered a rare life-zone. Their relative dryness means they are easily overrun by field fires, which ranchers light in order to burn off old pasture. Hardy grasses spring up in their wake, such as the imported African jaragua, which gives much of Guanacaste its African savannah-like appearance.

Along with the leafy trees, tropical dry forest features **palms** and even a few **evergreens**. At the very top of a good thick patch of dry forest you see the umbrella form of **canopy trees**, although these are much shorter than in the tropical rainforest. Dry forest is a far less complex ecosystem than the humid rainforest, which has about three or four layers of vegetation. Like temperate-zone deciduous forests, the tropical dry forest has only two strata. The ground shrub layer is fleshed out by thorn bushes and tree ferns, primitive plants that have been with us since the time of the dinosaurs. Unlike rainforest, dry forest has very few epiphytes (plants growing on the trees), except for bromeliads (the ones that look something like upside-down pineapple leaves). The most biologically diverse examples of tropical dry forest are in the lower elevations of Parque Nacional Santa Rosa, where the canopy trees are a good height, with many different species of deciduous trees. There are also some pockets of mangroves and even a few evergreens in the wetter parts of the park.

Tropical dry forests can support a large variety of **mammal life**, as in the Parque Nacional Santa Rosa–Parque Nacional Guanacaste corridor. Deer and smaller mammals, such as the coatimundi and paca, are most common, along with large cats, from the jaguar to the ocelot, provided they have enough room to hunt. You may see the endangered **scarlet macaw**, which likes to feed on the seeds of the sandbox tree, in a few remaining pockets of Pacific dry forest, including Lomas Barbudal and, further south, around Río Tarcoles and Carara (see p.303), itself a transition zone between the dry forests of the north and the wetter tropical cover of the southern Pacific coast. In addition, the staggering number and diversity of **insects** are of great interest to biologists and entomologists: there are more than two hundred types of bee in Lomas Barbudal, for example, and a large number of butterflies and moths in Parque Nacional Santa Rosa.

are punctuated by the thorny-looking **shoemaker's tree** and crisscrossed by rivers and the strips of deciduous woods that hug their banks. The reserve also features isolated examples of the majestic **mahogany** and **rosewood** trees, whose deep blood-red timber is coveted as material for furniture.

Lomas Barbudal is also rich in **wildlife**. If you don't spot a howler monkey, you'll at least likely hear one. And, this is practically the only place along the entire Guanacaste coast where you have a reasonable chance of seeing the **scarlet macaw**. Like Parque Nacional Santa Rosa to the north, Lomas Barbudal hosts an abundance of **insects** – some 200 to 300 **bee species** alone, around 25 percent of the species of bees in the entire world. Those allergic to stings or otherwise intolerant of insects might want to give Lomas Barbudal a miss; they're everywhere, including the aggressive Africanized bees (see p.223).

Practicalities

Although you could take a **taxi** (about $30 round-trip) to Lomas Barbudal from Bagaces, it's best reached with your own transport. Take the road north from Bagaces, and after about 7km follow the road off to the left; note that it's in pretty bad condition. The administration office lies 6km further, prettily set on the banks of the Río Cabuyo. You can **camp** ($2 per night), but bring your own water and food; there are no lavatories. There are also two swimmable rivers, a small network of trails designed and cleared by local volunteers, and a visitor centre.

Liberia and around

True to its name, the spirited provincial capital of **LIBERIA** (from *libertad*, meaning liberty) is distinctively friendly and progressive, its wide clean streets the legacy of the pioneering farmers and cattle ranchers who founded it. Known colloquially as the "Ciudad Blanca" (white city) due to its whitewashed houses, Liberia is the only town in Costa Rica that seems truly colonial in style and character. Many of the white houses still have their **puerta del sol** – corner doors that were used, ingeniously, to let the sun in during the morning and out in the late afternoon, thus heating and then cooling the interior throughout the day – an architectural feature left over from the colonial era and particular to this region.

At present, most travellers use Liberia simply as a jumping-off point for the national parks of **Rincón de la Vieja** and **Santa Rosa**, an overnight stop to or from the **beaches** of Guanacaste, or a break on the way to Nicaragua. However, Liberia is perhaps the most appealing town in Costa Rica, with everything you might need for a relaxing day or two – well-priced accommodation (although limited choice), a helpful tourist office and a couple of nice places to eat and drink. The nearby international airport delivers busloads of visitors to the western beaches, but Liberia happily remains unchanged: it's still the epitome of dignified (if somewhat static) provincialism, with a strong identity and atmosphere all its own.

Liberia also boasts several lively local **festivals**, including the **Fiestas Cívicas de Liberia** in early March. The festival has its origins as an annual livestock fair and is now celebrated over ten days with parades, bands, fireworks and bulls wreaking havoc on daring but alcohol-addled young locals. Most of the action takes place in the fairgrounds in the northwest corner of town. On July

25, **El Día de la Independencia** celebrates Guanacaste's independence from Nicaragua with parades, horseshows, cattle auctions, rodeos, fiestas and roving marimba bands. If you want to attend, make bus and hotel reservations as far in advance as possible.

Arrival and information

Liberia's international **airport** is connected to San José by regular Sansa and NatureAir flights; you can take a taxi from here into town ($5) unless you fancy a fifteen-minute walk from the terminal to the main road, where any eastbound bus will take you to town. Liberia's clean and efficient bus terminal is on the western edge of town near the exit for the Interamericana – it's a ten-minute walk at most from here to the centre of town. At the bus station is an elaborate list of departure times; these are pure fiction, so you must check with the ticket office. **San José** buses arrive at and depart from the Pulmitan terminal, a block southeast of the bus station. If you're coming by car, the exit off the Interamericana is at an intersection with traffic lights and three petrol stations – known as La Esquina de las Bombas (Gas Station Corner). Turning left (if coming from the south) brings you to the beaches, while a right takes you along the town's **Avenida Central**, lined with floppy mango trees. **Addresses** in Liberia are most often given in relation to the **church**, the **Parque Central**, or the large, white **Gobernación**, the regional government building across from the church on the corner of C Real and Av Central.

Liberia's faded but helpful **tourist office** (Mon–Sat 8.30am–noon & 2–5pm; ☎665-0135) is on C 1, five minutes' walk south of Parque Central. The staff (who speak English) will book hotels and place international phone calls. In the high season, especially, they also function partially as a **tour service**, using local operators. The office is a non-profit-making service, and any donations are appreciated.

The efficient **correo**, Av 3, C 8 (Mon–Fri 7.30am–6pm, Sat 7.30am–noon), is a bit hard to find: it's between Av 3 and Av 5 in the low-slung white house across from an empty square field bordered by mango trees. Liberia has a few **Internet cafés**. *Cybermania* (daily 8am–10pm), located in a small business centre on the north side of Parque Central, is efficient, friendly, air-conditioned and cheap, as is the handy *Planet Internet* (daily 8am–10pm) on Calle Real just off Parque Central. Both cost about $1 per hour. There are plenty of **banks**, many of them on Avenida Central, leading into town, several with ATMs. The Banco de Costa Rica, across from Parque Central, will change travellers' cheques. You can pick up the *Miami Herald* and *New York Times* newspapers from the Librería Universitaria on Av 1, 100m east of Parque Central.

Liberia is a useful place to hire a car; there are many operators, mostly along the road to the beaches – Payless is one of the cheapest. Most hotels will arrange car rental for you. It's definitely worth considering a four-wheel drive, as the potholed roads can easily cause a flat tyre in a smaller car; you should go for full insurance regardless.

Accommodation

Pleasant Liberia is a convenient place to spend the night along this northern stretch of the Interamericana. In the popular dry season, it's best to book a room in advance.

El Bramadero La Esquina de las Bombas ☎666-0371, ✉bramadero@racsa.co.cr. The setting, beside the fuel pumps on the Interamericana, isn't the loveliest, but it's convenient for the beaches and popular with Ticos. The rooms are fairly nondescript, but surprisingly quiet (try to get one at the back), and there's a decent open-air restaurant and a pool. A good bet if everything else is full. ❸

Las Espuelas On the Interamericana, 2km south of town ☎666-0144, ⊕www.bestwestern.com. Much the better of Liberia's two representatives of the Best Western chain, this low, hacienda-style hotel offers standard a/c comfort; rooms come with phone and cable TV. There's a nice pool, a restaurant that does a decent slab of steak, and a bar with a pool table. ❺

Guanacaste Av 1, 300m south of the bus station ☎666-0085, ℻666-2287, ⊕www.hicr.org. Popular, HI-affiliated hostel, with a traveller-friendly cafeteria-restaurant. The rooms are simple, clean and tidy; the doubles aren't a great value compared to the town's other options, but there are a few dorm places available ($8). The hostel fills up quickly, so book ahead. With an HI card you get a 15 percent discount, and you might wangle a further 10 percent with a student ID. The management organizes a daily transfer ($20) to Rincón de la Vieja and sells bus tickets to Nicaragua. ❷–❸

Hostal Ciudad Blanca Av 4, 200m south and 150m east of the Gobernación ☎666-3962. Spotless hotel in a stately rancher's mansion with

a small breakfast terrace/bar, and twelve modern, a/c rooms with TV, private bath and ceiling fans. Popular with American travellers bedding down before heading out to the beach. Breakfast included. ❹

Liberia C 0, 75m south of Parque Central ☎666-0161, ✉.hotelliberia@hotmail.com. Well-established, friendly youth-hostel-type hotel with a jolly papaya orange exterior. The bare and basic rooms with shared cold-water bathroom are set around a sunny but bare courtyard. The newer rooms in an annexe to the rear (❹) are better than the old ones and have their own bath, though they cost an extra $4. Popular with vacationing foreigners and Costa Ricans alike so a reservation and deposit are required in the high season. The hotel staff organize transport to Rincón de la Vieja. Visa accepted. ❷–❹

La Posada del Tope C 0, 150m south of the Gobernación ☎ & ℻666-3876. Popular, cheap budget hotel in a beautiful historic house. The six basic rooms with fan and shared showers in the old part of the hotel are a bit stuffy, but clean; the more modern rooms across the street in a new annexe cost only slightly more, come with cable TV, and are set around a charming courtyard. The shared bathrooms aren't great, but there's plenty of character here, as well as a friendly staff, parking and a rooftop telescope for star-gazing. The manager runs transport to Rincón de la Vieja for $10 per person round-trip, as well as trips to Palo Verde. Visa and MasterCard accepted. ❷

El Sitio On the road to the beaches, 200m west of La Esquina de las Bombas ☏666-1211, ⓦwww .bestwestern.com. Now part of the Best Western chain, this large motel-style hotel, shaded by huge Guanacaste trees, is a good option for families (despite a brash new casino on site), with a pool and restaurant. The large characterless rooms have a/c, TV and private bath. Buffet breakfast included. ❹

The town

Liberia's wide, clean streets are used more by cyclists and horsemen than motorists. It's pleasant to walk around in the shade provided by the mango trees, though in March and April watch out for the ripe fruit plopping down full-force at your feet. The town is arranged around a large **Parque Central**, officially called Parque Mario Cañas Ruiz, named after a 20th-century poet and musician whose songs paid tribute to *sabanero* culture. The Parque is dedicated to *el mes del anexión*, the month of the annexation (July), celebrating the fact that Guanacaste is not in Nicaragua. Liberia's Parque Central is one of the loveliest central plazas in the whole country, ringed by benches and tall palms that shade gossiping locals. On the eastern edge of the Parque is the town **church**, a contemporary structure whose startlingly modernist – some would say downright ugly – form looks a little out of place in this very traditional town.

Far more appealing is the colonial, mottled yellow **Iglesia de la Agonía** that sits about 600m away on Avenida Central at the eastern end of town. On the verge of perpetual collapse – it has had a hard time from successive earthquakes – it's almost never open, but try shoving the heavy wooden door and hope the place doesn't collapse around you if it gives way.

The most historic street in town is the **Calle Real** (marked as Calle Central on some maps). In the nineteenth century this street was the entrance to Liberia, and practically the entire thoroughfare has now been restored to its original colonial simplicity. Stately white adobe homes feature large windows with ornate wooden frames and wide overhanging eaves under which locals pass the evenings in cane armchairs.

Museo de Sabanero

Dusty mementoes of daily life on the old cattle ranches are on display at the small **Museo de Sabanero**, or Cowboy Museum (Mon–Sat 8.30am–noon & 2–5pm, donation suggested), housed in the same building as the tourist office. The small but interesting exhibition shows well-worn objects found in the big ranch houses, or *casonas*, that formed the nucleus of the ranch communities. Entering the museum from the tourist office, you pass an enormous wooden hacienda table and then the musty, low-lit world of the old adobe house. Here you'll see all the *sabaneros'* accoutrements made from taut cattle skins, including

Tours from Liberia

Several of Liberia's hotels, including *La Posada del Tope* and *El Sitio*, run trips to attractions in the surrounding area, including Rincón de la Vieja ($10–20), Palo Verde ($25–35) or the Guanacaste beaches. Outside town, **Safaris Corobicí** (☏669-6191, ℻669-0544, ⓦwww.nicoya.com), 5km before Cañas on the Interamericana, specialize in floating trips on the Río Corobicí ($37–60 depending on duration). Guides row while you watch the local inhabitants – howler monkeys, huge iguanas and caimans. They also lead an interesting 2–3-hour birdwatcher's tour ($35–45). Mot-mots, cuckoos, laughing falcons, osprey eagles and herons, including the endangered Jabirú stork, have all been spotted along the Corobicí.

bridles, chaps, boots and the distinctive high-backed saddle, kept in place by a lariat wound around the horse's tail. Also on show are twirling spurs, old hacienda chairs, lariats smoothed with age, elaborate whips, branding irons and several unidentifiable tools that look like instruments of bovine torture.

Eating, drinking and entertainment

Liberia has several **restaurants** that serve local dishes such as **natilla** (soured cream) eaten with eggs or *gallo pinto* and tortillas. For a real feast, try a **desayuno guanacasteco**, a hearty local breakfast of tortillas, sour cream, eggs, rice and beans, and sometimes meat. This is *sabanero* or, more properly, **criollo** food, to be worked off with hard labour. For rock-bottom cheap **lunches**, try the stalls at the bus terminal or head to one of the fried chicken places, the bar *Las Tinajas*, or soda *Rancho Dulce*. You can pick up Guanacastecan **corn snacks** from stalls all over town and at La Esquina de las Bombas (Gas Station Corner).

Enjoy a quiet beer at *Las Tinajas* or *Jauja* pizzeria. The town's one main **disco**, *Kurú*, about 200 metres west of the Interamericana down the road to the beaches, gets lively with salsa and merengue, especially on weekends and holidays. *Tsunami*, across the road and down a side street, is also popular and fills with young dancing locals on the weekends. The main Saturday evening activity, however, involves watching the locals parading around the Parque Central in their finery, having an ice cream, and maybe going to the movies at the **Cine Liberia**, located in the shopping mall 1km south of the main Interamericana intersection.

Restaurants, bars and sodas

La Cocina de José Av 2, C4/6, one block south and one-and-a-half blocks west of Parque Central. The setting of this Tico restaurant is nothing to write home about – the small concrete terrace makes it look like a bus shelter – but the cuisine completely transcends its humble surroundings. Juicy steaks come in at $8–9, and the *tilapia* fillets are exquisite ($6–8). Start off with a hearty bean soup or the imaginative house salad.

Los Comales C Real, Av 3/5, 200m north of the northeast corner of Parque Central. A typical Costa Rican soda, very popular with locals for its generous portions of tasty rustic food, with *gallos* and *pintos* costing a mere $2, and *casados* $3; there are also several rice dishes on offer.

Jauja Av Central, C8/10. One of the better restaurants in town, though very touristy. Large and tasty pasta dishes are a pricey $6-7, pizzas around

La cocina Guanacasteca: corn cooking

Corn is still integral to the regional cuisine of Guanacaste, thanks to the Chorotegas, who cultivated maize (corn) to use in many inventive ways. One pre-Columbian corn concoction involved roasting and grinding the maize, and then combining the meal-like paste with water and chocolate to make the drink *chicha*. Although you can't find this version of *chicha* any more you can still get **grain-based drinks** in Guanacaste, such as *horchata* (made with rice or corn and spiced with cinnamon), or *pinolillo* (made with roasted corn), both milky and sweet, with an unmistakably grainy texture.

Corn also shows up in traditional Guanacastecan snacks such as **tanelas** (like a cheese scone, but made with cornflour) and **rosquillas**, small rings of cornflour that taste like a combination between tortillas and doughnuts. You can buy these at roadside stalls and small shops in Liberia. Served throughout the country, **chorreados** crop up most often on menus in Guanacaste: they're a kind of pancake made (again) with cornflour and served with *natilla*, the local version of sour cream.

$7, and there are also typical steaks and fish dishes. It's all served in a pleasant, outdoor garden setting, although the big-screen TV can be off-putting.

Rancho Dulce C Real, Av 0/2, 50m south of the Gobernación. A reliable choice at any time of day, this small and lovable soda serves *casados* ($3), sandwiches, *empanadas* and *refrescos*. You can sit at the tiny outdoor stools (if you have a small bottom) or tables. A reliable choice at any time of day.

Rincón del Pollo Av Central, 50m west of Parque Central. A simple, open place where only three dollars will get you half a roast chicken served with tortillas and salad. They only serve soft drinks, but don't object if you want to bring in your own beverage.

Las Tinajas West side of Parque Central. Liberia's best bar, with regular live music, also serves basic *casados* and excellent hamburgers ($3). The outdoor tables on the verandah of this old house are a pleasant spot to watch the goings-on in the Parque while enjoying a *refresco* or beer, the latter available on tap and served in chilled glasses.

Parque Nacional Rincón de la Vieja

The beautifully dry landscape of **PARQUE NACIONAL RINCÓN DE LA VIEJA** (daily 8am–4pm; $6), about 30km northeast of Liberia, encompasses terrains varying from rock-strewn savannah to patches of tropical dry forest, culminating in the blasted-out vistas of the volcano crater itself. The land here is actually alive and breathing: Rincón de la Vieja's last major eruptions took place in 1995 and 1998, and were serious enough to evacuate local residents. The danger has always been to the northern side of the volcano, facing Nicaragua (the opposite side from the two entrance points), and the most pressing **safety** issue for tourists is to be aware that rivers of lava and hot

Moving on from Liberia

Liberia is a main regional **transport hub**, providing easy access to Guanacaste's parks and beaches, the Nicaraguan border and **San José** (11 direct Pulmitan de Liberia buses daily; 4hr 30min). San José buses leave from the Pulmitan terminal, a block southeast of the main bus station, which serves all other destinations.

If you're heading for **the border**, take one of the hourly buses to La Cruz or Peñas Blancas, the border's official name (1hr). Through buses from San José to Managua also stop here, although it can be tricky to get a seat; the *Hotel Guanacaste* sells bus tickets to Managua ($11 one-way). The bus station also sells tickets to Managua if there is a vacant seat, otherwise it's a question of jumping on the bus, paying the driver and hoping you can grab a seat when someone gets off.

For **Parque Nacional Santa Rosa** (40 min), take a La Cruz or Peñas Blancas bus. You should take the earliest bus possible to give yourself time for walking; ask the driver to let you off at Santa Rosa – it takes about an hour to walk from here to the park's administration centre. You can also reach the park by *colectivo* taxi ($15 per car), shared between four or five people. Catch one at the northwestern corner of Parque Central. *Colectivo* taxis are also a good value if you're heading to **Parque Nacional Rincón de la Vieja** or the lodges near Las Pailas ranger station (roughly $25 for four people). Arguably the best way to get to Rincón de la Vieja is to travel with one of the Liberia hotels – *La Posada del Tope*, *Hotel Liberia* and *Hotel Guanacaste* – which arrange transport to the park. All services are open to non-guests, though hotel guests get first option.

The more northerly of Guanacaste's **beaches** are served by direct buses. For Playa Hermosa and Playa Panamá, five buses leave daily (1hr); for Playa del Coco, six leave per day (1hr). Heading south, six daily buses serve **Tamarindo** (1.5–2hr); you can also easily get to **Santa Cruz** (hourly 5.30am–7.30pm; 1hr), from where you can hook up with buses to beaches further south. Buses for **Nicoya** (2hr) leave on the hour from 5am to 7pm, and those to **Puntarenas** (3hr) leave at 5am, 8.30am, 10am, 11am and 3pm.

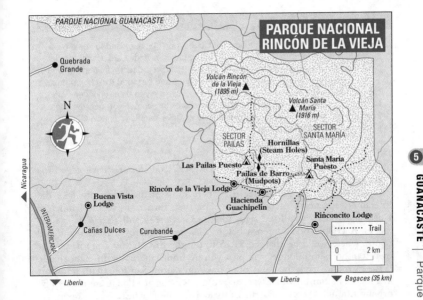

mud still boil beneath the thin epidermis of ground. While danger areas are clearly marked with signs and fences, you still have to watch your step: walkers have been seriously burned from crashing through this crust and stepping into mud and water at above-boiling temperatures.

With the right amount of caution, however, this is an enchanting place: brewing **mud pots** (*pilas de barro*) bubble, and puffs of steam rise out of lush foliage, signalling sulphurous subterranean springs. This is great terrain for **camping, riding** and **hiking**, with a comfortable, fairly dry heat, though it can get damp and cloudy at the higher elevations around the crater. **Birders**, too, enjoy Rincón de la Vieja, as there are more than two hundred species in residence.

Getting to the park

The local dry season (Dec–March especially) is the **ideal time** to visit Rincón de la Vieja, when the hiking trails and visibility as you ascend the volcano are at their best. The park has been split into two **sectors**: Sector Las Pailas ("cauldrons") and Sector Santa María, each with its own **entrance** and ranger station. The two are linked by an eight-kilometre walking trail. From Liberia most people travel through the hamlet of Curubandé, about 16km northeast, to the **Las Pailas** sector. The other ranger station, **Santa María**, lies about 25km northeast of Liberia. The **casona** that houses the ranger station here is a former retreat of US president Lyndon Baines Johnson.

Both routes to the park are along stony roads, not at all suitable for walking. People do, but it's tough, uninteresting terrain, and it's really more advisable to save your energy for the trails within the park itself. Options for getting here from Liberia are covered in the box on p.228 – transfers run by hotels such as *La Posada del Tope* are convenient and good value. **Hitching** is also an option if you can find a truck driver making a delivery, possibly at one of the gas stations at La Esquina de las Bombas on the Interamericana at Liberia. Alternatively, you could **rent a car** (you'll more or less need a 4WD) and stay in one of the

Driving along the Interamericana north of Liberia, don't be surprised to see a blue-suited *policía de tránsito* (traffic cop) or a light-brown-suited *guardia rural* (border police officer) leap out, kamikaze-like, into the highway directly in front of you – you'll need to stop and show your driver's licence and passport (which you must have on you at all times). These are routine checks, mainly to deter undocumented Nicaraguans from entering Costa Rica. The nearer the border you get, the more frequent the checks become. Make sure you drive carefully: knocking over a policeman is not a good move.

upmarket tourist lodges such as the *Hacienda Guachipelín* or *Rincón de la Vieja Lodge* (see opposite).

To get to the **Las Pailas sector**, where most of the lodges are, take the Interamericana north of Liberia for 6km, then turn right to the hamlet of Curubandé. Here you'll see signs for the *Guachipelín* and *Rincón de la Vieja* lodges. A couple of kilometres before *Guachipelín* there's a barrier and toll booth, where you'll be charged $1.75 to use the road. If you don't have your own transport, both lodges will pick you up from Liberia for an extra charge ($10–25 round-trip); they also offer **packages** from San José, with transport included. The **Santa María sector** and the Rinconcito Lodge are reached by driving through Liberia's Barrio La Victoria in the northeast of the town; ask for the *estadio* – the football stadium – from where it's a signed twenty-four-kilometre drive to the park.

Accommodation

The Rincón de la Vieja area boasts some very good **lodges**, most of which offer their own tours, either on horseback or by foot. There's a basic **campsite** near the Las Pailas puesto, and another slightly better equipped one at the Santa María puesto (both $2 per person), where there are lavatories and water, though you should take your own cooking utensils, food and water. If you have a sleeping bag, and ask in advance, you can also stay inside the musty bunk rooms in the Santa María ranger station (phone the ACG office at Santa Rosa for permission on ☎666-5051).

Borinquen Mountain Resort ☎690-1900, ⓦwww.borinquenresort.com. Upmarket, expensive lodge with its own spa centre, mudpools and sauna, set in stunning landscape at the skirts of Volcán Rincón de la Vieja. Accommodation is in luxurious villas and bungalows. There's a classy restaurant, full disabled access and facilities for kids. They also run horseback trips and ATV (all-terrain vehicle) excursions to the volcano. ❾
Buena Vista Lodge 31km northeast of Liberia ☎661-8158, ⓦwww.buenavistacr.com. A working cattle ranch – you can even ride with the cowhands if your horsemanship is up to it – with stupendous views over Guanacaste and some great trails through pockets of rainforest on the flanks of the volcano and up to the crater. Double rooms are housed in individual bungalows, many set around a small lake in which you can swim. A restaurant serves up wholesome meals, and

there are reasonably priced horseback and hiking tours available. If you're driving here, a 4WD is recommended; alternatively, you can arrange to be picked up from Cañas Dulces (accessible from Liberia by bus). ❹
Hacienda Guachipelín 5km beyond Curubandé on the edge of the park ☎666-8075, ⓦwww .guachipelin.com. A working ranch, the *Guachipelín* looks every inch the old cattle hacienda, with comfortable doubles in the main house. There's a fantastic swimming pool, and breakfast is included in the price. Attractions include a nearby waterfall, mud pots and some well-marked trails; guides are available for a variety of tours, including riding and hiking to the volcano. Pickups from Liberia can be arranged for a fee. ❺
Rinconcito Lodge In San Jorge ☎666-2764, Ⓔrinconcito@racsa.co.cr. The cheapest option close to the park, this farm is owned by a friendly

family and has plain but good-value cabinas with cold-water shared or private bathroom. The owners are a good source of advice on local transport, guides and directions, and can also arrange horse-riding, guided tours and pickups from Liberia (about $35 round-trip per car). Meals available (breakfast $3, lunch and dinner $5). ❸ **Rincón de la Vieja Lodge** 5km northwest of *Guachipelín* and 3.5km from the Las Pailas park

entrance; follow the signs ☎ & ⓕ661-8198, ⓦwww.rincondelaviejalodge.com. Popular lodge with simple, rustic accommodation, including doubles with private bath and hot water (❹), and bungalows decorated in attractive *sabanero* style (❺). There's a pool and reading area and the restaurant serves tasty, filling meals. Horse-riding, mountain-biking, a canopy tour and swimming at nearby waterfalls can all be arranged. ❻

Visiting the park

Costa Rica's most memorable national park is utterly dominated by the massive and majestic Volcán Rincón de la Vieja. The most direct approach to the crater and summit of the volcano is via the Las Pailas entrance, along a marked trail. From here, you can also take a circular walk that highlights some of the volcanic features, or walk to the Santa María station, 8km away. **Warning**: the trail to the summit is often closed due to low visibility or high winds, so it's definitely worth ringing ahead on ☎661-8139 to check conditions.

This is quite simply the best hiking in the country. A variety of elevations and habitats reveals hot springs, sulphur pools, bubbling mud pots, fields of *guaria morada* (purple orchids) – the national flower – plus a great smoking volcano at the top to reward you for your efforts. **Animals** in the area include all the big cats (but don't expect to see them), the shy tapir, red deer, collared peccary, two-toed sloth, and howler, white-faced and spider monkeys. There's a good chance you will see a brilliant flash of fluttering blue – this is the **blue morpho** butterfly, famous for its electric colours. **Birders** may spot the weird-looking three-wattled bellbird, the Montezuma oropendola, the trogon and the spectacled owl, among others.

Rincón de la Vieja is becoming more and more popular, and the trails may soon become over-walked. If you stay at one of the lodges and take their summit tours, either by horseback or on foot, you may pass through areas not covered in this section. Also, bear in mind that Rincón de la Vieja is an active volcano, and the trails described here may have been altered due to periodic **lava flows**. Before setting out, you should always check current conditions at one of the ranger stations, or call the Area de Conservación de Guanacaste (ACG) headquarters at the Santa Rosa National Park (☎666-5051, Spanish only). It's also advisable to carry all your **drinking water** – streams might look inviting, but often carry high concentrations of minerals (like sulphur) which can lead to extreme stomach upset if drunk.

The trails

From the Las Pailas puesto, you have several walking options. The most popular and least demanding trail heads east on a very satisfying six-kilometre circuit past many of the highly unusual natural features with which the park abounds, including a mini-volcano and "Pilas de Barro" **mud pots**; listen out for strange bubbling sounds, like a large pot of water boiling over. Mud pots, which should be treated with respect, are formed when mud, thermally heated by subterranean rivers of magma, seeks vents in the ground, sometimes actually forcing itself out through the surface in great thick gloops. It's a surreal sight: grey-brown muck blurping out of the ground like slowly thickening gravy. Another feature is the geothermal **hornillas** (literally, "stoves"), mystical-looking holes in the ground exhaling elegant puffs of steam. You almost expect to stumble upon the witches of *Macbeth*, brewing spite over them. Make sure not to go nearer than a metre or so, or you'll be steamed in no time. The combined effect of all these boiling holes is to make the landscape a bit like brittle Swiss cheese – tread gingerly and look carefully where you're going to avoid the ground crumbling underneath you. Many hikers have been scalded by blithely strolling too close to the holes. The trail also takes you through forest with abundant fauna and flora and be prepared to ford a couple of streams.

The highlight of the park, however, is the hike to the summit, a trail that heads north from Las Pailas. It's hard to get lost, but the top is 7.7km away, so you should start early to get up and down without hurrying too much. The walk takes you through forest similar to lower montane rainforest, densely packed, and lushly covered with epiphytes and mosses. Cool mist and rain often plague this section of the trail: if you are anywhere near the top and lose visibility, which can happen very suddenly, you're advised to stay away from the crater, whose brittle and ill-defined edges became more difficult to see, and consequently more dangerous, in cloudy weather.

At the **summit**, Rincón de la Vieja presents a barren lunar landscape, a smoking hole surrounded by black ash, with a pretty freshwater **lake**, Lago los Jilgueros, to the south. Quetzals are said to live in the forest that surrounds the lake, though you're unlikely to see them. When clear, the **views** up here are ample reward for the uphill sweating, with Lago de Nicaragua shimmering silver-blue to the north, the hump of the Cordillera Central to the southeast and the Pacific Ocean and spiny profile of the Nicoya Peninsula to the west. You can get hammered by wind at the top; bring a sweater and windbreaker.

From Las Pailas, trails also lead west to the *cataratas escondidas* (hidden waterfalls) and east to the Santa María station, along an eight-kilometre path. From Santa María, it's a more difficult and longer walk to the crater, but there are a number of other worthwhile trails, including the three-kilometre **Bosque Encantado** (Enchanted Forest) trail. It leads to a small forest and some hot springs next to a creek, which hikers love to leap into after a wallow in the springs, imitating a sauna effect. The temperature is usually just about right for soaking, but you should never jump into any thermal water without first checking current temperatures at the ranger station.

Parque Nacional Santa Rosa

Established in 1971 to protect a stretch of increasingly rare dry tropical forest, **PARQUE NACIONAL SANTA ROSA** (daily 8am–4pm; $6), 35km north of Liberia, is Costa Rica's oldest national park. Today it's one of the most popular in the country, thanks to its good trails, great surfing (though poor swimming) and prolific turtle-spotting opportunities. It's also, given a few official restrictions, a great destination for **campers**, with a couple of sites on the beach.

Santa Rosa has an amazingly diverse topography for its size of 387 square kilometres, ranging from mangrove swamp to deciduous forest and savannah. Home to 115 species of mammals (half of them bats), 250 species of **birds** and 100 of **amphibians** and **reptiles** (not to mention 3800 species of **moths**), Santa Rosa is a rich biological repository, attracting researchers from all over the world. Jaguars and pumas prowl the park, though you're unlikely to see them; what you may spot – at least in the dry season – are coati, coyotes and peccaries, often snuffling around watering holes.

The appearance of the park changes drastically between the **dry season**, when the many streams and small lakes dry up, trees lose their leaves, and thirsty animals can be seen at known waterholes, and the **wet months**, which are greener, but afford fewer animal-viewing opportunities. From July to November however, you may be able to witness hundreds of **Olive Ridley turtles** (*lloras*) dragging themselves out of the surf and nesting on Playa Nancite by moonlight; September and October are the months on which you are most likely to see them. Turtles arrive singly or occasionally in *arribadas*, a phenomenon unique to this species where thousands of females arrive en masse to lay their eggs. In an attempt to avoid the disturbances caused by big tour groups that have been a problem at places like Tortuguero, a maximum of twenty visitors are allowed access to the nesting area each day; reserve your place on ☎666-5051 or ask at the administration centre when you arrive. Though too rough for swimming, the picturesque **beaches** of Naranjo and Nancite, about 12km down a bad road from the administration centre, are popular with serious **surfers**. They're also great places to hang out for a while, or do a little camping and walking on the nearby trails.

PARQUE NACIONAL SANTA ROSA

N

Nicaragua (43 km) & La Cruz (24 km) ▲

INTERAMERICANA

Park Entrance

▶ *Liberia (35 km)*

Río Calera

Río Nispera

Administration Centre

Sendero Natural 'Indio Desnudo'

La Casona Campsite

La Casona Historical Museum

Playa Tule

Estación Biológica Nancite

Playa Nancite

Estero Real

Sendero Palo Seco

Río Poza Salada

Peña Bruja

Playa Naranjo Campsite

Bahía Naranjo

PACIFIC OCEAN

⚡ Mirador
--- Main trail
······· Broken trail

0   2 km

Visiting the park

Many of Santa Rosa's **trails** are intended for scientific researchers rather than tourists, and so are not well signed. If you do set off to walk, it's a good idea to hire a guide (about $10 per person); ask at the administration centre or, preferably, phone beforehand (☎666-5051) to arrange it. If you walk only one trail in the entire park, make it the very short (1km) and undemanding *sendero natural*, which provides an introduction to the unique features of the tropical dry forest. Curving around from the road just before the *casona*, it's signed as the **Sendero "Indio Desnudo"**, after the peeling-bark trees of the same name (also tongue-in-cheekily called "sunburned-tourist trees"). Along the trail you'll see acacia and **guapinol** trees, whose colloquial name is "stinking toe" on account of its smelly seed pods. Look out for monster iguanas hiding innocuously in tree branches, and for the ubiquitous bats.

From the administration centre a rough (but signposted) track leads past La Casona camping area, with several trails branching off along the way. Some of these may be restricted at any one time for research purposes; check first at the administration centre, however, as you can usually walk where you want as long as you let someone know. After about 5km you come to a fork, bearing left to Playa Naranjo, and right to Playa Nancite, both of them about 3km further on.

Playa Nancite is a lovely grey sand beach and when the tide has just gone out, it's as lustrous as a wet seal's skin. It is also the nesting home of the **Olive Ridley turtles**, a species which nests only here and at Ostional near Nosara on the Nicoya Peninsula (see p.261). With none of the large tour groups you find at other Costa Rican turtle beaches, it's a great place to watch the **arribadas**, during which up to eight thousand turtles – weighing on average around 40kg each – come ashore on any given evening, virtually covering the beach. According to estimates, more than eleven million eggs can be deposited by the turtles during a single *arribada*.

Due to rip tides, Playa Nancite is no good for swimming but, as is usually the case, it's good for **surfers**, with huge rolling, tubular waves. For the best surf, though, you should head for **Playa Naranjo**. Theoretically you can hike between the two (2hr) on a narrow trail across the rocky headland, which opens out on top into hot, dry scrub cover, but you have to watch the tide, since the trail crosses the deep Estero Real, the drainage point for two rivers. Ask for the *marea* (tidal times) from the administration centre before setting out.

La Casona

About 400m from the administration building is the formidable wooden and red-tiled homestead **La Casona** (Big House), one of Costa Rica's most famous historical sites. For many years it was the centre of a working hacienda until the land was expropriated for the national park in 1972. In an unbelievably mindless act, it was burned down in May 2001 by two poachers who were retaliating against arrests by park rangers. However, phoenix-like, it stands again after being lovingly (and painstakingly) reconstructed in less than a year – this time, with the addition of smoke alarms.

Information panels recount the various instances of derring-do which have occurred at La Casona, with resumés of the battles of March 20, 1856 (the confrontation between William Walker's filibusters and the Costa Rican forces; see p.238), of 1919 (against the Nicaraguans), and of 1955, against another Nicaraguan, the dictator Anastasio Somoza García, who ruled the country from 1936 until his assassination in 1956. His hulk of a tank can still be seen, rusting and abandoned, along a signed road just beyond the entrance hut.

La Casona, set around a flowering courtyard, is full of rustic character. It's now entirely given over to **exhibitions**, and you are free to clamber up and down the steps and wander around the dark rooms, which have a significant population of resident bats. Many of the exhibits were destroyed in the fire, but there's some information on the life of the notorious William Walker and the great battle of 1856, remnants of dead animals and archeological remains. At one side of La Casona, a stair path leads up to a viewpoint with a magnificent perspective of the twin volcanos of Rincón de la Vieja National Park.

Murciélago sector

Few tourists go to Santa Rosa's **Murciélago sector**, an area of reserve to the northwest of – and entirely separate from – the main sector of the national park. It's a kind of reforestation laboratory in which former cattle pasture is slowly being regenerated, though there's also a campsite and a beach that's safe for swimming. To get there, drive along the Interamericana from the main Santa Rosa entrance about 10km north then take the left turn 8km to the hamlet of **Cuajiniquil**. A poor road continues here another 9km to the ranger station (open daily 7am–7pm, joint entry with Santa Rosa or $6). Be sure to take the dirt road, not the paved one. You'll almost certainly need a 4WD, at least in the wet season, when there are two creeks to ford. At the ranger station you can camp ($2) and arrange meals with prior notification (at the Santa Rosa administration centre). Dirt roads lead from the Murciélago ranger station to a series of fine swimming beaches (this part is known as the **Area Recreativa Junquillal**), accessible by walking or by 4WD. The westernmost of these, **Playa Blanca**, a small white stretch of sand, is the prettiest and one of the most isolated and least visited in the country. There's a ranger station here, with a camping area, limited water and simple toilet facilities. **Border checks** (see p.232) are particularly vigilant in this area. As usual, have your passport and all other documents in order.

Just 30km from the border, Murciélago is home to the remains of the training grounds used by the CIA-backed **Contras** during the Nicaraguan civil war. They're overgrown and scrubby today, with no sign that anything was ever there. It was also the location of the famous "secret" airstrip built, on Oliver North's orders, in direct violation of Costa Rica's declared neutrality in the conflict. Originally given the go-ahead by President Alberto Monge, the airstrip was eventually destroyed under President Oscar Arias's subsequent administration – a unilateral action that led to the US reducing its financial and political support for Costa Rica.

Practicalities

Santa Rosa's **entrance hut** is 35km north of Liberia, signed from the Interamericana. After paying the park fee, pick up a map and proceed some 6km or so, taking the right fork to the **administration centre** (T666-5051, F666-5020), which also runs Guanacaste and Rincón de la Vieja national parks. As well as checking road conditions and getting your camping/turtle-watching permits, you can visit La Casona and make reservations (at least 3hr in advance) for a simple lunch in the *comedor*. The food – *casados* with fish, chicken or meat and salad – is good, and this is a great place to get talking to rangers or other tourists. From here a rough road leads to the beaches; to drive to these, even in the height of the dry season, you need a sturdy 4WD. The administration discourages any driving at all beyond the main park road; nevertheless, people – surfers, mainly – insist on doing so, and survive. Most park their vehicle at the administration centre and walk. One thing is for sure:

The great pretender: William Walker

Born in Tennessee in 1824, **William Walker** was something of a child prodigy. By the age of 14 he had a degree from the University of Nashville, notching up degrees in law and medicine just five years later before setting off to study at various illustrious European universities. However, upon his return to the US, Walker failed in his chosen professions of doctor and lawyer and, somewhat at loose ends, landed up in California in 1849 at the height of the Gold Rush. Here he became involved with the **pro-slavery** organization Knights of the Golden Circle, who financed an expedition, in which Walker took part, to invade Baja California and Mexico to secure more land for the United States. Undeterred by the expedition's failure, Walker soon put his mind to another plan. Intending to make himself overlord of a Central American nation of five slave-owning states, and then to sell the territory to the US, Walker invaded Nicaragua in June 1855 with mercenary troops. The next logical step was to secure territory for the planned eleven-kilometre canal between Lago de Nicaragua and the Pacific. Gaining much of his financial backing from Nicaraguan get-rich-quick militarists and North American capitalists who promptly saw the benefits of a waterway along the Río San Juan from the Pacific to the Atlantic, in 1856 William Walker, and several hundred mercenary troops, invaded Costa Rica from the north.

Meanwhile, Costa Rican president **Juan Rafael Mora** had been watching Walker's progress with increasing alarm and, in February 1856, declared war on the usurper. Lacking military hardware, Costa Rica was ill-prepared for battle, and Mora's rapidly gathered army of nine thousand men was a largely peasant-and-bourgeois band, armed with machetes, farm tools and the occasional rusty rifle. Marching them out of San José through the Valle Central, over the Cordillera de Tilarán and on to the hot plains of Guanacaste, Mora got wind that Walker and his band of three hundred buccaneers were entrenched at the **Santa Rosa Casona**, the largest and best-fortified edifice in the area. Although by now Mora's force was reduced to only 2500 (we can only guess that, in the two weeks that it took them to march from San José, heat exhaustion had left many scattered by the wayside), on March 20, 1856 they routed the filibusters, fighting with their *campesino* tools. Mora then followed Walker and his men on their retreat, engaging them in battle again in Nicaraguan territory, at **Rivas**, some 15km north of the border, where Walker's troops eventually barricaded themselves in another wooden *casona*. It was here – and not, as is commonly thought, at Santa Rosa – that **Juan Santamaría**, a nineteen-year-old drummer boy, volunteered to set fire to the building in which Walker and his men were barricaded, flushing them out, and dying in the process. Walker, however, survived the fire, and carried on filibustering, until in 1857 a US warship was dispatched to put an end to his antics which were increasingly embarrassing for the US government, who had covertly backed him. Undeterred after a three-year spell in a Nicaraguan jail, he continued his adventuring until being shot dead by the Honduran authorities the same year.

Later, Mora, no devotee of democracy himself, rigged the 1859 Costa Rican presidential election so that he could serve a second term – despite his military victories against Walker, there was strong popular opposition to his domestic policies – and was deposed later that year. He attempted a coup d'état, but was subsequently shot in 1860, the same year that his former adversary met his Waterloo in Honduras.

don't try to drive anywhere in the park (including the Murciélago sector to the north, and the road to Cuajiniquil, detailed on p.237) in the rainy season without asking rangers about the state of the roads. You could get bogged down in mud or stopped by a swollen creek. Before setting off, you can always phone the Area de Conservación de Guanacaste (ACG) headquarters (☎666-5051, Spanish only) to check the current state of the roads in the park.

If you're walking down to the beach, a ranger or fellow tourist will probably give you a ride, but on no account set out without **water** – a couple of litres per person, at least, even on a short jaunt. Particularly convenient are the easy-to-carry bottles of water with plastic handles sold at the gas stations on the road outside Liberia; stock up before you come. You can also buy drinks, including small bottles of water, at the administration centre.

Camping facilities at Santa Rosa are some of the best in the country. There are two sites, each costing $2 per person, payable as you arrive at the administration centre and valid for the length of your stay. The shady **La Casona** campground has bathrooms and grill pits, while **Playa Naranjo**, on the beach (and only open outside the turtle-nesting season), has picnic tables and grill pits, and a ranger's hut with outhouses and showers, plus, apparently, a boa constrictor in the roof. Wherever you camp, watch your fires (the area is a tinderbox in the dry season), take plastic bags for your food, do not leave anything edible in your tent (it will be stolen by scavenging coati) and, of course, carry plenty of water.

Parque Nacional Guanacaste

Located 36km north of Liberia on the Interamericana, much of **PARQUE NACIONAL GUANACASTE** was not long ago nothing more than cattle

PARQUE NACIONAL GUANACASTE

N

▲ Nicaragua (18 km)

La Cruz

Hacienda Los Inocentes

Río Mena

Río Aguitas

Río Chan

Río Orosi

Río Sapoá

Río Sontoli

Volcán Orosi (1487 m)

Sendero de los Indios

Río Las Haciendas

Río Pizote

Maritza Biological Station

Volcán Cacao (1659 m)

Sendero Cacao

Cacao Field Station

Cuajiniquil ▲

INTERAMERICANA

Río Tempisquito

Río San Josecito

1000

Río Gongora

1 ▶

0   2 km

..... Trail

▼ Liberia (33 km)

Quebrada Grande & ▼ Santa Clara Lodge

pasture. Influential biologist D.H. Janzen, editor of the seminal *Costa Rican Natural History*, who had been involved in field study for many years in nearby Santa Rosa, was instrumental in creating the park virtually from scratch in 1991. Raising over $11 million, mainly from foreign sources, he envisioned creating a kind of biological corridor in which animals, mainly mammals, would have a large enough tract of undisturbed habitat in which to hunt and reproduce.

The **Santa Rosa–Guanacaste** (and, to an extent, Rincón de la Vieja) **corridor** is the result of his work, representing one of the most important efforts to conserve and regenerate tropical **dry forest** in the Americas. Containing tropical wet and dry forests and a smattering of cloudforest, Parque Nacional Guanacaste also protects the **springwell of the Río Tempisque**, as well as the Ríos Ahogados and Colorado. More than three hundred species of **birds,** including the orange-fronted parakeet and the white-throated magpie jay, have been recorded here, while mammals lurking behind the undergrowth include jaguar, puma, tapir, coati, armadillo, two-toed sloth and deer. It's also thought that there are about five thousand species of moths and **butterflies**, including the giant owl butterfly.

The park is devoted to research rather than tourism, and the administration staff at Santa Rosa (see p.236) discourage casual visitors. There are three main research stations, and it is sometimes possible to stay at them if you show enough interest and contact the Santa Rosa administration centre well in advance. Apart from the primary rainforest that exists at the upper elevations, the park's highlight is an astonishing collection of pre-Columbian petroglyphs at a place called El Pedregal. A trail leads to the site from the Maritza field station.

Practicalities

Facilities at Guanacaste are still minimal. **Access** is very difficult, unless (as usual) you've got a Range Rover or some other tank of a vehicle. The road to Cacao field station, on the slopes of the volcano of the same name, leaves the Interamericana 10km south of the Santa Rosa turn-off. It leads to a hamlet called Potrerillos; once there, head for Quebrada Grande (on some maps called García Flamenco) and continue for about 8km. It's passable most of the way, but the boulders from hell appear 3km from the entrance; at this point you have to ditch non-4WD vehicles and walk. There's very basic **lodge** accommodation ($15 per person) at Cacao and Maritza field stations. Call the Santa Rosa administration (℡666-5051, ℻666-5020) to check if it's open. They'll try to discourage you, so make your interest clear. To reach Maritza station from the Interamericana, take a right turn opposite the left turn-off to Cuajiniquil (see p.237). It's about 15km on a poor road to the station. In addition to the path to the petroglyphs, there's also a trail that connects Maritza with Cacao station.

La Cruz, the haciendas and the border

Set on a plateau north of Parque Nacional Guanacaste, overlooking Bahía Salinas and the Pacific Ocean to the west, the tiny, sleepy town of **LA CRUZ** is the last settlement of any size before the border, just 20km away, and makes a reasonable stopover if you're heading up to Nicaragua. The views at sunset are incredible, and there are a couple of good **places to stay** in town, although if you're spending any length of time in the area you'd do better at one of the nearby tourist lodges (see box opposite).

Guanacaste is horse and cattle country, and what better way to experience the region than to stay on a working hacienda and do some riding. The attractive Italian-run ranch **Las Colinas del Norte** (☎679-9132, ℻679-9064; ❸–❹), 4km beyond La Cruz on the Interamericana, is staffed by amiable folk and makes for a good base to explore the area. They have rooms with air-conditioning and can arrange horseback trips and volcano tours. The airy restaurant (with a bar) serves up good pizza with home-made mozzarella and there's a pool.

The stunningly located **Los Inocentes Lodge** (☎679-9190, ⓦwww .losinocenteslodge.com), built in 1890, lies about 3km south of La Cruz; turn east off the Interamericana on a road signed to Santa Cecilia and the lodge is 17km along this road. The grounds have lots of wildlife and ample bird-watching opportunities. Horse-riding is the thing to do here – you can ride up Volcán Orosí, which hovers prettily above – and there's also a pool, small bar and restaurant with excellent food (included in the room rate). You can get here by bus; contact the owners for current bus schedules from La Cruz. ❻

The small, charming IYHA-affiliated **Santa Clara Lodge** (☎666-4054, ℻666-4047; ❹; HI members get a discount) is 7.5km south of the entrance to the Parque Nacional Guanacaste on the side road that leads to the park; follow the signs. Set on a working ranch and dairy farm, with resident *sabaneros* and lots of horses and cattle around, it's also a convenient base for visiting Guanacaste and Santa Rosa national parks. The rooms are tiny and sparsely furnished, but the lodge's atmosphere and authenticity make up for this. Horse-riding trips to nearby Volcán Orosí are available, and the owners can advise on transport to Santa Rosa.

In La Cruz is the quirky *Amalia's Inn* (☎669-9618, ℻679-9181; ❹), about 100m south of the town's Parque Central, with spacious rooms, a pool and a spectacular view over the bay. It's well worth paying extra for a room with a view. Casual, friendly *Cabinas Santa Rita*, across from the courthouse (☎679-9062, ℻679-9305), offers clean, simple rooms with shared or private bath (❷), along with more upmarket, air-conditioned doubles in an annexe at the back (❸); there's also secure parking. Eating options aren't so rosy – *La Orquidea* and *Thelma*, on the main road, are the town's best sodas but nothing to write home about. For more interesting fare, head to one of the hotels out of town or to the *Hotel Bella Vista* near the square, which has a bar, restaurant and fine views. You can check your email at BT, just east of the town square.

The Nicaraguan border: Peñas Blancas

Peñas Blancas (7am–8pm daily), the main crossing point into Nicaragua, is emphatically a border post and not a town, with just one or two basic sodas and no hotels. Aim to get here as **early** as possible, as procedures are ponderous and you'll be lucky to get through the whole deal in less than ninety minutes. If you come on a Ticabus, things are smoother – all passengers are processed together and have some priority. Both Costa Rican and Nicaraguan border officials are quite strict, and there are many checks to see that your paperwork is in order. Buses on both sides of the border are far more frequent in the morning. If you're arriving from Nicaragua, the last San José–bound bus leaves at 3.30pm (5.30pm Fri–Sun), and the last Liberia bus at 5pm. After that, the only alternative is to take a costly taxi.

Exit stamps are given on the Costa Rican side, where there is a restaurant and a helpful, well-organized Costa Rican **tourist office** (daily 6am–noon & 1–8pm). Money-changers are always on hand and can change colones, córdobas and dollars. After getting your Costa Rican exit stamp it's a short walk north to the barrier from where you can get one of the regular shuttle buses ($2), 4km north to the Nicaraguan shanty town of Sapoá, where you go through Nicaraguan *migración*.

An **alternative** way to cross into Nicaragua from Liberia is to take a Peñas Blancas service, then pick up a local bus to **Rivas**, the first Nicaraguan town of any size, 37km beyond the border. This might not be convenient if you are going all the way to Managua, but the formalities are far less cumbersome than on the Tica and SIRCA services. As there's so much regular local traffic and fewer (potentially visa-holding) foreigners on these buses, they are generally processed much more quickly.

The Guanacaste beaches

The **beaches of Guanacaste** are scattered along the rocky coastline that runs from Bahía Culebra in the north near Liberia to Sámara on the west of the Nicoya Peninsula. Few of those in the north could truthfully be called beautiful, and most are quite small, located in coves or sheltered bays that makes them good for swimming, and relatively safe – though they lack the "impressive expanse of Playas Flamingo and Tamarindo a bit further down the coast. The waters in the **Bahía Culebra** (marked on some maps as Playa Panamá) are some of the clearest and most sheltered in the country, with good snorkelling.

The landscape of the Nicoya Peninsula is changing rapidly and many of the northern beaches, such as Tamarindo and Playa Panamá, are being aggressively developed for mass tourism. The relatively new airport in Liberia exists mainly to service the package and charter market along this coast. Sprawling across nearly the entire Bahía Culebra is the **Papagayo Project** (see box p.244), the country's largest tourist development.

The signs of mass tourism lessen as you head further south towards **Parque Nacional Marino Las Baulas**, where droves of **leatherback turtles** come ashore to lay their eggs between October and February. If it's a peaceful beach-side break you want, however, best head down to **Sámara** or **Nosara** on the Nicoya Peninsula; for surfing, resorty **Tamarindo** is the spot. The beaches here have drawn foreign expatriates in pursuit of paradise, and these cosmopolitan enclaves are in sharp contrast to the rest of the region. The beaches of the southern part of the Nicoya Peninsula are covered in the Central Pacific and Southern Nicoya chapter.

It can take a long time to get to the Guanacaste coast from San José (4–5hr minimum, unless you fly) and in some places you feel very remote indeed. **Getting around** can take time, too, as the beaches tend to be separated by rocky headlands or otherwise impassable formations, with barren hilly outcroppings coming right down to the sea, carving out little coves and bays, but necessitating considerable backtracking inland to get from one to the other. Although bus connections with the capital are good, travelling from beach to beach on the peninsula by **bus** is tricky, and you'll have to ask locals to figure out the peninsular services, whose schedules are not formally published, but which locals will know. By far the most popular option is to **rent a car**, which allows you to beach-hop with relative ease. Roads are not bad, if somewhat potholed – you'll do best with a **4WD**, though this can prove expensive. Another possibility for couples or small groups is to **hitch**, as there's a fair amount of tourist traffic around here.

Bahía Culebra

Sheltered from the full force of the Pacific, the clear blue waters around **Bahía Culebra** boast some of the best beaches in the country for swimming and snorkelling. The calm waters quietly lap at the grey volcanic sands of **Playa Panamá**, the northernmost beach of the bay. Unusually for this dry, hot zone of Guanacaste, **Playa Hermosa**, on the southern edge of the bay, is blessed with soothing shade, calm waters and gorgeous sunset views of the Pacific and offshore islets. If you want to go **diving** off Playa Hermosa, contact *Diving Safaris* (☎672-0147, ⓦwww.costaricadiving.com) for trips or lessons. Both beaches are easily accessible by **car** from Liberia. Take the turn-off to the right just after the hamlet of Comunidad – signposted to Playas Hermosa, Panamá and Coco – and continue for several kilometres over the good paved road. There's another turn-off to Hermosa and Panamá on the right. Five daily buses head from Liberia to Playa Hermosa and Playa Panamá. From San José, there's also a direct daily bus to the two beaches (5hr) at the ungodly hour of 3.25am and returning 5am.

Practicalities

Bahía Culebra is dotted with upmarket hotels, many of them run by Italian companies. At the end of the Playa Panamá beach road, the *Fiesta Premier Resort* (☎672-0000, ⓦwww.fiestapremier.com; ❾) is a five-star all-inclusive complex that's so large you can hop on shuttle buses to get around. The quality of the service and buffet food has been highly recommended by readers. Up a steep dirt road off the southern access road to Playa Hermosa is *La Finisterra* (☎672-0293, ⓦwww.finisterra.net; ❾) a charming small hotel with a superb setting on the cliff at the southern end of the beach. Enjoy stunning sunset views, a swimming pool and warm hospitality. The restaurant offers tasty international dishes and breakfast is included in the price. The *Hotel Giardini di Papagayo* (☎672-0067, ⓦwww.grupopapagayo.com; ❼), well situated on a plateau overlooking Playa Hermosa, offers spanking new rooms decorated in the Californian–Spanish colonial vein favoured by upmarket hoteliers hereabouts. Rates include all meals, but you pay extra for sea views. Free snorkelling and kayaking trips are included. The all-inclusive gated *Hotel Occidental Costa Smeralda* (☎672-0193, ⓦwww.occidentalhotels.com/costasmeralda; ❾) has a lovely pool, good restaurant and efficient management; there's a two-night minimum stay.

A stone's throw from the beach, the budget *Iguana Inn* (☎672-0065; ❸), on the northern beach access road to Playa Hermosa, has simple, colourful rooms with fan and small hot-water bathroom. There's also a swimming pool and a well-equipped shared kitchen. *Playa Hermosa Inn* (☎672-0063 ⓕ672-0060; ❺–❻) sits just off the northern access road, and offers attractive if simple rooms with firm beds, fan (some have a/c) and hot-water bathrooms. There's a small swimming pool, and very attractive gardens leading down to the beach. Also off the northern access road, *El Velero* (☎672-1017, ⓦwww.costaricahotel.net; ❺–❼) is a friendly hotel with split-level rooms with balconies. Enjoy sea views from the lovely gardens that are filled with birds and lizards; a short path leads from the hotel down to the beach. There's also a good restaurant and a small pool. For the best cheap eats, head to *Pescado Loco*, opposite the *El Velero*; freshly caught fish costs $5–6 and roast chicken is $3.

Playa del Coco

Some 35km west of Liberia, with good road connections, **Playa del Coco** was the first Pacific beach to hit the big time with weekending Costa Ricans

The Papagayo Project

For several years now the entire Bahía Culebra area, encompassing Playas Panamá and Hermosa, has been under threat from the **Papagayo Project**, originally intended to be the largest tourist development in Central America, with no less than 14,000 rooms (there are currently a total of 13,000 hotel rooms in all of Costa Rica). Needless to say, the environmental impact of such a project on a relatively undeveloped region could be catastrophic. In 1994, the entire project ground to a halt, but it's now forging ahead, with several mega-resorts already opened. Golf courses, too, are underway – the latest craze of the moneymen behind the project, albeit a seemingly mad idea in this semi-arid landscape. Environmentalists fear that the enormous amount of water needed to maintain these golf courses will be taken from nearby wetlands, mangroves and other delicate habitats, and the locals are also worried that their water supplies may be curtailed.

from the Valle Central. The beach itself is nothing special, but it's kept clean by rubbish-collecting brigades organized by local residents, and the town's accessibility and budget accommodation make it a useful base to explore the better beaches nearby. It also has many good restaurants, all within walking distance, and is a good place from which to take a snorkelling or diving tour.

Arrival

A direct **bus** (5hr) leaves San José for Coco three times daily at 8am, 2pm and 4pm, returning at 4am, 8am and 2pm. You can also get to Coco on six daily local services from Liberia (1hr).

Accommodation

Coco has plenty of fairly basic **cabinas**, catering to weekending nationals and tourists. In the high season you should **reserve** for weekends, but you can probably get away with turning up on spec mid-week, when rooms may also be a little cheaper. In the low season bargains abound. There's **camping** ($3) at *Chopin* (☎391-5998), on the road heading right 100m before the beach.

Cabinas Catarina 100m before you reach the parquecito ☎670-0156. The most basic budget cabinas in town, and a good deal. Each cabina has a private bath with cold water only, and the friendly management will let you do laundry and cook meals in the small kitchen. ❸

Cabinas El Dorado On the beach, south of the parquecito ☎837-2726. Basic, inexpensive cabinas with cold showers and fan, right on the beach. Those nearer the sea are a little airier and have the advantage of being within earshot of the rolling waves. There's a bar and restaurant. ❸

La Flor de Itabo On the main road coming into town, about 1km from the beach ☎670-0011, ⊛www.flordeitabo.com. Tasteful, friendly and long-established hotel, decorated with lovely dangling shell mobiles and Guatemalan bedspreads. All rooms have private bath, a/c, hot water and TV; there are cheaper bungalows with fans only. There's also a fine on-site Italian restaurant, *Da Beppe*. ❺

Pato Loco Inn On the road coming into town, about 300m before the village ☎670-0145. The "Crazy Duck" offers nice airy rooms with private bath and fan (❻) or a/c (❼) – along with cordial, personal treatment. There are a couple of longstay apartments with kitchen, and there's Internet access for guests.

La Puerta del Sol Off the road leading to the right 100m before you reach the beach ☎670-0195, ⒻError670-0650. Friendly Italian-run retreat set in quiet gardens; rooms have a/c, phone and cable TV and a small terrace and lounge area. The thoughtfully arranged complex has a pool, gym and the *Sol y Luna* restaurant (see opposite) with top-notch Italian food. Breakfast is included in the price. ❻

B&B Villa del Sol 1km north of the village; turn right off the main road 150m before the beach ☎670-0085, ⊛www.villadelsol.com. Small, welcoming hotel in a quiet location with rooms set around a large plain grassy space – all have private bath with hot water and ocean views. Pleasantly decorated by the friendly French-Canadian owners, the hotel also has a large pool and tasty meals. ❻

Villa Flores Just before reaching the beach, head right up a dirt road; the hotel is 200 metres on your left ☎670-0269, ⓦwww.hotel-villa-flores .com. Quiet and comfortable, this newly spruced-up hotel has bright, cheerful rooms each with firm mattresses, private bath, hot water and a/c. The deluxe rooms upstairs are furnished with dark wood; the large balcony is a perfect spot to contemplate the spacious grounds or catch sea breezes. Breakfast is included in the rates, as is the warm hospitality. There's also a pool, Jacuzzi and small gym. ❺

Vista Mar Signposted turn 1km north of the village ☎ & ℱ670-0753, ℰhvistamar@racsa .co.cr. A good-value and nicely maintained hotel by the beach, with eight spacious and pleasantly decorated rooms, with shared or private hot-water bath, plus fan or a/c. There's a palm-fringed pool and a good restaurant serving Italian- and French-themed food. Breakfast included. ❸

The town

El Coco town spreads out right in front of the beach, with a tiny **parquecito** as the focal point. The minimal services include a miniscule **correo** (Mon–Fri 7.30am–5pm) and public **telephones** on either side of the parquecito. The Banco Nacional, on the main road as you enter town, will change dollars and travellers' cheques and has an **ATM**. **Taxis** gather by the little park on the beach. There's **Internet** access at Leslie's, in the same building as *Cabinas Catarina* (see opposite). A good supermarket, Luperón, is next to the Banco Nacional.

Playa del Coco is a popular **snorkelling** and **diving** centre: the staff at Rich Coast Diving (☎670-0176, ⓦwww.richcoastdiving.com), on the main road about 300m from the beach, speak English, organize snorkelling and scuba trips ($50–80 for a two-tank dive) and rent out mountain bikes. Deep Blue Diving (☎670-1004, ⓦwww.deepblue-diving.com), in the precinct of the *Coco Verde* hotel, runs similar trips.

Eating, drinking and nightlife

Coco has two very distinct types of places to eat and drink: those catering to Ticos and those that make some sort of stab at cosmopolitanism to hook the gringos. There's a lively nightlife, much of it emanating from the *Lizard Lounge* on the main street, an open bar with plenty of cocktails and shooters and moody bass beats. A little further up the street is *Banana Surf*, an upstairs bar with a balcony. At weekends, the *Cocomar Discoteca* by the beach gets hopping. A quietish but atmospheric bar is *La Vida Loca*, reached across a narrow footbridge 100m south of the park – look for the flashing cross.

Bar Coco Opposite the parquecito. A popular place in a prime position, *Bar Coco* offers good seafood lunches and dinners or just a beer in the evening.

Papagayo On the main drag, 100m before the beach. If it's fresh and available, you'll find it on the menu at Coco's best seafood restaurant, run by the family of the big shot of the local fishing fleet. The "catch of the day" will set you back $7, while a delectable mixed seafood platter comes in at $15. The fish are prepared in a wide variety of styles, but the quality is consistently excellent.

La Rana On the main road, 100m before the beach, on the left. Relaxing bar and restaurant serves Tico fare and Western burgers and steaks

– all at reasonable prices. Pleasant spot to grab a snack, chill out listening to music or catch the latest sporting events and news on the big screen.

Sol y Luna In the *Puerta del Sol* hotel. Expertly prepared Italian food, including home-made pasta seasoned with herbs, served in an attractive and intimate setting. The owners make a big effort to import the authentic ingredients, and there's also a decent wine selection. Mains dishes are $8–10.

Tequila Bar On the main road, near the parquecito. Although it looks a little ramshackle, the Mexican food here is high quality. Filling plates start at $5 and the Mexican owner extends a warm welcome to diners.

Playa Ocotal to Playa Conchal

Past the rocky headland south of Coco, the upmarket enclave of **PLAYA OCOTAL** is reached by taking the signed turn-off to the left 200m before reaching the beach at Coco. Ocotal and its surroundings have lovely views over the ocean and across to the Papagayo Gulf from the top of the headland, and the small beach is better for swimming than Coco, but the real attraction are the marlin and other "big game" fish that glide through these waters. Ocotal **hotels** are usually tied in with sports-fishing packages: one of the most highly rated is *El Ocotal* (℡670-0321, ⓦwww.ocotalresort.com; ❼), whose elegantly furnished rooms have TV, hammocks, air conditioning and fridges. Set on top of a hill, it has stunning views over the Pacific, and offers tennis and swimming as well as sports-fishing and scuba-diving packages. The best mid-range place to stay is the ultra-hospitable *Villa Casa Blanca* (℡670-0518, ⓦwww .informationcostarica.com; ❻), a small, quiet B&B that offers boat tours, deep-sea fishing, scuba diving to the Islas Murciélagos near Santa Rosa, and horse-riding trips. There's a charming bridged pool, a tennis court on the grounds and rates include breakfast.

Playas Flamingo and Brasilito

Despite its name, there are no flamingos at the upmarket and expensive gringo ghetto of **PLAYA FLAMINGO**, a place that feels more Florida or Cancún than Costa Rica – some of the big beach houses lining the white sands are owned by the odd movie star. It does, however, have the best beach on this section of the coast, with white sand, gentle breakers and picturesque rocky islets offshore. There's also great **sports-fishing**: almost all the resort-style hotels in the area cater to fishing enthusiasts or sun-worshippers on packages. It's approached along the road to the small, unappealing **PLAYA BRASILITO**, a scruffy beach with darkish sand; about 5km beyond it is Playa Flamingo's marina. This is more or less the centre of the community, with the larger **hotels** spread out along the beach. One of the largest is the *Flamingo Beach Resort* (℡654-4444, ⓦwww.resortflamingobeach.com; ❼); though it lacks character, it boasts a good pool, a restaurant, a casino and rooms with all the modern conveniences. *Flamingo Marina Resort* (℡654-4141, ⓦwww.flamingomarina .com; ❻) has modern rooms as well as enormous suites with Jacuzzis. There are several pools, a tennis court, a restaurant and tour service. Both hotels can arrange air charter service and will pick you up from the airstrip. A cheaper option – and pleasant hang-out spot – is *Mariner Inn* (℡654-4081, Ⓕ654-4042; ❹), which has clean and pleasant air-conditioned rooms and an appealing bar where fishermen's tall tales are swapped over cold beers and tasty burgers.

If you want to enjoy the beach but avoid the static and stand-offish atmosphere of Flamingo, head for **Playa Potrero** (just 3km before Playa Flamingo), a small cove that opens onto a decent crescent-shaped beach whose calm waters are good for swimming. You can camp at relaxed *Mayra's* (℡654-4213) right on the seashore; the friendly Italian-run *Bahía Esmeralda* (℡654-4480, ⓦwww.hotelbahiaesmeralda.com; ❹) is a good option too, with rooms located in a complex of cabins, plus a pool and a small restaurant. *Monte Carlo Beach Resort* (℡654-4674, ⓦwww.monte-carlo-beach-resort .com; ❺) has attractive air-conditioned bungalows with kitchen, a decent Italian restaurant and a pool.

The best budget option is in Brasilito: the relaxed *Hotel Brasilito* (℡654-4237, ⓦwww.brasilito.com; ❸–❹), right on the beach, has rooms that are sparsely furnished but with large beds, fans and hot-water bathrooms. In the same building, the reasonably priced *Perro Plano* restaurant serves typical regional fare as well as more eclectic choices such as Thai curries.

To reach Playas Flamingo and Brasilito by **car**, take the Liberia–Nicoya road to Belén, then turn right off the main road and follow a side road to the hamlet of Huacas, 25km beyond Belén, from where the beaches are signposted. Getting to Flamingo **from San José**, Tralapa runs direct buses (3 daily; 5hr). There are two buses daily from **Santa Cruz** (see p.255), arriving early in the morning or mid-afternoon at Brasilito, Flamingo and Potrero beach, several kilometres north.

Playa Conchal

Playa Conchal ("Shell Beach"), set in a steep broad bay a couple of kilometres south of Playa Brasilito and protected by a rocky headland, is an appealing pink-coloured beach, with mounds of tiny shells and quiet waters that are good for swimming and snorkelling. Set back from the beach between Playas Brasilito and Conchal is the huge *Melia Playa Conchal* (☎654-4123, ⓦwww .solmelia.com; ⑨), a plush Spanish-owned tourist complex, whose recent arrival has dramatically changed the character of the area from a sleepy low-key beach community to an exclusive resort boasting hundreds of suites and a golf course. To get to Conchal from Flamingo, you have to backtrack inland, turning right at the village of Matapalo. It's quicker to drive along the sand from Brasilito, but you'll need a 4WD or a tug-o-war team.

Parque Nacional Marino Las Baulas

On the Río Matapalo estuary between Conchal and Tamarindo, **PARQUE NACIONAL MARINO LAS BAULAS** (9am–4pm, open for guided night tours in season; $6, including tour; ☎653-0470) is less a national park than a reserve, created in 1995 to protect the nesting grounds of the critically endangered **leatherback turtles**, which come ashore here to nest from November to February. Leatherbacks have laid their eggs at **Playa Grande** for quite possibly millions of years, and it's now one of the few remaining such nesting sites in the world. The beach itself offers a beautiful sweep of light-coloured sand, and outside laying season you can surf and splash around in the waves, though swimming is rough, plagued by crashing waves and rip tides. Despite its proximity to an officially protected area, someone seems to have given developers carte blanche to build at Playa Grande. What effect this will have on the ancient nesting ground of the turtles remains to be seen. Meanwhile, *Rancho Las Colinas Golf and Country Club*, which includes an eighteen-hole golf course and over two hundred separate villas, is symptomatic of the lack of planning, the short-termism and the plain daftness (the golf course is located in an area with a long, hot dry season and a history of water shortages) that characterizes so much recent tourist development in Costa Rica.

Turtle nesting takes place only in season and at **night**, with moonlit nights at high tide being the preferred moment. Note that you are not guaranteed to see a nesting turtle on any given night, and it's definitely worth calling in at El Mundo de la Tortuga (see p.248) before your visit, both to see the informative exhibition and to ask if tides and weather are favourable for nesting – alternatively you could ask the rangers at the entrance hut.

Those who see a nesting are often moved both by the sight of the turtles' imposing bulk, and also by their vulnerability, as they lever themselves up on to the beach. Each female can nest up to twelve times per season, laying a hundred or so eggs at a time, before finally returning to the sea – after which she won't touch land again for another year. Eggs take about sixty days to hatch, and the female turtle **hatchlings** that make the journey from their eggs to the ocean down this beach will (if they survive) return here ten to fifteen years later to nest themselves.

While it's worth seeing a nesting, it's difficult not to feel like an intruder. Groups of up to fifteen people are led to each turtle by guides (some of them "rehabilitated" former poachers), who communicate via walkie-talkie – and if it's a busy night there might be several tour groups after the same turtle. When the guide locates a turtle ready to lay her eggs you trudge in a group along the beach and then stand around watching the leatherback go through her procreative duty, while from time to time the turtle will cast a world-weary glance in the direction of her fans. It's hard not to think it would be better for the turtle if everyone just stayed away and bought the video, although the viewing is well managed and fairly considerate, and the revenue does help to protect the turtles' habitat.

Around 200m from the park entrance, the impressive and educational **El Mundo de la Tortuga** exhibition (2pm–6pm, or until much later when turtles are nesting; $5; ☎653-0471) includes an audioguided tour in English and some stunning photographs of the turtles. You'll gain some insight into the leatherback's habitats and reproductive cycles, along with the threats they face and current conservation efforts. There's also a souvenir shop and a small café where groups on turtle tours are often asked to wait while a nesting turtle is located. It's open late at night – often past midnight – depending on demand and nesting times.

Practicalities

There are two official entrances to Playa Grande, though **tickets** to enter the reserve can only be bought at the southern entrance, where the road enters the park near the *Villa Baulas*. Playa Grande has in the past been a magnet for tour groups from upmarket Guanacaste hotels as well as day-trippers from Tamarindo and Coco. Nowadays, however, visitor numbers are regulated and you are no longer allowed to walk on the beach during nesting season (get the rangers to tell you stories of what people used to do to harass the turtles and you'll see why).

There are no bus services to the park. To **drive to Las Baulas**, take the road from Huacas to Matapalo, and turn left at the soccer field (a 4WD is recommended for this stretch during the wet season). Most people, however, visit the park by **boat** from Tamarindo, entering at the southern end rather than from the Matapalo road. Although most visitors to Las Baulas stay in Tamarindo, a few kilometres to the south, you'll find several excellent **hotels** at Playa Grande. *Bula Bula* (☎653-0975 ⊛www.hotelbulabula.com;⑤), in a splendid setting between Playa Grande and the river that runs behind the beach, offers ten rooms, plus some bungalows (sleeping 4–6). Excursions include kayaking, sports-fishing, horse-riding and mountain-biking. The restaurant serves fantastic food, particularly the large continental and Costa Rican breakfasts (included in the room rate). Right on the beach sits *Las Tortugas* (☎653-0423, ⊛www .cool.co.cr/usr/turtles; ⑤), the area's longest established hotel, with pool, restaurant and luxurious air-conditioned rooms and suites. The conscientious owners have kept the light the hotel reflects onto the beach to a minimum (turtle hatchlings are confused by light coming from land), and even showed the foresight to build so that the structure will block light from any future developments to the north. They also rent surfboards and can advise on turtle tours and horse-riding. Nestled among the trees on the beach is *Villa Baula*

The leatherback turtle

Leatherback turtles (in Spanish, *baulas*) are giant creatures. Often described as a relic from the age of the dinosaurs, they're also one of the oldest animals on earth, having existed largely unchanged for 120 million years. The leatherback's most arresting characteristic is its sheer size, reaching a length of about 2.4m and a weight of 540kg. Its front flippers are similarly huge – as much as 2.7m long – and it's these which propel the leatherback on its long-distance migrations (they're known to breed off the West Indies, Florida, the northeastern coast of South America, Senegal, Madagascar, Sri Lanka and Malaysia). Leatherbacks are also unique among turtles in having a skeleton that is not firmly attached to a shell, but which consists of a **carapace** made up of hundreds of irregular bony plates, covered with a leathery skin. It's also the only turtle that can regulate its own body temperature, maintaining a constant 18°C even in the freezing ocean depths, and withstanding immense pressures of over 1500 pounds per square inch as it dives to depths of up to 1200m.

Since the 1973 Convention on the International Trade of Endangered Species, it is illegal to harvest green, hawksbill, leatherback and loggerhead turtles. Unlike Olive Ridleys or hawksbills, leatherbacks are not hunted by humans for food – their flesh has an unpleasantly oily taste – though poachers still steal eggs for their alleged aphrodisiac powers. Even so, leatherbacks still face many human-created hazards. They can choke on discarded plastic bags left floating in the ocean (which they mistake for jellyfish, on which they feed), and often get caught in longline fishing nets or wounded by boat propellers – all added to a loss of nesting habitats caused by beachfront development and the fact that, even in normal conditions, only one in every 2500 leatherback hatchlings makes it to maturity.

The number of nesting females at Las Baulas alone dropped from 1646 in 1988 to 215 in 1997, although numbers are up slightly in the new millennium. At Las Baulas, authorities have established a hatchling "farm" to allow hatchlings to be born and make their trip to the ocean under less perilous conditions than would normally prevail, though this will not affect adult mortality, which is believed to be the root cause of the drop in leatherback numbers. The fall in population has been particularly blamed on longline fishing, while large-scale rubbish dumping, ocean contamination and other factors contributing to fertility problems are also cited.

You can **volunteer** on two leatherback conservation projects: Earthwatch have run conservation vacations on Playa Grande for a number of years, documenting numbers of nesting turtles and their activity patterns. On the Caribbean side of the country, the Leatherback Sea Turtle Research Project concentrates on saving its Caribbean nesting habitat. Contact **Earthwatch** (in the US: 3 Clock Tower Place, Suite 100, Box 75, Maynard, MA 01754, ☎1-800/776-0188, ⓦwww.earthwatch .org; in the UK: 267 Banbury Road, Oxford OX2 7HT, ☎01865/318838) or the **Leatherback Sea Turtle Research Project** (Bahía Culebra, CRESLI, Campus Box 1764, Southampton College of Long Island University, Southampton, NY 11968, ☎631/287-8223, ⓦwww.cresli.org).

(☎653-0493, ⓦwww.hotelvillabaula.com; ❺–❻) offering comfortable seaside rooms with ceiling fans, plus some attractive private bungalows, all with private bath and hot water (some also have fridge). There are two lovely pools on the grounds and a good restaurant serving Indonesian dishes.

Playa Tamarindo

Perennially popular **Tamarindo** stretches for a couple of kilometres over a series of rocky headlands, and attracts surfers and vacationing spring-breakers.

Sprawling and occasionally snobby, **TAMARINDO** village has a sizable foreign community and boasts a decent selection of restaurants, a lively beach culture (think beautiful young things parading up and down the sand) and a healthy nightlife, at least during high season. Many come here to learn to surf, and indeed the gentle breakers are an ideal training ground, but Tamarindo is the least Costa Rican of places – locals are completely outnumbered by the tourist and expat hordes. Even by its own trendy terms, Tamarindo is booming, with small complexes of shops springing up in the concrete mini-mall-style favoured hereabouts, while Internet cafés, restaurants and real-estate agents have now colonized the entire centre of the village, as foreigners rush in to snap up their plots in paradise, even if they're no longer the bargain they once were.

Arrival and information

You can **fly** into Tamarindo on NatureAir and Sansa, both of which have offices in town; **buses** arrive by the village loop at the end of the road. This loop effectively constitutes Tamarindo's small centre and is surrounded by restaurants and populated by new-age jewellery-sellers. There are many banks in town, several with ATMs, including the Banco Nacional, 500m north of the loop. They will also change dollars, although you'll be hard pressed to find anywhere that doesn't accept them as currency. There are **public telephones** at the loop and several **Internet cafés** (around $2 per hour), including Tamarindo.Net at the junction north of the loop. You can wash clothes at Lavandería Mariposa by Iguana Surf. The Supermercado Tamarindo and Supermercado Pelicano sell basic foodstuffs. For **getting around** the area, and out to Playa Langosta, you could rent a scooter or a mountain bike from Tamarindo Rental Tours, among other places. There are several places to rent a car, including Budget, Payless and Economy.

Accommodation

Many of Tamarindo's **hotels** are very good, if expensive. You can **camp** at the dusty and mediocre *Camping Punta de Madero* ($3) on the road to Playa Langosta, but the nicer beachside campsites have closed due to new government regulations. Playa Langosta's upmarket B&Bs and hotels offer a retreat from the sometimes hectic Tamarindo beachside scene, and are a fifteen- to twenty-minute walk from the heart of the action.

B&B Casa Sueca Playa Langosta ☎ & ℱ653-0021. Beautifully appointed and cosy apartments, all artistically decorated, with private bath, hot water, fans and breezy balconies. You can rent surfboards and get advice on local surf hot-spots. Good weekly discounts. ❺

B&B Sueño del Mar Playa Langosta ☎653-0284, ⓦwww.sueno-del-mar.com. Swing in a hammock on the ocean-facing verandah of this beautiful Spanish hacienda-style house, with tiled roofs and adobe walls. The charming and luxurious rooms all come with pretty tiled showers. Rates include a tasty and filling breakfast. ❼

B&B Villa Alegre Playa Langosta ☎653-0270, ⓦwww.villaalegrecostarica.com. Relaxing Californian-owned B&B, set in a quiet location on the beach in Playa Langosta. The five rooms,

with large, comfortable beds, are themed on different countries and brightly and tastefully decorated The generous breakfast is served on the verandah by the pool. Also available are a pair of villas (accommodating 2–5 people) with kitchen facilities. ❻–❼

Cabinas Marielos Tamarindo ☎ & ℱ653-0141. Basic rooms, light and clean, with fan, cold water and the use of a small kitchen, in pleasant and colourful grounds set back from }the main road. There are also rooms available with a/c, and a handful with hot-water bathrooms and fridge. The *dueña* is helpful and professional. ❸–❹

Cabinas El Mono Loco About 300m up the road to Playa Langosta ☎653-0238, ⓔelmonoloco@racsa.co.cr. Run by a relaxed Tico

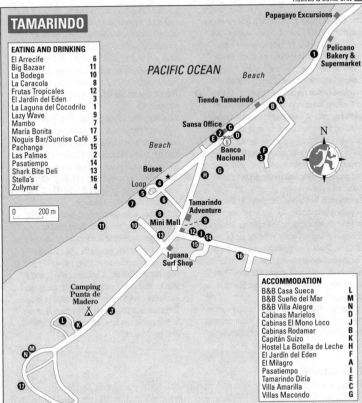

TAMARINDO

PACIFIC OCEAN Beach

Papagayo Excursions ◆

Pelicano Bakery & Supermarket ❶

Tienda Tamarindo

Sansa Office

Banco Nacional

Beach

Buses

Loop

Tamarindo Adventure

Mini Mall

Iguana Surf Shop

Camping Punta de Madero ⛺

0 — 200 m

N

EATING AND DRINKING

El Arrecife	6
Big Bazaar	11
La Bodega	10
La Caracola	8
Frutas Tropicales	12
El Jardín del Eden	3
La Laguna del Cocodrilo	1
Lazy Wave	9
Mambo	7
María Bonita	17
Noguis Bar/Sunrise Café	5
Pachanga	15
Las Palmas	2
Pasatiempo	14
Shark Bite Deli	13
Stella's	16
Zullymar	4

ACCOMMODATION

B&B Casa Sueca	L
B&B Sueño del Mar	M
B&B Villa Alegre	N
Cabinas Marielos	D
Cabinas El Mono Loco	J
Cabinas Rodamar	B
Capitán Suizo	K
Hostel La Botella de Leche	H
El Jardín del Eden	F
El Milagro	A
Pasatiempo	I
Tamarindo Diría	E
Villa Amarilla	C
Villas Macondo	G

GUANACASTE | Playa Tamarindo

5

family, this clean little hotel is set around a tranquil garden with a small plunge pool. There are dorm beds ($14 per person) as well as large simple rooms with a/c and hot water – try and get room 1, which receives considerably more sunlight than the others. Some rooms sleep up to seven, so it's good value for groups. The owners also rent bikes and prepare meals. ❺

Cabinas Rodamar Tamarindo ☎653-0109. A basic, friendly budget traveller's hangout, this motel-style compound set back from the main road has dark cabinas with cold-water bathroom, big beds and fan. The cheaper rooms with shared bathroom are a bit more spartan. There's a shared kitchen. ❷

Capitán Suizo Playa Langosta ☎653-0075, ⓦwww.hotelcapitansuizo.com. Popular, upmarket Swiss-run hotel set in spacious, landscaped grounds on the beach. The cabina-style rooms all have a balcony or terrace, fridge, ceiling fans

or a/c, bathtub, hot water and an outside shower. The palm-shaded pool is bigger than most, and the atmosphere friendly and relaxed. There's also a cocktail bar, beautiful beach views and a buffet breakfast. Prices in high season are $145–170, including taxes. ❼–❽

Hostel La Botella de Leche Tamarindo ☎653-0944, ⓦwww.labotelladeleche.com. Excellent backpacker hostel with comfortable bunk-bed accommodation in dorms. It's air-conditioned, sociable and has a well-equipped communal kitchen and spick-and-span shared cold-water bathrooms. It's designed with surfers in mind – you can rent and repair boards here, as well as arrange classes. It's very popular, and although the super-friendly *dueña* will do her utmost to squeeze you in, you'd be wise to reserve ahead. ❸

El Jardín del Eden On the hilltop behind the main road through town ☎653-0137, ⓦwww

.jardindeleden.com. Discreetly upmarket hotel in an exclusive hilltop position, with fine views over Tamarindo. Villas have all the usual amenities – a/c, fans, satellite TV, telephone and fridge – plus nice touches like tiled bathrooms and wicker chairs on the large private balconies. There's also a nicely landscaped pool, Jacuzzi, bar and an excellent French restaurant. Breakfast included. ⑥

El Milagro Tamarindo ⑦653-0042, ⓦwww .elmilagro.com. A long-time Tamarindo favourite, featuring nicely decorated cabinas with private hot-water bathroom and either fan (⑤) or a/c (⑥). Some rooms are generously proportioned, with French windows opening onto flowered terraces. The poolside restaurant serves great food. Breakfast included.

Pasatiempo Tamarindo ⑦653-0096, ⓦwww .hotelpasatiempo.com. Popular hotel with a relaxed and friendly atmosphere. The spotless rooms have ceiling fans and hot water – the larger rooms (sleeping 5) are a particularly good deal for groups. The atmosphere is homely, with hammocks strung outside the rooms and around the pool. There's also a lively restaurant and popular bar (that can get loud in high season). ⑤

Tamarindo Diriá On the beach in the heart of town ⑦ & ⑥653-0031, ⓦwww.tamarindodiria .co.cr. One of Tamarindo's oldest hotels, set in shady palm groves on the beach. Though it might look a bit worn, it obviously nabbed the village's prime location. Arranged around a good-sized swimming pool looking out to the ocean, the large – if slightly dated – rooms all have a/c, cable TV, telephone and private bath. Sea view rooms cost more, but it's worth the upgrade. There's a great seaside bar/restaurant. Breakfast included. ⑦

Villa Amarilla On the beachfront ⑦653-0038, ⓔcarpen@racsa.co.cr. A favourite spot for a quick beer on the beach between catching waves, this also has seven cabinas and a communal kitchen. Rooms are decked out in wood; the simpler ones have fridge, fan and shared bathroom (⑧). En-suite rooms have a/c and cable TV (④). There's a cheap and cheerful restaurant.

Villas Macondo Tamarindo ⑦ & ⑥653-0812, ⓦwww.villasmacondo.com. Tamarindo is sometimes overpriced, but this quiet, welcoming spot is a refreshing exception. The colourful cabinas, set around an enticing swimming pool, have comfortable beds, wooden ceilings and a little terrace strung with hammocks; the more expensive ones include cable TV, a/c and fridge. There are also apartments (⑥) with one or two bedrooms. Guests have access to a kitchenette with gas stove. ⑥

The town

Though fishing still plays a small part in the local economy, Tamarindo's transformation from village to beach resort has been rapid, with the usual associated worries about drugs and the loss of community. **Swimming** isn't great around Tamarindo, because of choppy waters and occasional rip tides. Most people are content to paddle in the rocky coves and tide pools south of the town. Tamarindo is, however, an ideal **surf** spot because of the reliable, but relatively gentle, waves and the beach attracts a combination of enthusiastic surfers and well-to-do Costa Ricans, who maintain vacation houses in the vicinity.

Beyond learning to ride a board, picking up the many pretty pastel-coloured shells that wash up on the beach, eating fresh fish and hanging out with fellow foreigners, there's little to keep you occupied in the village itself. In the evening, the main activity is watching the typically opulent **sunsets**, as the sun disappears into the Pacific just beyond the rocky headland that marks the southern end of the beach, but attention soon shifts to the bar with the cheapest drinks specials.

North of the Tamarindo river estuary begins the long sweep of Playa Grande (see p.247), where the **leatherback turtles** lay their eggs. Turtles also come ashore at Tamarindo, but in much smaller quantities. Officially, Tamarindo is within the boundaries of Las Baulas National Park, in so far as the ocean covered by the protected area extends out in an arc, encompassing Tamarindo beach. The Servicio de Parques Nacionales (National Parks Service) has bought up the beach south of Tamarindo to Playa Langosta, too, preventing further hotel development and allowing turtles to continue coming ashore along this entire stretch.

Surf schools

The Tamarindo area has always been a surfing paradise, and its credibility was upped several notches when Bruce Brown's seminal surfing docudrama Endless Summer II was partly filmed here. Most surfers ride the waves at Tamarindo, Playa Grande and adjacent Playa Langosta, an excellent surf beach a couple of kilometres to the south. The friendly and professional **Iguana Surf** (℡653-0148, ⓦwww .iguanasurf.net), 500m southwest along the road to Playa Langosta, will almost certainly have you standing on a board by the end of your first class; cost is around $30 including board rental. Another popular school is **Tamarindo Adventures** (℡653-0108, ⓦwww.tamarindoadventures.net). **Chica Surf** (℡827-7884, ⓔchicasu rfschoolcr@hotmail.com) is an all-girls school and surf shop just off the loop in the centre of town. All schools rent surfboards; typical prices are $20 for a day's rental of a long board, or $100 for a week. You can also rent boogie boards, windsurfing equipment and masks and snorkels.

Eating, drinking and nightlife

Tamarindo has a number of excellent, cosmopolitan restaurants, many serving delicious fresh seafood and also world and fusion cuisine. **Nightlife** centres on the restaurants and bars – a couple of them with pleasant beachfront locations – in the heart of the village. *Las Palmas*, 200m north of the loop, is a trendy spot to unwind and watch the sun set after a day in the surf. The spacious *Mambo* bar is the place to be on Thursday and Friday evenings; later in the night, the action continues at *La Bodega*, just to the south. On Saturdays, the scene shifts further south along the beach to *Big Bazaar*, which has more of a dance music vibe.

El Arrecife On the Tamarindo circle. A cheapish soda with filling and flavoursome rice dishes ($4–5). The ever-present *casado* ($4) won't leave you peckish.

La Caracola Just off the Tamarindo circle. Dig into Argentine-style steaks ($5-6), tasty salads ($4-5) or simpler *casados* ($5) at this relaxed restaurant with a beachfront vibe. They also serve cocktails. Closed Sat.

Frutas Tropicales Main road, at north end of town. One of the few genuinely cheap places in Tamarindo. The name says it all: all kinds of tropical fruit are on offer, including in the delicious fruit *refrescos*. They also serve good *casados* ($3.50) and hamburgers ($3) – and even rent out a couple of cabinas (④).

El Jardín del Eden In the *E Jardín del Eden* hotel. Romantic, upmarket (but reasonably priced) restaurant in tropical gardens serves high-quality French and Italian cuisine made with top-notch ingredients. The lobster, seafood brochettes and *pargo* (snapper) are all recommended. Count on spending around $30 per person.

Tours around Playa Tamarindo

Many operators in town run a popular two-hour **boat excursion** ($40 per person) that takes you around the river estuary where you might spot monkeys, birds and crocodiles. In leatherback nesting season (Nov to mid-Feb), you can head out on a **turtle tour** (about 2hr; $30 per person); trips leave in the evening, the exact hour depending on the tide. During the rest of the year, turtles also nest further south at Ostional Wildlife Refuge (see p.264), usually only on a couple of days each month, depending on the moon. A trip there and back costs around $40. Numerous Tamarindo operators run these and other trips; one of the most professional and helpful is **Costa Rica Paradise** (℡653-0031, ⓦwww.crparadise.com), also known as the Costa Rica Tourist Information Centre, just north of the turn-off to Playa Langosta.

La Laguna del Cocodrilo At the northern end of Tamarindo ☎653-0255. Classy Mediterranean restaurant in a palm-fringed garden (with resident crocodile) right on the beach. Starters include an exquisite tuna *carpaccio* ($6); for entrees, try the seafood, steak and other exotic offerings such as fried camembert in honey sauce and chicken stewed in a spicy beer sauce, all for $8–11. Stock up on picnic fare at the on-site French bakery.

Lazy Wave Opposite the entrance to Tamarindo resort, 100m up the Playa Langosta turn-off from the beach road. This outdoor restaurant may look casual, but it dishes up some of the best cooking in the region, if not the country. The very fairly priced menu (changes daily) is distinguished by the delicacy and inventiveness of its ingredients and flavours and includes sushi, seared tuna steaks and beef Wellington in giant portions. The bakery-patisserie is worth a visit, too.

María Bonita 1.5km south of Tamarindo on Playa Langosta ☎653-0933. Hospitable Caribbean restaurant that serves spicy chicken fillets ($6) as well as juicy baked fish dishes. It's also a popular drinking spot.

Noguis Bar/Sunrise Café On the Tamarindo loop. Casual café serves excellent breakfasts, with good breads, pastries and coffees, which you can either eat at the breezy seaside tables or take away, and fine snacks such as fish tacos and fresh fillets of fish.

Pachanga Near the *Pasatiempo* hotel. Turn left up towards Playa Langosta; as the road bends right, go straight ahead. Intimate, candlelit restaurant,

tastefully decorated and with a French-influenced gourmet menu. The fish tartar ($6) is exquisite, as is the snapper fillet ($11), but do consider the changing (and often enticing) daily specials. Closed Sun.

Pasatiempo In the *Pasatiempo* hotel. Perennially good and reasonably priced restaurant serves crowd-pleasers like Caesar salad ($4), a wonderfully succulent blackened fish with greens and chicken breast with mango stuffing ($8). If nothing else, try the superlative fruit cocktails and a few nibbles. Live music twice a week in high season.

Shark Bite Deli At the entrance to the Tamarindo Resort, 100 metres up the road to Playa Langosta. The imaginative, gourmet sandwiches are the best in town. There's also a book exchange.

Stella's Just beyond *Pachanga* restaurant. One of the town's best restaurants, with good Italian pasta ($4–7) and fresh fish cooked in excellent, inventive sauces. A large menu encompasses wood-oven pizzas and even – rare for Costa Rica – veal. Chicken stroganoff is a tasty choice; the seafood platter for two ($27) is a must for that special romantic meal. Attractive open dining area. Closed Sun.

Zullymar On the Tamarindo loop. Unbeatable beachfront location – everybody seems to come here for a drink while watching the sun go down – and good food, with main dishes for $7–10. Service is slow, so plan on sitting and watching the crabs scuttling across the sand while waiting. All will be forgiven, however, once your tasty *corvina* or *dorado* arrives. Inexpensive pizzas are served during the day only.

South from Tamarindo to Playa Junquillal

It's not possible to continue straight down the coast from Tamarindo: to pick up the road south you have to return a couple of kilometres inland to the hamlet of Villareal. Don't head south in the rainy season without a 4WD, and not at all unless you like crossing creeks – there are plenty on this stretch, and they can swell worryingly fast in the rain. In the dry months you should be

Moving on from Tamarindo

Two daily buses head to San José, departing just outside the Tamarindo resort at 3.30am and 5.45am (5.45am and 12.30pm on Sun; 6hr). Six buses travel to **Liberia** daily, leaving from outside the Tamarindo Internet Café on the loop. To head further south down the peninsula, take one of the six daily buses to Santa Cruz (1hr) and link up with buses to Sámara or Nosara from there. As always, bus timetables are likely to change.

Continuing down the west coast of the peninsula is much easier with your own transport. One option is Interbus (an a/c minibus service) that runs daily to destinations all over the country ($25 to San José; $38 to Monteverde) and will pick you up from your hotel in the morning. They can be reserved through various agents in town.

all right with any vehicle as far as the surfing beach of **Playa Avellana**, 11km south of Tamarindo, and then to Junquillal, 10km beyond, but it may not do the car any good, and further south the roads become discouragingly rough. There are a few surfers' hangouts where you can **stay** at Avellana, with spartan but good-value accommodation, though if you're not a surfer, you'll feel a bit out of it, and may prefer the more upscale option of *Cabinas Las Olas* (T658-8315, Eolassa@racsa.co.cr; ❺) set back from the beach with pleasant light bungalows and swinging hammocks among mangroves. At *Lola's on the Beach* you'll see Lola herself, a large porker splashing around in the surf.

Lovely **Playa Junquillal** has a long, relatively straight beach. It's ideal for **surfing**, pounded by breakers crashing in at the end of their thousand-kilometre journeys, but far too rough for swimming. If you're looking for seclusion and quiet, however, it's a great place to hang out for a few days – there's precious little to do, and nothing at all in the way of nightlife. There are several very good **hotels**, many perched up above the beach on a small cliff, with stupendous views. The friendly *Hotel Iguanazul*, 3km north of Playa Junquillal (T653-8123, Wwww.iguanazul.com; ❺), has a great setting overlooking the sea, with bright rooms decorated with indigenous art, plus its own pool, bar and restaurant with a lovely view of the beach. It offers fishing, diving and horseback tours, as well as excursions to Las Baulas. Call ahead to reserve and ask about road conditions, especially in the rainy season. The quiet *La Guacamaya Lodge*, 2km south of Junquillal (T & F653-8431, Wwww .guacamayalodge.com; ❺) features comfortable, semicircular rooms, lovely views, friendly management and a pool. Enchanting *El Castillo Divertido* (T658-8428, Ecastillodivertido@hotmail.com; ❹) is a small white turreted "castle" run by entertaining hosts. Rooms have fans and there's a bar, restaurant and rooftop terrace. The cheapest accommodation at Junquillal is the US-owned *Hotel Playa Junquillal* (T658-8432, Wwww.playa-junquillal.com; ❹). The rooms are basic, but reasonably furnished, with private bath and hot water. There's a small bar and restaurant, and the friendly management is very knowledgeable about walking and camping in the area. There's also a campsite in Junquillal itself, *Los Malinches* ($3 per person).

One **bus** daily arrives in Junquillal from San José (via Santa Cruz). This service currently gets you to Junquillal after dark: as with all the places along the west coast of Nicoya, make sure you book a room in advance. The bus returns to San José at 5am.

Santa Cruz

Generally regarded by travellers as little more than somewhere to pass through on the way from Liberia or San José to the beach, the sprawling town of **SANTA CRUZ**, some 30km inland from Tamarindo and 57km south of Liberia, is actually "National Folklore City". Much of the music and dance considered quintessentially Guanacastecan originates here, like the various complex, stylized local dances, including the "Punto Guanacasteco" ("*el punto*"), which rivals Scottish country dancing for its complexity and has been adopted as the national dance. That said, however, they're not exactly dancing in the streets of Santa Cruz; life is actually rather slow, much of it lived out in contemplative fashion on the wide verandahs of the town's old houses.

Unless the local *fiestas* are on (mid-January), Santa Cruz has little of interest to keep you in town any longer than it takes to catch the bus out. There isn't much in the way of services, either, apart from the **Banco Nacional** on the way into town. In the unlikely event that you need a **hotel**, choose from the

Diría (☎680-0080, ⑤680-0442; ❹), which has a pool and air-conditioned rooms with TV; or *Hotel La Estancia* (☎680-0476; ❸), whose rooms have TV and private bath and fans but can be stuffy. For **food**, join the locals at the popular *Coopetortillas*, a barn-sized tortilla-making cooperative just off the central plaza with its own restaurant that serves chicken, Guanacastecan *empanadas* and sweet cheese bread, as well as, of course, tortillas.

Santa Cruz is a regional **transport** hub, with good connections inland and to the coast. Two companies run daily buses to San José (5hr) from the bus terminal on the west side of the central plaza – the result is they depart more or less hourly. There are numerous local bus services to Liberia. A number of buses leave for **Tamarindo** including a direct service at 8.30pm (about 1hr) returning from Tamarindo at 6.45am. For **Junquillal** a bus leaves at 6.30pm and returns to Santa Cruz at 5am. You can also get to **Playas Flamingo** and **Brasilito**, via Tamarindo, with two services leaving daily at 6.30am and 3pm (1hr 30min) and returning to Santa Cruz at 9am and 5pm (call ☎221-7202 in San José or ☎680-0392 in Santa Cruz for schedule information).

Guaitíl

The one town in Guanacaste where you can still see crafts being made in the traditional way is **GUAITÍL** (12km east of Santa Cruz), well known throughout Costa Rica for its **ceramics**. On the site of a major Chorotega potters' community, the present-day artisans' cooperative (*cooperativo artesanía*) was founded more than twenty years ago by three local women whose goal was to use regional traditions and their own abilities as potters and decorators for commercial gain. Today the artisans are still mainly women, keeping customs alive at the distinctive, large, dome-shaped kilns, while the men work in agricultural smallholdings.

Every house in Guaitíl seems to be in on the trade, with pottery on sale in front of people's homes, on little roadside stalls and in the Artesanía Cooperative

---

Dance and music in Guanacaste

In their book *A Year of Costa Rican Natural History*, Amelia Smith Calvert and Philip Powell Calvert describe their month on Guanacaste's **fiesta** circuit in 1910, starting in January in Filadelfia, a small town between Liberia and Santa Cruz, and ending in Santa Cruz. They were fascinated by the formal nature of the functions they attended, observing: "The dances were all round dances, mostly of familiar figures, waltzes and polkas, but one, called '*el punto*' was peculiar in that the partners do not hold one another but walk side by side, turn around each other and so on."

At Santa Cruz, "All the ladies sat in a row on one side of the room when not dancing, the men elsewhere. When a lady arrived somewhat late then the rest of the guests of the company, if seated, arose in recognition of her presence. The music was furnished by three fiddles and an accordion. The uninvited part of the community stood outside the house looking into the room through the open doors, which as usual were not separated from the street by any vestibule or passage." The Calverts were also delighted to come across *La giganta*, the figure of a woman about 4m high; actually a man on stilts "with a face rather crudely moulded and painted". What exactly *La giganta* represented isn't known, but she promenaded around the streets of Santa Cruz in her finery, long white lace trailing, while her scurrying minders frantically worked to keep her from keeling over. *La giganta*, along with other oversized personalities, is still featured in nearly every large village fiesta, usually held on the local saint's day.

Chorotega pottery

The chief characteristics of **Chorotega pottery** are the striking black and red on white **colouring**, called *pataky*, and a preponderance of panels, decorated with intricate anthropomorphic snake, jaguar and alligator motifs. Archeologists believe that pieces coloured and designed in this way were associated with the elite, possibly as mortuary furniture for *caciques* (chiefs) or other high-ranking individuals. In the Period VI (an archeological term for the years between 1000 BC and 500 AD) the *murillo appliqué* style emerged, an entirely new, glossy, black or red pottery with no parallel anywhere else in the region, but curiously similar to pottery found on Marajó Island at the mouth of the Amazon in modern-day Brazil, thousands of kilometres away.

After the Conquest, predictably, pottery-making declined sharply. The traditional anthropomorphic images were judged to be pagan by the Catholic Church and subsequently suppressed. Today you can see some of the best specimens in San José's Museo Nacional (see p.85) or watch them being faithfully reproduced in Guaitíl.

Today, potters in Guaitíl use local resources and traditional methods little-changed since the days of the Chorotegas. To make the clay, local rock is ground on ancient metates, which the Chorotegas used for grinding corn. The pigment used on many of the pieces, curiol, comes from a porous stone that has to be collected from a natural source, a four-hour walk away, and the ceramic piece is shaped using a special stone, also local, called zukia. Zukias were used by Chorotega potters to mould the lips and bases of plates and pots; treasured examples have been found in Chorotega graves.

on the edge of the soccer field. Some of the houses are open for you to wander inside and watch the women at work. Wherever you buy, don't haggle and don't expect it to be dirt cheap, either. A large vase can easily cost $20 or $25. Bear in mind, too, that this is decorative rather than functional pottery, and may not be that durable.

Guaitíl is on the old road to Nicoya; to get there from Santa Cruz, head east on the smaller road instead of south on the new road; turn off to the left where you see the sign for Guaitíl.

Nicoya

Bus travellers journeying between San José and the beach towns of Sámara and Nosara need to make connections at the country town of **NICOYA**, inland and northeast of the beaches. Set in a dip surrounded by low mountains, Nicoya is the peninsula's main settlement. The town is permeated by an air of infinite stasis but is undeniably pretty, with a lovely **Parque Central** and its white adobe church (earthquake-battered, structurally unstable and currently closed), cascading bougainvillea and colourful plants. There's a considerable Chinese presence in the town and many of the restaurants, hotels and stores are owned by descendants of Chinese immigrants.

Practicalities

Eight **buses** a day arrive in Nicoya from San José, a journey of around six hours. Some take the slightly longer route via the road to Liberia, but most use the new Tempisque Bridge (see box p.250). Buses also arrive from a number of regional destinations, including Liberia (10 daily), Santa Cruz (16 daily), Sámara (3–6 daily) and Nosara (1 daily). Two buses head for Naranjo, from where you can catch the ferry to Puntarenas, or head further south towards Montezuma. Most buses arrive at Nicoya's spotless bus station on the southern edge of town, a short walk from the centre; the Liberia service pulls in across from the *Hotel Las Tinajas*.

The friendly *Hotel Jenny* (☎685-5050; ❸), 100m south of the Parque Central, is the cheapest **place to stay**, with old, basic, air-conditioned rooms with TV and phone. The *Hotel Las Tinajas* (☎685-5081; ❸), 100m northeast of Parque Central, is nicer, with dark rooms inside the main building and lighter cabinas around the back. Good **restaurants** include the *Cafetería Daniela*, 100m east of the Parque, for breakfast and pastries; the sodas by the Parque (*El Nuevo Horizonte* is the best) for large *casados*; and, for Chinese food, the *Restaurant El Teyet*, across from *Hotel Jenny*.

As usual, you'll find most **services** around Parque Central, including the **correo** and banks, several with ATMs. **Taxis** line up by the Parque, or call Coopetico (☎658-6226). There's an Internet café opposite *Hotel Jenny*, just south of Parque Central.

Main Highway, Santa Cruz, Río Tempisque Ferry & Playa Naranjo

NICOYA

Sámara & Nosara

ACCOMMODATION		EATING AND DRINKING	
Hotel Jenny	B	Cafetería Daniela	2
Hotel Las Tinajas	A	El Nuevo Horizonte	1
		Restaurant El Teyet	3

Playa Sámara

A road runs the 35km between Nicoya and the coast at Nosara, via Caimital, though it's only negotiable with a 4WD. Most drivers, and all buses, take the longer, paved route (marked as Route 150 on some maps) through **PLAYA SÁMARA**, from where you can loop north back up the coast. The scenery from Nicoya to Sámara, 30km south, is rolling, rather than precipitous, although there are a couple of particularly nasty corners, marked by crosses commemorating the drivers who didn't make it.

The Friendship Bridge

Opened in April 2003, the new Puente Tempisque connects the mainland with the Nicoya Peninsula. The bridge spans from near Puerto Moreno (17km east of the Nicoya–Carmona road) on the peninsula to a point 25km west of the Interamericana on the mainland. The 780-metre bridge (toll is 90¢) replaces a time-consuming ferry connection saving at least two hours in reaching places like Sámara. The bridge was a $26-million gift from the Taiwanese government as a reward for Costa Rica being one of some two dozen countries in the world that recognizes Taipei as the legitimate Chinese authority rather than Beijing. The bridge is partly held up by suspension cables connected to towers that, at 80m, make this expensive present the tallest structure in the country.

Arrival and information

Sansa and NatureAir **planes** from San José arrive at the airstrip 6km east of town at Carrillo, from where 4WD taxis make the trip to Sámara for about $6. The express **bus** from San José leaves daily at 12:30pm and 6:15pm, and arrives at Sámara some 5 hours later, stopping about 50m in front of the beach right at the centre of the village. The express bus **back to San José** leaves at 4am and 8.45am; there are also several daily buses **to Nicoya** (2hr).

You can buy tickets for some bus services from the Transporte Alfaro office (daily 7am–5pm) in the centre of the village, which also sells potato chips, suntan lotion and bottles of cold water and is home to the village's public telephone. Sámara's correo – a small shack really – 50m before the entrance to the beach, offers minimal services. There is nowhere to change money (other than at the large hotels) but nearly all establishments accept US dollars. A mobile ATM machine sometimes turns up in the village for much of the high season, but don't rely on it being there. Tropical Latitude, near the Hotel Casa del Mar, offers Internet access; for laundry, head for Lava Ya.

There aren't as many tours or other activities at Sámara as there are at other places on the peninsula, but Sámara Adventures (☎656-0655), on the beach-front road just south of the town centre, runs a variety of fishing and water sports excursions, as well as wildlife-spotting trips to the Ostional Reserve. Tío Tigre (☎656-0098) will instruct you in the art of sea-kayaking and they also run dolphin-watching cruises. Pura Vida (☎656-0273) arrange dives and PADI courses. Apart from hanging around the beach here, plenty of people head 6km south to Playa Carrillo (see p.261), an even more beautiful strip of palm-backed sand.

Accommodation

Staying in Sámara is getting pricier, with few cheap cabinas. Although during the low season most hotels can offer better rates than the ones listed here, on high-season weekends you should have a **reservation** no matter what price range. *Camping Coco*, on the beach, is clean and well run, with cooking grills, as is *Camping Playas Sámara*, at the north end of the beach, with toilets and showers (both $3 a night).

Aparthotel Mirador de Sámara First left as you come into Nicoya, and 100m up the hill from the *Marbella* ☎656-0044, ⓦwww.miradordesamara .com. Huge apartments (five–seven people) with large bathrooms, bedrooms, living rooms, kitchen and terrace, all with panoramic views of town and beach. The bar is in an impressive tower with spectacular sunset views, and there's a small pool with wooden sundecks. Good low-season and long-stay discounts. Better value for four or more people, rather than couples. ❻

B&B Casa Naranja Town centre ☎ & Ⓕ656-0220. This small, central hotel has three rooms (one with a/c) in a modern building. The very fair price includes a good French breakfast, and the attached bar-restaurant-creperie is highly recommended. ❸

Belvedere 100m down the road to Carrillo ☎ & Ⓕ656-0213, ⓦwww.samara-costarica.com. This wonderfully pleasant hotel has ten rooms and two

apartments with either a/c or fan (the latter $8 less), and all are brightly furnished in light wood, with mosquito nets and solar-heated water. There's also a Jacuzzi and swimming pool, and a good German breakfast is included. ❹

Cabinas El Ancla On the beachfront road 200m south of the centre ☎656-0254. Simply furnished rooms, with cold-water bathroom and fan, right on the beach. Upstairs rooms are a bit hotter but still better than the dark and oppressive downstairs rooms. Friendly *dueña* and good beachfront seafood restaurant. ❸

Casa del Mar 50m north of the entrance to beach on the left ☎656-0264, Ⓕ656-1029. Large, good-value rooms (although a bit sparsely furnished) close to the beach. The downstairs rooms are clean and white, but rather dark; ask for an upstairs room with shared bath and palm-fringed sea view. ❹

Giada About 100m before you come to the beach, on the left ☎656-0132, ⓦwww.hotelgiada.net.

Small hotel set around a compact pool, with spotless banana-yellow rooms, good beds, overhead fans, private baths and tiled showers – the upstairs rooms are better for views and breeze. There's also a friendly Italian restaurant. **❹**

Marbella First left as you come into town from Nicoya ⊤ & ℗656-0362. Fairly inexpensive hotel, with a tiny pool – for plunging rather than swimming – and ten rather dark, but brightly painted rooms, that come with either a/c or fan as well as cable TV. There's also an on-site restaurant. **❹**

Villas Playa Sámara On the road to Carrillo ⊤656-0372, ⓦwww.villasplayasamara.com. Upmarket resort, wildly popular amongst wealthy Costa Rican families, with both all-inclusive and accommodation-only tariffs. The well-built villas come with large, spacious kitchens and sitting rooms, and outside terrace and hammock but the whole effect (golf carts for your luggage; see-your-neighbour proximity) is a bit suburban, and the management could be more efficient – although the beachside setting at the quiet south end of the beach is lovely. **❼**

The town

Sámara, 30km southwest of Nicoya, is one of the peninsula's most peaceful and least developed beachside resorts. It also boasts some of the calmest waters, making it ideal for swimming. The long clean stretch of sand is protected by a reef about a kilometre out, which takes the brunt of the Pacific's power out of the waves. It's a great place to relax, and its distance from the capital makes it much quieter than the more accessible Pacific beaches, although the new Puente Tempisque means that many locals fear imminent overdevelopment. But for now, even at the busiest times, there's little action other than weekenders tottering by on stout criollo **horses** (available for rent at $5 per hour) and the occasional dune buggy racing up the sand. On Sundays, the town turns out in force to watch the local **soccer** teams who play on the village field as if they're Brazil and Argentina battling it out for the World Cup – even weekending Ticos shun the beach for the sidelines.

Eating, drinking and nightlife

Sámara has a couple of very nice places to **eat**, where you can also enjoy a cold beer by the lapping waves. **Nightlife** is quiet, except at weekends, when the dark *Tutti Frutti* disco on the beach gets going. It's open until 3am, and costs $1 to enter. A little further north is the much more pleasant *Las Olas*, a casual open beach bar with pool tables and a cheery vibe. By far the most peaceful and stylish spot for a drink is *La Vela Latina*, south of the centre on the beach where you can sip a daiquiri while relaxing on a rocking chair.

Ananas As you enter town from Nicoya. Pleasant café with incredibly tasty ice cream, fruit salads, juices, breakfasts and coffee-and-cake combinations. Open for breakfast, lunch and afternoon coffee only.

El Ancla On the beach. Waterside restaurant with extensive menu of fish dishes attracts plenty of holidaying Ticos who know good seafood when they smell it.

Las Brasas Town centre ⊤656-0546. Two-level restaurant with Spanish dishes such as paella or, of all things, an entire suckling pig (with advance notice). The fillet steaks ($9) are tasty, as is the guacamole, but the pasta dishes are nothing special.

La Casa de la Playa On the beach. Relaxing arty café and restaurant with healthy juices and salads. Seafood dishes include a tasty coconut curry ($7) or grilled prawns.

Creperie Naranja In *Casa Naranja* in town centre. Authentic French and North African cuisine served in a small outdoor garden lit with candles in the evening. The wide menu offers, among other things, savoury crepes ($3.50), French favourites like *duck à l'orange* ($5) and some incredible traditional cakes and desserts, flans, tarts and sweet crepes from $3 to $4 – pricey, but worth every penny.

East of Sámara

Aficionados of Pacific sunsets will want to head 6km east of Sámara to **Playa Carrillo**, a ninety-minute walk along flat sands. Known for its spectacular evening light and colours, palm-fringed Carrillo is also safe for swimming, though the fact that more and more people are setting up hotels and restaurants means the beach no longer has the sleepy, end-of-the-line feel it once had. Try the *Mirador* restaurant, just behind Playa Carrillo up on a hill, where you can enjoy a drink and a **meal** (though the food is rather plain) to the sound of crashing waves, while watching pastel mauves, pinks and oranges blend into each other as the sun goes down. Just behind the *Mirador* is a good budget **accommodation** option, the *Cabinas Colibrí* (☎656-0656; ❸); rooms have tiled floors, hot showers and above-average beds, and breakfast is included.

The stretch east of Carrillo is for off-road driving nuts only, and should not be attempted without a 4WD (make sure the clearance is high). You need a good **map**, because roads go haywire in this part of the peninsula, veering off in all directions, unsigned and heading to nowhere, some ending in deep creeks (unpassable even by Range Rovers and Land Rovers at high tide). The further south you go, the tougher it gets, as dirt roads switch inland and then through the hamlets of Camaronal, Quebrada Seca and Bejuco, all just a few kilometres apart but separated by frequent creeks and rivers. It's best not drive down here alone, as there's a very good chance you'll get stuck (rising to a virtual certainty in the rainy season, whatever vehicle you have) and settlements are few and far between. There are **filling stations** in Sámara and Cóbano: bring a spare can with you just in case, because the distance between the two, in total, is about 70km. Be sure also to carry lots of drinking water and food, and, if possible, camping gear. You can **camp** on the deserted beaches, and there are also a few budget and upmarket places to stay in the settlement of Playa San Miguel, about 30km southeast of Carrillo. The most luxurious option in the area, indeed in all of Costa Rica, is the isolated *Hotel Punta Islita* (☎656-0470, ⓦ www.puntaislita.com; ❽–❾), 8km south of Playa Carrillo. Hillside rooms have majestic views and the atmosphere is exclusive and facilities include a driving range, tennis courts, pools, restaurants and a canopy tour. Management can arrange snorkelling, mountain-biking and fishing trips.

North of Sámara: Nosara and around

The pretty drive from Sámara 25km northwest to the village of **NOSARA** runs along shady, secluded dirt and gravel roads punctuated by a few creeks. It's passable with a regular car (low clearance) in the dry season (though you'll still have to ford two creeks except at the very driest times of year), but you'll need a 4WD or high clearance in the wet. The road follows a slightly inland route; you can't see the coast except where you meet the beach at **Garza**, about ten minutes before Nosara. This little hamlet is a good place to stop for a *refresco* at the *pulpería*, and perhaps take a dip in the sea. Though most people drive to Nosara, you can also come on the daily **bus** from Nicoya or San José; there are also two buses from Playa Sámara.

NatureAir and Sansa **fly** daily to Nosara from San José, usually via Sámara, landing at the small airstrip. The San José **bus** comes in at the Abastecedor general store. There isn't much to the village itself but a soccer field, a couple of restaurants and a petrol station. The Tuanis tour agency and souvenir shop, near the soccer field, has Internet access and books for sale and rents bikes; they also have a useful noticeboard with local events.

The recorrido de toros

If you're in Nosara on a weekend in January or February, or on a public holiday like the first of May, be sure not to miss the **recorrido de toros** (rodeo). *Recorridos*, held in many of the Nicoya Peninsula villages, are a rallying point for local communities, who travel long distances in bumpy communal trucks to join in the fun.

Typically, the village *redondel* (bullring) is no more than a rickety wooden circular stadium, held together with bundles of palm thatch. Here local radio announcers introduce the competitors and list the weight and ferocity of the bulls, while travelling bands, many of them from Santa Cruz (see p.255), perform oddly Bavarian-sounding oom-pah-pah music at crucial moments in the proceedings. For the most fun and the best-seasoned rodeo jokes, sit with the band – usually comprising two saxophones, a clarinettist, a drummer and the biggest tuba known to man – but avoid the seat right in front of the tuba.

The *recorrido* usually begins in the afternoon, with "Best Bull" competitions, and gets rowdier as evening falls – after dark, a single string of cloudy white light bulbs illuminates the ring – and more beer is consumed. The *sabanero* tricks on display are truly impressive: the mounted cowboy who gallops past the bull, twirls his rope, throws it behind his back and snags the bull as casually as you would loop a garden hose, has to be seen to be believed. The grand finale is the bronco bull-riding, during which a sinewy cowboy sticks like a burr to the huge spine of a Brahma bull who leaps and bucks with increasing fury. During the intervals, local men and boys engage in a strange ritual of wrestling in the arena, taking each other by the forearm and twirling each other round like windmills, faster and faster, until one loses his hold and flies straight out to land sprawling on the ground. These displays of macho bravado are followed by mock fights and tumbles, after which everyone slaps each other cordially on the back.

The *recorrido* is followed by a dance: in Nosara the impromptu dance floor takes up the largest flat space available – the airstrip. The white-line area where the planes are supposed to stop is turned into a giant outdoor bar, ringed by tables and chairs, while the mobile disco rolls out its flashing lightballs and blasts out salsa, reggae and countrified two-steps. Wear good shoes, as the asphalt is super-hard: you can almost see your soles smoking after a quick twirl with a hotshot cowboy.

The atmosphere at these events is friendly and beer-sodden: in villages where there's a big foreign community you'll be sure to find someone to talk to if your Spanish isn't up to conversing with the *sabaneros*. Food is sold from stalls, where you can sample the usual *empanadas* or local Guanacastecan dishes such as *sopa de albóndigas* (meatball soup with egg).

Accommodation

Nosara has some excellent beachside **accommodation** if you've money to spend. The cheaper spots are in or near the village, but you'll need to rent a bike or count on doing a lot of walking to get to the ocean.

Almost Paradise Café and Cabinas On hill behind Playa Pelada ☏682-0173, ⓦwww.aventurapelada.com. Unpretentious, hospitable and tranquil rooms in a pink wooden bungalow perched above the village with stupendous views. Six spacious, comfortable rooms have private bath with hot water; there's also pool on the grounds, with howler monkeys and birds roaming around, and a restaurant that serves healthy, mainly vegetarian food. Breakfast is included. ❸

Blew Dog's Surf Club Behind Playa Guiones ☏682-0080, ⓦwww.blewdogs.com. Popular and relaxed spot designed with surfers in mind. Bungalows come with fan and fridge and some have a small kitchen. The restaurant serves gringo favourites and is inevitably throbbing to the sounds of Bob Marley. ❹

Cabinas Chorotega In the village, by the supermarket ☏682-0105. Pleasant cabinas with large rooms. Upstairs cabinas are best, though you'll have to climb an extremely steep staircase;

the cheaper ones have shared bath. There's also a relaxing communal terrace with rocking chairs. ❸

Café de Paris South end of Nosara, at the entrance to Playa Guiones ☎682-0087, ⊛www .cafedeparis.net. Well-appointed rooms set in bungalows arranged around the pool. All have private bath and hot water, and a choice of ceiling fans or a/c. Rooms range from standard doubles to suites with a/c, kitchen, fridge and a small rancho with hammocks. There's also Internet access and a fine restaurant. ❻

Casa Río Nosara Near the village on road to beaches ☎682-0117. Rustic and simple bungalows run by friendly travellers. There's hot water, a communal kitchen and also a dormitory where you can bed down for $5 per night. Owners organize horseback riding. ❷

Casa Romántica Behind Playa Guiones ☎682-0019, ⊛www.hotelcasaromantica.com. Clean and well-kept family-run hotel right on the beach. Bright rooms have hot water, fridge and terrace. There's also a family room (5 people), a pool and a fantastic restaurant. If you fly or take the bus, the owners will pick you up if you let them know in advance. ❺

Casa Tucan 200m east of Playa Guiones ☎ & ⊕682-0113, ⊜casatucan@nosara.com. Small,

eight-room hotel, with brightly decorated rooms (some with kitchen), sleeping up to five people; all have private bath, hot water, fridge, and fan or a/c. There's a good restaurant and bar, a new juice bar and a pool. Good low-season or longstay discounts. ❺

Lagarta Lodge Signposted from the village ☎682-0035, ⊛www.lagarta.com. Set in a small private nature reserve southwest of the village, this lodge has excellent birdwatching and stunning coastal views. The rooms above the pool overlooking the ocean boast one of the best panoramas in the country. Rooms have private bath, hot water and fridges. A healthy buffet breakfast (not included) as well as other meals is also available. ❻

Hotel Playas de Nosara On the hilltop between Playas Guiones and Pelada; follow the signs ☎682-0121, ⊛www.nosarabeachhotel.com. Dramatically situated hotel on a headland overlooking the beach and pine-clad coastline. Its stunning design includes a 360-degree observation lounge that from afar makes the structure look like a mosque. The large, clean, cool rooms with fans are priced according to the quality of the view (not all rooms overlook the beach).There's a pool but (so far, anyway) few other services. ❻

The town

Nosara is more of a widely scattered community than a village as such; it spreads along three beaches and the hinterland behind them. The centre, if you can call it that, is known as Bocas de Nosara and is set about 4km inland, backed by a low ridge of hills. The three beaches in the area – Nosara, Guiones and Pelada – are fine for **swimming**, although you can be buffetted by the crashing waves, and there are some rocky outcroppings. **Playa Guiones** is the most impressive of the beaches: nearly 5km in length, populated by pelicans, and with probably the best swimming, though there's precious little shade. The whole area is a great place to go beachcombing for shells and driftwood, and the vegetation, even in the dry season, is greener than further north. Some attempts have been made to limit development, and a good deal of the land around the Río Nosara has been designated a wildlife refuge.

In contrast to busier Sámara, the vast majority of people who come to Nosara are North Americans and Europeans in search of quiet and natural surroundings. Much of the accommodation is slightly upmarket, and the owners and managers are more environmentally conscious than at many other places on the peninsula. A local civic association keeps a hawkish eye on development in the area, with the aim of keeping Nosara as it is, rather than having it become another Tamarindo or Montezuma.

The atmosphere in Bocas de Nosara itself is shady and slow, with the sweet smell of cow dung in the air and excitable voices drifting out from the local Evangelical church. People are friendly, and Nosara is still low-key, though it does get busy in the high season when foreigners flock here in search of seclusion. The area around the village can be very confusing, with little dirt and gravel roads radiating in all directions. To counter the lost-tourist effect locals have erected copious signs – though there are so many at certain intersections that they simply add to the confusion. Resign yourself to driving around looking lost at least some of the time.

Eating and drinking

The Nosara area has experienced a mini-explosion of restaurants in the past few years. Many of them are very good, and prices are not as high as you might expect, given the area's relative isolation. There are a number of places in the **village**, most of them around the soccer field or on the road into town, though most of the better restaurants are huddled together near **Playa Guiones**, where the majority of tourists eat.

Almost Paradise Café In the hotel of the same name. Vegetarian food is served on an outside terrace with wonderful views.

Bambú Bar Next to the Abastecedor general store. A bit dark, and with pounding music, though it's still a decent place to have a beer and watch the kids kick balls around the soccer field.

Bar-restaurant Tucan Next to the *Casa Tucan* hotel. The menu features seafood in adventurous fruit-based sauces, chicken, pasta and steaks (all $7–12), served in a pleasant rancho strung with inviting hammocks and coloured lights. A new juice bar offers "create-your-own" drinks.

Blew Dog's Surf Club Behind Playa Guiones. Cheerful and relaxed bar and restaurant perfect for surfers to refuel after a long day. The food is unadventurous but filling and generous – burgers, grilled fish and pizza – and there's a decent bar where waves (what else?) are the main topic of conversation.

Café de Paris At the southern entrance to Playa Guiones. The brioche and pain au chocolat confirm this bakery as a bona-fide overseas département of France, while the pleasant poolside restaurant serves sandwiches and pizzas for lunch ($4–9).

Casa Romántica In the hotel of the same name. The most ambitious food in town, featuring a changing menu of fish, steak and pasta dishes ($7–10). There's a decent wine list, too – possibly the only good one in Nosara. Dining is in a small outdoor area, lit with candles at night.

Giardino Tropicale South end of Nosara, on the road towards Sámara ☏682-0258. Superior-quality real Italian pizza cooked in a wood oven and served in a pretty plant-strewn dining area

($6–9). Other well-crafted Italian dishes are also on offer, and there's takeaway.

Gilded Iguana Behind Playa Guiones. Upmarket gringo bar with Mexican food that attracts the local expats. Reasonably priced lunch specials, including filet of *dorado* ($5) and fish and chips ($3). Closed Mon, Tues & Sun.

La Luna Just below the Playa Nosara hotels. ☏682-0122. A lovable spot above Playa Pelada, with tranquil terrace tables overlooking the sea. The constantly changing menu features lip-smacking international dishes and seafood. Highlights include salads, home-made bread and also Thai soups and curries. Cheerful owners dream up some sinful desserts, including vanilla toffee pudding and chocolate fudge cake. Main dishes are $6–9.

Lagarta Lodge In the hotel of the same name. Although the changing menu is perfectly fine, it's the setting rather than the food that makes this place special, as you dine to the sound of the Pacific crashing gently below. The sociable seating arrangement has all guests sharing space around a big mahogany table – a good way to meet people. Closed Tues.

Marlin Bill's Playa Guiones. Fairly pricey but well-prepared grilled seafood (particularly tasty is the *corvina*, sea bass) served in a setting just above the growing village near Playa Guiones. Closed Sat & Sun.

Olga's Bar On Playa Pelada. Cold beer, good *casados* and fish, and ocean views, but watch the bill – they don't itemise your food and drinks. One of the best spots to watch the setting sun.

Soda Vanessa In Nosara village. A typical soda with filling *casados* for under $3, as well as other snack-style fare.

Refugio Nacional de Fauna Silvestre Ostional

Eight kilometres northwest of Nosara, **Ostional** and its chocolate-coloured sand beach make up the **REFUGIO NACIONAL DE FAUNA SILVESTRE OSTIONAL**, one of the most important nesting grounds in the country for **Olive Ridley turtles** who come ashore to lay their eggs between May and November. Even more thrilling are the *arribadas*, mass arrivals of up to ten thousand females, depending on the moon and tides. If you're in town during the first few days of the *arribadas,* you'll see local villagers with horses, carefully stuffing their big, thick bags full of eggs and slinging them over their shoulders. This is quite legal: villagers of Ostional and Nosara are allowed to harvest eggs, for sale or consumption, during the first three days of the season only. Don't be surprised to see them barefoot, rocking back and forth on their heels as if they were crushing grapes in a winery; this is the surest way to pick up the telltale signs of eggs beneath the sand. You can't swim comfortably at Ostional though, since the water's very rough and is plagued by sharks, for whom turtle nesting points are like all-you-can-eat buffets.

It takes about fifteen minutes to drive the gravel-and-stone road from Nosara to the refuge; alternately you can bike it or take a taxi (about $8–$10). There are a couple of places to stay and eat in the village.

Parque Nacional Barra Honda and around

The **PARQUE NACIONAL BARRA HONDA** (Dec–April daily 8am–4pm; $6), about 40km east of Nicoya and 13km west of the Río Tempisque, is popular with spelunkers for its forty-odd subterranean **caves**. A visit to Barra Honda is not for claustrophobes, people afraid of heights (some of the caves are more than 200m deep) or anyone with an aversion to creepy-crawlies.

The landscape around here is dominated by the **limestone plateau** of the Cerro Barra Honda, which rises out of the flat lowlands of the eastern Nicoya Peninsula. About seventy million years ago this whole area – along with Palo Verde, across the Río Tempisque – was under water. Over the millennia, the porous limestone was gradually hollowed out, by rainfall and weathering, to create caves and weird karstic formations.

The caves form a catacomb-like interconnecting network under the limestone ridge, but you can't necessarily pass from one to the other. Kitted out with a rope harness and a helmet with a lamp on it, you descend with a guide, who will normally take you down into just one. The **main caves**, all within 2km of each other and of the ranger station, are the Terciopelo, the Trampa, Santa Ana, Pozo Hediondo and Nicoa, where the remains of pre-Columbian peoples were recently found, along with burial ornaments and utensils thought to be over two thousand years old. Most people come wanting to view the huge needle-like **stalagmites** and **stalactites** at Terciopelo, or to see subterranean wildlife such as bats, blind salamanders, insects and even birds.

Down in the depths, you're faced with a sight reminiscent of old etchings of Moby Dick's stomach, with sleek, moist walls, jutting rib-like ridges, and strangely smooth protuberances. Some caves are big enough – almost cathedral-like, in fact, with their vaulting ceilings – to allow breathing room for those who don't like enclosed spaces, but it's still an eerie experience, like descending into a ruined subterranean Notre Dame inhabited by crawling things you can barely see. There's even an "organ" of fluted stalagmites in the Terciopelo cave; if knocked, each gives off a slightly different musical note.

Above ground, three short **trails**, not well marked, lead around the caves. It's easy to get lost, and you should walk them with your guide or with a ranger if there is one free, and take water with you. Some time ago, two German hikers attempted to walk the trails independently, got lost and, because they were not carrying water, died of dehydration and heat exhaustion.

The endangered **scarlet macaw** sometimes nests here, and there are a variety of ground mammals about, including anteaters and deer. As usual, you'll be lucky to see any, though you'll certainly hear howler monkeys.

Cave architecture

Created by the interaction of water, calcium bicarbonate and limestone, the distinctive cave formations of stalagmites and stalactites are often mistaken for each other. **Stalagmites** grow upwards from the floor of a cave, formed by drips of water saturated with calcium bicarbonate. **Stalactites**, made of a similar deposit of crystalline calcium bicarbonate, grow downwards, like icicles. Both are formed by water and calcium bicarbonate filtering through limestone and partially dissolving it. In limestone caves, stalagmites and stalactites are usually white (from the limestone) or brown; in caves where copper deposits are present colours might be more psychedelic, with iridescent greens and blues. They often become united, over time, in a single column.

Practicalities

You need to be pretty serious about caves to go spelunking in Barra Honda. Quite apart from all the planning, what with the entrance fee, the payment to the guide and the price of renting equipment ($25), costs can add up. It's obligatory to go with a guide, who will also provide equipment; to do otherwise would be foolhardy, not to mention illegal. You pay your entry fee at the ranger station, which will give you information and perhaps supply a guide, but to save a trip, it's worth checking conditions and availability of guides first, either at the ACT regional headquarters (see p.219) on the Interamericana or in Nicoya (see p.257). Anyone who wants to follow the **trails** at Barra Honda has to tell the rangers where they are intending to walk and how long they intend to be gone for.

If you speak Spanish, another good way to hook up with guides is to call Sr Olman Cubillo, president of the local community development association, at the Complejo Ecoturístico Las Delicias (☎685-5580) in **Santa Ana**, the nearest hamlet to the caves. Recommended by both the SPN and the ACT, he can also give you **local information** about food, lodging, camping and horseback tours.

Driving to Barra Honda is possible even with a regular car. From the Nicoya–Tempisque road, the turn-off, 13km before the bridge, is well signed. It's then 4km along a good gravel road to the hamlet of Nacaome (also called Barra Honda), from where the park is, again, signed. Continue about 6km further, passing the hamlet of Santa Ana until you reach the ranger station, where most people arrange to meet their guide.

There's a **campsite** inside the park, with picnic tables and drinking water ($2 per person), and good basic **rooms** at *Proyecto Las Delicias* (❷), in Santa Ana. Most people who come to Barra Honda, however, stay in Nicoya (see p.257), or across the Río Tempisque on the mainland.

Moving on from the Nicoya Peninsula

The construction of the Puente Tempisque (see p.258) has made this the main access route to and from the Nicoya Peninsula, replacing the old choice between the time-consuming ferry or the long drive around the cleft of the peninsula and then picking up the Interamericana at Liberia.

The ferry services from Playa Naranjo and Paquera in the southeast of the peninsula head for Puntarenas on the mainland, but are only really of interest if you want to visit the south of the peninsula anyway – places such as Montezuma and Mal País – as the road between Nicoya and Playa Naranjo is badly potholed and a dullish, somewhat featureless grind that won't save any time over using the bridge.

Travel details

Buses

Cañas to: Liberia (11 daily; 50min); San José (11 daily; 3hr 30min).

Junquillal to: San José (1 daily; 5hr); Santa Cruz (1 daily; 1hr 30min).

Liberia to: Bagaces (11 daily; 40min); Cañas (11 daily; 50min); Cuajiniquil (1 daily; 1hr 30min); La Cruz (14 daily; 1hr); Nicoya (10 daily; 2hr); Parque Nacional Santa Rosa (5 daily; 1hr); Peñas Blancas (6 daily; 2hr); Playa del Coco (6 daily; 1hr); Playa Hermosa (5 daily; 1hr); Playa Panamá (5 daily; 1hr); Puntarenas (5 daily; 3hr); San José (11 daily; 4hr 30min); Santa Cruz (14 daily; 1hr); Tamarindo (6 daily; 1hr30min–2hr).

Nicoya to: Liberia (10 daily; 2hr); Nosara (1 daily; 2hr); Playa Sámara (3–6 daily; 1hr30min); San José (8 daily; 6hr); Santa Cruz (16 daily; 40min).

Nosara to: Nicoya (1 daily; 2hr); Playa Sámara (2 daily; 40min); San José (1 daily; 6hr).

Peñas Blancas to: Liberia (6 daily; 2hr); San José (3 daily; 6hr).

Playa Brasilito to: San José (3 daily; 5hr); Santa Cruz (2 daily; 1hr 30min).

Playa del Coco to: Liberia (6 daily; 1hr); San José (3 daily; 5hr).

Playa Flamingo to: San José (3 daily; 5hr); Santa Cruz (2 daily; 1hr 30min).

Playa Hermosa to: Liberia (5 daily; 1hr); San José (1 daily; 5hr).

Playa Panamá to: Liberia (5 daily; 1hr); San José (1 daily; 5hr).

Playa Potrero to: San José (3 daily; 5hr); Santa Cruz (2 daily; 1hr 30min).

Playa Sámara to: Nicoya (3–6 daily; 1hr30min); Nosara (2 daily; 40min); San José (2 daily; 5hr).

San José to: Cañas (11 daily; 3hr 30min); Junquillal (1 daily; 5hr); Liberia (11 daily; 4hr); Nicoya (8 daily; 6hr); Nosara (1 daily; 6hr); Peñas Blancas (3 daily; 6hr); Playa Brasilito (3 daily; 5hr); Playa del Coco (3 daily; 5hr); Playa Flamingo (3 daily; 5hr); Playa Hermosa (1 daily; 5hr); Playa Panamá (1 daily; 5hr); Playa Potrero (3 daily; 5hr); Playa Sámara (3 daily; 5hr); Santa Cruz (5 daily; 5hr); Parque Nacional Santa Rosa (4 daily; 6hr); Tamarindo (2 daily; 6hr).

Santa Cruz to: Junquillal (1 daily; 1hr 30min); Liberia (14 daily; 1hr); Nicoya (16 daily; 40min); Playa Brasilito (2 daily; 1hr 30min); Playa Flamingo (2 daily; 1hr 30min); Playa Potrero (2 daily; 1hr 30min); San José (5 daily; 5hr); Tamarindo (6 direct daily; 1hr).

Tamarindo to: Liberia (6 daily; 1h30min–2hr); San José (2 daily; 6hr); Santa Cruz (6 direct daily; 1hr).

Flights

Sansa

San José to: Liberia (1 daily; 1h15min); Nosara (1–2 daily; 1h10min); Playa Sámara (Mon–Sat 1–2 daily; 1hr); Tamarindo (5–6 daily; 50min).

NatureAir

San José to: Liberia (3 daily; 1h15min); Nosara (1–2 daily; 1h10min); Playa Sámara (1 daily in high season; 1hr); Tamarindo (3 daily; 50min).

6

The Central Pacific and southern Nicoya

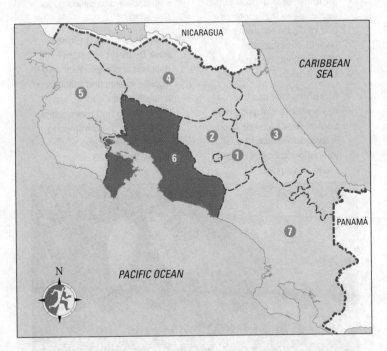

CHAPTER 6

Highlights

* **Reserva Monteverde Night Walk** Take an eerie night walk through the dense, verdant rainforest of the Monteverde Reserve – the intrepid guides catch bats, and introduce you to stick insects and frogs, and maybe even a tarantula. See p.283

* **Reserva Santa Elena** Search for the elusive quetzal in this lush reserve that protects one of Costa Rica's most perfect cloudforests and is maintained by local schoolchildren. See p.283

* **Morpho's** Discuss the day's wildlife sightings over *corvina* (sea bass) drizzled in avocado sauce at this atmospheric Santa Elena eatery. See p.285

* **Mal País** Ride the waves at this isolated surfing hang-out in the southwest of the Nicoya Peninsula. See p.302

* **Reserva Absoluta Cabo Blanco** Costa Rica's oldest piece of protected land features unique Pacific lowland tropical forest and is home to howler monkeys, sloths, deer and pelicans. See p.301

* **Manuel Antonio National Park** Relax on limestone-white beaches and explore tangled tropical forests and mangroves abundant with wildlife, from green turtles and rare squirrel monkeys to the shimmering green kingfisher and laughing falcon. See p.309

△ Scarlet macaw

6

The Central Pacific and southern Nicoya

The **Central Pacific** – though less of a geographical or cultural entity than other regions of Costa Rica – does boast several of the country's most popular tourist spots, including the number-one attraction, the **Reserva Biológica Bosque Nuboso Monteverde** (Monteverde Cloudforest Reserve), draped over the ridge of the Cordillera de Tilarán. Along with the nearby **Reserva Santa Elena**, Monteverde protects some of the last remaining pristine **cloudforest** in the Americas. **Southern Nicoya**, effectively cut off by bad roads and a provincial boundary from the north of the peninsula (covered in chapter 5), is part of **Puntarenas** province, whose eponymous capital, a steamy tropical port across the Gulf of Nicoya on the mainland, is the only town of any size in the entire area.

Some of the country's best-known **beaches**, several of which are easily accessible from San José, line the coasts of the Central Pacific and southern Nicoya. Each offers a distinct experience, from the coves of popular **Montezuma**, a former fishing village on the mainland coast, to the huge waves of **Jacó**, one of the best places to surf in the country. Further south, **Parque Nacional Manuel Antonio** has several extraordinary beaches, with white sands and azure waters.

With the exception of the cool cloudforest of Monteverde, the region is tropical, hot and drier than in the south of the country. Temperatures can be uncomfortably high all over the region, with a dry-season average of about 30°C. Even in the wet season, when Quepos and Manuel Antonio, in particular, often receive torrential afternoon rains, the temperatures don't cool down by much. Further north, the wet season is less virulent, though high in the clouds of Monteverde it can bucket down, especially in the afternoons. Even so, considering the number of visitors who descend on the Central Pacific during the dry season, visiting during the wet is a definite alternative. Hotels in Monteverde actually have space at this time, while prices in the Manuel Antonio area come down from the stratosphere – and although you might have to put up with a couple of hours' rain in the afternoon, you can still spend much of the day outdoors.

Two routes connect San José with Puntarenas and points south. The **Interamericana** (the main road) climbs over the Cordillera Central before dropping precipitously into the Pacific lowlands, levelling out at the town of Esparza,

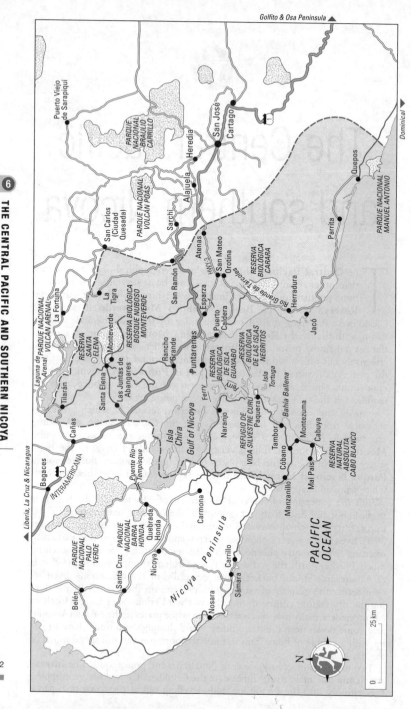

a few kilometres before the turn-off for Puntarenas, a total trip of about two hours. Many travellers who are aiming for Playa Jacó and Manuel Antonio choose the older road, Hwy-3, that passes Atenas and Orotina before heading south, skirting the **Reserva Biológica Carara**. Overall, Hwy-3 is a more pleasant experience, with great views and good roadside stalls at Orotina that sell fudge, nuts, *galletas* (cookies) and crafts. The road is in very good condition for most of the way between Orotina and Jacó, offering some of the least stressful driving in the country. By contrast, driving north from San José **to Monteverde** can often be quite an expedition. Although it's not far − just 180km − from San José, the final 35km is unpaved and in bad condition. Most car rental agencies won't allow you to take a regular car on this road in the wet season − as in much of Costa Rica, you'll need a 4WD at this time of year.

Most people cross over to the southern **Nicoya Peninsula** from Puntarenas on the ferries to Naranjo or Paquera. However, the new bridge across the mouth of the Río Tempisque (see p.258) has significantly shortened the drive. From Naranjo you can either continue south by car or north to Carmona and then up to Nicoya and Santa Cruz, but the roads aren't in great shape. From Paquera, you can take public transport down to Tambor and Montezuma.

Monteverde and around

Monteverde, though generally associated only with the eponymous cloudforest reserve, actually covers a much larger area, straddling the hump of the Cordillera de Tilarán between Volcán Arenal and Laguna de Arenal to the east and the low hills of Guanacaste to the west. Along with the reserve, you'll find the spread-out **Quaker** community of Monteverde, the neighbouring town of **Santa Elena**, with its own cloudforest reserve, and several small hamlets. The charms of these cloudforests are further magnified by the region's intangible quality of enchantment − a combination of tranquil beauty, invigorating weather and the area's odd mix of tidy Swiss-style farms and tropical botanical gardens.

The **Quaker** families arrived from Alabama in the 1950s. Monteverde's isolation suited them well in their desire for autonomy and, to a degree, seclusion. The climate and terrain proved ideal for dairy farming, which fast became the mainstay of the economy with the creation in 1954 of the local cheese factory, La Lechería. This region is now famous in Costa Rica for its dairy products, and you'll see a variety of these cheeses in most Costa Rican *supermercados*. Abroad, however, the Monteverde area is known for its pioneering private nature reserves. Of these, the Reserva Monteverde is the most popular, although the less-touristed Reserva Santa Elena offers an equally pristine cloudforest cover. In fact, because it receives fewer visitors, you may spot more animal and bird life at the Reserva Santa Elena and you'll certainly have more of the cloudforest to yourself. The Bosque Eterno de los Niños (Children's Eternal Rainforest), established with funds raised by schoolkids from all over the world, sits adjacent to the Monteverde Reserve.

Many travellers are also lured − and understandably so − by canopy tours which take visitors up into the high layers of the forest on ziplines and suspended bridges. Monteverde offers some of the best in Costa Rica and while the emphasis is far more on excitement than ecology, you can still appreciate the cloudforest ecosystem between adrenalin rushes.

If you want to avoid the crowds, try to come at the beginning or end of the wet season (May–Nov), when you get the double benefit of fewer visitors but decent weather. Near the reserve, accommodation tends to be expensive; prices

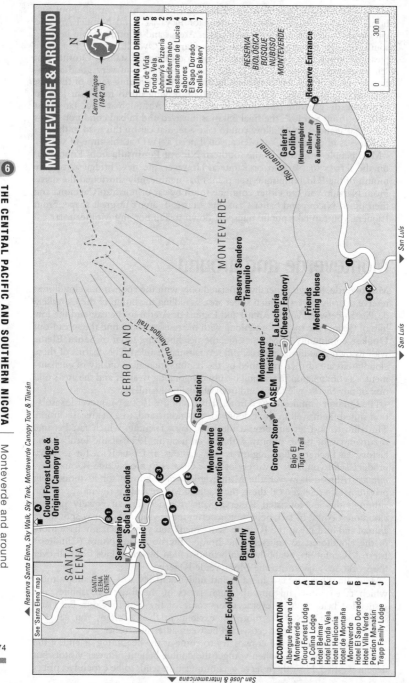

MONTEVERDE & AROUND

San José & Interamericana ▲

▲ *Reserva Santa Elena, Sky Walk, Sky Trek, Monteverde Canopy Tour & Tilarán*

See 'Santa Elena' map

Cerro Amigos (1842 m) ▲

SANTA ELENA

SANTA ELENA CENTRE

Serpentario

Soda La Giaconda

Clinic

Cloud Forest Lodge & Original Canopy Tour

Finca Ecológica

Butterfly Garden

CERRO PLANO

Gas Station

Cerro Amigos Trail

Monteverde Conservation League

Grocery Store

CASEM

Bajo El Tigre Trail

MONTEVERDE

Monteverde Institute

La Lecheria (Cheese Factory)

Reserva Sendero Tranquilo

Friends Meeting House

Río Guacimal

Galería Colibrí (Hummingbird Gallery & auditorium)

San Luis ▲

San Luis ▲

Reserve Entrance

RESERVA BIOLÓGICA BOSQUE NUBOSO MONTEVERDE

N

0   300 m

ACCOMMODATION
Albergue Reserva de Monteverde	G
Cloud Forest Lodge	A
La Colina Lodge	H
Hotel Belmar	D
Hotel Fonda Vela	K
Hotel Heliconia	C
Hotel de Montaña Monteverde	E
Hotel El Sapo Dorado	B
Hotel Villa Verde	I
Pensión Manakín	F
Trapp Family Lodge	J

EATING AND DRINKING
Flor de Vida	5
Fonda Vela	8
Johnny's Pizzeria	2
El Mediterraneo	3
Restaurante de Lucia	4
Sabores	6
El Sapo Dorado	1
Stella's Bakery	7

drop further away from the entrance. For a comprehensive preview of the area, visit the website Ⓦwww.monteverdeinfo.com, with background information on the flora and fauna of the cloudforest, plus details of tours and hotels.

Note that the **roads** to Monteverde are generally in poor condition. Partly to blame is the mountainous terrain, with a large soil run-off in the wet season that washes away the roads, and also the fact that these roads, like so many in Costa Rica, were built to serve small rural communities – and not the tens of thousands of visitors who make the journey up and down to see the reserve. While tour operators have regularly bemoaned the state of the roads up to the reserve, the **Monteverde Conservation League** (MCL) and the community in general have resisted suggestions to pave the road(s) to Monteverde, arguing that easier access would increase visitor numbers to unsustainable levels and threaten the integrity of local communities. In any case, Monteverdeans are fully aware that local businesses, especially hotels, benefit from visitors spending a night or two in the area. Whatever the future holds, it's unlikely that Monteverde will be ruined: the community is too outspoken and organized to let itself be overrun by its own success.

Information and accommodation

Santa Elena has all the facilities a weary traveller could hope for, making it a prime spot to gather information and plan exploration of the region. You'll soon have it staked out: the centre of town is basically three streets in a triangle. A Banco Nacional (with an ATM) sits at the northern apex. Several Internet cafés, including Pura Vida, are opposite the bank. *Chunches* sells espresso, snacks and secondhand paperbacks, and also has a laundry service (as do most of the area's lodgings). Santa Elena also has a well-stocked *supermercado* and a correo.

Accommodation

Santa Elena offers the area's cheapest accommodation, though you'll also find a couple of pensiones on the road to Monteverde. Most accommodation is basic, but you'll get a bed and heated water at least, and almost certainly a warm welcome. Locals run many of the small pensiones, and they usually offer an array of services, from home cooking and laundry to horse hire. Hotel **touts** often greet arriving buses in Santa Elena to pitch their budget pension; most are fine, so take your pick.

In contrast to Santa Elena, the majority of the hotels in and around the Monteverde community aspire to European mountain-resort facilities and atmosphere and tend to be expensive and packaged, appealing to those who like their wilderness deluxe. You'll certainly be comfortable in most of these places – large rooms, running hot water, orthopedic mattresses, and even saunas and Jacuzzis are the norm. These hotels often have a restaurant and, if you come on a package, meals may be included. The larger hotels sit amid extensive grounds with their own private trails into the surrounding woods. Most also have a small library and show slides of local flora and fauna. Aside from illustrated nature talks, nightlife within the hotels is low-key to non-existent – some have a small bar, and that's about it.

If you haven't come on a tour or with private transport, you'll have to do a lot of walking – at least 5km uphill from Santa Elena to either reserve or about 3km from many of the hotels in Monteverde to the Monteverde Reserve. There are regular buses to the reserves, however, and if you stick out your thumb, an obliging local or tourist will probably pick you up pretty quickly.

Getting to Monteverde independently **from San José** entails some pre-planning. Demand for the two daily buses is high, and in the dry season it's a good idea to buy your ticket a few days in advance. If you're travelling on the less-busy routes **from Puntarenas**, or from La Fortuna de San Carlos in the Zona Norte via Tilarán, you can probably get away with turning up on the spot. Wherever you arrive from, in the dry months you should **book a room** in advance – the larger, plusher hotels often fill up with tour groups for weeks at a time, and the cheaper ones also get booked solid. Give yourself at least three days in the area; one to travel to Monteverde, at least one to explore the reserve itself (two is better), and another to descend.

Air-conditioned Interbus shuttles run from San José to Monteverde ($30 round-trip). All the major operators offer tours (about $200 for two days) to Monteverde from San José, usually including two or three nights with accommodation, transport to and from the capital, and sometimes meals. The main difference between tours is the hotel they use in Monteverde and whether or not the reserve entrance fee ($6–8) is covered in the price. Another immensely popular travel connection is the "jeep–boat–jeep" trip (see box, p.288) between La Fortuna (at Volcán Arenal) and Monteverde, a spectacular and time-saving way to travel between two of the country's major attractions.

By car
Driving from San José to Monteverde takes about three and a half hours via the Interamericana – two hours to the turn-off (there's a choice of three – see below) and then roughly another ninety minutes for the final mountainous ascent. The question most drivers face is which **route** to take, and hardened 4WD veterans argue endlessly about which way features more exciting twists and turns and entails maximum shifting into four-by-four mode.

One route, sometimes called the Sardinal route, follows the Interamericana north from Puntarenas towards Liberia, branching off at the **Rancho Grande** to Monteverde. Local *taxistas* will swear on a book of lottery tickets that the best (and least-known) route is through **Las Juntas de Abangares** (see p.287),

Santa Elena and around

Albergue Ecológico Arco Iris Up a side street just east of the town centre ☏645-5067, ⊛www.arcoirislodge.com. Relax in spacious, well-appointed cabins (❹) amid quiet landscaped gardens near the town centre. You can also stay in cheaper rooms with bunkbeds (❸). Feast on a delicious breakfast ($5) of hearty German bread, granola, fresh fruit, eggs and toast. ❸–❹

Cabinas Don Taco 300m north of the Banco Nacional ☏645-5263, ⊛www.cabinasdontaco.com. This pleasant hotel has eight standard rooms (with shared balcony) and seven individual cabinas, each with hot-water bath, mini-refrigerator, TV and private balcony, some boasting fine views on a clear day. The hosts are warm and welcoming, there's laundry service and parking, and breakfast is included. ❸

Cabinas Vista Al Golfo 300m west of the church ☏645-6321, ⊛vistaalgolfo@hotmail.com. Monteverde's best budget accommodation has bright, clean, new rooms, some with bath. Enjoy breezes and fantastic views of the Gulf of Nicoya from the balcony and hang out with fellow travellers in the sociable shared kitchen. The cheery owners also organize tours. ❷

Pensión Colibrí Up a side street, east of the triangle ☏645-5682. In the heart of town, this simple, family-run pension is surprisingly peaceful, with surrounding greenery and a relaxing balcony. The small rooms have either shared or private hot-water baths. The owners rent horses and serve breakfast and lunchtime *casados*. ❷

Pensión El Sueño 25m east of supermarket ☏645-5021. Stay in cosy, rustic wooden rooms right in the heart of Santa Elena. The main building houses the cheaper rooms with shared bath, while modern, split-level en-suite rooms in the annex are about $10 more per person (❸). Start your day with a tasty breakfast cooked up by the friendly *dueños* (included for en-suite guests, otherwise $3); in the evening, stargaze from a leather rocking chair in the lounge. Ask about low-season discounts. ❷ a tiny town reached via a small road (labelled "145" on some maps) off the Interamericana. Once you've reached Las Juntas, drive past the main square, turn left and continue over a bridge; turn right, and follow the signs. The first 7km of this thirty-seven-kilometre road, via Candelaria, are paved but beware some spectacular hairpin bends. Higher up, you'll come across magnificent vistas of the entire Gulf and Peninsula of Nicoya. You can also reach Monteverde from **Tilarán**, near Laguna de Arenal. This forty-kilometre road is often very rough, but provides spectacular views over the Laguna de Arenal and Volcán Arenal (both covered in chapter 4).

Whichever route you take, you'll need a **4WD** in the rainy season, unless you're an expert at dodging large stones while fishtailing up and down hills. Indeed, some agencies will refuse to rent you a regular car to drive up to Monteverde in the rainy season.

By bus

All **buses** arrive first in Santa Elena; some then continue along the road to Monteverde, making their last stop at La Lechería (cheese factory). Most people arrive on one of the two direct services, departing at 6.30am and 2.30pm **from San José's** Tilarán terminal. The trip takes at least 3hr 30min, though it's often more like 5hr, especially in the rainy season. Be particularly vigilant when waiting to board the bus in San José for this is when thieves often prey on travellers. On the bus, keep all valuables on your person. Note that the afternoon service from San José arrives in Monteverde after dark. From **Tilarán**, you can catch the 12.30pm bus (3hr), but in the rainy season, this may stop a few kilometres short of Santa Elena, leaving you with no option but to walk the remainder of the way. From **Puntarenas**, a daily bus leaves for Santa Elena at 2.15pm (3hr).

The **Santa Elena bus stop** is next to the church, at the top of the town centre "triangle". If you are booked into one of the hotels on the road to the reserve, stay on the bus and ask the driver to drop you off. If you arrive on the bus from Puntarenas, arrange with your hotel to have a taxi ($5–6) meet you at the bus stop.

Pensión El Tucán 100m south of Banco Nacional ☏ & ℻645-5017. One of Santa Elena's more venerable budget lodgings, this pension has small rooms with shared hot-water bath. For classier digs (and double the price), stay in the cabins with private bath and balcony. **①–②**

Tina's Casitas 300m west of the church ☏645-5641 & 820-4821, ⓦwww.tinascasitas.de. Decorated with rustic flair by the environmentally conscious owner, Santa Elena's most tranquil budget accommodation offers cabinas with attractive wood furniture and Gulf of Nicoya views; some have private hot-water bath. **②**

Monteverde and around

Albergue Reserva Biológica de Monteverde At the entrance to the Monteverde Reserve; contact the Monteverde Conservation League on ☏645-5122. Accommodation is basic (dormitory bunk beds and shared bathroom) but there's an infectious environmental buzz about this lodge right inside the reserve. Often packed with

researchers and students (tourists are second priority), reservations are essential, and you'll need to pay half your room cost 45 days in advance. A berth costs $12 per person, $27 with meals. **③**

Cloud Forest Lodge 500m northeast of Santa Elena ☏645-5058 ⓦwww .monteverdecloudforestlodge.com. Set in 70 acres of primary and secondary forest high above Santa Elena, this secluded hotel is one of the classiest in the area but surprisingly low-priced. The well-appointed wood-panelled cabins have cable TV, a large private bathroom, and terraces with dizzying views over the Gulf of Nicoya. The hotel has its own five-kilometre system of trails and a 25 percent discount off the Original Canopy Tour, which starts here. It's best if you have your own transport, since it's a bit of a walk from the lodge to Santa Elena or Monteverde. **⑤**

La Colina Lodge About 2km before the reserve entrance ☏645-5009, ⓦwww.lacolinalodge.com. This handy, rustic spot near the reserve has simply decorated rooms with homely wooden furnishings. Rooms have private or shared bath, and some

have a balcony. You can camp on the grounds for $5 per person and also order dinner, mainly vegetarian home cooking.

Hotel Belmar Cerro Plano, 2km east of Santa Elena ☎645-5201, ⓦwww.hotelbelmar.net. The oldest of the area's many Swiss-style hotels, the perennially popular *Belmar* sits on a hillside above Cerro Plano, with sweeping views of the gulf. Pricier rooms are somewhat larger and equipped with a fan, rarely a necessity in blustery Monteverde. ⑤

Hotel Fonda Vela 2km before the reserve entrance ☎645-5125, ⓦwww.fondavela.com. Near the reserve amid quiet grounds, this lovely, old-fashioned hotel is expertly managed by an attentive staff. Newer suites aim for deluxe, with huge bathrooms and beautiful furniture while the older, rustic rooms lack a fan or a/c but have attractive wood-panelled walls and huge windows – the better to enjoy the astonishing views, particularly at sunset. Enjoy meals in the highly recommended restaurant. ⑥

Hotel Heliconia Cerro Plano ☎645-5109, ⓦwww .hotelheliconia.com. The comfortable rooms at this friendly hotel come with hot-water private bath but are quite simply furnished for the price. The more expensive cabins (⑥) and suites (⑦), higher up the hill and with better views, are slightly better value for money. The hotel also offers health treatments, from mud masks to massages, and you can enjoy fine Italian meals at the *Mediterraneo* restaurant. ⑥

Hotel de Montaña Monteverde 500m south of Santa Elena ☎645-5046, ⓦwww .monteverdemountainhotel.com. This well-maintained hotel, one of the first in the area, commands prime views over the Gulf of Nicoya. The pricier cabins (⑦) come with private balcony and better views over the gulf plus a minibar and phone. If you stay in the cheaper standard rooms (⑤), however, you still get access to the hotel's star amenities such as Jacuzzi, sauna and forest trails – plus you're cared for equally as well by the friendly management. ⑥

Quaker (*cuáquer*) settlers first arrived in remote Monteverde in the early 1950s. At that time, Monteverde was peopled by only a few Costa Rican farming families; there was no road, only an ox-cart track, and a journey to San José took several days. The Quakers bought and settled on some twelve square kilometres of mountainside, dividing the land and building their houses and a school.

Also called the Society of Friends, Quakerism is an altruistic, optimistic belief system that was founded by **George Fox** (1624–91), an Englishman born near Manchester. He instilled in his followers the importance of comporting oneself to encourage the goodness in others. Quakers are encouraged to see God in everybody, even those who are doing evil. A cornerstone of Quaker belief is **pacifism**. All war is seen as unlawful, as it impedes the call to bring out people's "inner light". From the beginning, Quakers placed themselves in opposition to many of the coercive instruments employed by the state and society, and they continue to embody a blend of the conservative, the non-conformist and absolute resistance to state control.

In 1656, Quakers arrived in the New World, where followers were initially subject to severe discrimination. The Quakers' deeply felt pacifism led to the exodus of several **Alabama** Quaker families from the US to Monteverde in the early 1950s. Harassed to the point of imprisonment for refusing the draft, the Quakers were drawn by Costa Rica's abolition of its army a few years earlier in 1948 – an extraordinary move under any circumstances, but particularly in Central America. The Quakers believed they would be able to live unmolested in this remote corner of a remote country.

Quakerism doesn't impose any obvious standards of dress or appearance upon its followers – you're not going to see the jolly old man from the oatmeal box sauntering by – nor does it manifest itself in any way that is immediately obvious to visitors, except for the area's relative lack of bars. The Quakers manage their **meeting houses** individually, with no officiating minister and purely local agendas. Gatherings focus on meditation, but anyone who is moved to say a few words or read simply speaks up, out of the silence. All verbal offerings in context are considered valid. The meeting houses welcome outsiders, who are never subject to being converted. In Monteverde, visitors can join meetings at the **Friends Meeting House**, held on Sundays and Wednesdays (look for announcements on the various community noticeboards). An excellent source of information on the Quakers and other pacifist groups in Central America is San José's **Centro de los Amigos para la Paz** (Friends Peace Centre; C 15, Av 6 bis, ☏233-6168), with leaflets and newspapers plus discussion groups and a small library and café.

Hotel El Sapo Dorado 500m east of Santa Elena ☏645-5010, ⓦwww.sapodorado.com. Take in stupendous views of the Gulf of Nicoya from these spacious, rustic wooden chalets perched on a hill. The mountain suites are set higher than the others, while the sunset suites lower down come with minibar, fridge and a terrace with views over the gulf. The restaurant serves tasty French fare. The golden toad it's named after hasn't, alas, been spotted for several years in the area. ❻

Hotel Villa Verde Near reserve entrance ☏645-5025, ⓦwww.hotelvillaverdecr.com. This comfortable hotel on peaceful grounds has simply furnished rooms (some a little dark) with hot-water private bath and a tasty breakfast. ❻

Pensión Manakín Cerro Plano ☏645-5080, ⓦwww.manakinlodge.com. This family pension with the forest as its backyard offers some of the best budget accommodation in the area, including rooms with shared (❸) or private bath (❹), dormitory bunk beds ($12 per person) and a cabin with a kitchenette. Guests also have access to a small gym, laundry service and Internet – and breakfast is included. ❸

Trapp Family Lodge Monteverde ☏645-5858, ⓦwww.trappfam.com. Within easy walking distance of the reserve, this attractive, wood-built lodge offers light and airy rooms with large windows – perfect for contemplating the cloudforest. Decent meals are served in the guests-only restaurant. (And in case you were wondering, the hotel has nothing to do with the Sound of Music.) ❺

Santa Elena and Monteverde villages

The influx of tourists in recent years to the cloudforest reserves has transformed the formerly peaceful enclave of **SANTA ELENA**, which now teems with dozens of new hotels, cabinas and restaurants. Just off the main road sprawls the settlement of **MONTEVERDE**, a seemingly timeless place where milk cans sit at the end of small dairy farm driveways to be collected, modest houses perch above splendid forested views, and farmers trudge along the muddy roads in sturdy rubber boots. La Lechería, or cheese factory, forms the heart of the community. It produces a range of European-style cheeses and, until the advent of tourism, was one of the area's main economic cogs. You can buy fresh cheese at the La Lechería shop (Mon–Sat 7.30am–4pm, Sun 7.30am–12.30pm), and also observe the cheese-making process on a two-hour tour (Mon–Sat 9am & 2pm; $8; reservations on T645-5436). Nearby, the Friends Meeting House, the centre for Quaker observance, welcomes interested visitors to participate in their meetings (10.30am on Sun, 9am on Wed). Along the Monteverde road is the arts and crafts collective CASEM with exhibits of local artists. Founded 20 years ago by eight women, CASEM has long played an important role in this small community, supporting over 140 local artisans.

The Monteverde Reserve

The **RESERVA BIOLÓGICA BOSQUE NUBOSO MONTEVERDE** (Monteverde Cloudforest Reserve; daily 7am–4pm; $12; T645-5122, Wwww .cct.or.cr) is one of the last sizeable pockets of primary cloudforest in Mesoamerica – and draws both foreigners and Costa Ricans in droves. The reserve was born out of a desire to protect the country's rapidly dwindling

The cloudforest

The primeval, other-worldly **cloudforest** – often described as a disturbingly impenetrable terrain of quetzals, jaguars and other near-mythical animals – enchants most visitors who walk beneath its gnarled canopy. The cloudforest's most obvious property is its dense, dripping **wetness**, and even in the dry season it looks as if everything has just been hosed down. Cloudforests are formed by a perennial near-100 percent humidity created by mists, produced here when the northeasterly trade winds from the Caribbean drift across to the high ridge of the continental divide, where they cool to become dense clouds that settle over this high-altitude forest.

The cloudforest can also be rather eerie, due to the sheer stacking and layering of vegetation, and the preponderance of **epiphytes**. Everything seems to be growing on top of each other, and you'll notice, walking the Monteverde and Santa Elena trails, that green mosses wholly carpet many trees while others seem to be choked by multiple layers of strangler vines, small plants, ferns and drooping lianas.

The **leaves** of cloudforest plants are often dotted with scores of tiny holes, as though they have been gnawed by insects that gave up after only a few millimetres. This is, in effect, exactly what happens. Many cloudforest plants can produce toxins to deter insects from eating an entire leaf or plant. The plants are able to produce these poisons because they harbour excess energy that would otherwise be used to protect themselves against adverse weather conditions, such as a prolonged dry season or heavy winds and rain. Insects in turn guard themselves by eating only a little of a leaf, and by sampling a wide variety, so that they are not overwhelmed by any one powerful toxin. For an in-depth look into cloudforests, check out *An Introduction to Cloudforest Trees*, by William Haber, Willow Zuchowski and Erick Bello, available at the reserve visitor centre and bookshops in San José.

pristine cloudforest. By 1972, homesteading in the Monteverde area had spread to the surrounding forest, and to prevent further destruction, a number of local residents along with two visiting American biologists established the reserve. The World Wildlife Fund provided funds to buy an additional five-and-a-half square kilometres and today the park encompasses ten square kilometres of protected land. It's administered by the non-profit Centro Científico Tropical (Tropical Science Centre) based in San José.

The reserve's sheer diversity of **terrain** – from semi-dwarf-stunted forest on the wind-exposed areas to thick, bearded cloudforest vegetation – results in truly memorable vistas from its various miradors. You can easily lose yourself in the views of dense, uninterrupted green, with the unimpeded wind whistling in your ears and no sign of human habitation as far as the eye can see. The Monteverde Reserve supports six different **life zones**, or eco-communities, hosting an estimated 2500 species of plants, more than 100 species of mammals, some 490 species of butterflies, and over 400 species of birds, including the quetzal.

Note that the cloudforest cover – dense, low-lit and heavy – makes it difficult to see, and many visitors leave the reserve disappointed that they have not spotted more wildlife. The amazing diversity of tropical plants and insects more than makes up for the elusive wildlife. Guided walks take you past thick mosses, epiphytes, bromeliads, primitive ferns, leaf-cutter ants and poison dart frogs. Plan on spending at least a full day in the reserve.

Temperatures are cool, as you would expect at this altitude: 15° or 16°C is not uncommon, though in the sun it often feels more like 22° to 25°. The average **rainfall** is 3000mm per year, and mist and rain move in quickly, so dress in layers, and be sure to carry an umbrella and light rain gear, especially after 10 or 11am. You should also bring **binoculars**, fast-speed **film** and **insect repellent**. You might get away without rubber boots in the dry season, but you'll most definitely need them in the wet. The reserve office (see below) rents out both boots and binoculars.

Practicalities

A **bus** leaves Santa Elena twice daily for Monteverde (Mon–Sat 6.15am & 1pm, returning at 11am and 4pm; $1); alternatively, a **taxi** costs about $6 per carload – try to get a group together to share. If you decide **to walk** (it takes about 90min), be aware that the road is uncomfortably dusty in the dry season, and that you'll encounter a surprising amount of traffic, though it gets quieter as you approach the reserve. The vegetation is more open along the road so **bird-spotting** opportunities are often just as good if not better than in the reserve, especially early in the morning.

The well-stocked **reserve office** at the entrance has a **visitor centre** where you can pick up maps (including a contour map of the area) and buy useful interpretative booklets for the trails. A small soda dishes out coffee, cold drinks and vegetarian *casados*. Near the reserve entrance, you can observe a wide variety of hummingbirds sipping from sugared water fountains at the **Galería Colibrí**, or Hummingbird Gallery (Mon–Sat 9.30am–4.30pm, Sun 10am–2pm). The auditorium sometimes hosts evening discussions by visiting academics and researchers, covering such broad themes as "gender issues in sustainable development" and "sex lives of lesser-known insects". Look for notices posted at the hotels, at the Galería Colibrí or in *Chunches* in Santa Elena.

The reserve imposes **a quota** of a maximum of 160 people allowed in the reserve at any given time. Although you're unlikely to be turned back because the quota has been reached, it's still a good idea to arrive early. In addition to the official **tours** organized by the reserve (see p.283), a number of excellent and experienced local guides can lead you through the reserve. Ask at your

Sights and sounds of Monteverde

Spotting a **quetzal** has become almost a rite of passage for visitors to Monteverde, and many zealous, binocular-toting birders come here with this express purpose in mind. This slim bird, with a sweet face and tiny beak, is extraordinarily colourful, with shimmering green feathers on the back and head, and a rich, carmine stomach. The male quetzal is the more spectacular, with a long, picturesque tail and fuzzy crown. About a hundred pairs of quetzals mate at Monteverde, in monogamous pairs, between March and June. During this period they descend to slightly lower altitudes than their usual stratospheric heights, coming down to about 1000m to nest in dead or dying trees, hollowing out a niche in which to lay their blue eggs. However, even during nesting season you're not guaranteed a glimpse; your best chance is on a guided tour. If you want to try on your own, arrive just after dawn, the most fruitful time to spot birds. Even though the office is closed at this time, you can enter the reserve trails and pay your entrance fee when you leave.

Other birds to look out for, particularly from March to August, are the **bare-necked umbrella bird** and the bizarre-looking **three-wattled bellbird** with three black "wattles", or skin pockets, hanging down from its beak. Even if you don't see one, you'll almost certainly hear its distinctive metallic call, which has been likened to a pinball machine. Some thirty types of hummingbird also flit about. Several types of endangered **cats**, including the puma, jaguar, ocelot, jaguarundi and margay, live in the reserve, which provides ample space for hunting. You likely won't come face to face with a jaguar but if you're lucky, you may hear the growl of a big cat coming out of the dense forest – usually unnerving enough to cure you of your desire to actually see one.

Ithomiid butterflies, better known as **clearwings**, have just that: transparent wings, fragile as the thinnest parchment. They abound in the reserve, especially on the Sendero Bosque Nuboso, feeding on dead insects, flower water and bird droppings. Another famous resident (now thought to be extinct) of the Monteverde area is the vibrant red-orange *sapo dorado*, or **golden toad**. First discovered here in 1964, the golden toad hasn't been spotted in many years but keep your eyes peeled.

hotel or pension. The reserve strongly advises that serious birders, wildlife spotters and those who would prefer to walk the trails in quiet avoid the **peak hours** of 8 until 11am, when the tour groups pour in.

Within the reserve, the **Albergue Reserva Biológica de Monteverde** (see p.277) offers bunk-bed accommodation. For overnight and long-distance hikers, there are three simple **shelter facilities** along the trails. The cost is about $5 per person per night, plus the entrance fee for each day you're in the reserve. The closest shelter is a two-hour hike from the reserve entrance. Shelters have beds and foam mattresses, drinking water, a basic shower, cooking utensils, a gas stove and, crucially, electricity. You must bring a sleeping bag, torch and food. The reserve office will give you the key and explain trail conditions and hiking times to each shelter.

The trails and tours

Most of the reserve's **trails** are contained in a roughly triangular pocket known as **El Triángulo**. They're clearly marked and easily walkable (at least in the dry season), and many of them are along wooden or concrete wiremesh-netted pathways; though this somewhat mars the feeling of hiking in real wilderness, it does prevent slipping and sliding on seas of mud.

The visitor centre at the reserve office has a good map of El Triángulo, with distances marked, and it also shows roughly where you pass the continental divide – there's no obvious indication when you're on the ground. If you're keen to plunge straight into the cloudforest, make for the self-guided Sendero Bosque Nuboso (2km). The forest canopy along this trail is literally dripping with moisture, each tree thickly encrusted with moss and epiphytes. You'll hear howler monkeys and a few flutters, but it's quite difficult to spot birds in this dense, dark cover. Your best bet for birdwatching is at the beginning of the trail, where the three-wattled bellbird and the bare-necked umbrella bird hang out.

The spongy terrain efficiently preserves animal tracks and in the morning especially you may spot marks of the agouti and coati. A small mirador, La Ventana (on the trail signed to Peñas Blancas), has vistas of the thickly forested hills on the other side of the continental divide. It's reached via a staircase of cement-laid steps that lead to a high, wild, wind-sculpted garden dotted with stunted vegetation and suspended over an amazingly green expanse of hills – a surreal place, with only the sound of wind as company. The Sendero El Camino (2km), higher in elevation than the others, is stony, deeply rutted in spots, and muddy.

The Río, Pantanoso and Chomogo trails, some quite steep and muddy, clamber up and down both sides of the continental divide. The Sendero El Puente features, as the name suggests, a 100-metre suspension bridge that takes you high up into the trees for great views of the cloudforest canopy.

Tours

The reserve runs excellent two- to three-hour **guided tours** ($15) at 7.30am sharp (with an additional tour at 8am if demand is high). Ask in your hotel or call the reserve office a day in advance on ☎645-5122 to secure a place. You can also strike out on your own as the trails are clearly marked, and the reserve office has detailed maps and booklets.

The fascinating, eerie **night walk** (2 hrs; $13) departs every evening at 7.30pm – you don't have to book for this tour, but turn up at the reserve office by 7.15pm to buy a ticket. (Those who are put off by the dark or creepy-crawlies might want to stick to the day tours). Many of the reserve's animals are nocturnal, and your chances of seeing one – albeit only as two brilliant eyes shining out of the night – are vastly increased after dark. You may spot tarantulas, toucans with their beaks tucked between their feathers, and some guides will even catch bats. Although the guides carry a powerful torch, it's useful to bring your own, as well as rain gear.

The Santa Elena Reserve

Less touristed than Monteverde, the **RESERVA SANTA ELENA** (daily 7am–4pm; $9; ☎645-5390, ⓦwww.monteverdeinfo.com/reserve), 6km northeast of Santa Elena, offers an equally memorable cloudforest experience. Poised at an elevation of 1650m, the three-square-kilometre reserve is higher than the

---

Volunteering in the reserves

Both the Santa Elena and Monteverde reserves depend significantly on **volunteer labour**. Activities include trail maintenance, teaching English and general conservation work. To volunteer, contact the reserve (☎645-5238, ⓦwww.cct.or.cr) for an application form. The minimum stay is two weeks; you'll be assigned tasks according to your experience and will generally be expected to work Monday to Friday from 7am to 4pm. Accommodation is free, but you pay $15 per day for food. Additionally, the CIEE (Council on International Educational Exchange; ⓦwww.ciee .org) offers a summer **education programme** in Monteverde, from about mid-June to mid-August, on tropical community ecology (in English).

Monteverde Reserve and boasts steeper, more challenging trails and a slightly better chance of seeing quetzals in season. Established in 1992, the self-funding reserve is supported mostly by entrance fees and donations and depends largely on volunteers, particularly foreign university students. The reserve is run by the local high school board, whose students help maintain the trails year-round.

The **visitor centre** at the entrance has maps of the twelve-kilometre trail network and a helpful leaflet on cloudforests, epiphytes, seed-dispersal patterns and some of the mammals you might see within the reserve. A small interpretative display written and illustrated by local schoolchildren documents the life of the cloudforest ecosystem and the history of the reserve itself. The highly recommended **guided tours** last between one and four hours. You can also rent **boots** at the centre and get coffee, cold drinks and sandwiches at the **cafeteria**.

The trails and tours

Santa Elena's four **trails** are confined to an area just east of the entrance. The easiest is the hour-long **Youth Challenge** trail with an observation tower at one end where, when not cloudy, you can sometimes see Volcán Arenal. The map from the visitor centre clearly states trail routes and distances, making it easy to navigate even the more difficult trails such as Sendero del Bajo, Sendero Caño Negro and Sendero Encantado. For the best chance of viewing Volcán Arenal, arrive as early as possible before cloud, mist and fog roll in to obliterate vistas.

Cut wood and mesh cover some trails, while others are unmade. Though the average temperature in the wet season is 18°C, it can feel cooler once the clouds move in. Guided nature walks ($15) head out at 7.30am and 11.30am daily; night tours ($15, inclusive of entrance fee) leave daily at 7pm. Strung along the entrance path are a line of hummingbird feeders that draw many of the multi-coloured birds.

Reserve practicalities

Getting to the Santa Elena Reserve from the village entails an arduous 6km walk over a boulder-strewn uphill road, but fortunately there are four daily buses ($3 round-trip). Buses depart from Santa Elena's Banco Nacional at 6.30am, 7am, 8am and noon, returning at 10.30am, 11.30am, 1pm and 3pm. You can pick up jeep-taxis ($6) on Santa Elena's main street or arrange for one at your hotel.

Eating, drinking and nightlife

In Santa Elena, you'll find a number of cheap soda-style eateries as well as a couple of classier options, some of which often require a reservation or standing in a queue. Most of the hotels between Santa Elena and the Monteverde Reserve have restaurants open to non-guests; some of the top-end hotels offer outstanding cuisine. The menus are usually fixed, and meals served at set times. The standard procedure is to drop by in person during the day, peruse the menu, and to make a booking if you like what you see. The strudel and brownies are delicious at the pleasant *Stella's Bakery* (closed evenings) opposite the CASEM cooperative in Monteverde. Get your rolls here and cheese just up the road at La Lechería, and it's picnic time.

Imbibing is kept to a minimum in the Quaker community of Monteverde – and even in gringo-packed Santa Elena. Most restaurants do have alcohol on the menu, but you'll detect a definite whiff of temperance in the air. That said, you can usually find folks slinging back beers at *Los Amigos* bar down a side street opposite the church in Santa Elena; later in the evening, the action moves to *Taberna* (open nightly until 2 or 3am), a lively and cheerful *discoteca* about 200 metres along the Monteverde road from the bottom of the Santa Elena triangle.

Santa Elena

El Campesino On the southern side of the Santa Elena triangle. Legions of stuffed toys hang from the ceiling at this quirky little eatery run by an expansive Tico and his young son. The menu features steaks and seafood for $5–7; take the owner's recommendations for specials of the day and you won't be disappointed.

Miramontes In the *Miramontes Hotel*, 2km northeast of Santa Elena off the road to the Santa Elena Reserve. If you're craving Swiss food and atmosphere, come to this cosy spot where you can happily tuck into gooey cheese fondue and tasty strudel.

Morpho's Opposite the Santa Elena supermarket. This stylish restaurant decorated with unusual hanging butterflies serves excellent dishes like *corvina al aguacate* (sea bass in avocado sauce), flavoursome steaks and tasty desserts. The mediocre Chilean wines are overpriced, but the main courses are a good deal at $4–8.

El Nido Across from Banco Nacional. Enjoy large *casados* ($3), lip-smacking sandwiches ($2–3) and tasty burgers at Santa Elena's best soda, a prime spot to observe the to-and-fro of people passing below. The *dueña* may seem grumpy at first, but she has a heart of gold.

Rainforest Café Opposite the Iglesia Santa Elena. This peaceful wood-furnished café with a balcony is just the spot to relax with a coffee – made with an espresso machine, no less – or a creamy milkshake. The tasty sandwiches also hit the spot.

El Tucán 100m south of Banco Nacional. Start your day with banana pancakes and other tasty gringo fare at this casual eatery in the *Pensión El Tucán*. You can also fill up on *casados* and pizzas. Closed lunch and Sunday.

Monteverde and around

Flor de Vida Cerro Plano. Enjoy forest views at this relaxed vegetarian café and restaurant that serves bagels, vegetable stir-fries ($5–7) and other international fare. Non-smoking.

Fonda Vela In *Hotel Fonda Vela*, Monteverde. Dig into succulent dinner specialities such as chicken in white wine and almonds ($11) at this large, casual restaurant serving French-influenced cuisine. For an intimate meal, there's also a more formal restaurant with a fireplace.

Johnny's Pizzeria Cerro Plano. With its superb food and service – and lovely candlelit colonial decor – it's no surprise this is one of the area's most popular restaurants with both tourists and locals. Tuck into pizza ($5–8) cooked in an open wood oven and pasta, meat and fish dishes, plus superior cocktails. During the day, hummingbirds sometimes alight in the quiet garden.

El Mediterraneo In the *Hotel Heliconia*, Cerro Plano. Dine on expertly cooked Italian dishes of fresh shellfish and grilled meats and also top-notch pizza. By Costa Rican standards, there's a wide, though scandalously overpriced, selection of wines.

Restaurante de Lucia Cerro Plano. For succulent grilled meats and delicious sea bass ($9), try this elegant restaurant with a good wine list.

Sabores Opposite the bullring in Cerro Plano. Sample the region's pure and natural dairy produce at this ice-cream parlour. Pick from a variety of flavours, including tropical fruit and coffee.

El Sapo Dorado In *Hotel El Sapo Dorado*, 500m east of Santa Elena. Take in jaw-dropping views over the Gulf of Nicoya at this classy restaurant with a romantic atmosphere. The food is a stab at gourmet French and dishes can be unreliable, but it's worth coming for the vistas alone. There are also plenty of vegetarian options including home-made spinach ravioli and tofu stir-fry. Open dinner only.

Horseback tours around Santa Elena

The efficient and friendly Desafío Expeditions (℡645-5874, ⓦ www.monteverdetours .com), opposite the *supermercado* in Santa Elena, specializes in scenic **horseback tours**. A two-hour ride through forest and farmland is $20, while a day-trip to the San Luís waterfalls is $49. Their four- to five-hour trip to La Fortuna includes horseback riding as well as vehicle and boat transfer for $65 per person. Sabine's Smiling Horses (℡645-5051, ⓦ www.horseback-riding-tour.com) also offers memorable journeys atop healthy, well-cared-for steeds. Owner Sabine knows the stunning countryside around Santa Elena well, and arranges trips that stop at various look-out points with **panoramic views** of the Pacific and the Nicoya Peninsula.

Entertainment

If you're around in February or March, you can attend the Monteverde Music Festival, featuring all sorts of groups from chamber orchestras to big bands. Performances are usually held at the Monteverde Institute near La Lechería in Monteverde, or the soccer field above Santa Elena. Performances are nightly and cost about $10. Shuttle buses sometimes head from Santa Elena to the performances – ask at your hotel. Monteverde Studios of the Arts (☎645-5434, in the US ☎800-370-3331, ⊛www.mvstudios.com) offers workshops from January to August in batik, ceramics, storytelling, travel writing, photography and yoga. Classes last about a week, and room and board can be arranged for an all-inclusive price.

Around Monteverde

The Reserva Sendero Tranquilo, a private reserve on the grounds of a local farm behind La Lechería in Monteverde, offers informative guided tours (7am–3pm, but phone ahead; $20; ☎645-5010) through primary- and secondary-growth forest. Learn about coffee-producing in Monteverde on the Cielo Verde Coffee Tour ($15 for a two-hour tour; ☎645-5641, ⊜tinascasitas@hotmail.com) where you can view each step in the production of the region's "black gold" on the well-managed organic farm Finca Cielo Verde, 2km west of Santa Elena. Call or stop by Tina's Casitas (see p.277) for more information.

Just outside Santa Elena, on the road to the Monteverde Reserve, sits the Serpentario (daily 9am–8pm; $8; ☎645-5238), with numerous slithering snakes, including deadly pit vipers and coral snakes, along with various other reptiles. Try to stop by late in the afternoon, when the serpents tend to be a

Canopy Tours

Canopy tours, pioneered in Monteverde, use techniques developed by spelunkers (cavers) and canyon rapellers so that visitors can experience the rainforest from a bird's-eye view. Having grappled up strangler figs to reach the top, you then whiz from platform to platform via pulleys strung on horizontal traverse cables. You're moving too fast to see much plant, animal or bird life – but it's definitely a thrill. Sky Trek (next to the Santa Elena bus station, ☎645-5238, ⊛www.skytrek.com), one of the most popular operators, offers the chance to zip along eleven high-tension cables suspended above the treetops. The longest **pulley-ride** is a whopping 770m. Tours (2hr 30min, $40) run between 7.30am and 3pm. The same company owns the popular Sky Walk (see below) and if you buy entrance to both, you'll save $10. Selvatura (☎645-5929, ⊛www.selvatura.com) also features memorable canopy tours as does Original Canopy Tour (at the Cloudforest Lodge, ☎645-5243, ⊛www.canopytour.com), who were the first to develop this style of excursion. Rates vary little between companies; with student ID you can usually save about $10.

For a different – but no less exhilarating – forest adventure, try Sky Walk (daily 7am–4pm; $15; ☎645-5238, ⊛www.skywalk.co.cr), an impressive series of **bridges** and paths located 3.5km along the road from Santa Elena towards the Santa Elena Reserve. Experience spectacular views – if not a touch of vertigo – as you walk across the wobbly structures over serious heights. Several bridges take you right alongside the canopy of tall trees, some of which have colonized the bridges, draping their woody lianas over the ramparts. Bring **binoculars**, for here's your chance to spot birds at their own level; you'll have to be much more sharp-eyed to see the howler monkeys who, judging from their enthusiastic grunting, live right along the trail.

little more active. Signposted on the other side of the road, the Ranario (Frog Pond; daily 9am–8.30pm; $8; ☎645-6320) is home to an array of colourful amphibians. As with the snakepit, your ticket is valid for multiple entries, and in this case it's well worth making a visit during the day and one at night, when different species emerge from beneath their lilypads. Both facilities include a guided tour in the price of admission.

The Bosque Eterno de los Niños (Children's Eternal Rainforest; $5), adjacent to the Monteverde Reserve, was initiated by Swedish schoolkids and encompasses cloudforest, rainforest and montane evergreen forest and harbours over fifty percent of known vertebrate species in the country. There are several trails, including the Sendero Bajo El Tigre, a short, unchallenging trek at a fairly low elevation with great views of the Gulf of Nicoya and spectacular sunsets. The guided twilight walk (daily at 5.30pm; $15) offers a memorable trek through the cloudforest.

The small settlement of **Cerro Plano**, just over a kilometre southeast of Santa Elena, consists mainly of hotels, but head down a signposted side road and you'll come to several interesting diversions. Walk among different butterfly species from around Costa Rica at the **Butterfly Garden** (daily 9.30am–4pm; $8; ☎645-5512), with four outdoor butterfly farms and a leafcutter ant colony. Try to arrive between 10am and 2pm when the butterflies are most active. The entry fee includes a guided tour of the farms, which begins in the on-site natural history museum. Nearby visit the Finca Ecológica, a wildlife reserve and organic farm (☎645-5554). A two-hour, guided twilight walk ($14) departs daily at 5.30pm and offers a good chance of seeing porcupines, armadillos, coatimundi, agoutis, grey foxes and a marvellous variety of insects and roosting birds. Also near Cerro Plano, the **Orchid Gardens** (daily 9am–5pm; $8) feature 400 different species of orchids, including the world's smallest.

Tilarán

Pleasant **TILARÁN** lies 40km northeast of Monteverde and roughly the same distance west of La Fortuna. The town's wide streets channel the vigorous breezes that breathe life into this otherwise lazy tropical hamlet. These same winds create the best **windsurfing** conditions in the country at the nearby Laguna de Arenal, 5km away. The *Hotel Tilawa* (☎695-5050, ⓦwww.hotel-tilawa.com; ❺), on the lakeshore east of town, has large rooms and cabinas and arranges windsurf and kitesurf rentals and lessons. After a day on the waves, enjoy home-brewed beer at the hotel bar. *Cabinas El Sueño* (☎695-5347; ❸), 150m northwest of the Parque Central, offers decent rooms with private bath and patio. *Hotel Naralit* (☎695-5393; ❸), just south of the church, has comfortable, spotless rooms. *La Carreta*, behind the church, serves up tasty Italian pasta dishes, pizzas and sandwiches on a breezy terrace.

Tilarán's bus station sits 100m north of the Parque Central. In addition to service to Santa Elena, there are **bus** connections west to Cañas and the Interamericana, from where you can head north to Liberia and the Guanacaste beaches, or south to Puntarenas. Two daily services travel east to La Fortuna, a bumpy but beautiful two-hour trip along the shores of Laguna de Arenal.

Las Juntas de Abangares

LAS JUNTAS DE ABANGARES, some 37km southwest of Santa Elena and 10km off the Interamericana, operated as a small gold-mining centre in the late nineteenth and early twentieth centuries. Commemorating the activities of the Abangares Gold Fields Company is the Ecomuseo de Oro, or Gold-mining Ecological Museum, just 5km from Las Juntas on a rough (4WD

Buses depart Santa Elena for **San José** daily at 6.30am and 2.30pm starting from the cheese factory in Monteverde. An extra service sometimes departs Santa Elena at 2pm Friday to Sunday; check the office next to the bus stop. One bus leaves Santa Elena daily at 6am for **Puntarenas** and at 7am for **Tilarán**. A bus also departs daily at 4.45am for the two-hour journey to **Las Juntas**, from where you can get to Liberia and points north in Guanacaste. If that's too early for you, take the San José-bound bus and ask to get off just after the bus turns onto the Interamericana, at the intersection for Chomes. From here, you can hail northbound buses to Liberia and elsewhere. Check at the Santa Elena bus station for **timetables** to all buses; you can buy tickets here Monday to Friday 5.45 to 11am and 1.30 to 5pm; and on weekends from 5.45 to 11am and 1.30 to 3pm. One of the more popular ways to travel to **La Fortuna**, near Volcán Arenal, is the jeep-boat-jeep trips, which usually take about two to three hours depending on the condition of the roads. Prices are competitive and hover around $15–20 one-way. The trip involves a ninety-minute jeep or minibus trip to the shores of Laguna de Arenal, then a spectacular trip across the water with the volcano looming above, and finally another jeep or bus transfer to La Fortuna. Desafío Expeditions (see box, p.285) and Pensión Santa Elena (☎645-5051) can arrange these trips.

only) little road. Exhibits include mining artefacts and dusty photographs of the area's mini gold boom. (It's not quite clear why the museum name includes "ecological", as gold mining has never been particularly known for respecting the environment.) The museum hours are daily between 6am and 5pm, but it's often closed; donations are gratefully accepted.

If you take the bus from Santa Elena to Monteverde, ask to be dropped off at the Ecomuseo, although you'll still have a thirty-minute walk from the fork in the road where the bus drops you off. If you're driving from Santa Elena, look for the fork on the left just before you hit the outskirts of Las Juntas, and the museum is signed from here. You'll need a 4WD for this last part of the journey; alternatively, you could leave your car in Las Juntas and hop in one of the 4WD taxis waiting at the rank around the corner from the church.

Puntarenas

Heat-stunned **PUNTARENAS**, 115km west of San José, has the look of raffish abandonment that haunts so many tropical port cities. What isn't rusting has long ago been bleached to a generic pastel. Old wooden buildings painted in faded tutti-frutti colours line the town's cracked, potholed streets and mop-headed mango trees provide the only shade from the relentless sun. It's hard to believe now, but in the 1800s this was a prosperous port – the export point for much of Costa Rica's coffee to England – and a popular resort for holidaying Ticos. Today most vacationing Costa Ricans have abandoned its dodgy beaches and somewhat tawdry charms in favour of the ocean playgrounds of Manuel Antonio and Guanacaste, and foreign tourists, who never spent much time here anyway, come only to catch a *lancha* or ferry across to southern Nicoya or to go on a boat trip to pristine **Isla Tortuga** – although in recent years the town's tourist trade has been somewhat revived by the daily visits of the giant **cruise ships** that call at the site of the old docks. Puntarenas carries on, however, as a working fishing town and a regional hub, with banks, businesses, hotels and transport facilities serving the populations of the southern Nicoya Peninsula and the Pacific coast.

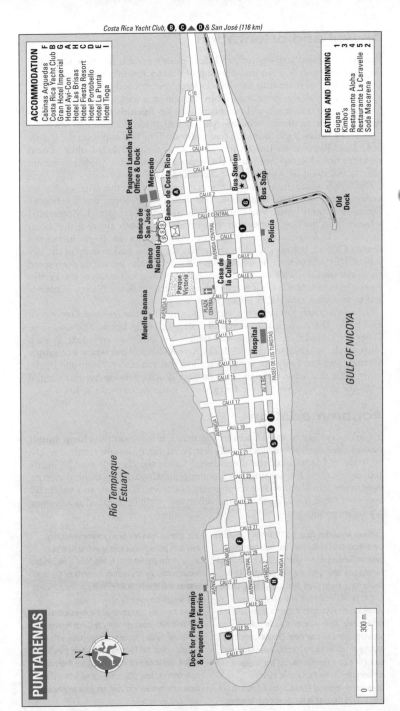

PUNTARENAS

Costa Rica Yacht Club, **B**, **C** ▲ **D** & San José (116 km)

ACCOMMODATION
Cabinas Arguedas	F
Costa Rica Yacht Club	B
Gran Hotel Imperial	G
Hotel Ayi-Con	A
Hotel Las Brisas	H
Hotel Fiesta Resort	C
Hotel Portobello	D
Hotel La Punta	E
Hotel Tioga	I

EATING AND DRINKING
Gugas	1
Kimbo's	3
Restaurante Aloha	4
Restaurante La Caravelle	5
Soda Macarena	2

Paquera Lancha Ticket Office & Dock

Mercado

Banco de Costa Rica

Banco de San José

Banco Nacional

Muelle Banana

Parque Victoria

Casa de la Cultura

PLAZA CENTRAL

Hospital

Bus Station

Bus Stop

Policia

Old Dock

GULF OF NICOYA

Río Tempisque Estuary

Dock for Playa Naranjo & Paquera Car Ferries

PASEO DE LOS TURISTAS

C.10

CALLE 8
CALLE 6
CALLE 4
CALLE 2
CALLE CENTRAL
CALLE 1
CALLE 3
CALLE 5
CALLE 7
CALLE 9
CALLE 11
CALLE 13
CALLE 15
CALLE 17
CALLE 19
CALLE 21
CALLE 23
CALLE 25
CALLE 27
CALLE 29
CALLE 31
CALLE 33
CALLE 35
CALLE 37

AVENIDA 3
AVENIDA CENTRAL
AVENIDA 1
AVENIDA 2
AVENIDA 4
AV. 4 BIS

N

0   300 m

Arrival and orientation

Puntarenas means "sandy point", and that's exactly what it is: a thin, island-like finger of sand pointing out into the Gulf of Nicoya, just five blocks across at its widest point, but more than sixty blocks long, and attached to the mainland by a narrow isthmus. You enter town from the east on a narrow isthmus road that follows the old train tracks and eventually becomes **Avenida Central**. The **Casa de la Cultura**, an orange colonial-style building, marks the centre of town.

Scores of **buses** arrive from San José every day. The bus stop is on the corner of C 2 and Paseo de los Turistas, just southeast of the Casa de la Cultura. **Local services** from Manuel Antonio and Quepos arrive here too, as do buses from Liberia and the daily service from Santa Elena.

The north shore runs along the estuary side, where the Gulf of Nicoya narrows into the Río Tempisque. The *lancha* to Paquera on the Nicoya Peninsula – from where you can head on to Playa Tambor and Montezuma – leaves from the busy docks near the *mercado*. The **south shore** is the site of the old docks, long abandoned by the container ships for the deeper harbour of Puerto Caldera, but now used by the cruise ships that pull in daily in the dry season. This side of town is worth a visit, if only for the serene, uninterrupted views out over the wide mouth of the Gulf of Nicoya and across to the Pacific. As you gaze out, to the right extends the southern tip of the Nicoya Peninsula and to the left, Costa Rica's long western coast.

The town centre lies just a few blocks northwest of the bus stop. Here you'll find banks, the municipal market and a slew of cheap hotels. The Banco de Costa Rica, Banco de San José and Banco Nacional, virtually next to each other on the north shore near the docks, have ATMs and **currency exchange.** Though you can easily get around on foot, you can always catch one of the many **taxis** that scoot through town or wave down a **bus** on Avenida Central – the last stop is in front of the **ferry dock** at the western end of town.

Accommodation

If you're catching an early *lancha* to Paquera, you may find the **cheap hotels** around the north shore docks quite handy. At night, however, this area can be seedy and at some of the more dismal hotels, the clientele may be drunk and/or not there for sleeping. Even considering Costa Rica's tropical climate, Puntarenas stands out as an exceptionally hot town. Wherever you stay, make sure your room has a **fan** that works, otherwise you'll be as baked as a ceramic pot by morning.

Cabinas Arguedas Av 0, C 27/29 ☏661-3508. It's but a short stroll to the ferry terminal from these basic yet well-equipped rooms with a/c and fridge. Parking and bike rental are also available. **③**

Costa Rica Yacht Club 3km east of town centre, next to *Hotel Portobello* ☏661-0784, ⓦwww .costaricayachtclub.com. If there's space (and there usually is), this pleasant yacht club will accommodate non-members. Simple rooms (**④**) come with hot water and access to a swimming pool. For a bit more (**⑤**) you get a/c, always a consideration in the Puntarenas swelter.

Gran Hotel Imperial Paseo de los Turistas, C 0/2 ☏661-0579. Housed in an old wooden building, this shabby hotel run by a quarrelsome family has dark but spacious rooms with private bath; some of the shared-bath rooms have a dilapidated wooden balcony. It's extremely handy for the bus station and also quite safe, as the police station is just across the road. **③**

Hotel Ayi-Con 50m south of the *mercado* on C 2 ☏661-0164. Catering mainly to Costa Ricans, this venerable budget option – cheap, clean, safe and central – near the Paquera dock offers a variety of rooms; the ones with shared bath are depressing cells with old fans (**②**) while rooms with a/c are more comfortable and have en-suite bathrooms with cold water. **③**

Hotel Las Brisas Paseo de los Turistas, C 31/33 ⊕661-4040,ⓔhbrisas@racsa.co.cr. Relax at this cheerful, clean waterfront hotel at the peninsula's western tip. Rooms come with cable TV, phone and a/c and some have balconies overlooking the Gulf of Nicoya. Splash about in the swimming pool and enjoy Greek fare at the breezy café. ❺

Hotel Fiesta Resort Playa Doña Ana, 10km southeast of Puntarenas ⊕663-0808, ⓦwww .fiestaresort.com. Costa Rican families frequent this all-inclusive hive of organized activity on brown-sand Playa Doña Ana. The beach isn't that clean, but the nicely landscaped pools – including a large children's wading pool – help make up for it. Management is friendly and prices include everything, including alcohol. Rooms have cable TV and a/c, and the buffet-style food is quite tasty. If you get bored you can always join the grannies in a salsa class. ❻

Hotel Portobello 3km east of the town centre on the estuary (north) side ⊕661-1322,

⊕661-0036. Set in landscaped gardens, this faded but charming hotel has decent en-suite rooms with hot water and a choice of a/c or sea breezes. Cool off in the swimming pools and take your meals at the decent restaurant. ❹

Hotel La Punta Av 1, C 35 ⊕661-0696. It looks a bit abandoned, but this simple hotel is close enough to the Paquera ferry for you to park your car in line the night before and stumble out of bed and onto the boat the next morning. Basic, reasonably priced rooms come with fan or a/c and there's also a small, leaf-strewn pool. ❹

Hotel Tioga Paseo de los Turistas, C 17/19 ⊕661-0271, ⓦwww.hoteltioga.com. One of the more elegant downtown hotels, with extra-friendly management and several grades of a/c rooms; those that face the sea have a balcony with lovely views (❽). You can also kick back in the soothing interior courtyard or around the pretty pool. Rates include breakfast in the cafeteria-style restaurant. ❺

The town

Though Puntarenas always appears to be slowly expiring in the equatorial sun, it seems to do so with affecting elegance – and its decaying streets exude a certain melancholy charm. The southerly promenade is optimistically called **Paseo de los Turistas**, though these days the only *turistas* to be seen are off the cruise ships or here on high-season weekends. A wide avenue, it's bordered on the town side with hotels and restaurants and a couple of discos, while the sea-facing side sports a long painted promenade – the colours, of course, long since faded by the sun. The **beach** itself used to be polluted; today, the sand at least looks clean and is backed by sparse landscaped greenery. An unsettling, metallic whiff, however, comes off the water, and the breezes do little to mitigate the intense heat. Still, you can relax at one of the beachside restaurants or kiosks and dig into good *pargo* (snapper) and other fresh fish while watching clouds drift in across the Gulf of Nicoya.

From the eastern end of the Paseo, the long, skinny finger of the old dock crooks out into the gulf. This is where bananas and coffee were loaded, before all the big shipping traffic shifted 18km down the coast to the deeper harbour of Puerto Caldera. The docks on the northern, **estuary** side, however, are a quite different matter, with a jungle of ketches and sturdy mini-trawlers testifying to a thriving fishing industry. Despite the aura of hot lassitude, lots of business is conducted in the few blocks surrounding the docks, especially in the hectic *mercado*, a cacophony of noise, people and pungent smells. Though safe enough during the day, it's best to avoid the docks at night.

West of the docks, the Parque Victoria is little more than a long, thin strip of green, bordered by red benches and a pretty, unusual stone church that looks like it might be more at home in England. A few metres south, the Casa de la Cultura (Mon–Fri 8am–noon & 1–4pm) exhibits evocative *fin-de-siècle* photographs documenting Puntarenas' lost prosperity. Sepia images of tough fishermen hang alongside photos of white-clad ladies whose husbands made their wealth from coffee exports. More interesting – and the pride of Puntarenas – is the

6

Moving on from Puntarenas

While the new bridge across the Río Tempisque north of Puntarenas has made access to the Nicoya Peninsula easier, **ferries** are still popular, particularly if you're heading to Montezuma and other places around the peninsula's southern tip. The ferry port sits at the northwestern end of Puntarenas, a fifteen-minute walk from the city centre. Buses (labelled "FERRY") run up and down Avenida Central from the centre. There are three ferry routes: Ferry Peninsular (℡641-0118) travels **to Paquera** (every two hours from 4am to 10pm; 1hr; passengers 80¢, cars $14). Navieras Tambor (℡661-2084) goes **to Tambor** (1.5hrs; passengers $1.50, cars $11) with departures at 4.30am, 8.30am, 12.30pm & 5.30pm. Ferry Naranjo (℡661-1069) travels **to Playa Naranjo** (1hr; passengers $1.50, cars $11) departing at 3.15am, 7am, 10.50am, 2.50pm, 5pm & 9pm. Paquera is closest to the popular southern Nicoya destinations and buses meet the Paquera boat and then head onwards to Montezuma. Note that there are regular minor changes to the ferry schedules. It can be a slow process buying a car ticket, so in high season arrive at least an hour before departure and park in the queue before purchasing your ticket. In addition to the ferry, two daily *lanchas* travel to Paquera; these speedier passenger-only boats leave from the dock near the *mercado* in the town centre at 11.30am and 4pm.

Buses depart every hour on the hour for **San José** from the bus terminal just off Paseo de los Turistas on C 2. The trip takes about two hours, depending on traffic. Buses to **Liberia** (7 daily; 3hr) and **Santa Elena** (daily at 2.15pm; 3hr 30min) also depart from here. For **Manuel Antonio** (4 daily; 2hr), take the Quepos bus service.

local museum (just east of Casa de la Cultura; Tues–Sun 9.45am–5.15pm), with a rundown of the region's archaeology, biology and history, focusing on the town's relationship with the sea that virtually surrounds it.

Eating, drinking and nightlife

Perhaps because of its history as a bona-fide resort, eating out in Puntarenas is more expensive than elsewhere in Costa Rica. Even fish – probably caught no more than a couple of hundred of metres away – can be pricey. Pick up a cheap meal and a *refresco* in the **mercado** – but avoid drinking anything made with the local water. Or, linger over a quiet drink or a seafood lunch at the beachside sodas and kiosks near the **old dock.**

If you've got money to spend, head for one of the well-above-average **restaurants** that line the western end of the Paseo de los Turistas. For **nightlife**, the Casa de la Cultura hosts concerts on summer weekends (Dec–April). Some of the larger hotels have discos that draw crowds on Saturday nights and holiday weekends and you can always enjoy drinks at the open-air **bars** along Paseo de los Turistas.

Gugas Av 2, C 0/1. Dig into fresh fish at this friendly, open (no walls, just a roof) bar and restaurant, one block back from the waterfront and not far from the bus station.
Kimbo's Paseo de los Turistas, C 7/9. This lively restaurant and bar serves *corvina* (sea bass) and beef stroganoff for around $6. Tico tourists pop in for drinks at night, when the music, from salsa and merengue to Costa Rican karaoke classics, cranks up.
Restaurante Aloha Paseo de los Turistas, C 19/21. Enjoy an evening drink and sea views and breezes at the outdoor tables of this popular restaurant featuring regular live music. The extensive, expensive menu offers a range of seafood dishes, including lobster, and also pizza.

Restaurante La Caravelle 100m west of *Restaurante Aloha* on the Paseo. For a welcome change from burgers and *casados*, tuck into fine French cuisine at this intimate, classy restaurant. The charming decor features a horse from a merry-go-round after which the restaurant is named. Closed Mon.

Soda Macarena At the bus stop. This small soda with ocean views serves up cheap, delicious fare, from fruit plates to toasted sandwiches; try their "Churchills", similar to a crushed-ice *granizado*, but made with ice cream.

The southern Nicoya Peninsula

The hour-long ferry trip from Puntarenas across the Gulf of Nicoya is soothing and slow-paced, with the boat purring through calm waters and past island bird sanctuaries. In the distance, the low brown hills of the Nicoya Peninsula are ringed by a rugged coastline and pockets of intense jungly green. If you're driving, you can opt to take the Tempisque Bridge across to the Nicoya Peninsula but the roads in the southern part of the peninsula are quite rough which means you'll save little time, if any, over the ferry.

Much of the southern peninsula has been cleared for farming, cattle grazing or, in the case of **Tambor** and **Montezuma**, given over to tourism. Friendly **Cóbano**, 6km inland from Montezuma, is the main town in the southwest of the peninsula, with a petrol station, post office, *guardia rural* and a few bars. You'll also find a Banco Nacional with an ATM – use it here because it's the only one in the area.

Most tourists pass straight through Cóbano on their way to Montezuma, one of Costa Rica's most popular beach hang-outs. The partly paved road to Montezuma, lined by acres of cattle pasture like much of the Osa Peninsula further south, offers a startling – and disconcerting – vision of the future of the deforested tropics. Once covered with dense primary Pacific lowland forest, today only stumps dot the fields. The red soil, unimpeded by the natural drainage of the felled forest cover, cuts rivulets down the hills. If you're searching for prime surf waves and a quieter beach scene than Montezuma, head further west to low-key Mal País.

Refugio Nacional de Vida Silvestre Curú

The small, semi-privately owned **REFUGIO NACIONAL DE VIDA SILVESTRE CURÚ** (☎661-2392; $5), 8km southwest of Paquera, protects a wide variety of flora, including many endangered **mangrove** species. A network of seventeen **trails** fans out through the reserve. Pick up a map and directions from the owners. A great variety of **wildlife** roams the deciduous forest areas. Due to the low number of visitors allowed in each day, the wildlife here at the reserve hasn't been frightened into hiding. You're likely to see or hear monkeys and agoutis – deer and wildcats also live here but are less forthcoming. At low tide the rocky tidal pools yield crabs and assorted shellfish. Pretty white-sand **beaches**, dotted with rocky coves and backed by exuberantly chaotic palm fronds, unfold along the reserve's coasts.

Practicalities

A number of **restrictions** govern visits to Curú. You cannot arrive here on your own, unannounced, but must call the owner, Señora Schutz, a week in advance, and let her know when to expect you, so she can make sure the gate is unlocked. Only thirty people are allowed in at any one time – students and field researchers have priority, and Curú's association with the University of Massachusetts means it's often booked solid. You can hire a guide for about $15 for a few hours. No **camping** is allowed, but you may sometimes find space available at the basic accommodation used by students and researchers. It's far easier, however, to use Tambor as your base and travel here by taxi or bus.

Tambor

Since 1992, when the Spanish hotel group Barceló unveiled its 400-room *Hotel de Playa Tambor*, the small village of **TAMBOR**, set in Bahía Ballena, has become synonymous with large-scale tourist-resort development. The hotel has been plagued by controversy since before it even opened, and throughout its construction the backers at times seemed wilfully bent on acting out every environmental and social gaffe possible. Barceló was convicted of both illegally draining and filling ecologically valuable mangrove swamps, similar to those protected by the nearby Curú Wildlife Refuge. They were also accused of violating Costa Rican law dictating that the first 50m of any beach is public property, with no development or habitation allowed. Despite an order ruling that the project be stopped, the government, in the end, appeared unwilling to close them down. Grupo Barceló now owns several other hotels throughout Costa Rica.

Despite the presence of the mega-hotel – set off by itself in the bay, with its own road, grounds and guards – the whole area remains rather remote. The **village** itself, surrounded on two sides by rising, thickly forested hills, exudes a friendly, laid-back vibe. A seal-grey, sandy beach stretches along a narrow horseshoe strip at the western end of the sheltered **Bahía Ballena** where, true to its name, you can sometimes spot *ballenas* (whales). If you fancy a trip out to Isla Tortuga (see below), enquire at the hotels or ask one of the local boatmen.

Isla Tortuga

One of the most popular day-trip destinations in Costa Rica, **Isla Tortuga** is actually two large (over three square kilometres in total) uninhabited islands, just off the coast of the Nicoya Peninsula near Paquera. Characterized by its poster-perfect white sands, palm-lined beaches and lush, tropical deciduous vegetation, it's certainly a picturesque place, offering quiet – during the week, at least – sheltered swimming and snorkelling. At the weekend, however, a number of tour operators and boats disgorge their loads of passengers, roughly at the same time and the same place, somewhat marring the islands' image as an isolated pristine tropical paradise.

Cruises to Isla Tortuga usually leave from Puntarenas and take between one and three hours' sailing time each way. There's plenty of opportunity for spotting **marine animals**, including large whale sharks, depending upon the season. You also pass by Negritos and Guayabo island sanctuaries, where swarms of **sea birds** nest. On the island there's time for lunch (usually included in the tour price) and **snorkelling**, followed by sunbathing or a little walking. Swimming in the warm water is perfectly safe.

The majority of visitors to Tortuga actually come on day-trips from San José. All in all, tours from the capital – including transport to and from Puntarenas – cost about $100, which is fairly steep, especially as you only get two to two-and-a-half hours on the island itself. One of the biggest operators is the fairly luxurious Calypso Tours (℡256-2727, ⊛www.calypsotours.com), who also run one-day catamaran cruises around the Gulf of Nicoya ($150, including all meals). A slower-paced, cheaper, and less regimented option is to take a tour from Tambor (see above) or Montezuma (see opposite).

Practicalities

Sansa and NatureAir fly into Tambor's **airstrip**, also used by the guests at the *Hotel de Playa Tambor*. The **Montezuma–Paquera bus** stops in the village, near the airstrip.

The beautifully situated budget hotel *Hotel Dos Lagartos* (℡683-0236; ❷–❸), by the beach, has a friendly staff and basic rooms with fans and a choice of private or shared bathroom. Nearby, the small, beachside *Hotel Tambor Tropical* (℡683-0011, Ⓦwww.tambortropical.com; ❾) is set on scenic grounds with a pool and Jacuzzi and offers comfortable hexagonal cabinas with kitchen. No children under 16 are accepted. The price includes breakfast, and they also arrange tours to Isla Tortuga and elsewhere. Three kilometres south of the village by the beach, the large *Hotel Tango Mar Beach Resort* (℡683-0001, Ⓦwww.tangomar.com; ❾) has comfortable cabins with private bath and a swimming pool and tennis courts. A small golf course (open to the public) unfolds behind one of area's nicest stretches of sand. Ask about the worthwhile weekly discounts and low-season bargains. Internet access is available.

Dine on fresh fish directly hauled in from the incoming boats at the pleasant **Restaurant Bahía Ballena Yacht Club** in the centre of the village on the beach. You can also enjoy cocktails in the lively bar with pool table.

Montezuma

The popular beach resort of **MONTEZUMA** lies about 40km southwest of Paquera, near the tip of the Nicoya Peninsula. Some three decades ago, a

MONTEZUMA

Ⓐ, Ⓑ, Cóbano & Paquera ▲

Ⓒ & Playa Grande ▲

Ⓓ Ⓕ ❶Ⓔ Ⓖ ✝ ❷ ❸ Librería Topsy

N

Ⓘ Abastecedor Montezuma Ⓗ

❹Ⓙ Bus Stop Montezuma Expeditions Chico's Shop

Laundry ★ ❺

Ⓚ Aventuras de Montezuma Tours ❻ ❼ Mini-market

Ⓛ Ⓑ

❾ Ⓜ

PACIFIC OCEAN

EATING AND DRINKING

Amor de Mar	P
Bakery Café	2
Chico's Bar	7
Cocolores	3
Iguana Café	5
El Jardín	4
Los Mangos	11
Luz de Mono	1
Moctezuma	8
El Parque	9
Playa de los Artistas	10
El Sano Banano	6

ACCOMMODATION

Amor de Mar	P
Horizontes de Montezuma	B
Hotel La Aurora	I
Hotel El Jardín	J
Hotel Luz de Mono	E
Hotel Lys	M
Hotel Los Mangos	O
Hotel Moctezuma	L
Hotel Montezuma Pacífico	F
Nature Lodge Finca Los Caballos	A
Hotel El Pargo Feliz	H
Pensión Jenny	K
Hotel Tajalín	G
Lucy	N
Luna Loca Hostel	D
El Sano Banano Beach Hotel	C

0   100 m

❿

Ⓝ

⓫Ⓞ

▼ Ⓟ, Cabo Blanco, Cabuya & Mal País

handful of foreigners seeking solitude fell in love with Montezuma and decided to stay. In those days, Montezuma was just a sleepy fishing village, largely cut off from the rest of the country. Today, Montezuma draws tourists galore, including backpackers, spring-breakers, honeymooners and tour groups. Virtually every establishment in town offers gringo-friendly food and accommodation and sells tours. Nevertheless, Montezuma still feels like a village because large-scale development has been kept to a minimum – and it's still a bit of an effort to get here.

Montezuma and the coast south to Cabo Blanco feature some of Costa Rica's loveliest coastline: leaning palms and jutting rocks dot the white-sand beaches. Here you can enjoy uninterrupted views of the Pacific, especially arresting on nights with a full moon or when the occasional lightning storm illuminates the horizon and silky waters. Inland, thickly forested hills, including rare Pacific lowland tropical forest, dominate the landscape.

Arrival and information

Buses pull in near *Chico's Bar* (see p.300) close to the beach. The **centre** of town consists of a beachfront road and a short sloping street leading up and inland from it. At the top of this street, a right turn takes you to Cóbano, while a left heads south towards Cabo Blanco.

On the main drag, the helpful multilingual folks at Aventuras de Montezuma (T & F642-0050, Eavenzuma@racsa.co.cr) offer the largest range of **tours**, services and information in town, including trips to Isla Tortuga ($40) and horse-riding on the beach and to local waterfalls ($25). They also have an **Internet** café, **international phone service** and can arrange **car** and **motorbike rental**. In the centre of the village, the **Montezuma Expeditions** kiosk rents out bicycles and motorbikes, and offers full-day trips to Isla Tortuga ($40, including breakfast and time for snorkelling); diving trips ($90, including equipment rental); and four-hour horse-rides to waterfalls ($25). They also arrange transfers to Cabo Blanco Reserve. The *El Sano Banano*, adjacent to Aventuras de Montezuma, has an Internet café by its restaurant for $3 per hour.

Chico's shop, near the mini-market, sells sunscreen, film, clothing and telephone cards, which you can use in the **telephones** outside (if the lines are working). For **newspapers** and a bookshop, try Librería Topsy on the beachfront road. Dollars are accepted everywhere, and many places will accept travellers' cheques. The nearest bank and ATM is up the road in Cóbano, 6km away, although it surely won't be too long until Montezuma gets a branch of its own.

Accommodation

Accommodation prices remain quite moderate in Montezuma because the village caters to a young, studenty crowd who can't afford the rates of, say, Manuel Antonio, and even prices in some of the more upscale hotels drop in low season by about $10–15. **Reservations** are highly recommended in the dry season, especially on weekends, and are essential over Christmas and Easter. Most times, though, if you arrive on a late bus without a reservation, there is bound to be somewhere to stay.

While convenient, staying in the **village** can be noisy, due to the shenanigans at *Chico's Bar* and the odd car pulling in and out of the village. Elsewhere you'll find it wonderfully peaceful, with choices out on the **beach**, on the road that heads southwest to the Cabo Blanco Reserve, and on the sides of the steep hill about 1km above the village. If you get bitten by the Montezuma bug (and many do) and decide you'd like to stay **long-term**, you'll see notices around town advertising houses for rent; most are located between Montezuma and Cabo Blanco or Mal País.

Camping is prohibited on the beach; instead, you can stay at one of the organized camping sites between Montezuma and Cabuya, on the road to the Cabo Blanco Reserve, where there are toilets, showers and barbecues.

In the village

Hotel La Aurora Montezuma ⊤642-0051, ⊛www.playamontezuma.net/aurora. Take your pick among sixteen varied rooms at this pleasant, environmentally conscious pension. The older ones (❹) come with fans, communal fridge, coffee- and tea-making facilities and shared bath. The new, slightly more expensive cabinas have a/c and private bath with hot water. There's also an apartment with its own kitchen and terrace and all guests have use of a well-equipped kitchen. ❹–❺

Hotel El Jardín At entrance to town on Cóbano road ⊤642-0548, ⊛www.hoteljardin.com. Relax in attractive, spacious cabins with wooden ceilings, tiled bathrooms and terraces with attractive leather rocking chairs. Some rooms come with fridges, while those upstairs have views over the town and sea. You can also cool off in the enticing pool. ❺

Hotel Luz de Mono Montezuma ⊤642-0090, ⊛www.luzdemono.com. This friendly hotel has well-appointed rustic stone villas and rooms, all with private bath, hot water, fridge, coffee maker and CD player (complete with Costa Rican music). Take your meals at the excellent Italian restaurant. ❻

Hotel Lys Just south of the centre ⊤642-0642. On the sand, this casual hotel draws budget travellers looking for a place to crash – and who aim on spending more time on the beach than indoors. Rooms are basic but scrubbed clean daily by the friendly owners. It fills quickly so ring ahead. ❷

Hotel Moctezuma By the beach in the centre of town ⊤ & ⓕ642-0058, ⊛www.playamontezuma .net/ecotours/hotel. Right in the thick of things, this hotel offers simple, gloomy rooms with cold shower, fan and shared bathroom in an old wooden building with a spacious balcony overlooking the sea. The new annexe across the street has brighter en-suite rooms with a small fridge. ❸

Hotel Montezuma Pacífico Near the church in the centre of town ⊤642-0204. The rooms are rather characterless but clean and quiet and come with a/c, hot water and breakfast. Try to get one of the front rooms which have decent views or a room with a balcony. ❹

Hotel El Pargo Feliz Montezuma ⊤642-0065. Very close to the beach, these plain cabinas have fan and cold-water private bath. You can lounge about in hammocks and relax in the small garden.

Reception is closed in the afternoons unless you ring ahead. ❸

Hotel Tajalin Montezuma ⊤642-0061, ⊛www .tajalin.com. In a quiet location near the centre of the village, basic rooms come with fan (❸) or a/c (❹); airy rooms on the top floor have sea views.

Luna Loca Hostel 200m north of the village on the road to Cóbano ⊤642-0390, ⊛www .playamontezuma.net/lunaloca. This friendly new backpacker hostel sits peacefully on a forested hillside, with a regular troupe of monkeys as visitors. There are three private rooms, but most beds are bunks ($10 per night, including breakfast) in clean dormitories fronted by a sociable balcony. There's a shared kitchen and TV lounge. ❸

Pensión Jenny Just west of town, up a path by the soccer field ⊤642-0306. One of the cheapest spots in town, but something of a last exit for the lost, to be used when everywhere else is booked. The management is pleasant enough and the rooms simple and sweaty, but the shared bathrooms and showers look like something out of a prisoner-of-war film. ❷

Around the village

Amor de Mar 600m southwest of the village on the beach, just across the bridge ⊤ & ⓕ642-0262, ⊛www.amordemar.com. This upmarket (for Montezuma) seafront hotel, well-managed by German owners, sits in pretty landscaped gardens on a rocky promontory. Hammocks hang between giant mango trees. The attractive selection of rooms come with and without bathroom; those upstairs and facing the sea are best, most of which come with verandah and ocean views. ❺

Horizontes de Montezuma 1.8km before Montezuma on the road from Cóbano ⊤642-0534, ⊛www.horizontes-montezuma.com. Perched in the hills above Montezuma, this small, distinctive, tropical-Victorian hotel has spacious, airy rooms with hot-water private bath and balcony looking over the jungle or ocean. There's a pool and a good restaurant and the owners offer intensive private Spanish lessons. ❺

Hotel Los Mangos About 500m down the road to Cabo Blanco ⊤642-0076, ⊛www.hotellosmangos .com. Expensive-looking but slightly dark bungalows (❺) on attractive grounds come with fan and large, hot-water showers; some have their own verandahs complete with rocking chairs. There's also a pool, Jacuzzi and decent restaurant. **④–⑤**

Lucy 500m south of the centre ☎642-0273. This Montezuma stalwart, still operating even though the government once attempted to have it torn down because it violates the *zona marítima*, which prohibits building on the first 50m of beach, offers clean, basic rooms with cold-water showers and an upstairs seaside terrace; a couple of rooms have private bath. The owner also offers a reasonable laundry service and runs a cheap eatery next door. **②**

Nature Lodge Finca Los Caballos 3km before Montezuma on the road from Cóbano ☎642-0124, ⓦwww.naturelodge.net. Set in tropical gardens with a small pool, this casual lodge has eight comfortable rooms with hot-water private bath. The owners offer highly recommended horse tours, as well as advice on birdwatching and local fauna and flora. The restaurant serves international cuisine prepared with organic ingredients. **⑤**

El Sano Banano Beach Hotel A fifteen-minute walk north of the village along the beach (your bags will be taken care of) ☎642-0638, ⓦwww.elbanano.com. One of Costa Rica's most characterful hotels, the truly special *El Sano Banano* offers secluded circular cabinas all with beachfront balconies and outside showers; some also have kitchenettes. The newer split-level apartments, perfect for families, boast beach views. There's a lovely freeform swimming pool with a waterfall, beautifully landscaped gardens and an ample sun terrace. Breakfast is included in the café in town. **⑤**

The village and around

It's Montezuma's atmosphere, rather than its activities, that draws visitors, and other than hanging out and sipping smoothies, there's not much to do in the village itself. Despite the inviting palm-fringed, white-sand beaches, swimming isn't very good immediately to the north of Montezuma – there are lots of rocky outcroppings, some hidden at high tide, and the waves are rough and currents strong. Your best bet is to head north of Montezuma along the lovely **nature trail** (1.5km; 30min) that dips in and out of several coves before ending at **Playa Grande**. Here, you'll find reasonable swimming, decent surfing and a small waterfall on the beach's eastern edge; some also sunbathe topless or nude, though this isn't particularly appreciated by local people.

A number of **waterfalls** lace Montezuma and its environs; the closest lies about a kilometre south down the road towards Cabo Blanco and then another 800m on a path (signposted to the *catarata*) through dense vegetation. Bring your swimsuit if you want to bathe, but always take care, especially in the wet season when flash floods may strike. Under no circumstances should you try to climb the waterfalls; many people have been injured – and even killed – in the attempt. Local tour operators lead **horse-rides** to falls that are otherwise difficult or impossible to reach on foot.

The single most popular excursion in town is to the **Cabo Blanco Reserve** (see p.301) for a morning of walking. Although you can do this by tour, you can also reach it by public transport or with your own 4WD (or fully insured 2WD in the dry season). If you enjoy **mountain biking,** ride the 9km down to Cabo Blanco, walk the trails and bike back in a day. Mind the height of the two creeks en route, however, as you might not get through them on your bike at high tide.

Always a draw is the popular **Isla Tortuga** (see box p.294), off the coast of the peninsula near Curú, where you can snorkel, swim safely in calm, warm, shallow waters and sunbathe. Several companies in town organize day-trips for about $40 per person; you can also approach local boatmen if there's a group of you, though make sure you establish exactly what is included in the price. If you do this, also be sure to take enough drinking water for the trip.

△ Montezuma waterfall

Eating, drinking and nightlife

Just a few years ago, all you could eat in Montezuma was fantastically fresh **fish**, practically straight off the hook. These days, the varied menus in town offer not just *comida típica* but a slew of tourist favourites like vegetarian pizza, granola, mango shakes and paella.

Nightlife in Montezuma centres on *Chico's Bar*, an interesting mix of local kids – who arrive packed in the back of pickups – and tourists guzzling from a surprisingly wide bar stock and shouting above the music. It closes at two, after which people tend to adjourn to the beach for some alfresco drinking. On Wednesdays, the action shifts to the *Shangrilá* on the grounds of the *Luz de Mono* hotel. More retiring types can take in the very popular video movie shows (in English) at the *El Sano Banano* restaurant nightly at 7pm; you have to spend at least $6 in the restaurant to get in.

Amor de Mar In *Amor de Mar* hotel. Enjoy beautiful oceanfront views while sampling light snacks, smoothies (made with home-made yoghurt) and superb breakfasts with delicious home-baked German bread.

Bakery Café Opposite *Luz de Mono* hotel. Despite staff who seem to have mistaken cool for arrogant, it's still worth stopping by for the tasty sandwiches and vegetarian dishes served on a soothing, shady terrace – perfect for lunch after a morning on the nearby beach.

Cocolores This intimate restaurant in a garden by the beach serves toothsome coconut fish curry ($6), Lebanese salad ($3.50) and a range of vegetarian dishes – all accompanied by home-made bread. Closed Mon.

Iguana Café Fill up on big, tasty sandwiches and wash it all down with good coffee. Get lunch to go and enjoy it on the beach.

El Jardín In the *Hotel El Jardín*. Choose from stuffed zucchini and burritos, veggie dishes, fish fillet in Mexican *ranchera* sauce and spaghetti and shrimp – plus good fruit drinks and espresso.

Luz de Mono In the *Luz de Mono Hotel*. Montezuma's most upmarket restaurant offers gourmet dining in a large airy rancho. The international menu features jumbo shrimp ($15) and hearty, delicious American breakfasts ($7.50). If you're counting your colones, skip the food and

go for the reasonably priced happy-hour cocktails (4–7pm).

Los Mangos Tuck into fresh Mediterranean-style cuisine – pastas, salads and seafood – at this poolside restaurant.

Moctezuma Look out to sea from beneath palm trees at this upstairs restaurant where the Spanish chef cooks great paella and seafood, especially the grilled or garlic fish. Sop it all up with hunks of fresh bread.

El Parque On the beach just south of the centre. This casual, open soda serves hearty Costa Rican dishes as well as burgers and sandwiches – and all at reasonable prices by Montezuma standards.

Playa de los Artistas About half a kilometre south of the village. Splash out on an unhurried outdoor candlelit dinner of classy Italian-inspired fish, steak and vegetable dishes (main courses hover around $10–12) at this rustic beachside restaurant. The tuna and snapper choices are recommended. Closed Sun.

El Sano Banano Come here for excellent American breakfasts and filling lunch and dinner specials, including the fillet of fish ($8), crepes, vegetarian pizzas and cannelloni with spinach, most of which feature organic produce. At the very least, try the incredible smoothies made with fresh fruit and yoghurt. They put on films every evening at 7pm so come early to get a seat.

Moving on from Montezuma

Aventuras de Montezuma (see p.296) sells tickets for NatureAir **flights** from Tambor to San José as well as air and bus transfers to other destinations in Costa Rica. A popular route to San José involves taking a launch to just outside Jacó for $30; from there, catch a cab to the Jacó bus station and connect with the frequent San José-bound buses. Slower but more convenient is the Interbus service that picks you up from your hotel in the morning and gets you to San José in about six air-conditioned hours ($35).

Cabuya and the Reserva Natural Absoluta Cabo Blanco

Nine kilometres south of Montezuma lies the Cabo Blanco Reserve and **CABUYA**, a pleasant town that draws a growing community of permanent foreign residents who enjoy the slow pace of life, relative isolation and unspoiled scenery. Cabuya is everything that Montezuma isn't, so if you're looking to escape the crowds and loll on secluded beaches, this is the place to come.

Reserva Natural Absoluta Cabo Blanco

RESERVA NATURAL ABSOLUTA CABO BLANCO (Wed–Sun 8am–4pm; $6; ☎642-0093, ⓦwww.caboblancopark.com), about a kilometre west of Cabuya, is Costa Rica's oldest protected piece of land, established in 1963 by Karen Morgenson, a Danish immigrant to Costa Rica, and her Swedish husband Olof. Until 1989, no visitors were allowed; even today, scientific researchers have priority, and the number of visitors remains low.

Cabo Blanco occupies an area of around twelve square kilometres, almost the entire southwestern tip of the Nicoya Peninsula. A unique biodiversity – including pockets of Pacific lowland tropical forest found nowhere else in Costa Rica – complements the reserve's natural beauty. Though hard to believe today, most of the reserve was pasture and farmland until the early 1960s. Since its inauguration, the reserve has been allowed to regenerate naturally; a small area of original forest that had escaped destruction served as a "genetic bank" for the reestablishment of the complex tropical forest that now fills the reserve.

It used to be said that animals in Cabo Blanco were less shy than in any other protected area in Costa Rica, perhaps due to the lack of visitors, though these days, as Montezuma's popularity increases, so do pressures on the reserve, to a degree few expected. The more people that have flooded in, the shyer the animals have become, and there's now talk of imposing daily limits on visitors – about forty, probably. The most frequently seen animals are howler monkeys, deer, sloths and squirrels, while agoutis and coati are also common, as are snakes – watch your step. The margay and the tamandua (anteater) are among the species that live here, but which you're unlikely to see. The best time for animal-spotting is any morning around 8am, or on Wednesday mornings, after the reserve has been closed for two days. Bird life is astonishingly plentiful down by the shore – you'll often see scores of pelicans and clouds of frigate birds, while brown boobies nest on the islands off the tip of the peninsula.

Pay your entrance fee at the **ranger hut**, and they'll supply you with a trail map that also outlines the history of the reserve and the species living here. A **trail** (5km; 2hr) leads from the entrance through tropical deciduous forest to **Playa Cabo Blanco** and **Playa Balsitas**, two lovely, lonely spots (in low season, anyway). Swimming, however, isn't great around here; be wary of the high tide (*marea alta*). Ask the ranger at the entrance when and where you'll likely get cut off if walking along the beach. It's also very **hot**: 30°C is not uncommon, so bring a hat, sunblock and plenty of water. No camping is allowed in the reserve, but you'll find plenty of places to stay in the village of Cabuya (see p.302), a twenty-minute walk from the park entrance.

Practicalities

The **roads** from Montezuma to Cabuya and Cabo Blanco are rough; you'll need a 4WD to get there yourself, except in the very driest time of year (and make sure you have full insurance on that hire car). Keep an eye out for the two creeks, which are deep at high tide. An old, road-hardened **bus** runs between Montezuma and Cabo Blanco, leaving from Montezuma's *parqueo* at 8am, 9.50am, 2.05pm, 4.10pm and 7.10pm, and returning from Cabo Blanco at 7.10am, 9.10am, 1.10pm, 3.20pm and 6.20pm daily, although sometimes it may not run in the rainy season. **Jeep-taxis** make the trip from Montezuma to Cabo Blanco for $10 per person.

As for accommodation, in Cabuya you'll find the welcoming *El Ancla de Oro* (T & F642-0369, Elamont@racsa.co.cr; ④). Rustic cabins, with mosquito nets and fans, sit among fruit trees and there are also self-catering bungalows. The restaurant dishes up dinner nightly, including delicious lobster served in garlic butter ($12) and cheaper but equally good *pargo* (red snapper). Fernando Morales' house (4km north of Cabuya, T642-0351) has basic rooms (②) and a pleasant campsite. Nearby, the *Hotel Cabo Blanco* (T & F642-0332; ④) is set right on a gentle beach with good swimming. Nine rooms come with fan or a/c, sleep up to four and cost a flat rate (and therefore are more economical for groups).

Playa Santa Teresa, Mal País and around

The long surf beach of **Playa Santa Teresa**, 12km southwest of Cóbano, and also accessible via a steep and bumpy road from Cabuya, lures an increasing number of travellers and has a smattering of cabinas, eateries and shops, as well as a couple of bars. The beach is backed by a straggly community that extends both ways along the oceanfront from the area's main landmark, *Frank's Place*. Turning south from here takes you along the **Mal País** ("Bad Land") section of the beach strip, which is quieter and more peaceful than Playa Santa Teresa. In Mal País, a pleasant mix of foreigners, particularly Italians, share the ample beach with a young surf crowd.

If you fancy learning how to ride a board, you'll find a number of schools, including Pura Vida (T640-0118), on the beach a couple of hundred metres north of the main intersection. Nearby, Pacific Divers (T640-0187, Wwww .pacificdivers-costarica-com) run PADI courses and guided dives, although visibility usually isn't great. You can also ride horses along the beach or on the jungle road to Cabo Blanco; try Horse Tours and Bikes (T640-0209) at the Mal País end of the beach.

North of Mal País lies **Manzanillo**, a great surfing beach on the western side of the peninsula with long waves similar to Playa Junquillal in the north. You'll find few facilities, though, and the beach may be deserted. In the rainy season, the drive isn't recommended; the creeks – at least a dozen of them – that cut the dirt road between Mal País, Manzanillo and Sámara are likely to be so high that you won't make it in anything less than a Land Rover or a large truck.

In fact, **roads** all over this part of the peninsula are confusing, in bad shape and liable to be nearly impassable in the rainy season. It's just about possible to get around in the dry season in a 4WD, however, with a good road map, some Spanish and camping gear. Some people, certainly locals, drive from Cóbano up to Carmona in the north, or from Manzanillo northwest to Sámara, but neither is an interesting enough drive to make it worth the trouble.

Practicalities

The relaxed gringo vibe at *Frank's Place* (T640-0096, Wwww.frankplace .com; ③) makes it one of the area's most popular places to bed down. The cheap rooms are decent if a little dark, while the more upmarket ones (⑤) come with private bath, a/c, kitchen and fridge. You can hang out on hammocks around the pool, and at the casual café-restaurant that makes après-surf stomach-fillers like tasty $3 *casados*. The hospitable *Blue Jay Lodge*

(☏640-0089, ⓦwww.bluejaylodgecostarica.com; ❺, includes a generous breakfast), south of the intersection, has intimate, widely spaced bungalows that sleep two to three people. Head up the hillside for the best bungalows, with ocean views and plenty of wildlife; for a relaxing break, cool off in their swimming pool. Camping is officially prohibited on the beach, but there are several sites that operate anyway, including *Victor* ($2.50 per person), 500m south of the intersection. Mal País's large expat population translates into a wide choice of eating places. Enjoy superb sunsets over succulent seafood at *Piedra del Mar*, on the beach south of the junction. *Bar Tabé*, just north of *Frank's Place*, gets lively at night. Also, regular beach parties draw revellers. Check www.malpais.net for more info. Two daily buses run between Cóbano and Mal País. A taxi will set you back around $13 (one-way).

South of Puntarenas

South of Puntarenas on the mainland, the coast road (sometimes signposted as the **Costañera Sur**) leads down to Quepos and continues, in various states of paving, south to Dominical (covered in Chapter 7). At first the landscape is sparse and hilly, with the coast coming into view only intermittently. The road improves considerably once you're past the huge trucks heading to the container port and refineries at hideous Puerto Caldera. About 30km southeast of Puerto Caldera, just across the wide mouth of the Río Tárcoles, is the **Reserva Biológica Carara**, known for its rich bird life. You'll find a number of lovely old places to stay nearby, much better than the run-of-the-mill hotels in the resort town of **Jacó** – and particularly handy if you're a birder who wants to get to the trails early. South of here, along the coast from the hamlet of Parrita to Quepos, unfolds a long corridor of African oil-palm plantations, a moody landscape of stout, brooding tree sentinels.

Reserva Biológica Carara and Río Tárcoles

The **RESERVA BIOLÓGICA CARARA** (daily 7am–4pm; $6; ☏383-9953), 90km west of San José, occupies a transition area between the hot tropical lowlands of Guanacaste and the humid, more verdant climate of the southern Pacific coast. Consequently, Carara teems with **wildlife**, much of it of the unnerving sort. Huge crocodiles lounge in the bankside mud of the Río Tárcoles, and snakes (19 out of Costa Rica's 22 poisonous species) slither about. Mammals include monkeys, armadillos, agoutis and most of the large felines, from the jaguar and puma to the ocelot and margay. **Birding** is excellent, and this is one of the best places in the country to see the brightly coloured **scarlet macaw** in its natural habitat. Most nights at twilight, anytime between 3pm and 5.30pm, they migrate from the lowland tropical forest areas to the swampy mangroves, soaring off in a burst of red and blue against the darkening sky. Among other birds that frequent the treetops, you may see toucans, trogons and guans, while riverside birds include herons, anhingas and storks. The best time to see **migratory birds** is, as usual, the dry season, from December to April.

Whatever time of year you visit, it's worth hiring a guide, who can take you into restricted areas where tourists aren't allowed on their own. Be aware that many day-tours from San José come here because it's only a two-and-a-half-hour-drive away. Serious birders are advised to stay overnight in the area, as early mornings offer famously more rewarding birdwatching than at any other time of day.

Practicalities

To get to Carara **from San José**, take the Orotina Highway and turn left at the long bridge over the Río Tárcoles. You'll see many cars parked at the entrance, just past the bridge, and even on the bridge itself, with birders training their binoculars on the river, or croc-spotters pointing at the lazing reptiles. There have been robberies on this bridge and some people advise that it is no longer safe to stop, although plenty do. The **ranger station**, with toilets and picnic tables, lies 3km from the bridge. Staff hand out basic maps and answer questions about the reserve's wildlife. The car park here has become a magnet for **thieves** breaking into unattended cars, and vehicles should be left in the guarded *parqueo* at the ranger station at the entrance. It's extremely **hot** in Carara, especially at midday, when it can reach 30°C. In the wet season, the area receives about 3000mm of rain per year.

Although camping is not allowed, you'll find a number of good **accommodation** options near Carara. They all offer **birding** tours – *Tarcol Lodge* is one of the premier birding destinations in the country – and several have excellent horse-riding and hiking opportunities. Though accessible to independent travellers, it's best to phone ahead and ask to be met off the buses from San José; some lodges also offer transport from the capital, or from nearby Jacó or Quepos.

Most serious birding tours from North America and the UK include Carara on their itineraries. In San José, Costa Rica Expeditions (℡257-0766, ⓦwww.costaricaexpeditions.com) offers all-inclusive tours with trained guides, transport and lunch for $99.

Hacienda Doña Marta Cascajal, near Orotina ℡653-6514, ℻239-9555. This family-run, working dairy farm has cabinas around a pool and tasty home-cooked meals. The surrounding forest and riverside land is perfect for horse-riding and birding trips; they also offer tours of the area with meals included. ❺

Tarcol Lodge 5km north of Tárcoles village on the south bank of the Río Tárcoles ℡267-7138, ⓦwww.ranchonaturalista.com. Pleasant, rustic *Tarcol* is dedicated to the needs of birdwatchers. At high tide, the lodge gets surrounded on three sides by water. When the tide retreats, the birds come out and literally hundreds of species descend upon the sandflats. Local tours, all meals and transport from San José are included in the lodge's prices. The owners also run the *Rancho Naturalista Lodge* near Turrialba (see p.138) and offer week-long packages split between here and Turrialba. ❺

Villa Lapas 500m east of the turn-off to Tárcoles village, signed from the Costañera Sur just past the Río Tárcoles bridge ℡637-0232, ⓦwww.villalapas.com. Set in landscaped gardens near the river, this peaceful, well-equipped resort hotel has large, pleasant a/c rooms and also mini-golf and a pool. The owners have established a small network of trails in the nearby private reserve – perfect for early morning birdwatching. Río Tárcoles and Carara both lie within walking distance from here, and you can enjoy meals at the fine restaurant. ❼

Jacó

Less than three hours from San José, this thriving beach resort sits in a hot coastal plain behind the broad **Playa Jacó**, the closest beach to the capital and an established seaside attraction that draws a mix of surfers, package tourists and Ticos on holiday. When covered in mist and backed by a spectacular Pacific sunset, the beach's wide, chocolate-coloured sands look quite attractive, and they're now a lot cleaner than they used to be, thanks to conscientious locals who organize clean-up brigades after heavy high-season weekends. You can

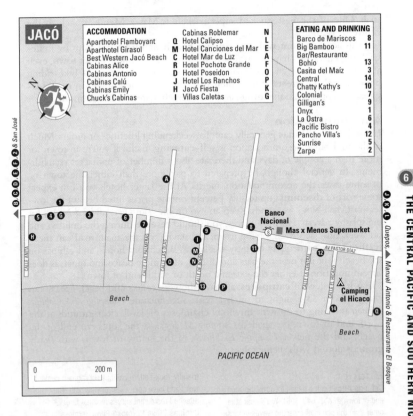

JACÓ

ACCOMMODATION

Aparthotel Flamboyant	Q
Aparthotel Girasol	M
Best Western Jacó Beach	C
Cabinas Alice	R
Cabinas Antonio	D
Cabinas Calú	J
Cabinas Emily	H
Chuck's Cabinas	I

Cabinas Roblemar	N
Hotel Calipso	L
Hotel Canciones del Mar	E
Hotel Mar de Luz	A
Hotel Pochote Grande	F
Hotel Poseidon	O
Hotel Los Ranchos	P
Jacó Fiesta	K
Villas Caletas	G

EATING AND DRINKING

Barco de Mariscos	8
Big Bamboo	11
Bar/Restaurante Bohío	13
Casita del Maíz	3
Central	14
Chatty Kathy's	10
Colonial	7
Gilligan's	9
Onyx	1
La Ostra	6
Pacific Bistro	4
Pancho Villa's	12
Sunrise	5
Zarpe	2

Banco Nacional

Mas x Menos Supermarket

Camping el Hicaco

Beach

Beach

PACIFIC OCEAN

0   200 m

swim at the long, spacious sandy beach although the water isn't the cleanest and you do have to watch out for rip tides.

Surfing aficionados not only have the steady waves of Jacó, but also the more challenging waves at the nearby beaches of Playa Hermosa, and Esterillos Este and Oeste, among others. While Jacó has numerous hotels and cabinas, reserve in advance in the high season (Dec–April), especially on weekends.

Arrival and orientation

Buses depart from the Coca-Cola bus terminal in San José (3hr; $2.25) daily at 7.30am, 10.30am, 1pm, 3.30pm and 6.30pm. From Puntarenas (1hr 15min), buses leave daily at 5am, 11am, 2.30pm and 4.30pm; from Quepos (1hr 15min–2hr) buses depart at 4.30am, 7.30am, 10.30am and 3pm. Buses stop at the extreme north end of the village at the Plaza Jacó mini-shopping centre.

Several **banks** on the main drag, including the Banco Nacional, accept foreign-issued credit cards and change travellers' cheques. You'll find several **car rental** agencies in town, including National, by the Banco Popular, and Payless, at the northern end of town. Many places rent out mountain **bikes**, **scooters**, **surfboards** (about $20 a day) and boogie boards ($10 a day). **Internet cafés** are all over town; Centro Computacional sits between Calle Hicaco and Calle Las Brisas, while Mexican Joe's is near the Banco Popular. Jacó has several laundromats, including Aquamatic at the southern end of the strip. One of the best stocked supermarkets is Mas x Menos, smack in the centre of Jacó.

Locals advise against **walking on the beach at night**: hold-ups by knife-wielding characters have been reported. Otherwise, strolling about town, even at night, should be safe, especially since a special contingent of bike-riding police patrol the streets. Part of their mandate is to crack down on the wide-spread use of recreational drugs, and snap searches are not uncommon.

Accommodation

Jacó's cheapest **cabinas** generally cater to weekending Josefinos or surfers. Much of the mid-range accommodation is **self-catering**, useful if you're in town for more than a couple of days, and there are also a number of upmarket establishments. In general, though, be prepared to pay more than either the town or, in some cases, the accommodation, merits. At the larger hotels you can expect some sort of **discount** (up to fifty percent on the prices listed below) for low-season (May–Nov) weekends. Keep an eye on the *Tico Times* and *La Nación* for big splashy adverts. For most places, you should **reserve** during the holidays and on weekends. Jacó is a growing town, and staying on the main road can mean **traffic noise**, particularly on busy weekends. Beachfront hotels, and cabinas on the beach (but not near the bars and discos), offer more peace and quiet, as does accommodation at either the extreme north or south end of town.

Jacó has a slew of **campsites**; all have showers, toilets and beach access and charge about $3 a night to pitch a tent. Sites include *Camping and Cabinas Mariott* (nothing to do with the hotel chain), set on level, clear grounds at the north end of town; the shaded *Camping Madrigal*, at the southern end of the beach; and the newer *Camping El Hícaco*, in the centre of town, with shady grounds dotted with picnic tables.

Budget

Cabinas Alice On the beach towards the southern end of town ☎ & ℱ 643-3061. You'll hear little other than the sound of crashing waves in these cabinas surrounded by beautiful beachfront grounds. All come with fan and hot water, while some also have a small kitchen with fridge and a small terrace. You can enjoy meals at the restaurant and splash about in the pool. ❸–❹

Cabinas Antonio At the north end of Jacó, near the San José bus stop ☎643-3043. Basic cabinas come with fridge, fans and hot-water private bathrooms, and there's a restaurant and pool. ❸

Cabinas Calú Calle de Bohío in the town centre ☎643-1107. Large, if a bit dark, rooms have hot-water private bathrooms; the central location can get noisy on weekends. The friendly owners also offer a laundry service. ❷

Chuck's Cabinas Calle Anita, near the beach at the northern end of town ☎643-3328. A relaxed surfing vibe pervades this unpretentious little spot with dormitory accommodation and simple rooms with cold-water bathrooms. You can also get your surfboard repaired and advice on waves. ❷

Cabinas Emily On the main road on the north side of town ☎643-3513. Filled with surfers, these friendly, rock-bottom cabinas sport green cement walls and have cold-water private bath. The attached restaurant serves regional fare. ❷

Cabinas Playa Hermosa Playa Hermosa, 7km south of Jacó ☎643-2640, ⓦwww .playahermosacr.com. Well-priced cabins come with fans and a swimming pool.

Cabinas Roblemar Calle Bohío near the beach off the middle section of the main drag ☎643-3558. This central but fairly quiet establishment has smallish cabinas with large comfortable beds; each pair of cabinas shares a simple kitchen and cold-water bathroom. ❸

Hotel Calipso At the southern end of the main strip ☎643-3208, ℱ643-3728. This sleepy, friendly hotel has simple rooms with shared cold-water bath and fan, a swimming pool and parking. ❸

Moderate

Aparthotel Flamboyant In town centre, in front of beach ☎643-3146, ℮flamboya@sol.racsa.co.cr. Stay right by the sand in these well-maintained apartments with hot-water bathroom, ceiling fans and kitchen. Relax in the Jacuzzi and pool and fill up on good meals at the restaurant. ❺

Auberge du Pélican Southern end of Playa Esterillos, signposted "Esterillos Este" from the main road ☏778-8105, ⓦwww.aubergepelican.com. This welcoming spot has a/c rooms with wooden floorboards and attractive furnishings in charming, palm-shaded grounds. Plus, there's a quality restaurant (breakfast is included), a pool table and a swimming pool. ❺

Hotel Mar de Luz In the town centre, on the landward side of the main drag ☏ & ⓕ 643-3259, ⓦwww.mardeluz.com. This well-kept, family-friendly hotel sits amid soothing, landscaped grounds away from the road. Colourful modern apartments (sleeping up to five) surround two large pools and a garden. Rooms come with TV, a/c, microwave and kitchenette, plus there's a lounge, games area and small library. ❺

Hotel Pochote Grande At the northern end of town ☏643-3236, ⓕ220-4979. Set around a tempting pool and landscaped grounds, well-kept, beachfront rooms have a/c, hot-water bathroom and fridge. The attached restaurant serves decent local food along with a number of German dishes. ❺

Hotel Poseidon Calle Bohío in the town centre ☏643-1642, ⓦwww.hotel-poseidon.com. Right in the centre of Jacó rises this renovated, two-storey white stucco hotel; good-sized rooms have all the modern conveniences including minibar and cable TV. The pool sports a swim-up bar and the on-site restaurant dishes out fine fare, including tender slabs of tuna with Asian-influenced sauces.

Hotel Los Ranchos In the centre ☏ & ⓕ643-3070. A variety of rooms, from upstairs loft rooms (some with kitchenettes) to two-storey bungalows with kitchens, sit around attractive gardens and a pool. ❹

Jacó Fiesta Just outside the southern end of town ☏643-3147, ⓦwww.jacofiesta.net. Located at the quiet southern end of the beach, this small hotel is older than the others, but rooms are clean with hot-water private bath, a/c, well-equipped kitchenettes and cable TV. There are several swimming pools and a decent attached restaurant. ❺

Expensive

Apartotel Girasol Calle Los Almendros at the southern end of town ☏ & ⓕ643-1591, ⓦwww.girasol.com. Relax right on the beach in these spacious, luxurious tiled apartments (sleeping up to four) with fan, a/c, a full kitchen and a cane-furnished lounge area. Take a break in the lovely swimming pool and garden. Service is friendly and there's secure parking. ❻

Best Western Jacó Beach North end of town ☏643-1000, ⓦwww.bestwestern.co.cr. This well-established resort offers plenty of facilities, including a big clean pool, restaurant, casino and weekend disco, plus kayaking, sports-fishing and sailing. Perfectly comfortable rooms, decorated in anonymous chain-hotel style, come with private bath, a/c and cable TV. ❻

Hotel Canciones del Mar On the beach in thecentre of town ☏643-3273, ⓦwww.cancionesdelmar.com. The colourful apartments in this appealing, bamboo-framed beachfront hotel come with large beds, patio and modern kitchen. Other pluses include an ample pool, breakfast (included in the price), worthwhile discounts for weekly and monthly stays and a hospitable welcome. ❻

Hotel Club del Mar Southern end of town ☏643-3194, ⓦwww.clubdelmarcostarica.com. On a quiet beach south of town sit these English-owned, luxury apartments with a family-friendly atmosphere and a huge range of amenities, including pool, restaurant, spa, small library and games room. ❼

Villas Caletas 8km north of Jacó, off the Costañera Sur ☏637-0606, ⓦwww.hotelvillacaletas.com. Perched on a clifftop above the Pacific, this is one of Costa Rica's finest boutique hotels. Luxurious, beautifully decorated individual villas sit amid landscaped grounds and offer stunning views, especially at sunset. The restaurant serves gourmet cuisine with prices to match. The grounds look like a film set, with a small Greek theatre and a pool with a view. A shuttle takes guests down the precipitous one-kilometre trail to the private beach. ❼

The town and around

Jacó straggles along a three-kilometre main road, a brash strip of shops, restaurants and hotels. Turning off from this main drag, a few streets lead to the sea but never quite make it, petering out in attractive palm groves or the beach. On high season weekends the main road becomes busy with traffic; bear this in mind if your hotel backs onto it.

The combination of beach-crazed weekending Josefinos and surfers – neither known for their sobriety or quietness – often transforms Jacó into too much of a party beach for many travellers. Jacó's nightlife is predictably hedonistic and sleazy, with young holidaymakers jostling for bar space with prostitutes and their clientele. That said, it can be eerily quiet in the low season, with only a few ecstatic French Canadians, recently liberated from the northern winter, scooting about on motor bikes.

Jacó also makes a good base for the many surfing beaches nearby (most of them better than Jacó). Little **Playa Herradura**, 7km north, has good beach breaks but hardly any accommodation, so most visit as a day-trip from Jacó. Just south of town, you'll find several wild, sparsely populated, wave-crashed beaches including **Playa Hermosa**, with a long stretch of darkish sand and a tempting break for surfers. About 25km further south stretches the long **Playa Esterillos**.

Surfers can rent boards at a number of competing places in Jacó; ask at *Hotel Los Ranchos* (see p.307) for advice and recommendations. Several locals offer lessons, including Gustavo Castillo (☎643-3574), an experienced surfer and teacher. Renting a **mountain bike** (about $10 a day) is handy for getting around this spread-out town.

You can easily reach the southern beaches from Jacó by car or by getting on a Quepos-bound bus and asking to be let off at the relevant stop. In the case of Esterillos Este, you'll have to walk just under a kilometre from the main road to the beach. Beware of parking at Playa Hermosa, as break-ins have been frequently reported.

A number of operators in town offer **tours** throughout the area, including to the nearby **Reserva Biológica Carara** and to **Isla Damas**, a small mangrove-dominated island where you can spot lots of monkeys. Jacó Adventures (100m south of *Restaurante Colonial*, ☎643-1049, ✉jacoadventures@playajaco.com) offers many excursions, including rafting trips on the Río Savegre ($89), day-trips to Isla Tortuga ($70; see p.294), and **kayaking** and **snorkelling** tours ($55). Their real speciality, however, is **sports-fishing**, with some of the best half- and full-day expeditions on the coast – a half day for four people starts at $240.

Eating and drinking

Jacó offers a surprisingly wide assortment of **restaurants** – many specializing in fresh seafood – to suit all budgets. For cold beer and tasty Mexican *bocas* (finger-foods like tacos and empanadas), stop by *Zarpe* **bar** at the north end of town. Enjoy a sunset drink right on the beach at *Bar y Restaurante Bohío*, with church-pew benches and tables under a ranch roof. The spacious, upstairs *Onyx* bar, across the bridge in the northern section of the main road, draws a happy young tourist crowd who socialize to pop and light dance music and play pool. The popular *Discoteca Central*, on the beach on Calle Central, charges $2.50 on weekends. Once it shuts, at 4 or 5 in the morning, revellers head around the

Moving on from Jacó

Buses to San José (3h; $2.25) depart from the stop at the north end of Jacó, near the Plaza Jacó shopping centre, daily at 5am, 7.30am, 11am, 3pm and 5pm. Here you'll also find the bus ticket office, behind the Banco de Costa Rica. Four daily buses stop in Jacó from Puntarenas at 6.15am, 12.15pm, 3.45pm and 5.45pm; these buses continue on to **Quepos** and **Manuel Antonio**. There may be extra bus services on holiday weekends, but if you intend to travel between Friday and Sunday, especially in high season (Dec–April) or on public holidays, try to buy your ticket at least three days in advance. Additionally, you always have the option of taking one of the air-conditioned minibuses that travel all over Costa Rica; a one-way trip to San José or the airport costs $21.

corner on the main road to the bar-restaurant *Pancho Villa's* to squeeze out the last few drops of the night.

Barco de Mariscos In town centre on the main road. This informal venue specializes in well-prepared fresh shellfish and fish dishes. They also run a popular café and ice-creamery next door.

Big Bamboo In town centre on the main road. Come here for tasty pizzas and *empanadas*. They also deliver (☎643-3706) – always handy when you've become a little too comfortable at your hotel's poolside terrace .

Casita del Maíz North end of town. Deservedly popular with locals, this casual soda serves up fine *casados* ($3) made with fresh ingredients.

Chatty Kathy's Opposite Mas x Menos supermarket. Breakfast on pancakes and delicious cinnamon rolls at this Canadian-owned upstairs café.

Colonial On the main road, near Calle de Bohío. Travellers and Ticos come to this tastefully designed bar-restaurant for drinks as well as main meals, including expensive but large and succulent steaks and burgers.

Gilligan's On the main road, a block south of the bridge. This quiet little restaurant offers just two or three daily specials, but they're always delicious,

and include imaginatively prepared fish or chicken dishes for $7–9.

Jammin' At Playa Hermosa, 7km south of Jacó. This relaxing rasta restaurant dishes up generous portions of surfer-friendly fare – burgers, quesadillas, sandwiches, salads, shakes and smoothies – for $6–8.

La Ostra On the main road, by the bridge. Try the fine fish and shellfish dishes, from refreshing ceviches ($3-6) and *corvina* (sea bass; $4) to succulent lobster, at this long-established *marisquería* (seafood restaurant) in a large quiet rancho next to a creek. Service is erratic.

Pacific Bistro At northern end of the strip. This small, quality restaurant with Asian-inspired decor and food specializes in superb salads and fish ($8–14 for main dishes). If you see tuna steak on the menu, don't pass it up.

Sunrise At northern end of the main road. The generous breakfasts (eggs, pancakes, muffins and fresh fruit and juices) at this friendly, relaxed café are so tasty and popular that the owners can afford to shut at midday and head for the beach.

Quepos and Parque Nacional Manuel Antonio

The small corridor of land between the old banana-exporting town of **Quepos** and the little community of **Manuel Antonio**, outside the **Parque Nacional Manuel Antonio**, has experienced one of the most dramatic tourist booms in the country in the last few years. Visitors descend in droves to experience the park's stunning, picture-postcard setting, with spectacular white-grey sand beaches fringed by thickly forested green hills. Outdoor activities abound, including walking the park's easy trails, whitewater rafting, ocean-cruising and horse-riding. The unique *tómbolo* formation of **Punta Catedral**, that juts out into the Pacific from the park, accounts for much of the region's allure. A rare geophysical phenomenon, a *tómbolo* results when an island becomes joined, over millennia, to the mainland through accumulated sand deposits. Other smaller islands, some of them no more than rocky outcroppings, dot the waters around Punta Catedral. As you watch a lavish sunset flower and die over the Pacific, it does seem as though Manuel Antonio may be one of the more charmed places on earth.

That said, the huge tourist boom has undeniably taken its toll on the whole area. The 7km from Quepos town to the national park entrance features an unbroken line of hotels and lodges and the sheer influx of visitors can reduce the park's main trails to conga lines. The Quepos area can also be pricey and over the years, budget travellers have often opted for the cheaper beaches at Montezuma or Tamarindo on the Nicoya Peninsula. Consequently, some

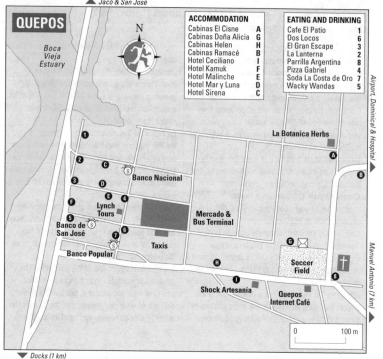

Jacó & San José

QUEPOS

*Boca
Vieja
Estuary*

N

ACCOMMODATION

Cabinas El Cisne	A
Cabinas Doña Alicia	G
Cabinas Helen	H
Cabinas Ramacé	B
Hotel Ceciliano	I
Hotel Kamuk	F
Hotel Malinche	E
Hotel Mar y Luna	D
Hotel Sirena	C

EATING AND DRINKING

Cafe El Patio	1
Dos Locos	6
El Gran Escape	3
La Lanterna	2
Parrilla Argentina	8
Pizza Gabriel	4
Soda La Costa de Oro	7
Wacky Wandas	5

La Botanica Herbs

Banco Nacional

Lynch Tours

Banco de San José

Mercado & Bus Terminal

Taxis

Banco Popular

Shock Artesanía

Soccer Field

Quepos Internet Café

Airport, Dominical & Hospital

Manuel Antonio (7 km)

0   100 m

Docks (1 km)

THE CENTRAL PACIFIC AND SOUTHERN NICOYA | Quepos and P. N. Manuel Antonio

hotels have dropped their rates, and now are merely expensive rather than overpriced.

Then there's the **road**: sometimes it's in good condition and at other times, deep potholes puncture the asphalt. Beyond the nondescript town of **Parrita**, the road runs through a surreal landscape of brooding African oil-palm plantations owned by United Brands. The rudimentary bridges along this stretch are periodically washed out and you may be subject to delays as you wait to cross yet another makeshift bridge. Along with the forests of oil palms, you'll pass a series of "company" villages, with identical two-storey bungalows on stilts, arranged around soccer fields. Bright blue once, but long since bleached to a uniform grey-green, the bungalows were originally built for the banana workers, before the fruit plantations were ravaged by Panamá disease in the 1950s. Today they're bunkhouses for oil-palm workers and managers.

Quepos

Arriving in **QUEPOS** from San José, Puntarenas or Jacó, it's immediately apparent that you've crossed into the lush, wetter southern Pacific region. Here, the vegetation grows thicker and greener than further north, and more often than not it has just started or finished raining. Backed up against a thick hill, with a muddy – and polluted – beach in front (obscured by the seaside road out to the old dock), Quepos can look pretty ramshackle. Disaffected youths linger on stone benches on the main drag or whiz their mountain bikes back and forth to the old banana docks. Quepos does, however, have plenty of hotels, bars and restaurants and it's a good place to meet fellow travellers. Most come for its proximity to the Parque Nacional Manuel Antonio and its beaches, 7km south. Compared to most of the establishments along the road to the park entrance, lodgings and restaurants in Quepos are affordable, and there are frequent buses to the park, making it the most useful base in the area.

The name "Quepos" derives from the indigenous language of the Quepoa people, part of the larger Borucas (or Bruncas, as they are sometimes called) people, who occupied this area for at least a thousand years before the arrival of Juan Vásquez de Coronado in 1563. After the invasion, the Quepoa went into a predictably swift decline due to disease and enslavement. Once a banana-exporting town, Quepos was severely hit by the Panamá disease, a devastating banana malady, which prompted United Fruit to pull out in the 1950s. The area has gone through something of a resurgence in recent decades, with the establishment of the African oil-palm plantations. It has also developed into one of the country's prime **sports-fishing** destinations, with the waters around these parts teeming with big, hard-fighting fish, including Spanish mackerel, sailfish, wahoo, yellowfin tuna, dorado, blue marlin, white-tip shark and cubera snapper. Posh sports-fishing boats anchor in Blue Bay in front of town and many small tour agencies cater more or less exclusively to sports-fishers.

Arrival

Buses leave San José's La Coca-Cola bus station for Quepos eight times daily. Express buses (3hr 30min) depart at 6am, noon, 6pm and 7:30pm. Regular buses (5hr) leave at 7am, 10am, 2pm and 4pm. Buses continue to Manuel Antonio, dropping you off at hotels on request. On weekends, holidays and any time during the dry season, you'll need to buy your bus ticket at least three days in advance, and your return ticket as soon as you arrive. All buses arrive in Quepos at the busy **terminal**, which doubles as the *mercado*, just one block east of the town centre. The Interbus **shuttle service** travels daily between San José and Quepos and Manuel Antonio ($25 one-way) using air-conditioned Mercedes minibuses. They leave San José at 9am and 1.30pm and return from Manuel Antonio at 8.30am and 2.30pm, picking you up from your hotel at each end. For reservations, call ☎283-5573 in San José, contact Lynch Tours in Quepos (☎777-1170, ⊛www.lynchtravel.com) or book on the Internet at ⊛www.interbusonline.com.

If you're driving to Quepos, note that it's easy to miss the town and find yourself out on an old abandoned dock with nowhere to go but the Pacific. The entrance to town is actually on the left-hand side, down a narrow slip road, just after you cross Puente Boca Vieja. From here, continue straight ahead until you reach the last street where you can turn left. Head about 1km further down this road and you'll see the winding uphill road to Manuel Antonio branching off to the right; it's signed, but easy to miss.

Due to the long drive and the condition of the roads, many fly from San José: this takes only twenty five minutes and, as Quepos residents like to point out, there are no pot holes in the sky. Ten daily **flights** (run by Sansa and NatureAir; $46–50 one-way) head to Quepos but the flights tend to be heavily booked up so reserve early. The airstrip lies 5km north of town; from here a minibus ($2–5) runs into Quepos and on to Manuel Antonio, dropping you off at your hotel.

Orientation and information

Tiny Quepos covers only about three blocks by four and its "downtown" consists of a main seaside road and a few blocks around it. The streets do have numbers, but nobody uses them. There's no official tourist office, although you can get **information** at Lynch Tours (see opposite). Shock Artesanía, on the south side of the soccer field, sells **maps** and laminated wildlife guides. For up-to-date town info, pick up *Quepolandia*, a free bimonthly English newsletter found at many local businesses.

To change **money** and **travellers' cheques**, head for the Banco Nacional, just northwest of the bus terminal; the attached ATM accepts Visa and Mastercard/Cirrus. Other banks also change travellers' cheques, as does Lynch Tours. The Banco de San José/Credomatic is the only place you can get cash advances on Mastercard, and is also open on Saturday mornings. Most businesses in town change dollars.

The **correo** (Mon–Fri 8am–5pm) sits at the eastern end of town. A plethora of places have **Internet** access, including Internet Tropical, in front of the *Hotel Malinche*, which also has international **phone** service, fruit *batidos* and toasted sandwiches. Quepos Internet Café, opposite the soccer field, has a happy hour and student discounts. For car rental, try Alamo by the soccer field.

Take precautions against **theft** in the Manuel Antonio area. Rental cars left on the street have become a favourite target so never leave anything of value in your car. Some hotels have secure parking or can point you towards a safe place to leave your vehicle. Never leave anything on the beach when swimming and, if you take the bus, don't let anyone else handle your luggage – best to keep it with you on the bus if possible. Wherever you stay, ensure your hotel room is locked at all times. It's also unwise to walk around at night in Quepos – especially alone – as the seawall area is a hangout for local drug users. Drugs have become a problem in the area and are blamed for many of the robberies from hotel rooms and cars.

In you're in need of **medical attention**, go to the excellent Hospital Dr Max Teran (☎777-0200) near the airport.

Accommodation

Cabinas El Cisne 200m north of the church ☎777-0719. Friendly folk run this casual spot with comfortable rooms equipped with refrigerator, TV, small kitchen and fan or a/c. ❸

Cabinas Doña Alicia On the northwest corner of the soccer field ☎777-0419. The cheery owners keep everything spotlessly clean at this budget hotel. Rooms (all sleep up to four) have comfortable double beds and cold-water private bath. They also have a few decently priced single rooms (a rarity in Quepos) and secure parking in the back. ❷

Cabinas Helen A block south and east of the *mercado* ☎777-0504. These clean, secure cabinas in the back of a family home are equipped with private bath, fridge and fans. They offer decent single rates, and there's also a small patio, parking and a laundry service. ❸

Cabinas Ramacé Opposite *Cabinas El Cisne* ☎777 -0590. Clean, if somewhat bare and sterile, cabinas (some with a/c) come with hot-water bathrooms and fridge. There's secure parking in the back. ❷–❹

Hotel Ceciliano Near football field on the south side of the street ☎777-0192. Darkish but clean and breezy cabinas come with fan and shared bath, while comfortable en-suite cabinas have a/c. ❷–❸

Hotel Kamuk On the western avenue ☎777-0811, ⓦwww.kamuk.co.cr. This airy *Best Western* hotel offers rooms with a/c, cable TV and phone. Pricier rooms (❻) boast balconies with sea views and there's a pool. The café and restaurant centres on seafood – they'll cook up the fish you catch – and they also serve sushi, pasta, chicken and steaks. ❺–❻

Hotel Malinche Just west of the *mercado* ☎ & ☎777-0093. This modern, motel-style hotel has basic but bright and comfortable a/c rooms (❺) with carpet, TV and balcony. Older downstairs rooms have ceiling fans. Neither come with hot water, but you'll hardly miss it in this climate. The friendly folks who run the hotel also arrange fishing charters. ❸

Tours and activities in the Quepos area

You'll find a wide range of **tours in the Quepos area**, most of which include equipment rental and guides, along with lunch and/or snacks. Many of the upmarket hotels have their own tour-service desk. In the town centre, the friendly and reputable Lynch Tours (℡777-1170, ⓦwww.lynchtravel.com) is an excellent source for unbiased information. They offer outings to Dominical, Corcovado and Bahía Drake either by bus or plane, and also arrange transfers to all over Costa Rica in air-conditioned Mercedes shuttle buses. Their many **local tours** include horse-riding trips to a waterfall ($55), sports-fishing ($450–1200 for a full day of offshore fishing), sea kayaking ($65), whitewater rafting ($70–98), rainforest canopy tours ($65) and perennially popular daytime or sunset cruises, some specifically to see dolphins ($65). Iguana Tours (near the soccer field, ℡777-1262, ⓦwww.iguanatours.com) run a variety of jungle tours.

Equus Stables (℡777-0001, ⓔhavefun@racsa.co.cr), on the road to Manuel Antonio, offers a two-hour sunset **horse-riding** tour ($35) on the beach and up into the mountains. As with elsewhere in the country, it's worth checking to see how the horses are treated and stabled before you ride, since overwork and abuse of horses is fairly widespread and a thorny issue among travellers and riding outfitters.

Several **sports-fishing** operators run tours, including Bluefin (℡777-2222, ⓦwww.bluefinsportfishing.com), with a full-day offshore charter ($600–850). Costa Rica Dreams (℡ & ⓕ777-0593) also runs well-organized tours. The *Hotel Malinche* (see opposite) can set you up with a recommended local fisherman.

Rafting operator Los Amigos del Río (℡777-0082) has an office between Quepos and Manuel Antonio – look for a large orange building on the left with inflatable rafts outside.

Try one of the popular **cruises** along the coast to Manuel Antonio. Sunset Sails (℡ & ⓕ777-1304 or book through Lynch Tours) offers four-hour sunset dolphin-watching (Dec–April only; $69) cruises in a classic wooden yacht. Enjoy stunning views of the coastline and offshore islands – and keep your eyes peeled for whales and sea turtles. Also popular are excursions to the Rainmaker Conservation Project (22km to the north; $45–65 for a half day) with a series of hanging bridges from which you can observe the jungle ecosystem.

Hotel Mar y Luna Just northwest of the *mercado* ℡777-0394. Central and friendly, this budget hotel has dark rooms with hot-water private bath and fans. Hang out on the plant-filled communal balcony and enjoy the free coffee. ❷
Hotel Sirena On first road to the left as you enter Quepos ℡777-0528, ⓕ777-0165. Comfortable rooms – those upstairs receive more light – come with private bath, hot water and a/c. There's also a small pool and a poolside bar and restaurant (breakfast is included in the price). Try one of their recommended sports-fishing or horse-riding tours. ❺

Eating and drinking

The **restaurants** in Quepos fall into two categories: gringo–owned and –geared eateries and those owned by locals and frequented by Ticos (and where you'll find the cheapest meals). **Fish** is predictably good – order grilled *pargo* or *dorado* and you can't go wrong. Mid-week, **nightlife** is more or less limited to excited fishermen debating the merits of burleys and tackle. On the weekends, *Wacky Wanda's* gets lively with a cheerful mix of tourists and locals who hang out in air-conditioned comfort until fairly late at night.

Cafe El Patio On the sea wall. When you're salivating for a real cup of coffee, look no further – the coffee here is among the best in the country. Try the delicious Queppuccino ($2) or buy a bag of roasted beans to take home. They also serve *refrescos* (in flavours like vanilla nut chill or iced raspberry mocha) and cakes, sell English-language newspapers and

Moving on from Quepos

Buses to Manuel Antonio (15 daily; 20min) depart from the terminal at the *mercado* between 5.30am and 9.30pm; slightly fewer run in the rainy season. Express bus service **to San José** (3hr 30min) departs at 6am, 9.30am, noon, 3pm and 5pm. Regular bus service (5hr) to San Jose leaves at 5am, 8am, 2pm and 4pm. Buses **to Puntarenas** (3hr) leave at 4.30am, 7.30am, 10.30am and 3pm; the Puntarenas bus will also drop you in Jacó (1hr 30min). When road conditions permit, buses also head south to Dominical and Uvita. **Taxis** line up at the rank at the south end of the *mercado*; the journey to Manuel Antonio costs $3–5. If you're **driving**, you can get to San Isidro, Golfito, the Osa Peninsula and other points in the Zona Sur via Dominical, 44km south of Quepos. Although the road is usually in terrible condition and you'll need a sturdy 4WD, it beats going all the way back to San José and taking the Interamericana south. For **plane** tickets and schedules to San José, visit Lynch Tours (see p.313).

magazines and accept US dollars and travellers' cheques.

Dos Locos Just southwest of the *mercado*. Enjoy large, healthy sandwiches and pseudo-Mexican cuisine, including fajitas, burritos and tacos, while taking in street views from the open dining area. Wash it all down with a margarita or two.

El Gran Escape On the sea wall. American-style breakfasts, decent (if fairly pricey) Mexican food and a good selection of drinks at the bar draws an overwhelmingly American fishing crowd. The pleasant, plant-filled seating area opens to the street – and weekend nights can get rowdy.

La Lanterna Opposite the Banco Nacional. A cut above your standard gringo pizza joint, this restaurant has a pleasant verandah and specializes in fine pizzas and classy if somewhat

minimalist Italian main dishes, including chicken marsala and saltimbocca, made with quality imported ingredients.

Parrilla Argentina Next to the church. Low on frills and high on quality, this is the best place in town for juicy Argentinian-style steaks. You can watch right from your table as the chef grills the hefty beef slabs. A *bife de chorizo* (a thick rump steak cut off the rib) will set you back about $11 but it should tide you over for quite a while.

Pizza Gabriel West of the *mercado*. This small, unpretentious restaurant with gingham tablecloths serves up simple, decently priced pizzas.

Soda La Costa de Oro Next to Banco Popular. Just about the best and cheapest soda in town, here you can nosh on fish *casados* ($2.50) amid a busy lunchtime crowd of locals and tourists.

Quepos to Parque Nacional Manuel Antonio

Southeast of Quepos, a seven-kilometre stretch of road winds over the surrounding hills, pitching up at the entrance to the village of **MANUEL ANTONIO** and the **Parque Nacional Manuel Antonio**. Manuel Antonio was one of the first places in the country to feel the effects of the 1990s tourist explosion. Drawn by its lavish beauty, hoteliers and businesses rushed into the area, and these days the entire road from Quepos to the park is lined with some sort of accommodation. The most exclusive – and expensive – hotels hide away in the surrounding hills, with lovely ocean and sunset views. The very best overlook Punta Catedral (Cathedral Point), which juts out picturesquely into the Pacific. Though you'll find some affordable places near the park entrance, and the occasional low-season discount, prices are high compared to the rest of the country.

The Manuel Antonio **bus** from San José continues beyond Quepos, dropping people off at their hotel along the road between the town and park entrance. La Buena Nota souvenir shop (☎777-1002), 5km east from Quepos between the *Hotel Karahé* and *Cabinas Piscis*, functions as the area's **information** centre and also sells film, foreign papers, magazines and locally made hand-crafted clothes.

You'll find **Internet access** in the unlikely setting of a restored railway car – brought all the way from northern Chile – in front of *La Cantina* restaurant across from the *Costa Verde* hotel. For **shopping**, the Sí Como No *artesanía* shop in Manuel Antonio stocks the work of local painters and craftsmen.

Manuel Antonio has several **language schools**, including the reputable Escuela de Idiomas d'Amore (T777-1143, Wwww.escueladamore.com) and the Centro de Idiomas del Pacífico (T777-0805, Wwww.cipacifico.com), housed in the *Cabinas Pedro Miguel*, whose Canadian owner offers personalized classes. A few San José schools offer a week's study here as part of their curriculum.

Accommodation

The hotels below are listed **in the order you encounter them from Quepos** – all are well signed from the road. More than anywhere else in this guide, our hotel choice is partial, representing the best value in each price range. Prices quoted are for high season and generally include tax and breakfast; in the low season and for longer stays some of these hotels offer discounts and it's worth asking and checking websites for special offers. **Reserve** well in advance – in the highest season, from December 1 to January 15, you should reserve as much as four months before arriving. You can take a **taxi** from Quepos to most of these hotels for a set fare of around $5. It's usually cheaper to hail taxis along the way because the driver may pick up a number of people on the road, making it cheaper for everyone.

Between Quepos and Manuel Antonio

Cabinas Pedro Miguel T777-0035, F777-0279. Backed by the rainforest, these comfortable Costa Rican-owned *casitas* come equipped with basic furnishings, mosquito nets and a kitchenette. Home to the Escuela del Pacífico language school, this friendly spot also has a small pool and a great cook-your-own restaurant (see p.317). Low-season and mid-week discounts are available, but book ahead. ❸–❺

Hotel Plinio T777-0055, Wwww.hotelplinio.com. Stay in comfortable, if a bit dark, rooms decorated in Guatemalan prints. Gaze out at spectacular sunsets from the raised platform beds of the highest rooms. Landscaped tropical gardens feature a pool and a four-kilometre nature trail, with great views from the top. Enjoy meals at the excellent restaurant. ❺

Aparthotel Mimo's T777-0054, Wwww.mimoshotel.com. Set around a pool, these large apartments with fan (❺) or junior suites with a/c (❻) all come with hot-water bathrooms and kitchenette. Laze away the day on outdoor hammocks and take your meals at the good Italian restaurant. Reasonable rates, especially in low season, include continental breakfast. ❻–❼

Hotel El Mono Azul T & F777-1954, Wwww.monoazul.com. Small but bright, clean rooms come with a fan (newer rooms have a/c) and a terrace. Across the road, villas sleep up to five. Splash about in the lovely swimming pools and dine in the excellent restaurant that serves a wide range of pizzas, mahi-mahi fillets, steaks, soups and salads. This hotel is also home to an innovative children's project to save local squirrel monkeys. Book in advance. ❺

Hotel Villa Teca T777-1117, Wwww.hotelvillateca.net. Relax on a tranquil hillside in smallish but cheerful bungalows surrounded by a flowering garden. There are a couple of pools, a decent Italian restaurant, generous low-season discounts and transfers to the national park. Prices include breakfast. ❺

Didi's B&B T777-0069, Wwww.didiscr.com. Kind hosts run this intimate, welcoming B&B with just three colourfully decorated rooms with cable TV and either fan or a/c. There's a Jacuzzi, fishing tours can be arranged and breakfast is included in the price. ❹

Hotel Las Tres Banderas T777-1284, Wwww.hoteltresbanderas.com. Set in a quiet wooded area, this welcome hotel has large double rooms (❺) that open onto a terrace or balcony overlooking the forest. Spacious suites (❻) have a kitchenette and sofa bed. There's a swimming pool and a restaurant that sometimes serves tasty Polish specialities for guests only (unless you call ahead to reserve a meal). ❺

Hotel La Colina T777-0231, Wwww.lacolina.com. Located on the near-vertical incline locals call "cardiac hill", this lovely hotel offers comfortable rooms with private bath and a/c; if your legs are up to it, apartments (**6**) higher up boast a fantastic 180-degree view of the jungle and sea. The hotel also has one of the better restaurants in the area, serving Costa Rican food with Italian and French influences, including an excellent *ceviche* and beef carpaccio. Breakfast is included and there's a pool. **5**–**6**

Hotel Flor Blanca ☎777-0032, ℗777-1633, ⓦwww.hotelflorblanca.com. One of the cheaper options on this luxury-strewn road, this simple hotel has plain, thin-walled rooms with private bath, fridge and a choice of fan or a/c. For what you get, it's far from a bargain but still less expensive than any of the neighbours and offers reasonable off-season discounts. **4**

Tulemar ☎777-0580, ⓦwww.tulemar.com. This luxury hideaway has fourteen beautiful octagonal bungalows built on stilts and set into the hillside, many with sweeping views over Punta Catedral – and prices to match (around $275 in high season but significantly cheaper in low season). The lovely bungalows are equipped with all the amenities, including a/c, VCR and TV, phones and well-equipped kitchenettes. Nature trails traverse the verdant grounds and there's also a large swimming pool. Breakfast is included. **8**

Hotel La Mariposa ☎777-0355, ⓦwww.lamariposa.com. Manuel Antonio's oldest luxury hotel offers villas set in lovely gardens around a pair of swimming pools. Take in Punta Catedral views from many of the rooms and enjoy excellent meals at the prestigious (and overpriced) restaurant which serves Mediterranean cuisine, including fresh yellowfin tuna and a delicious lobster bisque. Breakfast is included. **7**

Makanda-by-the-Sea ☎777-0442, ⓦwww.makanda.com. Surrounded by quiet gardens with ocean views, these elegant, luxury villas come with kitchenette and a balcony or terrace. Expect to pay about $265 per night. No children under 16 admitted and breakfast is included. **8**

Hotel El Parador ☎777-1414, ⓦwww.hotelparador.com. Stuffed with hundreds of imported antiques and suits of armour quietly oxidizing here in the tropics, the *Parador* has entered local legend for the scale of its luxuriousness. The sumptuous hillside villas, many with staggering views, come with cable TV, a/c and bathtubs. More spectacular vistas beckon from the pool and (expensive) restaurant. Reached via a long rough road, the hotel is enviably secluded but expensive to reach without a car – taxis can charge up to $10. Mind you, there's always the helipad. A lavish breakfast buffet is included. **8**

Villas El Parque ☎777-0096, ⓦwww.villaselparque.com. Self-catering rooms, suites and duplex villas, all with kitchen, balcony and screened dining area. Some also have a/c, and many boast views of the Pacific and Punta Catedral. **6**–**7**

Villas Nicolas ☎777-0481, ⓦwww.villasnicolas.com. Set high above the surrounding greenery, these friendly, classy rooms come with hot-water private bath and ceiling fans; some have kitchens and there's also a small pool. Rooms with views go for about $20 more. **5**–**6**

Sí Como No ☎777-0777, ⓦwww.sicomono.com. Enjoy beautiful views of the Pacific and Punta Catedral from this award-winning architectural complex set high on a hill. The hotel has solar-heated hot water, a Jacuzzi, two pools, swim-up bar, waterslide and a small cinema with nightly screenings (free to guests). Rooms (and prices) vary from well-appointed doubles ($190) to fully equipped villas ($220–240). The poolside *Rico Tico* grill serves excellent food, and breakfast is included. **8**

Hotel Villa Roca ☎ & ℗777-2335. This gay-friendly hotel sits on the slope of a steep terraced hill surrounded by peaceful foliage and fine ocean views. Nine rooms (**5**) and four luxurious apartments (**7**) all come with a/c. A leafy garden surrounds the pool and area tours can be arranged. **5**–**7**

Costa Verde ☎777-0584, ⓦwww.costaverde.com. Spacious, rustic rooms and studio apartments, all constructed out of beautiful hardwood, have balconies with terrific ocean views and lovely details like decorative tiles. It's friendly and professionally run and, quirkily, reception is in a train carriage. Ask for a room in the D block, which looks onto Punta Catedral and features some of the most stunning views in Manuel Antonio. Choose among three swimming pools with stupendous vistas and cap off the day with a fine meal in the restaurant. **6**

Manuel Antonio Village

Albergue Costa Linda ☎777-0304. This friendly backpacker spot has basic dorm rooms with shared cold-water bathrooms. There's also a comfort-food restaurant, with filling favourites like pancakes and spaghetti, as well as more upscale apartments that come with cable TV, kitchenette, fridge and a verandah. **2**–**4**

Cabinas Piscis ☎777-0046, ℮vivipisc@racsa.co.cr. One of the few budget places left in Manuel Antonio, these basic and dark but clean rooms have cement floors and cold-water shared or private bath. You can access the beach via a lovely garden and the small restaurant (open in high season only) serves sandwiches and juices. Student and group discounts are available, but it's popular, so book ahead. **2**–**3**

Cabinas Espadilla ☎777-2113, ⓦwww.espadilla
.com. Set in attractive gardens with a pool, these
pleasant, if somewhat overpriced, airy cabinas
have large beds, hot-water private bath, a kitchen
and fan or a/c. The cabinas are a better value for
groups of three to four people. ❺

Hotel Los Almendros ☎ & ⓕ777-0225. Near
the beach and park, this decent hotel has rooms
with hot-water bathroom and fan or a/c. There's
Internet access available and an open-air
Argentinian restaurant. ❹

Hotel Vela Bar ☎777-0413, ⓕ777-1071,
ⓔvelabar@maqbeach.com. This small hotel close
to the beach and park has basic but pleasant
rooms with private bath and fan or a/c and also
a small casita with kitchenette and lounge. ❹

Hotel Villabosque ☎ & ⓕ777-0401, ⓦwww
.hotelvillabosque.com. Stay in clean, bright rooms
in a whitewashed villa with wicker chairs, private
hot-water bath and a/c. There's also a pleasant
outdoor reading and TV area, a good restaurant
and bar and a small swimming pool. ❺

Eating and drinking

Eating in Manuel Antonio is notoriously expensive and the area's few reasonably
priced **restaurants**, such as *El Mono Azul* and *Mar y Sombra*, are understandably popular. The more upmarket hotels all have on-site restaurants, some are
excellent and most quite pricey. A number of Manuel Antonio places close or
have restricted hours in the rainy season – ask at La Buena Nota (see p.314)
for up-to-date info. At the more popular places – including *Plinio*, *Karola's* and
Vela Bar – call or stop by to make a **reservation**, especially on weekends and
during high season. For a lively night out, try the stylish **bar** and **nightclub**
Jungle Room, signposted just off the main road. *Cockatoo Bar* attracts a mixed
gay and straight crowd. If you fancy dancing inside a natural grotto, try the *Bat
Cave* near the *El Parador* hotel.

Between Quepos and Manuel Antonio

El Avión Near *Hotel Villa Roca* ☎777-3378. Dine
or drink inside an old aircraft once used for 1980s
arms-trafficking at the appropriately named "The
Plane" restaurant. In truth, dining is more enjoyable
in the open-air section, with sensational views, but
the whole place exudes character. The menu includes
corvina in avocado sauce and surf 'n turf specials.

Barba Roja Next to *Divisimar Hotel*, on the
road to Manuel Antonio, about 2.5km west of
park entrance. This friendly, perennially popular
restaurant dishes up top-quality American cuisine,
including grilled fish, nachos, steaks, chunky
burgers and desserts. Or, just come to nurse a
quiet drink while watching the sunset.

Café Milagro Opposite the *Barba Roja*. Start your
day with one of the best breakfasts in town, served
as bright and early as 6.30am. Enjoy delicious
pastries washed down with excellent locally roasted
coffee and a superlative cappuccino.

La Cantina Across from the *Costa Verde* hotel.
American-style open-air bar with live music most
nights and fresh but pricey seafood (fish dishes
for $8–10 or jumbo prawns for $15). If you're not
flush, just go for the beer and music. There's also
Internet access in an old railway carriage.

Karola's Near *Barba Roja*. Tuck into Mexican
cuisine – from burritos and seafood to vegetarian

dishes – and top it off with a macadamia nut pie
that has entered local food legend. Closed Wed
and in low season.

Pedro Miguel In *Cabinas Pedro Miguel*, signposted
as soon as you leave Quepos. Wonderful, open-air
do-it-yourself barbecue restaurant with rough-hewn
wooden tables and chairs, set right next to the
forest. Choose your cut of meat or fish, then cook it
on the outdoor grill. It's extremely popular, and loads
of fun. Open Dec–April only.

Plinio In *Plinio Hotel* ☎777-0055. Quite simply,
Plinio stands out as one of the best restaurants in
the country. The menu has a distinct Asian slant,
including aromatic Thai soups, curries, stir-fries
and a good selection of Chilean wines. Main dishes
cost $8–10. Hang out at the relaxed bar and enjoy
good music.

Rainforest Restaurant In *El Mono Azul* hotel.
Dig into generous plates of chicken and fish
or try their tasty hamburgers, sandwiches and
pizza. There's a nightly film (the dinner and movie
special costs $8). Check out the shop next to the
restaurant – all proceeds go to a local project
run by children to preserve the rainforest and the
squirrel monkey habitat.

Rico Tico Grill In *Sí Como No* hotel. Enjoy superb
cuisine, including succulent fish brochettes, along
with exceptional cocktails and chilled fruit drinks
while seated poolside with a view over the ocean.
Breakfast also hits the spot and, if you're up early

6

Lifeguards at Playa Espadilla

Until recently very few of Costa Rica's beaches had **lifeguards** (in Spanish, *guardavivas*). Like most South and Central American countries graced with good beaches, the nation lacks the resources to make them safe for swimmers. About two hundred people drown in Costa Rica every year – one of the highest rates in the world, and the country's second leading cause of accidental death after car crashes.

In 1993, members of the Quepos and Manuel Antonio business community contributed funds to form Costa Rica's first professional **surf rescue lifeguards**. This eleven-strong team of professionally trained locals who know the currents well has reduced the number of drownings to nearly zero. Before the lifeguards, the beach usually claimed between five to ten lives a year. Funds, donated by local businesses dependent on tourism, the US Lifesaving Association and the University of California's Ocean Initiative Group, are currently sufficient only to guard the beaches in **high season**, between December and April.

enough, comes with the added entertainment of squirrel monkeys and coatimundi that live in the trees in front of the restaurant.

Manuel Antonio village

Los Almendros In *Los Almendros* hotel. Try juicy grilled steaks and tasty Argentinian *empanadas* in this pleasant, open-air restaurant.

Café del Mar Right on the beach, this popular thatched *chiringuito* kiosk serves up salads and cold beers to thirsty swimmers and beach-goers. Chill-out music adds to the relaxing vibe.

Mar y Sombra Manuel Antonio village, 500m from the park entrance, on the beach. One of the most popular eateries in the village, the sprawling and

cheap *Mar y Sombra* sits in a shady palm grove on the beach and offers *típico* food including *casados* ($3) and the fried fillet of fish of the day, simply prepared in garlic and butter, with fried plantains and salad for $5. On the weekends, groove in the lively disco.

Restaurante Lobster Pulsing with music and occasionally live bands on the weekends, this cheerful terrace restaurant serves up fresh seafood, typical Costa Rican fare and ice-cold beer.

Vela Bar Manuel Antonio village. Dine on grilled fish, paella and an assortment of vegetarian dishes in this dark, thatched restaurant, the swankiest in the village.

Playa Espadilla

PLAYA ESPADILLA (also sometimes called Playa Primera or Playa Numero Uno) lies outside the park, just north of the park entrance near Manuel Antonio village. One of the most popular beaches in Costa Rica, Playa Espadilla boasts wide, smooth, light-grey sands and stunning sunsets. It's also quite dangerous and plagued by **rip tides** that travel between six and ten kilometres per hour. Even so, lots of people do swim here – or rather, paddle and wade – and live to tell the tale. Professional lifeguards now patrol in high season (see box, above), so it's considerably safer.

Parque Nacional Manuel Antonio

PARQUE NACIONAL MANUEL ANTONIO (Tues–Sun 7am–4pm; $7; ☎777-0644, ⓦwww.manuelantonio.com), some 150km southwest of San José as the crow flies, may be Costa Rica's smallest national park but it's by far one of the most popular. Considering the number of hotels and restaurants sidling up to the park's borders, one can easily imagine the fate that might have overtaken its limestone-white sands had it not been designated a national park in 1972. Even so, the park suffers from the high number of

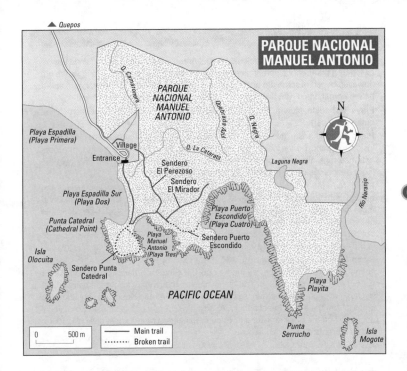

PARQUE NACIONAL MANUEL ANTONIO

Q. Camaronera

Quebrada Azul

Q. Negra

Playa Espadilla (Playa Primera)

Village

Entrance

Q. La Catarata

Sendero El Perezoso

Sendero El Mirador

Laguna Negra

Río Naranjo

Playa Espadilla Sur (Playa Dos)

Punta Catedral (Cathedral Point)

Playa Puerto Escondido (Playa Cuatro)

Sendero Puerto Escondido

Isla Olocuita

Sendero Punta Catedral

Playa Manuel Antonio (Playa Tres)

PACIFIC OCEAN

Playa Playita

0   500 m

——— Main trail
········· Broken trail

Punta Serrucho

Isla Mogote

N

visitors and frequently reaches its quota of eight hundred visitors at any one time. The park closes on Mondays to give the animals a rest and the rangers and trail maintenance staff a chance to work.

Covering an area of only 6.8 square kilometres, Manuel Antonio preserves not only the lovely **beaches** and the unique *tómbolo* formation of Punta Catedral, but also **mangroves** and humid tropical **forest**. Visitors can only visit the section of the park facing the sea. The eastern *montaña*, or mountain section, off-limits to the public, is regularly patrolled by rangers to deter poaching, which is rife in the area, and incursions into the park from surrounding farmers and *campesinos*.

Rangers at Manuel Antonio know their terrain well and are happy to talk to you about the park if they're not too busy, telling fond stories about boa constrictors, and the antics of the *monos tití*, or **squirrel monkeys**. Manuel Antonio is one of the few remaining natural habitats for the creatures, whose cuteness is their own nemesis. Highly sought-after as pets and for zoos, they used to be prime targets for poachers. Smaller than their primate cousins – the howler, white-faced, spider and capuchin monkeys – they have close-set bright eyes and a delicate, white-haired face. You might spot squirrel monkeys along the park trails or outside the park in the Manuel Antonio area. Local schoolchildren have set up a project to build overhead wooden "bridges" for the monkeys to cross the increasingly busy road from Manuel Antonio to Quepos. Contributions are welcome – ask at the *Mono Azul* hotel for details. Besides being quiet, you can also help the squirrel monkeys by not feeding them (for which you can be fined) or leaving any litter.

The beaches in the Parque Nacional Manuel Antonio can be confusing, since they're called by a number of different names. It's important to know which beach you're on, however, because some are unsafe for swimming. To be sure, ask the rangers about beach conditions. From the north to the south the beaches are as follows:

Playa Espadilla (see p.318; also called Playa Primera or Playa Numero Uno); outside the park.

Playa Espadilla Sur (also called Playa Dos or Playa Segunda) is the first beach inside the park, on the north side of Punta Catedral. The main trail from the park entrance runs along the back of this beach. While usually fairly calm, it's also the most dangerous in rough conditions. Beware the currents.

Playa Manuel Antonio (also called Playa Tres or Playa Blanca) is by far the best swimming beach. Immediately south of Punta Catedral, it's in a deeper and more protected bay than the others, though you can still get clobbered by the deceptively gentle-looking waves as they hit the shore – be careful getting in and out. Unfortunately it's quite narrow and can get crowded. The best time to come is in the early morning, before 10am.

Playa Puerto Escondido (also called Playa Cuatro) is a pretty, white horseshoe-shaped beach that can be reached along the Sendero Puerto Escondido. Don't set out for this beach without first checking with the rangers about the *marea* (tide) because at high tide you can't get across Playa Puerto Escondido, nor can you cross it from the dense forest behind. At best it will be a waste of time; at worst you'll get cut off on the other side for a few hours. Rangers advise against swimming here, as the currents can be dangerous.

You also have a good chance of seeing other **smaller mammals**, such as the raccoon, coati, agouti, two-toed sloth and white-faced capuchin monkey. The abundant **birdlife** includes the shimmering green kingfisher, the brown pelican, who can often be seen fishing off the rocks, and the laughing falcon. Beware the snakes that drape themselves over the trails and look like vines – be careful what you grab onto. Big iguanas hang out near the beaches, often standing stock-still for ten minutes at a time, providing good photo opportunities.

The **green turtle**, or llora, has probably nested in the Manuel Antonio area for thousands of years. At low tide at the south end of Playa Manuel Antonio, rangers can show you stones that they believe were used as turtle traps by the indigenous peoples of the area. Rangers have recently set up a project to preserve the area as a nesting ground for the green turtle to try and increase the species' dangerously low numbers.

The **climate** is hot, humid and wet, all year round. Though the rains ease off in the dry season (Dec–April), they never disappear entirely. The average year-round temperature is 27°C, and it can easily get to 30°C and above – take lots of water on the trails. There's usually a vendor selling water and soft drinks on Playa Manuel Antonio.

The trails

The **park entrance** marks the south end of Playa Espadilla. Manuel Antonio has a tiny system of short **trails**, all easy, except when it's rainy and they can get slippery. Nearest to the entrance lies the short **Sendero La Catarata** (500m) that leads to a small, pretty waterfall, after which the trail is named. From here, you can continue towards Playa Manuel Antonio on the main trail – check out the massive giant bamboo on the left-hand side. You may spot sloths in the eucalyptus trees that line the trail, and occasionally monkeys. The trail runs along the back of the long **Espadilla Sur** beach, also called **Playa Dos**. It's usually calm and less crowded than the main park beach, Playa Manuel Antonio, but isn't often supervised, so be careful of currents.

While many people flop down on the beaches once they reach the end of the main trail, it's worth pushing on and embarking on the **Sendero Punta Catedral** (1.4km), a loop around Punta Catedral with a wonderful view of the Pacific, dotted with jagged-edged little islands. Note that the hilly terrain means it can get treacherous at times, and rangers sometimes close it completely. After following the full loop of this trail, you'll come to the beachside trail that rings **Playa Manuel Antonio** (also known as Playa Tres or Playa Blanca), the park's best swimming beach and, predictably, the most crowded. At the end of Playa Manuel Antonio you can either go inland on the **Sendero El Mirador** (1.3km) or take a beachside trail, **Sendero Playa Gemalas y Puerto Escondido** (1.6km), that heads through relatively dense humid tropical forest cover, crossing a small creek before eventually reaching rocky Playa Puerto Escondido (Playa Cuatro). You can clamber across Playa Puerto Escondido at low tide – but check tide times with the rangers before leaving to avoid getting cut off.

Practicalities

Buses from Quepos and San José drop passengers off 200m before the park entrance. If you're staying at a hotel between the park and Quepos, and want to travel by **taxi**, it's cheaper to flag one down on the road rather than calling from the hotel. If you're driving, note that you'll be charged $2.50 to leave your car at one of the supervised lots on the road loop at the end of Manuel Antonio village, or anywhere on the main street.

There have been problems with **theft** in Manuel Antonio, usually as a result of people leaving valuables (like cameras) on the beach. The rangers, who often sit at the picnic tables, might be able to look after your stuff (though they do it only as a favour; it's not actually part of their job.) Take care also if walking alone in the park; a number of robberies have been reported. Although rangers often patrol the park, by law they can't deny entrance to the park to anyone. Both Playa Espadilla Sur and Playa Manuel Antonio have toilets and showers.

You can take guided **tours** with park-accredited guides for $15 per person. The informative guides speak English and have sophisticated binoculars to help spot animals. Enquire at the park entrance, or ask your hotel to ring the park office to reserve a guide. Be aware that when you leave your car in the parking area in Manuel Antonio village you may be approached by "guides" offering their services at the same price as the official park guides. These shysters have been known to rob their clients while in the park. The park-accredited guides carry photo ID, so ask to see it before hiring one on.

Travel details

Buses

Jacó to: Puntarenas (4 daily; 1hr 15m); Quepos (4 daily; 1hr 15min); San José (5 daily; 2hr 30min–3hr).

Montezuma to: Paquera (6 daily; 1hr); Cabo Blanco (5 daily; 20min).

Paquera to: Montezuma (6 daily; 1hr); Tambor (6 daily; 40min).

Puntarenas to: Liberia (7 daily; 3hr); Quepos

(4 daily; 3hr); San José (14 daily; 2hr); Santa Elena (1 daily; 3hr 30min).

Quepos to: Jacó (4 daily; 1hr 15min–2hr); Puntarenas (4 daily; 3hr); San Isidro (2 daily; 3hr 30min plus); San José (9 daily; 3hr 30min–5hr).

San José to: Jacó (5 daily; 2hr 30min–3hr); Manuel Antonio (5 daily; 3hr 30min); Santa Elena (2 daily; 4–5hr); Puntarenas (14 daily; 2hr); Quepos (9 daily; 3hr 30min–5hr).

Santa Elena to: Las Juntas (2 daily; 2hr); Puntarenas (1 daily; 3hr 30min); San José (2 daily; 4–5hr); Tilarán (1 daily; 3hr).

Tilarán to: Santa Elena (1 daily; 3hr).

Ferries

Naranjo to: Puntarenas (6 daily; 1hr 15min).
Paquera to: Puntarenas (14 daily; 1hr).

Puntarenas to: Paquera (14 daily; 1hr).
Puntarenas to: Naranjo (6 daily; 1hr 15m).

Flights (Sansa)

Quepos to: San José (6 daily high season, 3–4 in low season; 25min).
San José to: Quepos (6 daily high season, 3–4 in low season; 25 min); Tambor (2 daily; 30min).
Tambor to: San José (2 daily; 30min).

Flights (NatureAir)

Quepos to: San José (4 daily; 25min).
San José to: Quepos (4 daily; 25min); Tambor (2 daily; 30min)
Tambor to: San José (2 daily; 30min).

The Zona Sur

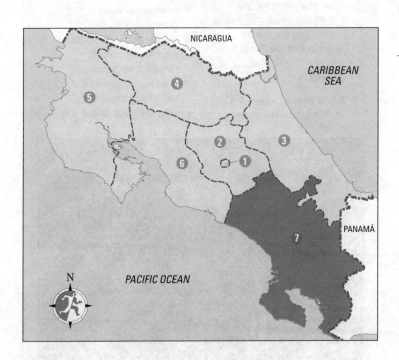

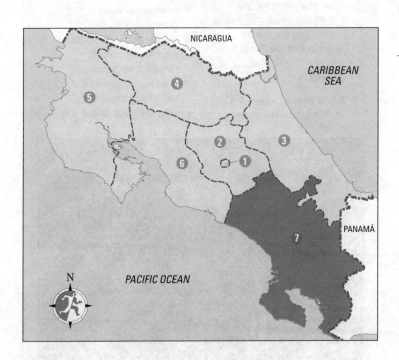

NICARAGUA

CARIBBEAN SEA

4

5

2

3

6

1

PANAMÁ

7

N

PACIFIC OCEAN

THE ZONA SUR

7

Highlights

△ Pineapples

The Zona Sur

osta Rica's **Zona Sur** (southern zone) is the country's least-known region, both for Ticos and for visitors, though tourism has increased significantly in recent years. The geographically diverse Zona Sur encompasses the high mountain peaks of the Cordillera de Talamanca at its northern edge, the agricultural heartland of the Valle de El General, the river-cut lowlands of the Valle de Diquis around Palmar and the coffee-growing Valle de Coto Brus, near the border with Panamá. The region is particularly popular with hikers, many of whom come to climb Cerro Chirripó in the Talamancas – one of the highest peaks in Central America – set in the chilly, rugged terrain of the **Parque Nacional Chirripó**. Experienced walkers also venture into the giant neighbouring **Parque Internacional La Amistad**, a UNESCO Biosphere Reserve and World Heritage Site that protects an enormous but largely inaccessible tract of land along Costa Rica's southern border.

Halfway down the region's Pacific coast, the **Playa Dominical** area was originally a surfing destination, but its tropical beauty now draws an ever-increasing number of visitors (not to mention property developers), especially since road improvements have made it accessible without a 4WD. Further south down the coast, the **Península de Osa** is the site of the **Parque Nacional Corcovado**, one of the country's prime rainforest hiking destinations, whose soaring canopy trees constitute the last chunk of tropical wet forest on the entire Pacific side of the Central American isthmus. The Península de Osa is also home to the remote and picturesque **Bahía Drake**, from where tours depart to the nearby **Reserva Biológica Isla del Caño**, scattered with the lithic spheres fashioned by the local Diquis. On the opposite side of the Golfo Dulce from the Península de Osa, near the border with Panamá, is **Golfito**, the only town of any size in the region, and one that suffered from an unsavoury reputation for years after the pull-out of the United Brands fruit company's banana operations in 1985. It has been attracting more visitors of late since being made a tax-free zone for manufactured goods from Panamá, though for foreign visitors it's more useful as a base from which to move on to the Península de Osa and Corcovado.

Despite the region's profusion of basic, inexpensive **accommodation**, you may find yourself spending more money than you bargained for simply because of the time, distance and planning involved in getting to many of the region's more beautiful spots – this is particularly true if you stay in one of the very comfortable private **rainforest lodges** in the Osa, Golfito and Bahía Drake areas. Many people prefer to take a package rather than travel independently, and travellers who stay at the rainforest lodges often choose to fly in. Bear

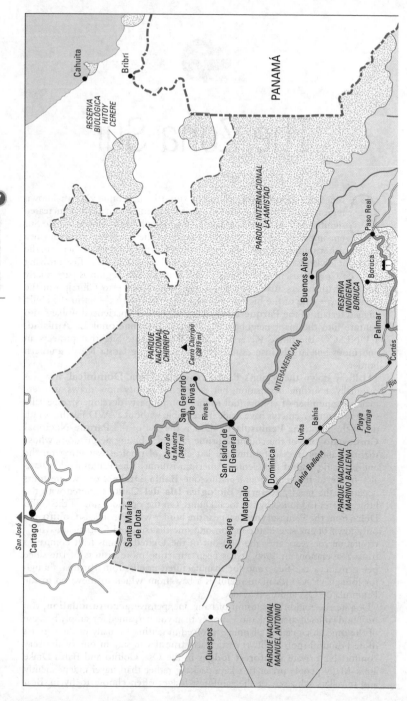

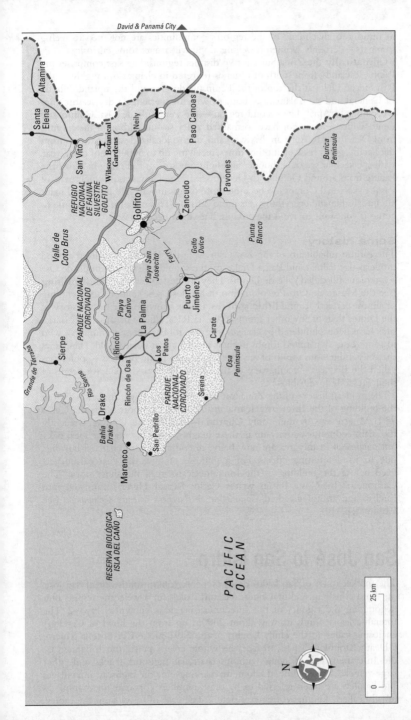

PACIFIC
OCEAN

in mind, too, that many of the region's communities are not used to seeing strangers – certainly women travelling alone will attract some curiosity.

Climatically the Zona Sur has two distinct regions. The first comprises the Pacific lowlands, from south of Quepos (covered in chapter 6) roughly to the Río Sierpe Delta at the top of the Península de Osa, and the upland Valle de El General and the Talamancas, both of which experience a dry season from December to April. The second region – the Península de Osa, Golfito and Golfo Dulce – does not have so marked a dry season (although the months from December to April are less wet) and, due to localized wind patterns from the Pacific, gets very wet at other times, receiving up to 5000mm of rain a year, with spectacular seasonal thunder and lightning storms cantering in across the Pacific from around October to December. In the rainy season, some parts of Parque Nacional Corcovado become more or less unwalkable, local mud roads are undrivable and everything gets more difficult. This makes it a good time to come if you want to avoid the crowds, but you'll need a 4WD.

Some history

The earliest inhabitants of the Zona Sur were the **Diquis**, who lived around modern-day Palmar and Bahía Drake, on the shoulder of the Península de Osa – a region still called Valle de Diquis. They are best known for **goldsmithing** (see the Museo de Oro Precolombino in San José, p.81) and for their crafting of almost perfectly round **lithic spheres**. Less is known of the early history of the Diquis than of any other group in Costa Rica, chiefly because their burial sites have been plundered by *huaqueros* (grave-robbers/treasure hunters), who in some cases dynamited tombs in their zeal to get at buried gold. These days the only indigenous group of any size in the area is the Borucas – sometimes called the Bruncas – a subgroup of the Diquis. (See box, p.358, for details of their Fiesta de los Diablos.)

The modern history of the Zona Sur has been defined by its isolation. Before the building of the **Interamericana** in the 1950s, transport across the Cerro de la Muerte was by mule only. **Charcoal-burning** was until very recently the main economic activity up in these heights, using the majestic local oaks, but *campesinos* in the area are now being discouraged from charcoal-burning, due to its deforesting effects. For a glimpse of how the charcoal-burners lived before the building of the Interamericana, read the short story "The Carbonero" by Costa Rican writer Carlos Salazar Herera, translated into English and anthologized in *Costa Rica: A Traveller's Literary Companion* (see Contexts, p.410).

San José to San Isidro

The market town of San Isidro de El General, 136km southwest of San José, sits amid a lush agricultural landscape, and makes for a welcome respite after negotiating the rigours of the Interamericana, also known as Hwy-2. The Interamericana winds its way about 2000m up from the bowl of Cartago's enclosing valley to the chilly heights of the 3491-metre Cerro de la Muerte ("Death Mountain") pass. In fact, the whole area is pretty much defined by the Interamericana, heaving with international transport trucks and other large vehicles. Yellow-topped kilometre markings line the highway, and villages and hamlets are often referred to by these numbers (Briseño, for example, is usually called "kilómetro treinta y siete"). The ease of travel from the capital, via Cartago, to San Isidro depends on the current condition of the highway. Rock- and mudslides are frequent and there have been isolated reports of drivers being flagged down and robbed by bandits, although this normally happens to intercontinental truckers rather than tourists. Still, it's not a good idea to drive at night – not just because of the chance of robbery, but more crucially because of reduced visibility. Fog, mist and rain are a constant threat at all times, and the road lacks shoulder or meridian markings. The biggest problem you'll likely face, though, are the long tailbacks caused by lack of overtaking opportunities. Ticos frequently risk life and limb passing large trucks on blind corners, but don't be tempted to follow suit – Costa Rica has one of the world's highest road-accident rates. Ardent quetzal spotters should note that the chilly approaches to the Cerro de la Muerte pass are the most reliable place to spot the birds, who like these untouched high-altitude cloudforests. Several places are well set up for spotting, which is best in nesting season (March–June).

About 60km south of San José, the *Albergue de Montaña Tapantí* (☎290-7641, ℱ232-0436; ❺) enjoys a fantastic setting high on a ridge, with warm and comfortable bungalow-like chalets equipped with private bath and hot water. The lodge also hosts unique small-scale **cultural tours** of the area, where for $10 you can spend the morning with a local *campesino* family (who receive the entire fee) and find out about local farming methods, tour smallholdings, perhaps do a bit of trout fishing and watch milk being churned into cheese.

Ten kilometres further, on a side road to the right at kilometre 70, the *Albergue Mirador de Quetzales* (☎ & ℱ 381-8456; ❸) is run by a local family

---

The Diquis

Very little is known about the history of the **Diquis region** before 1000 BC, though culturally it appears to have formed part of the Greater Chiriquí region, which takes its name from the province in southwestern Panamá. Archeologists date the famous **lithic spheres** (see box on p.340) from sometime between 1000 BC and 500 AD; between around 700 and 1600 AD the Diquis began fashioning **gold** pendants, breastplates, headbands and chains, becoming master goldsmiths within a hundred years or so. Between 500 and 800 AD drastic changes occurred in the culture of the Diquis. Archeologists attribute them to the impact of the arrival of sea-going peoples from Colombia or possibly the Andes – a theory borne out by their metates and pottery, which show llama or guanaco figures, animals that would have been unknown on the isthmus. In the Diquis's own artisanry, both the ingenious – often cheeky – goldwork and the voluptuous pottery display a unique humour as well as superlative attention to detail.

The Diquis were in a state of constant **warfare** among themselves and with foreign groups. Like the Chorotegas to the north in Greater Nicoya, they seem to have engaged in sacrifice, ritually beheading war captives. Huge metates unearthed at Barilles in Panamá show images of these rituals, while smaller crucible-like dishes – in which coca leaves, yucca or maize may have been crushed and fermented – suggest ritual inebriation.

The indigenous peoples of Zona Sur first met the Spaniards in 1522 when the cacique of the Térraba group graciously hosted Captain **Gil González** for a fortnight. González was on his way from near the present-day Panamá border, where his ship had run aground, to Nicaragua. Despite infirmity (he was in his fifties), he was walking all the way. The Diquis seem to have declined abruptly after this initial contact, most likely felled by influenza, smallpox, the plague and other diseases brought by Spanish settlers.

who have many of the quetzals' favourite trees on their land. They offer guided hikes and special quetzal-spotting outings at 6am daily ($6 per person). The *albergue* itself is cosy and reasonably priced, with an eight-room lodge (shared bathrooms) and several wooden cabinas with private baths. You can enjoy delicious home-cooked meals for about $10 extra.

A little less than 20km further on, a turn-off leads to the lovely hamlet of **San Gerardo de Dota** – you'll need a 4WD to get here, since the road down from the Interamericana is treacherously steep in parts. In the village, the *Hotel de Montaña Savegre* (☎740-1028, Ⓕ740-1027, ⓦwww.savegre.co.cr; ➎ including all meals) is well known among birders for the number of quetzals that nest on or near its property. The very friendly *dueños* have trail maps, can arrange guides (which cost extra) and offer bird-spotting tips, trout-fishing trips in the Río Savegre and horse-riding through the village. Close by, the *Trogon Lodge* (☎295-8181, Ⓕ239-7657, ⓦwww.grupomawamba.com; ➎) has comfortable cabins (despite being heated, they can still get chilly at night) and immaculate grounds, with several trout ponds and marked trails through the woods. There are also normally many quetzals to be seen around here (Marcelina Mata Martinez is a recommended birding guide). Both hotels offer a transfer service from San José. If you're on a tight budget, *Cabinas El Quetzal* (no phone; ➋) in the centre of the village has simple rooms in a family home.

San Isidro and the Valle de El General

The spectacular descent into **SAN ISIDRO DE EL GENERAL**, just 702m above sea level, brings you halfway back into tropical climes after the chilly ride over Cerro de la Muerte. In Costa Rica, San Isidro is regarded as an increasingly attractive place to live, with its clean, country-town atmosphere. While the Talamancas are a non-volcanic range – and the Valle de El General therefore lacks the incredibly fertile soils of the Valle Central – there is still considerable local agricultural activity, and pineapples grow particularly well. The town hosts an **agricultural fair** in the first week in February on the Parque Central, when farmers don their finery, put their produce up for competition and sell fresh food in the streets. May is the **month of San Isidro** – patron saint of farmers and animals – and is celebrated by fiestas, ox-cart parades, dog shows and the erection of gaudy ferris wheels. The town's one museum, the **Museo Regional del Sur** (Tues–Sat 8am–4.30pm in theory), is 75m northwest of the modern church on the Parque Central's eastern side. The **museum** is devoted to the *campesino* history of the area and features occasional displays of local artwork.

Practicalities

San Isidro's main **bus terminal** is adjacent to the town's central market at Av 6, C 0/2, but most buses from here head to local destinations. To and from San José, TRACOPA buses stop right on the Interamericana at the corner of C 2, while MUSA buses pick up passengers across the road. The Banco Nacional on the main square changes **travellers' cheques** and has an **ATM**, as does the Banco de Costa Rica on Av 4, C 0. There are two **Internet cafés** on the main square (BTC Internet and Brunca Café Internet) and you'll find the correo on C 1, Av 6/8.

Of the budget choices in town, the best **accommodation** is at the large *Chirripó*, C 1, Av 2/4 (☎771-0529; ➊), which has simple rooms with private bath and hot shower, a decent restaurant and free parking. The *Hotel del Sur* (☎771-3033, Ⓕ771-0527; ➍) is set in quiet, pleasant grounds about 6km

Moving on from San Isidro

If you're travelling **south** from San Isidro to Palmar (2 daily; 4hr), Golfito (2 daily; 5hr) or Paso Canoas (2 daily; 6hr), it's better to get a bus that originates in San Isidro rather than one that's coming through from San José, as they're often full and you could find yourself standing all the way to Panamá. If you want to try for one of the through-services, visit TRACOPA's ticket office (Mon–Sat 7am–4pm) at C 3 and the Interamericana; you can buy tickets if there are seats available, and schedules are posted telling you what time the buses pass through town. Buses for **Quepos** (4 daily; 3hr 30min) and **Dominical** (4 daily; 40min–1hr) leave from the terminal known locally as Y Griega, at the corner of C 2 and the Interamericana. Buses for **San Gerardo de Rivas** leave at 5am and 2pm (1hr 40min) from the El Mercado bus terminal at Av 6, C 0/2. For all local services, buy your ticket on the bus.

southwest of San Isidro on the Interamericana and has en-suite rooms, tennis courts, a swimming pool and a good restaurant.

The fresh and amazingly varied local produce is put to good use, and San Isidro has several worthwhile places to **eat**. The best place for breakfast is the café at the *Hotel Chirripó*, which serves *gallo pinto* and toast and eggs with excellent local coffee daily from 6.30am. Almost next door is the *Taquería Mexico Linda,* a brightly decorated and cheerful little café with delicious Mexican food. For superb seafood, try *Marisquería Marea Baja* on C 2, Av 4/6 or put together your own meal at the bustling Mercado Central on C 2, Av 4/6.

Information about the Parque Nacional Chirripó and Parque Internacional La Amistad is available from the regional office of the national parks service (Mon–Fri 8am–4pm; ☎771-3155, ☏771-3297, ✉acla-p@ns.minae.go.cr) at C 2, Av 4/6, south of the Parque Central. It's worth stopping off here to ask about current conditions and, if possible, to make reservations for Chirripó (see below). On C 4, Av 1/3 are the offices of **CIPROTUR** (☎771-6096, ☏771-2003, ⊛www.ecotourism.co.cr), a non-profit organization that promotes tourism in the Zona Sur. The helpful staff can book hotel rooms and answer queries and it's worth checking out their informative website before you set off.

Parque Nacional Chirripó

Some 20km northeast of San Isidro, **PARQUE NACIONAL CHIRRIPÓ** is named after the Cerro Chirripó, which lies at its centre – at 3819m the highest peak in Central America south of Guatemala. Ever since the conquest of the peak in 1904 by a missionary priest, Father Agustín Blessing (local indigenous peoples may of course have climbed it before), visitors have been flocking to Chirripó to do the same, finding accommodation in nearby **San Gerardo de Rivas**.

The park's terrain varies widely, according to altitude, from cloudforest to rocky mountaintops. Between the two lies the interesting alpine **páramo** – high moorland, punctuated by rocks, shrubs and hardy clump grasses more usually associated with Andean heights. Colours are muted yellows and browns, with the occasional deep purple. Below the *páramo* lie areas of **oak forest**, now much depleted through continued charcoal-burning. Chirripó is also the only place in Costa Rica where you can observe vestiges of the **glaciers** that scraped across here about thirty thousand years ago: narrow, U-shaped valleys, moraines (heaps of rock and soil left behind by retreating glaciers) and

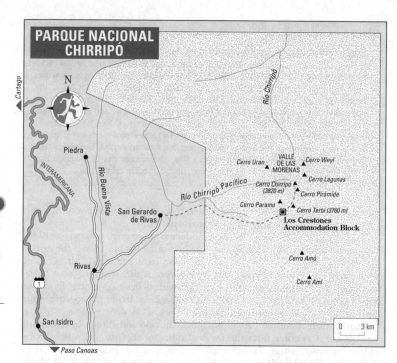

glacial lakes, as well as the distinctive **crestones**, or heavily weathered fingers of rock, more reminiscent of Montana than Costa Rica. The land is generally waterlogged, with a few bogs – take care where you step, as sometimes it's so chilly you won't want to get your feet wet.

Many **mammals** live in the park, and you may see spider monkeys as you climb from the lower montane to the montane rainforest. Your best bet for **bird-spotting** is in the lower elevations: along the oak and cloudforest sections of the trail you may spot hawks, trogons, woodpeckers and even quetzals, though in the cold and inhospitable terrain higher up, you'll only see robins and hawks.

The **weather** in Chirripó is extremely variable and unpredictable. It can be hot, humid and rainy between May and December, but is clearer and drier between January and April (the peak season for climbing the mountain). Even then, clouds may roll in at the top and obscure the view, and rainstorms move in very fast. The only months you can be sure of a dry spell are March and April. **Temperatures** may drop to below 0°C at night and rise to 20°C during the day, though at the summit, it's so cold that it's hard to believe you're just 9° north of the equator.

San Gerardo de Rivas

The tiny town of **SAN GERARDO DE RIVAS**, 17km northeast of San Isidro and 3km west of the park, is home to a park puesto and several very reasonably priced, friendly **places to stay**, and most climbers spend a night here before heading into the park; try to get somewhere with **hot water**, as it can get very cold at night. There are also a couple of attractive family-run hotels a few kilometres further back down the road towards San Isidro in the village of **Rivas**. Many of the places listed below rent out camping equipment like sleeping bags and cooking stoves. You'll find several decent places **to eat** in San Gerardo, the best of which is the *Restaurante El Bosque*, with tasty *bocas* as well as *casados*, table football and gorgeous views over the river below.

Accommodation

Albergue de Montaña Talari Rivas ⊤ & ⓕ 771-0341, ⓔtalaripz@racsa.co.cr. Eight neat en-suite rooms, set in twenty acres of tranquil riverside forest, with walking trails, a swimming pool and an excellent restaurant. They also offer reasonable packages to Chirripó ($215 for four nights). ❹

Albergue Vista al Cerro San Gerardo de Rivas ⊤373-3365 or 771-1866, ⓕ771-0341. Friendly guesthouse near the park entrance with immaculate dormitory accommodation and shared bathroom with hot water, plus a restaurant that opens at 3am for climbers wishing to make an early start; they also arrange tours. ❶

Cabinas El Descanso San Gerardo de Rivas ⊤375-3752, ⓔeldescanso@ecotourism.co.cr. Private house close to the ranger station with 12 basic rooms, a shared bathroom with hot water, an excellent vegetarian restaurant, horses for hire and free transport to the park entrance, 3km away. ❶

Hotel y Restaurante Roca Dura San Gerardo de Rivas ⊤771-1866, ⓔluisrocadura@hotmail.com. Seven smallish but clean rooms (one is built into the large slab of rock after which the hotel is named), some with private bath and hot water. The café and restaurant are a hive of activity. ❶–❷

Hotel y Restaurante Urán San Gerardo de Rivas ⊤388-2333, ⓕ771-1669, ⓦwww.hoteluran.com. Neat, tidy and convenient, the *Urán* sits just 75m from the start of the main Chirripó Trail. Thirteen small rooms come with shared bathrooms ($7) and eight slightly bigger ones have private bathrooms; all rooms have hot water. They offer free pick-up from the ranger station and the on-site restaurant serves up big platefuls of good, solid Tico food – the perfect preparation for a long day's hike. ❶

Rancho La Botija del Sur Rivas ⊤ & ⓕ770-2146. Eight cabinas with pretty bamboo ceilings, plus a fresh-water swimming pool and a viewing tower overlooking the farm's coffee and banana plantations. Several large stones carved with indigenous patterns have been discovered on the property, and can be seen on a daily tour (7am–9am; $5 per person). ❺

Visiting the park

Visiting the Parque Nacional Chirripó requires advance planning. First you have to **reserve a place**, since no more than forty hikers are allowed in the park at any one time, and demand far outstrips capacity in the popular travel seasons (around March and April, especially Easter, and Christmas) – although there are sometimes cancellations. When making reservations you should state your preferred dates, bearing in mind that it's not possible to book for the high season (which starts in January) before November 1. Most hikers find two or three nights sufficient. You may have to pay in advance (by money transfer) and in full – $15 for two days, $10 for every day after that plus $10 per night for accommodation.

To reserve a place, call or visit either the Fundación de Parques Nacionales office in San José (see p.68) or the regional parks office in San Isidro (see p.331). You can't officially make a reservation at the park's puesto in San Gerardo and if you turn up without one, you'll most likely be turned away. Even with a reservation you're required to check in at the puesto; this regulation also applies if you're heading for the camping trail that starts from Herradura.

If you're not camping you must stay in the **accommodation block** at Los Crestones, which has fifteen rooms (each sleeping four people), cold showers, a cooking area and a big sink where you can wash clothes. It's also now possible to **camp** in the park, although this takes a bit more planning. You'll need to make a special reservation, hire a local guide (obligatory; $25 per day for up to ten people; $50 for groups of 10–16) in the nearby hamlet of Herradura (ask at the *pulpería* for recommendations or the puesto in San Gerardo) and enter the park from Herradura. The trail to the summit of Chirripó via the campsite is longer and more arduous than the more common trek via the accommodation block at Los Crestones – you'll need a minimum of three days. Note if you're camping that no fires are allowed in the park; forest fires frequently devastate the area, some caused by improperly put-out campfires.

While Chirripó is hot at midday, it frequently drops to freezing at the higher altitudes at night. You should bring **warm clothing** (temperatures can fall to –7°C at night) and a proper **sleeping bag** (though these can be rented on-site), a blanket, water, food and a propane gas stove. A short list of clothing and other essentials might include a good pair of boots, socks, long trousers, T-shirt, shirt, sweater, woolly hat and jacket, lots of insect repellent, sunglasses, first aid (for cuts and scratches), gloves (for rocks and the cold), binoculars and a torch – the accommodation huts only have electricity between 6pm and 8pm.

Detailed contour **maps** of the park are available from the Instituto Geográfico (see p.18) in San José, who sell four maps covering the entire climb. Otherwise, the staff at the entrance puesto can supply you with an adequate map of the park, showing some altitude markings. You can also hire a horse to carry your gear up to the accommodation huts. The services of a **guide** can be useful and interesting in helping to identify local species and interpreting the landscapes you pass through – again, ask at the entrance puesto for recommendations.

Cerro Chirripó

Almost everyone who climbs Chirripó goes up to the accommodation huts first, rests there overnight, and then takes another day or two to explore the summit, surrounding peaks and *páramo* – it's not really feasible to climb Chirripó in one day. During high season, you'll have company on the path up the mountain, and the trail is well marked with signs stating the altitude and the distance to the summit. Watch out for **altitude sickness**, though; if you have made a quick ascent from the lowland beach areas, you could find yourself becoming short of breath, experiencing pins and needles, nausea and exhaustion. If this happens, stop and rest; if symptoms persist, descend immediately. The main thing to keep in mind is **not to go off the trail** or exploring on your own without telling anyone, especially in the higher areas of the park. Off the trail, definite landmarks are few, and it's easy to get confused.

The **hike** begins at 1219m and ends at 3819m, the summit. It's almost entirely uphill and so exhausting that you may have trouble appreciating the scenery. On the first day most hikers make the extremely strenuous fourteen-kilometre trek to the accommodation huts – reckon on a minimum of seven hours if you're very fit (and the weather is good), up to twelve hours or more if you're not. You may be able to hire a horse to carry your gear for you (around $60 per 20kg). On the second day you can make the huts your base while you hike to the summit and back, which is easily done in a day, perhaps taking in some of the nearby lagoons.

The walk begins in a cow pasture, before passing through thick, dark cloudforest, a good place to spot **quetzals** (March–May are the best months). After a relatively flat stretch of several kilometres, where you're likely to be plagued by various biting insects, you'll arrive at a **rest station** halfway to the accommodation huts. Some people stay here, splitting the hike into a less-taxing two days, but conditions are extremely rustic, with three sides open to the wind. The **Cuesta de los Arrepentidos** ("Hill of the Repentants", meaning you're sorry at this point that you came) is the real push, all uphill for at least 3km. At **Monte Sin Fé** ("Faithless Mountain"), about 10km into the trail, is another patch of tropical montane forest, more open than the cloudforest. Keep your eye out for the *refugio natural*, a big cave where you can sleep in an emergency, from where it's just 3km to the **accommodation huts**. At the huts, the land looks like a greener version of Scotland: bare moss cover, grasslands and a waterlogged area where the lagoons congregate. There are no trees, and little wildlife in evidence.

The **rangers** based up here are friendly, and in the high season (Jan–April) you can ask to accompany them on walks near the summit to avoid getting lost. Do not *expect* this, however, as it is not their job to lead guided walks. It's just ninety minutes' walk from the accommodation huts along a well-marked trail to **the summit** – there's a bit of scrambling involved, but no real climbing. You'll need to set off by dawn, as clear weather at the peak is really only guaranteed until 9 or 10am. There's also a little book in a metal box where you can sign your "I did it" message; bring a pen. From the top, if it's clear, you can see right across to the Pacific. However, you're above the cloud line up here, and the surrounding mountains are often obscured by drifting milky clouds.

Dominical

The popular surfing town of **DOMINICAL**, 44km southeast of Quepos and 25km southwest of San Isidro, may represent the face of things to come along this stretch of the Pacific coast. Previously a secluded fishing village, it has, since the recent paving of the coastal road and the laying down of electricity and phone lines, begun to expand dramatically. A glut of new hotels, shops and restaurants have opened in town, while the coastal areas to the south, still largely made up of unspoilt stretches of beach and rainforest, are rapidly being bought up by hungry property developers and hotel chains. The fear expressed by many locals is that the area is destined to become the country's next Manuel Antonio (see p.309). Should the proposed paving of the Quepos–Dominical road go ahead as planned in the next few years, then the arrival of full-scale mass tourism, and all its attendant environmental problems, is surely only a matter of time.

Today, Dominical stands on the cusp of change. Despite its recent growth, the town is still relatively small with just a few dirt-track roads, though lined with scores of (mainly American-owned) cabinas and budget hotels. Its emergence as a tourist destination has, however, been confirmed by the opening of a smart new **tourist office** (ⓔinfocenter@dominical.biz) in a purpose-built building at the northern edge of town. The office also has an Internet café and, perhaps most significantly for the area's future, the offices of the Central Pacific Land Company. In addition to providing information on the local area, the tourist office also holds a wealth of literature on the entire Zona Sur region making it well worth stopping by even if you're not planning on staying in Dominical.

Nowadays any vehicle *should* be able to make the trip to and around Dominical, although it makes sense to rent a 4WD if you want to explore the surrounding area. **From San José** it is more convenient and faster to come via San Isidro; **from Guanacaste** and the Central Pacific, it's best to take the largely unpaved (and very bumpy) road south from Quepos. **Buses** from Quepos arrive daily at around 6.30am and 3pm, and continue to San Isidro (2hr). Buses from San Isidro go on to Uvita. You can **change money** at the San Clemente Bar and Grill, which is also the town's post office.

Accommodation

There's a broad range of good accommodation in the Dominical area. In the town itself, most lodgings are basic and cater to the surfing community, but you'll also find a number of more upmarket places, usually owned by foreigners. The most expensive hotels include some wonderful hideaways, good for honeymooners, romantics and escapists. There are also a string of hotels and self-catering lodges along the coast road towards Uvita.

Dominical

Cabinas San Clemente Down the main street and on the beach to the right ☎787-0026, ⒻⓀ787-0158. Attractive en-suite rooms plus basic but very clean dormitories for the surfer crowd who relax on the hammocks strung up on the balcony facing the sea. Surf and boogie board rental available. ❶–❸

Cabinas Sun Dancer On the main street opposite the *Posada del Sol* ☎787-0189. Recently opened budget cabinas aimed squarely at the surfing community with basic, clean rooms, a small pool, the ubiquitous hammocks and a garden. They offer very cheap long-term rates. ❷

Diuwak Hotel & Beach Resort Just off the main street 50m from the beach in front of the ICE electrical sub-station. ☎787-0087, Ⓕ787-0089, ⓦwww.diuwak.com. A glimpse into Dominical's future, *Diuwak* is the town's latest mini-resort offering 18 well-equipped cabinas, all with private bath (some with a/c), extensive gardens, a supermarket, an Internet café, a tour service and private parking. ❺

Río Lindo On the right as you enter Dominical ☎787-0028, Ⓕ787-0078, ⓦwww.hotelriolindo .com. Ten comfortable rooms with private bathroom, some with a/c; there's also a pool, bar and whirlpool on the grounds and they offer horse and kayak tours. ❹

Tortilla Flats Next to *Cabinas San Clemente* on the beach ☎787-0033, Ⓔtortflat@racsa.co.cr. Popular surfers' hotel with brightly decorated en-suite rooms and a beachfront bar where crowds gather in the evening to watch the sunset. ❸

Villas Río Mar Down a track to the right as you enter the village ☎787-0052, Ⓕ787-0054, ⓦwww.villasriomar.com. Comfortable, upscale rooms in individual chalets, set in extensive terraced gardens with swimming pool, bar, tennis court and Jacuzzi. ❻

Around Dominical

Cabinas el Coquito del Pacífico 10km north of Dominical in the village of Matapalo ☎ & Ⓕ384-7220, Ⓔel-coquito@gmx.net. Comfortable rooms with private bath and fan, a bar-restaurant, a new swimming pool and direct access to a wide and mostly deserted white-sand beach, good for bathing (but ask about currents). ❺

Finca Brian y Milena 3km south of Dominical, on the road to Escaleras – take a steep left fork away from the coast ☎396-6206. A nice small-scale family farm, doubling as a wildlife sanctuary, experimental fruit farm, botanical garden and guest lodge. There's also good birdwatching and volunteer programmes. Most people arrive on packages, which include meals and hikes in the surrounding rainforest. Camping is also available. ❸

Hacienda Barú 1km north of Dominical on the road to Quepos ☎787-0003, Ⓕ787-0004, ⓦwww.haciendabaru.com. Comfortable self-catering chalets set in a beautiful private reserve comprising over three square kilometres of rainforest, mangroves and protected beach. Good for birders and orchid lovers – there are 250 varieties scattered around – plus there's a butterfly farm, turtle nursery and a fixed viewing platform set high in the forest canopy on-site; horse-riding and night tours are also available. Take time to chat with the hacienda's owner, Jack Ewing, a committed environmentalist with lots of local knowledge. ❺

Pacific Edge 3km south of Dominical; follow the signed left-hand fork ☎381-4369, Ⓕ771-8841, Ⓔpacificedge@pocketmail.com. Secluded, simple and comfortable, on a ridge 600m above the sea, with beautiful mountain and beach views. The four roomy chalets each have private shower and hammocks. Delicious meals, including bangers and mash (one of the owners is English), can be ordered in advance. ❺–❻

Roca Verde 1.5km south of Dominical ☎787-0036, Ⓕ787-0013, ⓦwww.hotelrocaverde. com. Ritzy small hotel in a wonderful position right on the beach. All rooms have en-suite bath, a/c and balcony, and there's also a swimming pool, table tennis and a restaurant with Tex-Mex and American food. ❻

The town

Dominical consists of a dusty, unpaved, unnamed main street (where you'll find most of the town's bars and restaurants) and a beachfront lined with hotels and surf schools. And that's about it – no park, no main square, no museums. In fact, there's no official town centre, unless you count the wooden building – housing the new tourist office and an Internet café – that greets you as turn off the highway. Dominical is expanding all the time, however, as more and more foreigners (principally but not exclusively Americans), lured by the promise of cheap accommodation and ever-improving facilities (not to mention the great surfing) decide to set up home and businesses here. The number of massage parlours and New Age remedy shops seems to grow exponentially by the month. Aside from the surfing, sunbathing and other beach-based activities (see box, p.338) there's not actually a great deal to do in the town itself. Events are staged throughout the year, usually catering to the sensibilities of the surfing crowd – Halloween and dance parties, film screenings and so on – the pick probably being the "Coast to Coast" race in March when hardy competitors attempt to make their way, by whatever means possible, from Limón to Dominical in just four days.

Eating and drinking

If you're self-catering, there are small **supermarkets** next to the tourist office, in the *Diuwak Resort* and just south of the town in the Plaza Pacífica shopping centre. Otherwise there's a handful of decent places to eat in and around the village as well as plenty of lively bars, the best being the beachfront *Tortilla Flats* with great views of the sunset over the Pacific.

Green Leaf Whole Foods Cafe On the main street, south and across from *Posada del Sol*. Surf culture is not the only piece of imported Americana the town has to offer. This California-style eatery serves up a healthy, organic, tofu-heavy, vegetarian menu. Very tasty soups. Closes at sundown.

Punta Dominical 5km south of Dominical; take a signed right fork down to the beach, which then winds up onto the rocky point above. Fancy Italian restaurant with excellent food and great sea views. They also have *cabinas* for rent.

San Clemente Bar and Grill On your left as you enter the village, just past the football pitch. Large,

breezy Tex-Mex restaurant popular with the surf crowd; there's a pool table and half-price cocktails on Tuesdays.

Soda Nanyoa On the main street opposite *Posada del Sol*. This pleasant, airy diner serves a hybrid menu catering to the town's cosmopolitan population: *gallo pinto* and *casados* for the local Ticos; nachos and Philly cheese steak sandwiches for the ever-present contingent of Americans.

Thrusters Towards the beach on the left. Large, barn-like bar with TV, pool tables, dart board, table football and an extensive range of drinks. Heats up on the weekends.

South of Dominical

The stretch of coast that runs south from Dominical to the lovely shallow bay at **Playa Tortuga** is one of the most pristine in Costa Rica. As a consequence, it's continually under siege from real-estate agents, who buy and sell plots of land as fast as they can persuade local fishermen and farmers to part with them. For the moment, though, this area encompasses a string of gloriously empty beaches as well as **Parque Nacional Marino Ballena** – fifty-six square kilometres of water around Uvita and Bahía created to safeguard the ecological integrity of the local marine life.

Dominical activities

Surfing is the big draw in Dominical, and thousands of visitors flock here every year to ride the big waves that crash on to the town's dark-sand beach. Dominical is home to half a dozen surf schools offering lessons for around $50 per person for a two-hour session. Try the Green Iguana Surf Camp just back from the seafront (☎787-0033, ⓦwww.greeniguanasurfcamp.com). As is usual with surfing beaches, the **swimming** varies from not great to downright dangerous, and is plagued by rip-tides and crashing surf. About twenty minutes' walk south along the beach brings you to a small cove, where the water is calmer and you can paddle and snorkel.

Don Lulo's Nauyaca Falls Tour (☎ & ⓕ787-0198, ⓦwww.ecotourism.co.cr /docs/nauyacawaterfalls; $80 per person including meals) makes for one of Costa Rica's best day excursions. The tour begins with a horseback ride to Don Lulo's home and small private zoo for breakfast, before continuing on horseback through lush rainforest with knowledgeable guides to the two cascades that make up the Nauyaca Falls – the principal one drops 46m into a sparkling pool where you can swim. A típico lunch cooked over an open flame completes the day. You'll need to reserve a place on the tour as far in advance as possible.

Equally popular, the private rainforest reserve at **Hacienda Barú** (see p.336) features tree-climbing trips where you winch yourself up extremely tall trees and also guided walks and an exhilarating canopy tour ($35), which involves swooping from platform to platform through primary rainforest on long steel cables, accompanied by guides who impart a wealth of forest folklore. Also recommended are the kayak and **snorkelling tours** (from $50 per person) to the Parque Nacional Marino Ballena and Isla del Caño run by Costa Rica Southern Expeditions (☎787-0100, ⓕ787-0203, ⓦwww.costarica-southern-expeditions.com).

Bahía Ballena and the Parque Nacional Marino Ballena

In the last decade or so, access to the lovely **BAHÍA BALLENA**, south of Dominical, has become relatively easy, but the tiny hamlets of **Bahía** and **Uvita** are still little-visited, and hardly geared up for tourism. Efforts to get here are amply rewarded, however, with wide beaches washed by lazy breakers, palms swaying on the shore, and a hot, serene and very quiet atmosphere. This will no doubt change, as more people discover Bahía Ballena, but for the time being it's extremely unspoilt.

There's not a lot to do here, but if you like hanging out on the beach, surfing and walking through rock shoals and along the sand, you'll be happy. At certain times of year (usually May–Oct), Olive Ridley and hawksbill **turtles** may come ashore to nest, but nowhere near to the same extent as elsewhere in the country. The beach is now regulated by volunteers working for the Parque Nacional Marino Ballena, who patrol the beaches at night warning off poachers. If you want to see the turtles, it's best to talk to the rangers at the park's puesto in Bahía village – whatever you do, remember the ground rules of turtle-watching: come at night with a torch, watch where you walk (partly for snakes), keep well back from the beach and don't shine the light right on the turtles. You may also see **dolphins** frolicking in the water. Ask around about **boat tours**, making sure that the boat has a good outboard motor and lifejackets on board, as you'll be out on the open Pacific; tours include snorkelling and sports-fishing trips, and visits to the Isla del Caño. With your own equipment you can snorkel to your heart's content directly off the beach.

There are two villages on Bahía Ballena. **Uvita**, which winds inland at the crossroads just north of the Río Uvita, is the slightly more developed of the two with a couple of decent **places to stay**, including the budget *Hotel Tucán* (☎743-8140, Ⓦwww.tucanhotel.com; ❶–❷), with backpacker-style dormitories, and the slightly more upscale *Balcón de Uvita* (☎743-8034, Ⓦwww.balcondeuvita .com; ❺) which has a celebrated Indonesian restaurant; take a left fork as you enter Uvita, but note that you'll need a 4WD to get there.

The tiny village of **Bahía**, right next to Uvita, is better situated, on the lovely beach next to the Parque Nacional Marino Ballena, but has a much more limited tourist infrastructure. There are a few budget hotels, namely *Villas Hegalua* (no phone; ❶) and *Cabinas Punta Uvita* (no phone; ❶). If you're keen on exploring the area in depth (and have the funds to finance it) your best bet is to book a stay at *La Cusinga Lodge* (☎770-2549, Ⓦ www.lacusingalodge .com; ❽), just past the Puente Uvita, one of the country's best eco-lodges and one of the few owned and run by Ticos. Occupying a gorgeous rainforest setting overlooking the Parque Nacional Marino Ballena, the lodge provides an important lesson in how to preserve the environment for both the benefit of tourists and the local community. Its seven cabinas have all been made from wood from the lodge's sustainable teak plantation; the food (served in a communal dining area) has usually been grown or caught locally; all the electricity is provided by solar and hydro power; and there's an education centre where local children can come and learn about the area. Trails lead through the rainforest (inhabited by howler and white-faced monkeys) and down to a beautiful stretch of quiet beach.

From San Isidro, **buses** leave C 1, Av 4/6 twice daily at 9am and 4pm, heading for Uvita and Bahía via Dominical (1hr 30min).

Parque Nacional Marino Ballena

Created in 1990, the **PARQUE NACIONAL MARINO BALLENA** protects an area of ocean off the coast of Uvita containing one of the biggest chunks of **coral reef** left on the Pacific coast. It's also the habitat of **humpback whales,** who come here from the Arctic and Antarctic to breed – although they are spotted very infrequently (Dec–April is best) – and **dolphins**. The main threats to the ecological survival of these waters is the disturbance caused by shrimp trawling, sedimentation as a result of deforestation (rivers bring silt and pollutants into the sea and kill the coral) and dragnet fishing, which often entraps whales and dolphins. On land, 1.1 square kilometres of sandy and rocky beaches and coastal areas are protected, as is **Punta Uvita** – a former island connected to the mainland by a narrow land bridge. **Services** here are minimal: there are park rangers, but no trails.

Playa Tortuga

Heading south on the coastal road, Highway 34 (also known as the Costanera Sur), you'll come to **PLAYA TORTUGA**, about halfway between Dominical and Palmar. A few years ago this beach won an award as the cleanest in Costa Rica: no wonder, as practically nobody made the bone-shaking trip out here back then. The road has improved and consequently Playa Tortuga sees more visitors these days, but still far fewer than other beaches in Costa Rica. You'll find a couple of very good **hotels** close to the beach: the recently expanded *Posada Playa Tortuga* (☎384-5489, Ⓦwww.hotel-posada.com; ❻) has comfortable rooms, a large swimming pool with Jacuzzi and an amazing view. *Villas Gaia* (☎ & ℱ256-9996, Ⓦwww.villasgaia.com; ❻) offers twelve brightly coloured cabinas, a pool and an attractive restaurant. It also has a range of tours including snorkelling at Isla Caño, boat tours of local mangrove swamps and microlight plane trips ($65).

Palmar to Bahía Drake

Some 30km south of Playa Tortuga, where Highway 34 joins the Interamericana, and about 100km north of the Panamá border, the small, prefab town of **PALMAR** serves as the hub for the area's banana plantations. This is a good place to see **lithic spheres** (see below), which are scattered on the lands of several nearby plantations and on the way to **Sierpe**, 15km south on the Río Sierpe. Ask politely for the "esferas de piedra"; if the banana workers are not too busy they may be able to show you where to look. Palmar is also a useful jumping-off point for the beautiful **Bahía Drake** and the secluded **Isla del Caño** biological reserve – both accessed via Sierpe – as well as for the Marenco/San Pedrillo ranger station. Set in a pretty bay, this ranger station is perhaps the most picturesque entrance to the **Parque Nacional Corcovado** (see p.352) on the Península de Osa.

Palmar is divided in two by the Río Grande de Térraba. **Palmar Sur** contains the airport, while most of the services, including hotels and buses, are in **Palmar Norte**. Osa Tours (☎786-7825, ℱ786-6534, ℰcatuosa@racsa.co.cr), in the Centro Comercial del Norte in Palmar Norte, has **tourist information**, can help with reservations and transport and also sells stamps; you can make international telephone calls and receive Western Union money transfers here too. The town's **accommodation** is very basic. *Casa Amarilla*, 300m east of the TRACOPA bus stop (☎786-7251; ❶), has clean rooms with private bath and fan; the upstairs ones have balconies and better ventilation. *Hotel Osa*, on Calle Principal, has simple budget rooms (☎786-6584; ❶).

From San José, TRACOPA **buses** run to Palmar Norte seven times daily and take five and a half hours, with the last one returning to the capital at 4.25pm. Buses for **Sierpe** leave Palmar Norte from the Supermercado Térraba (5 daily; 30min), with the first bus leaving at 7am.

Lithic spheres

Aside from goldworking, the Diquis are known for their precise fashioning of large stone **spheres**, most of them exactly spherical to within a centimetre or two – an astounding feat for a culture without technology. Thousands have been found in southwestern Costa Rica and a few in northern Panamá. Some are located in sites of obvious significance, like burial mounds, while others are found in the middle of nowhere; they range in size from that of a tennis ball up to about two metres in diameter.

The spheres' original function and meaning remain obscure, although they sometimes seem to have been arranged in positions mirroring those of the constellations. In many cases the Diquis transported them a considerable distance, rafting them across rivers or the open sea (the only explanation for their presence on Isla del Caño), indicating that their placement was deliberate and significant. (Ironically, some of the posher Valle Central residences now have stone spheres – purchased at a great price – sitting in their front gardens as lawn sculpture.)

You can see lithic spheres in the area around Palmar and also on Isla del Caño. Tours to Isla del Caño are available from the Quepos/Manuel Antonio area (see p.309) and Dominical hotels (see p.336).

Bahía Drake and around

BAHÍA DRAKE (pronounced "Dra-kay") is named after Sir Francis Drake, who anchored here in 1579. Today a favourite of yachters, the calm waters of the bay are dotted with flotillas of swish-looking boats. This is one of the most stunning areas in Costa Rica, with the blue wedge of Isla del Caño floating just off the coast, and fiery-orange Pacific sunsets. The bay is rich in marine life, and a number of **boat trips** offer opportunities for spotting manta rays, marine turtles, porpoises and even whales. You can also go hiking or horse-riding, or take a tour to **Isla del Caño**, about 20km off the coast of the Peninsula de Osa (and easily visible from Drake).

Bahía Drake and its tiny hamlet of **Agujitas** make a good base from which to strike out for the Parque Nacional Corcovado on the northwest of the Peninsula de Osa – the park's San Pedrillo entrance is within a day's walk, and hikers can combine serious trekking with serious comfort at either end of their trip by staying at one of the upscale rainforest eco-lodge-type hotels (see p.342) that have sprung up in recent years. Other than the lodges and a couple of inexpensive, locally run hotels in Agujitas, there are very few facilities here, though the village has a small *pulpería* with a radio phone and there's a medical clinic, Hospital Clínica Bíblica, on the beach.

Getting to Bahía Drake

Like many other places in Zona Sur, **getting to Bahía Drake** requires some planning. There are four choices: the really tough way, hiking in from Corcovado; the cheap way, by bus from San José and then by boat along the Río Sierpe; the bumpy way, by 4WD along the gravel and dirt road between Rincón and Drake; and the luxury way, flying from San José to Drake, and taking one of the many **packages** offered by hotels in the area. If you do this, transport to your lodge is taken care of. Both Sansa and NatureAir operate two daily flights to Drake Bay.

Travelling **independently**, you'll need to get a bus from San José to Palmar; depending on what time you get in, you can then either bed down in Palmar Norte for the night or get a local bus (see opposite) or taxi to **Sierpe** (about $12), where there are a few cabinas. If you're coming from San José and hoping to make it to Drake on the same day, you'll need to catch the 5am bus. In Sierpe, you must find a **boatman** to take you the 30km downriver to Bahía Drake, a journey of two hours. You need someone with experience, a motorized *lancha*, and lifejackets: ask Sonia Rojas at the *Fenix pulpería* to help you find someone or try the riverfront bar of the *Hotel Oleaje Sereno* or the *Bar Las Vegas*, both of which are popular hang-outs for boat captains. The going rate for a one-way trip to Drake is currently about $20 per person or around $65–85 per boatload (maximum usually eight). Some hotel *lanchas* will take independent

Visiting Corcovado from Agujitas

From Agujitas you can follow the beachside trail via Marenco to the San Pedrillo entrance of Parque Nacional Corcovado (see p.352) – a walk of around eight to twelve hours. You can camp at San Pedrillo, although the Fundación de Parques Nacionales much prefer that you let them know in advance if you want to do this by contacting the Puerto Jiménez office (☎735-5036, ℗735-5276). If you are staying at any of the Bahía Drake lodges, they should be able to contact the Puerto Jiménez office of Corcovado and make a reservation for you to stay and eat in San Pedrillo with the rangers.

travellers if there's room but be sure to arrive early; note that owing to fierce afternoon tides, the last *lancha* leaves at around 3.30pm.

The trip down mangrove-lined Río Sierpe is calm enough (you can spot monkeys, sloths and sometimes kingfishers), until you see the Pacific rolling in at the mouth of the river. The Sierpe is very wide where it meets the sea, and huge breakers crash in from the ocean, making it a turbulent and treacherous crossing (sharks reportedly wait here for their dinner). If the tide is right and the boatman knows his water, you'll be fine. All the *lanchas* used by the lodges have powerful outboard motors, and there's little chance of an accident; all the same, some find this part of the trip a bit hairy. Once you are out in Bahía Drake the water is calm.

Accommodation

Accommodation is clustered either in the tiny village of Agujitas itself, or on Punta Agujitas, the rocky point on the other side of Río Agujitas. Virtually all the eco-lodges listed below do a range of **tours**, from guided excursions to Corcovado to boating in Bahía Drake and trips to Isla del Caño. The larger lodges are accustomed to bringing guests on packages from San José and can include transport from the capital, from Palmar, or from Sierpe. The packages (and the prices given below) usually include three meals a day – there are few eating options in Bahía Drake otherwise. Although hoteliers say you can't **camp** in the Drake area, people do – if you want to join them, pitch your tent considerably and be sure to leave no litter.

Aguila de Osa Inn At the end of the village on Río Agujitas ⑦296-2190, ⑤232-7722, ⑩www.aguiladeosainn.com. Very posh sports-fishing lodge with a smart restaurant, landscaped gardens and thirteen beautifully decorated rooms, all with large tiled bathrooms. Tours are also available. ⑧

Cabinas Jade Mar In the village ⑦384-6681, ⑤786-7366. One of the few village cheapies, and a good place to stay if you want to get a taste of local life, with extremely well priced and pleasant, if basic, cabinas, kept very clean by the informative Doña Martha. All cabins have private bath (cold water only), and hearty meals are included in the price. Inexpensive tours to Corcovado and Isla del Caño are also available. ④

Corcovado Adventures Tent Camp 2km south of Agujitas ⑦385-9675, in San José ⑦289-3595, ⑩www.corcovado.com. En route to Parque Nacional Corcovado, this collection of well-screened and furnished tents (complete with beds and tables) sits on platforms on an isolated beach facing the sea. ⑤

Delfin Amor Eco Lodge Just beyond Punta Agujitas ⑦394-2632, ⑩www.divinedolphin.com. Tent-style accommodation, vegetarian food and a friendly community atmosphere in a small lodge specializing in encounters with wild dolphins for $35 for a full-day tour or $35 for a sunset tour. ⑤

Drake Bay Wilderness Resort Punta Agujitas ⑦ & ⑤770-8012, in San José ⑦256-7394, ⑩www.drakebay.com. The most established lodge

in the area, providing a buffer zone between tourist and wilderness with rustic, comfortable cabinas or, if you want to rough it a bit, well-appointed tents – both options are well-screened. There's hearty local food available, and the camp also has its own solar-heated water supply, night-time electricity, plus excellent snorkelling and canoeing. It's pricey at about $780 for three nights, but this includes air transfers from San José (and free laundry). ⑧

Hotel Pirate Cove About 5km outside Drake ⑦393-9449, ⑤786-9845, ⑩www.piratecovecostarica.com. Seven en-suite tent-style cabinas (including three very large family cabinas) in a lush rainforest overlooking a pristine two-kilometre stretch of beach. The excellent restaurant serves Costa Rican and European cuisine. Tours of Parque Nacional Corcovado and Isla del Caño are offered. ⑤–⑥

Jinetes de Osa Between Punta Agujitas and Agujitas ⑦385-9541, ⑩www.costaricadiving.com. Right on the area's main beach, this is one of the less expensive options in Bahía Drake. There's an on-site PADI dive school and most guests come here on dive packages. Accommodation, some of it en suite, is simple but comfortable, and prices include three meals a day. ④

La Paloma Lodge Punta Agujitas ⑦293-7502, ⑤ 239-0954. ⑩www.lapalomalodge.com. Beautiful, rustic rooms in thatched hilltop bungalows, with private bath, balconies and hammocks. The airy, two-storey bungalows are best, surrounded by forest and boasting spectacular views, particularly at sunset. *Pangas* (traditional canoes) are available for guests to paddle on the Río Agujitas behind the lodge, and there's also an attractively tiled swimming pool. Excellent service with friendly and helpful staff. ❼

Poor Man's Paradise Past Playa San Josecito, just beyond the San Pedrillo entrance on the way to Bahía Drake ☎771-4582, ⓕ771-8841, ⓦwww.mypoormansparadise.com. One of the most secluded lodges in what is, after all, a pretty secluded area. The tent-style cabinas are set in pretty gardens and have ocean views. A mixture of private and shared bathrooms are available and you can also camp on the grounds for $7 per person. Rates include three meals a day served in the lodge's lovely indigenous-style thatched roof restaurant. ❹

Proyecto Campanario Near Sierpe ☎282-5778, ⓕ282-0374, ⓦwww.campanario.org. Established by ex-Peace Corps volunteers, this remote field station, reachable via a three-day hike or by boat from Sierpe, offers courses in tropical ecology and tour "packages" for hardy eco-tourists not fazed by its isolation. Tours consist of short walks, long hikes or all-day expeditions to the Reserva Biológica Campanario or Parque Nacional Corcovado as well as trips to deforested and impacted areas to talk to local communities. They also offer snorkelling and scuba-diving excursions to the Isla del Caño. Seven-night "conservation camps" start at $876 and include accommodation, all meals and activities.

Rancho Corcovado On the beach in front of Agujitas ☎350-4866, ⓕ786-7366. Family-run hotel with beautiful views over the bay and simple, clean en-suite rooms. You can also camp on the grounds ($6 per person). Rates include full board. Camping and horse-riding tours are also available. ❹

Isla del Caño

The tiny **RESERVA BIOLÓGICA ISLA DEL CAÑO** sits placidly in the ocean some 20km due west of Bahía Drake. Just 3km long by 2km wide, the uninhabited island is the exposed part of an underwater mountain, thrown up by an ancient collision of the two tectonic plates on either side of Costa Rica. It's a pretty sight in the distance, and going there is even better – if you can afford it. You can't get there on your own, but a **tour** is usually included in the package price of the Bahía Drake lodges. Alternatively, tours are run by many operators in the Manuel Antonio area (see p.318) and, increasingly, from Dominical (p.335).

The island is thought to have been a burial ground of the Diquis, who brought their famed **lithic spheres** here from the mainland in large, ocean-going canoes. Your guide can take you hiking into the thick rainforest interior to look for examples near the top of the 110-metre high crest, and you'll certainly come across some as you wander around – they're lying about all over the place. Caño is also a prime **snorkelling** and diving destination. Underwater you'll see coral beds and a variety of **marine life**, including spiny lobsters and sea cucumber, snapper, sea urchins, manta rays, octopuses and the occasional barracuda. On the surface, porpoises and Olive Ridley turtles are often spotted, along with less frequent sightings of humpback and even sperm whales.

Golfito and around

The former banana port of **GOLFITO**, 33km north of the Panamanian border and 48km southeast of Palmar Norte, straggles for 2.5km along the water of the same name (*golfito* means "little gulf"). The town's setting is spectacular, backed up against steep, thickly forested hills to the east, and with the glorious Golfo Dulce – one of the deepest gulfs of its size in the world – to the west. The low shadow of the Peninsula de Osa shimmers in the distance, and everywhere the vegetation has the soft, muted look of the undisturbed tropics. It is also very **rainy**; even if you speak no Spanish, you'll certainly pick up the local expression *va a caer baldazos* – "it's gonna pour".

Golfito extends for ages without any clear centre, through stretches where the main road is hemmed in by hills on one side and the lapping waters of the *golfito* on the other. The town is effectively split in two – by a division in wealth as well as architecture. In the north is the **Zona Americana**, where the banana company executives used to live and where better-off residents still reside in beautiful wooden houses shaded by dignified palms. Here you'll find the tax-free **Depósito Libre**, an unaesthetic outdoor mall ringed by a circular concrete wall. Some two kilometres to the south of the Depósito, the **Pueblo Civil** (civilian town), is a very small, tight nest of streets – hotter, noisier and more crowded than the *zona*. It's here you'll find the *lancha* across the Golfo Dulce to Puerto Jiménez and the Península de Osa. Although the Pueblo Civil is perfectly civil in the daytime, be careful at night. Be wary of entering any bar with a sign positioned outside so that you can't see in – these are for professional transactions only.

Arrival and information

Buses from San José to Golfito (8hr) currently leave the TRACOPA terminal at 7am and 3pm. You should book your ticket in advance, particularly in December, when hordes of bargain hunters descend on the Depósito Libre to do their Christmas shopping. Buy your return ticket as soon as you disembark. You can also **fly** here with Sansa and NatureAir; the airstrip is in the Zona Americana. The Banco Nacional opposite the TRACOPA terminal changes **travellers' cheques** and gives cash advances on credit cards, but it's a tediously slow process. The **correo** (Mon–Fri 7.30am–5pm, Sat 8am–noon) is right in the centre of the Pueblo Civil. You'll find an **Internet café** on the main street next to the petrol station. You can catch a **water taxi** to Playa Cacao and other local destinations from the *muellecito* (ferry dock) just north of the gas station. Land–Sea Tours (T & F775-1614, Elandsea@racsa.co.cr), on the waterfront at the southern end of the *pueblo*, organizes a wide range of tours and has a book exchange and lots of local information.

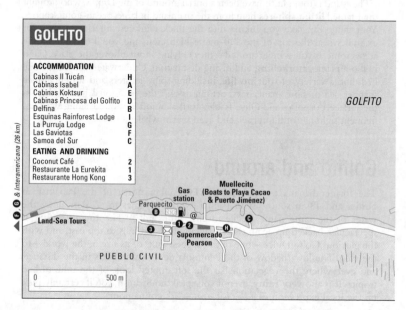

GOLFITO

ACCOMMODATION	
Cabinas Il Tucán	H
Cabinas Isabel	A
Cabinas Koktsur	E
Cabinas Princesa del Golfito	D
Delfina	B
Esquinas Rainforest Lodge	I
La Purruja Lodge	G
Las Gaviotas	F
Samoa del Sur	C

EATING AND DRINKING	
Coconut Café	2
Restaurante La Eurekita	1
Restaurante Hong Kong	3

GOLFITO

F, G, & Interamericana (26 km)

Land-Sea Tours

Parquecito

Gas station

Muellecito (Boats to Playa Cacao & Puerto Jiménez)

Supermercado Pearson

PUEBLO CIVIL

0   500 m

United Brands ("La Yunai")

Golfito's history is inextricably intertwined with the giant transnational **United Brands** – known locally as "La Yunai" – which first set up in the area in 1938, twenty years before the Interamericana hit town. The company built schools, recruited doctors and police and brought prosperity to the area, though "problems" with labour union organizers began soon afterwards, and came to characterize the relationship between company and town. What with fluctuating banana prices, a three-month strike by workers and local social unrest, the company eventually decided Golfito was too much trouble and pulled out in a hurry in 1985. The town declined and, in the public eye, became synonymous with rampant unemployment, alcoholism, abandoned children, prostitution and general unruliness.

Today, at the big old *muelle bananero* (banana dock) container ships are still loaded up with bananas to be processed further up towards Palmar. This residual traffic, along with tourism, has combined to help revive the local economy. Many visitors come to Golfito because it's a good base for getting to the Parque Nacional Corcovado by *lancha* or plane, and also a major **sports-fishing** centre. The real rescue, though, came from the Costa Rican government, who in the early 1990s established a **Depósito Libre** – or tax-free zone – in the town, where Costa Ricans can buy manufactured goods imported from Panamá without the 100 percent tax normally levied. Ticos who come to shop here have to buy their tickets for the Depósito 24 hours in advance, obliging them to spend at least one night, and therefore colones, in the town.

Accommodation

Golfito's accommodation, much of it basic and inexpensive, caters to Costa Ricans visiting the Depósito Libre. There are a couple of slightly smarter hotels too. Be warned that the sheer number of people coming to Golfito to shop, especially at Christmas, means that rooms are often booked in advance – if

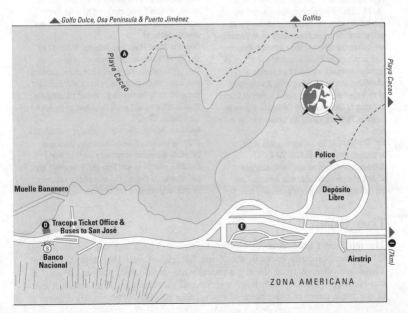

you don't have reservations try to get to town as early in the day as possible. You'll find several luxurious accommodation options along the coast north of Golfito. **Playa San Josecito**, 10km northwest of Golfito and accessible only by boat, has two upmarket eco-lodges, while further north along the coast at **Playa Cativo**, thirty minutes by boat from Golfito, you'll find one of the premier resorts in Costa Rica.

Golfito

Cabinas II Tucán On the main road, 50m north of the *muellecito* ☎775-0553. Basic but perfectly serviceable accommodation just north of the Pueblo Civil. The rooms all have private bath and fans and the owner is a great source of local information (and stories). Free parking available. ❶

Cabinas Koktsur Just south of the Depósito ☎775-1191. Basic but clean double rooms and friendly staff. No hot water. ❶

Cabinas Princesa del Golfito Opposite the Banco Nacional ☎775-0442. Small and friendly with pleasantly decorated, good-value rooms. Hearty Tico meals are served in the adjacent soda. ❶

Delfina In the Pueblo Civil ☎775-0043. Old house converted into a warren of widely varying rooms. Some are rather dark, while those at the back are quieter and overlook the water. The budget rooms (shared bath, ceiling fan) are better value than those with private bath and ancient, groaning a/c. Fills up on the weekends with Depósito visitors. ❶

Esquinas Rainforest Lodge La Gamba, about 7km from Km-37 on the Interamericana ☎ & ☏775-0901, ⓦwww.esquinaslodge.com. Friendly eco-lodge run by the Government of Austria as part of a model project combining development aid, nature conservation and rainforest research – all profits go to the local community. It's set in primary rainforest, with resident wildlife and on-site hiking and horse-riding trails. A wide range of packages are available, plus a variety of tours, including to Corcovado and the Wilson Botanical Gardens. Fantastic meals are included in the room rate. ❼

Las Gaviotas At the southern entrance to town ☎775-0062, ☏775-0544, ⓔlasgaviotas@hotmail.com. Well-equipped, if slightly shabby resort with nice views out over the gulf and the town's only swimming pool. The

somewhat barrack-like (but very affordable) rooms all have private baths with hot water, a/c and cable TV. The waterside rancho restaurant serves great local seafood. ❹

La Purruja Lodge 4km south of Golfito towards the Interamericana ☎775-1054, ⓦwww.purruja .com. Small family-run hotel set in lovely gardens, with spacious rooms, pool table and dart board. Camping and tours are also available. ❷

Samoa del Sur On the main road between the Zona Americana and the Pueblo Civil ☎775-0233, ☏775-0573, ⓔsamoasur@racsa.co.cr. Fourteen spacious but slightly gloomy rooms on the waterfront, with a large and rather raucous boat-shaped bar-restaurant (it's the bar of choice for US marines on shore leave). ❸–❹

Around Golfito

Cabinas Isabel (also known as *Cabinas Playa Cacao*) ☎382-1593, ⓔsabel@racsa.co.cr. These indigenous-style, thatched roof cabinas are right on the water. Though simply furnished, they're very comfortable with en-suite bathrooms and fans and there's a communal dining area. Jungle walks, no-frills fishing tours and trips out to the local mangrove swamps to see the crocodiles are also available. ❸

Dolphin Quest Playa San Josecito ☎775-1742, ☏775-0373, ⓦwww.dolphinquestcostarica.com. This upmarket eco-lodge has comfortable cabinas and suites set on extensive grounds with trails and tours, including horse-riding, kayaking and fishing. Book in advance and you'll be picked up by *lancha* from Golfito. ❺–❼

Rainbow Adventures Playa Cativo ☎1-800/565-0722, ⓦwww.rainbowcostarica.com. Luxurious, tastefully decorated individual chalets sit next to a beautiful, pristine beach. They serve excellent food and offer tours through the surrounding rainforest, as well as snorkelling and birdwatching. ❽

The town

Though there's little to do in Golfito, be sure to check out the old homes of the banana company execs in the Zona Americana near the Depósito Libre. These are obvious from their grandeur: wide-verandah'd, painted in jolly, if sun-bleached, colours, with huge screens and sun canopies. One row, just east of the main street in the centre of town (near the Banco Nacional) displays a particularly fine series of washed-out tropical hues – lime-green blends into faded oyster-yellow, followed by tired-pink and metallic-orange.

Immediately to the east of town, the tiny **Refugio Nacional de Fauna Silvestre Golfito** isn't easily accessible, although there are some trails up the steep hill, and fantastic views across the Golfo Dulce. The trail entrances tend to be overgrown and difficult to find, so ask around locally.

If you're in Golfito to **sports-fish**, the larger hotels can help arrange tours and tackle – the area is particularly rich in marlin and sailfish. **Swimming** is no good, however, as the bay is polluted, and you'll see oil in the water and various bits of floating refuse all around Golfito. Your best bet for a swim is to head across to Playa Cacao, or to move south down the Península Burica. Comprehensive and imaginative **tours** of the area, featuring activities such as jungle hikes, panning for gold and cave exploration, can be arranged through Land-Sea Tours (see p.344).

Less than a kilometre away across the *golfito*, **Playa Cacao** has good swimming, although the beach is a little grimy. You'll find a number of decent bars and restaurants nearby. You can get to Cacao by *lancha* from the *muellecito* in Golfito (around $4), or in the dry season drive a rough unfinished track from the turn-off right in front of the *guardia*, bearing left.

Eating and drinking

Golfito has plenty of **places to eat**. For *casados* and *platos del día* there are two groups of simple **sodas**: one near the Depósito Libre, catering to Ticos who have come to Golfito on shopping trips, and another, slightly better-value cluster on the main drag of the Pueblo Civil and in the surrounding streets. The *Coconut Café*, opposite the main dock, is both a nice place for a beer or a *refresco* and a great source of local information – the American owner seems to know just about everyone in Golfito. *Restaurante La Eurekita*, in the Pueblo Civil close to the post office, serves solidly *típico* food, very good burgers and has a nice breezy view of the water. *Restaurante Hong Kong*, also in the Pueblo Civil, is renowned for its excellent (and cheap) chow mein dishes.

Moving on from Golfito

Buses to San José leave daily at 5am and 1pm. Daily flights head to San José on Sansa and NatureAir, and are bookable through Land-Sea Tours. For **Corcovado**, you can either take the ferry across the Golfo Dulce to Puerto Jiménez (daily at 11am from the *muellecito*; 1hr 30min; $3), or a small plane to Jiménez (approx $100 for up to 5 people) – contact Alfa Romeo Aero Taxi's office at the airstrip, or call ☎755-1515, Ⓔcorcovadotaxi@racsa.co.cr. Daily buses to **Neily** and **San Vito** leave from in front of the *muelle bananero* where, in the dry season only, you can also pick up buses south to **Playas Zancudo** and **Pavones** (2hr 30min–3hr).

There are two ferry piers in Golfito, the old *muelle bananero* and the municipal dock, called the *muellecito*, near the Pueblo Civil. All boats are motorized *lanchas*, and prices seem to be about the same from either place. Whoever you go with, make sure there are lifejackets on board: the Golfo Dulce is usually calm, but winds can come up suddenly, causing unexpectedly high waves. A *lancha* departs Golfito daily at 11.30am **to Puerto Jiménez** (1hr 30min). Alternatively, **Land-Sea Tours** organizes transport in their boats to almost anywhere in the Golfo Dulce area, including Playa Cacao, Playa Cativo, Playa Zancudo and Puerto Jiménez – costs are competitive, but you'll get a much better price if you gather a group together.

Of the **hotel-restaurants**, *Las Gaviotas* has an all-you-can-eat barbecue ($10) on Friday and Saturday evenings from 6pm, with good meat dishes and a reasonable wine list, though its best feature is the waterside location on the *golfito*. The beachside bar and restaurant at the *Samoa del Sur* hotel is a pleasant spot for an evening beer or meal, with a menu featuring seafood and pizza ($5–8).

Playas Pavones and Zancudo

South of Golfito are a couple of very isolated **beaches** en route to the **Peninsula Burica**, a thin, pristine finger of land that's shared with Panamá. Ask anyone in town where you can swim, and they'll direct you to black-sand **PLAYA ZANCUDO**, 15km southeast of Golfito, facing the Golfo Dulce and bordered on one side by the Río Coto Colorado. Playa Zancudo also has a couple of professional sports-fishing outfits, while other local activities include surfing, river trips and excursions (run by *Cabinas Los Cocos*, see below) across the bay to the beautiful Casa Orchideas Botanical Gardens, reachable only by boat.

On summer weekends from December to April, Playa Zancudo sometimes fills with Zona Sur Ticos taking a beach break, but otherwise it's fairly low-key, except for a small colony of mainly US expats. It's a friendly place, perfect for unwinding, and there are several decent **places to stay**. *Cabinas Los Cocos* (℡776-0012, ⓦwww.loscocos.com; ❺) is the most upmarket with well-equipped cabinas – each with kitchen, fridge, screens, fans and hammocks – surrounded by dense tropical foliage. *Sol y Mar* (℡776-0014, ⓦwww.zancudo.com; ❸–❹) has groovy little huts in a garden by the beach and they offer sports-fishing trips. *Maria's* (℡776-0131; ❶) has very basic but good-value rooms above a restaurant. For **food**, *Estero Mar* serves tasty seafood or you can dine on gourmet French cuisine at *Sol y Mar*, which has a lively bar and popular volleyball competitions on Saturday afternoons. The usual array of sodas around town serve *casados* and other typical filling fare.

About 12km further south is **PLAYA PAVONES**, famed among surfers for having the longest continuous wave in the world – exactly how long, they do not divulge. The waves are biggest and best from May to November. Needless to say, the water's too rough for anything else and the community here largely consists of avid surfers. There are few facilities in Pavones other than basic cabinas for rent and a couple of nondescript bars.

You can reach both Pavones and Zancudo from Golfito by **lancha** (45min) or, in the dry season only (Jan–Sept), by **bus** (2hr 30min–3hr) from in front of the *muelle bananero*. **Driving** to the beaches takes a little over two hours from Golfito and entails crossing the Río Coto Colorado on a tiny ferry. You need a 4WD, whatever time of year; during the wet season it's worth checking the levels of the creeks and fords that you'll have to pass before you set out.

After another 10km or so south you come to **Punta Banco**, site of the beautiful *Tiskita Lodge* (℡296-8125, ⓕ296-8133, ⓦwww.tiskita-lodge.co.cr; ❼), a friendly, extremely comfortable rainforest lodge (that doubles as a biological research station) with cabinas overlooking the beach and a swimming pool on the grounds. Trails weave through the surrounding forest and birdwatching is good. You can also tour their fruit farm (the owner is an agronomist). They offer good-value packages, including flight from San José and three high-quality meals a day.

Península de Osa

In the extreme south of the country, the **Península de Osa** is an area of immense biological diversity, somewhat separate from the mainland. In the early years of the twentieth century, Osa was something of a **penal colony**; a place to which men were either sent forcibly or went, machete in hand, to forget. Consequently, a violent, frontierlands folklore permeates the whole peninsula, and old-time residents of **Puerto Jiménez** are only too happy to regale you with hosts of gory tales. Some may be apocryphal, but they certainly add colour to the place.

It was on the Península de Osa that the Diquis found **gold** in such abundant supply that they hardly had to pan or dig for it. Gold can still be found, as can the odd *orero* (goldminer/panner). When **Parque Nacional Corcovado** was established in the mid-1970s, substantial numbers of miners were panning within its boundaries, but the heaviest influx of *oreros* stemmed directly from the pull-out of the United Brands Company in 1985. Many were laid-off banana plantation workers with no other means of making a living. They resorted to panning for gold, an activity that posed a threat to the delicate ecosystem of the park – and a clear example of how the departure of a large-scale employer can lead to environmental destruction. In 1986 the *oreros* were forcibly deported from the park by the Costa Rican police. Today, several well-known international conservationist groups are involved in protecting and maintaining Osa's ecological integrity, and were recently successful in fighting off an attempt to establish a wood-chip mill here.

Few will fail to be moved by Osa's beauty. Whether you approach the peninsula by *lancha* from Golfito or Bahía Drake, on the Jiménez bus, or driving in from the mainland, you'll see what looks like a floating island – an intricate mesh of blue and green, with tall canopy trees sailing high and flat like elaborate floral hats. You'll also see a revealing picture of *precarista* (squatter) life on the country's extreme geographical margins. Since the mid- to late-1980s, the improvement of the road between Jiménez and Rincón has brought many families seeking land. Most have built simple shacks and cultivated a little roadside plot, burning away the forest to do so. They plant a few vegetables and a banana patch and may keep a few cattle. Soil here is classically tropical, with few nutrients, poor absorption and minimal regenerative capacity. In a few years it will have exhausted itself and the smallholders will have to cultivate new areas or move on.

You could feasibly explore the whole peninsula in four days, but this would be rushing it, especially if you want to spend time walking the trails and wildlife-spotting at Corcovado. Most people allot five to seven days for the area, taking it at a relaxed pace, and more if they want to stay in and explore Bahía Drake (see p.341). Hikers and walkers who come to Osa without their own car tend to base themselves in Puerto Jiménez – a place where it's easy to strike up a conversation, and people are relaxed, environmentally conscientious and not yet overwhelmed by tourism.

Puerto Jiménez

The relaxed town of **PUERTO JIMÉNEZ** – known locally simply as Jiménez – has plenty of places to stay and eat and good public transport connections. It caters mainly to the budget end of the spectrum, its basic

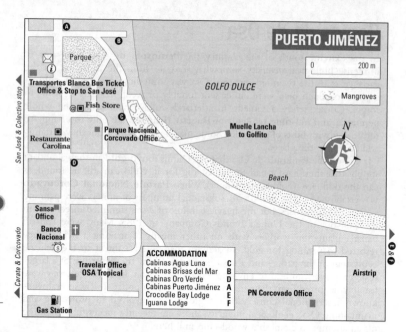

cabinas in a whole different class and price range from the luxury lodges (many American-owned) lining the road to Carate, 43km southwest. In this instance, at least, it seems that whatever money is being made from the preservation of Osa's ecological heritage (and there's plenty to be made), little of it is finding its way back to the local communities. From Jiménez, you can also take a *colectivo* truck, the local transport, to Carate from where it's possible to enter Corcovado (see p.352).

Arrival and information

Two **buses** arrive daily from San José (C 12, Av 7/9) via San Isidro (6am & noon; 10hr). Buses depart Jiménez for San Jose at 5am and 11am from the bus station just west of the soccer field where you can also buy tickets (open daily 7–11am & 1–5pm). A **lancha** departs Golfito daily at 11am (1hr 30min); another *lancha* returns to Golfito daily at 6am. You can **fly** in from San José with Sansa or NatureAir, or from Quepos with NatureAir. The new Banco Nacional, just north of the gas station, changes **travellers' cheques** and dollars. The correo, opposite the soccer field, has public phones and **Internet** access, as does Café Net El Sol on the main street.

The small **tourist information** office sits opposite the soccer pitch; they have Internet access and info on tours to Corcovado and Bahía Drake. The helpful Osa Tropical (☎735-5062, ⓕ735-5043, ⓔosatropi@racsa.co.cr), on the main road 50m north of the gas station, doubles as the local NatureAir and Sansa agent and has tour info and phone and fax services. Escondido Trex (☎ & ⓕ735-5210, ⓦwww.escondidotrex.co.cr), with an office in the *Restaurante Carolina* (see p.352), offers a wide range of tours, including hiking tours into Corcovado. For more unique excursions, contact biologist Andy Pruter of Everyday Adventures (☎ & ⓕ735-5138, ⓦwww.psychotours.com), who takes people on high adrenalin "psycho" tours that include climbing 45-metre fig trees, rappelling waterfalls and ocean kayaking ($45–75).

If you're planning a **trip to Corcovado**, the Oficina de Area de Conservación Osa (Mon–Fri 8am–noon & 1–4pm; ℡735-5036, (F)735-5276), facing the airstrip, is staffed by friendly rangers who can answer questions and arrange accommodation and meals at the park puestos (though you're advised to sort this out before you arrive – see p.355 for details).

The main form of local public transport, the *colectivo*, departs from the El Tigre supermarket in Jiménez to **Carate** ($10), twice daily (except Sundays in the dry season) at about 6am and 1.30pm. Note that it's an achingly bumpy drive and involves the careful negotiation of at least half a dozen small (and in the rainy season not so small) rivers. The *colectivo* will drop you off at any of the lodges between Jiménez and Carate, and will also pick you up on its way back to town if you arrange this in advance – ask the driver. If you don't get a place on the truck, a number of local taxi drivers have 4WDs; try Orlando Mesen (℡735-5627; approx $60 return to Carate). The *colectivo* also heads to **Bahía Drake** on Mondays and Fridays at noon (less frequently in the wet season) but confirm the times at the tourist office or at the El Tigre supermarket. Note that Puerto Jiménez is home to the only petrol station on the entire Península de Osa, so be sure to fill up before you leave.

Accommodation

Jiménez's **hotels** are reasonably priced, clean and basic. Though in the dry season it's best to reserve a bed in advance, this may not always be possible, as phone and fax lines sometimes go down. There are a few comfort-in-the-wilderness places **between Jiménez and Carate** around the lower hump of the peninsula, a couple of which make great retreats or honeymoon spots. These tend to be quite upscale; backpackers usually stay in Jiménez.

In Puerto Jiménez

Cabinas Agua Luna On the waterfront near the *lancha* pier ℡ & (F)735-5393, (E)agualu@racsa.co.cr. A range of comfortable waterfront accommodation, from basic rooms with fans (❷) to luxury rooms with cable TV, a/c and fridge. ❺

Cabinas Brisas del Mar On the waterfront, just east of the soccer field ℡735-5028. This basic backpacker complex overlooking the gulf offers a choice of dormitory-style rooms ($10) or slightly more comfortable double rooms ($40).

Cabinas Oro Verde On the main street ℡735-5241. Nine basic, clean rooms right in the middle of town, with restaurant, laundry service and friendly owners. ❶

Cabinas Puerto Jiménez On the way into town from the Interamericana ℡735-5090. Quiet cabinas next to the water, with simple, spotlessly clean and nicely furnished rooms. They're well screened, with bath and fan, though some can be dark – ask to see a few before you choose. ❶

Crocodile Bay Lodge 4km out of town towards Playa Platanares ℡735-5631, (F)735-5633, (W)www.crocodilebay.com. Luxury sports-fishing resort with swimming pool, Jacuzzi, landscaped gardens and a large pier. Very expensive package deals only. ❽

Iguana Lodge Follow the signs for 5km out of Jiménez to Playa Platanares ℡735-5205, (F)735-5436, (W)www.iguanalodge.com. Wonderful hotel run by very friendly US family with four two-storey cabinas in lovely gardens by the beach – all rooms face the sea and are attractively decorated. Rates include three delicious meals a day. ❼

Between Puerto Jiménez and Carate

The following are listed **in order of their distance from Puerto Jiménez** on the way to the park. All are signed from the road and include three meals a day in their room rates.

Lapa Ríos 20km south of Puerto Jiménez ℡735-5130, (F)735-5179, (W)www.laparios.com. One of the country's most comfortable and impressive jungle lodges, set in a large private nature reserve with excellent birdwatching. Rooms have big beds and mosquito nets, and, being built of locally sourced materials (bamboo furniture, hardwood floors, palm thatched roofs), blend nicely with the surrounding forest. There's also a huge thatched restaurant, complete with spiral staircase, and a swimming pool. ⑧

Bosque del Cabo Above Playa Matapalo, down a private road to the left off the Carate road ℡ & ℻735-5206, ⓦwww.bosquedelcabo.com. Run by a friendly American couple, this grand lodge has ten luxurious hardwood and stucco cabinas (several with magnificent ocean views) plus two even more luxurious houses that sleep up to six. The lodge sits on landscaped grounds with acres of rainforest and is very eco-friendly; all the electricity is supplied by solar and hydro power. There's also a very good restaurant and tours are available.⑦–⑧

Lookout Inn Just north of Carate, and very convenient to its airstrip ℡735-5931, ⓦwww .lookout-inn.com. An informal, fun atmosphere pervades at this beach house set on a rainforested hillside with three large rooms, swimming pool and beautiful ocean views. Tours are available. ⑥

Luna Lodge Set in the hills above Carate – call for a pick-up from the nearby Carate airstrip ℡380-5036, ⓦwww.lunalodge.com. Remote, tranquil and beautiful lodge with welcoming owners and staggering views over the surrounding virgin rainforest. Yoga classes take place on a specially built platform overlooking the jungle and there's healthy home-grown food available.⑦

Corcovado Tent Camp About a 45min walk along the beach from Carate (book via Costa Rica Expeditions, ℡257-0766, ℻257-1665, ⓦwww .costaricaexpeditions.com). Twenty self-contained and fully screened "tent-camps" elevated on short stilts in an amazing beachside location, with bedrooms and screened verandahs, communal baths and good local cooking. Packages are available, some including flights right to Carate, and they also offer guided tours around Parque Nacional Corcovado ($45–75) and horse-riding. ⑤

La Leona Tent Camp Just south of La Leona puesto ℡735-5705, ℻735-5704. Striking a balance between comfort and convenience, the La Leona complex of rustic-style tent cabinas is set right on the beach just a short walk from the entrance to Parque Nacional Corcovado. Though they can get uncomfortably hot, the tents are well-equipped and there's a very good restaurant (the price includes three meals a day). The lodge also offers a range of tours including crocodile-spotting, night hikes and rappelling. ⑤

The town

Despite its small size, lack of big city facilities and somewhat sleepy, down-at-heel appearance, Puerto Jiménez nonetheless has a distinctly cosmopolitan flavour to it, welcoming a constant flow of visitors by land, sea and air throughout the year. Most are backpackers looking for a cheaper route to Corcovado than that offered via Bahía Drake. It is, however, a transient cosmopolitanism. Puerto Jiménez has no permanent expat community in the manner of Dominical or Puerto Viejo. This is a place to pass through – not to linger. The main street, which runs for just a few hundred metres from the soccer field in the north to the petrol station in the south, represents the rather dusty heart of town.

Eating and drinking

The most popular place in town (particularly with tourists) is the funky little *Juanita's*, which does very reasonable Mexican food, including a very hot chili; it's a great place to hang out with a cool drink even if you're not in the mood for food. Other social spots include *Restaurante Carolina*, on the main drag, which has a *comida típica* menu (and also rents out cabinas) and the *Agua Luna* hotel's very popular Chinese restaurant and bar overlooking the bay.

Parque Nacional Corcovado

Created in 1975, **PARQUE NACIONAL CORCOVADO** (daily 8am–4pm; $7), 368km southeast of San José, protects a fascinating and biologically complex area of land, most of it on the peninsula itself. It also comprises the Parque Nacional Piedras Blancas on the mainland, which covers a diverse landscape, from evergreen primary forest to desolate beaches. Several dirt trails

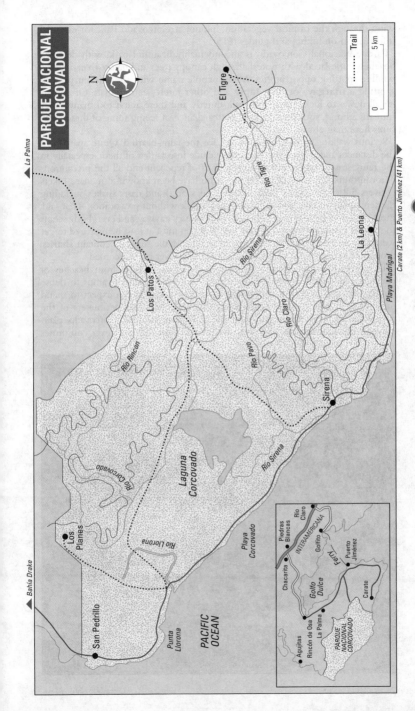

7

PARQUE NACIONAL CORCOVADO

N

▲ La Palma

▲ Bahía Drake

San Pedrillo

Los Planes

Río Corcovado

Punta Llorona

Río Llorona

Laguna Corcovado

Playa Corcovado

PACIFIC OCEAN

Río Sirena

Río Rincón

Los Patos

Río Pavo

Río Claro

Río Sirena

Sirena

Río Tigre

El Tigre

La Leona

Playa Madrigal

▶ Carate (2 km) & Puerto Jiménez (41 km)

········· Trail

0   5 km

Piedras Blancas

Río Claro

INTERAMERICANA

Golfito

Chacarita

Golfo Dulce

Puerto Jiménez

Ferry

Carate

Aguitas

Rincón de Osa

La Palma

PARQUE NACIONAL CORCOVADO

wind through the tropical vegetation; inquire at Corcovado Park for essential information on hiking and guides ($15).

Parque Nacional Corcovado is an undeniably beautiful park, with deserted beaches, some laced with waterfalls, high canopy trees and better-than-average wildlife-spotting opportunities. Many people come with the sole purpose of spotting a **margay**, **ocelot**, **tapir** and other rarely seen animals. Of course, it's all down to luck, but if you walk quietly and there aren't too many other humans around, you should have a better chance of seeing some of these creatures here than elsewhere.

Serious walking in Corcovado is not for the faint-hearted. Quite apart from the distances and the terrain, **hazards** include insects (*lots* of them, especially in the rainy season: take a mosquito net, tons of repellent and all the precautions you can think of), herds of peccaries – who have been known to menace hikers – rivers full of crocodiles (and, in one case, sharks) and nasty snakes, including the terciopelo and bushmaster, which can attack without provocation. That said, most of these are present elsewhere in the country anyway, and everybody seems to make it through Corcovado just fine. But you must at least be prepared to get wet, dirty and incredibly hot – bear in mind that the sea does contain **sharks**, though everyone swims in it and no attacks have ever been recorded.

The **terrain** in Corcovado (literally "hunchback") varies from beaches of packed or soft sand, riverways, mangroves and *holillo* (palm) swamps to dense forest, although most of it is at lowland elevations. Hikers can expect to spend most of their time on the beach trails that ring the outer perimeters of the peninsular section of the park. Inland, the broad, alluvial Corcovado plain contains the **Corcovado Lagoon**, and for the most part the cover constitutes

△ Corcovado National Park

the only sizeable chunk of tropical **premontane wet forest** (also called tropical humid forest) on the Pacific side of Central America. The Osa forest is as visually and biologically magnificent as any on the subcontinent: biologists often compare the tree heights and density here with that of the Amazon basin cover – practically the only place in the entire isthmus of which this can still be said.

The coastal areas of the peninsular section of the park receive at least 3800mm of **rain** a year, with precipitation rising to about 5000mm in the higher elevations of the interior. This intense wetness is ideal for the development of the intricate, densely matted cover associated with tropical wet forests; there's also a dry season (Dec–March). The inland lowland areas, especially those around the lagoon, can be amazingly **hot**, even for those accustomed to tropical temperatures.

Park practicalities

Unless you're coming to Corcovado with Costa Rica Expeditions and staying in their tent camp or the nearby La Leona Tent Camp, in the dry months, at least, you have to **reserve** in advance – this will include meals, camping space or lodging at the puesto of your choice (see p.356). The best way to do this is to fax the park's Puerto Jiménez office directly on ⑤735-5276 or, if you're already in the country, visit the Fundación de Parques Nacionales in San José (see p.68), who will fax or telephone Corcovado on your behalf. You'll have to specify your dates and stick to them. In the rainy season or off-peak times (generally between Easter and Christmas), it's possible to do all this at the park's office in Jiménez (see p.351), but the Fundación prefers that you go through their San José office. Be warned that the park is one of Costa Rica's most popular, and you'll need to book at least six weeks in advance or risk not getting in. It currently costs $2 per night to camp at the puestos, or $6 (plus a $2 reservation fee) to sleep in the comfortable accommodation block at Sirena puesto (see p.356). You can either take basic – rice and beans or fish – **meals** with the rangers ($3 for breakfast, $6 for lunch and dinner – pay in colones at the puesto) or bring your own food and utensils and use their stove.

It's suggested that you come in a group of at least two people, that you bring your own mosquito net, sleeping bag, food and water – though you can fill up at the beachside waterfalls and at the puestos – and be more or less experienced in hiking in this kind of terrain. If you can afford it, your best option is to hire a local guide, particularly useful to spot the recalcitrant wildlife. Ask at the Puerto Jiménez office for advice; Oscar Cortes Alfaro comes highly recommended.

Local guides

In recent years, a programme to train local men and women between the ages of 18 and 35 as **naturalist guides** has been initiated at Rincón de Osa, a village about 35km northwest of Jiménez, snug in the curve of the Golfo Dulce. The programme is typical in Costa Rica – Rara Avis and Selva Verde in Sarapiquí, among others, have similar schemes – enabling people not only to make a living from their local knowledge, but also to appreciate the many ways in which a rainforest can be sustainable. Guides are taught to identify some of the 367 or more species of birds recorded in the area, the 177 amphibians and reptiles, nearly 6000 insects, 140 mammals and 1000 trees – Corcovado's biodiversity makes for a lot of homework. They are also given lectures in tourism and tutored by working professional guides. If you wish to hire a local guide, ask in Rincón or at the Fundación Neotrópica office in San José for details. This arrangement works best if you are planning to hike around the Los Patos–Sirena Trail, as this has the nearest entrances to Rincón.

You should plan to hike early in the day – though not before dawn, due to snakes – and take shelter at midday. Corcovado is set up so that the rangers at each puesto always know how many people are on a given trail, and how long they are expected to be. If you are late getting back, they will go looking for you. This gives a measure of security but, all the same, take **precautions**. There have been no mishaps (like people getting lost) in the park of late, but always check with the rangers or ask around in Jiménez regarding current conditions. A few years ago things were tense between the *oreros* who still mine, some of them illegally, in and around Corcovado, and the rangers, whose job it is to stop them. Though no tourist has been hurt, the *oreros* may well be suspicious of strangers, and it's best not to walk alone just in case.

Incidentally, it's especially important when coming to Corcovado to brush up on your **Spanish**. You'll be asking the rangers for a lot of crucial information and few, if any, speak English. Bring a phrase book if you're not fluent.

The puestos

The *pulpería* in the village of **Carate**, about 43km from Jiménez, sells basic food-stuffs, though it's not cheap. You can also pitch your **tent** right outside; there's a minimal charge ($2 per tent per night) which covers the use of toilets and showers. From here it's a ninety-minute walk along the beach to enter Corcovado at the **La Leona** puesto, although you can stop off en route for refreshment at the Corcovado or La Leona tent camps (see p.352). It's then a sixteen-kilometre hike to **Sirena**, where you can stay for a day or two in the simple lodge, exploring the local trails around the Río Sirena. Sirena, the biggest puesto in the park, is also a research station, and often full of biologists. Hikers coming from the Bahía Drake area enter at **San Pedrillo** and walk the 25km to Sirena from there.

The small hamlet of **La Palma**, 24km northwest of Puerto Jiménez, is the starting point for getting to the **Los Patos** puesto. It's a twelve-kilometre walk to the park, much of it through hot lowland terrain. You need to arrive at Los Patos soon after dawn; if you want to stay in La Palma and get up early, *Cabinas Corcovado* (❶–❷) is a good bet. The **El Tigre** puesto, at the eastern inland entrance to the park, is a decent place to take breakfast or lunch with the ranger(s) before setting off on the local trails. To get there from Jiménez, drive 10km north and take the second left, a dirt track, signed to El Tigre and Dos Brazos. **All puestos** have camping areas, drinking water, information, toilets and telephone or radio-telephone contact. Wherever you enter, jot down the details of the **marea** (tides) which are posted in prominent positions. You'll need to cross most of the rivers at low tide – to do otherwise is dangerous. Rangers can advise on conditions.

The trails

The sixteen-kilometre trail from **La Leona to Sirena** runs just inland from the beach, which makes it easy to keep your bearings. You can only walk its full length at low tide; if you do get stuck, the only thing to do is wait for the water to recede. If you can avoid problems with the tides, you should be able to do the walk in five to six hours, taking time to look out for birds. The walking can get a bit monotonous, but the beaches are uniformly lovely and deserted, and you may be lucky enough to spot a flock of **scarlet macaws** in the coastal trees – a rare sight. You will probably see (or hear) monkeys, too. Take lots of sunscreen, a big hat and at least five litres of water per person – the trail gets very hot, despite the sea breezes.

The really heroic walk in Corcovado, all 25km of it, is from **Sirena to San Pedrillo**, the stretch along which you'll see the most impressive trees. It's a

What to see at Corcovado

Walking through Corcovado you'll see many lianas, vines, mosses and spectacularly tall trees – some of them 50 or 60m high, and a few more than 80m high. All in all, Corcovado's area is home to about a quarter of all the tree species in the country, including the **silkwood** (or *ceiba pentandra*), characterized by its height – thought to be the largest tree in Central America – and its smooth grey bark. One silkwood, near the Llorona–San Pedrillo section of the trail, is over 80m high and 3m in diameter. You'll also notice huge **buttresses**: above-ground roots shot out by the silkwoods and other tall canopy species. These are used to help anchor the massive tree in thin tropical soil, where drainage is particularly poor.

Corcovado supports a higher volume of **large mammals** than most other areas of the country, except perhaps the wild and rugged Talamancas. **Jaguars** need more than 100 square kilometres each for their hunting; if you are a good tracker you may be able to spot their traces within the park, especially in the fresh mud along trails and riverbeds. Initially they look identical to those made by a large dog, but the four toes are of unequal size (the outermost one is the smallest) and the fore footprint should be wider than its length. You might, too, see the **margay**, a spotted wildcat about the size of a large domesticated house cat, which comes down from the forest to sun itself on rocks at midday. The **ocelot**, a larger spotted cat, is even shyer, rarely seen for more than a second, poking its head out of the dense cover and then melting away into the forest again immediately.

With a body shape somewhere between a large pig and a cow, the **Baird's tapir** is an odd-looking animal, most immediately recognizable for its funny-looking snout, a truncated elephant-type trunk. Tapirs are very shy – and have been made even more so through large-scale hunting – and not aggressive, and you would have to be exceptionally lucky to see one here or anywhere. More threatening are the packs of white-collared **peccaries**, a type of wild pig, who in Corcovado typically group themselves in packs of about thirty. They are often seen along the trails and should be treated with caution, since they can bite you. The accepted wisdom is to climb a tree if they come at you threateningly, clacking their jaws and growling, though this, of course, means you have to be good at climbing trees, some of which have painful spines.

More common mammals that you'll likely spot are the ubiquitous **agouti** (also called paca), foraging in the underbrush. Essentially a large rodent with smooth, glossy hair, the agouti looks similar to a large squirrel. The **coati**, a member of the raccoon family, with a long ringed tail, is also sure to cross your path. Another mammal found in significant numbers in the park – and all over the peninsula – is the **tayra** (tolumuco), a small and swift mink-like creature. They will in most cases run from you, but should not be approached, as they have teeth and can be aggressive.

Among the park's resident **birds** is the **scarlet macaw**, around 300 of which live in the park – more, in terms of birds per square kilometre, than anywhere else in the country. Macaws are highly prized as caged birds and, despite the efforts of the SPN, poaching is still a problem in Corcovado, as their (relative) abundance makes them easy prey. Around the Río Sirena estuary, especially, keep an eye out for the **boat-billed heron**, whose wide bill gives it a lopsided quality. The big black **king vulture** can also be found in Corcovado; a forager rather than a hunter, it nevertheless looks quite ominous. There are many other smaller birds in Corcovado including, perhaps, the fluffy-headed **harpy eagle**. Though the harpy is thought to be extinct in Costa Rica, ornithologists reckon there's a chance that a few pairs still live in Corcovado, and in the Parque Internacional La Amistad on the Talamanca coast.

two-day trek, so you need a tent, sleeping bag and mosquito net, and you mustn't be worried by having to set up camp in the jungle. Fording the **Río Sirena**, just 1km beyond the Sirena puesto, is the biggest obstacle: this is the deepest of all the rivers on the peninsula, with the strongest out-tow current, and has to be crossed with care, and at low tide only – **sharks** come in and out in search of food at high tide. Be sure to get the latest information from the Sirena rangers before you set out.

About half of the walk is spent slogging it out on the beach, where the sand is more tightly packed than along the La Leona–Sirena stretch. Some hikers do the beach section of the walk well before dawn or after dark; there are fewer dangers (like snakes) at night on the beach and as long as you have a good torch with lots of batteries and/or the moon is out, this is a reasonable option. The second half of the walk – a seven-hour stint – is in the jungle, just inland from the coast. Beyond the jungle you come once more to the beach, at which point you are only about an hour away from the Río San Pedrillo and just 10km from Bahía Drake, easily walkable along the coast.

Less frequented than the track around the edge of the peninsula is the well-marked twenty-kilometre inland trail from **Los Patos to Sirena**. It takes you steeply uphill for some 5km into high, wet and dense rainforest, after which the rest of the walk is flat, but extremely hot. This is a trail for experienced rainforest hikers and hopeful **mammal**-spotters, giving you a reasonable chance of coming across, for example, tapirs, peccaries, margay, or the tracks of tapirs and jaguars. That said, some hikers come away very disappointed, having not seen a thing. It's a gruelling trek, especially with the hot inland temperatures (at least 26°C, with 100 percent humidity) and the lack of sea breezes, although there are crude shelters en route where you can rest in the shade (but not camp), but it is probably best avoided if you've not done much rainforest hiking before.

The **El Tigre** area, at the eastern inland entrance to the park, is gradually becoming more developed, with short walking trails being laid out around the puesto. These provide an introduction to Corcovado without making you slog it out on the marathon trails, and can easily be covered in a morning or afternoon.

The Borucas and the Fiesta de los Diablitos

Many indigenous peoples throughout the isthmus, and all the way north to Mexico, enact the **Fiesta de los Diablitos**, a resonant spectacle that is both disturbing and humorous. In Costa Rica the Borucas use it to celebrate New Year and to re-enact the Spanish invasion, with Columbus, Cortez and his men reborn every year. The fiesta takes place over three days and is a village affair: foreigners and tourists are not encouraged to come as spectators.

On the first day a village man is appointed to play the bull; others disguise themselves as little devils (*diablitos*), with burlap sacks and masks carved from balsa wood. The *diablitos* taunt the bull, teasing him with sticks, while the bull responds in kind. At midnight on December 30 the *diablitos* congregate on the top of a hill, joined by musicians playing simple flutes and horns fashioned from conch shells. During the whole night and over the next three days, the group proceeds from house to house, visiting everyone in the village and enjoying a drink or two of home brew (*chicha*). On the third day, the "bull" is ritually killed. The symbolism is indirect, but the bull, of course, represents the Spaniard(s), and the *diablitos* the indigenous people. The bull is always vanquished and the *diablitos* always win – which of course is not quite how it turned out, in the end.

Paso Real to Panamá

Twenty kilometres north of Palmar on the Interamericana is the ferry at **Paso Real**. From here you can either continue on the Interamericana or take the tiny car ferry and drive a little-touristed route along a paved road, which takes you through some spectacularly scenic country. The latter is little used by tourists except those few heading to the pretty mountain town of **San Vito**, the jumping-off point for the **Wilson Botanical Gardens** and **Parque Internacional La Amistad**.

Most people stick to the Interamericana, however, which switchbacks its way to the Panamá border following the wide and fast-running **Río Grande de Térraba**, cutting a giant path through the almost unbearably hot lowland landscape, its banks coloured red with tropical soils. Rainstorms seem to steamroller in with the express purpose of washing everything away, and you can almost see the river rise with each fresh torrent. The area is prone to landslides in the rainy season, when you can find yourself stranded by a sea of mud. The last section of the trip down to **Panamá** is through an empty border region in which the highway itself is the major feature.

Boruca and Reserva Indígena Boruca

About 12km past the turn-off for Buenos Aires on the Interamericana, and then 18km up a bad road, is the village of **BORUCA**. This is officially within an **indigenous reserve** and, technically, foreign tourists need a better reason to come than simply to look around. However, because of its proximity to the highway, tourists do occasionally turn up, usually looking to buy local **crafts**.

The women of Boruca make small tablecloths and purses on home-made looms, while the men fashion balsa-wood masks, some of which are expressly intended for the *diablitos* (little devils) ceremony (see box opposite) and procession that takes place on New Year's Eve. You can buy either from the artisans themselves or from the local cooperative, the Boruca Artesanías Group – it'll help if you have at least a working knowledge of Spanish. Local people have little other outlet for their crafts (you won't find them in the San José shops), so a visit can be a good way of contributing to the local economy; note that you'll need a 4WD to get here.

San Vito and the Wilson Botanical Gardens

The recently paved road from **Paso Real** to San Vito is steep and winding, with beautiful views. Just beyond Paso Real a tiny ferry (two cars only) crosses the Río Térraba on request. Even though the roads around here have improved, it's much easier with a 4WD to deal with occasional washouts and landslides, especially from May to November.

Settled largely by post-World War II immigrants from Italy, **SAN VITO** is a clean, prosperous agricultural town with a lovely setting in the Talamancas. At nearly 1000m above sea level it has a wonderfully refreshing climate, as well as great views over the Valle de Coto Brus below. The town is growing as Costa Ricans discover its qualities, and will soon be an important regional hub, though for now there's nothing to do around here but visit the nearby **Wilson Botanical Gardens** (daily 8am–4pm; $6), 6km to the south. The gardens are among the best in the country, and on the itineraries of many specialist birdwatching and natural-history tours. The huge tract of land is home to orchids, interesting tropical trees and exotic flowers such as heliconias. There's good **birding** too, on the paths and in the surrounding lands, with more than 300 species in total. They make an excellent day-trip if you happen to be in the area, but unless you have a keen interest in birds and regional and exotic flora it's probably not worth making a special trip from San José. You can **stay** at the gardens in bunkhouses (**❷**) or cabinas with private bath (**❻**). Students and researchers with ID get reduced rates. Contact the Organisation for Tropical Studies, or OTS (**☎**240-6696, **🖳**www.ots.ac.cr) for details; you must reserve in advance.

Parque Internacional La Amistad

Created in 1982 as a biosphere reserve, the **PARQUE INTERNACIONAL LA AMISTAD** (daily 8am–3.45pm; $7) is a joint venture by the governments of Panamá and Costa Rica to protect the Talamancan mountain areas on both sides of their shared border. Amistad also encompasses several **indigenous reserves**, the most geographically isolated in the country, where Bribrí and Cabecar peoples are able to live with minimal interference from the Valle Central. It is the largest park in the country, covering 2070 square kilometres of Costa Rican territory.

In 1983 Amistad was designated a World Heritage Site, thanks to its immense scientific resources. The Central American isthmus is often described as being a crossroads or filter for the meeting of the North and South American eco-communities; the Amistad area is itself a "biological bridge" within the isthmus, where an extraordinary number of habitats, life zones, topographical features, soils, terrains and types of animal and plant life can be found. Its **terrain**, while mainly mountainous, is extremely varied on account of shifting altitudes, and ranges from wet tropical forest to high peaks where the temperature can drop below freezing at night. According to the classification system devised by L.R. Holdridge (see Contexts). Amistad has at least seven (some say eight or nine) **life zones**, along with six transition zones. Even more important is Amistad's function as the last bastion of some of the species most in danger of **extinction** in both Costa Rica and the isthmus. Within its boundaries roam the jaguar and the puma, the ocelot and the tapir. Along with Corcovado on the Península de Osa, Amistad may also be the last holdout of the **harpy eagle**, feared extinct in Costa Rica.

Too bad for keen natural historians and animal-spotters, then, that the terrain is so rugged, for there is only limited access to Amistad. Indeed, only serious and experienced walkers and hikers should consider it a destination. There are few rangers in relation to the size of the area, and getting lost and/or running out of water and food is potentially fatal. Drinking from the many streams and rivers is not recommended, due to the presence of the giardia bacterium.

Park practicalities

If you are really serious about exploring La Amistad's limited (and often unmarked and uncleared) trails, contact the Fundación de Parques Nacionales office in San José (see p.68) in advance. They may be able to hook you up with a local guide who knows the area. The small hamlet of **Altamira**, 25km northeast of San Vito, functions as the park headquarters, with a puesto maintained by a full-time ranger who can provide information. You'll need a 4WD even to get here, whatever the season. From Altamira you can walk a demanding ten-kilometre-long trail, most of it uphill, to a flat ridge called **Las Tablas**, where it's possible to **camp**. Take water, tent and a three-season sleeping bag.

Near Las Tablas, bordering the park, *La Amistad Eco-Lodge*, 3km from the hamlet of Las Mellizas on the way to Sabalito (℡228-8671, ℻289-7858, 🅦www .laamistad.com; ❻) has comfortable rustic rooms. It's on the Montero family farm, which also grows organic coffee and has a few kilometres of trails in its surrounding woods – the Monteros can provide transport if you ask in advance.

Paso Canoas and the Panamanian border

Duty-free shops and stalls lining the Interamericana announce the approach to **PASO CANOAS**. As you come into town, either driving or on the TRACOPA or international Ticabus service, you'll pass the Costa Rican customs checkpoint, where everybody gets a going-over. Foreigners don't attract much interest, however; customs officials are far more concerned with nabbing Ticos coming back over the border with unauthorized amounts of bargain consumer goods.

To cross from Costa Rica into Panamá, most nationalities need a **tourist card**; UK citizens need only show their passport. Tourist cards should be collected in advance from the **Panamanian consulate**, or from the office of Copa, Panamá's national airline, in San José. Many people should also have a **visa** – Canadians, Australians and New Zealanders among them. You may also need a return ticket back to Costa Rica (or an onward ticket out of Panamá to another country), but bear in mind that immigration requirements frequently change, seemingly at whim, so always check with the Panamanian consulate before setting off.

The **migración** is on the Costa Rican side, next to the TRACOPA bus terminal. You'll have to wait in line, maybe for several hours, especially if a San José–David–Panamá City Ticabus comes through, as all international bus passengers are processed together. Arrive early to get through fastest. There's no problem **changing money**: there's a Banco Nacional on the Costa Rican side of the border and, beyond that, plenty of moneychangers. Note that Panamá has no paper currency of its own, and US dollars – called *balboas* – are used. It does have its own coins, equivalent to US coins, which are also in wide circulation. Also beware that you cannot take any **fruit or vegetables** across the border, even if they're for your lunch; they will be confiscated.

If you absolutely have to bed down in Paso Canoas, there are about a dozen rock-bottom budget **cabinas** and *hospedajes*. These are all extremely basic, with cell-like rooms, private bath and cold water. They can also be full on weekends. One place a cut above the pack is *Cabinas Interamericano* (℡732-2041; ❶), on a side road to the right after the TRACOPA bus terminal, heading towards the border. Rooms are not bad, and there's a restaurant.

DAVID, the first city of any size in Panamá, is about ninety minutes beyond the border. Buses run from the Panamanian border bus terminal every hour or so until 5pm. From David it's easy to pick up local services, including the Ticabus to Panamá City, which you can't pick up at the border.

Parque Nacional Isla del Coco

Five hundred kilometres southwest off Costa Rica's Pacific coast, the remote **PARQUE NACIONAL ISLA DEL COCO**, integrated into the national park system in 1978, is these days most famous as "Dinosaur Island" in

Steven Spielberg's blockbuster *Jurassic Park*. In the opening frames of the film, a helicopter swoops over azure seas to a remote, emerald-green isle: that's Coco. At 12km long and 5km wide, Coco is the only island in this part of the Pacific that receives enough rain to support the growth of **rainforest**. It also has an extraordinary wealth of **endemic species**: seventy plant species, sixty-four insect species, three spiders and four types of bird, all of which are found nowhere else in the world. Besides researchers and rangers, Coco has no human inhabitants.

Though evidence suggests that the island was known by pre-Columbian sea-going peoples from Ecuador and Colombia, in the modern age it was "discovered" by the navigator and sea captain Joan Cabezas in 1526. Attempts were made to establish a colony here in the early twentieth century, and nowadays wild descendants of the would-be settlers' pigs and coffee plants have upset the island's Galapagos-like ecosystem. Other threats include illegal fishing in its waters; the SPN has extremely limited resources for policing the island, as simply getting there by sea is so expensive. Besides biologists and divers, Coco attracts treasure hunters. It is said that over the centuries nefarious pirates buried bullion here, but in more than five hundred expeditions by tenacious treasure hunters, no one has yet found it. If you're interested in the island, contact the Fundación Amigos de La Isla del Coco (T256-7476, Wwww.cocosisland.org) which was founded in 1994 to help preserve the unique terrestrial and marine biodiversity of Coco.

Getting to Coco entails major expense. In the North American winter months the ship *Okeanos Aggressor* leaves from Puntarenas (T385-2628, Wwww.aggressor.com) for specialist ten-day **diving tours**. The price is about $3000 per person, excluding transport to Costa Rica and equipment rental, which is available once you arrive.

Travel details

Buses

Dominical to: Quepos (4 daily; 2hr); San Isidro (3 daily; 40min–1hr).
Golfito to: Playas Pavones and Zancudo (dry season only, 1 daily; 2hr 30min); San José (2 daily; 8hr).
Palmar to: San José (7 daily; 5hr 30min); Sierpe (5 daily; 30min).
Paso Canoas to: San Isidro (2 daily; 6hr); San José (6 daily; 9hr).
Playas Pavones and Zancudo to: Golfito (dry season only, 1 daily; 2hr 30min).
Puerto Jiménez to: San Isidro (2 daily; 5hr); San José (2 daily; 8–9hr).
Quepos to: Dominical (4 daily, 2hr).
San Gerardo de Rivas to: San Isidro (2 daily; 40min).
San Isidro to: Dominical (4 daily; 40min–1hr); Paso Canoas (2 daily; 6hr); Puerto Jiménez (3 daily; 5hr); Quepos (4 daily; 3hr 30min); San Gerardo de Rivas (2 daily; 1hr 40min); San José (16 daily; 3hr); Uvita (2 daily; 1hr 30min).
San José to: Golfito (2 daily; 8hr); Palmar (7 daily; 5hr 30min); Paso Canoas (6 daily; 9hr); Puerto Jiménez (2 daily; 8–9hr); San Isidro (16 daily; 3hr).
Sierpe to: Palmar (5 daily; 30min).
Uvita to: San Isidro (2 daily; 1hr 30min).

Lancha

Golfito to: Puerto Jiménez (daily at 11am; 1hr 30min), returning from Jiménez at 6am.

Flights

Golfito to: Puerto Jiménez (1 daily); San José (4 daily).
Puerto Jiménez to: Golfito (1 daily); San José (2–5 daily).
San José to: Golfito (5 daily); Palmar Sur (4 daily); Puerto Jiménez (3 daily).

Contexts

Contexts

A brief history of Costa Rica

The peopling of Costa Rica probably took place sometime around 10,000 BC, about 25,000 years after the first *Homo sapiens* had crossed the Bering Strait into what is now the Americas (though the only thing to support this tentative date is a single flint arrowhead excavated in the 1890s in Guanacaste). Archeologists know almost nothing of the various people who inhabited modern-day Costa Rica until about 1000 BC. Certainly no written records were left.

Costa Rica before the Spanish

Pre-Columbian Costa Rica was a contact zone – a corridor for merchants and trading expeditions – between the Mesoamerican empires to the north and the Andean empire to the south. Excavations of pottery, jade and trade goods, and accounts of cultural traditions, have shown that the pre-Columbian peoples of Costa Rica adopted liberally from both areas.

When the Spaniards arrived in Costa Rica in the early sixteenth century, it was inhabited by as many as 27 different groups or clans. Most clans were assigned names by the invaders, which they took from the **cacique** (chief) with whom they dealt. The modern-day Zona Norte was home to the **Catapas**, the **Votos** and the **Suerres**; the extreme south of the Talamancas held the **Cabécars** and the **Guayamís**, whose influence spread to the modern-day Zona Sur and the Osa Peninsula. In the nearby Valle de Diquis and Valle de El General were the **Térrabas** and their sub-group the **Borucas**. The Valle Central contained the **Huetars**. Modern-day Guanacaste was the most heavily populated and farmed area in pre-Columbian Costa Rica, home to the **Chorotegas** and the older Nicoyan peoples.

Many of these groups had affinities with their neighbours in Nicaragua to the north and Panamá to the south. The Chorotegas in particular showed signs of cultural inheritance from the Olmec peoples of southern Mexico, while those of the extreme south and Osa Peninsula had affinities with peoples in Panamá and Colombia.

About 1000 BC, most of these groups would have been involved in **subsistence farming**. They also existed in a state of almost constant warfare. However, unlike in the Mesoamerican states and in the Inca empire, where war and domination had led to the establishment of complex, far-reaching empires, in Costa Rica no one group gained ascendancy, and the political position of the clans seemed to remain more or less constant throughout the ages, with no group imposing its language or customs on the rest. One reason could be that although these groups were only too willing to go to **war**, they did not do so in order to increase their territory. Perennially low population density in ancient Costa Rica meant that there was plenty of land, and plenty of space into which persecuted or vanquished groups could escape. Like the forest-dwelling tribes in Amazonia to the south, these pre-Columbian peoples waged war to capture slaves, victims for potential sacrifice, marriage partners or simply for revenge.

As for **religion**, the clans were highly complex and specialized. Shamans were respected members of society, officiating at funerals, which were the most important rites of passage, especially in the Talamancan groups. Some clans had animal taboos that prevented them from hunting and killing certain beasts. The taboos neatly complemented each other: one group might not be able to hunt the tapir, for example, while the neighbouring clan in turn would be prohibited from hunting the main prey of another group. This delicate balance played itself out on various levels, promoting harmony between man and nature. Like everywhere from southern Mexico to Brazil, the jaguar was much revered among all the groups, and only hunted to provide shamans with pelts, teeth and other ritualistic articles.

Gender divisions were, to an extent, along familiar lines: men made war and performed religious duties, while women were confined to domestic roles. However, women of the Boruca group in the southwest went to war alongside men, and the Votos of the Zona Norte regularly had women chiefs. In many clans, the inheritance of names and objects was matrilineal.

People lived **communally** in stockaded villages – especially in the Talamancan groups – called **palenques** by the Spaniards. Whole groups, not necessarily related by kin, would live kibbutz-like in a village big house. They organized work "gangs" who would tackle labour projects, usually agricultural. In most cases land was held communally and harvests shared to ensure the survival of all. **Social hierarchy** was complex, with an ascending scale of **caciques** and shamans occupying the elite positions.

The Chorotegas in Guanacaste in particular developed a high level of **cultural expression**, possessing a written, symbol-based language, and harvesting and trading such diverse products as honey, natural dyes, and cotton.

Costa Rica "discovered"

On September 18, 1502, on his fourth and last voyage to the Americas, **Columbus** sighted Costa Rica. Battered by a storm, he ordered his ships to drop anchor just off Isla Uvita, 1km offshore from present-day Puerto Limón. The group stayed seventeen days, making minor forays into the heavily forested coast and its few villages. The indigenous peoples that Columbus met – as he could not fail to notice – were liberally attired in gold headbands, mirrored breastplates, bracelets and the like, convincing him of potential riches. In fact, the **gold** worn by those first welcoming envoys would have been traded or come to the peoples of the Caribbean coast through inter-tribal warfare. There was very little gold in the area known as the Atlantic watershed – the eastern slopes of the Cordilleras Central and Talamanca. Rather it came from the southwest of the country near the Valle de Diquis, over the near-impenetrable hump of the Cordillera de Talamanca. With dreams of wealth, Columbus sailed on, charting the entire coastal area from Honduras to Panamá, including Costa Rica, and naming it **Veragua**.

In 1506 King Ferdinand of Spain despatched **Diego de Nicuesa** to govern what would become Costa Rica. From the start his mission was beset by hardship, beginning when their ship ran aground on the coast of Panamá, forcing the party to walk up the Caribbean shore. There they met native people who, unlike those who had welcomed Columbus tentatively but politely with their shows of gold, burned their crops rather than submit to the authority of the Spanish. This, together with the impenetrable jungles, the creatures that lived there and tropical diseases, meant that the expedition had to be abandoned.

Next came **Gil González Davila**, in 1521–22, who concentrated on Costa Rica's Pacific coast, which offered safer anchorages. González and his men covered practically the entire length of Pacific Costa Rica on foot, baptizing as they went: the expedition priest later claimed that some 32,000 souls had been saved in the name of the King of Spain. The indigenous peoples, meanwhile, began a campaign of **resistance** that was to last nearly thirty years, employing guerrilla tactics, full-scale flight, infanticide, attacks on colonist settlements and burning their own villages. There were massacres, defeats and submissions on both sides, but by 1540 Costa Rica was officially a Royal Province of Spain, and a decade later, the Conquest was more or less complete. Most of the key areas of the country had been charted or settled, with the exception of the Talamanca region, which remained largely unexplored for centuries.

Indigenous people in the colonial period

During the first years of the Spanish invasion those indigenous Costa Ricans who grouped themselves in large settlements, like the Chorotegas, proved more easily subjected, and were carted off by the Spanish to work in the mines, build the first Costa Rican towns, or co-opted to general slavery in the guise of farmwork. The more scattered groups fared better, in the main exiling themselves to the rugged Talamancas. By then, however, the real conquerors of the New World had arrived: smallpox, influenza, and measles. In the seventeenth and eighteenth centuries huge pandemics swept the country, among them the so-called **Great Pandemic** of 1611–60, in which whole towns and villages disappeared virtually overnight. **Caciques** as well as commoners died, leaving groups without leadership. Although colonial censuses are notoriously inaccurate, in 1563 it is reckoned that an estimated

Gold, land and souls

The first Spanish accounts of Costa Rican indigenous peoples were made in the sixteenth century by "chroniclers", the official scribes who accompanied mapping and evangelical expeditions. In general these were either soldiers or missionaries who showed almost no talent for ethnography. Rather, they approached the pre-Columbian world as inventory-takers or suspicious accountants, writing terse and unimaginative reports liberally spiced with numbers and accounts of gold (although they found almost none). It was they who started the trend of portraying the cultures of the indigenous peoples of Costa Rica as "low" and underdeveloped; what they in fact meant was that there was little that could be expropriated for the Crown. Of the narratives which stand out is one by Columbus himself, who described the small welcoming party he received in 1502 in vivid and rather romanticized prose in his *lettera rarissima*, meant for the eyes of his sovereign.

Another, more important, account is by Gonzalo Fernández de Oviedo, whose comprehensive, nineteen-volume *Historía General de las Indias, Islas y Tierra Firme del Mar Oceano* was first published in 1535. Oviedo spent only ten or twelve days with the Chorotega peoples but he had a fine eye for detail, and recorded many aspects of the Chorotega diet, dress, and social customs. He also noticed that they spoke a form of Nahua, the language of the Aztecs and the lingua franca of Mesoamerica, an observation which has since convinced most historians of a direct cultural link between the empires to the north and the peoples of pre-Columbian Costa Rica and Nicaragua.

One of the first things the Spanish chroniclers noticed was that the indigenous peoples in the Talamancas in the southeast and the Greater Chiriquí in the southwest practised ritual sacrifice. Every full moon, prisoners captured in the most recent raid would be ritually beheaded. The Spanish, of course, were repelled, and so began the systematic baptism campaigns, and the destruction of indigenous "idolatry".

80,000 indigenous peoples lived in Costa Rica; by 1714 the official count was 999. Today there are only about 5000 indigenous people in the country out of a population of nearly 3.5 million. For more on the current status of indigenous people in Costa Rica, see p.376.

In 1560 **Juan de Cavallon** and **Juan Vásquez de Coronado** – the first true conquistadors of Costa Rica – succeeded in penetrating the Valle Central, the area that would become most significant in the development of the nation. As Cortés had done in Mexico, the Spaniards of Costa Rica took advantage of existing rivalries among the native groups and played them off against each other. In this way they managed to dominate the groups of the Pacific coast with the help of tribes from the Valle Central.

In the early years of the colony, the Spaniards quickly established the **encomienda**, a system widespread in the Spanish crown's Central American possessions that gave the conquistadors and their descendants the right to demand tribute or labour from the indigenous population. The **encomienda** applied to all indigenous males in Costa Rica between the ages of 18 and 50, and to a lesser extent to women. Quotas were set for the donation of foods such as cacao fruit, corn, chicken, honey and chilli peppers. Although these are all foodstuffs the settlers could have grown and harvested themselves, the capacity for the **encomienda** to enrich the colonies was immense. From the Spanish point of view, this was compensation for the risks and hazards involved in coming to the New World. As many people have said, no man came to America to be poorer than he was in Europe.

Costa Rica's indigenous peoples resisted servitude to the colonials quite fiercely, although (in the words of one **cacique**) they did get tired of "running around in the jungle and hiding all the time". Nor was there total acceptance of the way the native population was treated during this period. High-ranking clergymen protested to their Spanish overlords, and as early as 1542 the **New Laws**, influenced by the passionate appeals of Fray Bartolomé de las Casas, decreed that colonizers had a duty to "protect" the indigenous peoples, and in 1711 the Bishop of Nicaragua, Fray Benito Garret y Arlovi, informed on the governor of Costa Rica for his brutal policies. These decrees assuaged the conscience of the Spanish crown, but what happened on the ground in the colonies, of course, was quite a different matter.

The early settlers

It seems more appropriate to discuss Costa Rica's lack of colonial experience, rather than a bona fide colonization. In 1562, **Juan Vásquez de Coronado** became the second governor of Costa Rica. Coronado has always been portrayed as the good guy, renowned for his favourable treatment of the indigenous peoples. It was under his administration that the first settlement of any size or importance was established, and **Cartago**, in the heart of the Valle Central, was made capital of the colony. During the next century settlers confined themselves more or less to the centre of the country. The Caribbean coast was the haunt of buccaneers – mainly English – who put ashore and wintered here after plundering the lucrative Spanish Main; the Pacific coast saw its share of pirate activity too, most famously when Sir Francis Drake came ashore briefly in Bahía Drake in 1579.

This first epoch of the colony is remembered as one of unremitting **poverty**. Within a decade of its invasion Costa Rica was notorious throughout the Spanish empire for its lack of gold. The settlers and their descendants, unlike those to the north and the south, who became wealthy on the gold of the

Aztecs and Inca, never achieved their dreams of instant aristocracy. Instead, they were confronted with almost insuperable obstacles, including tropical fever, hunger, and belligerent natives. The Valle Central was fertile, but there was uncertainty as to what crops to grow. Coffee had not yet been imported to Costa Rica, nor had tobacco, so it was to subsistence agriculture that most settlers turned, growing just enough to live on. There were no export crops and no national markets for foodstuffs. Spanish fabrics, manufactured goods and currency became so scarce that by 1709 Valle Central settlers were forced to adopt cacao beans as currency. Goat's hair and bark were used as clothing fabrics, making your average eighteenth-century Costa Rican farmer look as wild and uncivilized as Romulus and Remus before the founding of Rome. In 1719, the governor of Costa Rica famously complained that he had to till his own land. To make matters worse, Volcán Irazú blew its top in 1723, nearly destroying the capital. With the emphasis on agriculture, and with little industry or trade, Costa Rica was unsurprisingly slow in founding urban settlements. In 1706, Cubujuquí (present-day Heredia) was established; in 1737, Villa Nueva de la Boca del Monte (later shortened, thankfully, to San José) was founded; and in 1782, it was the turn of Villa Hermosa (present-day Alajuela).

The tough yeoman **settler farmers** who survived in these conditions are the most distinct figures in Costa Rica's early colonial history, and their independent, though impoverished, state is widely believed to be the root of the country's modern-day egalitarianism. Recent historical works, however, concede that while everybody in the early days of the colony may have been equally poor, social distinctions still counted, and where they did not exist, were manufactured, albeit in a much less virulent form than in other Central American possessions of the Spanish crown.

Two other crucial factors went into the making of the modern nation. One was **coffee**, eventually to become Costa Rica's main export, a crop that requires many smallholders rather than large hacienda systems. Another factor in the unique development of the colony was **ethnic**: quite simply, the vast majority of peasants in Costa Rica were descendants of the Spanish colonists, rather than **indigenos** or **mestizos**, and as such were treated as equals by the ruling elite, who saw them as **hermaniticos**, or "little brothers".

Independence and prosperity

The nineteenth century was the most significant era in the development of Costa Rica. Initially, after 1821, when Central America declared **independence** from Spain, freedom made little difference to Costa Ricans. Although granted on September 15, 1823, the news did not reach Costa Rica until a month later, when a mule messenger arrived from Nicaragua to tell the astonished citizens of Cartago the good news. Rather than rejoicing in being freed from the Spanish – Spain had not paid much attention to the poor and isolated province anyway – a **civil war** promptly broke out among the inhabitants of the Valle Central, dividing the citizens of Alajuela and San José from those of Heredia and Cartago. This struggle for power was won by the Alajuela–San José faction, and **San José** became the capital city in 1823.

Costa Rica made remarkable progress in the latter half of the nineteenth century, building roads, bridges and railways and filling San José with neo-Baroque, European-style edifices. Virtually all this activity was fuelled by the **coffee** trade, bringing wealth that the settlers just a century earlier could hardly have dreamed of. The coffee story begins as early as 1808, when beans from Cuba or Jamaica – depending on which sources you believe – were

The history of banana-growing in Costa Rica is inextricably linked to the establishment of the railroads. Initially the brainchild of Costa Rican president Tomas Guardia, the San José–Puerto Limón railway – the "Jungle Train" – was built by American capitalist Minor Keith. From the outset in 1871, the idea behind the proposed railway was to establish an easy route for Valle Central coffee to reach the Caribbean coast, thus circumventing both the fluvial method of transporting the beans via the Río Sarapiquí, and the Puntarenas route, by which the crop had to travel around Cape Horn.

Almost immediately after construction began, however, the contractors faced a labour shortage. The lowlands of Limón Province have a particularly brutal climate: continuously hot, muggy, and lashed by heavy rain. Yellow fever, venomous serpents, raids by bands of indigenous peoples and general exhaustion conspired to fell much of the workforce, initially made up of Highlanders, imported Chinese "coolie" labour, and Italians. Due to economic conditions in Jamaica at the time, there was a ready pool of black labour. Between 1874 and 1891 some 11,000 Jamaicans arrived in Costa Rica. The Highland majority did not respond well to this immigration, largely on grounds of race. Costa Ricans thought of themselves as white and often compared themselves favourably with the darker-skinned inhabitants of neighbouring countries. It is generally held that for the first half of this century a law existed prohibiting the migration of Afro-Caribbeans to the Valle Central.

In 1890 the train finally sparked and puffed its way out of the capital. Minor Keith's involvement in the history of Costa Rica did not stop here, as he had ingeniously planted bananas along the tracks in order to help pay for the train's construction. The fruit flourished and, as new markets opened up in Europe and the US, it became an exportable commodity: Costa Rica was the first Central American republic to grow bananas in bulk. In 1899 Keith and a colleague founded the United Fruit Company. The company, or Yunai, as it was called locally, came to transform the social, political and cultural face of Central America – and of all the countries in which it operated, it had the biggest dealings in Costa Rica.

Opinions of the Yunai oscillate between the belief that it was a capitalist scourge that gave Costa Rica its Banana Republic burden, and that it was the saving grace of the nation. Almost from the beginning, United Brands – as it came to call itself – gained a reputation for anti-union practices, deserting entire areas once labour showed any signs of being organized. That said, the banana companies have always generally offered high salaries, and many Highlanders would spend a year or two working on the banana plantations with the express purpose of getting together enough money to start a small farm, although workers would more often spend their salaries – for many years given in redeemable scrip instead of cash – on drink and dissipation. To a degree this was a deliberate plan by the company to have their labour force continuously in hock and therefore pliable.

As long as the United Fruit Company provided a steady flow of jobs, there was no real temptation for the Jamaicans and their descendants to leave the Caribbean coast, where they had effectively transported their own culture intact. In isolated Limón they could retain their traditional food, Protestantism, and play West Indian games like cricket, preserving their culture in the face of a much larger Highland majority. They could also use their ability to speak English to advantage – often Afro-Caribbeans attained high-ranking positions in the *bananeros* because they could communicate with the American foremen in their own language.

When the plantations began to close down in Limón in 1925 as a result of the dreaded banana maladies Sigatoka and Panamá disease, the fortunes of the Jamaicans changed. In the face of a pestilence so virulent that plantations could only run for about two or three years, the United Fruit company had to look elsewhere in the country for possible locations for their operations. While keeping their Limón plantations open, in 1934 they began acquiring land and planting bananas in the area around modern-day Quepos in the Central Pacific, and Golfito in the Zona Sur. This spelled bad news for the Afro-Caribbean workers as, unbeknown to them, United Fruit had signed a contract with the Costa Rican government stipulating that employment preference be given to native Costa Ricans. When the contract became public in September 1930, racial tensions rose to boiling point in Limón. Afro-Caribbeans were caught, unable to afford the passage home to Jamaica on the one hand and prohibited from working elsewhere in the country on the other. It seems that United Fruit itself did not have any qualms about employing Afro-Caribbeans; quite the opposite. Rather it was the government, along with the white plantation workers and the Highland elite who felt most threatened, and who in 1933 petitioned Congress to prohibit the entry of blacks into the country "because they are of a race inferior to ours".

In 1934, the most virulent strike yet seen in the Costa Rican *bananeros* began. It was organized by Carlos Luis Fallas, labour activist and novelist, who had been exiled to Limón as a result of his militancy on behalf of labour organizations in the Valle Central. As historian Michael Seligson puts it, sending Fallas to the *bananeros* "was like throwing Brer Rabbit into the briar patch. For the judges Limón was the Siberia of Costa Rica; for Fallas, it was the Nirvana of union organizers." Fallas proved a brilliant organizer, though initially the proposals he put forward to the Company were quite mild, requesting things like malaria drugs, snakebite serum and payment in cash rather than scrip, which could easily be squandered. Nonetheless, the Company refused to recognize these proposals, and in August 1934 the strike began in earnest, tenaciously holding on in the face of physical harassment by the Company and police forces. For the next four years strikes and worker opposition raged on. In 1938 the Company finally pulled out of Limón Province for good, deserting it for the Pacific coast.

Left behind in the economic devastation and unable to migrate within the country in search of work, the Afro-Caribbean population either took up cacao cultivation, hacked out their own smallholdings or took to fishing or other subsistence activities. Overnight the schools, bunkhouses, American dollars, scrip economy, liquor and cigarettes disappeared, as did the US foremen and the ample plantation-style homes they had occupied. From about 1934 to 1970 the region was virtually destitute, without much of a cash economy or any large-scale employers. It is only now beginning to recover in terms of banana production – under the aegis of the national banana-franchise operators Standard Fruit Company – and only at considerable cost to the environment as more tropical forests are felled and more rivers polluted with the pesticides used on the fruit.

It is hard to appreciate the overwhelming presence that the Yunai wielded in communities until you have seen the schools and hospitals that it established, the plantation house-style accommodation it built for its managers and the rows upon rows of barrack-like houses it provided for its workers. You can get a flavour of this in the banana towns of Limón's Estrella Valley and on the road from Jacó to Quepos, where you pass through a long corridor of African palm oil farms, United Brands' only major remaining investment in Costa Rica. The Company also left its mark on the collective consciousness of the region. Carlos Luis Fallas' novels *Mamita Yunai* and *Gentes y gentecillas*, Garcia Marquez's *One Hundred Years of Solitude*, and Guatemalan Asturias's masterly *El Papa Verde* all document the power of the Company in the everyday life of the pueblitos of Central America.

first planted in the Valle Central. The plants thrived in the highland climate and by 1820 citizens of Cartago were being encouraged – ordered, even – to plant coffee in their backyards. But most significant in the early history of the coffee trade was the arrival in 1844 of English merchant **William Le Lacheur**. His ship, the **Monarch**, had emptied her hold of its cargo, and Le Lacheur arrived in the Pacific port of Puntarenas looking for ballast to take back to Liverpool. He travelled to the Valle Central where he secured a cargo of coffee beans, which he bought on credit, promising to return and pay in two years' time.

Until that point, most of Costa Rica's coffee had made its way to Chile, where it was mixed with a lower-grade South American bean, packaged for export under the brand of **Café de Valparaíso** and sent to England, taking the long way around Cape Horn. With Le Lacheur's shipment, however, British tastebuds were won round to the mellow, high-quality bean. A trading partnership began that saw the Costa Rican upper classes using Sheffield steel cutlery and Manchester linens for most of the 1800s.

The **coffee bourgeoisie** played a vital role in the cultural and political development of the country, and in 1848 the newly influential **cafetaleros** elected to the presidency their chosen candidate, Juan Rafael Mora. Extremely conservative and pro-trade, Mora came to distinguish himself in the battle against the American-backed filibuster William Walker in 1856, only to fall from grace and be executed in 1860 (see p.238).

The early twentieth century

The first years of the **twentieth century** witnessed a difficult transition towards democracy in Costa Rica. Universal male suffrage had come into effect during the last years of the nineteenth century, but class and power conflicts still dogged the country, with several **caudillo** (authoritarian) leaders, familiar figures in other Latin American countries, hijacking power. In general, however, these figures ended up in exile, and neither the army nor the church gained much of a foothold in politics. A number of radical labour initiatives were created during the 1920s, inspired by the Russian revolution, though for most of the twentieth century Costa Rica's successive administrations, whatever their political colour, have proved no friend of labour relations, beginning in 1924 when most **strikes** were outlawed. In 1931 the Communist party was formed, followed quickly by the National Republican party in 1932. The latter dominated the political scene for most of the 1940s, with the election in 1940 of the Republican (PRN) candidate **Rafael Calderón Guardia**, a doctor educated in part in Belgium and a devout Catholic.

It was Calderón who instigated the social reforms and state support for which Costa Rica is still almost unique in the region. In 1941 he established a new **Labour Code** that reinstated the right of workers to organize and strike, and a social security system providing free schooling for all. Calderón also paved the way for the establishment of the University of Costa Rica, health insurance, income security and assistance schemes, and thus won the support of the impoverished and the lower classes and the suspicion of the governing elites. One of those less than convinced by Calderón's policies was the man who would come to be known as **"Don Pepe"**, the coffee farmer **José Figueres Ferrer**, who denounced Calderón and his expensive reforms in a radio broadcast in 1941 and was then abruptly forced into exile in Mexico, from where he plotted his return.

The "revolution" of 1948 and after

The **elections of 1948** heralded the most eventful year of the twentieth century for Costa Rica. Constitutionally, Costa Rican presidents could not serve consecutive terms, so the election battle that year was between **Teodorico Picado**, widely considered to be a Calderón puppet, and **Otilio Ulate Blanco**, an ally of Figueres, who during two years in exile had become a heroic figure in some circles, returning to Costa Rica to play a key part in the **Acción Democrática**, a loose group of anti-Calderonistas. Ulate won the presidency, but the PRN won the majority in Congress – a fact that effectively annulled the election results.

For his part, **Figueres** was back on the scene and intent upon overthrowing Picado, who had stepped in and declared himself president in the face of the annulment. Figueres soon formed an opposition party, ideologically opposed to the PRN, calling them, somewhat ironically in view of the "republican" in their name, "communists". In March, **fighting** around Cartago began, culminating in an attack by the Figueres rebels on San José. To a degree, the battles were fought to safeguard the system of democratic election in the face of corruption, and in order to stem the clannishness and personality cults that dogged all Costa Rican political parties and presidential campaigns.

While Figueres' rebel forces were well equipped with arms, some supplied through CIA contacts, the militia defending president Picado was not: the national army consisted of only about 300 men at the time, and had to be supplemented by machete-wielding banana workers. Two thousand were dead by mid-April, when hostilities ceased. In May, the **Junta of the Second Republic** was formed, with Figueres as acting president, despite an after-the-fact attack from Nicaraguan Picado supporters in December.

Figueres wanted above all to engineer a complete break with the country's past, and especially the policies and legacies of the Calderonistas. Seeing himself as fighting both communism and corruption, he not only outlawed the PVP, the Popular Vanguard Party – formerly known as the Communist Party – but also nationalized the banks and devised a tax to hit the rich particularly hard, thus alienating the establishment. The new **constitution** drawn up in 1949 gave full citizenship to Afro-Caribbeans, full suffrage to women and abolished Costa Rica's army. In a way, the **abolition of the army** fitted with political precedents in Costa Rica. Nearly thirty years before, in 1922, former president Ricardo Jiménez Oreamuno had given a famous speech in which he said: "the school shall kill militarism, or militarism shall kill the Republic ... we are a country with more teachers than soldiers ... and a country that turns military headquarters into schools." Although the warming sentiment behind Jiménez's words is oft-repeated in Costa Rica, the truth is somewhat darker. Figueres' motives were not utopian but rather a pragmatic bid to limit the political instability that had been the scourge of so many Latin American countries, and an attempt to save valuable resources. Today, while the country still has no army, the police forces are powerful, highly specialized and, in some cases, heavily armed. **Paramilitary** organizations do exist. Chief among them is the Free Costa Rica Movement (MCRL), formed in 1961 and still active, which has allegedly been involved in a number of deeds more reminiscent of the Guatemalan army's death squads than the spirit of a harmonious and army-free Costa Rica.

In 1951 Figueres formed the **National Liberation Party**, or PLN, in order to be legitimately elected. He was a genius in drawing together disparate strands of society: when the elections came around the following year he got the agricultural smallholder vote, while winning the support of the urban working classes with his retention of the welfare state. At the same time he appeased the right-of-centrists with his essentially free-marketeering and staunch anti-communist stance.

The **1960s** and **1970s** were a period of prosperity and stability in Costa Rica, when the welfare state was developed to reach nearly all sectors of society. In 1977 the **indigenous bill** established the right of aboriginal peoples to their own land reserves – a progressive measure at the time, although indigenous peoples today are not convinced the system has served them well (see p.376). At the end of the 1970s, regional conflicts deflected attention from the domestic agenda, with the Carazo (1978–82) administration announcing its support for the FSLN revolutionary movement in Nicaragua, who had finally managed to despatch the Somoza family into exile.

Storm in the isthmus: the 1980s

Against all odds, Costa Rica in the 1980s and 1990s not only saw its way through the serious political conflicts of its neighbours, but also successfully managed predatory US interventionism, economic crisis and staggering debt. Like many Latin American countries, Costa Rica had taken out bank and government **loans** in the 1960s and 1970s to finance vital development. But in the early 1980s the slump in international coffee and banana prices put the country's finances into the red. In September 1981, Costa Rica defaulted on its interest payment on these loans, becoming the first third-world country to do so, and sparking off a chain of similar defaults in Latin America that threw the international banking community into crisis. Despite its defaults, Costa Rica's debt continued to accumulate, and by 1989 had reached a staggering US $5 billion, one of the highest per capita debt loads in the world.

To compound the economic crisis came the simultaneous escalation of the **Nicaraguan civil war**. During the entire decade Costa Rica's foreign policy – and to an extent its domestic agenda – would be overshadowed by tensions with Nicaragua and the US. Initially, the Monge PLN administration (1982–86) more or less capitulated to US demands that Costa Rica be used as a supply line for the Contras, and Costa Rica also accepted military training for its police force from the US. Simultaneously, the country's first agreement for a structural adjustment loan with the IMF was signed. It seemed increasingly clear that Costa Rica was on the path to both violating its declared neutrality in the conflicts of its neighbours and condemning its population to wage freezes, price increases and other side effects associated with the IMF restructuring.

In May 1984 the situation escalated with the events at the **La Penca** press conference, given by the US-backed Contra leader Edén Pastora. Held in a simple hut on the banks of the Río San Juan, the conference had minimal security. A bomb was apparently carried into the hut by a "Danish" cameraman and concealed within an equipment case, and was intended to kill all. Miraculously, an aide of Pastora's accidentally kicked the case over, so that when it was detonated the force of the blast went up and down instead of sideways, thus saving the lives of most of those within, including Pastora himself. Although nobody is quite sure who was behind the bombing, it seems that the point of the carnage was to implicate Managua, thus cutting off international support and destabilizing the Sandinista government further. Both the CIA and freelance Argentine terrorists have been implicated. The immediate effect was to shock the Costa Rican government and the international community into paying more attention to the deadly conflicts of Nicaragua and, by association, El Salvador and Guatemala.

The Arias peace plan

In 1986 PLN candidate **Oscar Arias Sánchez** was elected to the presidency, and Costa Rica's relations with the US and Nicaragua took a different tack. The former political scientist began to play the role of peace broker in the conflicts of Nicaragua, El Salvador and, to a lesser extent, Honduras and Guatemala, mediating between these countries and also between domestic factions within them. In October 1987, just eighteen months after taking office, Arias was awarded the Nobel Prize for Peace, attracting worldwide attention.

Arias's **peace plan** focused on regional objectives, tying individual and domestic conflicts into the larger picture: the stability of the isthmus. It officially called for a ceasefire, the discontinuation of military aid to the Contra insurrectionists, amnesties for political prisoners and for guerrillas who voluntarily relinquished the fight, and, lastly and perhaps most importantly, intergovernmental negotiations leading to free and fair elections. The peace plan began, rather than ended, with the awarding of the Nobel Prize, dragging on throughout 1987 and 1988 and running into obstacles as, almost immediately, all nations involved charged one another with non-compliance or other violations. The situation deteriorated when the US stationed troops in southern Honduras, ready to attack Nicaragua. Meanwhile, Washington continued to undermine Costa Rica's declared neutrality, requesting in April 1988 that Arias approve Costa Rican territory as a corridor for "humanitarian aid" to the Contras. The same month, Arias met with US President George Bush in Washington. Arias's diplomatic credibility enabled him to secure millions of dollars worth of American aid for Costa Rica without compromising the country politically. For its part, the last thing the US wanted was internal unrest in Costa Rica, its natural (if not entirely compliant) ally in the region.

However, while Arias had obviously stalled on the US using Costa Rica's northern border as a base from which to attack Nicaragua, he seemed to have fewer quibbles about what was happening in the south, in Panamá. In July 1989, CIA-supported anti-Noriega guerrilla forces (many of them ex-Contras) amassed along the Costa Rica–Panamá border in preparation for the US invasion of Panamá that would take place in December. Though Arias had gained the admiration of statesmen around the world, he proved to be less-than-popular at home. Many Costa Ricans saw him as neglecting domestic affairs, while increasing prices caused by the IMF's economic demands meant that conditions had not improved much in Costa Rica.

The 1990s

In 1990 the mantle of power fell to **Rafael Calderón Fournier** (son of Calderón Guardia), who, in the 1980s, had been instrumental in consolidating the opposition that became the free-marketeering Partido Unidad Social Cristiana, or PUSC. A year later, Costa Rica was rocked by its most powerful **earthquake** since the one that laid waste to most of Cartago in 1910. Centred in Limón Province, the quake killed 62 people and caused expensive structural damage. At the same time, nationals of El Salvador, Honduras, Guatemala and especially Nicaragua were looking to Costa Rica – the only stable country in the region – for asylum, and tension rose as the **refugees** poured in. In 1992 Costa Rica faced more trouble as it was brought to law in US courts for its failure to abide by international labour laws, a continuing black mark on the country's copybook for most of the twentieth century.

Until 1994, elections in Costa Rica had been relatively genteel affairs, involving lots of flag-waving and displays of national pride in democratic traditions. The elections of that year, however, were probably the dirtiest to date. The campaign opened and closed with an unprecedented bout of mudslinging and attempts to smear the reputations of both candidates, tactics which shocked many Costa Ricans. The PLN candidate – the choice of the left, for his promises to maintain the role of the state in the economy – was none other than **José María Figueres**, the son of Don Pepe, who had died four years previously. During the campaign Figueres was accused of shady investment rackets and influence-peddling. His free-market PUSC opposition candidate, Miguel Angel Rodríguez, fared no better, having admitted to being involved in a tainted-beef scandal in the 1980s. Figueres won, narrowly, though his term in office was plagued by a series of scandals. On a more positive note, in January 1995 a Free Trade agreement was signed with Mexico in order to try to redress the lack of preference given to Costa Rican goods in the US market by the signing of NAFTA. Costa Rica's economy received a further shot in the arm in 1996 when the communications giant INTEL chose the country for the site of their new factory in Latin America, creating thousands of jobs.

In February 1998 PUSC candidate **Dr Miguel Angel Rodríguez** was elected president, thus continuing the trend in Costa Rican politics for the past half-century, wherein power has been traded more or less evenly between the PLN and the PUSC. The new government committed itself to solving Costa Rica's most pressing problems, making improvements to the country's

Indigenous peoples in modern Costa Rica

Today you won't see much evidence of native traditions in Costa Rica. Only about one percent of the country's population is of aboriginal extraction, and the dispersion of the various groups ensures that they frequently do not share the same concerns and agendas. Contact between them, apart from through bodies such as CONAI – the national indigenous affairs organization – is minimal.

Although a system of indigenous reserves was set up by the Costa Rican administration in 1977, giving aboriginal peoples the right to remain in self-governing communities, titles to the reserve lands were withheld, so that while the communities may live on the land, they do not actually own it. This has led to government contracts being handed out to, for example, mining operations in the Talamanca area, leading to infringements on the communities themselves, which are further hampered by the presence of missionaries in settlements like Amubri and San José Cabécar. The twelve "Indian reserves" scattered around the country are viewed by their inhabitants with some ambivalence. As in North America, establishing a reservation system has led in many cases to a banishing of indigenous peoples to poor quality land where enclaves of poverty soon develop.

Although the persecution of native peoples in Costa Rica is nothing like as bad as in Guatemala, in recent years there have been a number of disturbing indigenous rights violations, many of them documented by CODEHUCA (Comisión para la defensa de los derechos humanos en centroamérica). At the same time there is growing recognition of the importance of preserving indigenous culture and of providing reserves with increased services and self-sufficiency. In 1994 the first indigenous bank was set up in Suretka, Talamanca, by the Bribrí and Cabecar groups, to counter the fact that major banks have often refused indigenous business and initiatives credit. In addition, indigenous groups from around the country, realizing that they need a cohesive voice and common agenda, have banded together to rent a building in San José to be used as the headquarters for a united movement.

dreadful road system top priority, but financing this and other major public works by private investment. Increasingly, courting private money and catering to foreign interests are the order of the day. Still, problems dog the economy in the shape of increasing balance of payments difficulties, as well as pressures on the banana market from Ecuador's growing competition – banana plantation labour in Ecuador costs $3 a day, compared to $18 in Costa Rica.

The new millennium

Rodríguez was succeeded in April 2002 by Abel Pacheco de Espriella, a psychiatrist also from the PUSC; it was the first time that party had been re-elected. One of the key issues Pacheco has faced is **CAFTA**, the Central American Free Trade Agreement that has alarmed anti-globalization movements worldwide and aroused widespread fear in Costa Rica of the definitive erosion of the advanced social system that has been in place in the country for the last half-century. The son of a banana farmer, Pacheco was initially wary of the accord, but finally added Costa Rica's name to those of all the other Central American nations. At the time of writing, the agreement was being considered by the US Senate. If passed, it would certainly mean the end of Costa Rica's nationalized insurance system, and two of the country's key export industries, bananas and coffee, on which so much of the economy rides, would face heavy competition from the lower wages of other Central American countries. Plantation labour in Costa Rica costs as much as six times that of Honduras or Nicaragua.

In recent years, the government has managed to claw back the inflation rate, currently around nine percent, and population growth has slowed; this is vital, for Costa Rica has the highest rural population density in Latin America, and there is tremendous **pressure for land**. Unsurprisingly, the prognosis for the *campesino*, that now nearly forgotten former backbone of the country, is not good, as peasant agriculture becomes increasingly anachronistic in the face of the big banana, coffee, palmito and pineapple plantations. Furthermore, the burden of the welfare state in Costa Rica has become increasingly difficult for the state to carry. High external debts to service the country's respected system of social welfare mean that a staggering thirty percent of the government budget goes on keeping up interest payments to foreign banks. However, the nation's high literacy and life expectancy rates pay tribute to the relative success of the system over the last few decades and provide a strong platform for progress in the new century.

Despite the country's impressive system of national parks, the forecast for the **environment** is blackened by the authorities' continuing strategy of attracting large hotel and development groups. While **tourism** is a vital part of the nation's economy, other countries have found to their cost that summer visitors are notoriously fickle, and today's fashionable gated resort hotel can easily become tomorrow's five-star white elephant. Treading the fine line between preserving Costa Rica's social system and creating a more stable economic foundation, and developing the tourist sector in a sustainable and sensible way, seem to be the key challenges facing the nation in the early years of the third millennium.

Landscape and wildlife

New World animals are believed to have crossed from Asia via the Bering Strait land bridge and migrated steadily southward through North America, evolving on the way. Because of Costa Rica's own celebrated position as a land bridge between the temperate Nearctic zone to the north and the Neotropics to the south, its varied animal life features tropical forms like the jaguar, temperate-zone animals like the deer, and some unusual, seemingly hybrid combinations such as the coati.

Habitats

Although roughly the size of West Virginia, Nova Scotia, or Wales, Costa Rica has nearly as many **habitats** as the whole of the US, including forests, riverside mangroves, seasonal wetlands and offshore marine forms such as coral reefs. Costa Rica has a remarkably varied **terrain** for its size, ranging from the plains of Guanacaste, where there is often no rain for five months of the year, to the Caribbean lowlands, thick-forested and deluged with a liberal 6000mm of precipitation annually. In terms of **elevation**, too, the country possesses great diversity: from the very hot and humid lowlands of Corcovado, the terrain rises within 150km to the chilly heights of Cerro Chirripó, at 3819m.

Life zones

Because Costa Rica's territory is almost bewilderingly varied, with similar geographical features found in many different places, it makes sense to speak of **life zones**, a detailed system of categorization referring primarily to forest habitats, developed in 1947 by biologist L.R. Holdridge to describe particular characteristics of terrain, climate and the life they support. Although he conceived the system in Haiti, with temperature and rainfall being the main determinants, this system has been used to create ecological maps of various countries, including Costa Rica. To read more about the cloudforest see p.280; for the dry forest, turn to p.224.

The most endangered of all the life zones in Costa Rica is the **tropical dry forest**, which needs about six dry months a year. Most trees in a tropical dry forest are deciduous or semi-deciduous; some lose their leaves near the end of the dry season, primarily to conserve water. They are less stratified than rainforests, with two layers rather than three or four, and appear far less dense. Orchids flower in the silver and brown branches, and bees, wasps and moths proliferate. Animal inhabitants include iguanas, white-tailed deer and some of the larger mammals, including the jaguar. The best examples are in the northwest, especially **Guanacaste** and **Santa Rosa** national parks.

The **tropical wet forest** is home, metre per metre, to the greatest number of species of flora and fauna, including the bushmaster snake and tapir, along with jaguar and other wild cats. Here the canopy trees can be very tall (up to 70 or even 80m) and, true to its name, it receives an enormous amount of rain – typically 5000–6000mm per year. Found in lowland areas, tropical wet forest is now confined to large protected blocks, chiefly the **Sarapiquí–Tortuguero** area and the large chunk protected by **Corcovado National Park** on the Osa Peninsula.

Premontane wet forests are found upon many of Costa Rica's mountains. Some trees are evergreen and most are covered with a thick carpet of moss. These forests typically exist at a high altitude and receive a lot of rain: the cover in **Tapantí National Park** in the southwest Valle Central is a good example, as is **Braulio Carrillo**, which has all five of the montane life zones within its boundaries. Many of the same animals that exist in the tropical wet forest exist here, along with brocket deer and peccaries.

Perhaps the most famous of Costa Rica's life zones are the tropical lower montane wet forests, or **cloudforests**, which occur in very isolated patches, mainly south of Cartago and on the Pacific slopes of the Cordillera de Tilarán. The cloudforest hosts many bromeliads, including orchids, and has an understorey thick with vines; its animal life includes tapirs, pumas and quetzals. Costa Rica's best known cloudforest is at **Monteverde**.

Tropical montane rainforest occurs at the highest altitudes; the tops of **Poás** and **Irazú** volcanoes are good examples. Although large mosses and ferns can be seen, much of the vegetation has a shrunken, or dwarfed aspect, due to the biting wind and lofty altitude. Animals that live here include the Poás squirrel (endemic to that volcano) and some of the larger birds, including raptors and vultures.

At the very top of the country near **Cerro Chirripó** is the only place you'll find **tropical subalpine rain páramo**, inhospitably cold, with almost no trees. Costa Rica is the northern frontier of this particular Andean type of *páramo*. Except for hardy hawks and vultures, birds tend to shun this cold milieu, although at lower elevations you may spot a quetzal.

Mangroves, wetlands and rivers

The **mangrove** is an increasingly fragile and endangered ecosystem that occurs along tropical coastlines and is particularly vulnerable to dredging: both the Papagayo Project in Guanacaste and the *Tambor Beach Hotel* in the Central Pacific have been accused of irresponsibly draining mangroves. With their extensive root system, mangrove trees are unique for their ability to adapt to the salinity of seaside or tidal waters, or to areas where freshwater rivers empty into the ocean. Because they absorb the thrust of waves and tides, they act as a buffer zone behind which species of aquatic and land-based life can flourish unmolested. Meanwhile, the beer-coloured mangrove swamp water is like a nutritious primordial soup where a range of species can grow, including crustaceans and shrimp as well as turtles, caimans and crocodiles, and their banks are home to a range of bird life.

Birds and reptiles are especially abundant in the country's remaining **wetlands**, which are typically seasonal, caused by the flooding of rivers with the rains, only to shrink back to pleated mud flats in the dry season. The **Caño Negro** seasonal wetlands in the Zona Norte and the Río Tempisque, within the bounds of **Palo Verde National Park** in Guanacaste, are the prime wetlands in Costa Rica.

Despite increasing silting and pollution caused largely by the banana plantations, Costa Rica's **rivers** support a variety of life, from fish, including the tarpon, to migratory birds, crocodiles, caimans and freshwater turtles. The waterways that yield the best wildlife-watching are the Tortuguero canals and the Ríos San Juan, Sarapiquí, Sierpe, and the Río Tárcoles in the Carara Biological Reserve on the central Pacific coast.

Marine habitats

Costa Rica's **coral reefs**, never as extensive as those in Belize, are under threat. Much of the **Caribbean coast** was seriously damaged by the 1991 earthquake, which heaved the reefs up above the water. The last remaining ones on this side of the country are at **Cahuita** and a smaller one further south at **Manzanillo** in the Gandoca–Manzanillo Wildlife Refuge. Though the Cahuita reef has been under siege for some time by silting caused by clearing of land for banana plantations, and pesticides used in banana cultivation, you can still see some fine – extremely localized – specimens of moose horn and deer horn coral. On the **Pacific coast** the most pristine reef is at **Bahía Ballena**, protected within Costa Rica's first marine national park, and also the reef that fringes Isla del Caño, about 20km offshore from the north coast of the Osa Peninsula.

Wildlife

C

It is a source of constant woe for guides in Costa Rica to have to deal with tourists who have paid their national park entrance fees and then expect to be reimbursed in kind by seeing a tapir, jaguar or ocelot. Many of the country's more exotic **mammals** are either nocturnal, endangered, or made shy through years of hunting and human encroachment. Although encounters do occur, they are usually brief, with the animal in question dipping quietly back into the shadows from which it first emerged. That said, however, it's very possible you will come into (usually fleeting) contact with some of the smaller and more abundant mammals.

Despite its reputation, Costa Rica does not have Central America's most diverse vertebrate fauna – that honour goes to Guatemala. However, Costa Rican **insects** and **birds** are particularly numerous, with 850 species of birds (including migratory ones) – more than the US and Canada combined. Costa Rica is also home to a quarter of the world's known **butterflies** – more than in all Africa – thousands of moths, and scores of bees and wasps.

Birds (*pájaros, aves*)

Bird life, both migratory and indigenous, is abundant in Costa Rica and includes some of the most colourful birds in the Americas: the **quetzal**, the **toucan** and the **scarlet macaw**. Many are best observed while feeding. Guides often point out quetzals, for instance, when they are feeding from their favoured **aguacatillo** tree, and you might catch a glimpse of the hummingbird hovering over a bright flower as it feeds on its nectar.

It's only fair that any discussion of birds in Costa Rica starts with the one that so many people come to see: the brilliant green and red **quetzal**. With a range historically extending from southern Mexico to northern Panamá – more or less the delineations of Mesoamerica – the dazzling quetzal was highly prized by the Aztecs and the Maya. In the language of the Aztecs, *quetzali* means, roughly, "beautiful", and along with jade, the shimmering, jewel-coloured feathers were used as currency in Maya cities. The feathers were also worn by Maya nobles to signify religious qualities and social superiority, and formed the headdress of the plumed serpent Quetzalcoatl, the supreme Aztec god.

Hunting quetzals is particularly cruel, as it is well known that the bird cannot (or will not) live in captivity, a poignant characteristic which has made it a symbol of freedom throughout Mesoamerica. The male in particular – who possesses the distinctive feather train of up to 1.5m long – is still pursued by poachers, and the quetzal is further endangered due to the destruction of its favoured cloudforest habitat. These days the remaining cloudforests (particularly Monteverde) are among the best places to try to see the birds (March–May is best), although they are always difficult to spot, in part due to shyness and in part because the vibrant green of their feathers, seemingly so eye-catchingly bright, actually means that they blend in well with the wet and shimmering cloudforest. Quetzals are officially protected in Costa Rica in Braulio Carrillo and Volcán Poás national parks in the Valle Central, in Chirripó in the Zona Sur, and in Monteverde.

The increasingly rare **scarlet macaw** (*lapa*), with its liberal splashes of red, yellow and blue, was once common on the Pacific coast of southern Mexico and Central America. The birds, which are monogamous, live in lowland forested areas, but these days your only chance of spotting them is in Corcovado National Park on the Osa Peninsula, and perhaps the Carara Biological Refuge in the Central Pacific, Palo Verde National Park or Lomas Barbudal Biological Refuge in Guanacaste. They are usually spotted in or near their nesting holes (they nest in tree trunks), in the upper branches, or while flying high and calling to one another with their distinctive raucous squawk.

Parakeets are still fairly numerous and are most often seen in the lowland forested areas of the Pacific coast. You're also likely to see the **chestnut-mandibled** and **keel-billed toucans** (*tucánes*), with their ridiculous but beautiful banana-shaped beaks. The chestnut-mandibled is the largest; their bills are two-tone brown and yellow. Keel-billed toucans have the more rainbow-coloured beaks and are smaller, which is sometimes taken advantage of by their larger cousins, who may drive them away from a cache of food or hound them out of a particular tree. At other times, though, both types seem to commune quite happily. Other than humans, the toucan is thought to have few predators. They can be found in both higher and lower elevations, but in Costa Rica you are most likely to see them in the Caribbean lowlands, particularly the Sarapiquí area. They are most often spotted at dawn and in the afternoon as early as 4pm or 4.30pm – although dusk is best – sitting in the open upper branches of secondary forest. They also often fly low over the road from Guápiles to Las Horquetas.

In the **waterways** and **wetlands** of the country, most birds you see are **migratory** species from the north, including herons, gulls, sandpipers and plovers. Larger marine birds – pelicans and frigatebirds for example – come from much further afield, often making the journey from New Zealand or Cape Horn. Most migratory species are in residence between January and April, though a few arrive as early as November. The seasonal lagoons of the **Río Tempisque** basin in Guanacaste are home to the largest diversity and number of freshwater birds – both migratory and resident, in Central America. **Caño Negro** in the Zona Norte is another rewarding area for bird-watching.

Permanent residents of Costa Rican river areas include **cormorants**, and **anhingas** (sometimes called "snakebirds" in English, due to their sinuous necks). **Anhingas** are fishermen, impaling their prey on the knife-point of their beaks before swallowing. The elegant, long-limbed white **ibis** often stands motionless on river-level branches and banks; harder to spot and more endangered is the giant **jabirú stork**, most often seen in Caño Negro and on the Río Tempisque in Palo Verde National Park.

Travelling the Tortuguero canals or on the Río Sierpe down to Bahía Drake on the Osa Peninsula you are likely to see a **kingfisher** (*martín pescador*). The green kingfisher, with its deep forest-green back and distinctive crown is particularly lovely. The largest colony of the Nicaraguan **grackle** (*zanate*) makes regular appearances in Caño Negro; the only place in Costa Rica where these dark, crow-like birds nest. Other water birds include **brown pelicans** (*buchón*) and the pretty pink **roseate spoonbills**, found mainly in the Río Tempisque basin, where you can also see huge clumps of nesting **night-herons** (*cuacu*). The most common bird, and the one you're likely to come across hiking or riding in cattle country, is the unprepossessing grey-white **egret** (*garça*).

Of the raptors (hawks and eagles) the **laughing falcon** (*guaco*), found all over the country, probably has the most distinct call, which sounds exactly like its Spanish name. The "laughing" bit comes from a much lower-pitched variation, which resembles muted human laughter. The laughing falcon preys on reptiles, including venomous snakes, biting off the head before bringing the body back to its eyrie, where it drapes it over a branch, sings a duet with its mate, and proceeds to dine. The sharp-eyed, mottled brown **osprey** eagle still has a reasonably good species count, despite the blows that deforestation has dealt to its rainforest habitat. You're most likely to see ospreys patrolling the skies of the canals between Barra del Colorado and Limón or in the Gandoca–Manzanillo Wildlife Refuge. The **harpy eagles** have not fared so well, and are thought to be locally extinct, due to widespread destruction of their favoured upper-canopy habitat. There is a chance that some may still live and hunt in the interior of Corcovado National Park on the Osa Peninsula, or within the rugged La Amistad International Park in the south of the country. Their bushy crowns give them a tousled look, rather than the usual fierce appearance of raptors, and they have a delicate, hooked beak.

You're unlikely to see much of owls, as they are nocturnal, but the **tropical screech owl** (*sorococa*) is commonly heard, even in the suburbs of San José, with its distinctive whirring call that builds to a screech or laugh as it takes flight. The unremarkable brown **oropéndola**, relative of the oriole, is best-known for its distinctive basketweave nest, which looks like a lacrosse net and droops conspicuously from tree limbs all over the country, especially in the Valle Central and Chirripó.

Hardly anyone gets through a day or two in Monteverde or Santa Elena without at least hearing the distinctive, metallic call of the **three-wattled bellbird**. If you catch a glimpse of them you'll find that they look even stranger than their clunk-sounding clarion call, with three worm-like black sacks hanging off their beak. Monteverde is also a good place to watch the antics of the tiny thumb-sized **hummingbirds** (*colibrís*), who buzz about like particularly swift, engorged bees. Thanks to their wings' unusual round hinges, hummingbirds can feed on flower nectar while actually hovering. They are numerous in Costa Rica, and some local types, like the purple-throated hummingbird, are particularly pretty.

The shrunken-shouldered **vulture** (*zópilote*) is not usually considered of interest to birders. That said, it is the one bird that almost everyone will see at some point, hanging out opportunistically on the side of major highways waiting for rabbits and iguanas to be thumped beneath the wheels of a passing vehicle.

Mammals (*fauna, animales*)

Costa Rica's **mammals** range from the fairly unexotic (at least for North Americans and Europeans) white-tailed deer (*venado cola blanca*) and brocket deer (*cabra de monte*), via the seemingly antediluvian, such as Baird's tapir or "mountain cow" (*danta*), to the preternatural or semi-sacred jaguar (*tigre*).

Now an endangered species, the **jaguar** is endemic to the New World tropics and has a range from southern Mexico to northern Argentina. Although it was once common throughout Central America, especially in the lowland forests and mangroves of coastal areas, the jaguar's main foe has long been man, who has hunted it for its valuable pelt and because of its reputation among farmers as a predator of calves and pigs. It is easily tracked, due to its distinctive footprint. Incredibly, the hunting of jaguars for sport was allowed right up until the 1980s, although the trade was hampered by the fact that it is illegal to import the pelts into most countries, including the US. Though you won't see a jaguar in the wild, one of the sorriest sights in Costa Rica is the captive jaguar – in a hotel's private zoo, for example – typically kept in small cramped cages where it can do little but pace back and forth. Considered sacred by the Maya, jaguars are a very beautiful mid-sized cat; nearly always golden with black spots, and much more rarely a sleek, beautiful black. They feed on smaller mammals such as agoutis, monkeys and peccaries, and may also eat fish and birds. Not to be confused with the jaguar, the **jaguarundi** is a small cat, very rarely seen, ranging in colour from reddish to black. Little studied, the jaguarundi has short legs and a low-slung body, and is sometimes confused for the tayra, or tropical mink. They are swift and shy, and although they live in many lowland areas and forests, are very rarely encountered by walkers.

Along with the jaguar, the tapir is perhaps the most fantastical form inhabiting the Neotropical rainforest, where it is called **Baird's tapir**. A distant relative of the rhinoceros, the tapir also occurs in the tropics of southeast Asia. Rather homely, with eyes set back on either side of its head, the tapir looks something between a horse and an overgrown pig, with a stout grey-skinned body and a head that suggests an elephant with a truncated trunk. Their antediluvian look comes from their prehensile snout, small ears, and delicate cloven feet. Weighing as much as 300 kilograms and vegetarian, they are extremely shy in the wild, largely nocturnal, and stick to densely forested or rugged land: consequently they are very rarely spotted by casual rainforest walkers. The tapir has proved to be very amiable in captivity, and is certain to be unaggressive should you be lucky enough to come upon one. Like the jaguar, its main foe is man, who hunts it for its succulent meat. Nowadays the tapir is protected to a degree in the national parks and preserves.

All Costa Rica's cats have been made extremely shy through centuries of hunting. The one exception, since its pelt isn't big enough to make it a worthwhile target, is the small, sinuous-necked **margay** (*tigrillo*), with its complex black-spotted markings and large, inquisitive eyes. It has been known to peek out of the shadows and even sun itself on the rocks. The **ocelot** (*manigordo*) is similar, somewhere between the margay and jaguar in size, but is another animal you are very unlikely to see. Of all the cats, the sandstone-coloured **mountain lion** (*puma*) is said to be the most forthcoming. It's a big animal, and although not usually aggressive towards humans, should be treated with respect.

Some of the animals you are more likely to see – because of their abundance and diurnal activity – look like outsize versions or variations on temperate-zone mammals: the **agouti** or **paca** (*tepezcuintle*), a large water-rodent, for example, or the mink-like **tayra** (*tolumuco*), who may flash by you on its way up a tree. Notable for its lustrous coat and snake-like sinuosity, the tayra can be fierce if cornered. The Neotropical **river otter** (*nutria*) is an altogether friendlier creature, although extremely shy. The **coati** (often mistakenly called *coatimundi*; *pizote* in Spanish) looks like a confused combination of a racoon, domestic cat and an anteater. There is also a tropical **racoon** (*mapache*) that looks like its northern neighbour, complete with eye mask. Nearly all of these are foragers and forest-floor dwellers.

The **peccary** (*saíno*), usually described as a wild pig or boar, comes in two little-differentiated species in Costa Rica: collared or white-lipped. They can be menacing when encountered in packs, when, if they get a whiff of you – their sight is poor so they'll smell you before they see you – they may clack their teeth and growl a bit. The usual advice, especially in Corcovado National Park where they travel in groups as large as thirty, is to climb a tree. However, peccaries are not on the whole dangerous and in captivity have proved to be very affectionate, rubbing themselves against you delightedly at the least opportunity.

You may well see an **anteater** (*hormiguero*) vacuuming an anthill at some point. Of the two species that inhabit Costa Rica, you're much more likely to see the **northern tamandua**, although it is largely nocturnal. It hunts ants, occasionally bees, and termites, digging into nests using its sharp claws and inserting its proboscis-like snout into the mound to lick up its prey. Far rarer, the **silky anteater** is arboreal, a lovely golden in colour, and hardly ever seen.

Costa Rica is home to four species of monkey. Most people can expect to at least hear, if not see, the **howler monkey** (*mono congo*), especially in the lowland forests: the male has a mechanism in its thick throat by which it can make sounds which resemble those from a gorilla. Their whoops are most often heard at dawn or dusk. The **white-faced or capuchin** (*carablanca*) **monkey** is slighter than the howler, with a distinctly humanoid expression on its delicate face. This, combined with its intelligence, often consigns it to being a pet in a hotel or private zoo. In the wild, it's also the most curious of the monkeys, often descending to the lower branches of trees to get a better look at the strange pinkish creatures staring up at them. The **spider monkey** (*araña*) takes its name from its spider-like ability to move through the trees employing its five limbs – the fifth is its prehensile tail, which it uses to grip branches. A troupe of spider monkeys making their leaping, gymnastic way through the jungle (usually following a well-worn trail known as a 'monkey highway') is a particularly impressive sight. The **squirrel monkey** (*mono tití*) is presently only found in and south of Manuel Antonio National Park. Their delicate grey and white faces have long made them attractive to pet owners and zoos, and consequently they have been hunted to near extinction in Costa Rica. However, they are extremely gregarious – though they can be easily put off by too many people tramping through Manuel Antonio – and you may well catch sight of one.

Two types of **sloth** (*perezoso*) live in Costa Rica: the **three-toed** sloth, active by day, and the nocturnal **two-toed** sloth. True to their name, sloths move very little during the day and have an extremely slow metabolism. They are excellently camouflaged from their main predators, eagles, by the algae that often covers their brown hair. In the first instance at least they are very difficult to spot on your own; a guide will usually point one out. Scan the V-intersections in trees, particularly the middle and upper elevations: from a distance they resemble a ball of fur or a hornet's nest. Sloths present something of a mystery in their defecating habits, risking life and limb to descend to the forest floor, once a week, to defecate. Their sharp taloned claws are best suited to the arboreal universe, and outside the tree limbs they are a bit lost, exposing themselves to predation by jaguars and other animals. No one has yet come up with a solid hypothesis as to this irrational behaviour.

Costa Rica has many species of **bats** (*murciélagos*), which literally hang out sleeping on the underside of branches, where they look like rows of small grey triangles. In Tortuguero, you may see a **fishing bat** skimming the water, casting its aural net in front in search of food: being blind, it fishes by sonar. For the best bat-viewing opportunities, head to Barra Honda caves on the Nicoya Peninsula, where they roost in huge numbers.

Amphibians and reptiles
(*anfíbios, reptiles*)

There are many, many **frogs** (*ranas*) and **toads** (*sapos*) in Costa Rica. Though they seem vulnerable – small, and with few defences – many tropical frogs look after themselves by secreting poison through their skin. Using some of the most powerful natural toxins known, the frog can directly target the heart muscle of the predator, paralyzing it and causing immediate death. As these poisons are transmittable through skin contact, you should never touch a Costa Rican frog. Probably the best-known, and most toxic, of the frogs, is the colourful **poison dart frog**, usually quite small, and found in various combinations of bright red and blue or green and black. Even the innocuous-looking **shore** or **beach frog** can shoot out a jet of toxins; while it may not be fatal to humans, it can kill heedless cats and dogs who try to pick it up in their mouths.

The more common ways in which tropical frogs defend themselves are through camouflage (usually mottled brown, green or variations thereon – they blend perfectly into the tropical cover) or by jumping, a good method of escape in thick ground cover. Jumping also throws snakes – who hunt by scent, and are probably their most prevalent predator – off track. You will most likely see frogs around dusk or at night; some of them make a regular and dignified

Guises and disguises

Rainforest fauna and flora have an elaborate repertoire of ruses, poisons and camouflages that they put to a variety of uses, from self-protection to pollination. Many tropical animals are well known for their gaudy colour, which can mean one of two things: warning potential predators to keep away, or flaunting an invulnerable position at the top of the food chain. Particularly notable are the birds that inhabit the rainforest canopy: toucans, parakeets and scarlet macaws, not to mention the resplendent quetzal. Unfortunately, while flaunting the fact that they have hardly any predators, these beautiful birds make themselves vulnerable to perhaps the most threatening adversary of them all: humans. Advertising toxicity is another ingenious evolutionary development. The amazingly colourful poison dart frogs are a case in point, as is the venomous coral snake. These reptiles give the "keep away" signal loud and clear to potential predators, some of whom, after successive bad experiences, build up a species memory and cease preying upon them.

Some animals are camouflage experts. Again, camouflage serves one of two purposes: to be able to hide in order to ensnare prey, or to hide in order to avoid predators. The predatorial jaguar looks exactly like the mottled light of the ground floor of the rainforest, making it easier to both hide and hunt, while the clear-winged butterfly literally disappears into the air. Sloths, too, hide from their attackers, with a greasy green alga growing on their fur, making them look even more like the clump of leaves that they already resemble.

Then there are the mimics, usually insects, which have an evolutionary ability to look like something which they are not. The asilidae family in particular features many mimics: flies impersonate wasps and wasps disguise themselves as bees, all in the pursuit of safety or predation.

procession down paths and trails, sitting motionless for long periods before hopping off again. The chief thing you'll notice about the more common frogs is their size: they're much stouter than temperate zone frogs. Look out for the gaudy **leaf frog** (*rana calzonudo*), star of many a frog calendar. Relatively large, it is an alarming bright green, with orange hands and feet and dark blue thighs. Its sides are purple, and its eyes are pure red, to scare off potential predators.

Travelling along or past Costa Rica's waterways, you may well see **caimans** and **crocodiles**. Crocs hang out on the muddy banks, basking in the sun, while the smaller, shyer caimans will sometimes perch on submerged tree branches, scuttling away at your approach. Both are under constant threat from hunters, who sell their skin to make shoes and handbags. Your best chance of seeing either is in Tortuguero. Pot-bellied **iguanas** are the most ubiquitous of Costa Rica's lizards, as common here as chickens are in Europe or the US. Masters of camouflage, they can occasionally be spotted on the middle and lower branches of trees and on the ground. Despite their dragon-like appearance, they are very shy, and if you do spot them, it's likely that they'll be scurrying away in an ungainly fashion. In wetlands and on rivers, watch out for a tiny form skittering across the water: this is the **"Jesus Christ" lizard** (*basilisk*), so-called for its web-like foot and speed, which allows it to "walk" on water.

Costa Rica is home to a vast array of **snakes** (*serpientes*, *culebras*). Many of them, both venomous and non-venomous, are amazingly beautiful: this can be appreciated more if you see them in captivity than if you come across one in the wild. That said, the chances of the latter happening – let alone getting bitten – are very slim. Snakes are largely nocturnal, and for the most part far more wary of you than you are of them.

Out of 162 species found in the country, only 22 are venomous. These are usually well camouflaged, but some advertise their danger with a flamboyance of colour. One such is the highly venomous **coral** (same in Spanish) snake which, although retiring, is easily spotted – and avoided – with its bright rings of carmine red, yellow and black. The **false coral** snake, which is not venomous, looks very similar; a guide or a ranger will be able to point out the subtle differences. Of all the Costa Rican snakes the **bushmaster** (*matabuey*) is the one of which even guardaparques are afraid. The bushmaster, whose range extends from southern Mexico to Brazil, is the largest venomous snake in the Americas – in Costa Rica it can reach a size of nearly 2m. The most aggressive of snakes, it will actually chase people, if it is so inclined. The good news is that you are extremely unlikely to encounter one, as it prefers dense and mountainous territory – Braulio Carrillo, the Sarapiquí region and Corcovado, for example – and rarely emerges during the day.

Once the inhabitant of the rainforests, the fer-de-lance or **terciopelo** has adapted quite well to cleared areas, grassy uplands, and even some inhabited stretches, although you are far more likely to see them in places which have heavy rainfall (like the Limón coast) and near streams or rivers at night. Though it can reach more than 2m in length, the terciopelo ("velvet") is well camouflaged and very difficult to spot, resembling a big pile of leaves with its grey-black skin with a light crisscross pattern. Along with the bushmaster, the terciopelo is one of the few snakes who may attack without provocation. They are usually killed when encountered, due to their venom and fairly healthy species count. These are the ones you'll see coiled in jars of formaldehyde at rainforest lodges, often on display beside the supper table.

The very pretty **eyelash viper** (*bocaracá*) is usually tan or green, but some-times brilliant yellow when inhabiting golden palm fruit groves. Largely arboreal and generally well camouflaged, it takes its name from the raised scales around its eyes. They are quite venomous to humans and should be given a wide berth if seen hanging from a branch or negotiating a path through the groves.

Considering the competition, it's not hard to see why the **boa constrictor** (*boa*) wins the title of most congenial snake. Often with beautiful semi-triangular markings, largely retiring and shy of people, the boa is one of the few snakes you may see in the daytime. Although they are largely torpid, it is not a good idea to bother them. They have big teeth and can bite, though they are not venomous and are unlikely to stir unless startled. If you encounter one, either on the move or lying still, the best thing is to walk around it slowly, giving it a good 5m berth.

For more details on precautions when dealing with snakes, see p.22 in Basics.

Insects (*insectos, bichos*)

Costa Rica supports an enormous diversity of insects, of which the **butterflies** (*mariposas*) are the most flamboyant and sought after. Active during the day, they can be seen, especially from about 8am to noon, almost anywhere in the country. Most adult butterflies take their typical food of nectar – usually from red flowers – through a proboscis. Others feed on fungi, dung and rotting fruit. Best-known, and quite often spotted, especially along forest trails, is the fast-flying **blue morpho**, whose titanium-bright wings seem to shimmer electrically. Like other garish butterflies, the morpho uses its colour to startle or shock potential predators. Far more difficult to spot, for obvious reasons, is the **clear-winged butterfly**.

Of the annoying insects, you'll surely get acquainted with **mosquitos** (*zancudos*), a few of which carry malaria and dengue fever (see p.21). In hot, slightly swampy lowland areas such as the coastal Osa or the southern Nicoya peninsulas, you may also come across **purrujas**, similar to blackflies or midges. They can inflict itchy bites, as can the **chiggers** (*colorados*) that inhabit scrub and secondary growth areas, attaching themselves to the skin, leech-like, in order to feed. Though not really bothersome, the **lantern fly** (*machaca*) emits an amazingly strong mint-blue light, like a mini-lightning streak – if you have one in your hotel room you'll know it as soon as you turn out the light.

The ant kingdom is well represented in Costa Rica. Chief among the rainforest salarymen are the **leaf-cutter ants**, who work in businesslike cadres, carrying bits of leaf to and fro to build their distinctive nests. The ones to watch out for are the big **bullet ants** that resemble moving blackberries (their colloquial name is **veinticuatro** – "24" – meaning that if you get bitten by one it will hurt for 24 hours). Endemic to the Neotropics, carnivorous **army ants** are often encountered in the forest, typically living in large colonies, some of more than a million individuals. They are most famous for their "dawn raids", when they pour out of a hideaway, typically a log, and divide into several columns to create a swarm. In this columnar formation they go off in search of prey – other ants and insects – which they carry back to the nest to consume.

Among the many **bees and wasps** (*abejas, avispas*) are aggressive **Africanized bees**, which migrated from Africa to Brazil and then north to Costa Rica, where they have colonized certain localities. Although you have to disturb their nests before they'll bother you, people sensitive or allergic to bee-stings should avoid Palo Verde National Park.

Marine life

Among Costa Rica's **marine mammals** is the sea cow or **manatee** (*manatí*), elephantine in size, lumbering, good-natured and well-intentioned, not to mention endangered. Manatees all over the Caribbean are declining in number, due to the disappearance and pollution of the fresh- and saltwater riverways in which they live. In Costa Rica your only reasonable chance of seeing one is in the Tortuguero canals in Limón Province, where they sometimes break the surface. At first you might mistake it for a tarpon, but the manatee's overlapping snout and long whiskers are quite distinctive.

Five species of **marine turtle** nest on Costa Rica's shores. Nesting takes place mostly at night and mostly in the context of *arribadas*: giant invasions of turtles who come ashore in their thousands on the same beach (or spot of beach) at a certain time of year, laying hundreds of thousands of eggs. Greens, hawksbills and leatherbacks come ashore on both coasts, while the Olive Ridley comes ashore only on the Pacific. The strange blunt-nosed **loggerhead**, which seems not to nest in Costa Rica, can sometimes be seen in Caribbean coastal waters.

The **green turtle**, long-prized for the delicacy of its flesh, has become nearly synonymous with its favoured nesting grounds in Tortuguero. In the 1950s it was classified as endangered, and, thanks in part to the protection offered by areas like Tortuguero, is making a comeback. Some greens make Herculean journeys of as much as 2000km to their breeding beaches at Tortuguero, returning to the same stretch year after year. *Arribadas* are most concentrated in June and October. Green turtles are careful nesters: if a female is disturbed by human presence she will go back to the ocean and return only when all is clear.

The **hawksbill** (*carey*), so-named for its distinctive down-curving "beak", is found all over the tropics, often preferring rocky shores and coral reefs. It used to be hunted extensively on the Caribbean coast for its meat and shell, but this is now banned. Poaching does still occur, however, and you should avoid buying any tortoiseshell that you see for sale. Hawksbills do not come ashore in *arribadas* to the extent that green turtles do, preferring to nest alone.

Capable of growing to a length of 5m, the **leatherback** (*baula*) is the largest reptile in the world. Its "shell" is actually a network of bones overlaid with a very tough leathery skin. Though it nests most concentratedly at the Parque Nacional Las Baulas on the western Nicoya Peninsula, it also comes ashore elsewhere, including Tortuguero on the Caribbean coast. The **Olive Ridley** (*lora, carpintera* – also called Pacific Ridley) turtle nests on just a few beaches, among them Playa Nancite in Santa Rosa National Park and Ostional near Nosara on the Nicoya Peninsula. They come ashore in massive *arribadas*, and, unusually, often nest during the day. Olive Ridley eggs are as prized as any, but its species count seems to be fairly healthy. Among the freshwater **turtles** (*tortugas*) in Costa Rica is the **yellow turtle** (*tortuga amarilla*), most often seen in Caño Negro. The **black river turtle** and the **snapping turtle**, about whom little is known (except that it snaps), also inhabit rivers and mangrove swamps, and may occasionally be spotted on the riverbanks.

Though **dolphins** (*delfines*) and **whales** thread themselves through the waters of the Pacific coast, it is rare to see them. Dolphins are sighted in the Manuel Antonio and Dominical areas: for the best chance of a glimpse, take a boat trip at the Ballena Marine National Park. Getting to see a **whale** (*ballena*) is even harder. Though around Dominical, Bahía Drake and Isla del Caño, both sperm and humpback whales may be around in April and May, they are not dependable in their arrivals.

Fish (*pezes*)

Costa Rica is one of the richest sports-fishing grounds in the Neotropics. The best-known big-game fish in Costa Rica is the startlingly huge white **tarpon**. Other big fish prized for their fighting spirit are **snook**, **marlin**, and **wahoo** – all of which ply the waters of Barra del Colorado, Quepos and Golfito on the Pacific coast, and Playa Flamingo in Guanacaste. More laid-back are the **trout** (*trucha*) and **rainbow bass** (*guapote*) that live in the freshwater rivers and in Laguna de Arenal. Costa Rica also features a few oddities and evolutionary throwbacks, including the undeniably homely **garfish**, which inhabits the Caño Negro wetlands and the canals of Limón Province. Snorkellers will see a number of exotic fish, including enormous, plate-flat **manta rays** and the **parrotfish**, so-called less for its rich colouring than for its distinctive "beak" (actually a number of tiny teeth, welded together) which is used to munch coral. There's another set of teeth at the back of the mouth that then grinds the coral down in order to digest it. Many of the white-sand beaches throughout the Caribbean, including the one just south of Cahuita, are the result of aeons of coral excreted by these fish. Other sea creatures include stingrays, oysters, sponges, ugly moray eels, sea urchins, starfish, spiny lobsters, and fat, slug-like **sea cucumbers** that lie half submerged in the sea bed, digesting and excreting sand and mud.

Sharks are generally found on beaches where turtles nest, especially along the northern Caribbean coast, on Playa Ostional in the Nicoya Peninsula – although not further south in Playas Nosara – and in the waters surrounding Corcovado.

The tropical rainforest

M any myths are perpetuated about the rainforest: that it is a representation of disorder (a natural chaos); that it is full of loud and startling sounds; that it is thick and impenetrable as well as mysterious. Along with these ideas, conveyed through fiction, poetry and the more colourful representations of the first European explorers of the tropics, go the colonial notions that it is a world unfinished, awaiting the seed of civilization, and it is in itself valueless and unprofitable.

Meanwhile, it's likely that in just forty years' time the world's rainforests may not exist at all outside officially protected areas. Throughout the 1980s Costa Rica had one of the highest rates of deforestation in the world. So much of Costa Rica's forest is being logged, cleared or otherwise destroyed that it is estimated that Costa Rica will soon not only have no forests left outside the protected areas, but will actually be importing timber: until twenty years ago, bringing wood to Costa Rica would have been the equivalent of taking coals to Newcastle.

The horizontal universe

Tropical forests exist only in a thin band roughly ten degrees on either side of the equator. Their main characteristic is the diversity of life they support, being home to around 40 to 50 percent of all living things on earth (barring marine ecosystems). But in biological terms, the tropical rainforest is still the Great Unknown. Scientists have catalogued fewer than one in six of their two million species, and it is often said that we know less about the workings of the rainforest than we know about the surface of the moon.

Though "rainforest" describes the typically diverse, typically wet tropical forests you encounter in most areas of Costa Rica, there are minute differences in altitude and climate. The unifying factor is, of course, rain. To qualify, a true rainforest must receive more than 2000mm annually, dispersed relatively equally throughout the year – many receive as much as 5000mm or 6000mm. Most of what is discussed below pertains to **primary rainforest** (*bosque primario*), which has not been disturbed for several hundreds, or even thousands, of years. **Secondary growth** is the vegetation that springs up in the wake of some disturbance, like cutting, cultivation or habitation.

A tropical rainforest is characterized by the presence of several layers. At its most complex it will have four layers: the **canopy**, about 40–70m high, at the very top of which are **emergent** trees, often flat-topped; the **subcanopy** beneath the emergent trees, followed by the **understorey** trees, typically 10–20m in height; and finally the **shrub**, or ground, layer. Each level is interconnected by a mesh of horizontal lianas and climbers.

The canopy often looks like a moth-eaten umbrella opened over the lower layers. The chief function of these very tall trees is to **protect** the layers below and to filter light. In very harsh downpours or tropical storms, it is the canopy that takes the brunt of the driving wind and rain, and sometimes lightning, often being lashed about like a cat-of-nine-tails in the process. Sometimes they may be felled in particularly violent storms, falling with a great crash and creating a hole in the upper layer through which light filters to feed the understorey below.

Up to 50 percent of the rainforests' mammalian population may at some point live in the trees, compared to about 15 percent of mammals in temperate-zone forests. The majority of the animals, especially insects, remain most of the time in a specific layer of the forest; some never leave their particular "floor". Species loss – in some cases leading to local extinction, as with the canopy-dwelling harpy eagle – takes place when the rainforest is felled, in part because many animals are not able to adapt to the new topography: they need their floor in order to survive.

Rainforest vegetation has a muffled quality. Mosses beard trees, vines and lianas seemingly strangle their host trees, and huge clumps of plants sprout from the armpits formed by tree branches. This results from **co-** or **interdependency** (sometimes called "mutuality"), another distinct feature of the tropical rainforest. Over millennia, birds and plants have had the entire year in which to engage in ecological interactions, unlike in the temperate zones, where winter shuts both plants and animals down for part of the year.

Rainforest **epiphytes**, plants that grow on other plants, present an example of **commensualism**, a form of symbiosis in which one species profits from its association with another without harming or benefiting the host. Sometimes the relationship is more parasitic, with the epiphyte taking nutrients from its hosts, as is the case with **bromeliads**, which resemble the leafy top of a pineapple turned upside down and stuck on a tree. **Orchids** are the flowering parts of these pineapple-like "weeds", as are pineapples. Bromeliads' leaves trap moisture; otherwise they take their nutrients from their host.

Co-evolution is where two species evolve more or less together due to mutual influence. Flowering plants and their insect pollinators are the best example you'll see in the rainforest. Birds, too, are important in this game of mutual survival. Hummingbirds, for example, pollinate flowers by picking up small quantities of pollen when they insert their long beaks into the flower to drink nectar, then transporting it to another flower. Some plants and birds build tight-knit relationships; deep flowers are pollinated only by long-beaked hummingbirds, more shallow ones by shorter-billed birds.

Experiencing the rainforest

Among the celebrated but false characteristics attributed to rainforests are **giganticism** and **density**. In reality, most rainforest tree trunks are thin, with the taller trees seeming to rise emaciated into the sun, sprouting like mushrooms atop the other layers in their search for light. Neither is primary rainforest as impenetrable as many visitors expect. It's actually roomy on the ground. Most growth goes on above your head – what the German explorer Alexander von Humboldt called "a forest above a forest". It's the **secondary forest**, which grows up after the destruction of primary growth, that is bushy and hard to penetrate.

During the day the primary forest cover can be quite **light**, except in perennially misty cloudforests or when it is raining. It's true that aside from secondary growth or where a tree has crashed, leaving a hole in the canopy, about 90 percent of the sunlight is captured by the upper layers before it reaches the ground. But when the sun is out, the rainforest light is almost bright in its translucence, a "light darkness", that is neither day nor night; rather as if a mesh of cheesecloth has been thrown over your head.

The true tropical rainforest is also not that **colourful**, unless you take into account incrementally differing shades of green and bark. Most orchids, for instance, grow in the upper canopy, as much as 40m above the ground, although you may see flashes of red in the form of heliconias, smiling-lip-shaped red flowers that grow in symmetrical bunches at eye level or lower.

Rather than hearing frightening screeches and feeling yourself being watched from all corners by the unseen eyes of tapirs and jaguars, you are likely to feel unexpectedly lonely in the largely **silent** tropical rainforest. Most walkers, unless they are trained or with a guide, do not see very much at all of other living creatures. Almost every living thing inside a tropical rainforest is shy of humans and/or well camouflaged, and many spend their days in semi-torpor or completely hidden. During the day it can be very quiet, except for birds and howler monkeys, two of the more voluble rainforest-dwellers. Once twilight begins to fall, though, the buzz and hum of the tropical forest crescendos noticeably, with the intertwined croaks of frogs, the mating calls of toads, the whirr of crickets and the night cries of birds.

Among the most fantastic of the rainforest trees is the **walking palm**, whose finger-like roots are prehensile; in fact, they can actually move. If it is so inclined, the palm can "walk" more than 1m in its lifetime in search of water, stepping over inconvenient obstacles like logs. **Strangler vines** initially look disturbing; a sort of arboreal version of the boa constrictor that doesn't strangle, but rather out-competes host trees for light, eventually dehydrating them to death. Everywhere in the rainforest you will see dried-up, hollowed-out dead trees surrounded by the healthy stranglers they once supported. The loops of **lianas and vines** – stranglers and otherwise – are amazingly intricate, spiralling endlessly into complex **pas-de-deux**.

One of the most startling characteristics of some rainforest trees is their **buttresses**, which help anchor the tree in thin soil where runoff is considerable. These sometimes massive above-ground roots have bark that ranges from cement-hard to long peeling strips, called **exfoliating bark**. Some trunks also have huge **spines** that look as though they could have defended a medieval garrison. These are a protective mechanism, making it difficult for animals or humans to climb the tree.

Rainforest destruction

What the large-scale **destruction** of the rainforest will mean in terms of climatic change and the chemical composition of the air is not known. We do know, however, that the tropical rainforest performs vital photosynthesizing processes, affects **weather** patterns, and mitigates the greenhouse effect and a range of other changes occurring as a result of humankind's misuse of its environment. Tropical forests, particularly those at higher altitudes, do the usually richer lowland soils a big favour by acting as **watersheds** and absorbing most of the tremendous rainfall of the tropical climate. Without them, lowland agricultural soils would be washed away by torrents of water. Each year in Costa Rica about 725 million tons of **topsoil** are lost to wind erosion and water runoff – 83 percent of this happens in areas cleared and put under pasture. When it's bucketing down in the Valle Central in October, visitors will have a hard time believing that Costa Rica has a problem with water supply, or even desertification, as is the case in Guanacaste, but the watershed deterioration caused by deforestation has put the country at risk from both.

Many of the lower orders of living things that inhabit rainforests, like fungi and bacteria, have provided **medicine** with some of its most effective treatments against serious illnesses – good arguments, in human terms, for preserving the rainforest and the medical secrets it may divulge. Also lost when rainforests are felled are forest-dwelling indigenous **peoples** and their cultures. **Animals** and birds, including jaguars, tapirs, macaws, toucans and quetzals, lose their habitats or are hounded out into the open where they are easily killed by hunters.

The reason that such destruction takes place is, quite simply, that there is serious **money** to be made from the felling of tropical forests. **Loggers** fell the forest for the hardwoods it yields, using them to make expensive furniture prized for its durability and beauty. The most famous endangered hardwoods are mahogany and purpleheart, whose names evoke their lovely deep-blooded colour. Meanwhile, the big old oak trees of the cloudforests are used for timber and charcoal. Although the major deforesters often have the implicit support of the national government because they are earners of much-needed foreign currency or foreign investment, they do not have total *carte blanche*. Loggers need a government permit, and the export of many rare tropical hardwood species is prohibited. But between a certain level of corruption and illegality, logging still takes place: the Costa Rican Forestry Office reckons that illegal cutting of rainforest trees accounted for 80 percent of forest losses between 1989 and 1991, and travellers who spend any amount of time on the nation's highways can expect at some point to find themselves stuck behind a slow-moving truck loaded with massive tree trunks swathed in chains – these are tropical hardwoods, trees hundreds or even thousands of years old, that are being lost for good.

Other perpetrators fell the trees for the land the forest stands on. **Bananas**, another large foreign-currency earner, only grow well in the hot, wet tropical lowlands. Other major agro-exports include coffee, tea and macadamia nut plantations, all grown for the foreign market. **Cattle-ranchers** have been clearing areas of rainforest for years. The first horses and cows were brought to Costa Rica by the Spanish as early as 1561. By 1950, approximately an eighth of the country was under pasture. The cattle industry in Costa Rica grew rapidly from the 1960s to the 1980s, largely funded by loans from the US to encourage lower-grade beef production and by rising beef prices on the international market. During much of the 1980s Costa Rica was the world's biggest exporter of beef to the US.

Cattle ranching takes up more land and yields less than any other type of farming and ranches create little local employment in comparison to banana or coffee plantations. The tropical soils of the pasture the cattle feed on are exhausted quickly, usually within three to ten years. By 1983 about 30 percent of the country was pastureland, much of it abandoned. Of all the forests cut during the 1960s and 1970s to make way for the growth of the cattle industry, about 90 percent are not regenerable. Meanwhile, since the late 1980s, tastes, both domestic and foreign, have changed, and the consumption and price of beef has dropped to such an extent that the future of large-scale cattle ranching seems in doubt.

Despite this, cattle continue to feature heavily in Costa Rica – especially in Guanacaste, where the cowboy and hacienda culture reigns supreme. Many haciendas have turned to non-traditional activities like tourism and have scaled down their herds in order to concentrate on the new trade, although in aspect and essence they remain working cattle farms. At the other end of the scale, the smallholder keeps cattle as a way of safeguarding against the risks of subsistence-level agriculture. Cows can be milked, slaughtered or sold, and in hard times – or in an inflationary economy such as Costa Rica's – they are a good investment for the *campesino*.

Another big threat to the survival of the tropical forest is **agriculture**. The very act of felling the rainforest renders the soil useless after a couple of years. Rainforest soils are, in fact, very poor in nutrients. The complex, dense appearance of the trees represents an attempt to compensate for this, as they have to build a store of crucial chemicals above ground, in their leaves and bark. When a rainforest tree is felled by a storm or by wind and comes crashing down, the nutrients are recycled by the ground vegetation within a matter of weeks (rather than months, as in the temperate zone). In this way essential chemicals are kept in constant exchange. These chemicals are located in the thin uppermost layer of soil – the humus – which is easily washed away, turned over for cultivation, or tramped into nonexistence by cows' hooves. The main exponent of slash-and-burn techniques in Costa Rica is usually the *precarista*, or squatter *campesino*, victim of unequal land distribution and poverty.

Costa Rica has the highest rural population density in Latin America, so there is tremendous pressure on **land**. Until the second half of this century, deforestation came under the legal definition of "improvement of the land", and the state still encourages deforestation by allowing the *campesino* to establish title to isolated patches of "unwanted" land, usually in remote areas, if he clears or otherwise "improves" it. (This is not just a Costa Rican phenomenon: in the eighteenth century, pioneer settlers to Canada and the United States were granted title to land according to the same criteria.) The effects of this colonization are most conspicuous along the roadsides and in the smaller communities of the Zona Norte, where you see smallholders' shacks built on poor, stump-studded land, dotted with the odd banana tree, vegetable patches, and a few cattle and pigs.

Archeologists and biologists speculate that the pre-Columbian isthmus peoples used the slash-and-burn method to plant crops of maize and *pejiballe*, and that this did not do long-term damage to the regenerative capacities of complex forest systems (for more on this, see p.220). Rather it is large-scale colonization, followed by burning, that ensure the rainforest will never recover. Burning renders long-term cultivation of anything from grasses to carrots impossible, as it definitively destroys the humus at the topmost layer of the former rainforest soil.

Forests of the future

Any real solutions to the problem of deforestation – rather than the preservation of existing forests – appear complex or unattainable. Historically, the blame for the near-total deforestation of the Central American isthmus lies with the conquistadors, who, in the search for domestic wealth, disrupted indigenous forms of sustainable cultivation to grow export crops, effectively turning the country into a coffee-and-banana republic. The concerns of the domestic elites and the consumer demands of the countries that import Costa Rican goods make it difficult to break the pattern. In what is essentially a third-world country, with little economic room for manoeuvre, it seems Costa Rica's rainforest can no longer just exist; instead, it must pay its own way in order to survive. In short, it must become **sustainable**.

A recent development in the sustainable use of rainforests is the entry of large **pharmaceutical** companies into the conservation effort. INbio (National Institute of Biodiversity) was founded in San José in 1989 as the first institute of its kind in the world, and is devoted to taking an entire inventory of Costa Rica's species, and training locals in species collection procedures. Many lower-order rainforest flora like fungi and bacteria are thought to possess potential anti-cancer, rheumatoid, and hypertension agents. INbio has recently signed a lucrative contract with Merck, one of the world's largest pharmaceutical companies, who have guaranteed that INbio (and the state) will receive "royalties" on any drugs successfully developed from samples INbio sends for investigation.

Debt payments and ecological concerns can even be successfully intertwined in **"debt-for-nature"** swaps. A complex arrangement still in the pioneering stage, this scheme allows organizations like the World Wide Fund for Nature to purchase a piece of Costa Rica's foreign debt, usually at a discount. Costa Rica's government in return issues short-term government bonds. The funds raised by selling these bonds to investors are funnelled into conservation. For the first world foreign banks and organizations who participate, debt-for-nature is seen in purely economic terms: an investment in the environment. Philosophically speaking, though, some justify it as the Third World being "paid back" for the First World's ravages, including carbon monoxide emissions and the deforestation that has long been encouraged by the markets and tastes of the developed world.

Conservation and tourism

Costa Rica is widely seen as being at the cutting edge of worldwide conservation strategy, an impressive feat for a tiny Central American nation. At the centre of Costa Rica's internationally applauded conservation effort is a complex system of national parks and wildlife refuges, which protect a full 25 percent of its territory, one of the largest percentages of protected land among Western-hemisphere nations. These statistics are used with great effect to attract tourists and, along with Belize, Costa Rica has become virtually synonymous with ecotourism in Central America.

On the other hand, the National Parks Service does not possess the funds to protect adequately more than half the boundaries of these areas, which are under constant pressure from logging and squatters (*precaristas*), and to a lesser extent from mining interests. In addition, the question uppermost in the minds of conservationists and biologists is what, if any, damage is being caused by so many feet walking through the rainforests.

Conservation in the New World tropics

The **traditional view** of conservation is a European one of preserving, museum-like, pretty animals and flowers; an idea that was conceived and upheld by relatively wealthy Old World countries in which the majority of the forests have long-since disappeared. In the contemporary world, this definition of conservation no longer works, and certainly not in the New World tropics, besieged as they are by lack of resources, huge income inequities, legislation that lacks bite, and the continual appetite of the world market for tropical hardwoods, not to mention the Old World zeal for coffee and picture-perfect supermarket fruits.

There's a leftist perspective on conservation that sees an imperialistic, bourgeois and anti-*campesino* agenda among the large conservation organizations of the North. By this reckoning, saving the environment is all very well but does little for the day-to-day realities of the 38 percent or so of Costa Rica's population who live below the poverty line. These people have, in many cases, been made landless and impoverished by, for instance, absentee landowners speculating on land (in the Zona Norte and in Guanacaste) or by the pulling-out of major employers like the United Fruit Company (in the Zona Sur near Golfito and on the Osa Peninsula). Many are left with simply no choice but to engage in the kind of activity – be it gold-panning or slash-and-burn agriculture – which is universally condemned by conservationists in the North.

Conservation in Costa Rica

Costa Rica has a long history of conservation-consciousness, although it has taken different forms and guises. As early as 1775, laws were passed to limit the destructive impact of *quemas*, or brush-burning. Meanwhile, a vogue developed in Europe for **botanical gardens**. The period from 1635 to 1812 saw the birth of some of Europe's most splendid gardens – including London's Kew Gardens, founded in 1730. Scientists-cum-adventurers in search of knowledge and botanists in search of flora descended upon the Neotropics.

The bulk of **preservation laws** were passed after 1845, concurrent with Costa Rica's period of greatest economic and cultural growth. That said, most of this legislation was directed at protecting resource extraction rather than the areas themselves – to guard fishing and hunting grounds and to conserve what were already seen as valuable timber supplies. In 1895 laws were passed protecting water supplies and the establishment of *guardabosques* (forest rangers) to fight the *quemas* caused by the regular burning of deforested land and pasture by cattle-ranchers. The forerunners of several institutions later to be important to the development of conservation in Costa Rica were founded by the end of the nineteenth century, including the Museo Nacional and the Instituto Físico Geográfico.

Much of the credit for helping establish Costa Rica's system of national parks has to go to **Olof Wessberg** and **Karen Morgenson**, longtime foreign residents who in 1963, largely through their own efforts, founded the Reserva Natura Absoluta Cabo Blanco near their home on the southwest tip of the Nicoya Peninsula. Wessberg and Morgenson helped raise national consciousness through an extensive campaign in the mid-1960s, so that by the end of the decade there was broad support for the founding of a national parks service. In 1969 Santa Rosa National Monument and Park was declared, and in 1970 the SPN (Servicio de Parques Nacionales) was officially inaugurated. Spearheaded by a recently graduated forester, Mario Boza, the system developed slowly at first, as the law which established Santa Rosa really existed only on paper: neighbouring farmers and ranchers continued to encroach on the land for pasture and brush-burning as before.

Although it remains a mystery, the murder of Olof Wessberg in 1975 on the Osa Peninsula is an illustration of the powerful interests that are thwarted by conservation. Wessberg was conducting a preliminary survey in Osa to assess the possibility of a national park there (the site of modern-day Corcovado). Although his assailant – the man who had offered to guide him – was caught, a motive was never discovered and the crime has not been satisfactorily solved.

Nonetheless, despite the pressures of vested interests, the Costa Rican conservation programme moved forward in the early 1980s with the founding of **Minae** (Ministerio del Ambiente y Energía), the government body entrusted with the overall control of the country's ecological resources. In 1988, the Arias government drafted a national conservation strategy, and, soon after his election victory in 1994, president José María Figueres boldly proclaimed, "We will build a constructive alliance with nature." This took the form of trying to bring together all the various conservation efforts taking place throughout the country under direct government control. For decades, much of the most important conservation work had been undertaken by privately (often foreign) funded initiatives and so, in 1996, the Costa Rican Nature Reserve Network was founded which for the first time brought the country's disparate patchwork of privately owned reserves and refuges (of which there are more than 100) under the control of a single administrative body subject to the same rules and regulations as state-owned parks. The Costa Rican government continues to welcome privately funded conservation programmes as they help to remove some of the financial burden from the beleaguered state coffers, which struggle to raise the revenue necessary to maintain the national parks. Moves to siphon off funds from non-national park related tourism have led to some uneasy stand-offs between the government and the tourist office and for the time being money continues to be in short supply. A solution needs to be found, however. Visitor numbers are continuing to rise placing increasing burdens on the parks, all of which require extra staff. Ideally the government would like to purchase more lands for preservation but as yet has still to find much of the money owed to landowners deprived of their land when the national parks were created.

National parks are now such an entrenched part of Costa Rica's landscape that they might be taken to have always been there. In fact most have been established in the last twenty-five years and the process of creating them is not always smooth. Tortuguero National Park (see p.172) on the Caribbean coast is a case in point.

Turtle Bogue (the old Miskito name for Tortuguero) had always been isolated. Even today access is by fluvial transport or air only, and before the dredging of the main canal in the 1960s it was even more cut off from the rest of the country. Most of the local people were of Miskito or Afro-Caribbean extraction, hunting and fishing and living almost completely without consumer goods. There was virtually no cash economy in the village, with local trade and barter being sufficient for most people's needs.

In the 1940s, lumbering began in earnest in the area. A sawmill was built in the village, and during the next two decades the area experienced a boom. The local lumber exhausted itself by the 1960s, but in the twenty-year interim it brought outsiders and a dependence on cash-obtainable consumer goods. Simultaneously, the number of green sea turtles began to decline rapidly, due to overfishing and egg harvesting, and by the 1950s the once-numerous turtle was officially endangered. The alarm raised by biologists over the green turtle's precipitous decline paved the way for the establishment, in 1970, of Tortuguero National Park, protecting 30 of the 35 kilometres of turtle-nesting beach and extending to more than 200 square kilometres of surrounding forests, canals and waterways. The establishment of this protective area put former sources of income off-limits to local populations, and villagers who had benefited from the wood-and-turtle economy either reverted to the subsistence and agricultural life they had known before or left the area in search of a better one. Nowadays, over thirty years after the park was officially established, many locals make a good living off the increasing amount of tourism it brings, especially those with their own independent businesses, although others are relegated to low-paid positions in hotels and other services.

The establishment of the Tortuguero National Park effectively broke the boom-and-bust cycle so prevalent in the tropics, whereby local resources are used to extinction, leaving no viable alternatives after the storm has passed. In Tortuguero the hardwoods have made a bit of a comeback, and the green turtle's numbers

Eco-paradise lost: pesticides and pollution

There are, however, flaws in this Garden of Eden. Chief among them is the importance of the **agro-export** economy. The growth of the large-scale agro-industries depends on a continual supply of cheap labour and land, and the **pollution** wreaked by the pesticides used in banana plantations – the country's major agro-export – is becoming an increasing threat. Foreign consumers attach an amazing level of importance to the appearance of supermarket bananas and pineapples, and about 20 percent of potentially dangerous pesticides used in the cultivation of bananas serve only to improve the look of the fruit and not, as it is often thought, to control pestilence. Travellers who pass through banana plantations in Costa Rica or who take river trips, especially along the Río Sarapiquí, can't fail to notice the ubiquitous blue plastic bags. The pristine appearance of Costa Rican bananas is due largely to the fact that they grow inside these pesticide-lined bags, which make their way into waterways where they are fatally consumed by fish, mammals (such as the manatee) or iguanas. In the Río Tempisque basin armadillos and crocodiles are thought to have been virtually exterminated by agricultural pesticides.

C

CONTEXTS | Conservation and tourism

are up dramatically from their low point in the 1950s and 1960s. Considering the popularity of the national park and its lagoons and turtle tours, there's no doubt that conservation and protection of Tortuguero's wildlands can have lasting benefits to locals. Unfortunately, it's becoming increasingly difficult for the park authorities to protect the environment, promote tourism without adversely affecting the environment and ensure it is of a sufficient level to support the livelihoods of local people. In order to protect the well-being of the turtles, the main attraction for the majority of visitors, the park authorities have introduced a number of stringent regulations, the most significant being to restrict the number of people allowed on to the beach during the laying season to just 400 per day. Everyone must be off the beach by midnight and all visitors must be accompanied by a certified guide. Most guided tours are provided by the upmarket lodges lining Tortuguero Canal but there are also over a hundred certified guides working out of Tortuguero village itself. Owing to the restrictions on the number of visitors, not all of them can find work each night, and guides that are idle for several nights have been known to try and sneak visitors on to the beach. If caught, the usual punishment is for the guide to have their licence revoked for anything up to two weeks, which obviously leaves them impoverished and perhaps even more willing to break the rules.

Consequently, a campaign to get the authorities to allow more people on the beach for longer is underfoot, arguing that 400 is just an arbitrary figure and that, so long as the visitors remain a safe distance from the turtles, it doesn't matter how many people are on the beach. It's easy to understand why people struggling to make a living from the eco-tourism industry would benefit from the rule change but equally easy to see that such an alteration would harm the turtles (which, in turn, would lead to a decline in tourism). So far, the authorities have remained firm – as they have regarding the ban on lucrative midnight tours through the park's canals that used a searchlight to pick out the native wildlife (much of which is nocturnal). So powerful were these searchlights that they were temporarily blinding many of the animals; a great many died, and the decision was taken to ban the night tours. Some local people are campaigning to have them reintroduced in a 'managed' way, however, and whether or not a tiny community like Tortuguero can absorb high levels of tourism and still retain its ecological and cultural integrity remains to be seen.

Animals are not alone in being at risk from pesticides. In 1987 a hundred Costa Rican plantation workers sued Standard Fruit, Dow Chemical and Shell Oil for producing a pesticide that is a known cause of sterility in banana-plantation workers. Although the workers' claims were upheld in US courts, the companies have appealed. Since then several harmful pesticides have been banned, although every year six percent of all Costa Rican banana workers present claims for incidents involving exposure to pesticides – the highest such rate in the world.

Conservation initiatives

In recent years Mario Boza, a prominent conservationist, has been advocating a strategy of **macro-conservation**. By uniting concerns and "joining up" chunks of protected land, he argued, the macro-areas will allow larger protected areas for animals who need room to hunt, like jaguars and pumas. Most of all, they will allow countries to make more effective joint conservation policies and decisions. Macro-conservation projects currently include the Proyeto Paseo Pantera ('the path of the panther', the idea being to create an unbroken stretch of jungle throughout all of Mesoamerica), El Mundo Maya (Belize, El

Salvador, Guatemala, Honduras and Mexico), Si-a-Paz (Nicaragua and Costa Rica) and La Amistad International Park and Biosphere Reserve (Costa Rica and Panamá).

Arguably, however, the most revolutionary change in conservation management, and the one most likely to have the biggest pay-off in the long term, is the shift toward **local initiatives**. Some projects are truly local, such as the tiny grassroots organization TUVA and its selective logging of naturally felled rainforest trees on the Osa Peninsula, or the ecotourism co-operative of Las Delicias in Barra Honda on the Nicoya Peninsula.

Another initiative, even more promising in terms of how it affects the lives of many rural-based Costa Ricans, is the creation of **"buffer zones"** around some national parks. In these zones *campesinos* and other smallholders can do part-time farming, are allowed restricted hunting rights and receive education about the ecological and economic value of the forest. Locals may be trained as nature guides, and *campesinos* may be given incentives to enter into non-traditional forms of agriculture and ways of making a living which are less environmentally destructive.

In recent years Costa Rica's **waste disposal problems** have given the country a garbage nightmare, culminating in a scandal in 1995 over the overflowing of the Río Azul site, San José's main dump. The government fully recognizes the irony of this – rubbish lining the streets of a country with such a high conservation profile – and in an admirable, typically Tico grass-roots initiative, legions of schoolkids are now sent on rubbish-collecting after-school projects and weekend brigades. Even more ingenious is the national movement that sends Costa Rican schoolchildren to national parks and other preserves as **volunteers** to work on conservation projects during school holidays, thus planting the seeds for a future generation of dedicated – or at least aware – conservationists.

Conservation organizations in Costa Rica

The following list represents just a sample of the large number of conservation organizations working in Costa Rica, and there are many more local operations in addition. For details of voluntary conservation opportunities in Costa Rica, see p.54.

Fundación Neotropica, Aptdo 236-10002, Frente al Colegio de Ingenieros y Arquitectos, Curridabat, San José (☎253-2130, ☎253-4210, ⊕www.neotropica .org). Well-established organization that works with several small-scale and (typically) local conservation initiatives in Costa Rica. Their Curridabat office sells posters, books and T-shirts in aid of funds. Accepts donations.

Fundación Amigos de la Isla del Coco, Aptdo 276-1005, Barrio México, San José (☎ & ☎256-7476, ⊕www.cocosisland.org). Organization set up in 1994 to raise funds to preserve the unique flora and fauna of the remote Isla del Coco (also known as 'Dinosaur Island' because it featured in the film *Jurassic Park*), one of UNESCO's World Heritage Sites.

World Wide Fund for Nature (⊕www.wwfca.org), 1250 24th St NW, Washington DC, 20037 USA (☎202/293-4800); 90 Eglington Ave E, Suite 504, Toronto, Ontario M4P 2Z7 (☎416/489-8800); Panda House, Weyside Park, Godalming, Surrey GU7 1XR (☎01483/26444). The fund is a major donor to wildlife preservation schemes throughout Central America including, in Costa Rica, projects in Monteverde and Tortuguero. The organization's Costa Rican headquarters is located at: Central American Program Office, 7170 CATIE, Turrialba (☎556-1383, ☎556-1737).

Tourism

Around 700,000 tourists a year come to Costa Rica – mostly from the US, Canada and Europe – an incredible number, considering that the population of the country itself is only a little over three million. In 1994, revenue to Costa Rica from tourism was $700 million or more, surpassing earnings by banana exports for the first time in the country's history. In the North American winter months of December to March, it is estimated that the country's hotel rooms are at near-100 percent occupancy. Ten years ago it seemed unlikely that this small Central American country, peaceful but off the beaten track, would attract so many visitors. Along with the considerable charms of the country itself, its popularity today is linked with the growing trend toward eco-tourism.

If managed properly, low-impact **eco-tourism** is one of the best ways in which forests, beaches, rivers, mangroves, volcanos and other natural formations can pay their way – in *dólares* – while remaining pristine and intact. However, eco-tourism is a difficult term to define. It was often seen in relation to what it was not: package tourism, wherein visitors have limited contact with nature and with the day-to-day lives of local people. But as more and more organizations and businesses hijack the "eco" prefix for dubious uses, the authentic eco-tourism experience has become increasingly difficult to pin down. One of the best attempts has been put forward by ATEC, the Talamancan Eco-tourism and Conservation Association, which seeks to promote, as it says, "socially responsible tourism" by integrating local Bribrí and Afro-Caribbean culture into tourists' experience of the area, as well as giving residents pride in their unique cultural heritage and natural environment. Their definition is:

> Eco-tourism means more than bird books and binoculars. Eco-tourism means more than native art hanging on hotel walls or ethnic dishes on the restaurant menu. Eco-tourism is not mass tourism behind a green mask.
>
> Eco-tourism means a constant struggle to defend the earth and to protect and sustain traditional communities. Eco-tourism is a cooperative relationship between the non-wealthy local community and those sincere, open-minded tourists who want to enjoy themselves in a Third World setting and, at the same time, enrich their consciousness by means of significant educational and cultural experience.

There are more cynical views. For some, eco-tourism is a PR concept with a nice ring, but all in all no less destructive or voyeuristic than regular (package-holiday) tourism. Most, though, argue that if people are going to travel, they may as well do so in a low-impact manner that reduces destruction of the visited environment, and promotes cultural exchange.

Several pioneering projects in Costa Rica have set out to combine tourism with sustainable methods of farming, rainforest preservation, and scientific research. Some of these, like the Rainforest Aerial Tram and the Monteverde Cloudforest Reserve, are the most advanced of their kind in the Americas, if not the world. Not only does the Aerial Tram provide a fascinating glimpse of the tropical canopy – normally completely inaccessible to human eyes – but also offers a rare safe and stable method for biologists to investigate this little-known habitat. Income from visitors is funnelled into maintaining and augmenting the surrounding reserve. Monteverde, meanwhile, merely in preserving a large piece of complex tropical forest, gives scientists a valuable stomping ground for taxonomic study. Tourism is just one of the main activities in the reserve, which has been a research ground for tropical biologists from all over the world, and provides revenue for maintenance and, hopefully, future expansion.

The huge growth of tourism in the country worries many Costa Ricans, even those who make their living from it. Is it just a fad that will fade away, only to be replaced by another unprepared country-of-the-moment? What – if any – are the advantages of having an economy led by tourism instead of the traditional exports of bananas and coffee? Furthermore, how do you reconcile the need to attract enough visitors to make tourism economically viable whilst ensuring that this tourism remains low-impact? It's a problem made all the more difficult by ongoing arguments between two of the main organizations charged with managing the country's eco-tourism industry: MINAE – the government body that directly controls the country's network of national parks – and the Costa Rican Tourist Board (Instituto Costarricense de Turismo or ICT). Whereas MINAE is, despite severe underfunding, widely seen as having done a reasonably good job in ensuring that tourism doesn't overwhelm the parks' fragile ecosystems, the ICT is often regarded as putting commercial interests above environmental ones. In contrast to the somewhat impoverished state of MINAE, the ICT makes a lot of money out of tourism, much of it derived from the three percent tax collected on every occupied hotel room. This has led some to accuse the ICT of being more concerned with generating new accommodation (and thus money) than with the possible impact the increase in visitors could have on the environment and local communities. The head of MINAE even went so far as to initiate a public row with the ICT who, he claimed, were using the lure of the national parks to increase the amount of tourist revenue but were failing to donate enough of this revenue towards the parks' upkeep. When the ICT refuted these claims and refused to give the parks any more money, the head of MINAE responded by threatening to close the national parks to all visitors. The ICT, realising the devastating effect this would have on tourist revenue, backed down and increased its contributions.

The question of who pays for Costa Rica's environmental well-being is one that continues to provoke fierce debate. Though the government actively welcomes contributions from foreign sources, many Costa Ricans are alarmed by what they see as the virtual purchase of their country by foreigners. Though many hotels and businesses are still Costa Rican-owned and managed, entire

---

Ecotourism codes of conduct

Though well-meaning, ecotourism **codes of conduct** can seem preachy and presumptuous. Still, in any attempt to define the term, or to go any way towards understanding its aims, it's useful to know what the locally accepted guidelines are. The Asociación Tsuli, the Costa Rican branch of the Audubon Society, has developed its own short code of conduct for "Environmental Ethics for Nature Travel":

- Wildlife and natural habitats must not be needlessly disturbed.
- Waste should be disposed of properly.
- Tourism should be a positive influence on local communities.
- Tourism should be managed and sustainable.
- Tourism should be culturally sensitive.
- There must be no commerce in wildlife, wildlife products or native plants.
- Tourists should leave with a greater understanding and appreciation of nature, conservation and the environment.
- Tourism should strengthen the conservation effort and enhance the natural integrity of places visited.

areas on the Pacific coast may as well be plastered with "Se Vende" signs as the government gears itself up to sell off yet more national resources and industries in its quest for foreign investment. It remains to be seen what effect this might have on small communities and local cultures.

At times the government seems bent on turning the country into a high-income tourist enclave. North Americans and Europeans will still consider many things quite cheap, but Costa Rica is already the most expensive country to visit in the region, and recently the tourism minister was quoted in the national press as saying that he had no qualms about discouraging "backpackers" (meaning budget tourists) from coming to Costa Rica. Better-heeled tourists, the thinking goes, not only make a more significant investment in the country dollar for dollar, but are more easily controlled, choosing in the main to travel in tour groups or to stay in big holiday resorts such as the Papagayo Project in Guanacaste and the *Hotel Playa Tambor* on the Nicoya Peninsula.

However, tourists with a genuine concern and interest in the country's flora, fauna and cultural life can choose from a variety of places to spend their money constructively, including top-notch rainforest lodges that have worked hard to integrate themselves with their surroundings. And those who want to rough it can still do so heroically in places like Corcovado and Chirripó. For now, at least, Costa Rica is one of the few countries in the world where eco-tourism can viably outlast and out-compete other, potentially more damaging, types of tourism.

Books

The most comprehensive volumes written on Costa Rica tend to be about **natural history** – many make better introductions to what you'll see in the country than the glossy literature pumped out by the government tourist board and most guidebooks. Frustratingly, many of the most informative works on both natural and cultural history are out of date or out of print (designated "o/p" in the list below). You'll find a number of the titles listed below in San José bookshops, but don't expect to see them elsewhere in the country.

Those interested in **Costa Rican fiction** (which is alive and well, although not extensively translated or known abroad) will have much richer and varied reading with some knowledge of Spanish. Costa Rica has no single internationally recognized towering figure in its national literature, and in sharp contrast to other countries in the region the most sophisticated and best-known writers in the country are women. Carmen Naranjo is the most widely translated, with six novels and two short-story collections (plus some of the country's most prestigious literary awards) to her name, but there are a number of lesser-read writers, including the brilliant Yolanda Oreomuno, and an upsurge of younger women, tackling contemporary social issues like domestic violence and alcoholism in their fiction and poetry. The publication in the 1930s of Carlos Luis Fallas' seminal novel *Mamita Yunai*, about labour conditions in the United Fruit Company banana fields of Limón Province, sparked a wave of "proletarian" novels, which became the dominant form in Costa Rican fiction until well into the 1970s. Until recently Costa Rican fiction also leant heavily on picturesque stories of rural life with some writers – usually men – drawing on the country's wealth of fauna. There are a number of *cuentos* (stories), fable-like in their simplicity and not a little ponderous in their symbolism, featuring turtles, fish and rabbits as characters.

Travel narratives

Peter Ford *Tekkin a Waalk* (UK, Flamingo, o/p). Journalist Ford was based in Managua for most of the terrible 1980s. After that his idea of a holiday seems to have been to "tek a waalk" (as it's called in the local patois) along the eastern coast of the isthmus. In the very short part of the book that deals with Costa Rica, Ford's boatmen overshoot the river entrance to Greytown, Nicaragua, and end up in the northeastern Costa Rican village of Barra del Colorado, much to the chagrin of the *migración* – Ford must be one of the few people ever to be deported from Costa Rica.

Paul Theroux *The Old Patagonian Express: By Train through the Americas* (US, Houghton Mifflin/ UK, Penguin). Somewhat out of date (Theroux went through over twentyfive years ago), but a great read nonetheless. Laced with the author's usual tetchy black humour and general misanthropy, the descriptions of his two Costa Rican train journeys (neither of which still runs) to Limón and to Puntarenas remain apt – as is the account of passing through San José, where he meets American men on sex-and-booze vacations.

Culture and folk traditions

Roberto Cabrera *Santa Cruz Guanacaste: una aproximación a la historia y la cultura popular* (San José, Ediciones Guayacán). The best cultural history of Guanacaste, written by a respected Guanacastecan sociologist. Verbal snapshots of nineteenth- and twentieth-century hacienda life, accounts of bull riding, and details of micro-regional dances such as the *punto guanacasteco* (adopted as the national dance), *El torito* and the veiled dance.

⊡ **Paula Palmer** *What Happen: A Folk History of the Talamanca Coast* (San José, Ecodesarrollos). The definitive – although now dated – folk history of the Afro-Caribbean community on Limón Province's Talamancan coast.

Palmer first went to Cahuita in the early 1970s as a Peace Corps volunteer, later to return as a sociologist, collecting oral histories from older members of the local communities. Great stories and atmospheric testimonies of pirate treasure, ghosts and the like; complemented by photos and accounts of local agriculture, foods and traditional remedies.

Paula Palmer, Juanita Sánchez and Gloria Mayorga *Taking Care of Sibö's Gifts* (San José, Editorarama). Manifesto for the future of Bribrí culture, ecological survival of the *talamanqueña* ecosystems and a concise explication of differing views of the land and people's relationship to it held by the *ladinos* and Bribrí on the KéköLdi indigenous reserve.

Conservation

⊡ **Catherine Caulfield** *In the Rainforest* (US, University of Chicago Press). One of the best introductions to the rainforest, dealing in an accessible fashion with many of the issues covered in the more specialized titles. Her chapter on Costa Rica is a wary elucidation of the destruction that cattle ranching in particular wreaks, as well as an interesting profile of the farming methods used by the Monteverde community.

Marcus Colcheser and Larry Lohmann (eds) *The Struggle for Land and the Fate of the Forests* (US & UK, Zed Books). A volume of essays that divides rainforest issues into general theoretical discussions, followed by case studies. Although Costa Rica is covered only in passing, the chapter on Guatemala introduces relevant points, while the brief and accessible history of agrarian reform in Latin America puts the *campesino* and

landlessness issues of Costa Rica in context.

Luis Fournier *Desarrollo y perspectivas del movimiento conservacionista costarricense* (San José, EDUCA). Seminal, if dry, survey of conservation policy from the dawn of the nation until present, by one of Costa Rica's most eminent scientists and conservationists.

Susanna Hecht and Alexander Cockburn *The Fate of the Forest: Developers, Destroyers and Defenders of the Amazon* (US, Schocken, o/p/UK, Penguin). The best single book readily available on rainforest destruction, this exhaustive volume is written with a sound knowledge of Amazonian history. The beautiful prose dissects some of the more pervasive myths about rainforest destruction, and it's comprehensive enough to be applicable to any forested areas under threat in the New World tropics.

William Weinberg *War on the Land: Ecology and Politics in Central America* (US & UK, Zed Books). Just one chapter, but a good one, devoted to Costa Rica. While not failing to congratulate the country for its conservation achievements, the author also reveals the internal wranglings of conservationist policy.

History and current affairs

Tony Avirgan and Martha Honey *La Penca: On Trial in Costa Rica, the CIA vs. the Press* (San José, Editorial Porvenir). Avirgan, a journalist and longtime resident of San José, was wounded at the La Penca news conference bombing in 1984. After this, he and Honey sunk their teeth into the dark underbelly of US/CIA politics and operations in the area during the years of the Nicaraguan Civil War. In contrast to her more recent and more definitive book (see below), Honey concludes here that the attack was carried out by the CIA.

Mavis Hiltunen Biesanz, Richard Biesanz, Karen Zubris Biesanz *The Ticos: Culture and Social Change in Costa Rica* (US, Lynne Reiner). An intriguing blend of quantitative and qualitative research, supported by personal interviews with many Costa Ricans, this book seeks to get under the skin of Costa Rican society, examining (amongst other things) government, class and ethnic relations, the family, health and sport, and managing to be rigorous and anecdotal at the same time.

Richard Biesanz, Karen Zubris Biesanz and Mavis Hiltunen Biesanz *The Costa Ricans* (US, Prentice Hall, o/p). Rather outdated generalizations and idealizations about the Costa Rican "character". However, though descriptive rather than analytical, many of the authors' observations and conclusions, especially about sexual conduct, inequality and marriage, ring true.

* **Tjabel Daling** *Costa Rica In Focus: A Guide to the People, Politics and Culture* (US, Interlink/UK, Latin America Bureau). The most authoritative and up-to-date country guide, entertainingly illustrated with bits of Costa Rican current life, such as billboards and labels. The text offers an especially clear-eyed cultural and social analysis.

Steven Palmer and Iván Molina (eds) *The Costa Rica Reader* (US, Duke University Press). One of the best introductions to the country for the general reader, this book features more than fifty texts by Costa Ricans, from essays and memoirs to histories and poems, interspersed with photographs, maps, cartoons and fliers.

Omar Hernandez, Eugenia Ibarra and Juan Rafael Quesada (eds) *Discriminación y racismo en la historia costarricense* (San José, Editorial de la Universidad de Costa Rica). Most of these essays are written in the language and form of legal case studies, but nonetheless provide a history of the racial bias of legal discrimination in Costa Rica, and that of ethnicity in human rights abuses. Interesting counterpoint to Costa Rica's reputation for harmonious social relations, although probably only of use to specialists and those with a particular interest in race issues.

Martha Honey *Hostile Acts – US Policy in Costa Rica in the 1980s* (US & UK, University of Florida Press). Those sceptical of elaborate conspiracy theories may have their minds changed by this exhaustively researched, weighty volume detailing the US's "dual diplomacy" against Costa Rica in the 1980s. In this heroic volume Honey concludes that the La Penca bomber was a leftist Argentine terrorist with connections to Nicaragua's Sandinista government.

Silvia Lara and Tom Barry *Inside Costa Rica* (US, Inter-Hemispheric Resource Center/UK, Latin America Bureau). One title that will bring you up to date with most aspects of the country, although it has little to say about tourism, conservation, and culture. Left-leaning, argumentative and analytical, the authors refuse to toe the party line on Costa Rica, and though the style is factual and somewhat dry, it is enlivened by flashes of humour and apt, well-supported conclusions.

Michael A. Seligson *Peasants of Costa Rica and the Development of Agrarian Capitalism* (US & UK, University of Wisconsin). The best single history available in English, although only a university or specialist library will have it. Much

wider in scope than the title suggests, this is an excellent intermeshing of ethnic and racial issues, economics and sociology along with hard-core analysis of the rise and fall of the Costa Rican peasant.

Various *Between Continents, Between Seas: Precolumbian Art of Costa Rica* (US, Harry Abrams, o/p). Produced as a catalogue to accompany the exhibition that toured the US in 1982, this is the best single volume on pre-Conquest history and craftsmanship, with illuminating accounts of the lives, beliefs and customs of Costa Rica's pre-Columbian peoples as interpreted through artefacts and excavations. The photographs, whether of jade pendants, Chorotega pottery or the more diabolical of the Diquis' gold pieces, are uniformly wonderful.

Elías Zamora *Acosta etnografía histórica de Costa Rica, 1561 y 1615* (Spain, Universidad de Sevilla). Hugely impressive archival research that reconstructs the economic, political and social life in the province in the years immediately following the Spanish invasion. A masterwork, distressingly difficult to get hold of.

Wildlife, natural history and field guides

Paul H. Allen *The Rainforests of the Golfo Dulce* (US, Stanford University Press). Obviously a labour of love, this is the best descriptive account of the lush rainforest cover found in the southwest of the country. It's a scientific book, with complete taxonomic accounts, although still very readable and with interesting photographs.

⊡ **Les Beletsky** *Costa Rica: Ecotraveller's Wildlife Guide* (Academic Press). This readable wildlife and natural history handbook, written by a professional wildlife biologist,

is a good compromise between a guidebook and a heavy field guide. The text is accompanied by photos and drawings; the plates showing species with photos of their typical habitats are particularly useful. Includes detailed information on about 220 bird, 50 mammal and 80 amphibian and reptile species.

Mario A. Boza *Costa Rica's National Parks* (available in San José from Editoral Heliconia). Essentially a coffee-table book, this informed volume is a great taster for what you will find in the national parks.

The text is in Spanish and English, and there are uniformly stunning photographs.

A.S. and P.P. Calvert *A Year of Costa Rican Natural History* (US, Macmillan). Although now very old – the year in question is 1910 – this is a brilliant, insightful and charmingly enthusiastic travelogue/natural history/autobiography by American biologist and zoologist husband and wife team. It features much, much more than natural history, with sections such as "Blood Sucking Flies", "Fiestas in Santa Cruz" and "Earthquakes". The best single title ever written on Costa Rica – the only problem is finding it. Try good libraries and specialist bookstores.

Stephen E. Cornelius *The Sea Turtles of Santa Rosa National Park* (San José, Fundación de Parques Nacionales, o/p). Field guide to the four species of marine turtles who nest in Santa Rosa, and elsewhere. Full of detail about marine turtles' habits, but difficult to find.

Philip J. De Vries *The Butterflies of Costa Rica and their Natural History* (US & UK, Princeton University Press). Much-admired volume, really for serious butterfly enthusiasts or scientists only, but illustrated with beautiful colour plates so you can marvel at the incremental differences between various butterflies.

Louise H. Emmons and François Feer *Neotropical Rainforest Mammals – a Field Guide* (US, University of Chicago Press). Not written specifically for Costa Rica, but most mammals found in the country are covered here. Huge but portable, with more than 300 illustrations, and useful for identifying the flash of colour and fur that speeds past you as you make yet another fleeting contact with a rainforest mammal.

Joseph Franke *Costa Rica's National Parks* (Mountaineers Books). A park-by-park discussion of the system of national parks and wildlife refuges, with detailed information on hiking and trails, as well as a topographical and environmental profile of each park. Useful if you're intending to spend any time hiking in more than one or two parks.

Daniel H. Janzen *Costa Rican Natural History* (US, University of Chicago Press). The definitive reference source, with accessible, continuously fascinating species-by-species accounts, written by a highly influential figure, involved on a policy level in the governing of the national parks system. The introduction is especially worth reading, dealing in a cursory but lively fashion with tectonics, meteorology, history and archeology. Illustrated throughout with gripping photographs. Available in paperback, but still doorstep-thick.

Michael W. Mayfield and Raphael E. Gallow *The Rivers of Costa Rica: A Canoeing, Kayaking and Rafting Guide* (US, Menasha Ridge Press). An essential book for serious white-water rafters and river or sea kayakers. Stretch-by-stretch and rapid-by-rapid accounts of the best rafting rivers south of the Colorado, including the Reventazón and Pacuaré.

Sam Mitchell *Pura Vida: The Waterfalls and Hot Springs of Costa Rica* (US, Menasha Ridge). Jolly, personably written guide to the many little-known waterholes, cascades, and waterfalls of Costa Rica. Complete with detailed directions and accounts of surrounding trails. Available in English in San José.

Donald Perry *Life Above the Jungle Floor* (Simon & Schuster, o/p). Nicely poised, lyrical account of biologist Perry's trials and tribulations in conceiving and mounting his Rainforest Aerial Tram (see p.127). Most of the book deals with his time at Rara Avis, where he conceived and tested his tram prototype, the Automated Web for Canopy Exploration.

F. Gary Stiles and Alexander F. Skutch *A Guide to the Birds of Costa Rica* (US, Cornell University Press/ UK, Black Press). All over Costa Rica you'll see guides clutching well-thumbed copies of this seminal tome, illustrated with colour plates to aid identification. Hefty, even in

paperback, and too pricey for the amateur, but you may be able to pick up good secondhand copies in Costa Rica.

Allen M. Young *Sarapiquí Chronicle: A Naturalist in Costa Rica* (Smithsonian Institute Press, o/p). Lavishly produced book based on entomologist Allen M. Young's twenty years' work in the Sarapiquí area and featuring a well-written combination of autobiography, travelogue and natural science, centring on the insect life he encounters.

Fiction

Miguel Benavides *The Children of Mariplata* (UK, Forest Books). A short collection of even shorter stories, most of which are good examples of fable-like or allegorical Costa Rican tales. Many are written in the anthropomorphized voice of an animal; others, like "The Twilight Which Lost its Colour" describe searing slices of poverty-stricken life.

Carlos Cortés *Cruz de Olvido* (México, Alfaguara). Told in the macho, exhausted and regretful tone of a disillusioned revolutionary, this novel charts the return of a Costa Rican Sandinista supporter from Nicaragua to his home country, where "nothing has happened since the big bang". The narrative marries the narrator's humorous disaffection with boring old Costa Rica and his investigation into the bizarre, excessively symbolic death of his son.

Fabián Dobles *Ese Que Llaman Pueblo* (San José, Editorial Costa Rica). Born in 1918, Dobles is Costa Rica's elder statesman of letters. Set in the countryside among *campesinos*, this is a typical "proletarian" novel.

Fabián Dobles *Years Like Brief Days* (UK, Peter Owen/UNESCO). The first novel by Dobles to be

translated into English, this epistolary story is told in the form of a letter written by an old man to his mother, describing the village he grew up in and his eventful life.

Carlos Luis Fallas *Mamita Yunai: el infierno de las bananeras* (San José). Exuberant, full of local colour, culture and diction: this entertaining, leftist novel depicting life in the hell of the banana plantations is a great read. It's set in La Estrella valley in Limón Province, where Fallas, a pioneering labour organizer in the 1930s and 1940s, was instrumental in forcing the United Brands conglomerate to take workers' welfare into account.

Joaquín Gutiérrez *Puerto Limón* (San José, Editorial Costa Rica). One of the best of the "proletarian" genre, written by one of the nation's foremost literary figures, who was also a prominent journalist. While very much focused on the gritty realism of labour conditions in mid-twentieth century Costa Rica, the writing is lyrical and beautifully simple.

Amanda Hopkinson (ed) *Lovers and Comrades: Women's Resistance Poetry in Central America* (US,

Interlink/UK, Women's Press, o/p). Heartfelt contributions by Costa Rican poets Janina Fernandez, Eulalia Bernard and Lily Guardia. Poems such as Bernard's "We are the nation of threes" shows that Costa Rican poetry is no less political and no less felt than the more numerous contributions from the countries torn by war in the 1980s.

▣ **Enrique Jaramillo Levi** (ed) *When New Flowers Bloomed: Short Stories by Women Writers from Costa Rica and Panamá* (US, Latin American Literary Review Press). Collection of the best-known Costa Rican women writers, including Rima de Vallbona, Carmen Naranjo, Carmen Lyra and Yolanda Oreamuno. Most of the stories are from the late 1980s, with shared themes of domestic violence – a persistent problem in Costa Rica – sexual and economic inequality, and the tyrannies of female anatomy and desire. Look out especially for Emilia Macaya, a younger writer.

Tatiana Lobo *Assault on Paradise* (US, Curbstone Press). Costa Rica's first great historical novel tells the story of the arrival of the Spaniards in Costa Rica and, as the title indicates, their destruction of the land and life of the indigenous peoples they encountered.

Carmen Naranjo *Los perros no ladraron* (1966), *Responso por el niño Juan Manuel* (1968), *Ondina* (1982) and *Sobrepunto* (1985). In keeping with a tradition in Latin American letters but unusually for a woman, Naranjo has occupied several public posts, including Secretary of Culture, director of the publishing house EDUCA and Ambassador to Israel. She is widely considered an experimentalist and her novels can be found in Costa Rica, and her collection of stories *There Never Was Once Upon a Time* (US, Latin

American Literary Review Press) is available in English.

Yolanda Oreamuno *La ruta de su evasión* (San José, EDUCA). Oreamuno had a short life, dying at the age of 40 in 1956. By the time she was 24, however, she had distinguished herself as the most promising writer of her generation with her novel *Por Tierra Firme*. Technically brilliant, she is a great *scénariste*, with a continually surprising lyrical style. *La ruta* concerns a child sent to look for his father, who has disappeared, possibly on a drinking binge. The search is both actual and spiritual; the novel a complex weave of themes.

Barbara Ras *Costa Rica: A Traveller's Literary Companion* (US, Whereabouts Press). This is probably the most accessible starting point for readers interested in Costa Rican literature, with flowing and well-translated stories arranged by geographical zone. The best stories are also the most heartrending – read "The Girl Who Came from the Moon" and "The Carbonero" for a glimpse of real life beyond the tourist-brochure images.

Yasmin Ross *La flota negra* (México, Alfaguara). Originally a journalist from Mexico, Ross has made Costa Rica her home and in *La flota negra* has written one of the best-received novels set in Costa Rican in recent years. It takes as its starting point the story of the Black Star Line, the shipping company that brought so many of the Caribbean immigrants whose descendants now make up the population of Limón, along with Marcus Garvey's visit to the province.

Anachristina Rossi *La loca de Gandoca* (San José, EDUCA). One of the most popular novels to be published in Costa Rica in recent years, Rossi's book is really "faction", documenting in businesslike prose and with tongue firmly in cheek the bizarre and byzantine wranglings over the Gandoca-Manzanillo refuge, including the surveying of the indigenous Bribrí KéköLdi reserve.

Rosario Santos (ed) *And We Sold the Rain: Contemporary Fiction from Central America* (US, 7 Stories Press/UK, Ryan Publishing). Put together in the late 1980s, this collection attempts to show the faces of real people behind the newspaper headlines about guerrillas and militaries during the political conflicts of that decade. There are Costa Rican stories by Samuel Rovinski, Carmen Naranjo and Fabian Dobles.

Rogelio Sotela (ed) *Escritores de Costa Rica* (San José, Lehmann, o/p). Outdated, out-of-print and inaccessible in all but the best libraries, nevertheless this is still the definitive volume of Costa Rican literature up until the 1940s. Several fascinating sections, including one devoted to folklore. Much dreadful poetry, though.

Rima de Vallbona *Flowering Inferno: Tales of Sinking Hearts* (US, Latin American Literary Review Press). Slim volume of affecting short stories by one of Costa Rica's most respected (and widely translated) writers on social life, customs, and the position of women.

Language

Language

Language

Although it is commonly said that everyone speaks English in Costa Rica, it is not really the case. Certainly many who work in the tourist trade speak some English, and there are a number of expats who speak anything from English to German to Dutch, but the people you'll meet day to day speak only Spanish. The one area where you will hear English widely spoken is on the Caribbean coast, where many of the Afro-Caribbean inhabitants are of Jamaican descent, and speak a distinctive regional Creole.

If you want to get to know Costa Ricans, then, it makes sense to acquire some Spanish before you arrive. Ticos are polite, patient and forgiving interlocutors, and will not only tolerate but appreciate any attempts you make to speak their language. The rules of pronunciation are pretty straightforward. Unless there's an accent, all words ending in l, r and z are stressed on the last syllable, all others on the second last. Unlike in the rest of Latin America, in Costa Rica the final "d" in many words sometimes gets dropped; thus you'll hear "usté" for "usted" or "¿verdá?" for "¿verdad?" Other Costa Rican peculiarities are the ll and r sounds. All vowels are pure and short.

A somewhere between the A sound in "back" and that in "father".

E as in "get".

I as in "police".

O as in "hot".

U as in "rule".

C is soft before E and I, hard otherwise: cerca is pronounced "serka".

G works the same way: a guttural H sound (like the ch in "loch") before E or I, a hard G elsewhere: gigante becomes "higante".

H is always silent.

J the same sound as a guttural G: jamón is pronounced "hamon".

LL may be pronounced as a soft J (as in parts of Chile and Argentina) instead of Y: ballena (whale) becomes "bajzhena" instead of "bayena".

N is as in English, unless it has a tilde (accent) over it, when it becomes NY: mañana sounds like "manyana".

QU is pronounced like the English K.

R is not rolled Scottish burr-like as much as in other Spanish-speaking countries: carro is said "cahro", with a soft rather than a rolled R.

V sounds more like B: vino becomes "beano".

Z is the same as a soft C: cerveza is thus "servesa".

A Costa Rican dictionary

Mario Quesada Pacheco *Nuevo diccionario de Costarriqueñismos* (San José, Editorial de la Universidad Tecnológica de Costa Rica). An entertaining, illustrated dictionary of slang and *dichos* (sayings) for Spanish-speakers interested in understanding heavily argot-spiced spoken Costa Rican Spanish. It's a fascinating compendium, giving the regional location of word usage and sayings, what age group uses them, and some etymology. It also reveals a wealth of localisms developed to describe local phenomena – witness, for example the number of different words for "wasp".

Useful expressions and vocabulary

Basics

Yes, No	Sí, No	Open, Closed	Abierto/a, Cerrado/a
Please	Por favor	With, Without	Con, Sin
Thank you	Gracias	Good, Bad	Buen(o)/a, Mal(o)/a
Where, When?	¿Dónde, Cuando?	Big, Small	Gran(de), Pequeño/a
What, How much?	¿Qué, Cuánto?	More, Less	Más, Menos
Here, There	Aquí, Allí	Today, Tomorrow	Hoy, Mañana
This, That	Este, Eso	Yesterday	Ayer
Now, Later	Ahora, Más tarde		

Greetings and responses

Hello, Goodbye	Hola, Adiós	Not at all/ You're welcome	De nada
Good morning	Buenos días		
Good afternoon/ night	Buenas tardes/ noches	Do you speak English?	¿Habla (usted) inglés?
See you later	Hasta luego	I don't speak Spanish	(No) Hablo español
Sorry	Lo siento/ discúlpeme	My name is...	Me llamo...
Excuse me	Con permiso/perdón	What's your name?	¿Como se llama usted?
How are you?	¿Cómo está (usted)?		
I (don't) understand	(No) Entiendo	I am English/ Australian	Soy inglés(a)/ australiano(a)
What did you say?	¿Cómo?		

Needs and directions

I want	Quiero	It's fine, how much is it?	¿Está bien, cuánto es?
I'd like	Quisiera		
Do you know...?	¿Sabe...?	It's too expensive	Es demasiado caro
I don't know	No sé	Don't you have anything cheaper?	¿No tiene algo más barato?
There is (is there)?	(¿)Hay(?)		
Give me...	Deme...	Can one...?	¿Se puede...?
(one like that)	(uno así)	..camp (near) here?	¿...acampar aquí (cerca)?
Do you have...?	¿Tiene...?		
..the time	..la hora	Is there a hotel nearby?	¿Hay un hotel aquí cerca?
..a room	..un cuarto		
..with two beds/	..con dos camas/	How do I get to...?	¿Por dónde se va a...?
..double bed	..cama matrimonial		
It's for one person	Es para una persona	Left, right, straight on	Izquierda, derecha, derecho
(two people)	(dos personas)	Where is...?	¿Dónde está...?
..for one night	..para una noche	..the bus station	..el estación autobuses
(one week)	(una semana)		

..the nearest bank	.. el banco más cercano	What time does it leave (arrive in...)?	¿A qué hora sale (llega en...)?
..the post office	..el correo	What is there to eat?	¿Qué hay para comer?
the toilet	..el baño/servicio	What's that?	¿Qué es eso?
Where does the bus to... leave from?	¿De dónde sale el autobus para...?	What's this called in Spanish?	¿Como se llama éste en español?
I'd like a (return) ticket to..	Quisiera un tiquete (de ida y vuelta) para...		

Useful accommodation terms

Ceiling fan	Abanico	Double bed	Cama matrimonial
Hot water	Agua caliente	Single bed	Cama sencillo
Cold water	Agua fría	Check-out time (usually 2pm)	Hora de salida
Air conditioned	Aire-acondicionado		
Shared bath	Baño colectivo/ compartido	Taxes	Impuestos
		Desk fan	Ventilador

Numbers, days and months

1	un/uno/una	200	doscientos
2	dos	201	doscientos uno
3	tres	500	quinientos
4	cuatro	1000	mil
5	cinco	2000	dos mil
6	seis	1990	mil novocientos noventa
7	siete		
8	ocho	1991	..y uno
9	nueve	first	primero/a
10	diez	second	segundo/a
11	once	third	tercero/a
12	doce		
13	trece	Monday	lunes
14	catorce	Tuesday	martes
15	quince	Wednesday	miércoles
16	diez y seis	Thursday	jueves
20	veinte	Friday	viernes
21	veintiuno	Saturday	sábado
30	treinta	Sunday	domingo
40	cuarenta		
50	cincuenta	January	enero
60	sesenta	February	febrero
70	setenta	March	marzo
80	ochenta	April	abril
90	noventa	May	mayo
100	cien(to)	June	junio
101	ciento uno	July	julio

August	agosto	November	noviembre
September	septiembre	December	diciembre
October	octubre		

A Costa Rican menu reader

Basics

Aceite	Oil	Frijoles	Beans
Aceitunas	Olives	Huevos	Eggs
Ajo ("al ajillo")	Garlic (in garlic sauce)	Leche	Milk
		Queso	Cheese
Cebolla	Onion	Salsa	Sauce
Cilantro	Coriander		

Meat (carne), fish (pescado) and seafood/shellfish (mariscos)

Atún	Tuna	Langosta	Lobster
Bistec	Steak	Lomito	Cut of beef (filet mignon)
Cerdo	Pork		
Corvina	Sea bass	Pargo	Red snapper
Jamón	Ham	Trucha	Trout

Fruits

Anona	Custard fruit; sweet, thick ripe taste: one of the best fruits in the country	Guayaba	Guava; very sweet fruit, usually used for making spreads and jams
Carambola	Starfruit	Limón	Lemon
Cas	Pale flesh fruit with sweet-sour taste	Mamones chinos	Spiny-covered red or yellow fruits that look diabolical but reveal gently flavoured lychee-type fruit inside; somewhat like peeled green grapes, but sweeter and more fragrant. Usually sold in small bags of a dozen on street corners or buses
Chinos	Usually used for refrescos		
Fresas	Strawberries		
Granadilla	Passion fruit; small yellow fruits, sharp and sweet		
Guanábana	Soursop; very large green mottled fruit, with sweet white flesh tasting like a cross between a mango and a pear; mostly found on the Caribbean coast	Maracuyá	Yellow fruit with bitter taste, often used in refrescos; delicious when sweetened

Moras	Blackberries
Naranja	Orange
Papaya	Papaya/pawpaw; large round or oblong fruit with sweet orange flesh. Best eaten with fresh lime juice, and very good for stomach bugs
Pejibaye	A Costa Rican speciality, you'll find this small green-orange fruit almost nowhere else. Like its relative, the coconut, it grows in bunches on palm trees: the texture is unusual, as is the nutty flavour
Piña	Pineapple
Sandía	Watermelon
Tamarindo	A large pod of seeds, covered in a sticky, light-brown flesh; the unique taste – at once tart and sweet – is best first sampled in a refresco
Zapote	Large sweet orange fruit, with a dark-brown outer casing

Vegetables

Aguacate	Avocado
Chayote	Resembling a light-green avocado, this vegetable is tender and delicate when cooked, and excellent in stews and with meat and rice dishes
Fruta de pan	Breadfruit; eaten more as a starch substitute than a fruit
Hongos	Mushrooms
Palmito	Heart-of-palm; the inner core of palm trees, usually eaten on salads, with a somewhat bitter taste and fibrous texture
Plátanos	Plantains; eaten sweet
Zanahorias	Carrots

Typical dishes (*platos*)

Arreglados	Meat and mayonnaise sandwiches on greasy bread buns
Arroz…	Rice…
…con pollo	…with chicken
…con carne	…with meat
…con pescado	…with fish
…con mariscos	…with seafood
…con camarones	…with shrimps/prawns
Bocas	Small snacks, usually eaten as an accompaniment to a beer
Casado	Plate of meat or fish, rice and salad, sometimes served with fried plantains
Ceviche	Raw fish, usually corvina, "marinated" in lime juice, onions, chillies and coriander
Chicarrones	Pork rinds
Chilasquilas	Tortillas and beef with spices and battered eggs
Empanadas	Meat or vegetable patties
Frijoles molidos	Mashed black beans with onions, chilli peppers, coriander and thyme
Gallo pinto	"Painted rooster"; breakfast dish of rice and beans
Gallos	Small sandwiches
Pan de maíz	Corn bread; white rather than yellow

Picadillo	Potatoes cooked with beef and beans		flour, chicken or pork, olives, chillies and raisins all wrapped in a plantain leaf
Sopa negra	Black-bean soup with egg and vegetables		
Tacos	Tortilla filled with beef or chicken, cabbage, tomatoes and mild chillies	Tortilla	Thin, small and bland bread, served as an accompaniment to meals and, especially in Guanacaste, breakfast
Tamal	One of the best local specialities, usually consisting of maize		

Desserts

Cajeta	Dessert made of milk, sugar, vanilla and sometimes coconut	Queque seco	Pound cake
		Tamal asado	Cake made of corn flour, cream, eggs, sugar and butter
Helado	Ice cream		
Milanes	Delicate chocolate fingers	Tres leches	Boiled milk and syrup-drenched cake
Queque	Cake		

Regional dishes

Caribbean	
Pan bon	Sweet glazed bread with fruit and cheese
Patacones	Plantain chips, often served with frijoles molidos (see above)
Rice and beans	Rice and beans cooked in coconut milk
Rundown	Meat and vegetables stewed in coconut milk

Guanacaste	
Chorreados	Corn pancakes
Horchata	Hot drink made with corn or rice and flavoured with cinnamon
Natilla	Sour cream
Olla de carne	Rich, hearty meat stew
Pinolillo	Milky corn drink
Rosquillas	Corn doughnuts
Tanelas	Scone-like corn snack

El idioma and tiquismos

Costa Rican Spanish is a living language full of flux and argot. Local slang and usage are often referred to as **Tiquismos** (from *Costarriqueñismos*, or Costa Ricanisms) or, as Costa Ricans will say when enlightening the foreigner as to their meaning, "*palabras muy ticas*". Some of the expressions and terms discussed below may be heard in other countries in the region, especially in Nicaragua and El Salvador, but still they are highly regional. Others are purely endemic, including *barbarismos* (bastardizations) and *provincialismos* (words particular to specific regions of Costa Rica).

The noun "Tico" used as a short form for Costa Rican comes less from a desire to shorten "Costarriquense" than from the traditional trend toward

diminution which is supposed to signal classlessness, eagerness to band together and desire not to cause offence. In Costa Rica the common Spanish diminution of "ito" – applied as a suffix at the end of the word, as in "herman*ito*"; "little brother" – often becomes "itico" ("herman*itico*"). That said, you hear the -ito or -itico endings less and less nowadays.

Costa Rican Spanish often displays an astounding **formality** that borders on servility. Instead of "*de nada*" ("you're welcome") many Costa Ricans will say, "*para servirle*", which means, literally, "I'm here to serve you". When they meet you, Costa Ricans will say "*con mucho gusto*"; "it's a pleasure", and you should do the same. Even when you leave people you do not know well, you will be told "*que le vaya bien*" ("may all go well with you").

Nicknames and a delight in the informal mix with a quite proper formal tone used in spoken Costa Rican Spanish. Nicknames centre on your most obvious physical characteristic: popular ones include *flaco/a* (thin); *gordo/a* (fat), and *macho/a* (light-skinned). Terms of endearment are also very current in popular speech; along with the ubiquitous *mi amor*, you may also get called *joven*, young one.

Intimate address

It's difficult to get your head round forms of **second-person address** in Costa Rica. Children are often spoken to in the "usted" form, which is technically formal and reserved for showing respect (in other Spanish-speaking countries children are generally addressed as "tú"). Even friends who have known each other for years in Costa Rica will address each other as "usted". But the single most confounding irregularity of Costa Rican speech for those who already speak Spanish is the use of **"vos"** as personal intimate address – generally between friends of the same age. Many people on a short trip to the country never quite get to grips with it.

Now archaic, "vos" is only used widely in the New World in Argentina and Costa Rica. It has an interesting rhythm and sound, with verbs ending on a kind of diphthong-ized stress: vos sabés, vos queres (you know, you want), as opposed to *tu sabes/usted sabe* or *tu quieres/usted quiere*. If you are addressed in the "vos" form it is a sign of friendship, and you should try to use it back if you can. It is an affront to use "vos" improperly, with someone you don't know well, when it can be seen as being patronizing. Again, Costa Ricans are good-hearted in this respect, however, and put errors down to the fact that you are a foreigner.

Everyday expressions

Here are some everyday **peculiarities** that most visitors to Costa Rica will become familiar with pretty quickly:

¡achará! expression of regret: "what a pity", like "*¡qué lástima!*"

adiós "hi", used primarily in the *campo* (country) when greeting someone on the road or street. Confusingly, as in the rest of Latin America, *adiós* is also "goodbye", but only if you are going away for a long time.

¿diay? slightly melancholic interjection in the vein of "ah, but what can you expect?"

fatal reserved for the absolutely worst possible eventuality: "*esta carretera para Golfito es fatal*" means "the road to Golfito is the very worst".

feo literally "ugly", but can also mean rotten or lousy, as in "*Todos los caminos en Costa Rica están muy feos*" ("All the roads in Costa Rica are in really bad shape").

maje literally "dummy", used between young men as an affirmation of their friendship/maleness: it's used like "buddy, pal" (US) or "mate" (UK). There is no equivalent for women, unfortunately.

pura vida perhaps the best-known *tiquismo*, meaning "great" "OK", or "cool".

que mala/buena nota expression of disapproval/approval – "how uncool/great".

Luck and God

Both **luck** and **God** come into conversation often in Costa Rica. Thus you get the pattern:

"¿Cómo amaneció?"	"How did you sleep?"
	(Literally, "how did you wake up?")
"Muy bien, por dicha, ¿y usted?"	"Very well, fortunately, and you?"
"Muy bien, gracias a Dios."	"Very well, thank God."

Also, you will hear *dicha* and *Dios* used in situations that seem to have not much to do with luck or divine intervention: "*¡Qué dicha que usted llegó!*" ("What luck that you arrived!"), along with such phrases as "*Vamos a la playa esta fin de semana, si Dios quiere*" ("We'll go to the beach this weekend, God willing"). Even a shrug of the shoulders elicits a "*¡Dios sabe!*" "God only knows." And the usual forms "*hasta luego*" or "*hasta la vista*" become in Costa Rica the much more God-fearing "*Que Dios le acompañe*" ("may God go with you").

"Where is your boyfriend?"

"*¿Dónde está su novio?/padres?*" ("Where is your boyfriend/family?") is a query women, especially those travelling alone, will hear often. **Family** is very important in explaining to many Costa Ricans who you are and where you come from, and people will place you by asking how many brothers and sisters you have, where your family (*padres*) live, whether your *abuela* (grandmother) is still alive... It's a good idea to get to grips with the following:

madre/padre	mother/father
abuelo/abuela	grandfather/grandmother
hija/hijo	daughter/son
hermano/hermana	brother/sister
tía/tío	aunt/uncle
prima/primo	cousin

Glossary

abastecedor a general store, usually in a rural area or *barrio* (neighbourhood) that keeps a stock of groceries and basic toiletries.

agringarse (verb) to adopt the ways of the gringos.

agua potable drinking water.

aguacero downpour.

ahorita "right now" (any time within the coming hour).

area de acampar camping area.

area restringido restricted area.

bárbaro fantastic, cool (literally "barbaric").

barrio neighbourhood (usually urban).

bomba petrol station.

botica pharmacy.

burro can refer to the animal (donkey), but is usually an adjective denoting "really big", as in "*vea este bicho sí burro*": "come see this really big insect".

campesino peasant farmer, smallholder.

campo literally countryside, but more often in Costa Rica "space", as in "seat" when travelling. Thus "*¿Hay un campo en este autobus?*": "is there a (free) seat on this bus?"

cantina bar, usually patronized by the working class or rural labouring class.

capa rain gear, poncho.

carro car (not *coche*, as in Spain).

cazadora literally, huntress; a beaten-up old schoolbus that serves as public transport in rural areas.

chance widely used anglicism to denote chance, or opportunity; like *oportunidad*.

chiquillos kids; also *chiquititos*, *chiquiticos*.

chivo cute.

chorreador sack-and-metal coffee-filter contraption, still widely used.

choteo quick-witted sarcasm, something Costa Ricans admire, provided it's not too sharp-tongued.

colectivo An open-back truck used as a form of public transport in some rural, remote areas such as the Osa Peninsula.

conchos yokels, hicks from the sticks.

cordillera mountain range.

dando cuerda colloquial expression meaning, roughly, to "make eyes at", in an approximation of sexual interest (men to women, hardly ever the other way around).

entrada entrance.

evangélico usually refers to anyone who is of a religion other than Catholic, but particularly Protestant even if they are not evangelical. Such religions are also called *cultos*, belying a general wariness and disapproval for anything other than Catholicism.

finca farm or plantation.

finquero coffee grower.

foco flashlight/torch.

gambas buttresses, the giant above-ground roots that some rainforest trees put out.

gaseosa fizzy drink.

gasolina petrol.

gringo not-at-all pejorative term for a North American. A European is usually *europeo*.

guaca pre-Columbian burial ground or tomb.

güisqui whisky (usually bad unless imported, and astronomically expensive).

hacienda big farm, usually a ranch.

hospedaje very basic *pensión*.

humilde humble, simple; an appearance and quality that is widely respected.

ICT Instituto Costarricense de Turismo, the national tourist board.

indígena an indigenous person; preferred term among indigenous groups in Costa Rica, rather than the less polite *índio* (Indian).

invierno winter (May–Nov).

jornaleros day labourers, usually landless peasants who are paid by the day, for instance to pick coffee in season.

mal educado literally, badly educated; a gentle if effective insult, especially useful for women harassed by hissing, leering men.

malecón seaside promenade.

marimba type of large xylophone played mainly in Guanacaste. Also refers to the style of music.

mestizo person of mixed race indigenous/Spanish; not usually pejorative.

metate pre-Columbian stone table used for grinding corn, especially by the Chorotega people of Guanacaste. Many of the archeological finds in Costa Rica are metates.

MINAE the ministry in charge of the national parks system.

mirador lookout or viewing platform.

morenos offensive term for Afro-Caribbeans. The best term to use is *negros* or *Limonenses*.

muelle dock.

Neotrópicos Neotropics: tropics of the New World.

Nica Nicaraguan, from *Nicaragüense*.

palenque a thatched-roofed longhouse inhabited by indigenous people; more or less equivalent to the Native North American longhouse.

pasear to be on vacation/holiday; literally, to be passing through.

peligro danger.

peón farm labourer, usually landless.

personaje someone of importance, a VIP, although usually used pejoratively to indicate someone who is putting on airs.

PLA National Liberation Party, the dominant political party.

precarista squatter.

puesto post (ranger post).

pulpería general store or corner store. Also sometimes serves cooked food and drinks.

purrujas spectacularly annoying, tiny biting insects encountered in lowland areas.

PUSC Social Christian Unity Party, the opposition party-of-the-moment.

rancho palm-thatched roof, also smallholding.

redondel de toros bullring, not used for bull-fighting but for local rodeos.

refresco drink, usually made with fresh fruit or water, sometimes fizzy drink, although this is most often called *gaseosa*.

regalar (verb) usually to give, as in to give a present, but in Costa Rica the usual command or request of "*deme uno de estos*" ("give me one of those"), becomes "*regáleme*". Thus "*regáleme un cafecito, por favor*": "could you give me a coffee?".

rejas security grille, popularly known in English as The Cage: the iron grille you see around all but the most humble dwellings in an effort to discourage burglary.

sabanero Costa Rican cowboy.

salida exit.

sendero trail.

soda cafeteria or diner; in the rest of Central America it's usually called a *comedor*.

temporada season: *la temporada de lluvia* is the rainy season.

temporales early morning rains in the wet season (mainly in the Valle Central).

terreno land, small farm.

UCR Universidad de Costa Rica (in San Pedro, San José).

UNA Universidad Nacional (in Heredia).

verano summer (Dec–April).

Rough
Guides
advertiser

GREEN TORTOISE
ADVENTURE TRAVEL

Belize • Guatemala
Nicaragua
Costa Rica • Panama

**BUDGET CAMPING TRIPS IN
CENTRAL AMERICA**

1-415-956-7500 www.greentortoise.com

ROUGH GUIDES ADVERTISER

Visit us online

roughguides.com

Information on over 25,000 destinations around the world

- **Read** Rough Guides' trusted travel info

- **Share** journals, photos and travel advice with other readers

- Get exclusive Rough Guide **discounts** and travel **deals**

- Earn membership points every time you contribute to the
  Rough Guide **community** and get **free** books, flights and trips

- Browse thousands of CD reviews and artists in our **music** area

ROUGH GUIDES ADVERTISER

Rough Guides travel...

UK & Ireland
Britain
Devon & Cornwall
Dublin
Edinburgh
England
Ireland
Lake District
London
London DIRECTIONS
London Mini Guide
Scotland
Scottish Highlands &
    Islands
Wales

Europe
Algarve
Amsterdam
Amsterdam
    DIRECTIONS
Andalucía
Athens DIRECTIONS
Austria
Baltic States
Barcelona
Belgium & Luxembourg
Berlin
Brittany & Normandy
Bruges & Ghent
Brussels
Budapest
Bulgaria
Copenhagen
Corfu
Corsica
Costa Brava
Crete
Croatia
Cyprus
Czech & Slovak
    Republics
Dodecanese & East
    Aegean
Dordogne & The Lot
Europe
Florence
France

Germany
Greece
Greek Islands
Hungary
Ibiza & Formentera
Iceland
Ionian Islands
Italy
Languedoc & Roussillon
Lisbon
Lisbon DIRECTIONS
The Loire
Madeira
Madrid
Mallorca
Malta & Gozo
Menorca
Moscow
Netherlands
Norway
Paris
Paris DIRECTIONS
Paris Mini Guide
Poland
Portugal
Prague
Provence & the Côte
    d'Azur
Pyrenees
Romania
Rome
Sardinia
Scandinavia
Sicily
Slovenia
Spain
St Petersburg
Sweden
Switzerland
Tenerife & La Gomera
Tenerife DIRECTIONS
Turkey
Tuscany & Umbria
Venice & The Veneto
Venice DIRECTIONS
Vienna

Asia
Bali & Lombok
Bangkok
Beijing
Cambodia
China
Goa
Hong Kong & Macau
India
Indonesia
Japan
Laos
Malaysia, Singapore &
    Brunei
Nepal
Philippines
Singapore
South India
Southeast Asia
Sri Lanka
Thailand
Thailand's Beaches &
    Islands
Tokyo
Vietnam

Australasia
Australia
Melbourne
New Zealand
Sydney

North America
Alaska
Big Island of Hawaii
Boston
California
Canada
Chicago
Florida
Grand Canyon
Hawaii
Honolulu
Las Vegas
Los Angeles
Maui
Miami & the Florida

Keys
Montréal
New England
New Orleans
New York City
New York City
    DIRECTIONS
New York City Mini
    Guide
Pacific Northwest
Rocky Mountains
San Francisco
San Francisco
    DIRECTIONS
Seattle
Southwest USA
Toronto
USA
Vancouver
Washington DC
Yosemite

**Caribbean
& Latin America**
Antigua & Barbuda
Antigua DIRECTIONS
Argentina
Bahamas
Barbados
Barbados DIRECTIONS
Belize
Bolivia
Brazil
Caribbean
Central America
Chile
Costa Rica
Cuba
Dominican Republic
Ecuador
Guatemala
Jamaica
Maya World
Mexico
Peru
St Lucia
South America

ROUGH GUIDES ADVERTISER

Rough Guides are available from good bookstores worldwide. New titles are
published every month. Check www.roughguides.com for the latest news.

...music & reference

Trinidad & Tobago

Africa & Middle East
Cape Town
Egypt
The Gambia
Jordan
Kenya
Marrakesh
  DIRECTIONS
Morocco
South Africa, Lesotho
  & Swaziland
Syria
Tanzania
Tunisia
West Africa
Zanzibar
Zimbabwe

Travel Theme guides
First-Time Around the
  World
First-Time Asia
First-Time Europe
First-Time Latin
  America
Skiing & Snowboarding
  in North America
Travel Online
Travel Health
Walks in London & SE
  England
Women Travel

Restaurant guides
French Hotels &
  Restaurants
London
New York
San Francisco

Maps
Algarve
Amsterdam
Andalucia & Costa del Sol
Argentina

Athens
Australia
Baja California
Barcelona
Berlin
Boston
Brittany
Brussels
Chicago
Crete
Croatia
Cuba
Cyprus
Czech Republic
Dominican Republic
Dubai & UAE
Dublin
Egypt
Florence & Siena
Frankfurt
Greece
Guatemala & Belize
Iceland
Ireland
Kenya
Lisbon
London
Los Angeles
Madrid
Mexico
Miami & Key West
Morocco
New York City
New Zealand
Northern Spain
Paris
Peru
Portugal
Prague
Rome
San Francisco
Sicily
South Africa
South India
Sri Lanka
Tenerife
Thailand

Toronto
Trinidad & Tobago
Tuscany
Venice
Washington DC
Yucatán Peninsula

**Dictionary
Phrasebooks**
Czech
Dutch
Egyptian Arabic
EuropeanLanguages
  (Czech, French,
  German, Greek, Italian,
  Portuguese, Spanish)
French
German
Greek
Hindi & Urdu
Hungarian
Indonesian
Italian
Japanese
Mandarin Chinese
Mexican Spanish
Polish
Portuguese
Russian
Spanish
Swahili
Thai
Turkish
Vietnamese

Music Guides
The Beatles
Bob Dylan
Cult Pop
Classical Music
Country Music
Elvis
Hip Hop
House
Irish Music
Jazz
Music USA

Opera
Reggae
Rock
Techno
World Music (2 vols)

History Guides
China
Egypt
England
France
India
Islam
Italy
Spain
USA

Reference Guides
Books for Teenagers
Children's Books, 0–5
Children's Books, 5–11
Cult Fiction
Cult Football
Cult Movies
Cult TV
Ethical Shopping
Formula 1
The iPod, iTunes &
  Music Online
The Internet
Internet Radio
James Bond
Kids' Movies
Lord of the Rings
Muhammed Ali
Man Utd
Personal Computers
Pregnancy & Birth
Shakespeare
Superheroes
Unexplained
  Phenomena
The Universe
Videogaming
Weather
Website Directory

ROUGH GUIDES ADVERTISER

Also! More than 120 Rough Guide music CDs are available from all good book
and record stores. Listen in at www.worldmusic.net

Rough Guide Maps, printed on waterproof
and rip-proof Yupo™ paper, offer an
unbeatable combination of practicality,
clarity of design and amazing value.

CITY MAPS

Amsterdam · Barcelona · Berlin · Boston · Brussels · Dublin
Florence & Siena · Frankfurt · London · Los Angeles
Miami · New York · Paris · Prague · Rome
San Francisco · Venice · Washington DC and more...

COUNTRY & REGIONAL MAPS

Andalucía · Argentina · Australia · Baja California · Cuba
Cyprus · Dominican Republic · Egypt · Greece
Guatemala & Belize · Ireland · Mexico · Morocco
New Zealand · South Africa · Sri Lanka · Tenerife · Thailand
Trinidad & Tobago Yucatán Peninsula · and more...

US$9.99   Can$13.99   £5.99

Athens

Lisbon

London

1843533146

1843533154

1843530937

Paris

San Francisco

Venice

1843533170

1843533189

1843533537

PUBLISHED AUGUST 2004

Amsterdam

Antigua & Barbuda

Barbados

1843533065

1843533197

1843533200

Marrakesh

New York City

Tenerife & La Gomera

1843533219

1843533227

1843533235

US$10.99 · Can$15.99 · £6.99

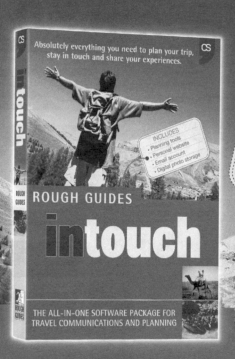

Absolutely everything you need to plan your trip, stay in touch and share your experiences.

INCLUDES
• Planning tools
• Personal website
• Email account
• Digital photo storage

ROUGH GUIDES

intouch

THE ALL-IN-ONE SOFTWARE PACKAGE FOR TRAVEL COMMUNICATIONS AND PLANNING

ROUGH GUIDES

A NEW CONCEPT IN TRAVEL

ROUGH GUIDES SOFTWARE
Share your adventures on the move

Rough Guides have launched **intouch**, a new all in one software package for planning your trip and staying in touch with people back home before, during and after your travels.

Create an itinerary and budget using on-screen information and maps, and take advantage of the diary to keep family and friends informed of your whereabouts.

The diary can be linked to your mobile phone so that you can send a text message, **intouch** will automatically send an email or cheap SMS to those listed on your account.

You can also post photos and diary entries online and then download them to make a journal on your return.

Rough Guides **intouch** is easy to install and you don't need to take anything with you – just hit the synchronize button and then use it from any internet café in the world.

Rough Guides **intouch** includes:
Planning tools
Free email address
Free personal website
Digital photo storage   And much more......

£5 OFF your purchase of Rough Guides **intouch** if you buy online at www.roughguidesintouch.com reference code: Rough Guide Books

Recommended retail price £24.99 available through leading retailers e.g. WH Smith, Waterstones and PC World

STANF☀RDS
EXPLORE DISCOVER INSPIRE

The world's finest map and travel bookshops

Explore

Discover

Inspire

Maps

Travel Guides

Illustrated Books

Travel Literature

World Atlases

Globes

World Wall Maps

Climbing Maps & Books

Maritime Maps & Books

Historical Maps

Instruments

Children's

**Stanfords Flagship Store
12-14 Long Acre
Covent Garden
London
WC2 9LP
(T) 020 7836 1321**

**39 Spring Gardens
Manchester
M2 2BG
(T) 0161 831 0250**

**29 Corn Street
Bristol
BS1 1HT
(T) 0117 929 9966**

**International Mail Order
Department
+44 (0)20 7836 1321**

www.stanfords.co.uk

Inspiring exploration and discovery for 150 years

NORTH SOUTH TRAVEL

Great discounts

North South Travel is a small travel agent offering excellent personal service. Like other air ticket retailers, we offer discount fares worldwide. But unlike others, all available profits contribute to grassroots projects in the South through the NST Development Trust Registered Charity No. 1040656.

Great difference

For **quotes** or queries, contact Brenda Skinner or her helpful staff. Recent **donations** made from the NST Development Trust include support to Djoliba Trust, providing micro-credit to onion growers in the Dogon country in Mali; assistance to displaced people and rural communities in eastern Congo; a grant to Wells For India,

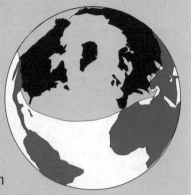

which works for clean water in Rajasthan; support to the charity Children of the Andes, working for poverty relief in Colombia; and a grant to the Omari Project which works with drug-dependent young people in Watamu, Kenya.

ROUGH GUIDES ADVERTISER

Tel/Fax 01245 608 291.
Email brenda@northsouthtravel.co.uk
Website www.northsouthtravel.co.uk

North South Travel,
Moulsham Mill,
Parkway,
Chelmsford,
Essex CM2 7PX,
UK

Don't bury your head in the sand!

Take cover!

with Rough Guide Travel Insurance

Worldwide cover, for Rough Guide readers worldwide

UK Freefone **0800 015 09 06**
Worldwide **(+44) 1392 314 665**
Check the web at
www.roughguides.com/insurance

ROUGH GUIDES

Insurance organized by Torribles Insurance Brokers Ltd, 21 Prince Street, Bristol, BS1 4PH, England·

small print and

Index

A Rough Guide to Rough Guides

In the summer of 1981, Mark Ellingham, a recent graduate from Bristol University, was travelling round Greece and couldn't find a guidebook that really met his needs. On the one hand there were the student guides, insistent on saving every last cent, and on the other the heavyweight cultural tomes whose authors seemed to have spent more time in a research library than lounging away the afternoon at a taverna or on the beach.

In a bid to avoid getting a job, Mark and a small group of writers set about creating their own guidebook. It was a guide to Greece that aimed to combine a journalistic approach to description with a thoroughly practical approach to travellers' needs —a guide that would incorporate culture, history and contemporary insights with a critical edge, together with up-to-date, value-for-money listings. Back in London, Mark and the team finished their Rough Guide, as they called it, and talked Routledge into publishing the book.

That first *Rough Guide to Greece*, published in 1982, was a student scheme that became a publishing phenomenon. The immediate success of the book – with numerous reprints and a Thomas Cook prize shortlisting – spawned a series that rapidly covered dozens of destinations. Rough Guides had a ready market among low-budget backpackers, but soon also acquired a much broader and older readership that relished Rough Guides' wit and inquisitiveness as much as their enthusiastic, critical approach. Everyone wants value for money, but not at any price.

Rough Guides soon began supplementing the "rougher" information about hostels and low-budget listings with the kind of detail on restaurants and quality hotels that independent-minded visitors on any budget might expect, whether on business in New York or trekking in Thailand.

These days the guides – distributed worldwide by the Penguin group – offer recommendations from shoestring to luxury and cover more than 200 destinations around the globe, including almost every country in the Americas and Europe, more than half of Africa and most of Asia and Australasia. Our ever-growing team of authors and photographers is spread all over the world, particularly in Europe, the USA and Australia.

In 1994, we published the *Rough Guide to World Music* and *Rough Guide to Classical Music*; and a year later the *Rough Guide to the Internet*. All three books have become benchmark titles in their fields – which encouraged us to expand into other areas of publishing, mainly around popular culture. Rough Guides now publish:

- Travel guides to more than 200 worldwide destinations
- Dictionary phrasebooks to 22 major languages
- History guides ranging from Ireland to Islam
- Maps printed on rip-proof and waterproof Polyart™ paper
- Music guides running the gamut from Opera to Elvis
- Restaurant guides to London, New York and San Francisco
- Reference books on topics as diverse as the Weather and Shakespeare
- Sports guides from Formula 1 to Man Utd
- Pop culture books from *Lord of the Rings* to Cult TV
- World Music CDs in association with World Music Network

Visit **www.roughguides.com** to see our latest publications.

SMALL PRINT

Rough Guide credits

Text editor: AnneLise Sorensen
Layout: Jessica Subramanian
Cartography: Manish Chandra
Picture research: Mark Thomas, JJ Luck, Harriet Mills
Proofreader: Stewart J. Wild
Editorial: **London** Martin Dunford, Kate Berens, Helena Smith, Claire Saunders, Geoff Howard, Ruth Blackmore, Gavin Thomas, Polly Thomas, Richard Lim, Clifton Wilkinson, Alison Murchie, Sally Schafer, Karoline Densley, Andy Turner, Ella O'Donnell, Keith Drew, Edward Aves, Andrew Lockett, Joe Staines, Duncan Clark, Peter Buckley, Matthew Milton, Daniel Crewe; **New York** Andrew Rosenberg, Richard Koss, Chris Barsanti, Steven Horak, AnneLise Sorensen, Amy Hegarty
Design & Pictures: London Simon Bracken, Dan May, Diana Jarvis, Mark Thomas, Jj Luck, Harriet Mills, Chloë Roberts; **Delhi** Madhulita Mohapatra, Umesh Aggarwal, Ajay Verma, Jessica Subramanian, Amit Verma

Production: Julia Bovis, Sophie Hewat, Katherine Owers
Cartography: **London** Maxine Repath, Ed Wright, Katie Lloyd-Jones, Miles Irving; **Delhi** Manish Chandra, Rajesh Chhibber, Jai Prakesh Mishra, Ashutosh Bharti, Rajesh Mishra, Animesh Pathak, Jasbir Sandhu, Karobi Gogoi
Online: **New York** Jennifer Gold, Suzanne Welles, Benjamin Ross; **Delhi** Manik Chauhan, Narender Kumar, Shekhar Jha, Rakesh Kumar
Marketing & Publicity: **London** Richard Trillo, Niki Hanmer, David Wearn, Chloë Roberts, Demelza Dallow; **New York** Geoff Colquitt, Megan Kennedy, Milena Perez
Custom publishing and foreign rights: Philippa Hopkins
Finance: Gary Singh
Manager India: Punita Singh
Series editor: Mark Ellingham
PA to Managing Director: Megan McIntyre
Managing Director: Kevin Fitzgerald

SMALL PRINT

Publishing information

This fourth edition published April 2005 by **Rough Guides Ltd**,
80 Strand, London WC2R 0RL.
345 Hudson St, 4th Floor,
New York, NY 10014, USA.
Distributed by the Penguin Group
Penguin Books Ltd,
80 Strand, London WC2R 0RL
Penguin Putnam, Inc.
375 Hudson St, NY 10014, USA
Penguin Group (Australia)
250 Camberwell Rd, Camberwell
Victoria 3124, Australia
Penguin Books Canada Ltd,
10 Alcorn Ave, Toronto, Ontario,
Canada M4V 1E4
Penguin Group (New Zealand)
Cnr Rosedale and Airborne Roads
Albany, Auckland, New Zealand
Typeset in Bembo and Helvetica to an original design by Henry Iles.

Printed and bound in China

© Jean McNeil 2005

No part of this book may be reproduced in any form without permission from the publisher except for the quotation of brief passages in reviews.

448pp includes index
A catalogue record for this book is available from the British Library

ISBN 1-84353-429-0

The publishers and authors have done their best to ensure the accuracy and currency of all the information in **The Rough Guide to Costa Rica**, however, they can accept no responsibility for any loss, injury, or inconvenience sustained by any traveller as a result of information or advice contained in the guide.

1 3 5 7 9 8 6 4 2

Help us update

We've gone to a lot of effort to ensure that the fourth edition of **The Rough Guide to Costa Rica** is accurate and up-to-date. However, things change – places get "discovered", opening hours are notoriously fickle, restaurants and rooms raise prices or lower standards. If we've got it wrong or left something out, we'd like to know, and if you can remember the address, the price, the time, the phone number, so much the better.

We'll credit all contributions, and send a copy of the next edition (or any other Rough Guide if you prefer) for the best letters. Everyone who writes to us and isn't already a subscriber will receive a copy of our full-colour thrice-yearly newsletter. Please mark letters: **"Rough Guide Costa Rica Update"** and send to: Rough Guides, 80 Strand, London WC2R 0RL, or Rough Guides, 4th Floor, 345 Hudson St, New York, NY 10014. Or send an email to **mail@roughguides.com**

Have your questions answered and tell others about your trip at **www.roughguides.atinfopop.com**

Acknowledgements

Joe Fullman: Thanks to Karla Arias for all her help in San José, Geinier Guzman for fighting the good ecological fight, Jim and Alison Dobbins for walking the mean streets of Tortuguero with me, Greg Ingram for translating, driving and generally being a great companion and most of all to Nic Mainwood for being wonderful, reading through my stuff and learning enough Spanish to understand what *Te Amo* means.

Andy Symington: Many thanks to all the obliging folk in Costa Rica who gave generously of their time and information during the research process, and also to all the people involved in the planning and editing stages at Rough Guides. I am as ever grateful to family and friends for their support and understanding, and particularly to Martin Davies for his excellent company despite getting off so lightly.

The editor would like to thank the RG Delhi team for top-notch typesetting; Katie Lloyd-Jones and Manish Chandra for their mapmaking expertise; Mark Thomas, Jj Luck and Harriet Mills for their thorough picture research; Stewart Wild for his vigilant proofreading; Nicky Agate for a fine index; Chris Barsanti and Steven Horak for their informative, engaging answers to my questions; Richard Koss for his generous assistance throughout; and Andrew Rosenberg for overall direction.

SMALL PRINT

Readers' letters

Thanks to all the readers who have taken the time to write in with comments and suggestions (and apologies for any errors, omissions or misspellings):

Margaret Andersen, Ingo Dumke, Corey Galstan, Susan Nguyen, Dena James, Jeff Provenzano, Glenn P. Rajaram, G. Boyd Reid, Rick Schwolsky, Thomas Simpson, Frank Tool, Klaus Vanselow, Rosemary Vase.

Photo credits

Cover Credits

Small front lower picture Hummingbirds © Getty (Imagebank)

Main front picture Glass Frog © Getty (Imagebank)

Back top picture Osa Peninsula © Getty (Imagebank)

Back lower picture Church © Alamy

Small front top picture Volcán Arenal © Getty (Stone)

Colour introduction

Beach, Manuel Antonio National Park © Robert Francis/South American Pictures

Surfer, Mal País © Britt Dyer/South American Pictures

Flower in Rincón de la Vieja National Park © Chris Barton

Evening street scene, Liberia © Ian Cumming/AXIOM

Eyelash viper © J. Sparshatt/AXIOM

Mangoes, Paquera, Nicoya Peninsula © A. Hampton/Travel Ink

Coffee bushes, Nicoya Peninsula © Chris Barton

Typical Costa Rican bus © Ian Cumming/AXIOM

Things not to miss

01 Teatro Nacional, San José © Diego Ferrari

02 Visitors to Monteverde Cloudforest Preserve © Gary Braasch/Getty Images

03 Playa Cocles © Diego Ferrari

04 Calle Real, Liberia

05 Sports-fishing © Tony Arruza/CORBIS

06 Oropéndola bird nests © D. Maybury/TRIP

07 Daytime eruption of Volcán Arenal © R. Powers/TRIP

08 Carnival, Puerto Limón

09 Coffee © Courtesy of Costa Rican Tourist Board

10 Santa Rosa National Park © Ian Cumming

11 Museo de Jade © Diego Ferrari

12 Santa Elena Cloudforest © Diego Ferrari

13 El Sano Banano © Courtesy of El Sano Banano

14 Poás Volcano © Courtesy of Costa Rican Tourist Board

15 Cowboys watering herd, Guanacaste © Jevan Berrange/South American Pictures

16 Manuel Antonio National Park © Robert Francis/South American Pictures

17 Xandari Plantation Inn © Macduff Everton

18 Black-sand beach at Corcovado National Park © Ian Cumming

19 Scarlet macaws, Costa Rica © David Stoecklein/CORBIS

20 Baird's tapir © Ian Cumming/AXIOM

21 Tortuguero Canal © Diego Ferrari

22 Rincón de la Vieja National Park © Martin Rogers/CORBIS

23 Precolumbian nose ring, Museo de Oro Precolombino © CORBIS

24 White-faced Capuchin monkey, Manuel Antonio National Park © J. Sparshatt/AXIOM

25 American Crocodile, Tortuguero National Park © Adrian Hepworth/NHPA

26 Irazú Volcano © Diego Ferrari

27 Whitewater rafting, Pacuaré River © Courtesy of Costa Rican Tourist Board

28 Leatherback turtle nesting in sand, Costa Rica © Kevin Schafer/CORBIS

29 Fruit, San Jose market © Gary Braasch/CORBIS

30 Sunset at Playa Samara © Diego Ferrari

Black and white photos

Parque Central, San Jose © Jose Fuste Raga/CORBIS (p.64)

San José advertisement © Ian Cumming/AXIOM (p.71)

Volcan Poás © Robert Francis/South American Pictures (p.106)

Raking drying coffee, near Heredia © Robert Francis/South American Pictures (p.129)

Creole cookery © Trevor Wood/Stone/Getty Images (p.142)

Tortuguero National Park © Kevin Schafer/CORBIS (p.175)

Green iguana © Rebeccca Whitfield/South American Pictures (p.182)

Painted fruit stand © Gary Braasch/CORBIS (p.214)

Horseman, Guanacaste © Ian Cumming/AXIOM (p.222)

Scarlet macaw © Robert Francis/South American Pictures (p.270)

Montezuma Waterfall © Martin Rogers/CORBIS (p.299)

Pineapples © Juan Carlos Ulate/Reuters/CORBIS (p.324)

Corcovado National Park © Ian Cumming/AXIOM (p.354)

Index

Map entries are in colour

Map symbols

maps are listed in the full index using coloured text

▄▄ ▄▄ ▪	International boundary		@	Internet
─ ─ ─	Chapter division boundary		(i)	Tourist office
▭①▭	Carretera Interamericana		◉	Accommodation
═══	Major road		▣	Restaurant
═══	Minor road		⋏	Campsite
───	Unpaved road		♠	Mountain refuge/Lodge
········	Pedestrianized street		★	Bus stop
▬▬	Railway line		⛽	Fuel station
─────	Path		Ⓢ	Bank
··········	Trail		⊠	Post office
─ ─	Ferry route		⊥	Garden
───	River		♦	Museum
‿	Bridge		✈	Airport (general)
كنتللنا	Reef		✗	Airport (domestic)
/|\	Hill shading		➕	Church
▲	Peak		▬	Building
⌓	Cave		⁺₊⁺	Christian cemetery
⚭	Waterfall		▨	Park
♦	Place of interest		▦	Beach
∴	Ruin			